# A MASTERY APPROACH TO
# WordPerfect®
## VERSION 5.1

## NITA HEWITT RUTKOSKY
Pierce College
Puyallup, Washington

**PARADIGM**

PRINTED WITH
SOY INK

**To all the business educators that gave me input and suggestions for organizing this textbook.**

Developmental Editor . . . . . . . . . . . . . . . . . . . . . . . . Elizabeth Sugg
Copy Editor . . . . . . . . . . . . . . . . . . . . . . . . . . . . . Carol Danielson
Illustrator . . . . . . . . . . . . . . . . . . . . . . . . . . . . . . . . . Brad Olsen
Composition . . . . . . . . . . . . . . . . . . . . . . . . . . . Patricia Maxfield
Cover Design . . . . . . . . . . . . . . . . . . . . . . . . . Tessing Design, Inc.

This product was composed using WordPerfect, version 5.1.

WordPerfect is a registered trademark of WordPerfect Corporation.
Hewlett-Packard is a registered trademark of Hewlett-Packard Inc.
IBM is a registered trademark of International Business Machines.

**Library of Congress Cataloging-in-Publications Data**

Rutkosky, Nita Hewitt
      A mastery approach to WordPerfect, version 5.1 / Nita Hewitt
 Rutkosky.
       p.  cm.
      Includes index.
      ISBN 1-56118-082-3
      1. WordPerfect (Computer program)  2. Word processing--Computer
 programs.    I. Title.
 Z52.5.W65R878  1991
 652.5'536--dc20                     91-15610
                                    CIP

© 1991 by Paradigm Publishing Inc.
280 Case Avenue, Saint Paul, Minnesota 55101

Printed in the United States of America

10 9 8

# TABLE OF CONTENTS

## USING WORDPERFECT

When you prepare for a successful business career, you need to acquire the necessary skills and qualifications essential to becoming a productive member of the business community. Microcomputer systems are prevalent in many business offices, and students will encounter employment opportunities that require a working knowledge of computers and computer software.

Microcomputers, with the appropriate software, are used by businesses in a variety of capacities. One of the most popular uses of a microcomputer system is word processing—the creation of documents.

Word processing certainly belongs in the business office, but it is also a popular application for home computer use. People will want to learn word processing to write personal correspondence, keep personal records, provide support for a home-based business or cottage industry, write terms papers and reports, and much more.

This textbook provides students with the opportunity to learn word processing for employment purposes or home use and to fully utilize a microcomputer as a word processor. WordPerfect®, Version 5.1 software and an IBM® or IBM-compatible microcomputer system must be available to students to practice the functions and procedures of the program. WordPerfect needs to be installed on a hard-drive system, network system, or installed on floppy disks. To properly install the program, please refer to the Getting Started section of the WordPerfect, Version 5.1, Reference Manual.

## LEARNING WORDPERFECT

*A Mastery Approach to WordPerfect, Version 5.1* instructs students in the theories and practical applications of one of the most popular word processing software programs—WordPerfect. The textbook is designed to be used in beginning and advanced word processing classes and provide approximately 75 to 100 hours of instruction.

The textbook is divided into six units each containing several chapters. Each chapter contains performance objectives, material introducing and explaining new concepts and commands, a chapter summary, and a student study guide. Several hands-on computer exercises to be completed at the computer illustrate new commands step by step. Performance Assessments reinforce acquired skills while providing practice in decision-making and problem-solving. In addition, mastery assessments are included at the end of each unit.

The performance objectives let you know what you can expect to learn and what you can expect to be doing upon completion of the chapter. Each chapter introduces a new theory, including functions and commands, and provides examples and explanations to assist learning. A summary is included to highlight the main points of the chapter and provide a quick reference to key presses. You are provided with a study guide designed to help you assess your understanding of the material presented in the chapter. The last section of each chapter contains exercises to be completed at the computer. The last exercises in each chapter, called Performance Assessments, require that you prepare documents without step-by-step instructions. Simulation exercises at the end of each unit provide hands-on computer exercises that require you to make decisions about document preparation and formatting. These practical exercises provide ample opportunity to practice new functions and commands as well as previously learned material.

## MANIPULATING WORDPERFECT

There are two types of WordPerfect commands used in this text. If keys are to be pressed sequentially, a comma separates the two keys. For example,

```
Home, right arrow
```

command indicates that the Home key is pressed and released and then the right arrow key is pressed and released. A plus symbol (+) is used for commands where the first key is held down while the second key is being pressed. For example, to execute the

```
Alt + F7
```

command, the Alt key is held down and then the F7 key is pressed. After the F7 key is pressed, the Alt key may be released.

WordPerfect commands can be executed from the keyboard or with a mouse. The directions for each method are contained in this text. Many commands can be executed by pressing a number or a letter from the keyboard. For example, to print a document from the directory, the number 4 or the letter P will send the document to the printer. Both the number and the letter for commands are included in this text. Directions will use terminology such as "choose 4 or P for Print," and "choose 1 or L for Line." The method for executing commands from the mouse are also included. The mouse directions are preceded by the icon, **M**, and are set in italics. If you are using a mouse, please refer to Appendix A: Mouse, before beginning chapter 1.

# UNIT 1

## BASIC CHARACTER AND LINE FORMATTING

In this unit, you will learn to adjust characters and lines in the creation of simple office documents, such as business memorandums and letters.

# CHAPTER 1

## MICROCOMPUTER EQUIPMENT

### PERFORMANCE OBJECTIVES

Upon successful completion of chapter 1, you will be able to operate a word processing system, maintain storage devices, and save and retrieve a WordPerfect document.

### HARDWARE AND SOFTWARE

This textbook provides you with instruction on a word processing program using a microcomputer system. The program you will learn to operate is the software. Software is the program of instructions that tells the computer what to do. The computer equipment you will use is the *hardware*. Put simply, software makes the hardware operate.

You will be learning to operate a software program called WordPerfect®. There are hundreds of software programs written to turn your microcomputer into a word processor; WordPerfect is one of the most popular.

Even though you will learn to operate the functions and commands of WordPerfect, many procedures and theories you will practice can apply to other word processing programs. By learning one word processing program, you learn what you can and cannot do with a word processor and the terminology that is particular to word processing. These general concepts will transfer to other systems and programs.

### WHAT YOU NEED TO OPERATE WORDPERFECT

This textbook instructs you in the functions and commands of WordPerfect, Version 5.1. You will need an IBM PC or an IBM-compatible computer to operate WordPerfect. This computer system should consist of the CPU, monitor, keyboard, printer, and disk drives. If you are not sure what equipment you will be operating, check with your instructor.

The illustration in figure 1-1 shows you an IBM Personal Computer System. Following the illustration is an explanation of the components.

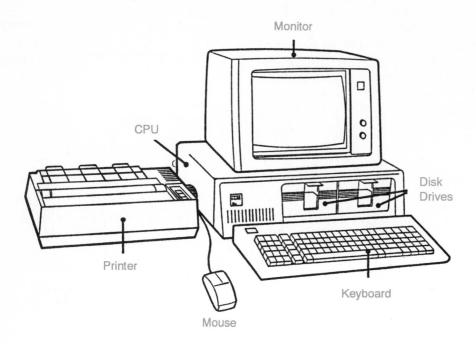

Monitor

CPU

Disk
Drives

Printer

Mouse

Keyboard

**Figure 1-1: IBM Personal Computer System**

## CPU

CPU stands for Central Processing Unit. The CPU is the *Brain* intelligence of the computer. All the processing occurs in the CPU. Silicon chips, which contain miniaturized circuitry, are placed on boards and plugged into slots within the CPU. Whenever an instruction is given to the computer, that instruction is processed through the circuitry in the CPU. The Central Processing Unit, in simple terms, is a central location where information is processed.

## Monitor

The monitor is a piece of equipment that looks like a television screen. The monitor displays the information of a program and what is being input at the keyboard. The monitor may also be referred to as the VDT (Video Display Terminal) or screen.

Monitors can vary in the amount and color of text they display. For word processing, a monitor is needed that displays 80 characters horizontally and at least 15 to 20 lines vertically. When you have a WordPerfect document displayed on the screen, you will be able to see up to 80 characters horizontally and 24 lines vertically.

Monitors can display text in different colors: green, amber, white, black, and even multicolors.

## Keyboard

To create word processing documents quickly and efficiently, you need a keyboard to input the information. Keyboards for microcomputers vary in the number and location of their keys. Microcomputers have the alphabetic and numeric keys in the same place as the keys on a typewriter. The symbol keys, however, may be placed at a variety of locations, depending on the manufacturer.

In addition to letters, numbers, and symbols, most microcomputer keyboards have function keys, cursor movements keys, and a ten-key pad. Some keyboards have the cursor movement keys combined with the ten-key pad; others have them separate.

Look at the keyboards shown in figure 1-2 to see examples of two microcomputer keyboards.

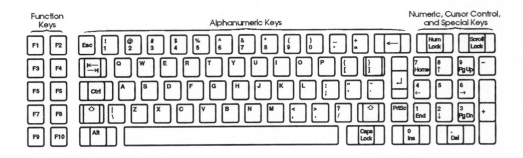

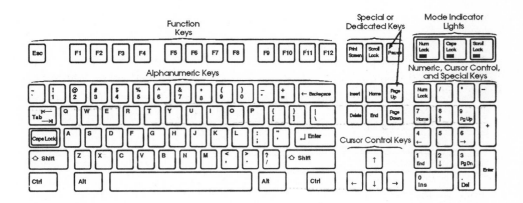

Figure 1-2: Microcomputer Keyboards

The function keys on the IBM PC in the upper illustration are the ten keys located to the left of the regular keyboard. On the right side of the keyboard is a group of keys with various functions. They are generally referred to as screen numeric keys and can be used as cursor movement keys, deletion keys, and number keys. If you press the Num Lock key, they can be used as a ten-key pad.

The keyboard in the lower illustration contains the same keys — function, cursor movement, and screen numeric keys — as the upper illustration. The difference is that the keyboard in the lower illustration has the function keys at the top of the keyboard and the cursor movement keys are separate and are located between the regular keyboard and the screen numeric keys.

Look at the keyboard you will be using to see how closely it matches either keyboard in the illustrations.

## Disk Drives

Depending on the computer system you are using, the WordPerfect program is saved on a disk, saved on a hard drive, or saved as part of a network system.

A disk drive spins a floppy disk and reads information from the disk. There are two types of disk drive systems — floppy-drive and hard-drive. WordPerfect operates more quickly and efficiently on a hard-drive system (or a network system) than a floppy-drive system.

If you are using WordPerfect on a floppy-drive system, you must have two disk drives available. WordPerfect Version 5.1 will operate on a floppy-drive system if the drives are 720k or larger. The WordPerfect program disks are sequentially inserted in one drive and a blank formatted disk on which documents will be saved is inserted in the second drive. If you are using a hard-drive system (or a network system), the WordPerfect program is saved on the hard drive (or part of the network). With a hard-drive (or *C – Hard Drive* network) system, you will need a blank formatted disk on which to save documents.

## Printer

When you create a document on the screen, it is considered *soft* copy. If you want a *hard* copy of the document, you need to have it printed on paper. To print documents, you will need to access a printer.

Printers are either impact or nonimpact. Impact printers have a mechanism that strikes the paper to create text. Nonimpact printers use a variety of methods — heat, ink-jet, laser — to print characters. These printers are much quieter and faster than impact printers; they are generally also more expensive than impact printers.

Two types of impact printers are dot matrix and character. A dot matrix printer forms text with a series of dots, and produces *draft quality* copy. A character printer prints fully formed characters and produces *letter quality* *(looks better)* copy.

## Mouse

WordPerfect, Version 5.1 may be operated completely from the keyboard or with a separate piece of equipment called a mouse. A mouse sits on a flat surface next to the computer and is operated with the left or right hand. When you install WordPerfect, Version 5.1 with a mouse, a rectangle displays on the screen and is moved by the mouse. For instructions on using a mouse, refer to Appendix A.

## DISKS AND DISK MAINTENANCE

To operate WordPerfect you should have your own disk on which to save documents. You will probably be using a 5 1/4-inch or 3 1/2-inch disk. To ensure that the information stored on a disk will always be there when you want to retrieve it, you need to follow certain rules of disk maintenance. If you are using a 5 1/4-inch or a 3 1/2-inch disk, follow these rules:

1.  Do not expose your disk to extreme heat or cold.
2.  Do not wipe or clean the magnetic surface.
3.  Keep the disk away from food, liquids, and smoke.
4.  Never remove a disk from the disk drive when the drive light is on.

If you are using a 5 1/4-inch, follow these additional rules:

1.  Do not touch the exposed surfaces of your disk.
2.  Do not use paper clips or rubber bands on the disk.
3.  Always keep your disk in the protective envelope when it is not in use.
4.  Do not write on a disk with a pencil or ballpoint pen. If you need to write on the disk label, use a felt-tip pen.
5.  Keep disks away from magnets and magnetic fields. They can erase the information you have stored.
6.  Store disks in an upright position when they are not being used.

The disk that you will be using for document storage must be formatted. Formatting is a process that establishes tracks and sectors in which to store information on the disk and to prepare the disk to accept data for the disk operating system being used. The procedure for formatting disks is presented in Appendix B.

## WORDPERFECT TEMPLATE

The WordPerfect Corporation includes a template with the WordPerfect program that identifies the commands from the function keys. The template is placed around the function keys to provide a visual aid. The WordPerfect, Version 5.1 template is shown in figure 1-3.

When the template is placed over the function keys, you do not need to memorize commands. Each function key has four levels: the function key by itself, Alt key plus the function key, Shift key plus the function key, and Ctrl key plus the function key. (This is explained further in Chapter 3.) The commands are written on the template in different colors. The colors identify the level of the function key, as indicated below:

BLACK     = Function key by itself
BLUE      = Alt plus function key
GREEN     = Shift plus function key
RED       = Ctrl plus function key

The WordPerfect template is a very useful tool that provides a quick reference to the WordPerfect commands.

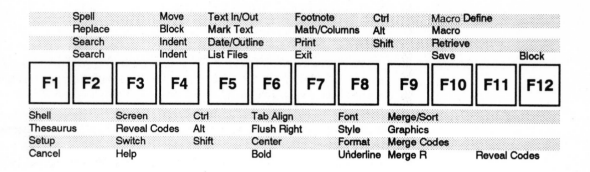

**Figure 1·3: WordPerfect Template**

## CREATING A WORDPERFECT DOCUMENT

Six basic steps are completed when working with a word processing system to create a document. The steps are

1. enter the program,
2. key in the information to create the document,
3. save the document on the disk,
4. bring the document back to the screen and make any necessary edits (changes),
5. save the revised document on the disk, and
6. print a hard copy of the document.

In this chapter, you will be provided with the information necessary to complete all the steps except 4. At the end of this chapter, you will complete several exercises and practice the steps. Let us take a look at the steps to creating a WordPerfect document.

## Operating WordPerfect on a Floppy-drive System

When you sit down at your computer, you will follow basic operating steps. These will need to be completed every time you begin working with WordPerfect. The steps completed vary depending on the microcomputer system configuration.

To operate WordPerfect on a floppy-drive system, complete the following steps:

1. Insert the WordPerfect #1 disk into Drive A. To insert a disk into disk drives that are stacked, you want the label on the disk facing up. If your drives are side by side, you want the label facing left. Drive A is usually either the top drive or the left drive. Gently push the disk into the drive until it is all the way in. You may need to close the disk drive door.

2. Insert your formatted work disk into Drive B. Follow the same disk inserting instructions as in step 1. (The procedure to format a disk is described in Appendix B.)

3. Turn on the CPU. The location of the on/off switch for computers varies. It may be in the back right corner or in the front left corner. Check to see where your power switch is. Depending on your system, you may also need to turn on the monitor and the printer.

4. When the computer is turned on, the disk drive is activated and information on the disk is read into the computer's memory. The first information loaded is the Disk Operating System (DOS). When DOS is present, you will get a message on the screen telling you today's date and asking you to enter the new date. The screen will look similar to this:

```
Current date is Tue 1-01-1980 [your date may vary]
Enter new date:_
```

The blinking underline after the date is called the cursor. The cursor indicates the position of the next character entered. The cursor is ready for you to enter the new date. The date must be entered as month, day, and year. If today's date is September 25, 1992, it would be entered in this form:

```
09-25-92
```

When you have entered the new date, you must press the Enter key (sometimes called the Return). When you press Enter, you tell the computer to accept the information keyed in. (When entering the date you do not need to enter the day of the week.)

When you press Enter after keying in the date, the following message appears on the screen:

```
Current time is 0:00:52.78 [your time may vary]
Enter new time:_
```

At this message, enter the time. Enter the time in hours and minutes. You do not need to include seconds or hundredths of a second. For times in the P.M., military time is required (just add 12 to the time). If the current time is 2:45 P.M., you would enter the following:

```
14:45 [press Enter]
```

When you have completed these steps you will get a message on the screen that looks like this: **A>**.

This is called the A prompt.

5.  The **A>** indicates that the computer will read information from Drive A. If you are using a dual disk drive system, you will need to let the computer know that the documents you create will be saved on the work disk in Drive B. This is called changing the logged disk drive. With the cursor resting after the **A>**, log to Drive B by keying in B:, then pressing Enter. When you press the Enter key you are telling the computer to accept the information or command you have keyed in on the screen. After you press the Enter key, you will see this on your screen:

```
A>B:
B>_
```

This message indicates that the disk drive has been changed to B and anything you save will be kept on that drive. Now you are ready to load the WordPerfect program. The command to load WordPerfect is WP. But remember the WordPerfect program is in Drive A. Therefore, the command to load WordPerfect is A:WP and press Enter. This is what you should key in at that **B>**:

```
B>A:WP [press Enter]
```

6.  It takes about 4 to 6 seconds for WordPerfect to load. When it is loaded, you will see a WordPerfect copyright screen. In the middle of the screen the following message is displayed:

```
Insert diskette labeled "WordPerfect 2" and press
any key
```

7.  Take the WordPerfect #1 disk out of Drive A and insert WordPerfect #2. Press any key on the keyboard (such as the spacebar). In a few seconds the WordPerfect copyright screen is removed and replaced by a "clear" screen. You are now ready to begin keying in a document.

## Operating WordPerfect on a Hard-drive System

The operating instructions for a hard disk drive system vary slightly from the instructions given earlier. To operate WordPerfect from a hard drive, complete the following steps:

1.  Turn on the computer.
2.  Key in the date if necessary (use the procedure for entering the date that is described earlier). Press Enter.
3.  Key in the time if necessary (use the procedure described earlier). Press Enter.
4.  Insert your formatted work disk in Drive A.
5.  At the **C>**, key in **A:** and press Enter.
6.  At the **A>**, key in **C:\WP51\WP** and press Enter.

### Operating WordPerfect on Other Systems

Operating WordPerfect on your computer system may vary from these instructions. If necessary, ask your instructor for the specific steps to load WordPerfect, and write the steps here:

_____

_____

_____

_____

_____

_____

## THE WORDPERFECT SCREEN

When you load WordPerfect you will be presented with a clear screen. At this point, you are ready to key in a document. A document is any information you choose—for instance, a letter, memo, report, term paper, or table. The WordPerfect screen is shown in figure 1-4.

Doc 1 Pg 1 Ln 1" Pos 1"

Figure 1-4: WordPerfect Screen

### Cursor

The blinking underline in the upper left corner of the screen is the cursor. The cursor indicates the location of the next character entered at the keyboard.

### Status Line

At the bottom right corner of the screen is the status line. It tells you the document in which you are working (explained in a later chapter) and the page number. It also identifies the location of the cursor by line and position. Line and position locations are displayed in inches. As you key in information, the cursor moves across the screen, and the status line changes to always display the cursor position.

### Margins and WordPerfect Defaults

You do not have to tell WordPerfect to do certain things; they are built in by the programmers and are called program defaults. A default is something that automatically occurs every time you load WordPerfect. For example, at a clear screen you are automatically given a one-inch left margin (indicated by 1" on the status line) and a one-inch right margin. You did not have to set these margins; they are WordPerfect defaults.

### Word Wrap

As you key in text, you do not need to press the Enter key at the end of each line. WordPerfect wraps words around to the next line. A word is wrapped to the next line if it begins before the right margin and continues past the margin. The only times you need to press Enter are to end a paragraph, create a blank line, or end a short line. Even when word wrap is used, text can be adjusted, if necessary.

## SAVING A DOCUMENT

When you have completed a document, the information will need to be saved on the disk. When a document is keyed in for the first time and is displayed on the screen, it is only a temporary document. If you turn off the computer, or if the power goes off, you will lose the information and have to rekey it.

Only when you save a document on the disk is it saved permanently. Every time you load WordPerfect and your work disk, you will be able to bring the document back to the screen.

To save the document on your work disk, press the F7 function key (**M** *Click on File, then Exit*). The F7 key is one of the ten function keys located to the left of the regular keyboard or one of the twelve function keys above the regular keyboard. When you press F7 (or **M** *Click on File, then Exit*) you will see the following message at the bottom left corner of the screen:

**Save document?  Yes (No)**

WordPerfect is asking if you want to save the document and is giving you two choices — yes and no.  WordPerfect assumes you want to save the document and is answering the question with yes. If you did not want to save the document, you would key in an **N** over the Y (**M** *Click on No*). But in this case, you do want to save the document, so you would press the Enter key or key in a **Y** for yes (**M** *Click on Yes*). When you do this the message changes to:

```
Document to be Saved:_
```

To respond to this message, you must know how to name documents.

### Naming a Document

WordPerfect saves a document with the name you give it. The name can be from one to eight characters in length and may contain letters, numbers, or both. (A name can include either upper- or lowercase letters.) The document name may not contain spaces.

You can extend your document name past eight characters by adding a period to the end of the document name. This is called an *extension*. After the period, you can use up to three more characters. When you have entered the document name, press the Enter key.

A message telling you that the document is being saved will appear at the bottom of the screen. This process takes only a few seconds. When the document is saved, you will get this message:

```
Exit WP? No (Yes)
```

### Exiting WordPerfect

If you want to create another document with WordPerfect, press the Enter key or key in an **N** for no (**M** *Click on No*). If you are finished for the day and are ready to exit, key in a **Y** for yes (**M** *Click on Yes*). When a C> (or other drive letter) appears on the screen, take your disk out of the disk drive, and turn off the computer. Always exit the WordPerfect program before turning off the computer.

## DOCUMENT RETRIEVAL

After you have saved a document on the disk, you may want to bring it back to the screen to make revisions. If you have exited WordPerfect, you need to enter the program again. Follow your instructions until you have a clear screen. At the clear screen, press the List key, F5 (**M** *Click on File, then List Files*). When you press F5 (**M** *Click on File, then List Files*), the following message appears in the bottom left corner of the screen:

```
Dir A:\*.* [The drive letter may vary.]
```

The cursor is resting under the A (or other drive letter). This message tells you that WordPerfect will display files (documents) saved on the disk in Drive A. Press the Enter key (**M** *Click the right mouse button*) and you will be presented with the directory of Drive A. The directory tells you many important things. It lists the time and date a document was created, the current disk drive, and how much free space remains on the disk. It also lists all documents saved on the disk followed by the amount of disk space each document occupies.

At the bottom left corner is a list of commands available to you. The first command is **1 <u>Retrieve</u>**. To retrieve a document to the screen, move the cursor (which appears in the directory as a solid bar) with the cursor movement keys (located on the right side of the keyboard) until it rests on the document you want to bring to the screen. Choose 1 or R for Retrieve to retrieve the document to the screen. The document is brought to the screen, where you can make changes. Whenever changes are made to a document, remember to save the document on the disk again. If you do not, you will lose all your changes.

(*Note*: Make sure you have a clear screen before you retrieve a document. You can retrieve one document into another document accidentally, and you want to avoid this situation for now.) *Do not retrieve into current document.*

## COMPUTER EXERCISES

You will be completing hands-on exercises at the end of each chapter. These will provide you with the opportunity to practice the techniques presented in the chapter. In the beginning chapters, the text will be typewritten and presented in arranged form. To provide you with realistic situations, documents in later chapters may be presented in unarranged or handwritten form.

In the exercises at the end of this chapter, you will be creating and saving several short documents. Press the Enter key only to end a short line or create a blank line between paragraphs. Let the word wrap feature wrap text to the next line within a paragraph.

The WordPerfect screen will display approximately 24 lines of text at one time. When more than 24 lines of text are entered, the text scrolls off the top of the screen. When this happens, the text is not lost or deleted. When the document is saved, all the text is saved — not just 24 lines.

## CHAPTER REVIEW

### Summary

- Computer equipment is called the hardware. The program used to operate the computer is called the software.
- A computer system generally consists of five items: monitor, CPU, disk drive(s), keyboard, and printer. In addition, a mouse can be used to perform WordPerfect functions.
- A monitor displays the information of a program and what is being input at the keyboard. Monitors vary in the amount and color of text displayed.
- Microcomputer keyboards have letter and number keys in the same location as keys on a typewriter. However, the location of symbol keys varies.
- There are two types of drives — floppy-drives and hard-drives.
- The printer produces hard copy. Text on the screen is called soft copy.
- There are different kinds of printers, which vary in price, speed, and quality of print.
- Disks need to be handled responsibly to ensure that the information saved can be read by the disk drive.

- A disk must be formatted to save WordPerfect documents.
- The WordPerfect program includes a template that identifies the commands from the function keys.
- In a document, the cursor appears as a blinking underline and indicates the position of the next character to be entered on the screen.
- The status line indicates the document in which you are working and the current position of the cursor — page, line, and position.
- Document names can be from one to eight characters long and can contain letters, numbers, or both. By adding a period, you can extend the document name by three characters.
- WordPerfect automatically wraps text to the next line as you key in information.
- The WordPerfect screen can display approximately 24 lines of text at one time.
- You should always exit WordPerfect before turning off the computer.
- WordPerfect has many default settings that occur every time you load the program.

## Loading, Creating, and Saving Review

1. Turn on the computer.
2. Key in the date and press Enter.
3. Key in the time and press Enter.
4. Insert the WordPerfect #1 disk in Drive A and close the drive door.
5. Insert your formatted work disk in Drive B and close the door.
6. At the **A>**, key in **B:** and press Enter.
7. At the **B>**, key in **A:WP** and press Enter.
8. At the WordPerfect copyright screen, take out the WordPerfect #1 disk and insert the WordPerfect #2 disk. Press any key on the keyboard.
9. At the clear screen, key in your document.
10. Save the document by pressing F7 (**M** *Click on File, then Exit*).
11. At the **"Save document? Yes (No)"** question, press Enter.
12. At the **"Document to be Saved:"** prompt, enter the name of your document and press Enter.
13. At the **"Exit WP? No (Yes)"** question, press Enter if you want to continue working with WordPerfect; key in a **Y** for yes if you are done and want to exit the program.

## Document Retrieval Review

1. Follow the loading instructions until you have a clear screen.
2. Press F5, for List Files.
   **M** *Click on File, then List Files.*
3. When **Dir A:/*.*** appears at the bottom of the screen, press Enter.
   **M** *Click on the right mouse button.*
4. Move the cursor until it is located on your document.
5. Choose 1 or R for Retrieve to retrieve the document to the screen.

✓ **STUDY GUIDE FOR CHAPTER 1**

Provide a brief description of the following terms:

1.   Monitor: _A piece of equipment that looks like a television screen which displays the input_

2.   CPU: _The brain of the computer_

3.   Disk Drives: _Where the information is read. There are two types - hard drive & floppy drive_

4.   Printer: _It prints the information on the screen (softcopy) onto paper (hard copy)_

5.   Keyboard: _Means of inputting information into the computer with letters & number keys on it._

Circle the items in the list below that are valid file names:

|  |  |
|---|---|
| DOC 1 | JOHANNSEN |
| (12345) | (LETTER.18) |
| (BUS23) | LTR 2 |
| (X7ER34) | DOC.1008 |
| (REPORT33.LTR) | (12345.REP) |
| (3) | 18.LETTER |

**True/False:** Circle the letter T if the statement is true; circle the letter F if the statement is false.

| | | | |
|---|---|---|---|
| 1. | Software is the list of instructions that tells the computer how to operate. | (T) | F |
| 2. | CPU stands for Control Processing Unit. | T | (F) |
| 3. | A microcomputer keyboard has the alphabetic and numeric keys in the same location as a typewriter. | (T) | F |
| 4. | Text displayed on the screen is hard copy. | T | (F) |
| 5. | Your work disk must be formatted before you can save documents on it. | (T) | F |
| 6. | When a document is saved on the disk, it is saved only temporarily. | T | (F) |
| 7. | You should always exit WordPerfect before turning off the computer. | (T) | F |
| 8. | The status line appears in the upper right corner of the screen. | T | (F) |
| 9. | The cursor appears on the screen as a blinking underline and indicates the position of the next character entered. | (T) | F |

10. The status line indicates the current position of the cursor. T (F)

11. You should press the Enter key to end every line in a document. T (F)

## HANDS-ON EXERCISES

### Exercise One

1. Follow the instructions in this chapter to load the WordPerfect program.
2. At a clear screen, key in the text in figure 1-5. Do not worry about mistakes. You will learn how to correct errors in chapter 2.
3. When you are done keying in the text, save the document and name it CH01EX1 by completing the following steps:
   A. Press the Exit key, F7.
    *Click on File, then Exit.*
   B. At the **Save document? <u>Yes</u> (<u>No</u>)** question, press Enter or key in a **Y** for Yes.
   C. At the **Document to be Saved** message, key in **CH01EX1**, then press Enter.
   D. At the **Exit WP? <u>No</u> (<u>Yes</u>)** question, key in a **Y** for Yes.

---

```
The WordPerfect program, produced by WordPerfect Corporation, is
the top-selling word processing program for microcomputers.
WordPerfect was designed in the early 1980s and has been selling
well in the business community since that time.

To continually improve the quality of the program, WordPerfect
Corporation updates the WordPerfect program and markets a new
version every 18 to 24 months.
```

---

Figure 1-5: Exercise One

### Exercise Two

1. Follow the instructions in this chapter to load the WordPerfect program.
2. At a clear screen, key in the information in figure 1-6.
3. Save the document and name it CH01EX2 by completing the following steps:
   A. Press the Exit key, F7.
    *Click on File, then Exit.*
   B. At the **Save document? <u>Yes</u> (<u>No</u>)** question, press Enter or key in a **Y** for Yes.
   C. At the **Document to be Saved** message, key in **CH01EX2**, and press Enter.
   D. At the **Exit WP? <u>No</u> (<u>Yes</u>)** question, key in an **N** for No.

---

```
WordPerfect contains a wide variety of features and functions
that make it one of the most powerful word processing programs.
WordPerfect includes basic features such as word wrap, typeover,
and line and page formatting, as well as more advanced features
such as macros, styles, and tables.

The word wrap feature automatically wraps any word to the next
line that begins before the right margin and continues past the
```

margin. With this feature the WordPerfect user does not have to press the Enter key at the end of each line or make end-of-line hyphenation decisions.

Figure 1-6: Exercise Two

**Exercise Three**
1.  At a clear screen, display the list of documents and retrieve CH01EX1 to the screen by completing the following steps:
    A.  Press the List key, F5.
        **M** *Click on File, then List Files.*
    B.  Press Enter.
    C.  With the directory on the screen, move the cursor to CH01EX1 and choose 1 or R for Retrieve.
2.  Exit CH01EX1 without saving it by completing the following steps:
    A.  Press the Exit key, F7.
        **M** *Click on File, then Exit.*
    B.  **At the Save document?** question, key in an **N** for No.
    C.  **At the Exit WP?** question, press Enter or key in an **N** for No.

**Exercise Four**
1.  At a clear screen, display the list of documents and retrieve CH01EX2 to the screen by completing steps similar to those listed in exercise 3, step 1.
2.  Exit CH01EX2 without saving it by completing steps similar to those listed in exercise 3, step 2.

## PERFORMANCE ASSESSMENTS

**Assessment One**
1.  At a clear screen, key in the text in figure 1-7.
2.  Save the document and name it CH01PA1.

In a WordPerfect document, the status line, displayed in the lower right corner of the screen, indicates the current location of the cursor. The location of the cursor is identified by document, page, line, and position.

Inch measurements are used to indicate the location of the cursor by line and position. At a clear screen, the cursor is located on line and position one inch. This is because WordPerfect provides a one-inch top margin on a page along with a one-inch left margin.

Figure 1-7: Assessment One

**Assessment Two**
1.  At a clear screen, key in the text in figure 1-8.
2.  Save the document and name it CH01PA2.
3.  Exit WordPerfect.

---

As you learn to operate WordPerfect, you will learn such functions as cursor movement, inserting and deleting, blocking, search and replace, creating headers and footers, and much more.

A popular feature of WordPerfect is a spelling checking program called "Speller." Speller operates by matching words in a document with words in the Speller program. If a match is found, the word is passed over. If a match is not found, Speller stops at the word and offers correct spelling possibilities. In addition to Speller, WordPerfect also includes a thesaurus program that lets you look up synonyms and antonyms for specific words.

With WordPerfect's macro feature, you can save frequently used terms or formats and recall the term or format with a few keystrokes. This feature saves time when you are formatting documents.

WordPerfect also includes a math feature that will calculate data in columns or rows and a Tables feature that lets WordPerfect operate as a spreadsheet.

You will have many opportunities to practice using these and other WordPerfect features.

---

**Figure 1-8: Assessment Two**

# CHAPTER 2

## *PERFORMANCE OBJECTIVES*

Upon successful completion of chapter 2, you will be able to create and edit a simple WordPerfect text document.

### CURSOR MOVEMENT

Now that you are able to create WordPerfect documents, let us look at how you make changes or corrections to text. To add or delete text, you need to be able to move the cursor to certain locations in a document without erasing the text it passes through. For example, if you key in three paragraphs and then notice an error in the first paragraph, you need to move the cursor through lines of text without causing them to be deleted.

When you type on a typewriter, you move the typing position indicator by pressing either the space bar (to move to the right) or the Backspace key (to move to the left). If you press one of these keys on a word processing keyboard, you either insert text (with the space bar) or delete text (with the Backspace key).

To move the cursor without interfering with text, use the cursor movement keys that are located to the right of the regular keyboard. In the illustration shown in figure 2-1, you can see keys marked with left, right, up, and down arrows.

If you press the up arrow, the cursor moves up one line. If you press the other arrow keys, the cursor moves in the direction indicated on the key. If you hold the keys down, they become continuous-action keys and the cursor moves quickly.

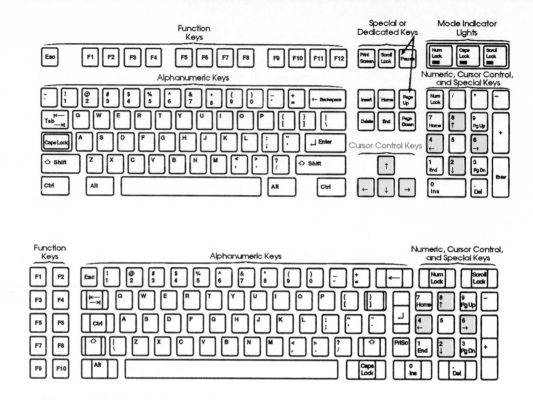

**Figure 2-1: Cursor Movement Control Keys**

## Cursor Movement by Word

You can also move the cursor in other ways. By holding the Ctrl key down and pressing the right arrow key, you can move the cursor one word to the right. You can move the cursor one word to the left by holding the Ctrl key and pressing the left arrow key. These keys are also continuous action. This is a quick way to move through a line of text. (*Note:* In this textbook, the plus sign (+) will be used to refer to commands that require you to press two keys at once. Thus "Ctrl + right arrow" means that you hold the Ctrl key down while you press the right arrow key.) *next word*

## Cursor Movement to End of Line

To move the cursor quickly to the end of the line on which the cursor is resting, press the End key.

## Cursor Movement by Screen

The cursor can be moved quickly around the screen if you press the Home key, let it up, and then press one of the cursor movement keys. If you want to move quickly to the top of the screen, press the Home key and then the up arrow. If you want to move quickly to the end of the line, press the Home key and then the right arrow. This works the same for the bottom of the screen (Home, down arrow) and the beginning of the line (Home, left ar-

*Home
Home
up takes to
beg. of
document*

*Home
Home
Home
Takes to beg.
before any
codes.*

row). (*Note*: In this textbook, the comma will be used to denote keys that are to be pressed sequentially in a command.)

As mentioned in chapter 1, the screen will display approximately 24 lines of text at one time. If you want to scroll through a document screen by screen, press the Home key and then the down arrow key. This moves the cursor to the bottom of the screen. If you press Home, down arrow again, the cursor moves 24 lines. Scrolling text a screen at a time is a good way to proofread documents: Read a screen; then press Home, down arrow to bring up the next screen.

### Cursor Movement by Page

When you begin working with longer documents (documents several pages long) you will find the Page Up and Page Down keys quite useful. When you press the Page Down key, the cursor moves to the beginning of the next page. With Page Up, the cursor moves to the beginning of the previous page. This is a quick way to move through a document. If the cursor is located on page 3, line 6", and you press Page Up, the cursor moves to page 2, line 1". If you press Page Up again, the cursor moves to page 1, line 1".

### Cursor Movement to Beginning and End of Document

WordPerfect also includes commands to move quickly to the beginning or end of a document. Press the Home key twice and the up arrow and the cursor moves to the beginning of the document. Press the Home key twice and the down arrow and the cursor moves to the end of the document. These are particularly useful commands in long documents.

If you move the cursor to the beginning of a document, the cursor may not be moved to the beginning of format codes. To make sure that the cursor is moved to the beginning of a document, press Home, Home, up arrow.

### Cursor Movement to Specific Page

WordPerfect includes a Go To command that allows you to move quickly to a specific page within a document. The Go To command is Ctrl + Home. When you press Ctrl + Home, WordPerfect displays the prompt **Go To** in the bottom left corner of the screen. Key in the page number you desire and press Enter. WordPerfect will move the cursor to the beginning of that page.

### Cursor Movement with the Mouse

Instructions for using the mouse are included in Appendix A. The mouse can be used to move the regular cursor to specific locations in the document. To do this, move the mouse cursor to the location where you want the regular cursor to appear, then click the left button on the mouse.

### Scrolling with the Mouse

The mouse can be used to scroll through a document. To do this, hold down the right mouse button, then drag the mouse to the edge of the screen. For example, to scroll down the document, hold down the right button on the mouse and move the mouse cursor to the bottom of the screen. With the mouse cursor at the bottom of the screen, scrolling will continue until you release the mouse button or you reach the end of the document. Scrolling up will continue until you reach the top of the document; scrolling left will continue until you reach the beginning of the line; and scrolling right will continue until you reach the end of the line.

## INSERTING TEXT

Once you have created a document, you may want to insert information you forgot or have since decided to include. When you load the WordPerfect program and start working with a clear screen, you are automatically in the "insert-on" mode. This means that anything you key in will be inserted instead of typed over existing text.

If you want to insert or add something, leave the insert in the on mode. If, however, you want to key over something, turn the insert off by pressing the Insert key. When you press this key, the message **Typeover** appears in the bottom left corner of the screen. Typeover will stay in effect until you press the Insert key again or until you exit WordPerfect.

There are many toggle keys in WordPerfect such as the insert key. You use the same key to turn the insert mode off and on. A toggle key has two conditions — on or off. If insert is on, you can turn it off by pressing the Insert key. If the insert is off, you can turn it on by pressing the Insert key.

Whether you edit a document with insert on or off depends on the changes you need to make. You might find that you do not need to turn insert off very often. At other times, you may turn it off for most of your edits.

## DELETING TEXT

When you edit a document, you may want to delete text. You may want to delete just one character or several lines. WordPerfect offers a wide variety of deletion commands.

### Deleting a Character

You can delete a character using the Backspace key or the Delete key. When you press the Backspace key, you delete the character to the left of the cursor. By pressing the Delete key, you delete the character under which the cursor is located.

### Deleting a Word

To delete a word, make sure the cursor is located somewhere within the word, hold the Ctrl key and press the Backspace key (Ctrl + Backspace). The entire word, including any punctuation, will be deleted. Any text to the right of the cursor will move in to fill the gap.

WordPerfect also includes word boundary commands. These commands allow you to delete a partial word. To delete characters from the cursor location to the beginning of the word, press Home, Backspace. To delete characters from the cursor location to the end of the word, press Home, Delete.

### Deleting a Line

You can delete text to the end of the line by holding the Ctrl key and pressing End. This will delete all text from the cursor to the end of the line. If you want to delete the entire line, you must have the cursor located on the first character of that line, then use Ctrl + End.

### Deleting Several Lines

WordPerfect has a command that allows you to perform a function any number of times. When you press the Esc key, the message **Repeat Value = 8** appears at the bottom of the screen. By default, the program will repeat any command eight times. If you want to delete four lines, follow these steps:

1. Make sure the cursor is located at the beginning of the lines you want to delete. Press the Escape key and the **Repeat Value = 8** message appears in the bottom left corner of the screen.

2. Key in a **4** over the **8** (because you want to delete just four lines, not eight).

3. Press the Ctrl + End. This tells WordPerfect you want to delete to the end of line four times.

### Deleting to the End of Page

If you are keying in a document and decide to remove the last paragraph, you can use the end-of-page deletion command. To delete to the end of page, place the cursor at the beginning of the text you want deleted and press Ctrl + Page Down. Before the text is deleted, you get the **Delete remainder of page? No (Yes)** message at the bottom left corner of the screen.

WordPerfect is asking this question to make sure you really want to delete the text and answering the question with No. If you want to remove the text to the end of the page, key in a **Y** for Yes.

With this command you can remove a character, a line, several lines, paragraphs, or an entire page. You control the amount of text deleted by your placement of the cursor.

### Deleting with the Block Command

The Block command together with the Backspace or Delete key can be used to delete specific amounts of text. To delete blocked text, complete the following steps:

1. Move the cursor to the beginning of text to be deleted, then access the Block command with Alt + F4 or F12. 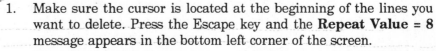 *toggle key*
   **M** *Click on Edit, then Block.*

2. Move the cursor to the end of the text to be deleted.

3. Press the Backspace or Delete key.

4. At the **Delete Block** question, key in a **Y** for Yes.

When you answer Yes at the Delete Block question, the blocked text is deleted and the Block command is turned off.

If you turn on the Block command and then decide you want to turn it off, press Alt + F4 or F12 again (**M** *Click on Edit, then Block*). The Cancel key, F1, will also turn off the Block command.

## AUTOMATIC ADJUST FEATURE

As you move around a document making changes, you will notice the text automatically adjusting itself. If you delete several words in a line, the text to the right of the line moves in to fill in the gap. This leaves you with blank spaces at the right of the line. By pressing the up or down arrow key, the text will automatically adjust itself to the left and right margins.

Later in this book you will learn how to adjust your text to make hyphenation decisions. Until then, WordPerfect is wrapping the words to the next line and not asking you to hyphenate.

## SPLITTING AND MERGING PARAGRAPHS

With insertion and deletion commands paragraphs can be easily split or merged. To split a large paragraph into two smaller paragraphs, place the cursor on the first letter where the new paragraph is to begin and press Enter twice. The first Enter takes the text to the next line. The second Enter inserts a blank line between the paragraphs.

To merge two paragraphs into one, you need to delete the spaces between them. There are a few methods for doing this. One is to place the cursor on the first character of the second paragraph and press the Backspace key until the paragraphs merge. Another method is to place the cursor two spaces past the period at the end of the first paragraph and press the Delete key until the paragraphs merge. When you merge the two paragraphs, the new paragraph will be automatically adjusted.

## CANCEL KEY

You may find that you occasionally strike the wrong function key or command. Or you may think you want to complete a function and then change your mind in the middle of the process. These situations are easily remedied by using the Cancel key, F1.

In addition to canceling a command, this key can also be used to restore deleted text. WordPerfect retains in memory the last three deletions made in one editing session. If you decide you want to restore text, move the cursor to the position where you want text inserted and press F1. The **Undelete 1 Restore; 2 Show Previous Deletion: 0** message appears at the bottom of the screen. Directly above this message will be the text last deleted in reverse video. You have two choices: Restore the text by pressing 1 or R for Restore, or have WordPerfect display the other two deletions in memory by pressing 2 or S for Show Previous Deletion.

## PRINTING YOUR DOCUMENT

The computer exercises you will be completing require that you make a hard copy of the document. Remember that soft copy is a document displayed on the screen and hard copy is a document printed on paper.

There are several ways to print a document. For now, you will learn to print from the directory. In a later chapter, other methods for printing will be introduced.

After saving a document, complete the following steps to print the document on paper:

1. Turn the printer on. (Ask your instructor for specific information about your printer.)

2. With the WordPerfect program loaded, press F5 (**M** *Click on File, then List Files*), then Enter to bring a list of your documents to the screen.

3. Move the cursor (remember that it appears as a solid bar) until it rests on the document you want to print.

4. From the prompts displayed at the bottom of the screen, choose 4 or P for Print to indicate that you want to print.

5. At the **Page(s): All** prompt, press Enter. (You will learn how to print specific pages in a later chapter.)

6. When printing is complete, you may exit WordPerfect or continue working with documents.

As you key in the information on the screen, you will notice that the left margin is even but the right margin appears jagged. However, when you print a document, it will have an even, or justified, right margin. A WordPerfect default is that documents will print with the left and right margins justified. (In a later chapter, you will learn how to change margin justification.)

## HELP KEY

WordPerfect offers a feature that lets you learn about the different functions of the program. This feature is an on-screen reference manual containing information on all WordPerfect commands.

The on-screen reference manual can be used to augment information you already have about a particular function or it can be used to learn a new function. The on-screen reference manual is accessed with the Help key, F3 (**M** *Click on Help, then Help*). When you access Help, the document in which you are working is removed from the screen and is replaced by the screen shown in figure 2-2.

```
Help              License #:  WP510381773          WP 5.1   11/06/89


     Press any letter to get an alphabetical list of features.

          The list will include the features that start with that letter,
          along with the name of the key where the feature is found.  You
          can then press that key to get a description of how the feature
          works.


     Press any function key to get information about the use of the key.

          Some keys may let you choose from a menu to get more information
          about various options.  Press HELP again to display the template.











     Selection: 0                             (Press ENTER to exit Help)
```

**Figure 2-2: Help Screen**


You have four choices with this menu. You can press any alphabetic key
and WordPerfect will display features that begin with that letter. You can
press a function key and WordPerfect will display information about that
particular function. You can press the Help key, F3, again to display the
WordPerfect template. Or you can press Enter to exit Help and return to
your document.

If you want more information about the Insert key, press Insert and the
information shown in figure 2-3 will appear on the screen.


```
Insert/Typeover

     Switches between insert mode and typeover mode.  (WP starts in insert
     mode.)

     Insert mode: Characters are inserted at the location of the cursor.
          Existing characters are pushed to the right to make room for new
          ones.

     Typeover mode: Replaces existing characters.  However, you cannot type
          over function codes while in this mode.  If you come to a function
          code, it will be pushed to the right, along with any text following
          it, to make room for the new characters.  The tab key will move the
          cursor and not insert a tab.  The backspace key will replace the
          character to the left with a space.







     Selection: 0                             (Press ENTER to exit Help)
```

**Figure 2-3: Insert/Typeover Help Screen**

To learn more about features or commands, press the appropriate key and WordPerfect will display information about that function. When you are through with Help, press either the space bar or the Enter key to exit the program.

The Help feature is context-sensitive. WordPerfect will provide screen information on any function or command in which you are currently working. For example, if you have a menu displayed and press F3 (M *Click on Help, then Help*), information about that menu will appear on the screen.

At the end of this chapter you will complete an exercise that requires you to use the Help key and learn more about particular functions. Although you will not be required to use the Help key in future exercises, feel free to use it whenever you want to as you work through this text. It is a useful source of information.

## CHAPTER REVIEW

### Summary

- The cursor movement keys are used to move the cursor throughout the document without interfering with text.
- The cursor can be moved by character, word, screen, or page and from beginning to end of a document.
- Many WordPerfect keys are toggle keys. You use the same key to turn a toggle function on and off.
- The WordPerfect default is for insert to be on. Insert can be turned on and off with the Insert key. When insert has been turned off, the message **Typeover** appears in the bottom left corner of the screen.
- Text can be deleted by character, word, line, several lines, and partial page.
- If changes are made to a document, WordPerfect automatically adjusts text to the margin settings.
- Paragraphs can be split or merged by using the Enter key or Deletion commands.
- Functions can be ended or discontinued with the Cancel key, F1. The Cancel key can also be used to restore previous deletions. WordPerfect keeps the last three deletions in memory.
- The directory provides one method for printing a document. By default, WordPerfect prints documents with a justified right margin. On the screen, however, text will appear unjustified at the right margin.

### Cursor Movement Review

| | |
|---|---|
| Arrow keys | Move cursor in the direction indicated |
| Ctrl + right arrow | Move cursor one word right |
| Ctrl + left arrow | Move cursor one word left |
| End | Move cursor to end of line |
| Home, up arrow | Move cursor to top of screen |
| Home, down arrow | Move cursor to bottom of screen |

## Cursor Movement Review

| | |
|---|---|
| Home, right arrow | Move cursor to end of line |
| Home, left arrow | Move cursor to beginning of line |
| Page Up | Move cursor to beginning of previous page |
| Page Down | Move cursor to beginning of next page |
| Home, Home, up arrow | Move cursor to beginning of document |
| Home, Home, down arrow | Move cursor to end of document |
| Home, Home, Home, up arrow | Move cursor to beginning of document and before any format codes |
| Ctrl + Home, #, Enter | Move cursor to a specific page in document |

## Deletion Commands Review

| | |
|---|---|
| Backspace | Delete character left of cursor |
| Delete key | Delete character under which cursor is located |
| Ctrl + Backspace | Delete word (including punctuation) |
| Home, Backspace | Delete word from cursor to beginning |
| Home, Delete | Delete word from cursor to end |
| Ctrl + End | Delete to the end of line |
| Escape, #, Ctrl + End | Delete x number of lines beginning at cursor position (you determine number) |
| Ctrl + Page Down | Delete text from cursor to end of page |

## Commands Review

| | Keyboard | Mouse |
|---|---|---|
| Help | F3 | Help, Help |
| Block command | Alt + F4 or F12 | Edit, Block |
| List | F5 | File, List Files |

## STUDY GUIDE FOR CHAPTER 2

Match the terms or functions with the correct definition by writing the letter of the term in the space next to the definition.

A. Insert key
B. Arrow keys
C. Escape key
D. Delete key
E. Ctrl + End
F. Alt + F4 or F12
G. Ctrl + left arrow
H. End key
I. Backspace key

J. Home, down arrow
K. Page Down key
L. Home, up arrow
M. Home, Backspace
N. Ctrl + Backspace
O. Ctrl + right arrow
P. Page Up key
Q. Home, left arrow
R. Home, Delete

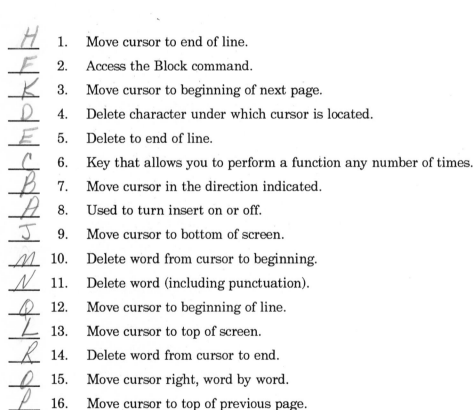

H  1. Move cursor to end of line.

E  2. Access the Block command.

K  3. Move cursor to beginning of next page.

D  4. Delete character under which cursor is located.

E  5. Delete to end of line.

C  6. Key that allows you to perform a function any number of times.

B  7. Move cursor in the direction indicated.

A  8. Used to turn insert on or off.

J  9. Move cursor to bottom of screen.

M  10. Delete word from cursor to beginning.

N  11. Delete word (including punctuation).

Q  12. Move cursor to beginning of line.

L  13. Move cursor to top of screen.

R  14. Delete word from cursor to end.

O  15. Move cursor right, word by word.

P  16. Move cursor to top of previous page.

**True/False:** Circle the letter T if the statement is true; circle the letter F if the statement is false.

1.   You can use the Delete or Backspace key to delete text.                              (T)    F

2.   The cursor movement keys lets you move through your document        (T)    F
     without deleting text.

3.   The WordPerfect default is for Insert to be in the off mode.                T    (F)

4.   As you make changes to your document, WordPerfect automatically       (T)    F
     adjusts the text to the left and right margins.

5.   You can split a paragraph in two by pressing the Enter key twice.        (T)    F

6.   Insert is always off when editing documents.                                    T    (F)

7.   The Backspace key deletes the character to the right of the cursor.      T    (F)

## PROOFREADERS' MARKS

In two of the exercises in this chapter, you will be required to edit documents that contain proofreaders' marks. Proofreaders' marks are listed and described in Appendix C.

## HANDS-ON EXERCISES

### Exercise One

1.   Load WordPerfect.

2.   At a clear screen, key in the text in figure 2-4.

3.   As you enter text, use the cursor movement, and insert/delete functions to correct errors.

4.   When the text is entered, complete the following steps to practice cursor movement:

     A. Move the cursor to the top of the screen by pressing Home, up arrow.

     B. Move the cursor character by character with the right arrow until it reaches the end of the line. (Remember, this is a continuous-action key if you hold it down.)

     C. Move the cursor word by word with Ctrl + right arrow until it is located at the end of the first paragraph.

     D. Move back through the first paragraph word by word (Ctrl + left arrow) until the cursor is located at the beginning of the first paragraph.

     E. Move the cursor to the end of the line by pressing Home, right arrow.

     F. Move the cursor to the last line of your text by pressing Home, down arrow.

     G. Move the cursor to the beginning of the document with Home, Home, up arrow. Move it to the end with Home, Home, down arrow.

5.   Save your document on the disk by following the instructions in chapter 1. Name the document CH02EX1.

6.   Print CH02EX1 following the instructions in this chapter. Remember, your hard copy will print with the right margin justified.

The WordPerfect Corporation, situated in Orem, Utah, was founded by
two men, Alan Ashton and Bruce Bastian.  In 1976, Bruce Bastian, a
student at Brigham Young University and leader of the marching
band, met Alan Ashton, a trumpet player and science professor at
the university.   They shared mutual interests in music and
computers.

In 1978, Ashton and Bastian formed a company they named Satellite
Systems, Inc.  Like many young companies, it did not do well at
first, and Bastian went to work for another company. While working
at the other company, he designed a word processing program to be
operated on minicomputers.

---

**Figure 2-4: Exercise One**

**Exercise Two**

1. Retrieve CH02EX1 to the screen.
2. Make the corrections as indicated by the proofreaders' marks in figure 2-5.
3. Save your document on the disk. Name the document CH02EX2.
4. Print CH02EX2.

---

The WordPerfect Corporation, situated in Orem, Utah, was founded by
two men, Alan Ashton and Bruce Bastian.  In 1976, Bruce Bastian, a
student at Brigham Young University and leader of the marching
band, met Alan Ashton, a trumpet player and science professor at
the university.   They shared *discovered* mutual interests in music and
computers.

In 1978, Ashton and Bastian formed a *new* company they named Satellite *the company*
Systems, Inc.  Like many young companies, it did not do well at
first, and Bastian went to work for another company.  While working
at the other company, *then* he designed a word processing program to be
operated on minicomputers. *which*

---

**Figure 2-5: Exercise Two**

**Exercise Three**

1. Key in the text in figure 2-6. Correct any errors.
2. Save the document on the disk and name it CH02EX3.
3. Print CH02EX3.

After working for a different company for less than a year, Bruce
Bastian and Alan Ashton get together again and complete a word
processing program they named SSI*WP.  The program was written to
operate on Data General Equipment.

In 1979, Ashton and Bastian named their company Satellite Software,
Inc., and began marketing their word processing program, SSI*WP.

In the early 1980s, IBM began marketing a personal computer.
Ashton and Bastian saw this as an opportunity to market their word
processing program.  In 1982, they rewrote their SSI*WP program to
operate on a personal computer and named the new program
WordPerfect.

**Figure 2-6: Exercise Three**

**Exercise Four**
   1.   Retrieve CH02EX3 to the screen.
   2.   Make the changes as indicated by the proofreaders' marks in figure 2-7.
   3.   Save this document on the disk and name it CH02EX4.
   4.   Print CH02EX4.

After working at the other for a different company for less than a year, Bruce
Bastian and Alan Ashton get together again and completed a word
processing program they named SSI*WP.  The program was written to
operate on Data General Equipment.  ^SSI*WP

no ¶ In 1979, Ashton and Bastian named their company Satellite Software,
Inc., and began marketing their word processing program, SSI*WP.

In the early 1980s, IBM began marketing a personal ^micro computer.
Ashton and Bastian saw this as an opportunity to market their word
processing program.  In 1982, they rewrote their SSI*WP program to
operate on a personal ^micro computer, and named the new program
WordPerfect.  They

**Figure 2-7: Exercise Four**

**Exercise Five**
   1.   Press the Help key, F3.
        **M** *Click on Help, then Help.*
   2.   Press the Insert key and read the information about insert and typeover.
   3.   Press the Delete key and read the information displayed on the screen.
   4.   Press the Backspace key and read the information.

5. Press Ctrl + End and read the information about the Delete-to-End-of-Line command.
6. Press Enter to exit Help.

## PERFORMANCE ASSESSMENTS

**Assessment One**
1. At a clear screen, key in the handwritten text in figure 2-8.
2. Save the document and name it CH02PA1.
3. Print CH02PA1.

---

When Ashton and Bastian were writing the word processing program SSI*WP to operate on micro-computers, they enlisted the help of the secretaries for the City of Orem. The secretaries provided constant input on WordPerfect as it was being written. This user input helped make WordPerfect a powerful and logical word processing program.

By 1983, WordPerfect nudges ahead of WordStar in sales. Up to that year, WordStar had been the leading word processing software program for microcomputers.

In 1986, Ashton and Bastian officially change the name of their company to WordPerfect Corporation. A company that began with just two people, now employs over a thousand.

---

**Figure 2-8: Assessment One**

**Assessment Two**
1.   Retrieve CH02PA1 to the screen.
2.   Make the changes indicated by the proofreaders' marks in figure 2-9.
3.   Save the document and name it CH02PA2. Print CH02PA2.

*While*
~~when~~ Ashton and Bastian were writing the ~~word~~ ~~processing~~ program SSI*WP to operate on micro-computers, they enlisted the help of the secretaries for the City of Orem. The secretaries provided constant input on WordPerfect as it was being written. This user input helped make WordPerfect a powerful and ~~logical~~ word processing program.
*well-constructed*

By 1983, WordPerfect nudges ahead of WordStar in sales. Up to that year, WordStar had been the leading word processing software program for microcomputers.

In 1986, Ashton and Bastian officially change the name of their company to WordPerfect Corporation. A company that began with just two people, now employs over a thousand. In the late 1980s, WordPerfect Corporation moved into the international market.

**Figure 2-9: Assessment Two**

# CHAPTER 3

## CHARACTER FORMATTING

## *PERFORMANCE OBJECTIVES*

Upon successful completion of chapter 3, you will be able to enhance single-page business letters and reports with basic character formatting features.

### FUNCTION KEYS

As you work with WordPerfect, you will learn many functions and commands. WordPerfect has more than 300 commands, most of which are performed by the functions keys located at the left or top of the keyboard. The function keys have four levels:

1. Function key (alone)
2. Alt + function key
3. Shift + function key
4. Control + function key

The template fits around or above the function keys and identifies the function key commands.

Some of the function keys can be used to apply special formatting to characters. In this chapter you will learn how to apply underlining, boldfacing, and centering formatting to text and to key in text in capital (uppercase) letters.

### UNDERLINING

Underlining text with a typewriter is a simple procedure—type the text, backspace to the beginning of the text to be underlined, and type in the underline symbol. This same procedure does not work with WordPerfect. If you key in text to be underlined, move the cursor to the beginning of text and key in the underline symbol, the text will be moved forward to the right (insert mode) or erased (typeover mode).

The F8 function key is used to underline text with WordPerfect. Press F8 before and after text to be underlined. For example, to underline the word *immediately*, complete the following steps:

1.   Press the F8 function key once.
2.   Key in **immediately**.
     Ⓜ *Click on Font, Appearance, then Underline.*
3.   Press the F8 function key again.

*F8*
*Underline*

The F8 function key that has two conditions—on and off. The first time you press F8, the underline function is activated. When you press F8 again, it is turned off. The text you key in after pressing F8 appears on the screen either underlined or in a different color, depending on the monitor, for easy identification. Also, when the underlining feature is on, the number after **Pos** in the status line appears underlined or in a different color.

You can identify the text to be underlined because it appears differently on the screen. What is not visible are the special embedded codes. To display the underline codes, access Reveal Codes. Reveal Codes is a useful feature that lets you see format changes made to a document. To display the Reveal Codes screen, press Alt + F3 or F11 (Ⓜ *Click on Edit, then Reveal Codes*). In Reveal Codes, the ruler line is inserted approximately 11 lines from the top of the screen. The screen displays eleven lines of text above the cursor and the same eleven lines of text below. The text above the ruler line appears normally. The text below is the same as above, except special codes have been added. Figure 3-1 shows an example of a document in Reveal Codes:

*F11*
*Reveal*
*codes*

*also*

```
 WordPerfect contains a wide variety of features and functions
 that make it one of the most powerful word processing programs.
 WordPerfect includes basic features such as word wrap, typeover,
 and line and page formatting, as well as more advanced features
 such as macros, styles, and tables.




 A:\3-1                                          Doc 1 Pg 1 Ln 2" Pos 1"
{     ▲     ▲     ▲     ▲     ▲     ▲     ▲     ▲     ▲     }     ▲     ▲
 WordPerfect contains a wide variety of features and functions[SRt]
 that make it one of the [UND]most powerful[und] word processing programs.[SRt]
 WordPerfect includes basic features such as word wrap, typeover,[SRt]
 and line and page formatting, as well as more advanced features[SRt]
 such as macros, styles, and tables.[HRt]




 Press Reveal Codes to restore screen
```

**Figure 3-1: Reveal Codes Document**

The cursor appears above the ruler line as usual (a blinking underline). Below the ruler line the cursor displays as a rectangle. The cursor can be moved through text and codes with the cursor movement commands. Codes and text can be deleted with the Backspace key or the Delete key. The Backspace key deletes the character or code to the left of the cursor. The

Delete key deletes the character on which the cursor is located. When the cursor is moved to a code, it expands to the entire code. For this reason, press the Delete key just once to delete the entire code.

Special codes appear in Reveal Codes that identify functions and commands. At the end of lines you may notice the code **[SRt]**. This code indicates a soft return, which is an end of line created by word wrap. Another symbol, **[HRt]**, identifies a hard return and indicates that the Enter key has been pressed.

In Reveal Codes the code **[UND]** identifies the beginning of underlined text and the code **[und]** identifies the end. The underlined word, *immediately*, looks like this in Reveal Codes:

```
[UND]immediately[und]
```

If, after underlining, you change your mind, access Reveal Codes and delete one of the underlining codes. Underlining codes are paired codes: If one code is deleted, the other is also removed.

## BOLDFACING

Boldfacing is a feature that allows you to emphasize or accentuate words and enhance the printed document. When text is boldfaced, it is printed darker than surrounding text.

Boldfacing with WordPerfect is accomplished in the same manner as underlining. To identify text to be boldfaced, press the F6 function key, key in the text, then press F6 to turn off boldfacing. The text that is to print boldfaced will appear brighter than other text on the screen or it will appear in a different color. The position number in the status line will also appear brighter or in a different color.

For example, to boldface the words *exciting and challenging*, complete the following steps:

1. Press the F6 function key once.
   **M** *Click on Font, Appearance, then Bold.*
2. Key in **exciting and challenging**.
3. Press the F6 function key again.

In Reveal Codes, the code **[BOLD]** identifies the beginning of boldfacing and the code **[bold]** identifies the end. The boldfaced words *exciting and challenging* look like this in Reveal Codes:

```
[BOLD]exciting and challenging[bold]
```

To remove boldfacing, access Reveal Codes and delete one of the boldfacing codes.

## CENTERING

Text can be centered between the left and right margins with the Center command, Shift + F6 (**M** *Click on Layout, Align, then Center*). When you access the Center command, the cursor automatically moves to the center of the screen. Text moves left one space for every two characters keyed in. If you make a mistake while keying text, backspace and rekey it. This will not interfere with the centering process. For example, to center the heading FORMATTING COMMANDS, complete the following steps:

1. Access the Center command with Shift + F6.
   **M** *Click on Layout, Align, then Center.*
2. Key in **FORMATTING COMMANDS**.
3. Press Enter.

When you press Enter at the end of the text, the centering feature is deactivated. The next line you key in will begin at the left margin as usual. If you want the next line centered, access the Center command.

In Reveal Codes, the code **[Center]** identifies the beginning of centered text and the **[HRT]** code identifies the end. The centered heading FOR-MATTING COMMANDS looks like this in Reveal Codes:

```
[Center]FORMATTING COMMANDS[HRt]
```

### Centering at a Specific Location

The center feature can also be used to center text around a specific location on the line. To center at a specific location, move the cursor to the location on the line you want text centered, access the Center command with Shift + F6 (**M** *Click on Layout, Align, then Center*), and key in the text.

## ALL CAPS

To key in text in all uppercase letters, press the Caps Lock key. Caps Lock is a toggle key. Press the key once to activate the caps lock function; press it again to turn it off. If you are not sure whether it is on or off, you can tell by looking at the status line.

The status line appears in the bottom right corner of the screen when you are working in a document. If the cursor is located at the beginning of a document, the status line will look like this:

```
Doc 1 Pg 1 Ln 1"      Pos 1"
```

Usually the **Pos** (for position) displays with the letter **P** in uppercase and the **o** and **s** in lowercase. When Caps Lock is activated, the **Pos** changes to **POS**.

## CREATING PRINT FEATURES WITH EXISTING TEXT

So far you have learned how to boldface, underline, center, and capitalize text as it is being entered. If you decide after you have keyed the document that you want one of these special features applied to the text, you must use a different procedure.

Underlining, boldfacing, or capitalizing existing text requires the use of the Block command. Centering existing text can be accomplished with the Block command or with another method.

### Underlining, Boldfacing, and Centering

To underline, boldface, or center text already displayed on the screen, position the cursor on the first character of the text to be underlined, boldfaced, or centered, and access the Block command, Alt + F4 or F12 (**M** *Click on Edit, then Block*). The blinking message **Block on** appears in the bottom left corner of the screen. Identify text to be included in the block by moving the cursor with the cursor movement keys. If you want just one word blocked, move the cursor until it is positioned one character past the word. As the cursor moves, you will notice that the affected text is highlighted or displayed in a different color.

After you have moved the cursor to include all the text, press the underline key, F8, the boldface key, F6, or the Center command, Shift + F6 (**M** *Click on Layout, Align, Center*). This turns the special feature on and turns off the Block command. If you press the Center command, the message **[Just: Center]**? <u>N</u>o (Yes) displays at the bottom of the screen. To center, key in a **Y** for yes.

The same text can be boldfaced, underlined, and centered. You must, however, complete three separate block functions. For example, to boldface, underline, and center the heading NEWSLETTER, complete the following steps:

1. At a clear screen, key in the word NEWSLETTER, then press Enter.
2. Move the cursor to the beginning of the word (the N in NEWSLETTER).
3. Access the Block command with Alt + F4 or F12.
   **M** *Click on Edit, then Block.*
4. Press the down arrow key once to move the cursor below the word and block it.
5. Press F6 to turn on boldfacing. (This also turns off the Block command.)
   **M** *Click on Font, Appearance, then Bold.*
6. Move the cursor to the N in NEWSLETTER and access the Block command with Alt + F4 or F12.
   **M** *Click on Edit, then Block.*
7. Press the down arrow key once to block the word.
8. Press F8 to turn on underlining.
   **M** *Click on Font, Appearance, then Underline.*
9. Move the cursor to the N in NEWSLETTER and access the Center command with Shift + F6.
   **M** *Click on Layout, Align, then Center.*
10. Press the down arrow key once.

The other method for centering existing text requires that the line including text to be centered ends in a hard return. Move the cursor to the beginning of the line, press Shift + F6 and then press the down arrow key. When you access the Center command (**M** *Click on Layout, Align, Center*), the text moves to the middle of the screen but is slightly off center. When the down arrow key is pressed, the text is centered between the left and right margins.

## CHANGING TO ALL UPPERCASE OR LOWERCASE

To change previously keyed text into either all uppercase or lowercase letters, the text must first be blocked. Access the Block command with Alt + F4 or F12 (**M** *Click on Edit, then Block*), move the cursor to highlight the block, then access the Switch command with Shift + F3. When you access the Switch command, the following message appears at the bottom of the screen:

1 <u>U</u>ppercase; 2 <u>L</u>owercase: <u>0</u>

If you want to change to all uppercase, choose 1 or U for Uppercase. If you want all lowercase, choose 2 or L for Lowercase. When switching from uppercase to lowercase, all letters (expect the first word in a sentence) will become lowercase. WordPerfect cannot distinguish proper names. To change the case of blocked text with the mouse, complete the following steps:

**M**  1.  *Block the text to be converted.*
      2.  *Click on Edit, then Convert Case.*
      3.  *Click on To Upper to convert to uppercase, or click on To Lower to convert to lowercase.*

## CHAPTER REVIEW

### Summary

- Use the F8 function key to underline text. Press F8 to turn on underlining, key in text, then press F8 to turn off underlining. Text to be underlined appears in reverse video or a different color on the screen. (**M** *Click on Font, Appearance, then Underline*).

- Press the F6 function key before and after text to be boldfaced. Boldfaced text appears brighter or in a different color on the screen. (**M** *Click on Font, Appearance, then Bold*).

- To center text, press Shift + F6 (**M** *Click on Layout, Align, then Center*), key in the text, then press Enter.

- When text has been boldfaced, underlined, or centered, special symbols are embedded in the document. These symbols can be viewed in Reveal Codes.

- To key in text in all uppercase letters, press the Caps Lock key. When Caps Lock is activated, the **Pos** in the status line changes to **POS**.

- To underline, boldface, or center existing text, use the Block command. Turn on the Block command with Alt + F4 or F12 (**M** *Click on Edit, then Block*), highlight text and press either F8 to underline, F6 to boldface, or Shift + F6 (**M** *Click on Layout, Align, then Center*) to center.

- To change text to all uppercase or lowercase letters, block the text and access the Switch command with Shift + F3. Choose 1 or U for Uppercase or 2 or L for lowercase. (**M** *Block the text to be converted, and click on Edit, then Convert Case. Click on To Upper to convert to uppercase, or click on To Lower to convert to lowercase.*)

- To center existing text, make sure the line ends in a hard return, press Shift + F6 (**M** *Click on Layout, Align, then Center*), and then press the down arrow.

## Commands Review

|                      | Keyboard          | Mouse                          |
|----------------------|-------------------|--------------------------------|
| Boldface key         | F6                | Font, Appearance, Bold         |
| Underline key        | F8                | Font, Appearance, Underline    |
| Center command       | Shift + F6        | Layout, Align, Center          |
| Uppercase function   | Caps Lock key     |                                |
| Block command        | Alt + F4, or F12  | Edit, Block                    |
| Reveal Codes function| Alt + F3, or F11  | Edit, Reveal Codes             |

## Codes Review

| Beginning of underlined text | [UND]    |
|------------------------------|----------|
| End of underlined text       | [und]    |
| Beginning of boldfaced text  | [BOLD]   |
| End of boldfaced text        | [bold]   |
| Beginning of centered text   | [Center] |
| End of centered text         | [HRt]    |

## STUDY GUIDE FOR CHAPTER 3

Write the letter next to the correct term or function that matches the definition.

A.  Shift + F6
    **M** *Layout, Align, then Center*

E.  **[Center]**

I.  F8

B.  Caps Lock key

F.  Alt + F3, or F11

J.  **[bold]**

C.  **[UND]**

G.  **[BOLD]**

K.  Alt + F4 or F12
    **M** *Edit, then Block*

D.  F6

H.  **[und]**

L.  **[HRt]**

____  1.  In Reveal Codes, identifies the beginning of underlined text.

____  2.  Accesses Reveal Codes.

____  3.  In Reveal Codes, identifies the end of boldfaced text.

____  4.  Center command.

____  5.  In Reveal Codes, identifies beginning of centered text.

____  6.  Block command.

____  7.  In Reveal Codes, identifies the end of underlined text.

____  8.  Activates uppercase function.

____  9.  In Reveal Codes, identifies the end of centered text.

____  10.  Boldface key.

____  11.  In Reveal Codes, identifies the beginning of boldfaced text.

____  12.  Underline key.

**True/False:** Circle the letter T if the statement is true; circle the letter F if the statement is false.

1.  The **Pos** message on the status line appears in all capital letters when Caps Lock is on.                                                    T     F

2.  You can delete underlining or boldfacing in Reveal Codes.                        T     F

3.  When you press the Enter key at the end of text, the centering feature is deactivated.                                                            T     F

4.  The same text cannot be underlined and boldfaced.                                T     F

5.  Before boldfacing existing text, the text must first be blocked.                T     F

## HANDS-ON EXERCISES

*Note*: In some of the exercises in this and other chapters, you will be required to create a business letter. Refer to Appendix D for the proper format for two types of business letters.

The date in a business letter is keyed in somewhere between 2 and 2 1/2 inches from the top of the page. When a document is printed, WordPerfect automatically leaves a 1-inch margin. (You will learn how to change this setting in a later chapter.) In the following exercises, press the Enter key six times before keying in the date. This will cause the cursor to move to Line 2 inches and print the date 2 inches from the top of the page.

At the end of a letter, the initials of the person keying in the letter are inserted. In this text, the initials appear in the exercises as "xx." Key in your own initials in lowercase letters where you see the "xx."

Identifying document names in correspondence is a good idea because it lets you retrieve the document quickly and easily at a future date. In this textbook, the document name is identified after the reference initials.

### Exercise One

1.  At a clear screen, press Enter six times to move the cursor to Line 2 inches.
2.  Key in the letter displayed in figure 3-2. Boldface and underline the text as indicated. Press the tab key to indent before keying in the types of printers and underline as indicated.
3.  Save the letter and name it CH03EX1. Print CH03EX1.

### Exercise Two

1.  At a clear screen, press Enter six times to move the cursor to Line 2 inches.
2.  Key in the letter displayed in figure 3-3. Use the Center command to center the names of the integrated programs.
3.  Save the letter and name it CH03EX2. Print CH03EX2.

### Exercise Three

1.  Retrieve CH03EX2 to the screen.
2.  Block the names of the integrated programs and boldface them by completing the following steps:
    A.  Move the cursor to the P in Powerhouse.
    B.  Turn on the Block command with Alt + F4 or F12.
        **M** *Click on Edit, then Block.*
    C.  Move the cursor to the blank line below Super Planner.
    D.  Press F6 to apply boldfacing to the blocked text and turn off the Block command.
        **M** *Click on Font, Appearance, then Bold.*
3.  Save the letter and name it CH03EX3. Print CH03EX3.

September 27, 1992



Ms. Jackie Hazelton
238 Sunset Avenue
Spokane, WA  99302

Dear Ms. Hazelton:

Our company received your letter requesting information on types of
printers.  Omega Tech is available to assist in the purchasing of
computer equipment.  There are three main types of printers:

> **Dot matrix**
> **Letter quality**
> **Laser**

Each category of printer has its own special characteristics.
There are many brands in each category.  Prices range from under
$100 to over $5,000.

Dot matrix printers are at the lower end of the price scale.  Some
have two print modes: draft and letter quality.  Draft prints at
speeds of 50 characters per second (cps) to over 300 cps.  The
higher the quality, the slower the speed.

Letter quality printers, sometimes referred to as daisy wheel
printers, are slower than dot matrix printers.  Generally, the
faster the speed, the more expensive the printer.

Laser printers are the most expensive of the three and also the
fastest.  The print quality of laser printers is very high and they
are also quiet.

For further information, please stop by our store and we can
demonstrate a variety of printers.

Sincerely,



Devon McKenna
Manager

xx:CH03EX1

Figure 3-2: Exercise One

September 29, 1992


Mr. Elliot Lehmen
12204 South 152nd Street
Spokane, WA 99302

Dear Mr. Lehmen:

Our company received your letter requesting information on integrated software programs. Integrated software has become very popular with owners of personal computers. Many businesses use integrated programs and consider them to be excellent management tools. Many new programs are available today and include the following:

Powerhouse
Manager Plus
ExecPlan
Timesaver
Enhancer
Integrator
Super Planner

If you would like a demonstration of the programs, please stop by our store at your convenience.

Sincerely,



Harold Vonstein
Assistant Manager

xx:CH03EX2

---

Figure 3-3: Exercise Two

**Exercise Four**
1.  Retrieve CH03EX2 to the screen.
2.  Block the names of the integrated programs and change them to all uppercase letters by completing the following steps:
    A. Move the cursor to the P in Powerhouse.
    B. Turn on the Block command with Alt + F4 or F12.
       **M** *Click on Edit, then Block.*
    C. Move the cursor to the blank line below Super Planner.

     D. Access the Switch command with Shift + F3. From the prompt that displays at the bottom of the screen, choose 1 or U for Uppercase.
       **M** *Click on Edit, Convert Case, then To Upper.*

3.   Save the letter and name it CH03EX4. Print CH03EX4.

## Exercise Five

1.   Retrieve CH03EX2 to the screen.
2.   Move the cursor to the beginning of the integrated program names and access Reveal Codes. Delete the **[Center]** code before each program name.
3.   Block the program names and underline them.
4.   Save the letter and name it CH03EX5. Print CH03EX5.

## PERFORMANCE ASSESSMENTS

## Assessment One

1.   At a clear screen, key in the report as shown in figure 3-4. Use the center, boldface, and Caps Lock key as shown in the figure.
2.   Save the report and name it CH03PA1.  Print CH03PA1.

## Assessment Two

1.   Retrieve CH03PA1 to the screen.
2.   Delete the boldfacing codes before the three headings What can Northwestern do for you?, How is Northwestern different from a commercial bank?, and What is the loan process?
3.   Block each heading and change the text to all uppercase letters.
4.   Save the report and name it CH03PA2. Print CH03PA2.

## NORTHWESTERN REVOLVING FUND

### What can Northwestern do for you?

Northwestern Revolving Fund is a nonprofit tax exempt organization that promotes community development by providing loans to a select group of borrowers. Northwestern concentrates on providing loan capital to geographic areas that are underserved by the banking industry, to businesses that are new or need small loans, and to organizations owned by or benefiting women, minorities, or low-income people.

### How is Northwestern different from a commercial bank?

The commercial banking industry has standards for determining small-business credit-worthiness. Many banks tend to rely primarily upon credit analysis for the basis of their loan decision. Unlike commercial banks, Northwestern is regulated as a registered security. By not being regulated as a commercial bank, Northwestern has been able to develop a more balanced approach to lending. Although Northwestern's approach includes credit analysis, it also incorporates a more thorough market and management review of the application.

### What is the loan process?

**Preapplication:** Your initial inquiry by phone or mail to Northwestern must include a description of your business and of yourself. Tell us what your business or project is about, how many dollars you need, what the loan proceeds will be used for, and available sources of collateral.

**Application form:** Northwestern will try to learn as much as possible about your business or project to tailor a loan package that will satisfy both you as the borrower and Northwestern as the lender. On the application form, we need information that includes three years of financial history, financial projections for the number of years a loan is requested, and market descriptions and your market strategies.

**Application assistance:** Northwestern provides general assistance in structuring the application proposal. However, for legal reasons, Northwestern cannot perform the detailed assistance that may be necessary. Therefore, we will arrange assistance at no charge for you from other organizations that specialize in small business consultation.

Figure 3-4: Assessment One

# CHAPTER 4

## LINE FORMATTING

## PERFORMANCE OBJECTIVES

Upon successful completion of chapter 4, you will be able to enhance single-page business memorandums and letters with basic character formatting features.

### FORMAT COMMAND

The Format command contains selections that affect the appearance of the document. To access the Format command, press Shift + F8 (**M** *Click on Layout*). When you access the Format command, the Format menu is displayed with four submenus — Line, Page, Document, and Other. One basic format change you may want to make to a document is to change the left and right margins.

### Margins on the Default Ruler Line

When you worked with documents in previous chapters, did you notice that the status line changed as the cursor moved across the screen? When you begin creating a document with WordPerfect, you are given a default ruler line that has a left margin of 1 inch and a right margin of 1 inch. When you get to the right margin, WordPerfect automatically wraps text down to the next line.

A standard piece of paper is 8 1/2 or 8.5 inches wide. WordPerfect leaves the first inch blank on the paper for the left margin and the last inch blank on the paper for the right margin. When you are keying in a document and the cursor reaches Position 7.5", any text keyed after this will wrap to the left margin. The default settings give you a 6 1/2-inch typing line.

### Changing Margins

Even though the default ruler line may be appropriate for many documents, there will be occasions when you need to shorten or lengthen margins. WordPerfect provides a command to do this.

To change the left and right margin settings, complete the following steps:

1. Access the Format command with Shift + F8.
2. Choose 1 or L for Line (**M** *Click on Layout then Line*) and the Format: Line menu is displayed as shown in figure 4.1

```
Format: Line

    1 - Hyphenation                          No

    2 - Hyphenation Zone - Left              10%
                          Right              4%

    3 - Justification                        Full

    4 - Line Height                          Auto

    5 - Line Numbering                       No

    6 - Line Spacing                         1

    7 - Margins - Left                       1"
                  Right                      1"

    8 - Tab Set                              Rel: -1", every 0.5"

    9 - Widow/Orphan Protection              No


Selection: 0
```

**Figure 4-1: Format: Line Menu**

3. At the Format: Line menu, choose 7 or M for Margins and the cursor moves to the 1" setting after Left.
4. Key in a new margin setting. Margin settings can be set by inches as well as tenths and hundredths of inches. For example, you can set a 2-inch left margin with 2; a 2 1/2-margin with 2.5; and a 2 7/8-inch margin with 2.88.
5. After keying in the new left margin setting, press Enter. This moves the cursor to the right margin setting. Key in the new right margin setting and press Enter.
6. Press F7 to return the cursor to the document.

If you change margins after entering text, you will find that the text automatically adjusts to the new settings from the position of the cursor to the end of the document or until another margin setting is encountered. If you change margins at the beginning of the second paragraph, all text from the second paragraph to the end of the document will adjust to the new settings. The first paragraph will remain at the original settings. This lets you have many different margin settings throughout a document.

## Reveal Codes

If margin settings have been changed, they will appear in Reveal Codes. If you change the left margin to 1.5 inches and the right to 1.5 inches, they will display as **[L/R Mar:1.5",1.5"]** in Reveal Codes.

If you want to delete the margin code, position the cursor on the code and press Delete. Or you can move the cursor to the right of the code and press the Backspace key. If you delete all margin codes, text will automatically readjust to the default settings of 1 inch.

### Ruler Line

In Reveal Codes, the ruler line appears as a bar across the screen. The left and right margins appear on the ruler line as brackets ([,]), and triangles indicate preset tab stops. WordPerfect automatically provides a tab stop every half inch. These tabs are part of the default ruler line. If the left or right margins are set in a position where there is a preset tab, the bracket is changed to a brace ({,}).

## MARGIN INDENTS

By now you are familiar with the word wrap feature of WordPerfect. This ends lines and wraps the cursor to the next line. If you want several lines of text to be inserted at the first tab stop, you must use the Indent key or the Indent command to get lines to wrap to a tab stop. The Indent key indents text from the left margin only, whereas the Indent command indents text from the left and right margins.

### Indent Key

To use the Indent Key, position the cursor at the left margin of the paragraph to be indented and press F4 (**M** *Click on Layout, Align, then Indent F4*). This causes the cursor to move to the first tab stop. As text is keyed in, it will wrap to the first tab stop rather than the left margin. The indent stays in effect until the Enter key is pressed. The F4 key (**M** *Click on Layout, Align, then Indent F4*) must be pressed again to turn Indent back on.

Text will be indented a tab stop each time the Indent key is pressed. Using the default ruler line, which contains tab stops every half inch, text can be indented 1 1/2 inches from the left margin by pressing F4 three times. The paragraph shown in figure 4-2 was created by completing the following steps:

---

```
1.    The Indent key, F4, can be used to create indented
      paragraphs. In this paragraph, the number 1 and the
      period were keyed in and then the Indent key, F4, was
      pressed. The Indent key causes the text to wrap to the
      first tab stop.
```

---

Figure 4-2: Indented Paragraph

1.  Position the cursor at the left margin.
2.  Key in **1** then the period.
3.  Press F4.
    **M** *Click on Layout, Align, then Indent F4.*
4.  Key in the paragraph.

## Indent Command

Shift + F4 is also an Indent command (**M** *Click on Layout, Align, then Indent Shift-F4*). With this command, text can be indented from the left and the right margins. For example, using the default ruler line, text can be indented a half inch from the left and right margins by accessing the Indent command once or indented 1 inch from each margin by accessing the Indent command twice. The paragraph shown in figure 4-3 was created by pressing Shift + F4 two times (**M** *Click on Layout, Align, then Indent Shift-F4 two times*).

```
The Indent command, Shift + F4, causes text to
wrap  to  a  tab  stop  rather  than  the  left
margin. Text will be indented from the left
margin  as  well  as  the  right  margin.
```

Figure 4-3: Paragraph Indented from Both Margins

When the Indent key or Indent command are used to indent text, additions and deletions can be made and the text will adjust correctly. If the Tab key is used to indent this type of text, the indention may wrap to the middle of a line when adjusting, causing extra spaces to appear in the middle of the line.

## Creating Hanging Paragraphs

WordPerfect includes a command to allow the left margin to be released temporarily. This is similar to the margin release key found on a typewriter. With margin release and the indent key, you can create hanging paragraphs. A hanging paragraph is one in which the first line begins at the left margin and the remaining lines are indented as shown in figure 4-4.

The hanging paragraph shown in figure 4-4 was created by completing the following steps:

1. Position the cursor at the left margin, then press F4.
   **M** *Click on Layout, Align, then Indent F4.*
2. Press Shift + Tab to release the left margin. This moves the cursor one tab stop left (in this case, the left margin).
   **M** *Click on Layout, Align, then Margin Rel.*
3. Key in the paragraph.

```
This  is  an  example  of  a  hanging  paragraph.  This  paragraph  was
      created  using  the  Indent  key,  F4,  and  the  margin  release
      command,  Shift + Tab.
```

Figure 4-4: Hanging Paragraph

## JUSTIFICATION

The WordPerfect default is to print documents with the left and right margins even, or justified (although the text appears ragged at the right margin on the screen). The justification of text in a paragraph can be changed with the Justification selection from the Format: Line menu. To change the justification of text in a paragraph complete the following steps:

1. Access the Format: Line menu with Shift + F8, then choose 1 or L for Line.
   **M** *Click on Layout, then Line.*

2. At the Format: Line menu, choose 3 or J for Justification and the prompt **Justification: 1 <u>L</u>eft; 2 <u>C</u>enter; 3 <u>R</u>ight; 4 <u>F</u>ull** appears at the bottom of the screen.

3. Make a selection from this prompt, then press F7.

At the Justification prompt, choose 1 or L for Left to justify text at the left margin but leave it uneven or ragged at the right margin. The following paragraph is left justified:

The Format menu contains a variety of selections that affect the appearance of the document. How a document looks when printed is called the format.

Choose 2 or C for Center to center each line in a paragraph between the left and right margins, which results in both the left and right margins being uneven or ragged. The following paragraph is center justified:

The Format menu contains a variety
of selections that affect the
appearance of the document. How a
document looks when printed is
called the format.

Choose 3 or R for Right to justify the right margin and leave the left margin ragged. The following paragraph is right justified:

The Format menu contains a variety
of selections that affect the
appearance of the document. How a
document looks when printed is
called the format.

The last selection, Full, is the default setting and justifies text at the left and right margins.

Changes in justification can be made throughout a document. When a change is made, a code is inserted in the document that can be seen in Reveal Codes. Changes made to justification affect text from the location of the code to the end of the document or until another justification code is encountered. Justification changes affect only the document in which you are working. If you save a document and begin a new one, justification reverts to the default setting of Full.

There are two methods for changing justification with the mouse. The first method, mentioned earlier, is to click on Layout, then Line to display the Format: Line menu. The other method is to click on Layout, then Justify. This inserts a submenu on the screen with the selections Left, Center, Right, and Full. Click on the justification desired.

## LINE SPACING

The WordPerfect documents you have created have been single spaced. The information keyed in was wrapped down to the next line unless you pressed the Enter key. There may be occasions when you may want to change to another spacing, such as double or triple spacing.

To change the spacing in a document, complete the following steps:

1. Access the Format: Line menu with Shift + F8, then choose 1 or L for Line.
   **M** *Click on Layout, then Line.*
2. Choose 6 or S for Line Spacing.
3. Key in the new line spacing setting and press Enter.
4. Press F7.

Line spacing can be set in whole numbers or decimal numbers. For example, you can enter numbers such as **1.5** for line and a half spacing, or **2.2** for two and two-tenths line spacing. You can enter up to five numbers after the decimal point. WordPerfect will, however, only use two numbers after the decimal point.

WordPerfect does not display text in partial lines. Instead, your text will display to the next whole number. For example, if you enter **1.5**, text will appear double spaced on the screen, If you enter **2.5**, text will appear triple spaced on the screen. Text will print properly, however, if your printer is capable of partial line spacing.

When changes are made to line spacing, a code is inserted in the document that can be seen in Reveal Codes. Line spacing codes can be deleted in Reveal Codes. If a line spacing code is deleted, WordPerfect reverts to the default setting of single spacing. Line spacing changes affect text from the location of the code to the end of the document or until another line spacing code is encountered.

## CHAPTER REVIEW

### Summary

- The function keys have four levels: They can be used alone or in conjunction with the Alt, Shift, and Ctrl keys.
- The WordPerfect default ruler line has a left and right margin of 1 inch.
- Change margins at the Format: Line menu. Text automatically adjusts to new margin settings. A document may contain several different margin settings. Margin settings are saved with a document.
- The Reveal Codes command displays format changes made to a document. Format codes can be deleted with either the Backspace key or the Delete key.

- The Indent key, F4 (**M** *Click on Layout, Align, then Indent F4*), wraps text to a tab stop. The Enter key ends the indent. Shift + F4 (**M** *Click on Layout, Align, then Indent Shift + F4*) indents text from the left and right margins. Shift + Tab (**M** *Click on Layout, Align, then Margin Rel*) releases the margin and moves the cursor to the first tab stop to the left of the left margin.
- The Justification selection from the Format: Line menu has a default setting of Full. At this setting, the left and right margins of text will print evenly. This setting can be changed to Left, Center, or Right.
- The Line Spacing selection from the Format: Line menu has a default setting of 1. At this setting, text is single spacing. This can be changed to a half or whole number. The WordPerfect screen will not display text in half lines; instead the text is displayed to the next whole number.

### Commands Review

|                     | **Keyboard**        | **Mouse**                         |
| ------------------- | ------------------- | --------------------------------- |
| Format: Line menu   | Shift + F8, 1 or L  | Layout, Line                      |
| Indent key          | F4                  | Layout, Align, Indent F4          |
| Indent command      | Shift + F4          | Layout, Align, Indent Shift - F4  |
| Margin Release      | Shift + Tab         | Layout, Align, Margin Rel         |

### Symbols Review

| [        | = Left margin setting            |
| -------- | -------------------------------- |
| ]        | = Right margin setting           |
| {        | = Left margin set on tab stop    |
| }        | = Right margin set on tab stop   |
| Triangle | = Tab stop                       |

## STUDY GUIDE FOR CHAPTER 4

Function keys have four levels. Which keys should you press to access each of the levels?

1. _____

2. _____

3. _____

4. _____

**Completion**: In the space provided at the right, indicate the correct symbol, term, or number for the explanation.

1.   Indicates the right margin on the ruler line.                              _____

2.   Indicates a preset tab stop.                                              _____

3.   Indicates the left margin on the ruler line.                              _____

4.   Indicates the right margin on a preset tab stop on the ruler              _____
     line.

5.   The default left margin setting.                                          _____

6.   The default right margin setting.                                         _____

7.   Accesses the Format command.                                             _____

8.   Name of the function key used to view special codes                       _____
     embedded in a document.

9.   Command to indent text from the left and right margins.                   _____

10.  Command to release the margin.                                           _____

**True/False**:  Circle the letter T if the statement is true; circle the letter F if the statement is false.

| | | | |
|---|---|---|---|
| 1. | Function keys have three levels. | T | F |
| 2. | Most of WordPerfect's commands are performed through the function keys. | T | F |
| 3. | By default, the line length is six inches. | T | F |
| 4. | A standard piece of paper is 8 1/2 inches wide. | T | F |
| 5. | The WordPerfect default ruler line has a tab stop every half inch. | T | F |
| 6. | Margin settings are saved with a document. | T | F |
| 7. | Margin settings can be deleted in Reveal Codes. | T | F |
| 8. | In Reveal Codes, this symbol **[SRt]** indicates that the Enter key has been pressed. | T | F |

9.   If margins are changed after text has been entered, text will automatically        T      F
     adjust from the position of the cursor to the end of the document.

10.  The Indent function wraps text to a tab stop.                                        T      F

11.  Shift + F4 indents text from the left margin only.                                   T      F

## HANDS-ON EXERCISES

*Note*: In some of the exercises in this and other chapters, you will be creating memorandums. Refer to Appendix E for the correct placement and spacing of memorandum.

### Exercise One

1.   At a clear screen, change the left and right margins to 1.5 inches by completing the follow-
     ing steps:
     A. Access the Format command with Shift + F8.
     B. From the Format menu, choose 1 or L for Line.
        **M** *Click on Layout, then Line.*
     C. At the Format: Line menu, choose 7 or M for Margins.
     D. Key in **1.5** and press Enter.
     E. Key in **1.5** and press Enter.
     F. Press F7.
2.   Key in the memorandum headings as shown in figure 4-5. Key in **DATE:** and press the Tab
     key once to move the cursor to Position 2 inches. Tab to Position 2 inches after keying in
     the other headings (**TO:**, **FROM:**, and **SUBJECT:**). The Tab key properly aligns the
     information after each heading.
3.   Key in the remainder of the memorandum.
4.   Save the memorandum and name it CH04EX1. Print CH04EX1.

### Exercise Two

1.   At a clear screen, change the left and right margins to 1.5 inches.
2.   Change justification to Left by completing the following steps:
     A. Access the Format: Line menu with Shift + F8, then choose 1 or L for Line.
        **M** *Click on Layout, then Line.*
     B. At the Format: Line menu, choose 3 or J for Justification.
     C. From the prompts that display at the bottom of the screen, choose 1 or L for Left.
     D. Press F7.
3.   Key in the memorandum headings as shown in figure 4-6. Align the information after the
     headings by using the Tab key.
4.   After keying in the information after SUBJECT, press Enter three times. Change the line
     spacing to double by completing the following steps:
     A. Access the Format: Line menu with Shift + F8, then choose 1 or L for Line.
        **M** *Click on Layout, then Line.*
     B. At the Format: Line menu, choose 6 or S for Line Spacing.
     C. Key in **2** and press Enter.
     D. Press F7 to return the cursor to the document and insert the line spacing code.
5.   Key in the remainder of the memorandum.
6.   Save the memorandum and name it CH04EX2. Print CH04EX2.

DATE:        October 1, 1992

TO:          Alyce Hersch

FROM:        Devon McKenna

SUBJECT:     Demonstration


For the past several months, we have been receiving daily
telephone calls regarding desktop publishing programs.
Customers are interested in previewing desktop publishing
programs before making a purchase.

To accommodate these daily requests, I would like you to
design a desktop publishing demonstration area in the
northeast corner of the store.  This area should include
three or four of the most popular desktop publishing
programs operating on both IBM and Macintosh computers.

I would like this demonstration area to be set up by the
end of next week.  If you need assistance, talk to Elsie
Levens.

xx:CH04EX1

Figure 4-5: Exercise One

DATE:        October 2, 1992

TO:          Dan Yamada

FROM:        Kelly O'Malley

SUBJECT:     Larson vs. Runyon


While preparing for the personal-injury case Larson vs.

Runyon, I discovered that more research is needed. I

would like you to research the issue of liability as it

pertains to tire damage caused by road surfaces.

Please have the research to my office by October 10.

XX:CH04EX2

**Figure 4-6: Exercise Two**

### Exercise Three
1.  At a clear screen, key in the letter shown in figure 4-7. To indent the enumerated items, complete the following steps:
    A.  Key in the number and the period.
    B.  Press F4.
       **M** *Click on Layout, Align, then Indent F4.*
    C.  Key in the paragraph.
    Repeat the same steps for each enumerated item.
2.  Boldface the heading after each enumerated item as indicated in the figure.
3.  Save the letter and name it CH04EX3. Print CH04EX3.

### Exercise Four
1.  At a clear screen, change the left and right margins to 1.5 inches.
2.  Change the Justification to Left.
3.  Key in the memorandum shown in figure 4-8. Use the Indent command, Shift + F4 (**M** *click on Layout, Align, then Indent Shift-F4*) to indent the quoted paragraph.
4.  Save the memorandum and name it CH04EX4. Print CH04EX4.

### Exercise Five
1.  At a clear screen, key in the letter shown in figure 4-9. Complete the following steps to create the hanging paragraphs:
    A.  At the left margin where the hanging paragraph is to begin, press the Indent key, F4.
       **M** *Click on Layout, Align, then Indent F4.*
    B.  Access the Margin Release command with Shift + Tab.
       **M** *Click on Layout, Align, then Margin Rel.*

October 4, 1992


Mrs. Maxine Giroux
5401 Rainier Drive
Spokane, WA  99302

Dear Mrs. Giroux:

Choosing a computer for personal and business use can be
frustrating and a little overwhelming.  We would like to provide
you with information to alleviate some of that frustration.  A
computer system generally consists of the following five
components:

1.   **CPU:**  The CPU (Central Processing Unit) processes information
     and is considered the intelligence of the computer.

2.   **Monitor:**  The monitor displays the information of a program
     and also displays what is being entered at the keyboard.

3.   **Keyboard:**  The keyboard is used to input information into the
     computer. In addition to letters, numbers, and symbols, most
     keyboards contain function keys, cursor movement keys, and a
     ten-key pad.

4.   **Disk Drives:**   The disk drive spins a disk and reads
     information from it.

5.   **Printer:**   A printer prints a hard copy of a document.
     Printers vary in speed, quality of print, and price.

We have several computer systems operating at our store.  Please
come in any time for a free demonstration.

Sincerely,



Harold Vonstein
Assistant Manager

xx:CH04EX3

Figure 4-7: Exercise Three

```
DATE:      October 12, 1992

TO:        Harold Vonstein

FROM:      Devon McKenna

SUBJECT:   Dvorak Keyboard


In a monthly computer periodical, I ran across an
article on the Dvorak keyboard.  I thought you might be
interested in sharing the following quote from the
article with the participants in your Dvorak keyboard
workshop:

     In the course of an eight-hour day, a Qwerty
     typist's fingers travel the equivalent of 16
     miles on the keyboard, while a Dvorak
     typist's fingers will travel only 1 mile.

I thought this information was interesting, and perhaps
the participants in your workshop will too.

xx:CH04EX4
```

Figure 4-8: Exercise Four

October 14, 1992



Mr. Nate Coburn
12445 South 43rd Street
Spokane, WA   99302

Dear Mr. Coburn:

The Rontech Corporation has just released a new, high-quality dot
matrix printer called the Rontech III.  This state-of-the-art, 24-
pin printer offers exceptional speed and sharpness in either letter
quality or draft style.  The Rontech III includes many additional
features.

You can choose from a wide variety of print enhancements, including
        Bold, Italic, Underlining, Subscript, Superscript, and Double
        Width.

The 24-pin print head produces sharp, crisp draft characters and
        letter quality characters that look like they came from a
        laser printer.

There are built-in connectors for both parallel and serial
        interface cables, so there is no need for extra options or
        modifications.

You can select either the letter quality or draft style with a
        touch of the front panel.

Come to our store and see the Rontech III.  We are sure you will be
as excited about this new printer as we are.

Sincerely,



Devon McKenna
Manager

xx:CH04EX5

Figure 4-9: Exercise Five

## PERFORMANCE ASSESSMENTS

**Assessment One**

1. At a clear screen, change the Justification to Left and the line spacing to double.
2. Key in the report shown in figure 4-10. Center and boldface text as indicated in the figure. Press the Enter key twice after the heading (this creates a quadruple space between the heading and the body of the report).
3. Save the report and name it CH04PA1. Print CH04PA1.

---

### THE EVOLUTION OF THE TYPEWRITER

The first recorded patent for a "typing machine" was issued to Henry Mill by Queen Ann of England. Henry Mill developed his machine in the early 1700s. However, the model he designed could not be turned into a workable model, and so it was never marketed.

The first marketable typewriter was designed by Christopher Latham Sholes, a newspaper editor, printer, and politician. Because his model was marketed, he is given credit for inventing the typewriter. In the early 1870s, the E. Remington and Sons Company bought Sholes' design and produced and manufactured the Remington Model No. 1 typewriter.

Sholes chose a design for the typewriter keys that slowed down the typist. He did this by placing commonly used keys in separate sections of the keyboard. This was done to ensure that the mechanical type bars would have enough time to fall back into place before the next keystroke had a chance to jam two bars together. Sholes' design is now commonly called the Qwerty keyboard, after the first six letters on the top alphabetic row.

Touch typing was not common until about twenty-five years after the introduction of the typewriter. In Cincinnati, Ohio,

in 1888, two men competed against each other in a typing competition.  One man, Louis Taub, used two fingers to type; the
other, Frank McGurrin, used all ten.  McGurrin had memorized the
keyboard layout and did not have to look back and forth between
his fingers and the text.  McGurrin won that competition.

---

Figure 4-10: Assessment One

**Assessment Two**
   1.  At a clear screen, create the reference page shown in figure 4-11 with the following
       specifications:
       A.  Change the Justification to Left.
       B.  Change the line spacing to double.
       C.  Center, boldface, and underline text as indicated in the figure.
       D.  Create a hanging paragraph for each reference.

   2.  Save the document and name it CH04PA2.  Print CH04PA2.

---

**REFERENCES**

Adler, N. J. (1990).  Contact hypothesis in ethnic relations.

   Psychological Bulletin, 71, 319-42.

Blake, R. R., Shepard, H. A., & Mouton, J. S. (1974).

   Understanding the process of acculturation for primary

   prevention.  Unpublished manuscript, Queen's University,

   Psychology Department, Kingston, Ontario.

Casmir, F. L. (1991).  Stereotypes and schemata.  In W. B.

   Gudykunst, L. P. Stewart, & S. Ting-Toomey (Eds.),

   Communication, Culture, and Organizational Process

   (pp. 48-67).  Beverly Hills:  Sage.

Hofstede, G. H. (1990).  Some theoretical and practical problems

   in multinational and cross-cultural research on

organizations.  In P. Joynt & M. Warner (Eds.), <u>Managing in</u>

<u>Different Cultures</u> (pp. 11-22).

Negandhi, A. R. (1989).  The mediating person and cultural

identity.  In S. Bochner (Eds.), <u>The Mediating Person</u> (pp.

37-52).  Cambridge:  Schenkman.

Porter, L. W., & Smith, F. J. (1985).  Organizational psychology.

In H. C. Triandis & R. W. Brislin (Eds.), <u>Handbook of</u>

<u>Crosscultural Psychology:  Vol. 5, Social Psychology</u>

(pp. 281-334).  Boston:  Allyn and Bacon.

Figure 4-11: Assessment Two

# CHAPTER 5

## PERFORMANCE OBJECTIVES

Upon successful completion of chapter 5, you will be able to enhance single-page business memorandums and generate two-column tables with tabs.

### TABS

The default ruler line contains preset tab stops every half inch. In some situations these tab stops may be appropriate. In others, you may need to create your own tab stops.

### Tab Key

To move the cursor to a preset tab stop, press the Tab key. On some keyboards the key may be labeled "TAB"; on others, it may be labeled with left- and right-pointing arrows. When the Tab key is pressed, the cursor moves to the nearest tab stop to the right.

### Tab Line

To make changes to the default tab line, complete the following steps:

1.  Access the Format: Line menu with Shift + F8, then choose 1 or L for Line.
    **M** *Click on Layout, then Line.*
2.  Choose 8 or T for Tab Set.
3.  Delete previous tabs with Control + End.
4.  Set new tabs.
5.  Press F7 twice.

When you choose the Tab selection from the Format: Line menu, the tab line shown in figure 5-1 displays at the bottom of the screen.

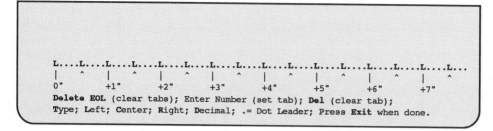

Figure 5-1: Tab Line

The **L** on the tab line indicates preset tab stops. There is a preset tab every
half inch up to 8.5 inches. The tab line displays to 54.5 inches. Below the
tab line is information on how to set and delete tab stops.

## Deleting Tabs

If you want to create tabbed text, you may need to delete some or all of the
previous tabs. To delete tabs in a specific location, display the tab line and
move the cursor with the cursor movement keys until it is located on the
tab to be deleted. Press either the Backspace key or the Delete key to
remove the tab. The **L** on the tab line disappears, indicating that the tab is
no longer in effect.

To clear all tabs, move the cursor to the beginning of the tab line and
press Ctrl + End. This deletes tabs to the end of the line.

## TYPES OF TABS

Eight types of tabs can be set on the tab line: left, center, right, decimal,
and left, center, right, and decimal with preceding leaders (periods).

## Left Tab

The left tab is the most common and is the WordPerfect default. The **L** on
the tab line indicates a left tab. Text keyed in at a left tab will align along
the left edge. The text in figure 5-2 was created with a left tab set at +3" on
the tab line.

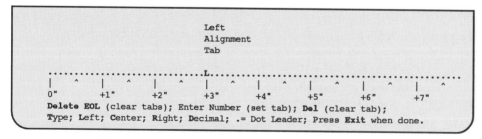

Figure 5-2: Left Alignment Tab

### Center Tab

A center tab centers text so there is an equal number of characters on the left and right of a particular setting. A center tab appears as a **C** on the tab line. The text in figure 5-3 was created with a center tab at +3" on the tab line.

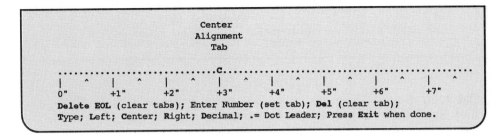

Figure 5-3: Center Alignment Tab

Notice that there is an equal (within a character) amount of text on either side of +3".

### Right Tab

The **R** on the tab line indicates a right tab. Text keyed in at a right tab aligns text along the right edge. The text in figure 5-4 was keyed in with a right tab at +3" on the tab line.

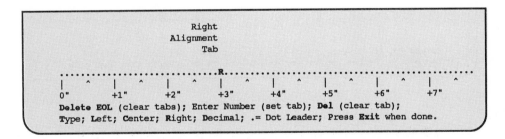

Figure 5-4: Right Alignment Tab

The text moves left as it is keyed in. It continues to move left until either the Enter or Tab key is pressed.

### Decimal Tab

The decimal tab is used to align numbers at a decimal point. The **D** on the tab line identifies a decimal tab. The text in figure 5-5 was keyed in with a decimal tab set at +3".

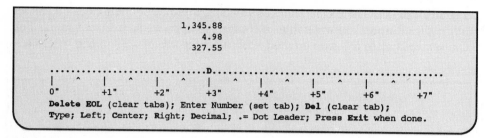

Figure 5-5: Decimal Tab

With the decimal setting numbers can be properly aligned.

### Tabs with Preceding Leaders

WordPerfect includes a feature that allows you to set tabs that are preceded by leaders (periods). The four kinds of tabs — left, center, right and decimal — can be set with preceding leaders. To understand how these tabs work, look at figure 5-6. The first column was set as a regular left tab. The second column was set as a right tab with preceding leaders:

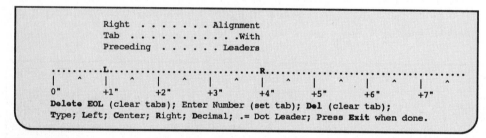

Figure 5-6: Tabs with Preceding Decimals

When the Tab key is pressed to move to the second column the leaders are automatically inserted.

### SETTING TABS

There are two methods for setting a left tab. If you know the measurement of the tab you want to set, key in the number and press Enter. Enter numbers as whole numbers or decimal numbers. For example, if you want a left tab set at 2 inches, key in a **2** and press Enter. If you want a tab set at 3 1/2 inches, key in **3.5** and press Enter. You can also enter numbers such as 2.1, 2.2, 4.6, 6.8 and so on. Another method is to move the cursor along the tab ruler line to the setting desired and key in an **L**.

The other tabs are set in a similar manner. Move the cursor to the desired setting, then key in a **C** for a center tab, an R for a right tab, or a D for a decimal tab. To set a tab with a preceding leader, key in a period followed by an L, C, R, or D. A tab with preceding leaders appears on the tab line in reverse video, for easy identification.

After all of your tabs are set on the tab line, press F7 twice to return to the document.

### Tab Types

With WordPerfect, Version 5.1, tabs can be set that are measured from the left margin or the left edge of the page. Tabs that are set measured from the left margin are called *relative tabs*. Tabs that are set measured from the left edge of the page are called *absolute tabs*.

Relative tabs are the default for Version 5.1. With relative tabs, the left margin displays as 0. Positions to the right of the left margin are displayed as positive numbers preceded by the plus sign. Positions to the left of the left margin are negative numbers and are preceded by the minus sign. With relative tabs, the distance between tab settings and the left margin remain the same regardless of what changes are made to the document.

With absolute tabs, the left edge of the page displays as 0. Positions to the right are positive numbers but do not display with the plus sign.

To change the type of tabs (absolute or relative), complete the following steps:

1.  Access the Format: Line menu with Shift + F8, then choose 1 or L for Line.
    **M** *Click on Layout, then Line.*
2.  Choose 8 or T for Tab Set.
3.  At the tab line, choose T for Type.
4.  From the prompt that displays at the bottom of the screen, choose 1 or A for Absolute, or 2 or R for Relative to Margin.
5.  Delete or set tabs.
6.  Press F7 twice.

### Setting Multiple Tabs

WordPerfect has a feature that lets you set several tabs at regular intervals. To set tabs at a consistent interval, at the tab line enter the setting for the first tab stop, followed by a comma and the interval number. For example, if you want tabs set every inch beginning at 2, key in **2,1** and press Enter. If you want tabs set every half inch beginning at 3.5 inches, key in **3.5,.5** and press Enter. Delete the previously set tabs first or they may interfere with the new tab settings.

If no tab exists at the beginning setting, left tabs will be set. If you want different kinds of tabs, key in the appropriate letter at the initial setting and enter the value for the tab interval as you normally would. For example, if you want right tabs set every 1.5 inches beginning at 3 inches, set a right tab at 3", key in **3,1.5** and then press Enter.

### SETTING UP COLUMNS USING WORDPERFECT

Columns of text or data in a document are usually centered between the left and right margins to provide a balanced look. A variety of methods can be used to determine the position of columns on the page. In a WordPerfect document, the simplest way to determine column positions is the use the *key line* method. To use this method, complete the following steps:

1.  Identify the longest entry in each column.
2.  Determine the number of spaces between columns.
3.  Access the Center command.

4.  Key in the longest entry in the first column and press the space bar the number of desired spaces between columns. Continue this procedure until all columns and spaces between columns have been entered.

5.  Position the cursor on the first letter of the first word in column one and record the number of that position. Continue this procedure for each column.

6.  Because WordPerfect, Version 5.1 sets relative tabs by default, subtract the left margin from each column position and record these new numbers.

7.  Delete the key line by moving the cursor to the beginning of the line and pressing Ctrl + End.

8.  Access the tab line, clear all previous tabs, and set new tabs at the positions recorded.

Suppose that you wanted to set the following columns in a document:

Dan East               Program Manager    Personnel
Kristin Osborn         Director           Sales
Tracy Harris           Director           Accounting

To position the columns using the key line method, complete the following steps:

1.  Identify the longest entry in each column. (In this example, the longest entries are Kristin Osborn, Program Manager, and Accounting.)

2.  Determine how many spaces you want between each column. Generally, six to ten spaces between columns are appropriate. Some columns may require more and others may require less. (In this example, use six spaces to separate the columns.)

3.  At a clear screen, access the Center command with Shift + F6.
    **M** *Click on Layout, Align, then Center.*

4.  Key in **Kristin Osborn**, then press the space bar six times.

5.  Key in **Program Manager**, then press the space bar six times.

6.  Key in **Accounting**.

7.  Position the cursor on the K in Kristin, check the status line, and record the position measurement. (In this example, it is 1.7 inches.)

8.  Position the cursor on the P in Program and record the position on the status line. (In this example, it is 3.7 inches.)

9.  Position the cursor on the A in Accounting and record the position on the status line. (In this example, it is 5.8 inches.)

10. Subtract the left margin measurement from the column positions to determine the tab positions. (If the left margin was set at the default of 1 inch, tabs are set at the following positions: first column, 1.7 − 1 = 0.7; second column, 3.7 − 1 = 2.7; third column, 5.8 − 1 = 4.8.)

11. Delete the key line by moving the cursor to the beginning of the line and pressing Ctrl + End.

12.  Set the tabs on the tab line by completing the following steps:
     A.  Access the Format: Line menu with Shift + F8, then choose 1 or
         L for Line.
         **M** *Click on Layout, then Line.*
     B.  Choose 8 or T for Tab Set.
     C.  At the tab line, clear previous tabs with Ctrl + End.
     D.  Key in **0.7** and press Enter.
     E.  Key in **2.7** and press Enter.
     F.  Key in **4.8** and press Enter.
     G.  Press F7 twice.
13.  Key in the column information. Use the Tab key to move the cursor
     to the tab stops.

If columnar entries are aligned at a decimal point, right, or centered,
consideration must be given to the tab position. The key line method can be
used for decimal, right, and center tabs. The difference is in determining the
tab position. After the key line has been entered, move the cursor to the
decimal point, to the right of the entry, or to the center of the entry, and record
that position on the status line. Use this measurement and complete the
remaining steps in the key line method.

## Column Headings

If the column heading is the longest line in the column, use it when creating
the key line. Column headings that are shorter than the column entries can
be visually centered above the entries. To do this, key in the column entries
first, leaving blank lines above the columns for the headings. After the column
entries have been keyed in, move the cursor above the columns, visually
determine the center of the columns, then key in the headings.

If there is only one column, the column heading can be centered above the
column by completing the following steps:

1.  Key in the column entries, then go back and insert blank lines
    above the column for the heading.

2.  Move the cursor to the first position of the column.

3.  Space over once for every two characters, spaces, and so on, in the
    longest entry in the column.

4.  Access the Center command with Shift + F6.
    **M** *Click on Layout, Align, then Center.*

5.  Key in the column heading.

Centering column headings over columns works for text that is set in the
default font (10-pitch Courier). Later in this textbook, you will learn to change
the font in the document. When the font is changed, the column heading may
appear centered on the screen but may print off-center.

For this reason, businesses are accepting column headings that are aligned
at the tab setting. This means that if you set left tabs for three columns across
the page, the column headings are entered at the left tab settings rather than
centered. One of the reasons aligning a heading at the tab setting is becoming
acceptable is because it saves time when you create a document.

### Reveal Codes

When you are working with tabs, always check the settings by displaying the Reveal Codes screen. You should see codes indicating any changes made to the default tab line. If you find settings you do not want, you can delete them by using either the Backspace key (to delete to the left of the cursor) or the Delete key (to delete the code where the cursor is located).

## CHAPTER REVIEW

### Summary

- To access the tab line, press Shift + F8, choose 1 or L for Line (**M** *Click on Layout, then Line*), then choose 8 or T for Tab Set.
- On the default tab line, left tab stops are set every half inch.
- On the tab line, L indicates a left tab; C identifies a center tab; R indicates a right tab; D, a decimal tab; and L, R, or D in reverse video indicates a tab with preceding leaders.
- Move the cursor to a preset tab stop with the Tab key.
- Before setting tabs for tabulated material, you will usually need to delete the default tab settings. To delete all previous tabs, move the cursor to the beginning of the tab line and press Control + End.
- Any changes to the tab line will appear in Reveal Codes.

### Tab Deletion Review

With the tab line displayed on the screen, there are two methods for deleting tab stops:

1. To delete a single tab stop, move the cursor with the cursor movement keys to the position where the tab is to be removed, and press either the Backspace key or the Delete key.
2. To delete all tabs, move the cursor to the beginning of the tab line and press Ctrl + End.

### Tab Selection Review

1. To set a left tab, key in the number (whole number or decimal number) and press Enter. Or move the cursor to the setting desired and key in an **L**.
2. To set a center, right, or decimal tab or a left, center, right, or decimal tab with preceding leaders, move the cursor to the setting desired and key in one of the following:
   C for center tab
   R for right tab
   D for decimal tab
   Period followed by L for left tab with leaders
   Period followed by C for center tab with preceding leaders
   Period followed by R for right tab with leaders
   Period followed by D for decimal tab with leaders
3. To set a series of tab stops at regular intervals, key in the number at which the interval is to begin, a comma, and the interval desired.

## STUDY GUIDE FOR CHAPTER 5

Completion: In the space provided at the right, indicate the correct command, term, or number.

1. How many inches apart are tabs set by default? _____

2. You can delete tab stops with the Delete key and which other key? _____

3. What letter indicates a default tab setting? _____

4. You can clear all tabs by pressing Ctrl plus what key? _____

5. What key moves the cursor to a preset tab stop? _____

6. What letter indicates a center tab on the tab line? _____

7. What letter indicates a decimal tab on the tab line? _____

8. What letter indicates a right tab on the tab line? _____

9. With the tab line displayed, what must be entered to set a right tab with preceding leaders? _____

**True/False:** Circle the letter T if the statement is true; circle the letter F if the statement is false.

1. To create tabulated material, you may need to delete previous tabs.  T  F

2. WordPerfect has a feature that allows you to set tabs at intervals.  T  F

3. In the key line method of determining columns, identify the shortest entry in each column  T  F

4. Preceding leaders are dashes.  T  F

5. In the key line method of determining columns, subtract the left margin from the column position before setting tabs.  T  F

## HANDS-ON EXERCISES

**Exercise One**
1. At a clear screen, make the following changes:
   A. Change the left and right margins to 2 inches.
   B. Change the justification to Left.
   C. Delete all tabs and set left tabs at +1 and +2.2 inches. To do this, complete the following steps:
      (1) Access the Format: Line menu with Shift + F8, then choose 1 or L for Line.
          **M** *Click on Layout, then Line.*
      (2) Choose 8 or T for Tab Set.
      (3) Delete tabs from the location of the cursor to the end of the line by pressing Ctrl + End.
      (4) Key in **1** and press Enter.
      (5) Key in **2.2** and press Enter.
      (6) Press F7 twice to return the cursor to the document.

2.  Key in the business letter shown in figure 5-7. (Press Enter six times before keying in the date. Use the Tab key to move the cursor to preset tabs.)
3.  Save the letter and name it CH05EX1. Print CH05EX1.

---

October 19, 1992



Mrs. Marie Montgomery
Angleton School District
234 Pine Street
Spokane, WA  99302

Dear Mrs. Montgomery:

The members of the vocational education
program at the Angleton School District made
a wise decision when they decided to add an
integrated microcomputer applications class
to the curriculum.

The following is a list of the six best-
selling integrated software programs. I got
the information from a current computer
periodical.

    No. 1       Manager Plus
    No. 2       ExecPlan
    No. 3       Enhancer
    No. 4       Super Planner
    No. 5       Timesaver
    No. 6       Powerhouse

I hope this is the information you need to
make your final decision about software.

Sincerely,



Harold Vonstein
Assistant Manager

xx:CH05EX1

---

Figure 5-7: Exercise One

## Exercise Two
1. At a clear screen, key in the headings and the first two paragraphs of the memorandum shown in figure 5-8.
2. With the cursor below the second paragraph, delete previous tabs and set left tabs at +0.5 and +5.5 inches. Set a center tab at +3.7 inches.
3. Key in the remainder of the memorandum shown in figure 5-8.
4. Save the memorandum and name it CH05EX2. Print CH05EX2.

```
DATE:      November 10, 1992

TO:        All Personnel

FROM:      Janet Weiss, Director of Personnel

SUBJECT:   Personnel Department


For the past six months, the Personnel Department has gone through
reorganization.   The reorganization  is  now  complete,  and  the
employees of the department are available to provide a variety of
services to the personnel of Puget Sound Semiconductor.

Please stop by our department and meet the employees and discover
what services the department can provide.  I am pleased to announce
the names and titles of the employees in the department.

        Janet Weiss         Director of Personnel      Step 6
        John White Cloud        Personnel Manager       Step 5
        Darlene Evans           Benefits Manager        Step 5
        Maria Valdez        Recruitment Coordinator     Step 4
        Brett Weinstein     Compensations Specialist    Step 3
        Duardo Carollo      Administrative Assistant    Step 2
        Ann Watanabe        Administrative Assistant    Step 2
        Robin Simmons           Receptionist            Step 1

xx:CH05EX2
```

Figure 5-8: Exercise Two

## Exercise Three
1. At a clear screen, change the left and right margins to 1.5 inches and the justification to Left.
2. Key in the headings and the first paragraph of the memorandum shown in figure 5-9.
3. With the cursor below the first paragraph, delete previous tabs and set a left tab at +0.5 inches and a right tab with preceding leaders at +5 inches.
4. Key in the remainder of the memorandum in figure 5-9.
5. Save the memorandum and name it CH05EX3. Print CH05EX3.

```
DATE:      October 6, 1992

TO:        All Personnel

FROM:      Janet Weiss, Director of Personnel

SUBJECT:   Reorganization of Personnel Department


Puget   Sound   Semiconductor   is   in   the   process   of
reorganizing  the  Personnel  Department.   The  company  is
changing  the  focus  of  the  department  to  provide  more
services to employees.  The department has created a new
career  path  for  employees  interested  in  the  personnel
field.   The  new  job  categories  are  listed  below:

         Step 1 . . . . . . . . . . . . . Receptionist
         Step 2 . . . . . . . Administrative Assistant
         Step 3 . . . . . . . Compensations Specialist
         Step 4 . . . . . . . Recruitment Coordinator
         Step 5 . . . . . . . . . . Benefits Manager
         Step 5 . . . . . . . . . . Personnel Manager
         Step 6 . . . . . . . . Director of Personnel

xx:CH05EX3
```

Figure 5-9: Exercise Three

## Exercise Four

1.  At a clear screen, change the left and right margins to 1.5 inches. Change the justification to Left.
2.  Key in the headings and the first paragraph of the memorandum shown in figure 5-10.
3.  With the cursor below the first paragraph, delete previous tabs and set a left tab at +1 inch and a decimal tab at +4 inches.
4.  Key in the remainder of the memorandum.
5.  Save the memorandum and name it CH05EX4. Print CH05EX4.

```
DATE:       December 4, 1992

TO:         Victoria Palmas, Director of Finances

FROM:       Janet Weiss, Director of Personnel

SUBJECT:    Personnel Department Billing


Personnel charges for the month of November have been
determined.  Please bill each department as indicated.

            Media Production        $1,200.45
            Public Relations           200.50
            Engineering                895.65
            Accounting                  29.55

Please send a copy of all invoices to the Personnel
Department.

xx:CH05EX4
```

Figure 5-10: Exercise Four

## Exercise Five

1. At a clear screen, key in the headings and the first paragraph of the memorandum shown in figure 5-11.
2. With the cursor below the first paragraph, delete previous tabs and set a left tab at +0.5 inches, a decimal tab with preceding leaders at +3.3 inches, and a right tab with preceding leaders at +6 inches.
3. Key in the remainder of the memorandum.
4. Save the memorandum and name it CH05EX5. Print CH05EX5.

DATE:        January 10, 1992

TO:          Devon McKenna, Manager

FROM:        Pamela Rousseau, Accountant

SUBJECT:     Monthly Net Profits


The monthly net profits for Omega Tech have been calculated.  The
following table shows the net profit, along with the increase or
decrease compared to the same month from the previous year.

```
        January  . . . . . .  $5,688.50  . . . . .  Increase 3%
        February . . . . . . . 3,896.25  . . . . . Decrease 12%
        March  . . . . . . . . 5,490.44  . . . . .  Increase 1%
        April  . . . . . . . . 3,789.20  . . . . .  Decrease 2%
        May  . . . . . . . . . 4,590.33  . . . . .  Increase 6%
        June . . . . . . . . . 3,990.55  . . . . .  Decrease 3%
        July . . . . . . . . . 5,399.00  . . . . .  Increase 9%
        August . . . . . . . . 5,566.25  . . . . . Increase 10%
        September  . . . . . . 4,775.80  . . . . .  Increase 4%
        October  . . . . . . . 5,220.85  . . . . .  Increase 3%
        November . . . . . . . 4,102.55  . . . . .  Decrease 2%
        December . . . . . . . 6,983.50  . . . . .  Increase 3%
```

xx:CH05EX5

---

Figure 5-11: Exercise Five


## PERFORMANCE ASSESSMENTS


### Assessment One

1.  At a clear screen, change the left and right margins to 1.5 inches. Change the justification to Left.
2.  Key in the headings and the first paragraph of the memorandum shown in figure 5-12.
3.  With the cursor below the first paragraph, use the key line method to determine the tab settings for the columns. Space eight times between columns. Set left tabs for both columns.
4.  Key in the column entries at the tab settings. Key in the remainder of the memorandum.
5.  Save the memorandum and name it CH05PA1. Print CH05PA1.

```
DATE:      December 18, 1992

TO:        Elsie Levens

FROM:      Devon McKenna

SUBJECT:   Window Displays


During the first quarter of the next year, I would like
a variety of window displays highlighting popular
software programs.  I have tentatively planned the
following displays:

        January        Integrated software
        February       Desktop publishing software
        March          Database software

Let me know what equipment and supplies you will need
to complete these displays.

xx:CH05PA1
```

Figure 5-12: Assessment One

## Assessment Two

1. At a clear screen, change the left and right margins to 1.5 inches. Change justification to Left.
2. Key in the headings and the first paragraph of the memorandum shown in figure 5-13.
3. With the cursor below the first paragraph, use the key line method to determine the tab settings for the columns. Space ten times between columns. Set a left tab for the first column and a decimal tab for the second column. (Be sure to get the position measurement of the decimal for the second column.)
4. Key in the column entries at the tab settings. Underline the entries in the first column and boldface the entries in the second column. Key in the remainder of the memorandum.
5. Save the memorandum and name it CH05PA2. Print CH05PA2.

DATE:       February 4, 1992

TO:         Payroll Department

FROM:       Janet Weiss, Director of Personnel

SUBJECT:    Overtime Hours


I have computed the overtime hours for the employees of
the Personnel Department.  The hours cover the month of
January.

        Maria Valdez          10.5 hours
        Brett Weinstein       4.0 hours
        Robin Simmons       14.0 hours
        Ann Watanabe        9.0 hours

Please include the overtime pay in the employees'
February paycheck.

xx:CH05PA2

**Figure 5-13: Assessment Two**

# PERFORMANCE MASTERY

## *UNIT PERFORMANCE*

In this unit, you have learned to adjust characters and lines in the creation of simple office documents, such as memorandums and letters.

## MASTERY ASSIGNMENTS

**Assignment One**

1. At a clear screen, key in the information shown in figure U1-1 in an appropriate memorandum format. You determine the following:
   A. Margins
   B. Justification
   C. Indentions
   D. Correct spelling (proper names are spelled correctly)
   E. Correct grammar and usage
2. Save the memorandum and name it U01MA1. Print U01MA1.

---

DATE: October 23, 1992; TO: Kim Chun, Vice President; FROM: Janet Weiss, Director of Personel; SUBJECT: New Employe Orientation

For the past three months, I have been monitering the New Employee Orientations conducted by the staff of the Personnel Department. After careful consideration of my observasions, I would like to make some changes in how the orientation is operated. My suggested changes include:
1.  Offer New Employee Orientation the first and third Monday of ever month.
2.  Begin the orientation at 8:30 a.m. and end at 4:30 p.m. with an hour for lunch between 12:00 and 1:00 p.m.
3.  Rotate the responsabilities for the orientation among the staff members of the Personnel Department.
4.  Invite administraters to attend the orientations as guest speakers.
Up to this point, New Employee Orientation has been conducted on an as-needed basis. This causes confusion and a lack of coordenation between the Personnel Department and the other departments in the company. Please look over my suggestions and let me know what you think.
xx:U01MA1

---

**Figure U1-1: Assignment One**

**Assignment Two**

1. At a clear screen, key in the information shown in figure U1-2 in an appropriate business letter format. You determine the following:
   A. Margins
   B. Justification
   C. Correct spelling (proper names are spelled correctly)
   D. Correct grammar and usage
2. Save the business letter and name it U01MA2. Print U01MA2.

---

October 2, 1993

Mr. Dan S. Yamada
Attorney at Law
800 Fourth Avenue
Suite 350
Seattle, WA 98002

Dear Mr. Yamada:

Business at Cheney Manufacturing has increased steadily this past year. To try and meet the demands of our customers, we are attempting to lease or purchase additional warehouse space in the south end of Seattle.

I have talked with several property management companies about lots and/or warehouses that are for lease or purchase. One of the leasing agreements I received from AB Properties is enclosed. Please look over this lease agreement and give me your impressions and suggestions.

There are several warehouses for sale in the Georgetown area. Do you recommend leasing or buying? What do you think would be the best course of action for Cheney Manufacturing?

Please respond as soon as you can. We need the additional space as soon as possible

Sincerely,


Charles R. Pruitt
President

---

**Figure U1-2: Assignment Two**

## Assignment Three

1. At a clear screen, key in the information shown in figure U1-3 in an appropriate memorandum format. You determine the following:
   A. Margins
   B. Justification
   C. Tab settings for columns
   D. Correct spelling (proper names are spelled correctly)
   E. Correct grammar and usage
2. Save the business memorandum and name it U01MA3. Print U01MA3.

DATE: October 15, 1992; To: All Directors; FROM: Terry Preston, Vice President; SUBJECT: Needs Assessement Survey

The needs Assessment Survey is compleated and ready for distribution. The survey is designed to establish the present and future needs of employees in the following areas:
1. Equipment     2. Office space
3. Sceduling     4. Staffing        (list)

A member of my support staff, Angela Stansburg, will administer the survey to employees in each department on the following dates:

Personnel . . . . . . . . . . . . October 19, 1992
Sales . . . . . . . . . . . . October 23, 1992
Research + Development . . . . . November 2, 1992
Facilities Management . . . . . . . November 4, 1992
Finances . . . . . . . . . . . . November 9, 1992

# The results of the survey will be available approximatly one month after the survey has been administered. Hopefully, I will present the results at the directors' meeting in December.    xx : U01MA3

Figure U1-3: Assignment Three

## Assignment Four

1.  At a clear screen, create the table shown in figure U1-4. You determine the following:
    A.  Centering and boldfacing
    B.  Tab settings
    C.  Correct spelling
    D.  Correct grammar and usage
2.  Save the table and name it U01MA4. Print U01MA4.

---

*Needs Assessment Survey*

| Department | Date | Room | Time |
|---|---|---|---|
| Personnel | 10/19/92 | 315 | 9:00 – 10:30 |
| Sales | 10/23/92 | 120 | 1:00 – 2:30 |
| Research & Development | 11/02/92 | 222 | 2:00 – 3:30 |
| Facilities Management | 11/04/42 | 120 | 9:00 – 10:30 |
| Finances | 11/09/92 | 315 | 2:00 – 3:30 |

**Figure U1-4: Assignment Four**

# UNIT 2

## BASIC PAGE FORMATTING

In this unit, you will learn to create and proof full-page and multiple-page business documents, such as letters and reports.

# CHAPTER 6

## SPELLER/THESAURUS

## *PERFORMANCE OBJECTIVE*

Upon successful completion of chapter 6, you will be able to proof all types of business text documents with the WordPerfect Speller and Thesaurus programs.

### DICTIONARY/SPELLING PROGRAMS

In the past few years, word processing programs have added many useful and sophisticated features. One of the most popular is a *spell checking* program. A spell checking program includes a list of thousands of words that is checked against a document created with the word processor. *Speller* is the name WordPerfect uses for its spell checking program.

### WHAT IS SPELLER?

Speller is a spell program that operates with WordPerfect and contains over 125,000 words. It actually contains three dictionaries: a common word list, a main word list, and a supplemental list that you can compile with words you have selected.

The common word list contains approximately 2500 of the most commonly used words in the English language. When Speller runs a check on a document, it checks the most common words first. This can be accomplished quickly and speeds up the checking process. If Speller has not matched all the words in the document, it moves to the main dictionary. Finally, Speller checks words against the supplemental dictionary.

### WHAT SPELLER CAN DO

Speller operates by comparing words in a document with the words stored in its dictionary. If the word matches, Speller moves on. If there is no match for the word, Speller stops and offers you several choices. With the Speller dictionary, you can check a word, a page, or an entire document.

When checking a document, Speller stops and highlights a word if its spelling does not match another word that exists in the dictionary. Text is highlighted when typographical errors such as transposed letters occur. Speller also highlights double word occurrences and words that contain numbers.

If you find yourself using certain proper names on a regular basis, Speller allows you to add them to the supplemental dictionary. Speller checks words against this dictionary and does not stop if a match is found.

Speller offers you several options when it finds a word that is not in any of its dictionaries. You can

1.    skip the word, leaving it in its original form;
2.    add the word to the Speller supplemental dictionary;
3.    edit the word to correct its spelling;
4.    look up words with similar beginnings; or
5.    look up words with similar phonetic pronunciation.

In addition to these features, Speller also lists the total number of words in a document. When Speller has checked the document, the message **Word Count: [number of words here] Press any key to continue** appears at the bottom of the screen.

## WHAT SPELLER CANNOT DO

A small number of words in the Speller dictionaries are proper names. You will find that most proper names in your documents do not appear in any of the dictionaries. Speller does not find a match for most proper names and so it highlights these words for correction. (Remember, however, that Speller allows you to add commonly used proper names to the supplemental dictionary.)

Speller does not identify words that are spelled correctly but used incorrectly. For example, if you key in *their* instead of *there*, Speller finds a match for *their* and does not stop for it to be corrected.

If a word is spelled incorrectly but that incorrect spelling matches another word, Speller does not highlight it. For example, if you want the word *crease* in a document but you keyed it in as *cease*, it is passed over. Speller matches *cease* with a word in its dictionary and assumes it was spelled correctly.

If you understand the limitations of a Speller, it can be of great assistance. However, the job of proofreading is not eliminated.

## THE SPELL COMMAND

To operate Speller, access the Spell Command with Ctrl + F2 (**M** *Click on Tables, then Spell*) and the prompt **Check: 1 Word; 2 Page; 3 Document; 4 New Sup. Dictionary; 5 Look Up; 6 Count: 0** appears at the bottom of the screen.

### Word, Page, and Document

The first three choices let you check a word, a page, or the entire document for spelling errors.

### New Supplemental Dictionary

When completing a spell check, WordPerfect searches the common word and main dictionaries first, then checks the supplemental dictionary. The supplemental dictionary is automatically created when Speller is first used and is a file that is used to store words that you add to the dictionary. You can create a different file as the supplemental dictionary by choosing 4 or N for New Sup. Dictionary from the Spell command prompt, keying in the name of the new document, and pressing Enter.

### Look Up

The Look Up choice lets you look up individual words (whether or not they are used in your document). If you are not sure of the correct spelling, you can use either the question mark or the asterisk as wild card characters. The question mark stands for a single letter, and the asterisk stands for a sequence of letters.

For example, let's say that you are not sure of the correct spelling for the word *separate*. You are not sure if it is spelled *seperate* or *separate*. You can look it up by choosing 5 or **L** for Look Up from the Spell command and keying in **sep?rate**. This causes Speller to list all words that are spelled with **sep_rate**.

Or, if you do not know the correct spelling for the word *submissive*, choose 5 or **L** for Look Up from the Spell command and then key in **subm***. Speller lists all words that begin with **subm** on the screen. You can check the list to find the correct spelling of submissive.

### Count

As mentioned earlier, Speller will give a count of the total number of words in a document when it has completed a spelling check. You can also get a count of words without running a check by choosing 6 or C for Count from the Spell command.

### SPELLING CHECK

To spell check the entire document, complete the following steps:
1.  Retrieve a document to the screen.
2.  Access the Spell command with Ctrl + F2. (If you are operating WordPerfect on a floppy-drive system, take the work disk out of Drive B and insert the Speller disk.)
    **M** *Click on Tools, then Spell.*
3.  From the prompt that displays at the bottom of the screen, choose 3 or D for Document.
4.  Make corrections as needed.
5.  When the spell checking is complete, WordPerfect displays the word count of the document with the message **Press any key to continue**. Press any key on the keyboard, such as the space bar.

When running a spell check, if Speller does not find a match for a word in the dictionaries, the word is displayed in reverse video. The prompt **Not Found: 1 Skip Once; 2 Skip; 3 Add Word; 4 Edit; 5 Look Up; 6 Ignore Numbers: 0** appears at the bottom of the screen.

In the middle of the screen, a double line of dashes appears and a list of suggested replacements that Speller has found is displayed. Each replacement is preceded by a letter. If the correct spelling is among the list displayed by Speller, key in the letter in front of that word. Speller inserts this word over the incorrectly spelled word and continues checking the rest of the document.

### Skip

The first and second choices from the prompt let you skip over a word that is spelled correctly. For instance, Speller does not have all proper names in the dictionaries. If Speller stops at a proper name and you know it is spelled correctly, choose 1 or 2 and it will be left alone. The first choice skips only that occurrence of the word. If the word appears later in the document, Speller stops and highlights it again. The second choice tells Speller to skip all occurrences of that word in the document.

### Add

The third choice, Add, is used to add words to the supplemental dictionary. This option is convenient if your documents contain frequently used words or proper names that are not in either of the dictionaries. By adding them to the dictionary, Speller will find a match and pass them by. This saves you time during a spelling check.

### Edit

The fourth option, Edit, lets you leave Speller temporarily and make corrections to the word. After corrections are made, press F7 to return to Speller.

### Look Up

With Look Up, you can look up the spelling of specific words. When you are not exactly sure how something is spelled, you can key in part of a word and use the asterisk to indicate a sequence of letters or the question mark to indicate one letter. Speller will display a list of all words that match the sequence.

### Ignore Numbers

The last choice from the prompt, **Ignore Numbers**, tells Speller to ignore words that contain letters and numbers. If a word contains a number, Speller will stop on that word. Speller will not, however, stop on a word that contains only numbers. For example, Speller will not stop at a Zip Code such as 99302, but will stop on a parts numbers such as HX345. If you do not want Speller to stop at words containing numbers, choose 6 from the prompt.

## DOUBLE WORDS

If a double word occurs in a document, Speller will stop during a spell check, highlight both words, and display the prompt **Double Word: 1  2 Skip;  3 Delete 2nd; 4 Edit; 5 Disable Double Word Checking** at the bottom of the screen. If you want the double word to remain in the document, choose either 1 or 2. The third choice is used to delete the second occurrence of the word. The Edit choice lets you temporarily exit Speller to edit your document, and the last choice turns off the double word checking.

## CHECKING A DOCUMENT WITH SPELLER

Let us look at an example to see how this operation is completed. Suppose the following text was saved as a document named SPELL.CHK:

```
Speller is a supplimental program than operates
with WordPerfect.  It allow you to cheek words
in your document with words in a dictionery.
Terry Morgenstein, administrative assistant,
states that Speller is a "life saver."
```

To run a spelling check on this document, follow these steps:

1. Retrieve SPELL.CHK to the screen.

2. Access the Spell command with Ctrl + F2. On a floppy-drive system, remove the work disk from Drive B and insert the Speller disk. **M** *Click on Tools, then Spell.*

3. From the prompts at the bottom of the screen, choose 3 or D for Document. Speller flashes the **\* Please Wait \*** message and begins checking.

4. The word *supplimental* is highlighted and one possible replacement is displayed on the screen. Key in an **A** to replace *supplimental* with the correct spelling.

5. Speller skips over the words *allow* (which should be *allows*) and *cheek* (which should be *check*) because it has found matches in its dictionary.

6. Speller highlights *dictionery* and displays one option for replacement. Key in an **A** to replace the word.

7. *Terry*, even though it is a proper name, is found in the Speller dictionary and is passed over.

8. Speller highlights *Morgenstein* but does not list any possible replacements because it cannot find anything that closely resembles this word. Choose 1 to skip this word.

9. The checking is complete. Speller displays the following message: **Word Count: 34  Press any key to continue.**

10. If you are using a floppy-drive system, take out the Speller disk in Drive B and insert your work disk.

The exercises at the end of this chapter will provide you with several opportunities to practice using Speller. Although subsequent chapters will not specifically request the use of Speller, try to develop the habit of checking each document after it is created.

The best way to use Speller is to create a document, check it with Speller, and then proofread it for content. You will need to proofread the document for correct use of words, verb endings, grammar, and other areas.

## THESAURUS

WordPerfect contains a synonym-finding feature called Thesaurus. The word *thesaurus* is defined as a dictionary of synonyms. This is exactly what WordPerfect's Thesaurus does for you — it provides you with a list of synonyms for a specific word. Synonyms are words that have the same or nearly the same meaning. With the Thesaurus program, the clarity and precision of business communications can be improved. Thesaurus can be used as a supplement to the Speller program or it can be used alone to improve a written document.

## WHAT THESAURUS CAN DO

WordPerfect's Thesaurus looks up synonyms for specific words and also provides a list of antonyms. Antonyms are words with opposite meanings. When the Thesaurus program is used to look up a specific word, four lines of the document stay at the top of the screen and the rest of the screen displays synonyms and antonyms.

The synonyms are divided into three categories: nouns, verbs, and adjectives (if appropriate). If one of the words listed is more appropriate than the word you used in a document, you can easily make a replacement.

## OPERATING THESAURUS

To operate the Thesaurus program, display a document on the screen and move the cursor to the word that you want to look up. Access the Thesaurus command with Alt + F1 (**M** *Click on Tools, then Thesaurus*). If you are using a floppy-drive system, take the work disk out of Drive B, and insert the Thesaurus disk. If the word you are looking up is in the Thesaurus, a list of synonyms and antonyms is displayed on the screen. In addition, a prompt with four selections appears at the bottom of the screen.

To understand how Thesaurus operates and what options are available, look at the example in figure 6-1. You have created a report and, after reading it, decide that the word *document* has been overused. You would like to find other words that can be substituted. Place the cursor on the word *document*, and access the Thesaurus command with Alt + F1 (**M** *Click on Tools, then Thesaurus*). Four lines of the document are displayed at the top of the screen and the rest of the screen appears as shown in figure 6-1.

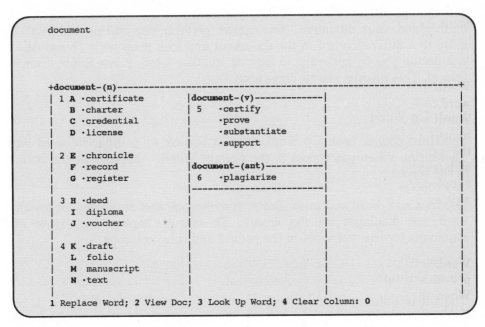

Figure 6-1: Thesaurus Operation

Thesaurus has displayed a list of noun and verb synonyms for *document*, as well as one antonym. The prompt at the bottom of the screen includes four choices.

## Replace Word

The first choice is used to replace one of the synonyms or antonyms found by Thesaurus for the word in the document. To make a replacement, choose 1 and the message **Press letter for word** _ appears at the bottom of the screen.

Most of the entries listed on the screen are labeled with letters. Key in the letter of the word you have chosen to replace your original word. When this happens, the word is replaced and the list of synonyms and antonyms disappears from the screen.

In the example above, the second column does not have letters next to the words. If you want to use one of the words in the second column, press the right arrow key. This causes the letters to disappear from the first column and appear in the second. The left and right arrow keys cause the letters to shift left and right. The up and down arrow keys, as well as the Page Up and Page Down keys cause the words to move up and down. The up and down arrow keys are useful when the list of synonyms and antonyms is too long to be viewed at one time.

Several of the synonyms for *document* have a dot in front of them to indicate that they are **headwords**. A headword is a word having its own list of alternatives. Thesaurus contains approximately 10,000 headwords with an overall amount of 150,000 words. If you press the letter next to a headword, a list of synonyms replaces whatever is in the second column. This lets you view two lists of synonyms at the same time.

### View Document

The second choice, View Doc, lets you temporarily leave Thesaurus and move about your document. You cannot perform any editing but you can move to a different word in the document and look it up with Thesaurus. If you decide you do not want to look up another word, press Enter, Exit, or Cancel. This returns you to Thesaurus.

### Look Up Word

The third choice, Look Up Word, is used to look up a different word with Thesaurus. When you choose 3, the prompt **Word:** _ appears at the bottom of the screen.

Key in a new word and press Enter. If synonyms and antonyms for another word are displayed on the screen, Thesaurus displays synonyms and antonyms for the new word in the second and third columns.

### Clear Column

The Clear Column choice is useful with the Look Up Word choice. If you want to look up another word with Thesaurus, Clear Column clears the previous entries and provides you with blank columns.

## CHAPTER REVIEW

### Summary

- Speller is a spelling program that operates with WordPerfect and contains approximately 125,000 words.
- Speller has three dictionaries: a common word list, a main word list, and a supplemental list.
- Speller operates by comparing words in a document against words stored in its dictionaries.
- Speller checks a word, page, or document for misspellings.
- Speller provides you with a word count for a document.
- Speller does not identify words that are spelled correctly but used incorrectly, nor does it identify misspellings that match other words in its dictionaries.
- Speller stops and highlights many proper names for correction. Frequently used proper names can be stored in the supplemental dictionary.
- Speller lets you skip a word, create a new supplemental dictionary and add words to it, edit a word, and look up words with similar beginnings.
- During a spell check, Speller highlights double word occurrences as well as words containing numbers.
- WordPerfect's Thesaurus program contains a list of synonyms and antonyms for many common words.

- Synonyms are divided into three categories: nouns, verbs, and adjectives. Depending on the word, Thesaurus may display only nouns, only verbs, or only adjectives, or it may display a combination of all three.
- To operate Thesaurus, display a document, move the cursor to the word you want to look up and access the Thesaurus command with Alt + F1 (**M** *Click on Tools, then Thesaurus*). (On a floppy-drive system, take the work disk out of Drive B and insert the Thesaurus disk before accessing the Thesaurus command.)
- When Thesaurus displays synonyms and antonyms on the screen, a dot in front of a word indicates that it is stored in Thesaurus.
- The right and left arrow keys are used to move the letters in front of words back and forth between columns. The up and down arrow keys and Page Up and Page Down keys are used to display words that do not fit on the screen.

## Commands Review

|                     | Keyboard | Mouse            |
|---------------------|----------|------------------|
| Spell Command       | Ctrl + F2 | Tools, Spell     |
| Thesaurus Command   | Alt + F1  | Tools, Thesaurus |

## STUDY GUIDE FOR CHAPTER 6

**True/False:** Circle the letter T if the statement is true; circle the letter F if the statement is false.

1.   Speller contains more than 135,000 words.                                    T     F
2.   Speller highlights all typographical errors.                                 T     F
3.   Speller eliminates the need for proofreading.                                T     F
4.   Access the Spell Command with Ctrl + F2 (**M** *Click on Tools, then Spell*).     T     F
5.   The common word list contains approximately 3,000 words.                     T     F
6.   In Look Up, the asterisk stands for a single letter.                         T     F
7.   In Look Up, the question mark stands for a sequence of letters.              T     F
8.   Thesaurus operates with WordPerfect.                                         T     F
9.   Antonyms are words with the same or similar meaning.                         T     F
10.  Synonyms are divided into two categories: nouns and adverbs.                 T     F
11.  Access the Thesaurus Command with Alt + F1 (**M** *Click on Tools, then Thesaurus*).     T     F
12.  When a list of synonyms and antonyms is displayed, the left and right arrow     T     F
     keys move the letters in front of the words.
13.  You can look up a different word after Thesaurus has displayed a list of     T     F
     synonyms and antonyms for a previous word.

Circle the words in the paragraph below that Speller will highlight for correction.

Least month the Data Processing Department circalated a questionaire too each department in the company reqeusting input on the types of reports need. The questionaire contained specefic information adn was used to design a new database program. The new program reguires the use of standerdized abbrevitions. The Data Processing Department will be issuing memos in the near future listing the new abbreviations.

Using the same paragraph, circle the incorrect words that Speller would not highlight.

Least month the Data Processing Department circalated a questionaire too each department in the company reqeusting input on the types of reports need. The questionaire contained specefic information adn was used to design a new database program. The new program reguires the use of standerdized abbrevitions. The Data Processing Department will be issuing memos in the near future listing the new abbreviations.

## HANDS-ON EXERCISES

### Exercise One

1.  At a clear screen, change the left and right margins to 2 inches and change the justification to Left.
2.  Key in the memorandum shown in figure 6-2. (Key in the text as written, including incorrect and misspelled words. You will make corrections in the following exercise.)
3.  Save the memorandum and name it CH06EX1. Print CH06EX1.

---

DATE:       November 10, 1992

TO:         Maria Valdez

FROM:       Janet Weiss

SUBJECT:    Recruitment Meeting


The union negotiations last week have
effected my schedule this week and I will not
be abel to meet with you Friday.  I would
like to rescedule our meeting for next week.
Any day next week is fine accept Thurday.

Please call me at your convinience to
reschedule the meeting.

xx:CH06EX1

---

Figure 6-2: Exercise One

**Exercise Two**

1.  Retrieve CH06EX1 to the screen. Complete a spelling check with Speller and decide whether to skip words or make corrections.
2.  Proofread the memorandum and make any corrections that were not highlighted by Speller.
3.  Save the memorandum and name it CH06EX2. Print CH06EX2.

**Exercise Three**

1.  At a clear screen, change the left and right margins to 1.5 inches and change the justification to Left.
2.  Key in the letter shown in figure 6-3. (Key in the text as written, including incorrect and misspelled words. You will make corrections in the following exercise.)
3.  Save the letter and name it CH06EX3. Print CH06EX3.

---

December 4, 1992


Ms. Devon McKenna
Omnitech
250 Center Street
Spokane, WA  99302

Dear Ms. McKenna:

Thank your for the information about personnel computers.  The letters and broshures you have send have provided me with a basic knowledge of computer systems.

I would like to visit your store in the next weak to see a demonstration of two microcompouter systems, the Rontech System 80 and the CompuPlus.  I would prefer either erly morning on Tuesday or late afternoon on Wenesday.

Give me a call at my office.  The number is 555-4433. If you have any more materials on the Rontech System 80 or the CompuPlus, I will pick it up when I visit.

If I do not here from you by teh end of this week, I will give you a call.

Sincerely yours,


Grace Fenmore

xx:CH06EX3

---

**Figure 6-3: Exercise Three**

## Exercise Four

1. Retrieve CH06EX3 to the screen. Complete a spelling check with Speller and decide whether to skip words or make corrections.
2. Proofread the letter and make any corrections that were not highlighted by Speller.
3. Save the letter and name it CH06EX4. Print CH06EX4.

## Exercise Five

1. At a clear screen, key in the letter shown in figure 6-4. (Key in the text as written, including incorrect and misspelled words. You will make corrections in the following exercise.)
2. Save the letter and name it CH06EX5. Print CH06EX5.

December 8, 1992


Mr. Charles Pruitt, President
Cheney Manufacturing
625 Parkway Plaza
Seattle, WA  98116

Dear Mr. Pruitt:

Re:  Cheney Manufacturing, Articles of Incorporation

I am in the process of perparing Articles of Incorporation for Cheney Manufacturing.  There are some questions to be answered before they can be competed.  Please answer the questions below providing as much detail as possibly.

1.    What are the names and addresses of the Executive Board for Cheney Manufacturing?
2.    When will the first meeting of the Executive Board for the corporation be held?
3.    What is the anticapated gross profit for 1992 for the corporation?
4.    What is the corporate address for Cheney Manufacturing?

Please send the answers to this questions by next week.  I will be out-of-town the week of December 20 - 26 and want to get the Articles of Incorporation competed before then.

Very trully yours,

MORENO, YAMADA, & SCHWARTZ



James D. Schwartz
Attorney at Law

xx:CH06EX5

Figure 6-4: Exercise Five

**Exercise Six**

1.  Retrieve CH06EX5 to the screen. Complete a spelling check with Speller and decide whether to skip words or make corrections.
2.  Proofread the letter and make any corrections that were not highlighted by Speller.
3.  Save the letter and name it CH06EX6. Print CH06EX6.

**Exercise Seven**

1.  At a clear screen, change the left and right margins to 1.5 inches and change the justification to Left.
2.  Key in the letter in figure 6-5.
3.  Save the letter and name it CH06EX7. Print CH06EX7.

---

December 10, 1992



Ms. Christy Roberts
12443 South 166th
Spokane, WA 99302

Dear Ms. Roberts:

Choosing the right word processing program can be difficult.  Let us help you make that choice.  Our company offers a wide choice of word processing programs, and our employees can explain the advantages and disadvantages of each.

For example, you may want to choose the popular WordPerfect word processing program, or you might decide an integrated program is what you need for your company.

Let us help you choose the software program that fits your personal and business needs.

Sincerely,


Devon McKenna
Manager

xx:CH06EX7

---

Figure 6-5: Exercise Seven

## Exercise Eight

1.  Retrieve CH06EX7 to the screen.
2.  The letter contains the words *choose* and *choice* several times.  To make the letter read better, use Thesaurus to replace a choose and/or choice in a few locations with appropriate synonyms.  (You decide which occurrences should be replaced with what synonyms.)
3.  Save the letter and name it CH06EX8. Print CH06EX8.

## Exercise Nine

1.  At a clear screen, change the left and right margins to 1.5 inches and change the justification to Left.
2.  Key in the letter in figure 6-6.
3.  Save the letter and name it CH06EX9. Print CH06EX9.

---

June 10, 1992


Mr. and Mrs. Ralph D'Arcy
12340 North 43rd Street
Salem, OR  98332

Dear Mr. and Mrs. D'Arcy:

We are pleased to announce that your daughter, Alicia, has won the outstanding student award at Green Lake High School.  Please accept our congratulations to you and your daughter.

We are pleased to see the award going to a student at our high school.  Alicia is an outstanding student and is well-deserving of this award.

Congratulations on the outstanding job you have done raising Alicia!

Sincerely,


Jo Collinsworth
Principal

xx:CH06EX9

---

**Figure 6-6: Exercise Nine**

**Exercise Ten**

1. Retrieve CH06EX9 to the screen.
2. The letter contains several occurrences of the words *please* and *outstanding*. To make the letter read better, use Thesaurus to replace a few occurrences of these two words with appropriate synonyms.
3. Save the letter and name it CH06EX10. Print CH06EX10.

## PERFORMANCE ASSESSMENTS

Beginning with Performance Assessment One, information in exercises in this and future chapters may not be displayed with proper formatting or spacing. You will be required to enter the information correctly. Refer to appendices C and D for proper formatting of business letters and memorandums. Include all parts of a memorandum or business letter including reference initials and document name.

**Assessment One**

1. At a clear screen, key in the information in figure 6-7 in an appropriate business letter format. You determine the margins and justification. Space the elements in the letter correctly. Key in the incorrect and misspelled words as written.
2. Complete a spelling check with Speller and decide whether to skip words or make corrections. Proofread the letter and make any corrections that were not highlighted by Speller.
3. Save the letter and name it CH06PA1. Print CH06PA1.

---

December 14, 1992

Mr. James D. Schwartz
Attourney at Law
800 Forth Avenue
Seattle, WA  98002

Dear Mr. Schwartz:

Re:  Cheney Manufacturing, Articals of Incorporation

Thank you for attending to the Articals of Incorporation in such a timely manner.  Hopefuly, the articals can be signed by the first of the year.

The names and addresses of the Executive Board for Cheney Manufacturing is:  Charles Pruitt, President, 625 Parkway Plaza, Seattle, WA 98116; Jamie Monier, Vice President, 625 Parkway Plaza, Seattle, WA 98116; and Larry Souza, 12689 - 132nd Street East, Woodinville, WA 98763.

The fist meeting of the Executive Board for Cheney Manufacturing will be heald on Febuary 2, 1993.

We have made only tenative projections of the gross profit for Cheney Manufacturing. Currently, the projections for gross profit for 1993 is $150,000.

The corprate address for Cheney Manufacturing is 625 Parkway Plaza, Seattle, WA 98116.

I hope this gives you enugh information to prepare the Articals of Incorporation.

Sincerly yours,


Charles Pruitt
President

xx:CH06PA1

---

Figure 6-7: Assessment One

**Assessment Two**

1. At a clear screen, key in the first page of a report shown in figure 6-8. Center, boldface, and indent text as displayed.
2. Complete a spelling check with Speller and decide whether to skip words or make corrections. Proofread the report and make any corrections that were not highlighted by Speller. (There are no intentional mistakes in the text in figure 6-7.)
3. Using Thesaurus, find appropriate synonyms for the following words in the report: *formation, earnest,* and *dubious* in the first paragraph; *repudiated* and *crucial* in the second paragraph (watch verb endings); and *prolific* and *arenas* in the third paragraph (watch noun endings).
4. Save the report and name it CH06PA2. Print CH06PA2.

---

## A BRIEF HISTORY OF A COMMUNITY IN ACTION

**THE WAR ON POVERTY YEARS: 1964-1969**

In the spring of 1964, before Congress passed the Economic Opportunity Act, a group of Central Area residents and friends began formation of a comprehensive anti-poverty proposal. Many civil rights leaders were pessimistic about the government funding any earnest social change, and many social service administrators were dubious about grass roots involvement. But once War-On-Poverty legislation was actually passed, interest intensified in this action plan for what would soon be christened the "Central Area Program."

Around the country, most Economic Opportunity grants went to expand established agencies. CAP became the first totally new, community-inspired program in the country to receive funding. Now, a quarter of a century later, it holds the distinction of being the oldest surviving, independent agency launched in that era. The now popular myth that the War-On-Poverty was a failure is repudiated by the productive history of the vast majority of people who shared in the formative years of CAP. Equally crucial has been the changed image of the Central Area.

In those prolific years, CAP became the service arm of the Tacoma civil rights movement and grew to over 300 employees in the summer of 1967. It encompassed a huge corps of volunteers that developed a broad network of cooperative community groups. The major arenas of service and action included:

**INTELLECTUAL:** After-school and evening homework help and education enrichment for some 10,000 "latch-key kids" and other youth in eleven Central Area Study Centers (1965-67). A parent outreach program assisted mothers and fathers promote the motivation and academic progress of their children. A joint CAP/Tacoma Public School "Counseling Bank" helped alienated students and parents reconcile with the public schools.

**EMPLOYMENT:** CAP job counseling, referral, and training projects assisted thousands of unemployed and under-employed heads-of-households, teenagers, welfare mothers, school dropouts, exconvicts, new immigrants, victims of racism, and socially, mentally, and physically handicapped persons. Approximately 500 youth and adults filled earn-while-you-learn positions in regular and special "crash" programs. Trainees and paraprofessionals constituted the majority of workers in the Beautification, Action Education, Community Organization, Day Care, Performing Arts, Study Center and Youth departments.

**YOUTH INVOLVEMENT:** The Youth Department promoted leadership and social career skill development through Senior High and Junior High Teen Councils. They operated a self-help Job Line, organized summer festivals and other recreational activities, fostered interschool and intercommunity conflict resolution sessions, and participated in extensive career counseling.

Figure 6-8: Performance Assessment Two

# CHAPTER 7

## PAGE FORMATTING

## PERFORMANCE OBJECTIVES

Upon successful completion of chapter 7, you will be able to create text heads and tables and present heads, tables, and text information in different positions on a page.

### VERTICAL PAGE ALIGNMENT

Until now, the documents you have created have been less than one page in length. In this chapter you will create documents that are several pages long. WordPerfect assumes that you will use standard-sized paper, which is 8.5 inches wide and 11 inches long. By default, WordPerfect leaves a 1-inch top margin and a 1-inch bottom margin. This allows a total of 9 inches of text to be printed on a standard page.

As you create a long document, you will notice that when the cursor nears Line 9.83", a row of hyphens is automatically inserted at the next line (Line 10"). This line is called a *page break*. The line below the page break is the beginning of page 2. The page break occurs after 10 inches because WordPerfect leaves the first inch of the paper blank and prints text on the next 9 inches.

### PAGE BREAKS

WordPerfect's default settings break each page near Line 10". However, there are several selections from the Format: Line, Format: Page, and Format: Other menus that may affect the location of page breaks.

#### Top and Bottom Margins

The top and bottom margin defaults are 1 inch. These settings are displayed on the Format: Page menu. To change the top and bottom margin settings, complete the following steps:

1. Access the Format: Page menu with Shift + F8, then choose 2 or P for Page.
   **M** *Click on Layout, then Page.*
2. From the Format: Page menu, choose 5 or M for Margins.
3. Key in the new top margin setting using inch measurements, then press Enter.
4. Key in the new bottom margin setting using inch measurements, then press Enter.
5. Press F7.

When the top and/or bottom margins have been changed, WordPerfect inserts a code in the document that can be viewed in Reveal Codes. If you change the top and bottom margins to 2 inches, the code displays as **[T/B Mar:2",2"]** in Reveal Codes.

When either or both margin defaults are changed, the default page break is also changed. For example, if the top margin is changed to 2 inches, WordPerfect inserts a page break every 8 inches. (Eleven inches minus 2 inches for the top margin and 1 inch for the bottom margin equals 8 inches.)

## Widow/Orphan

The last selection on the Format: Line menu is **Widow/Orphan Protection**. An orphan is the first line of a paragraph that appears at the bottom of a page while the rest of the paragraph is taken onto the next page. A widow is the last line of a paragraph that appears at the top of a page. **Widow/Orphan Protection** keeps at least 2 lines of a paragraph together at all times.

The default is for the Widow/Orphan Protection to be off. This means that WordPerfect inserts page breaks without considering whether a widow or orphan has occurred. When working with long documents, you will usually want this feature turned on. WordPerfect then takes the first line of a paragraph to the next page or breaks the page a line sooner so that a minimum of two lines of a paragraph fall at the top of a page.

To turn Widow/Orphan Protection on, complete the following steps:

1. Access the Format: Line menu with Shift + F8, then choose 1 or L for Line.
   **M** *Click on Layout, then Line.*
2. Choose 9 or W for Widow/Orphan Protection.
3. Key in a **Y** for Yes.
4. Press F7.

## Conditional End of Page

The Conditional End of Page feature tells WordPerfect to keep a certain number of lines together and not to insert a page break. For example, if you create a table that is 20 lines long, you may decide that it should not be divided between two pages. To identify the table as a block that should not be divided, move the cursor to the line above the table and insert a Conditional End of Page command by completing the following steps:

1.  Access the Format: Other menu with Shift + F8, then choose 4 or O for Other.
    **M** *Click on Layout, then Other*.
2.  Choose 2 or C for Conditional End of Page.
3.  At the prompt "**Number of Lines to Keep Together**", key in **20** and press Enter.
4.  Press F7.

The following message appears in Reveal Codes: **[Cndl EOP:20]**. If a page break falls within the 20 lines, WordPerfect breaks the page before the table, taking it in its entirety to the next page.

### Inserting Your Own Page Breaks

WordPerfect's default settings break each page at Line 10". If you have turned on Widow/Orphan Protection, inserted a Conditional End of Page command, or changed the top or bottom margins, the page break may vary. Even with these features, however, page breaks may appear in undesirable locations. To remedy these occurrences, you can insert your own page break. When you do so, the default page break disappears and is replaced by yours.

The WordPerfect page break appears as a hyphenated line. The page break you insert appears as a double hyphenated line. This makes it easy to see whether the page break was inserted by you or WordPerfect. The default page break is called a *soft page break* and a page break you insert is called a *hard page break*. Soft page breaks automatically adjust if text is added or deleted from a document. A hard page break does not adjust and is therefore less flexible than a soft page break. If you add or delete text from a document with a hard page break, check the break to determine whether it is still in a desirable location.

To insert a page break, move the cursor to the position where you want the page to break, hold down the Ctrl key, and press Enter. You will see a double hyphenated line inserted to indicate your page break. You may need to move the cursor up or down a few lines to see your page break replace the original page break.

Always check page breaks in a document. Some breaks require a judgment call that only you can make.

## CENTER PAGE

The **Center Page (top to bottom)** selection from the Format: Page menu is used to center text vertically on the page. You may, for example, want to vertically center the title page of a report, a short letter or memo, a table, or illustration.

To center text vertically on the page, complete the following steps:

1.  Key in the text.
2.  Move the cursor to the very beginning of the page. The cursor must be positioned before any text and codes.
3.  Access the Format: Page menu with Shift + F8, then choose 2 or P for Page.
    **M** *Click on Layout, then Page*.
4.  Choose 1 or C for Center Page (top to bottom).

5. Key in a **Y** for Yes.
6. Press F7.

Text will print centered on the paper but will not appear centered on the screen.

## CHAPTER REVIEW

### Summary

* Standard-sized stationery is 8 1/2 inches wide by 11 inches long. The top and bottom margins are 1 inch, which allows 9 inches of text on the page. WordPerfect inserts a page break at 10 inches.
* Widow/Orphan Protection is off by default. It can be turned on at the Format: Line menu. With Widow/Orphan Protection on, WordPerfect takes the first line of a paragraph to the next page or breaks the page one line sooner to allow two lines of a paragraph to go to the next page.
* The Conditional End of Page from the Format: Page menu, lets you identify a block of text that is to be kept as a unit and not divided by a page break.
* You can insert your own page break with Ctrl + Enter. The page break you insert appears as a double hyphenated line across the screen.
* Text can be vertically centered on the page with the Center Page (top to bottom) selection from the Format: Page menu.

### Commands Review

| | Keyboard | Mouse |
|---|---|---|
| Format: Line menu | Shift + F8, 1 or L | Layout, Line |
| Format: Page menu | Shift + F8, 2 or P | Layout, Page |
| Format: Other menu | Shift + F8, 4 or O | Layout, Other |
| Hard page break | Ctrl + Enter | |

## STUDY GUIDE FOR CHAPTER 7

**True/False:** Circle the letter T if the statement is true; circle the letter F if the statement is false.

1.  WordPerfect always breaks pages in a desirable location.                    T     F

2.  A widow is the last line of a paragraph that is taken to the top of a page.  T     F

3.  You can insert your own page breaks in a document.                          T     F

4.  The Widow/Orphan protection is on by default.                              T     F

5.  Conditional End of Page tells WordPerfect to keep a certain number of lines   T     F
    together.

6.  The WordPerfect page break appears as a double hyphenated line on the screen.  T     F

7.  The page break inserted by WordPerfect is considered a hard page break.      T     F


**Completion:** In the space provided at the right, indicate the correct number, symbol or term that answers the question.

1.  How many vertical inches are there on a standard sheet of          _____
    paper?

2.  The WordPerfect default gives you a page break after what          _____
    line?

3.  What do you press to insert your own page break?                   _____

4.  What do you press to access the Format: Page menu?                 _____

5.  What is the top margin default?                                    _____

6.  What do you press to access the Format: Other menu?                _____

7.  What is the bottom margin default?                                 _____

8.  What do you press to access the Format: Line menu?                 _____


## HANDS-ON EXERCISES

**Exercise One**

1.  Retrieve CH06PA2 to the screen.
2.  Move the cursor to the end of the document and add the paragraphs shown in figure 7-1. Indent the paragraphs with the Indent key, F4 (**M** *Click on Layout, Align, then Indent F4*).
3.  Move the cursor to the beginning of the document and change the line spacing to double. (Check the document and make sure there is a quadruple space between the title and first heading and a double space between all others lines.)
4.  Save the document and name it CH07EX1. Print CH07EX1.

**COMMUNITY ORGANIZATION:** Community organizers working door to door helped establish over 22 neighborhood self-help councils. The councils worked on such issues as a north-south bus on 23rd Avenue, getting street signs and lights at dangerous intersections, blocking the Emerald Expressway, and securing a fair share of government services. Communitywide special-interest organizations were mobilized and assisted, such as the ADC Motivated Parents, Tenants Association, and groups to deal with discrimination by police, business, and unions. Thousands of citizens were mobilized to participate in the array of Central Area Programs (CAPs), voter registration, voluntary school transfer program, and other training and employment opportunities.

**FAMILY SUPPORT SERVICES:** Day care centers were established in four churches. They enabled more than 150 limited-income and single parents to leave their children in safe, intellectually stimulating, and enjoyable settings while they worked or received training at CAP.

**VOLUNTEERS AND OUTREACH:** Aided by a full-time, unpaid volunteer coordinator, CAP activists and CAP staff members diligently recruited, oriented, trained, or worked alongside dozens of VISTA volunteers, students on field placements, and thousands of community volunteers. They worked from a few hours to many years as Study Center tutors, neighborhood advocates, performers, day care training specialists, fund raisers, resource providers, publicists, and artists. This was a reciprocal relationship providing those who gave a chance to develop their talents and their capacity for sharing.

**Figure 7-1: Exercise One**

## Exercise Two

1.  Retrieve CH07EX1 to the screen.
2.  Insert a hard page break with Ctrl + Enter at the left margin of the paragraph that begins "INTELLECTUAL: After-school and..." (Before inserting the page break, access Reveal Codes and position the cursor on the indent code.)
3.  Save the report and name it CH07EX2. Print CH07EX2.

## Exercise Three

1.  Retrieve CH07EX1 to the screen.
2.  With the cursor at the beginning of the document, change the top and bottom margins to 1.5 inches by completing the following steps:
    A.  Access the Format: Page menu with Shift + F8, then choose 2 or P for Page.
        **M** *Click on Layout, then Page.*
    B.  Choose 5 or M for Margins.
    C.  Key in **1.5** and press Enter.
    D.  Key in **1.5** and press Enter.
    E.  Press F7.

3. Move the cursor a double space above the paragraph that begins "YOUTH INVOLVE-MENT." (The cursor should be located on the last line of the paragraph that begins EMPLOYMENT.)

4. Insert a Conditional End of Page command for 14 lines by completing the following steps:
   A. Access the Format: Other menu with Shift + F8, then choose 4 or O for Other.
      **M** *Click on Layout, then Other*.
   B. Choose 2 or C for Conditional End of Page.
   C. Key in **14** and press Enter.
   D. Press F7.

5. Save the report and name it CH07EX3. Print CH07EX3.

## Exercise Four

1. At a clear screen, create the title page shown in figure 7-2. Boldface and center each line. Press the Enter key the number of times indicated in brackets.

2. Move the cursor to the beginning of the document. Access Reveal Codes, make sure the cursor is resting before any codes, then insert a Center Page code by completing the following steps:
   A. Access the Format: Page menu with Shift + F8, then choose 2 or P for Page.
      **M** *Click on Layout, then Page*.
   B. Choose 1 or C for Center Page (top to bottom). Key in Y for Yes.
   C. Press F7. (The text will not appear centered on the screen but will print centered on the page.)

3. Save the title page and name it CH07EX3. Print CH07EX3.

---

**CENTRAL AREA PROGRAM**
[Press Enter 15 times]

**A BRIEF HISTORY OF A COMMUNITY IN ACTION**
[Press Enter 15 times]

**by Dianna Cook, CAP Historian**

---

Figure 7-2: Exercise Four

## Exercise Five

1. Retrieve CH04PA1 to the screen.

2. Move the cursor to the end of the document and add the information shown in figure 7-3.

3. Move the cursor to the beginning of the document and turn Widow/Orphan Protection on by completing the following steps:
   A. Access the Format: Line menu with Shift + F8, then choose 1 or L for Line.
      **M** *Click on Layout, then Line*.
   B. Choose 9 or W for Widow/Orphan Protection.
   C. Key in a **Y** for Yes.
   D. Press F7.

4. Save the report and name it CH07EX5. Print CH07EX5.

A professor of statistics at the University of Washington, August Dvorak, designed a new keyboard arrangement, which he called the Dvorak keyboard. He patented his design in 1936.

Professor Dvorak conducted research in motion studies. Based on his research, he determined that the standard keyboard (Qwerty) was designed to slow down the typist. He designed his own keyboard based on the statistics he gathered.

As he watched people type, he noticed that the left hand was used more than the right hand and that the typist's fingers frequently had to jump up and down over the middle row of letters, greatly slowing the speed.

Professor Dvorak decided it would be easier to type if the most frequently used letters were placed in the middle row of keys--commonly called the home row keys. In the home row, he put vowels on the left hand and the most commonly used consonants on the right hand. The top row contained the next most commonly used letters, and the bottom row contained those least used.

With his arrangement of keys, Dvorak claimed that 70 percent of the typing would be done in the home row and 35 percent of the most commonly used words could be typed using only the home row. The result of this arrangement meant there was almost no finger motion.

In her article, "The Dvorak Keyboard," WSBEA Quarterly, Cecilia Shearson states, "In an average work day, a Qwerty typist's fingers travel the equivalent of about 16 miles on the keyboard while a Dvorak typist's fingers will travel about one mile."

Professor Dvorak asserted that the Qwerty typist's fingers travel from 12 to 20 miles in an average work day, whereas the Dvorak typist's fingers travel just over a mile. The lack of precision made it difficult to deduce an exact ratio. However, Dvorak stated that finger motions were reduced by more than 90 percent, implying a distance ratio of 10 to 1.

Figure 7-3: Exercise Five

## PERFORMANCE ASSESSMENTS

### Assessment One

1. Retrieve CH07EX5 to the screen.
2. Access Reveal Code and delete the [W/O On] code.
3. Delete one of the hard returns between the title and the body of the report. (This should leave a double space between the title and the body of the report.)
4. Move the cursor to the left margin of the paragraph that begins "A professor of statistics...," and insert a hard page break.
5. Save the report and name it CH07PA1. Print CH07PA1.

**Assessment Two**

1.  At a clear screen, key in the table shown in figure 7-4. Use the key line method to determine the tab settings. Boldface and center text as displayed.
2.  Move the cursor to the beginning of the document and insert a Center Page (top to bottom) code.
3.  Save the table and name it CH07PA2. Print CH07PA2.

---

**SALARY INCREASES**

**Effective January 1, 1993**

| Name | Increase | New Salary |
|------|----------|------------|
| Nona Lancaster | $   800 | $32,400 |
| Carl Gasperez | 1,200 | 30,250 |
| Deanna Dimico | 1,400 | 33,800 |
| Greg Acosta | 350 | 31,550 |
| Sue Yi | 900 | 33,600 |
| Faye Youngchild | 1,000 | 34,000 |
| Claire Rozell | 650 | 35,500 |

---

Figure 7-4: Assessment Two

# CHAPTER 8

## BLOCK OPERATIONS

### PERFORMANCE OBJECTIVE

Upon successful completion of chapter 8, you will be able to manipulate blocks and columns of text between areas of different business documents.

### CUT AND PASTE

In this chapter you will learn a procedure that is time-consuming to do on a typewriter but is quickly and neatly accomplished on a word processor. Many documents must be heavily revised, and these revisions can include moving, copying, or deleting blocks of text. This kind of editing is generally referred to as *cut and paste*. WordPerfect refers to this as a *block operation* or *block function*.

Documents created on typewriters may need revisions that require cutting and pasting with scissors and glue. The final product must then be completely retyped. With a word processor, a document can be revised on the screen and the text does not have to be rekeyed.

When cutting and pasting, you work with blocks of text that can be as small as one character or as large as an entire page or document. Once the text has been identified as a block, it can be

1. moved to a new location,
2. copied to a new location,
3. deleted from the document,
4. appended to a different document,
5. saved to a separate document, and
6. printed.

## MOVE COMMAND

The **Move** command, Ctrl + F4 (**M** *Click on Edit, then Select*), is used to move, copy, delete or append text that appears in a document as a sentence, paragraph, or page. When you access the Move command with Ctrl + F4, the prompt

**Move: 1 Sentence; 2 Paragraph; 3 Page; 4 Retrieve: 0**

appears at the bottom of the screen.

The first three choices let you move text by sentence, paragraph, or page. The fourth choice is used to retrieve text.

If you want to move a sentence, position the cursor on any character (or blank space) within the sentence and then choose 1 or S for Sentence. The sentence appears in reverse video. WordPerfect knows where a sentence begins and ends by looking for periods, exclamation points, and question marks. (**M** *Position the cursor within the paragraph and click on Edit, Select, then Sentence.*) click on Edit, Select, then Sentence.)

To move an entire paragraph, position the cursor anywhere within the paragraph and choose 2 or P for Paragraph. The paragraph will be highlighted in reverse video. WordPerfect identifies a paragraph as one hard return (Enter) to the next. (**M** *Position the cursor within the paragraph and click on Edit, Select, then Paragraph.*)

To move a page, choose 3 or A for Page (**M** *Click on Edit, Select, then Page*). WordPerfect will highlight the page where the cursor is located. WordPerfect defines a page as any text between page breaks.

After you have decided on the amount of text to be moved and have chosen a sentence, paragraph, or page, the prompt changes to

**1 Move; 2 Copy; 3 Delete; 4 Append: 0**

The Move command not only lets you move text; you can also choose to copy, delete, or append text. If you choose 1 or M for Move, the highlighted text disappears from the screen and remains in temporary memory until it is retrieved to the document, new text is moved or copied, or WordPerfect is exited. If you choose 2 or C for Copy, the text stays in its original location, an exact copy is placed in temporary memory, and an exact copy is inserted into a new location. The third choice lets you delete a sentence, paragraph, or page from a document. The last selection, Append, lets you move blocked text to a new or different document.

If you move or copy, WordPerfect displays the message **Move cursor; press Enter to retrieve** in the lower left corner of the screen.

To retrieve the text, move the cursor to the location where it is to be inserted, and press Enter. The text is inserted into the document without deleting existing text. WordPerfect automatically adjusts text if necessary.

As an example, suppose you keyed in a document with three paragraphs. After reading the paragraphs, you decided that the second paragraph should come before the first paragraph. To change the location of the paragraphs, complete the following steps:

1.   Move the cursor to the second paragraph.
2.   Access the Move command with Ctrl + F4.
3.   Choose 2 or P for Paragraph.
     **M** *Click on Edit, Select, then Paragraph.*
4.   Choose 1 or M for Move.
5.   Move the cursor to the first character of paragraph 1.
6.   Press Enter.

Follow the same basic steps to copy text to a new location in a document. At step 4, choose 2 or C for Copy, instead of 1 or M for Move.

If you delete text with the Move command, the text is removed from the screen and is placed in temporary memory. The text can be retrieved to the screen with Cancel, F1. The Cancel key can be used to "undelete" the last three deletions. So, if the text you deleted with the Move command is one of the last three deletions you have completed, access Cancel, F1, and restore the text.

If you chose to append a sentence, paragraph, or page that has been selected with the Move command, WordPerfect will display the message **Append to: _** Key in the name of the document you want the text appended to and press Enter. If it is an existing document on the disk, WordPerfect inserts the appended text at the end of the document. If you key in a new document name, WordPerfect creates a new document. For example, to append a paragraph in the document displayed on the screen into a document on the disk named REPORT, follow these steps:

1. Move the cursor anywhere within the paragraph to be appended.

2. Access the Move command with Ctrl + F4 and choose 2 or P for Paragraph.
   **M** *Click on Edit, Select, then Paragraph.*

3. With the paragraph selected, choose 4 or A for Append.

4. At the **Append to:** prompt, key in **REPORT** and press Enter.

The highlighting on the paragraph disappears and the paragraph stays in the original document with a copy being appended to the REPORT document.

## BLOCK COMMAND

The methods described above are used to move, copy, delete, or append a sentence, paragraph, or page. To move, copy, delete, or append an amount of text that does not fit into these categories, you need to use the Block command together with the Move command.

To highlight text with the Block command, access the command with Alt + F4 or F12 (**M** *Click on Edit, then Block*) and the message **Block on** flashes in the bottom left corner of the screen. Move the cursor through the text to be highlighted either with the cursor movement keys and commands, the mouse (**M** *Click, hold down the left button and drag*), or a variety of other methods. As the cursor moves through text, the text it passes through is changed to reverse video. Text can be quickly highlighted with the following methods.

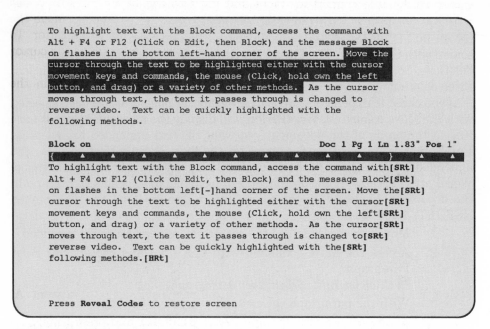

Figure 8-1: Block Command

## Blocking Text by Paragraph, Sentence, or Specific Character

If you want a paragraph blocked, move the cursor to the beginning of the paragraph, access the Block command, and press Enter. This moves the cursor to the end of the paragraph. To block a sentence, move the cursor to the first character of the sentence, access the Block command and press the period. This moves the cursor to the next period and blocks the sentence. Keying in any other character moves the cursor to the next occurrence of that character in the text.

## Canceling the Block Command

The Block command can be canceled with either the Cancel key, F1, or the Block command. If you change your mind or you block the wrong text, press F1, Alt + F4 or F12 (**M** *Click on Edit, then Block*) and the blocking is deactivated.

## Moving Text with the Block Command

To move a block of text that does not fit into the category of sentence, paragraph, or page, block the text first with the Block command, and then access the Move command with Ctrl + F4. The prompt **Move: 1 _B_lock; 2 _T_abular _C_olumn; 3 _R_ectangle: _0_** appears at the bottom of the screen.

Choose 1 or B for Block to tell WordPerfect that you are working with a block of text. The other two selections are used for columns established with tab stops and rectangles. When you choose 1 or B, the prompt changes to **1 _M_ove; 2 _C_opy; 3 _D_elete; 4 _A_ppend: _0_**

This is the same prompt as the one you see when using just the Move command. Choose 1 or M for Move and the message **Move cursor; press Enter to retrieve** displays in the lower left corner of the screen. Move the cursor to the location where you want the text inserted and press Enter. To move blocked text with the mouse, click on Edit, then Move. Move the cursor where you want the text inserted and press Enter.

To move a partial page of a document to another location within the document, follow these steps:

1.  Move the cursor to the beginning of text to be moved.
2.  Access the Block command with Alt + F4 or F12.
    **M** *Click on Edit, then Block.*
3.  Move the cursor to the end of text to be moved.
4.  Access the Move command with Ctrl + F4.
5.  Choose 1 or B for Block.
6.  Choose 1 or M for Move.
    **M** *Click on Edit, then Move.*
7.  Move the cursor to the new location and press Enter.

Follow the same basic steps to copy text to a new location in a document. At step 6, choose 2 or C for Copy, instead of 1 or M for Move.

If you delete text with the Block and Move commands, the text is removed from the screen and is placed in temporary storage. The text can be retrieved to the screen with Cancel, F1, as described earlier in this chapter.

You can also append text that has been blocked. The steps to append text to a different document are similar to the ones described earlier in the chapter. To append text that does not fit into the category of sentence, paragraph, or page, into a document named REPORT, follow these steps:

1.  Move the cursor to the beginning of text to be moved.
2.  Access the Block command with Alt + F4 or F12.
    **M** *Click on Edit, then Block.*
3.  Move cursor to the end of text to be moved.
4.  Access the Move command with Ctrl + F4.
5.  Choose 1 or B for Block.
6.  Choose 4 or A for Append.
    **M** *Click on Edit, Append, then To File.*
7.  At the **Append to:** prompt, key in **REPORT** and press Enter.

The highlighting on the text disappears and the text remains in the original document with a copy being appended to the REPORT document.

## SWITCH DOCUMENTS

WordPerfect lets you create or edit two documents at the same time. At a clear screen, the status line in the bottom right corner of the screen appears as **Doc 1 Pg 1 Ln 1"  Pos 1"**. Doc 1 indicates that you are currently working in Document 1. You can switch to Document 2 with the Switch command, Shift + F3 (**M** *Click on Edit, then Switch Document*). When you use this command, the text in Document 1 disappears and is replaced by a clear screen. The status line appears as **Doc 2  Pg 1  Ln 1"  Pos 1"**.

With the Switch command, you do not have to exit or save a document before moving on to another. For example, Document 2 can be used to practice commands or functions without interfering with the text in Document 1. Document 2 can also be used to create forms or tables with special tabs and formats that can then be moved into Document 1. If you are working in a long document and need to create a short memo or letter, you can switch to Document 2, create the memo, and return to Document 1 for further work.

### Moving and Copying Between Two Documents

Text that is created in Document 1 can be moved or copied to Document 2. Text can also be moved or copied from Document 2 to Document 1. For example, to move a table you created in Document 2 to Document 1, complete the following steps:

1. At a clear screen, switch to Document 2 with Shift + F3.
   **M** *Click on Edit, then Switch Document.*
2. Create the table.
3. Highlight the table with the Block command, access the Move command, and choose 1 or M for Move.
4. Switch back to Document 1 with Shift + F3.
   **M** *Click on Edit, then Switch Document.*
5. Move the cursor to the location where the table is to be inserted and press Enter.

Text can be copied between Documents 1 and 2 in a similar manner. Save text in Document 2 as you ordinarily would. If you create text in Document 2 and then switch back to Document 1, when you save Document 1, WordPerfect asks if you want to save Document 2.

## COLUMNAR TEXT

When the Block command is activated, the cursor highlights text as it moves through the document. As the cursor moves down the screen, all text from the left to the right margin is highlighted. If you want to move, copy, delete, or append one of several columns in a document, the text must be identified as a column.

When blocking columns of text, specific tab stops must be established on the tab ruler line to align columns. If the default tab line is used to set up columns, the Tab key may need to be pressed several times to move the cursor to a column setting. When tabbing in this manner, tab codes are inserted in the document and can interfere with the column blocking process. For this reason, you should set tab stops on the tab ruler line when creating columns rather than using the default tabs.

### Moving Columnar Text

To move a column of text in a document, move the cursor to any character on the first line of the column and access the Block command. Move the cursor to any character in the last entry of the column and access the Move command with Ctrl + F4. The prompt **Move:   1 Block; 2 Tabular Column; 3 Rectangle: 0** appears at the bottom of the screen.

Choose 2 or C for Tabular Column. If you are using a mouse, block the column and click on Edit, Select, then Tabular Column. When you choose Tabular Column, the block highlighting changes. The column and the space in front of the column is highlighted, eliminating highlighting on the other columns, and the prompt changes to **1 <u>M</u>ove; 2 <u>C</u>opy; 3 <u>D</u>elete; 4 <u>A</u>ppend: <u>0</u>**.

To move the column to a new location, choose 1 or M for Move. The column that is highlighted and the spaces in front of it are removed from the screen and stored in temporary memory. Any columns to the right move over to fill in the gap. Move the cursor to the location where you want the column to appear and press Enter.

As an example, suppose that three columns were keyed in with left tab stops set at Positions 1", 2.8", and 4.9" on the tab ruler line.

| | | |
|---|---|---|
| January | Shipping | V48678 |
| February | Publicity | X74565 |
| March | Engineering | C37455 |
| April | Accounting | T38443 |

To move column 2 to the right of column 3, follow these steps:

1. Move the cursor to any character on the first line of column 2.
2. Access the Block command with Alt + F4 or F12.
   **M** *Click on Edit, then Block.*
3. Move the cursor to any character in the last entry of column 2.
4. Access the Move command with Ctrl + F4 and choose 2 or C for Tabular Column.
   **M** *Click on Edit, Select, then Tabular Column.*
6. Choose 1 or M for Move.
7. Move the cursor one space after the first column entry in the second column and press Enter.

The columns will look like this:

| | | |
|---|---|---|
| January | V48678 | Shipping |
| February | X74565 | Publicity |
| March | C37455 | Engineering |
| April | T38443 | Accounting |

## COPYING COLUMNAR TEXT

Copying a column is very similar to moving a column. To copy a column, complete the following steps.

1. Move the cursor to any character on the first line of the column and access the Block command with Alt + F4 or F12.
   **M** *Click on Edit, then Block.*
2. Move the cursor to any chracter in the last entry of the column, access the Move command with Ctrl + F4, and choose 2 or C for Tabular Column.
   **M** *Click on Edit, Select, then Tabular Column.*
3. Choose 2 or C for Copy.
4. Move the cursor to the position where the column is to be copied and press Enter.

The text stays in its original position and a copy is inserted in the new location.

Using the three columns from the earlier example, copy column 1 below the three columns by completing the following steps:

1. Move to the end of the document and press the Enter key two times. (This is to make sure that you will be able to move the cursor below the columns.)

2. Move the cursor to the first line of column 1.

3. Access the Block command with Alt + F4 or F12.
   **M** *Click on Edit, then Block.*

4. Move the cursor to the last entry of column 1.

5. Access the Move command with Ctrl + F4 and choose 2 or C for Tabular Column.
   **M** *Click on Edit, Select, then Tabular Column.*

6. Choose 2 or C for Copy.

7. Move the cursor to the left margin a double space below the columns and press Enter.

The columns will look like this:

| | | |
|---|---|---|
| January | V48678 | Shipping |
| February | X74565 | Publicity |
| March | C37455 | Engineering |
| April | T38443 | Accounting |

January
February
March
April

## DELETING AND APPENDING COLUMNAR TEXT

To delete a column of text, move the cursor to the first entry of the column and access the Block command. Move the cursor to the last entry of the same column, access the Move command with Ctrl + F4, and choose 2 or C for Tabular Column (**M** *Click on Edit, Select, then Tabular Column*). At the next prompt, choose 3 or D for Delete. The column deleted is removed from the screen and any columns to the right move over to fill in the gap.

As an example, to delete the second column in the columns above, complete the following steps:

1. Move the cursor to the first line of column 2.

2. Access the Block command with Alt + F4 or F12.
   **M** *Click on Edit, then Block.*

3. Move the cursor to the last entry of column 2.

4. Access the Move command with Ctrl + F4 and choose 2 or C for Tabular Columns.
   **M** *Click on Edit, Select, then Tabular Column.*

5. Choose 3 or D for Delete.

The column is removed from the screen and column 3 moves over to fill in the gap. The columns look like this:

| January  | Shipping    |
|----------|-------------|
| February | Publicity   |
| March    | Engineering |
| April    | Accounting  |

January
February
March
April

Columns may also be appended to a document on the disk or into a new document. To append a column, follow the steps described above, except choose 4 or A for Append. Key in the file name and press Enter.

## CHAPTER REVIEW

### Summary

- A block of text can be defined as one character or as an entire page or document.
- The Move command is used to move, copy, delete, or append a sentence, paragraph, or page.
- Text to be moved with the Move command is stored in temporary memory. It remains in memory until it is retrieved to the document, new text is moved or copied, or WordPerfect is exited.
- To move, copy, delete, or append text that does not fit into the category of sentence, paragraph, or page, the text must be blocked with the Block command before accessing the Move command.
- With the Block command on, you can press Enter to block a paragraph or the period to block a sentence. When you press any character on the keyboard, the cursor moves to the first occurrence of that character in the text.
- If, during the middle of blocking text, you change your mind, you can use the Cancel key, F1, Alt + F4 or F12 (M *Click on Edit, then Block*), to deactivate blocking.
- You can create or edit two documents at the same time. WordPerfect identifies them as Document 1 and Document 2. To switch between the two documents, use the Switch command, Shift + F3 (M *Click on Edit, then Switch Document*).
- A column of text can be moved, copied, deleted, or appended with Block and Move commands.
- To move, copy, delete, or append columnar text, columns must be created with tabs set on the tab line.

### Commands Review

|                 | Keyboard          | Mouse                 |
|-----------------|-------------------|-----------------------|
| Move command    | Ctrl + F4         | Edit, Select          |
| Block command   | Alt + F4 or F12   | Edit, Block           |
| Switch command  | Shift + F3        | Edit, Switch Document |

## STUDY GUIDE FOR CHAPTER 8

**True/False:** Circle the letter T if the statement is true; circle the letter F if the statement is false.

1.  A block of text may be as small as one character or as large as an entire page.     T     F

2.  When text is moved, it remains in its original position and a copy is inserted in     T     F
    a new location.

3.  A paragraph is one hard return (Enter) to the next.     T     F

4.  If necessary, WordPerfect adjusts text that has been inserted.     T     F

5.  Text appended to a different document is removed from its original position.     T     F

6.  When a column is deleted, any columns to the right move in to fill the gap.     T     F


**Completion**: In the space provided at the right, indicate the correct number, symbol, term or command for the explanation.

1.  Press these keys to access the Move command.                    _____

2.  The Move command is used to move a sentence, a paragraph, or     _____
    this.

3.  Press these keys to access the Switch command.                  _____

4.  Turn off the Block command with Alt + F4, F12 or this key.       _____


## HANDS-ON EXERCISES

### Exercise One
1.  At a clear screen, key in the business letter shown in figure 8-2. Use an appropriate format
    for the letter. Boldface and underline text as displayed. Use the Indent command to indent
    the paragraphs below **Price, Speed, and Graphics Capabilities.**
2.  Save the letter and name it CH08EX1. Print CH08EX1.

### Exercise Two
1.  Retrieve CH08EX1 and make the following changes:
    A.  Delete the first paragraph in the letter.
    B.  Move **Price** and the paragraph below it beneath the **Speed** paragraph.
    C.  Add the following heading and paragraph below the Speed paragraph:

    ### Print Modes

    > Many dot matrix printers have two print modes—draft and letter
    > quality. The draft mode is the fastest.

2.  Check the spacing of the letter. Delete or add lines between paragraphs as needed.
3.  Save the revised letter and name it CH08EX2. Print CH08EX2

January 23, 1993

Mr. John Avey
2301 South First Street
Spokane, WA   99302

Dear Mr. Avey:

We received your letter regarding dot matrix printers.  We have
gathered some information that will help you decide on the type of
printer you want for your business.

Dot matrix printers have been improving in the past few years.
Some qualities of dot matrix printers include the following:

## Price

When compared to other types of printers, dot matrix
printers are at the lower end of the price scale. Prices
begin below $100 and move upward.

## Speed

Dot matrix printers are more versatile and up to 10 times
faster than character printers.  Printing speed ranges
from 50 to over 300 characters per second (cps).

## Graphics Capabilities

A standard feature on most dot matrix printers is the
ability to place a dot at any position on the page.  This
feature lets dot matrix printers print graphics.

We will be sending you information on character and laser printers.

Sincerely,

Harold Vonstein

xx:CH08EX1

**Figure 8-2: Exercise One**

**Exercise Three**
1. Retrieve CH07EX1 to the screen. Access Reveal Codes and delete the code for double line spacing.
2. Make the changes indicated by the proofreaders' marks shown in figure 8-3. (When moving the indented paragraphs, make sure the Indent code is included.)
3. Save the report and name it CH08EX3. Print CH08EX3.

# A BRIEF HISTORY OF A COMMUNITY IN ACTION

## THE WAR ON POVERTY YEARS: 1964-1969

In the spring of 1964, before Congress passed the Economic Opportunity Act, a group of Central Area residents and friends began formation of a comprehensive antipoverty proposal. Many civil rights leaders were pessimistic about the government funding any earnest social change, and many social service administrators were dubious about grass roots involvement. But once War On Poverty legislation was actually passed, interest intensified in this action plan for what would soon be christened the Central Area Program or CAP.

Around the country, most Economic Opportunity grants went to expand established agencies. CAP became the first totally new, community-inspired program in the country to receive funding. Now, a quarter of a century later, it holds the distinction of being the oldest surviving, independent agency launched in that era. The now-popular myth that the War On Poverty was a failure is repudiated by the productive history of the vast majority of people who shared in the formative years of CAP. Equally crucial has been the changed image of the Central Area.

In those prolific years, CAP became the service arm of the Tacoma civil rights movement and grew to more than 300 employees in the summer of 1967. It encompassed a huge corps of volunteers that developed a broad network of cooperative community groups. The major arenas of service and action included the following:

**INTELLECTUAL:** After-school and evening homework help and education enrichment for some 10,000 latch-key kids and other youth in eleven Central Area Study Centers (1965-1967). A parent outreach program assisted mothers and fathers in promoting the motivation and academic progress of their children. A joint CAP/Tacoma Public School "Counseling Bank" helped alienated students and parents reconcile with the public schools.

*[handwritten note in margin: move below youth involvement]*

**EMPLOYMENT:** CAP job counseling, referral, and training projects assisted thousands of unemployed and underemployed heads of households, teenagers, welfare mothers, school dropouts, ex-convicts, new immigrants, victims of racism, and socially, mentally, and physically handicapped persons. Approximately 500 youth and adults filled earn-while-you-learn positions in regular and special "crash" programs. Trainees and paraprofessionals constituted the majority of workers in the Beautification, Action Education, Community Organization, Day Care, Performing Arts, Study Center and Youth departments.

**YOUTH INVOLVEMENT:** The Youth Department promoted leadership and social career skill development through Senior High and Junior High Teen Councils. They operated a self-help job line, organized summer festivals and other recreational activities, fostered interschool and intercommunity conflict resolution sessions, and participated in extensive career counseling.

**COMMUNITY ORGANIZATION:** Community organizers working door to door helped establish over 22 neighborhood self-help councils. The councils worked on such issues as a north-south bus on 23rd Avenue, getting street signs and lights at dangerous intersections, blocking the Emerald Expressway, and securing a fair share of government services. Community wide special-interest organizations were mobilized and assisted, such as the ADC Motivated Parents, Tenants Association, and groups to deal with discrimination by police, business, and unions. Thousands of citizens were mobilized to participate in the array of Central Area Programs (CAPs), voter registration, voluntary school transfer program, and other training and employment opportunities.

**FAMILY SUPPORT SERVICES:** Day care centers were established in four churches. They enabled more than 150 limited income and single parents to leave their children in safe, intellectually stimulating, and enjoyable settings while they worked or received training at CAP.

**VOLUNTEERS AND OUTREACH:** Aided by a full-time, unpaid volunteer coordinator, CAP activists and CAP staff members diligently recruited, oriented, trained, or worked alongside dozens of VISTA volunteers, students on field placements, and thousands of community volunteers. They worked from a few hours to many years as Study Center tutors, neighborhood advocates, performers, day care training specialists, fund raisers, resource providers, publicists, and artists. This was a reciprocal relationship providing those who gave a chance to develop their talents and their capacity for sharing.

*delete*

*move below Employ- ment*

Figure 8-3: Exercise Three

## Exercise Four

1.  At a clear screen, key in the information shown in figure 8-4. Center and boldface the title. Do not enter the information in brackets at the end of the form.

2.  Block the text (including the title) and copy it a triple space below the last line.

3.  Block all the text and copy it a triple space below the last line. Continue copying text until the form has been repeated nine times. After all the forms are copied, check the soft page break and determine whether it is in a desirable location. If it is not, insert your own page break with Ctrl + Enter between forms, not within.

4.  Save the forms document and name it CH08EX4. Print CH08EX4.

**STUDENT IDENTIFICATION**

NAME _____   DATE _____

STREET ADDRESS _____

CITY _____   STATE _____ ZIP _____

QUARTER ENROLLED _____   NUMBER OF CREDITS ____
[Press Enter three times.]

Figure 8-4: Exercise Four

**Exercise Five**

1.  At a clear screen, key in the headings and first paragraph of the memorandum shown in figure 8-5. Use an appropriate memorandum style. Do not key in the information in brackets. Switch to Document 2 and create the tabbed information. Use the key line method to determine the tab settings. Block the tabbed information and copy it to Document 1. (When you block the tabbed information, include the Tab Set code.)

2.  Save the memorandum and name it CH08EX5. When WordPerfect asks if you want to exit Document 1, key in **Y** for yes. This switches you to Doc2. Save Doc2 and name it CH08DOC2. Print CH08EX5 and CH08DOC2.

DATE:   January 24, 1993; TO:   Janet Weiss, Director of Personnel;
FROM:   Valerie Pagano, Supplies Department; SUBJECT:   Stationery
Supplies

At the beginning of this year, we switched to a new wholesale
supply company. This company is offering stationery supplies at
reduced rates for bulk orders. The list below indicates the
supplies we are ordering and the percentage of savings.

[Switch to Document 2, set up appropriate tab settings, and key in the following text.]

| No. 6 Envelopes | $1.25 per carton | 20% discount |
| No. 10 Envelopes | $1.89 per carton | 18% discount |
| Bond paper, white | $3.25 per ream | 14% discount |
| Bond paper, cherry | $3.40 per ream | 17% discount |
| Letterhead stationery | $3.89 per ream | 15% discount |

[Copy the tabbed information, including the tab set code, switch to Document 1, and insert below the first paragraph.]

We will be ordering supplies next week.  Please let me know by the
end of this week what you want to order and the quantity.

Figure 8-5: Exercise Five

**Exercise Six**

1.   At a clear screen, delete previous tabs and set new left tabs at +0.6, +3.2, and +5.2 inches.
2.   Key in the letter shown in figure 8-6 in an appropriate business letter format.
3.   Save the letter and name it CH08EX6. Print CH08EX6.

---

January 24, 1993

Mr. Kosal Mao
12443 43rd Avenue East
Spokane, WA  99302

Dear Mr. Mao:

As a valued customer of Omega Tech, we want you to be the first to
hear about our storewide sale.  We are cutting prices on all types
of computer supplies.  Our sale will be going on the entire month
of February.  Each week we will spotlight a special item.  The
following information lists the special item, the week it is on
sale, and the percentage of markdown.

```
        Computer paper          February 1-7       40% off
        Computer ribbons        February 8-14      30% off
        Educational programs    February 15-21     25% off
        Floppy disks            February 22-28     25% off
```

Come in early and take advantage of our incredibly low prices.  As
a preferred customer of Omega Tech, you qualify for our special
"early bird" prices, which take effect January 30.

Sincerely,

Devon McKenna
Manager
xx:CH08EX6

---

Figure 8-6: Exercise Six

**Exercise Seven**

1.   Retrieve CH08EX6 to the screen.
2.   Reverse the second and third columns of the tabbed information.
3.   Save the letter and name it CH08EX7. Print CH08EX7.

**Exercise Eight**

1.   Retrieve CH08EX7 to the screen.
2.   Delete the last column indicating the week of the sale.
3.   Save the letter and name it CH08EX8. Print CH08EX8.

**Exercise Nine**

1. At a clear screen, key in the memorandum shown in figure 8-7 in an appropriate memorandum style. Use the key line method to determine the tab settings for the tabbed information.
2. Save the memorandum and name it CH08EX9. Print CH08EX9.

---

DATE: May 2, 1993; TO: Terry Preston, Vice President; FROM: Heidi Schueler, Director of Sales; SUBJECT: Financial Report

The following list shows the net profits for the employees of the Sales Department.

| Name | January | February | March |
|------|---------|----------|-------|
| Nona Lancaster | $  845 | $ 1,286 | $  923 |
| Carl Gasperez | 743 | 823 | 886 |
| Deanna Dimico | 1,004 | 1,208 | 995 |
| Greg Acosta | 948 | 878 | 850 |
| Sue Yi | 732 | 874 | 855 |
| Faye Youngchild | 1,485 | 1,533 | 1,332 |
| Claire Rozell | 806 | 732 | 783 |

xx:CH08EX9

---

Figure 8-7: Exercise Nine

**Exercise Ten**

1.  Retrieve CH08EX9 to the screen.

2.  Delete the January column heading and the column of numbers below it. Add the following April column to the right of the March column:

<u>April</u>
$ 972
793
1,012
819
724
1,326
820

3.  Save the revised memorandum and name it CH08EX10. Print CH08EX10.

## PERFORMANCE ASSESSMENTS

**Assessment One**

1.  Retrieve CH07EX5 to the screen. Access Reveal Codes and delete the **[Line Spacing:2]** code. (This will cause the report to be single spaced.)

2.  Make the changes indicated by the proofreaders' marks in figure 8-8.

3.  Save the report and name it CH08PA1. Print CH08PA1.

---

### THE EVOLUTION OF THE TYPEWRITER

The first recorded patent for a "typing machine" was issued to Henry Mill by Queen Ann of England. Henry Mill developed his machine in the early 1700s. However, the model he designed could not be turned into a workable model, and so it was never marketed.

The first marketable typewriter was designed by Christopher Latham Sholes, a newspaper editor, printer, and politician. Because his model was marketed, he is given credit for inventing the typewriter. In the early 1870s, the E. Remington and Sons Company bought Sholes' design and produced and manufactured the Remington Model No. 1 typewriter.

Sholes chose a design for the typewriter keys that slowed down the typist. He did this by placing commonly used keys in separate sections of the keyboard. This was done to ensure that the mechanical type bars would have enough time to fall back into place before the next keystroke had a chance to jam two bars together. Sholes' design is now commonly called the Qwerty keyboard, after the first six letters on the top alphabetic row.

*move to end*

Touch typing was not common until about twenty-five years after the introduction of the typewriter. In Cincinnati, Ohio, in 1888, two men competed against each other in a typing competition. One man, Louis Taub, used two fingers to type; the other, Frank McGurrin, used all ten. McGurrin had memorized the keyboard layout and did not have to look back and forth between his fingers and the text. McGurrin won that competition.

A professor of statistics at the University of Washington, August Dvorak, designed a new keyboard arrangement, which he called the Dvorak keyboard. He patented his design in 1936.

Professor Dvorak conducted research in motion studies. Based on his research, he determined that the standard keyboard (Qwerty) was designed to slow down the typist. He designed his own keyboard based on the statistics he gathered.

*copy to beginning*

As he watched people type, he noticed that the left hand was used more than the right hand and that the typist's fingers frequently had to jump up and down over the middle row of letters, greatly slowing the speed.

Professor Dvorak decided it would be easier to type if the most frequently used letters were placed in the middle row of keys--commonly called the home row keys. In the home row, he put vowels on the left hand and the most commonly used consonants on the right hand. The top row contained the next most commonly used letters, and the bottom row contained those least used.

*delete*

With his arrangement of keys, Dvorak claimed that 70 percent of the typing would be done in the home row and 35 percent of the most commonly used words could be typed using only the home row. The result of this arrangement meant there was almost no finger motion.

In her article, "The Dvorak Keyboard," WSBEA Quarterly, Cecilia Shearson states, "In an average work day, a Qwerty typist's fingers travel the equivalent of about 16 miles on the keyboard while a Dvorak typist's fingers will travel about one mile."

Professor Dvorak asserted that the Qwerty typist's fingers travel from 12 to 20 miles in an average work day, whereas the Dvorak typist's fingers travel just over a mile. The lack of precision made it difficult to deduce an exact ratio. However, Dvorak stated that finger motions were reduced by more than 90 percent, implying a distance ratio of 10 to 1.

---

Figure 8-8: Assessment One

**Assessment Two**

1. At a clear screen, key in the memorandum in figure 8-9 in an appropriate memorandum style. You determine the margins and justification. Make the changes indicated by the proofreaders' marks. Use the key line method to determine the tab settings for the tabbed information. (Before copying the department names a double space below the names, insert hard returns between the names and the last paragraph. If hard returns are not entered, the copied names may merge with the last paragraph.)

2. Save the memorandum and name it CH08PA2. Print CH08PA2.

---

DATE:   March 4, 1993; TO: Kim Chun, Vice President, Operations;
FROM: Director of Personnel; SUBJECT:   Department charges

The charges assessed each department of Puget Sound Semiconductor
for the month of February are listed below.

*(handwritten insertions: "3 1" after "month"; "and March" above; "^" marks)*

| | *February* | *$2,002.83* |
|---|---|---|
| Engineering | $1,205.45 | *937.64* |
| Accounting | 897.55 | *1,032.87* |
| Data Processing | 1,450.50 | *2,568.72* |
| Legal | 576.85 | *496.13* |
| Maintenance | 650.00 | *589.19* |
| Supplies | 642.25 | *1,589.02* |
| Administration | 1,205.60 | |

*(handwritten: "copy to one blank line below" bracket on left; "March" with arrow below the list)*

The figures have been sent to the Finance Department.  If you would
like to discuss the charges, please contact me.

---

Figure 8-9: Assessment Two

# CHAPTER 9

## PRINTING

## PERFORMANCE OBJECTIVE

Upon successful completion of chapter 9, you will be able to control printing features for simple business documents.

### PRINT MENU

The Print and the Print: Control Printer menus can be used to control many aspects of printing. To bring the Print menu to the screen, access the Print menu with Shift + F7 (**M** *Click on File, then Print*) and the text in figure 9-1 appears on the screen.

```
Print

    1 - Full Document
    2 - Page
    3 - Document on Disk
    4 - Control Printer
    5 - Multiple Pages
    6 - View Document
    7 - Initialize Printer


Options

    S - Select Printer                  PostScript (Additional)
    B - Binding Offset                  0"
    N - Number of Copies                1
    U - Multiple Copies Generated by    WordPerfect
    G - Graphics Quality                Medium
    T - Text Quality                    High




Selection: 0
```

Figure 9-1: Print Menu

The first selection from the Print menu is used to print the current document displayed. To use this selection, complete the following steps:

1. Retrieve a document to the screen.
2. Access the Print menu with Shift + F7.
   **M** *Click on File, then Print.*
3. Choose 1 or F for Full Document.

The second selection, Page, lets you print the page where the cursor is located. To use this selection, complete the following steps:

1. Retrieve a document to the screen and move the cursor to the page to be printed.
2. Access the Print command with Shift + F7.
   **M** *Click on File, then Print.*
3. Choose 2 or P for Page.

The third selection from the Print menu, Document on Disk, lets you print any document that is saved on the disk. When you choose 3 or D for Document on Disk, the prompt **Document name:** _ appears at the bottom of the screen.

At this prompt, key in the name of the document to be printed, press Enter, and the prompt changes to **Page(s) All:** _.

If you want to print the entire document, press Enter. You can also specify particular pages to be printed. The following table illustrates your options for printing pages (X, Y, and Z denote page numbers):

| **Entry** | **Action** |
|-----------|-----------|
| Enter | Entire document printed |
| X | Page X printed |
| X- | Page X to end of document printed |
| X-Y | Pages X through Y printed |
| -X | Beginning of document through page X printed |
| X,Y | Pages X and Y printed |
| X-Y,Z | Pages X through Y and Z printed |

The hyphen is used to identify a range, and the comma is used to identify specific pages. As illustrated in the last entry, the hyphen and comma can be used in the same print job. With these options, you can print as little or as much of a document as you wish. You can also identify specific pages for printing when you print from the directory.

If you want to print specific pages of the document currently displayed on the screen, choose 5 or M for Multiple Pages from the Print menu. At the **Page(s)** prompt, key in the page numbers to be printed and press Enter. For example, to print pages 2 through 5 and page 8 of the document currently displayed on the screen, complete the following steps:

1. Access the Print command with Shift + F7.
   **M** *Click on File, then Print.*
2. Choose 5 or M for Multiple Pages.
3. Key in **2-5,8** and press Enter.
4. Press F7 to return the cursor to the document.

## CONTROL PRINTER MENU

When a document is printing, the Print: Control Printer menu displays information about the document as well as offering printing selections. To display the menu, access the Print command with Shift + F7 (**M** *Click on File, then Print*), then choose 4 or C for Control Printer. The Print: Control Printer menu displays on the screen as shown in figure 9-2.

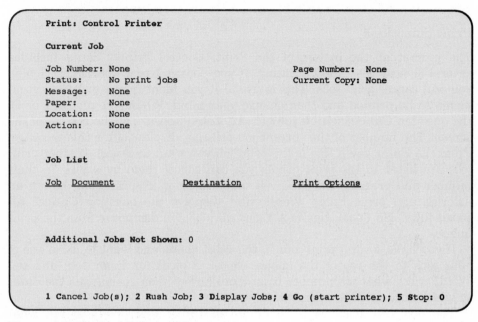

```
Print: Control Printer

Current Job

Job Number: None                         Page Number:  None
Status:     No print jobs                Current Copy: None
Message:    None
Paper:      None
Location:   None
Action:     None


Job List

Job  Document              Destination        Print Options




Additional Jobs Not Shown: 0




   1 Cancel Job(s); 2 Rush Job; 3 Display Jobs; 4 Go (start printer); 5 Stop: 0
```

Figure 9-2: Control Printer Menu

The Print: Control Printer menu includes three sections: Current Job, Job List, and print selections at the bottom of the menu.

### Current Job

As a document begins printing, information about the print job is displayed in the **Current Job** section of the menu. This information includes the number of the job being printed, the status (such as printing or waiting for a "Go"), the current page being printed, which copy (if you are printing more than one), and any messages. It also includes information on the type of paper, such as standard 8.5-by-11-inch, the location of the print job, and any actions to be taken.

When a document is printing, keep an eye on the **Current Job** section of the menu. Any specific instructions or messages about your job will be displayed in this section. For instance, if you are using hand-fed paper, you should hear the computer beep after you have entered the document name and page numbers. Display the Print: Control Printer menu and you will see a message in the **Status** and **Message** sections that tells you to insert paper and press G. If you are printing and something does not seem to be working correctly, the first place to look is the **Current Job** section. WordPerfect may be trying to tell you what is wrong or what needs to be done.

### Job List

The print queue is at the bottom of the Print: Control Printer menu under the **Job List** section. This displays the job number, document name, destination, and print option selected for the job (continuous, hand-fed, or sheet feeder).

WordPerfect numbers the print jobs beginning with 1 each time the program is loaded. Several documents can be identified for printing. They are listed in the print queue and are numbered consecutively.

### Print Selections

The prompt at the bottom of the Print: Control Printer menu includes several choices that affect printing. If you choose 1 or C for Cancel Job(s), you will cancel print jobs. This is useful if you identify one or more documents to be printed and then change your mind. When you choose 1 or C, the question **Cancel which job? (\*=All Jobs)** appears at the bottom of the screen. The number of the current job printing displays after this message. Press the Enter key if this is the print job you want to cancel. If other print jobs are listed in the print queue, you can cancel them by keying in their number and pressing Enter. If you want all print jobs canceled, key in an asterisk and press Enter. WordPerfect displays the question **Cancel all print jobs? No (Yes)**. Key in a **Y** and all jobs will disappear from the print queue.

If you have several print jobs in the print queue and want to move one of your jobs to the top of the queue, choose 2 or R for Rush Job, and tell WordPerfect what job number it is. WordPerfect then rearranges the order in which documents are printed.

The Job List displays a maximum of three print jobs. To see what additional print jobs are in the print queue, choose 3 or D for Display Jobs. The menu disappears and is replaced by a complete listing of the documents to be printed.

If your document is to be printed on hand-fed paper, you will need to become familar with the Go command. When your document has been identified for printing, the computer beeps and asks you to insert paper in the printer and then choose 4 or G. The Go command tells the printer to start or resume printing.

Choose 5 or S for Stop if you want to stop the printer. You can then resume printing by choosing 4 or G for Go, or you can cancel the print job by choosing 1 or C for Cancel Job(s).

## PRINT OPTIONS

Access the Print menu with Shift + F7 (**M** *Click on File, then Print*). There are several options available at the bottom half of this menu.

### Select Printer

The first option, Select Printer, is used to identify the type of printer being used. When a printer is selected, a printer definition file is saved on the WordPerfect disk. To select a printer, refer to the WordPerfect reference manual.

### Binding

The Binding option is used to shift text to the right on odd-numbered pages and to the left on even-numbered pages. This allows room on two-sided copies for holes to be punched. To use this option, display the Print menu with Shift+ F7 (**M** *Click on File, then Print*), and choose B. When you choose B, the cursor moves to the 0" setting. Key in the new setting and press Enter. Press F7 to return the cursor to the document.

### Number of Copies

The Number of Copies option from the Print menu lets you print more than one copy of a document. To print more than one copy, complete the following steps:

1. Access the Print Command with Shift +F7.
   **M** *Click on File, then Print.*
2. Choose N for Number of Copies.
3. Key in number of copies to be printed and press Enter.
4. Press F7 to return the cursor to the document.

The number of copies will remain at the new setting until you change it. If you do not want multiple copies of each document printed, access the Print menu and change the number of copies back to one.

### Multiple Copies Generated by

The Multiple Copies Generated by option lets you determine if multiple copies of a document are to be generated by WordPerfect or by the printer. This feature works when you are operating WordPerfect on a network system. You can have the network generate the copies rather than WordPerfect.

### Graphics Quality

The Graphics Quality option from the Print menu is used to change the quality of print when printing graphics. This can be changed to Do Not Print, Draft, Medium, or High. When Graphics Quality is chosen from the Print menu, the prompt **Graphics Quality: 1 Do Not Print; 2 Draft; 3 Medium, 4 High: 3** appears at the bottom of the screen. The first choice is used in a situation where you want text printed but not graphics. The other choices give you draft, medium or high graphics quality. When a new graphics quality is chosen, it stays in effect until it is changed again. Some printers may not use some of the graphics quality choices

### Text Quality

Many dot matrix printers can print in a variety of modes such as draft and letter quality. The Text Quality option from the Print menu lets you identify the mode of printing. When a printer is selected, WordPerfect sets up a default Text Quality setting. To change this setting, complete the following steps:

1.  Access the Print command with Shift + F7.
    **M** *Click on File, then Print.*
2.  Choose T for Text Quality.
3.  Make a choice from the Text Quality prompt.
4.  Press F7 to return the cursor to the document.

When Text Quality is chosen from the Print menu, the prompt **Text Quality: 1 Do Not Print; 2 Draft; 3 Medium; 4 High: 3** appears at the bottom of the screen. The first choice is for printers that are not capable of printing text and graphics in one pass, or for a situation in which you want graphics printed in a document but not the text. The other choices give you draft, medium, or high text quality. When a new text quality is chosen, it stays in effect until it is changed again. Some printers may not use some of the text quality choices listed. Check your printer to determine whether it uses any or all of these text qualities.

### View Document

The View Document selection from the Print menu is used to see how a document or a page will appear when printed. This is particularly useful for special features such as headers, footers, or footnotes, which do not appear on the screen but do print.

When you choose 6 or V for View Document from the Print command, WordPerfect displays the page on which the cursor is located with the prompt **1 100%  2 200%  3 Full Page  4 Facing Page: 3** displayed at the bottom of the screen.

The third choice, Full Page, is the default. This can be changed to 100% or 200%. With either of these selections, WordPerfect will display a portion of the page where the cursor is located, and the text can be easily read.

If you are working in a document of more than two pages, you can view two pages at one time — the page where the cursor is located and the facing page. To display facing pages, complete the following steps:

1.  Position the cursor on an even numbered page (the left page of a book).
2.  Access the Print command with Shift + F7.
    **M** *Click on File, then Print.*
3.  Choose 6 or V for View Document.
4.  Choose 4 for Facing Pages.

When you ask WordPerfect to display facing pages, the page where the cursor is located (even number) along with the next page (odd number) are displayed together on the screen. This lets you determine whether page breaks occur in a desirable location and how text flows from one page to the next.

When you are viewing a document, some of the cursor movement commands are available. For example, you can press the Page Down and Page Up keys to display different pages in the document. Or you can view the beginning and ending pages of a document with Home, Home, up arrow and Home, Home, down arrow.

When you are done viewing the document, press F7 to return the cursor to the document.

### Initialize Printer

The Initialize Printer option from the Print menu is used only if you have a printer with soft fonts that are marked with an asterisk. Initialize Printer loads the soft fonts into the printer. Use this feature each time you turn on the printer. For more information on initializing the printer, see the WordPerfect reference manual.

## PRINT SCREEN

If you want a hard copy of the information displayed on the screen, access the Print Screen command with Shift + Prt Sc. (The location of the Prt Sc key varies with keyboards.)

When you press Shift + Prt Sc, the entire contents of the screen, including the status line and any prompts displayed, are printed. This provides you with a quick way of seeing the screen contents on paper.

## PRINTING BLOCKED TEXT

Many print methods limit you to printing an entire document, a page, specific pages, or the screen contents. If you want to print a specific amount of text (such as two paragraphs, half a page, or a page and a half), use the Block command.

To print blocked text, complete the following steps:

1. Move the cursor to the beginning of text to be printed and access the Block command with Alt + F4 or F12.
   **M** *Click on Edit, then Block.*
2. Move the cursor to the end of text to be printed and access the Print command with Shift + F7.
   **M** *Click on File, then Print.*
3. At the prompt **Print block <u>No</u> (<u>Yes</u>)**, key in a **Y** for Yes.

The blocked text is sent to the printer and the block highlighting is turned off.

### Printing the Directory

The directory contains a list of all documents saved on the disk. At times, you may need a hard copy of the directory, for record-keeping or other purposes. To print the directory, complete the following steps:

1. Press F5.
   **M** *Click on File, then List Files.*
2. Press Enter to display the directory.
3. With the directory displayed, access the Print command with Shift + F7.

## CHAPTER REVIEW

### Summary

- Choose 1 or F for Full Document from the Print menu to print the document displayed on the screen. Choose 2 or P for Page to print the page where the cursor is located. Print a document on the disk with 3 or D for Document on Disk.
- When you print a document from the disk, you can print the entire document or specific pages of the document. When identifying specific pages, use the hyphen to specify a range and the comma for specific pages.
- Choose 4 or C for Control Printer from the Print menu to access the Print: Control Printer menu. The Print: Control Printer is divided into three sections: Current Job, Job List, and print selections.
- The print selections from the Print: Control Printer menu, include 1, Cancel Job(s); 2, Rush Job; 3, Display Jobs; 4, Go (start printer); and 5, Stop.
- Information about a document currently being printed displays in the **Current Job** section of the Print: Control Printer menu. This includes the Job Number, Page Number, Status, Current Copy, type of paper and any messages or actions.
- The **Job List** section of the Print: Control Printer menu (also called the print queue) displays the print jobs.
- Print jobs are numbered consecutively, beginning with 1 each time WordPerfect is loaded.
- The Options section of the Print menu includes selections to choose a printer, change the binding width, print more than one copy of a document, and change the text and graphics quality.
- The View Document selection from the Print menu displays a document on the screen as it will appear when printed. You can view the full page, 100% or 200% of the text on the page, or facing pages.
- The Print Screen command, Shift + Prt Sc, prints the contents of the screen including the status line and any prompts displayed.
- Use the Block command and the Print command to print specific amounts of text.
- To print the directory, display the directory on the screen and access the Print command with Shift + F7.

### Commands Review

|                       | **Keyboard**      | **Mouse**    |
|-----------------------|-------------------|--------------|
| Print Command         | Shift + F7        | File, Print  |
| Block command         | Alt + F4 or F12   | Edit, Block  |
| Print Screen Command  | Shift + Prt Sc    |              |

## STUDY GUIDE FOR CHAPTER 9

List the three sections of the Print: Control Printer menu.

1. _____

2. _____

3. _____


When the Print: Control Printer menu is displayed on the screen, a prompt appears at the bottom of the screen. Provide a brief description of the following selection numbers from this prompt.

1. _____

2. _____

3. _____

4. _____

5. _____


Suppose that a 15-page report is saved on your disk. The selections listed in Column 1 are entered when printing the document. Use the space provided in Column 2 to explain exactly which pages will be printed.

| Selection | Pages Printed |
|:---:|:---:|
| -7 | _____ |
| 2-8 | _____ |
| 10- | _____ |
| 2-6,8 | _____ |
| 7,9,13,15 | _____ |
| 2 | _____ |

## HANDS-ON EXERCISES

### Exercise One

1.  Retrieve CH07EX1 to the screen.
2.  Move the cursor to the beginning of page 2. Print page 2 by completing the following steps:
    A.  Access the Print command with Shift + F7.
        **M** *Click on File, then Print.*
    B.  Choose 2 or P for Page.
3.  Exit the document without saving it.

**Exercise Two**

1. At a clear screen, print pages 1 and 3 of CH07EX1 by completing the following steps:
   A. Access the Print command with Shift + F7.
      **M** *Click on File, then Print.*
   B. Choose 3 or D for Document on Disk.
   C. At the **Document name**: prompt, key in **CH07EX1** and press Enter.
   D. At the **Page(s): (All)** prompt, key in **1,3** and press Enter.
2. Exit the document without saving it.

**Exercise Three**

1. Retrieve CH07EX1 to the screen.
2. Block the paragraph on Youth Involvement and print it by completing the following steps:
   A. Move the cursor to the beginning of the Youth Involvement paragraph and access the Block command with Alt + F4 or F12.
      **M** *Click on Edit, then Block.*
   B. Move the cursor to the end of the Youth Involvement paragraph.
   C. Access the Print command with Shift + F7.
      **M** *Click on File, then Print.*
   D. At the **Print block: No (Yes)** prompt, key in a **Y** for Yes.
3. Exit the document without saving it.

**Exercise Four**

1. Retrieve CH07EX1 to the screen.
2. Move the cursor to the beginning of page 3, and print the screen contents with Shift + Prt Sc.
3. Exit the document without saving it.

**Exercise Five**

1. At a clear screen, access the Print command with Shift + F7 (**M** *Click on File, then Print*). Choose 3 or D for Document on Disk and identify CH05EX1 for printing. (After entering CH05EX1, press Enter at the **Page(s): (All)** prompt. Then immediately display the Print: Control Printer menu by choosing 4 or C for Control Printer. At this menu, stop printing by choosing 5 or S for Stop. Press F1 to return to the Print menu.) Identify the following documents for printing:
   A. CH05EX2
   B. CH06EX1
   C. CH06EX2
2. Choose 4 or C for Control Printer to display the Print: Control Printer menu, then choose 3 or D for Display Jobs. Print the screen contents with the Print Screen command, Shift + Prt Sc.
3. Press the space bar to return to the Print: Control Printer menu, then choose 2 or R for Rush Job. Identify CH06EX2 as a rush job to be printed first. (If the Job List displays the document as (Disk File), identify the last print job as a rush job.)
4. Choose 3 or D for Display Jobs to display all print jobs. Print the screen contents.
5. Press the space bar to return to the Print: Control Printer menu and cancel all print jobs. To do this, choose 1 or C for Cancel Job(s), key in an asterisk (*), then key in a **Y** for Yes.
6. With the Print: Control Printer menu displayed on the screen, print the screen contents.
7. Check the Print: Control Printer menu for any messages after Action. You may have to press G to clear the menu. (If the menu is not cleared of messages, you may not be able to print future documents.)

## PERFORMANCE ASSESSMENTS

### Assessment One

1. Retrieve CH05EX4 to the screen.
2. Print the document with the Full Document selection from the Print menu.
3. Exit the document without saving it.

### Assessment Two

1. Retrieve CH07EX5 to the screen.
2. Block and print the second paragraph on the first page.
3. Print page 2 of the document.
4. Exit the document without saving it.

# PERFORMANCE MASTERY

## *UNIT PERFORMANCE*

In this unit, you have learned to create and proof full-page and multiple-page business documents, such as business letters and reports.

## MASTERY ASSIGNMENTS

### Assignment One

1. At a clear screen, create the business report shown in figure U2-1. You determine the following:
   A. Margins
   B. Justification
   C. Line spacing
   D. Boldfacing
   E. Indentions
   F. Columns
   E. Correct spelling (use Speller; proper names are spelled correctly)
   G. Correct grammar and usage
   H. Page breaks
2. Save the report and name it U02MA1. Print U02MA1.

---

PACIFIC COUNSELING ASSOCIATION

ANNUAL REPORT

Mission Statement

The mission of the Pacific Counseling Association is to provide the following services:

1. To serve as a preventitive mental health center serving the ethnic minority community.
2. To assume a social, political, and educational responsibility to the ethnic minority community at large on issue affecting the community.
3. To provide mental health training with the goal of enhancing the awareness and sensativities of mental health professionals to ethnic minority issues.

Outpatient Program

PCA had been serving a wide spectrum of clients through broadly based programs since its beginning in 1963. In 1981, the statewide mental health system directed that government funded services be for the priority population of acutely, chronically mentally ill, and seriously disturbed. This shift encouraged us to explore how we would continue to serve the broader population and their needs seperately from the government defined priority population.

The Outpatient Program was established in 1981 to serve the non-priority client population which does not meet the criteria for acute, chronic, or serious mental illness. These are indaviduals able to function in the world and maintain appropriate social and interpersonal skills without intensive therapy and support. Clients are generally dealing with a wide range of problems that are usually more transisional in nature. Often, the focus is insight oriented with clients making changes in their interactions with family, in relationships, and within themselves. The average client in the outpatient program is in therapy for 6 to 9 months. This program offers individuals, couples, family and group psychotherapy. Clients can access support and pychiatric services as needed. The program is staffed by a core of contract therapists, volunter therapists and graduate interns.

During the decade of the 90's, *~enineties,*~ the outpatient program will continue to focus on the needs of the non-priority population with increased focus on serving more youth, older adults and families. *move above Outpatient*

Graduate Internship Program

PCA's Graduate Internship Program was developed in the early 1980's. The association's work provided a rare and dynamic opportunity to formalate and pass on new therapeutic models that addressed their specialized needs. Today, academic supervisors from area universities recognize and recommend our program for its outstanding quality.

The internship program offers two placements, three times a year, for graduate students in counseling, psychology, and social work. Placements are for nine months, 16-20 hours per week. Specialized training in psycho-social assesment, psychodiagnostics, crisis intervention, and minority issues are offered. Because of the program's reputation, between five and eight students apply each session for the two available positions.

Manager: Rita Davison, M.A., Clinical Director

Graduate Interns:
     George Harkness        Sidney Keele
     Jackie Slayton         Marianno Castillo
     Sarath Ben             Tina Gabretti
     Joel Gordon            Kim Purcell

**Figure U2-1: Assignment One**

## Assignment Two

1. At a clear screen, create a title page for the report created in assignment one. Use today's date for the date of the report. You determine
   A. Margins
   B. Positioning of elements on the page
2. Save the title page and name it U02MA2. Print U02MA2.

# UNIT 3

## BASIC DOCUMENT FORMATTING

In this unit, you will learn to create, revise, and maintain standard business letters and reports.

# CHAPTER 10

## PERFORMANCE OBJECTIVES

Upon successful completion of chapter 10, you will be able to begin and adjust page numbering in one document or between a variety of documents.

### PAGE NUMBERING

WordPerfect, by default, does not print numbers on pages. For documents such as memos and letters, this is appropriate. For longer documents, however, page numbers may be needed.

WordPerfect includes several options for numbering documents at the **Format: Page menu**. Page numbers can appear in various locations on the page and can be turned on and off in the same document. In addition, WordPerfect has a selection that lets you force an even or odd number on a page; turn on page numbering and change the beginning number; and suppress a page number on a specific page.

#### Numbering Pages in a Document

To turn on page numbering in a document, complete the following steps:

1. Access the Format: Page menu with Shift + F8, then choose 2 or P for Page.
   **M** *Click on Layout, then Page.*
2. Choose 6 or N for Page Numbering.
3. At the Format: Page Numbering menu, choose 4 or P for Page Number Position.
4. At the Format: Page Number Position menu (displayed in figure 10-1), choose a number to indicate the location of the page number.

5.   Press F7 to return the cursor to the document.

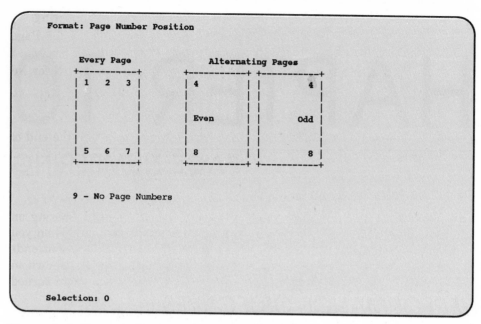

Figure 10-1: Format: Page Number Position Menu

The Format: Page Number Position menu, shown in figure 10-1, is a visual display of the locations where page numbers can be inserted in a document. For example, if you choose 1, page numbers appear at the upper left corner of each page. Selection 6 prints page numbers at the bottom center of each page. Selections 4 and 8 are used for alternating page numbers. Use these selections to print odd page numbers at the right margin and even page numbers at the left margin. One use for this function is in the creation of bound materials that are printed on both sides. The page number appears at the margin farthest from the binding.

When a document includes page numbering, WordPerfect subtracts two lines from the total number of lines printed on a page. One line is subtracted for the page number and the other to separate the page number from text. Page numbers do not appear on the screen, only on the printed copy.

## Page Numbering in Reveal Codes

Page numbers do not appear on the screen, but codes are inserted in the document that may be seen in Reveal Codes. If page numbering is turned on at the bottom center of each page, the code **[Pg Numbering:Bottom Center]** can be seen in Reveal Codes.

## Selective Page Numbering

Page numbering can be turned off in a document where page numbering was previously turned on. To do this, complete the following steps:

1.  Move the cursor to the page where numbering is to be turned off
    and access the Format: Page menu with Shift + F8, then choose 2
    or P for Page.
    **M** *Click on Layout, then Page.*
2.  At the Format: Page menu, choose 6 or N for Page Numbering.
3.  At the Format: Page Numbering menu, choose 4 or P for Page
    Number Position.
4.  At the Format: Page Number Position menu, choose 9 or N for No
    Page Numbers.
5.  Press F7 to return to the document.

Page numbering will remain off from the location of the cursor to the end of
the document or until a Page Numbering On code is encountered.

## Suppress Page Numbering

WordPerfect includes a feature that lets you suppress page numbering on
specific pages. This is different from turning page numbering off. When you
turn page numbering off in a document, it stays off until the document ends
or until numbering is turned back on. With the suppress feature shown in
figure 10-2, the page number is turned off for that specific page and turned
back on again for the other pages.

To suppress a page number on a specific page, complete the following steps:

1.  Move the cursor to the beginning of the page where the number is
    to be suppressed, and access the Format: Page menu with Shift +
    F8, then choose 2 or P for Page.
    **M** *Click on Layout, then Page.*
2.  At the Format: Page menu, choose 8 or U for Suppress (this page
    only), and the **Format: Suppress (this page only)** menu as shown
    in figure 10-2 displays on the screen.
3.  At the Format: Suppress (this page only) menu, choose 4 or P for
    Suppress Page Numbering.
4.  Key in a **Y** for Yes.
5.  Press F7 to return to the document.

```
Format: Suppress (this page only)

    1 - Suppress All Page Numbering, Headers and Footers

    2 - Suppress Headers and Footers

    3 - Print Page Number at Bottom Center    No

    4 - Suppress Page Numbering               No

    5 - Suppress Header A                      No

    6 - Suppress Header B                      No

    7 - Suppress Footer A                      No

    8 - Suppress Footer B                      No




    Selection: 0
```

**Figure 10-2: Format: Suppress Menu**

The Print Page Number at Bottom Center selection from the Format: Suppress (this page only) menu can be used to print the page number at the bottom of the first page of a title page or report with the remaining page numbers appearing in the location identified at the Format: Page Number Position menu.

## NEW PAGE NUMBER

When page numbering is turned on, pages are numbered beginning with 1. The beginning page number can be changed at the Format: Page Numbering menu, shown in figure 10-3. To begin page numbering with a number other than 1, complete the following steps:

1. Access the Format: Page menu with Shift + F8, then choose 2 or P for Page.
   **M** *Click on Layout, then Page.*
2. Choose 6 or N for Page Numbering.
3. Choose 1 or N for New Page Number.
4. Key in the new beginning page number and press Enter.
5. Press F7 to return the cursor to the document.

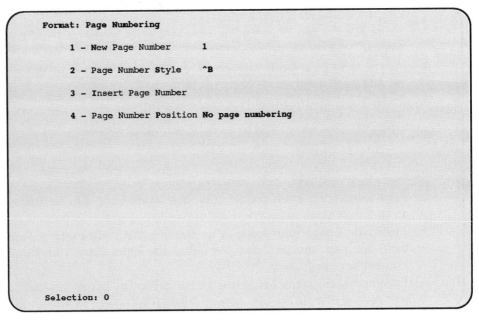

**Figure 10-3: Page Numbering Menu**

The new page number can be entered as an Arabic numeral (1, 2, 3, etc.) an uppercase Roman numeral (I, II, III, etc.), or a lowercase Roman numeral (i, ii, iii, etc.).

The other selections from the Format: Page Numbering menu let you customize the appearance and location of page numbering. The second selection, Page Number Style, is used to determine how the page number appears in the document. For example, this selection can be used to include the word *Page* before the page number. The code, ^B, indicates the page number. To enter this at the selection, hold down the Ctrl key and press the letter B. Do not use Shift + 6 to create the caret (^) symbol.

The Insert Page Number selection inserts the ^B (or whatever you entered at the New Page Number Style selection) in the document at the location of the cursor. WordPerfect then prints the page number in that location when the document is printed.

The last selection from the Format: Page Numbering menu is used to indicate the position of the page number on the page. When you choose 4 or P, the Format: Page Number Position menu is displayed.

## FORCE ODD/EVEN PAGE

WordPerfect includes a feature that can be used to force an even page number on a page that would otherwise be numbered odd, or to force an odd number on a page that would be even. Let us say, for example, that a page in a report is numbered 22 and you want to insert a table or another aid. You can tell WordPerfect to number the page with an odd number and it will number with the next higher number.

If you want to force an odd number on page 22 of a document, complete the following steps:

1. Move the cursor to the beginning of page 22 and access the Format: Page menu with Shift + F8, then choose 2 or P for Page. **M** *Click on Layout, then Page.*

2. From the Format: Page menu, choose 2 or O for Force Odd/Even Page.

3. At the prompt **1 O̲dd; 2 E̲ven: 0̲**, choose 1 or O for Odd to force an odd page number.

4. Press F7 to return the cursor to the document.

## CHAPTER REVIEW

### Summary

- Page numbering is off by default. Page numbering can be turned on in a document in a variety of locations.
- Alternating page numbers can be created. With alternating numbers, odd page numbers are printed at the right margin and even numbers are printed at the left.
- Page numbering may be turned on and off in the same document.
- By default, WordPerfect prints Arabic numbers. Upper- and lowercase Roman numerals can also be printed.
- By default page numbers begin with one. This can be changed to a different number at the Format: Page Numbering menu.
- An even or odd page number can be changed to a different number at the Format: Page menu. An even or odd page number can be forced in a document at the Format: Page menu.
- At the Format: Suppress (this page only) menu, you can suppress page numbers on a specific page and print a page number at the bottom center of a specific page.

### Command Review

| | Keyboard | Mouse |
|---|---|---|
| Format: Page menu | Shift + F8, 2 or P | Layout, Page |

## STUDY GUIDE FOR CHAPTER 10

WordPerfect numbers pages in a variety of locations. The Format: Page Number menu shows eight methods. Describe them below.

1. _____

2. _____

3. _____

4. _____

5. _____

6. _____

7. _____

8. _____

**True/False**: Circle the letter T if the statement is true; circle the letter F if the statement is false.

1. WordPerfect prints page numbers by default.      T    F

2. You can print odd page numbers at the right margin and even page numbers at the left margin.      T    F

3. WordPerfect will print page numbers in many different locations on the page.      T    F

4. Page numbering can be turned on and off within the same document.      T    F

5. Page numbers appear on the screen.      T    F

6. The WordPerfect default page numbering is Roman numerals.      T    F

7. When a document contains page numbering, WordPerfect subtracts three lines from the total number of lines printed on a page.      T    F

8. Page numbers can be suppressed on specific pages.      T    F

## HANDS-ON EXERCISES

### Exercise One

1. Retrieve CH07EX1 to the screen.
2. Turn on page numbering and number pages at the bottom center of the page by completing by following steps:
   A. With the cursor at the beginning of the document, access the Format: Page menu with Shift + F8, then 2 or P for Page.
      **M** *Click on Layout, then Page.*
   B. Choose 6 or N for Page Numbering.
   C. Choose 4 or P for Page Number Position.
   D. At the Format: Page Number Position menu, choose 6.
   E. Press F7 to return the cursor to the document.
3. Save the report and name it CH10EX1. Print CH10EX1.

## Exercise Two

1. Retrieve CH10EX1 to the screen.
2. Access Reveal Codes and delete the **[Pg Numbering: Bottom Center]** code.
3. Turn on page numbering and number pages in the bottom right corner of the page.
4. Save the report and name it CH10EX2. Print CH10EX2.

## Exercise Three

1. Retrieve CH07EX5 to the screen.
2. Turn on page numbering and number pages at the bottom of every page, alternating left and right.
3. Save the report and name it CH10EX3. Print CH10EX3.

## Exercise Four

1. Retrieve CH07EX1 to the screen.
2. Change the left and right margins to 1.5 inches.
3. With the cursor at the beginning of the document, turn on page numbering and number pages in the upper right corner of the page.
4. Move the cursor to the beginning of page 3. Turn off page numbering from page 3 to the end of the document by completing the following steps:
   A. Access the Format: Page menu with Shift + F8, then choose 2 or P for Page.
      **M** *Click on Layout, then Page.*
   B. Choose 6 or N for Page Numbering.
   C. Choose 4 or P for Page Number Position.
   D. At the Format: Page Number Position menu, choose 9 or N for No Page Numbers.
   E. Press F7 to return the cursor to the document.
5. Save the report and name it CH10EX4. Print CH10EX4.

## Exercise Five

1. Retrieve CH07EX5 to the screen.
2. With the cursor at the beginning of the document, turn on page numbering and number pages in the lower left corner of the page.
3. Move the cursor to the beginning of page 2 and suppress the page number for page 2 only by completing the following steps:
   A. Access the Format: Page menu with Shift + F8, then choose 2 or P for Page.
      **M** *Click on Layout, then Page.*
   B. Choose 8 or U for Suppress (this page only).
   C. At the Format: Suppress (this page only) menu, choose 4 or P for Suppress Page Numbering.
   D. Key in a **Y** for Yes.
   E. Press F7 to return the cursor to the document.
4. Move the cursor to the beginning of page three and force an even number by completing the following steps:
   A. Access the Format: Page menu with Shift + F8, then choose 2 or P for Page.
      **M** *Click on Layout, then Page.*
   B. Choose 2 or O for Force Odd/Even Page.
   C. Choose 2 or E for Even.
   D. Press F7 to return the cursor to the document.
5. Save the report and name it CH10EX5. Print CH10EX5.

**Exercise Six**

1. Retrieve CH07EX5 to the screen.
2. With the cursor at the beginning of the document, turn on page numbering and number pages at the bottom center of each page.
3. Change the beginning page number to 6 by completing the following steps:
   A. Access the Format: Page menu with Shift + F8, then choose 2 or P for Page.
      **M** *Click on Layout, then Page.*
   B. Choose 6 or N for Page Numbering.
   C. Choose 1 or N for New Page Number.
   D. Key in **6** and press Enter.
   E. Press F7 to return the cursor to the document.
4. Save the report and name it CH10EX6. Print CH10EX6.

## PERFORMANCE ASSESSMENTS

**Assessment One**

1. At a clear screen, make the following changes:
   A. Change the line spacing to double.
   B. Change the left and right margins to 1.5 inches.
   C. Change the justification to Left.
   D. Turn on page numbering and number pages in the lower right corner of the page.
2. Key in the information shown in figure 10-4.
3. Save the report and name it CH10PA1. Print CH10PA1.

**Assessment Two**

1. Retrieve CH10PA1 to the screen.
2. Delete the **[Pg Numbering:Bottom Right]** code and insert a code to number pages at the top, alternating left and right.
3. Move the cursor to the beginning of page 2 and force an odd number.
4. Move the cursor to the beginning of page 4 and suppress the page numbering.
5. Save the report and name it CH10PA2. Print CH10PA2.

Researchers at a prestigious university in the United States designed a research project to study how people control their actions. They chose typing because it was easy to find people at all ranges of skill, from those who had never typed to professionals who had accumulated thousands of hours of practice.

The researchers made some interesting discoveries. They found that beginning typists do not increase their speed and knowledge by typing nonsense drills; rather, they should start typing normal prose as soon as possible. They also discovered that typists should not maintain an even rhythm while typing. The time between keystrokes for an expert typist at 100 wpm could range from 20 to 280 milliseconds.

The researchers were aware of the popular story that Sholes had deliberately designed the Qwerty keyboard to slow typists down because early typists tended to jam keys that were struck too quickly in succession. The researchers saw a number of problems with this story. First, common letter pairs are no farther apart than uncommon letter pairs on the Qwerty keyboard. Second, widely separated letter pairs are usually typed faster because they can be typed by alternating hands. Third, the Qwerty layout was fixed long before touch typing became popular.

In their project, the researchers compared the Qwerty keyboard with the Dvorak arrangement, and they admitted that the Dvorak was a better arrangement. Their statistics, however, showed an increase in efficiency of only about 5 to 10 percent. They stated that the claims of improvements of 50 percent or more in typing speeds were probably due in part to the typist's enthusiasm for a novel keyboard.

A group of individuals reading about the findings of the research project and hearing of the claims by Dvorak supporters decided to try to verify or refute the ratios often quoted. They wrote a software program to study finger motion as typists entered a passage of text. The program made no determination of typing speed. It only computed the distance of finger travel. Using this program, the group found that the ratio of Qwerty finger-travel distance to Dvorak distance fell consistently in the range between 1.4 to 1 and 1.6 to 1. They found this to be far less than the ratio of 10:1 or 16:1. The group that designed the software program felt that this discrepancy was not caused by their choice of text material.

The group picked a typical day in a business office. They assumed that a typist would be producing 70 words per minute for 50 minutes each hour for eight hours of typing. This would add up to 28,000 words. Using a table they had established to measure finger travel in inches, they estimated that the ratio of total distance for the Qwerty keyboard was 1.65 and the Dvorak keyboard was 1.18. They saw that their findings differed significantly from ratios obtained by other sources.

**Figure 10-4: Assessment One**

# CHAPTER 11

## STANDARDIZED TEXT/WINDOWS

## PERFORMANCE OBJECTIVES

Upon successful completion of chapter 11, you will be able to create standardized text blocks and use them to create personalized business letters.

### STANDARDIZED TEXT

Many companies require documents that contain standard information. Paragraphs or entire documents can be standardized. Legal, medical, real estate, insurance, and other agencies produce this type of document. For example, wills, life insurance policies, and real estate contracts all require standardized text.

*Standardized text* is the term used to refer to information that remains the same. Some word processors and word processing programs may use the terms *document assembly, boilerplate,* or *standardized documents.*

To create these types of documents on a typewriter, you must retype the same information over and over again. This repetitive typing is eliminated when you use a word processor.

### SAVING STANDARDIZED TEXT

Standardized text comes in many forms: It can be a word, phrase, line, group of lines, paragraph, group of paragraphs, an entire page, or many pages. Standardized text can include a company address, list of corporation officers, signature block, statistical table, notary signature block, or other text. The list is practically limitless.

To better understand this feature, let us look at an example. In Exercise One, you will create personalized letters to send to people who have applied for positions with Puget Sound Semiconducter. The letters you create will use personalized text—date, name, and address—along with standard paragraphs.

Once the paragraphs have been saved, a business letter can be quickly constructed. In Exercise One you will create five personalized letters in less time than it would take to key in each letter. Some time is required to establish standardized text; once this is done, however, future documents are created much more quickly.

There are two methods for saving standard text. The first is to save a document just as you have been doing. The other method is to use the Block command.

### Save

If you know in advance what information or text is standard, you can save it as an individual document. You should determine how to break down the information based on how it will be used. Should the text be stored by paragraph, by several paragraphs, or by line? These are the questions you need to answer before saving text. If you choose to save one paragraph of standardized text, for example, you would key in the paragraph at a clear screen and save it as you would any other document.

### Block Command

When you create a document and then realize that the information you are keying in will be needed for future documents, you can save it with the Block command. For example, if you decide a particular paragraph should be saved, access the Block command, and then highlight the paragraph. Once the block is highlighted, press the Save key with F10 (**M** *Click on File, then Save*), and the prompt **Block name:** appears at the bottom of the screen. Key in the name under which you wish the text to be saved and press Enter. The blocked text is saved, and the highlighting is removed from the screen. To see whether the text was saved correctly, you may want to display the directory. The document name should appear in the directory in alphabetical order.

## RETRIEVING STANDARD TEXT

To create a personalized document that contains standard text, begin with a clear screen. Key in personalized text as needed. When you reach the point where standardized text is to be inserted, access the Retrieve command with Shift + F10 (**M** *Click on File, then Retrieve*), and the prompt **Document to be Retrieved: _** appears at the bottom of the screen.

Key in the name you have given the standard text and press Enter. WordPerfect searches through the directory, locates the document, and brings a copy to the screen.

### Format Changes in Standard Text

When a document is retrieved to the screen, WordPerfect brings the entire document to the screen, including any format changes. For example, if the standard text was saved with left and right margins of 2 inches, it is brought to the screen in that form.

## WINDOWS

WordPerfect's Switch feature, explained in an earlier chapter, lets you create or edit two documents at the same time. To move between Document 1 and Document 2, you use the Switch command, Shift + F3 (**M** *Click on*

*Edit, then Switch Document*). When you use the Switch command, you see only one document at a time.

WordPerfect's Windows feature, like Switch, lets you create or edit two documents. The difference is that Windows lets you see both documents at the same time. With the Windows feature, you split the screen horizontally a specified number of lines, then retrieve a different document into each window. Also, the screen can be split into two windows with the same document retrieved into each window. This is useful in long documents in which you might want to view one location in a document while editing in another location.

### Splitting the Screen

To use the Windows feature, complete the following steps:

1.  Access the Screen command with Ctrl + F3.

2.  From the prompt that displays at the bottom of the screen, choose 1 or W for Windows.
    **M** *Click on Edit, then Window.*

3.  At the prompt, **Number of lines in this window:** 24, key in the number of lines desired in the top window and press Enter. (If you want the screen split in half, key in **12**. If the mouse menu bar is visible at the top of the screen, the number of lines after the prompt is 23. If there is a separator line, there are 22.)

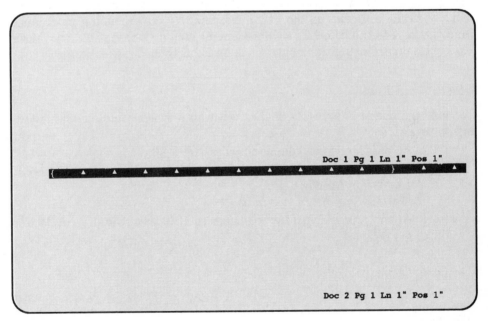

Figure 11-1: Screen: Windows

WordPerfect splits the screen horizontally, with Document 1 the top document and Document 2 the bottom document. The screen is split by the ruler line. On the ruler line, the triangles indicate tab stops, left and right brackets ([ ]) indicate the left and right margin, and left and right braces ({ }) indicate the left and right margins set on a tab stop.

Retrieve a document or documents into each window in the normal manner. To move between windows, access the Switch command with Shift + F3 (**M** *Click on File, then Switch Document*). The triangles in the ruler line point to the document where the cursor is located. If the cursor is located in Document 1, the triangles point up. If the cursor is located in Document 2, the triangles point down.

### Moving Text Between Windows

Information can be moved from a document in one window to a document in the other window. To move information from one window to another, complete the following steps:

1.  Highlight the information to be moved with the Block command, Alt + F4 or F12.
    **M** *Click on Edit, then Block.*
2.  Access the Move command with Ctrl + F4.
3.  Choose 1 or B for Block.
4.  Choose 1 or M for Move.
    **M** *Click on Edit, then Move.*
5.  Access the Switch command with Shift + F3.
    **M** *Click on Edit, then Switch Document.*
6.  Move the cursor to the location where the information is to appear and press Enter.

Use the same basic steps to copy information from a document in one window to a document in the other window. If you are using commands from the keyboard, choose 2 or C for Copy at step 4 (rather than 1 or M for Move). If you are using the mouse, click on Edit, then Copy at Step 4.

### Closing windows

To close the windows and return the screen to normal, complete the following steps:

1.  Access the Screen command with Ctrl + F3.
2.  From the prompt that displays at the bottom of the screen, choose 1 or W for Windows.
    **M** *Click on Edit, then Window.*
3.  At the prompt **Number of lines in this window**, key in **24** and press Enter.

## CHAPTER REVIEW

### Summary

- Many businesses require documents that contain standardized text. Standardized text may also be called *document assembly, boilerplate,* or *standardized documents.*
- Standardized text can be as small as a word or as long as an entire document.
- Standardized text can be saved as a regular document or saved with the Block command.

- To save standardized text as a separate document, key in the document at a clear screen and save it in the normal manner.
- To save standardized text within a document, block the text with the Block command, press F10 for save (**M** *Click on File, then Save*), name the block, and press Enter.
- To retrieve standard text to the screen, access the Retrieve command with Shift + F10 (**M** *Click on File, then Retrieve*).
- Standard text will be retrieved to the screen with any format codes that were inserted when it was originally saved.
- The Windows feature lets you create or edit two documents and view them at the same time. Windows splits the screen horizontally with the ruler line.
- In Windows, the top screen is Document 1 and the bottom screen is Document 2. Move between windows with the Switch command. The triangles on the ruler line point to the window that contains the cursor.
- Information can be moved or copied from a document in one window to a document in the other window.

## Commands Review

|  | Keyboard | Mouse |
|---|---|---|
| Save Key | F10 | File, Save |
| Exit key | F7 | File, Exit |
| Block command | Alt + F4 or F12 | Edit, Block |
| Switch command | Shift + F3 | Edit, Switch Document |
| Retrieve command | Shift + F10 | File, Retrieve |
| Screen command | Ctrl + F3 | Edit, Window |

## STUDY GUIDE FOR CHAPTER 11

**True/False:** Circle the letter T if the statement is true; circle the letter F if the statement is false.

| | | | |
|---|---|---|---|
| 1. | Standardized text may consist only of paragraphs. | T | F |
| 2. | Documents containing standardized text can also include personalized text. | T | F |
| 3. | Access the Retrieve command with Ctrl + F10 (**M** *Click on Edit, then Retrieve*). | T | F |
| 4. | A document that consists of standardized text will be listed in the directory. | T | F |
| 5. | When standardized text is retrieved to the screen, it does not include any format codes. | T | F |
| 6. | The Windows features splits the screen vertically. | T | F |
| 7. | Access the Screen command with Ctrl +F3 (**M** *Click on File, then Window*). | T | F |

In the space provided below, explain the steps you would follow to save the last paragraph as standardized text. (*Hint:* Use the Block command.)

The surrender value of a policy may be less than or greater than the total premiums paid.

The monthly life income illustrated using current annuity rates is not guaranteed. Rates are subject to change.

Values illustrated reflect any deductions made for applicable state premium taxes.

_____

_____

_____

_____

_____

Explain the steps you would follow to retrieve the paragraph you have just saved and insert it between the two paragraphs below.

Illustrated values for Flexible Premium Retirement Annuity policies reflect an annual service charge.

For a policy with a one-year rider, costs illustrated for term insurance are based on current rates charged.

_____

_____

_____

_____

_____

## HANDS-ON EXERCISES

**Exercise One**

1. At a clear screen, key in each paragraph in figure 11-2 as separate documents. Name the first document P1, the second document P2, and so on. Do not key in the numbers of the paragraphs as part of the standardized text.

*Note*: If you are using low density 5 1/4-inch disks, you may run out of space in your directory for new documents. (If you are saving documents on another storage device you do not need to be concerned about this.) You will need to delete documents from some of the beginning chapters. Chapter 13 provides information on how to delete documents. At this time, check with your instructor for specific information on how to delete the following documents from your disk:

     All documents from chapter 1
     All documents from chapter 2, except CH02EX2
     All documents from chapter 3, except CH03EX3
     All documents from chapter 8, except CH08EX6
     All documents from chapter 10

P1     Thank you for your interest in Puget Sound Semiconductor.  We
        have received your application and resume.

P2     Puget Sound Semiconductor is not hiring at this time.  The
        Personnel Department will, however, keep your application on
        file for the next six months.  If, after that time, you are
        still interested in employment with our company, please submit
        another application.

P3     Puget Sound Semiconductor is in the process of hiring
        additional personnel in your area of expertise.  Your
        application and resume are being reviewed, and you will be
        contacted within two weeks.

P4     If your qualifications and experience meet the job
        requirements, the Personnel Department will schedule a time
        for a personal interview.

P5     Our company is projecting 20 percent growth in the next two
        years.  With the expansion of the company, we anticipate an
        increase in personnel.  Within the next year, positions in
        your area of expertise will be opening.

P6     Your interest in Puget Sound Semiconductor is appreciated.  We
        look forward to hearing from you in the future.

P7     We look forward to meeting with you to discuss your
        qualifications and potential employment with our company.

P8     Sincerely,


        Janet Weiss, Director
        Personnel Department

        xx:CHX1

**Figure 11-2: Exercise One**

2.   You will be creating several documents using these standardized paragraphs. For all documents you create, change the left and right margin to 1.5 inches and change justification to left.

3.   At a clear screen, press Enter six times, type the date at the left margin, and press Enter five times. Key in the following address and salutation at the left margin:

        Mrs. Jeraldine Saunders
        2453 196th Street East
        Tacoma, WA  98445

        Dear Mrs. Saunders:

Double space after the salutation. Retrieve the following paragraphs to the screen: P1, P2, P5, P6 and P8 (in that order).

4. Save the document and name it CH11LTR1. Print CH11LTR1.
5. Create the following documents in the same way you created CH11LTR1 (change the margins to 1.5 inches and the justification to Left). Save and print each document.

CH11LTR2

```
Mr. Raymond Jaworski
243 Madrigale Lane
Yelm, WA 98465

Dear Mr. Jaworski:

P1, P3, P4, P7, P8
```

CH11LTR4

```
Ms. Simone LeJeune
18114 60th Street West
Graham, WA 98345

Dear Ms. LeJeune:

P1, P2, P6, P8
```

CH11LTR3

```
Ms. Joy Makepeace
547 Yesler Avenue
Seattle, WA 98422

Dear Ms. Makepeace:

P1, P3, P4, P7, P8
```

CH11LTR5

```
Mr. Jose Vasquez
65 East First
Sumner, WA 98380

Dear Mr. Vasquez:

P1, P3, P4, P7, P8
```

**Exercise Two**

1. Key in the paragraphs in figure 11-3 with the WordPerfect default settings and save each one as a separate document. Name the documents PARA1, PARA2, PARA3, and so on. Boldface the introductory words of each paragraph.

---

**Nonpayment of Premium.** If a premium is not paid by the end of the grace period, this policy will lapse. All insurance will terminate at the time of lapse if the policy has no cash value or dividend values. If the policy has cash value or dividend values, insurance will continue only as provided in the Options Upon Lapse provision, and any insurance or benefits provided by riders or dividends will terminate.

**Surrender for Cash.** Instead of having any insurance continued after lapse, the Owner can surrender this policy for its cash value and dividend values, less any loan, as provided in the Cash Value provision.

**Payment of Premiums.** Premiums are payable during the lifetime of the Insured at the Home Office or at any Central Service Office. Each premium is payable on or before its due date as shown in the Premium Schedule. The premium for this policy can be paid at annual, semiannual, or quarterly intervals at the Company's premium rate in effect as of the date of issue for that interval. The interval can be changed by paying the correct premium for the new interval. Premiums can be paid by any other arrangement made available by the Company.

**Grace Period.** A grace period of 31 days after the due date is allowed for payment of a premium. During this time, the insurance provided by the policy continues.

**Cash Value.** The cash values for this policy at the end of selected policy years are as shown in the Table of Guaranteed Values; if premiums have been paid in accordance with the Premiums section, there are no dividend values, and there is no loan. The cash value at any other time depends on the date to which premiums have been paid and on the length of time since the preceding policy anniversary. Upon request, the Company will furnish information about the amount of cash value available. If a premium is not paid, the cash value will not decrease during the three months after the due date of that premium. During the 31 days after a policy anniversary, the cash value of any extended insurance or paid-up insurance will not decrease.

**Loan Value.** The Owner can borrow against the sole security of this policy for any amount up to the loan value. On a policy anniversary, premium due date, or during a grace period the loan value is the cash value, plus any dividend values, less any loan and accrued interest. At any other time, the loan value is the amount which, with interest, will equal the loan value on the next policy anniversary or the next premium due date, if earlier. Extended insurance has no loan value.

**Loan Interest.** Interest accrues daily on the loan at 8 percent unless a lower loan interest rate for this policy is established for any period by the Company. Interest is compounded annually and is due on each policy anniversary or on the date of death, lapse, surrender, reinstatement, loan increase or loan repayment, or on any other date designated by the Company. Interest not paid when due becomes part of the loan and will also bear interest.

**Loan Repayment.** All or part of the loan, including accrued interest, can be repaid at any time before the Insured's death or the surrender of the policy. An unpaid loan will be deducted from any policy proceeds that become payable. If the policy is being continued under the Options Upon Lapse provision, an unpaid loan deducted in determining the extended or paid-up insurance may not be repaid unless the policy is reinstated. However, that loan will not be deducted again in determining any policy proceeds payable before reinstatement. If the unpaid loan, including accrued interest, exceeds the sum of the cash value and any dividend values of the policy, all insurance will terminate 31 days after the date the Company mails a notice of termination to the last known address of the Owner and of any assignee of record.

**Annual Dividend.** As long as this policy is in force (except as extended insurance), it is eligible to share in the divisible surplus of the Company. The policy's share, if any, is determined annually by the Company. It is payable as a dividend on the policy anniversary if all premiums due prior to that anniversary have been paid. It is not expected that a dividend will be payable on this policy before its second anniversary.

**Automatic Dividend Option.** If no option has been elected in the application or in a written notice to the Company, dividends will be applied to provide paid-up additions.

**Dividend Values.** Dividend values are the cash value of any paid-up additions and any dividend accumulations.

**Dividend Options.** The Owner can elect to have future dividends applied under several options or can change a previous election by written notice to the Company.

---

Figure 11-3: Exercise Two

2. You will create two different documents using the standardized paragraphs you have saved. Create the first document as follows:
   A. At a clear screen, make the following changes:
      (1) Change the top margin to 1.5 inches.
      (2) Change the line spacing to double.
      (3) Number pages at the bottom center of each page.
   B. Center and boldface the title POLICY AGREEMENT.
   C. Press Enter twice after the title and retrieve the following documents to the screen: PARA5, PARA3, PARA6, PARA9, PARA7, PARA1, PARA11.
   D. Save the document and name it CH11POL1. Print CH11POL1.
3. Create the second document as follows:
   A. At a clear screen, make the following changes:
      (1) Change the left and right margins to 1.5 inches.
      (2) Change the line spacing to double space.
      (3) Change the justification to Left.
      (4) Number pages at the top right margin.
   B. Center and boldface the title, LIFE INSURANCE POLICY. Boldface and center the subtitle, Premium Schedule.
   C. Press enter twice, then retrieve the following documents to the screen: PARA10, PARA4, PARA2, PARA8, PARA6, PARA12, PARA1.
   D. Save the document and name it CH11POL2. Print CH11POL2.

## Exercise Three

1. At a clear screen, split the screen into two windows by completing the following steps:
   A. Access the Screen command with Ctrl + F3.
   B. From the prompt that displays at the bottom of the screen, choose 1 or W for Windows.
      **M** *Click on Edit, then Window.*
   C. At the prompt **Number of lines in this window: 24**, key in **12** and press Enter.
2. With the cursor located in Document 1, retrieve CH11POL1 to the screen.

3.  Move the cursor to Document 2. To do this, access the Switch command with Shift + F3 (**M** *Click on Edit, then Switch Document*). With the cursor located in Document 2, retrieve CH11POL2 to the screen.

4.  Highlight the first paragraph, Automatic Dividend Option, in Document 2 using the Block command. With the first paragraph blocked, copy it to the end of CH11POL1 in Document 1 by completing the following steps:
    A.  Access the Move command with Ctrl + F4.
    B.  Choose 1 or B for Block, then 2 or C for Copy.
        **M** *Click on Edit, then Copy.*
    C.  Access the Switch command with Shift + F3.
        **M** *Click on Edit, then Switch Document.*
    D.  Move the cursor to the end of Document 1 and press Enter to retrieve the copied paragraph.

5.  With the cursor in Document 1, highlight the first paragraph, Cash Value, with the Block command. With the first paragraph blocked, move it to the end of Document 2.

6.  With the cursor located in Document 2, save the document and name it CH11POL4. At the **Exit doc 2?** prompt, key in a **Y** for Yes.

7.  With the cursor located in Document 1, save the document and name it CH11POL3. When WordPerfect asks if you want to exit WordPerfect, key in an **N** for No.

8.  With the cursor located in Document 1, close the window by completing the following steps:
    A.  Access the Screen command with Ctrl + F3.
    B.  Choose 1 or W for Window.
        **M** *Click on Edit, then Window.*
    C.  Key in **24** and press Enter.

9.  Print CH11POL3 and CH11POL4.


## PERFORMANCE ASSESSMENTS


**Assessment One**

1.  Retrieve CH07EX1 to the screen.

2.  Block the paragraph that begins with INTELLECTUAL and save it as a separate document named SERV1. (Include the Indent code in the block.)

3.  Block the following paragraphs and give them the name indicated:
    | | |
    |---|---|
    | EMPLOYMENT | SERV2 |
    | YOUTH INVOLVEMENT | SERV3 |
    | COMMUNITY ORGANIZATION | SERV4 |
    | FAMILY SUPPORT SERVICES | SERV5 |
    | VOLUNTEERS AND OUTREACH | SERV6 |

4.  Exit CH07EX1 without saving it.

5.  At a clear screen, create the business letter shown in figure 11-4. Retrieve the standard paragraphs to the screen in the order indicated. (Check to make sure the page break is in a desirable location.)

6.  Save the business letter and name it CH11PA1. Print CH11PA1.

February 3, 1993

Ms. Annabeth DeRoest, Coordinator
Community Social Services
200 King Building
Seattle, WA 98110

Dear Ms. DeRoest:

The Central Area Program provides a variety of social services to
the residents of central Seattle.  Since the early 1960s, CAP has
designed and implemented programs to meet the specific needs of the
community.

At the present time, a number of service programs are operating at
the CAP facility.  The programs include

     SERV2
     SERV4
     SERV6
     SERV1
     SERV3
     SERV5

We would be honored to have you tour our facility and participate
in some of the service programs.

Sincerely,



Lowell Cook
Director

---

Figure 11-4: Assessment One

**Assessment Two**
  1. At a clear screen, make the following changes:
     A. Change the left and right margins to 1.5 inches.
     B. Delete previous tabs and set new left tabs at +0.4, +0.8, and +1.2.
  2. Key in the first section of an outline as shown in figure 11-5. Boldface and center informa-
     tion as displayed and use the Tab or Indent key to indent the information after the
     numbers and letters.

## OUTLINE

```
I.   A Brief History of a Community in Action

     A.   The War-on-Poverty Years: 1964-69
          1.   Intellectual
          2.   Community Organization
          3.   Youth Involvement
          4.   Employment
          5.   Volunteers and Outreach
```

Figure 11-5: Assessment Two

3. Split the screen into two windows of equal size.
4. Move the cursor to Document 2 and retrieve CH07EX1.
5. Using the outline in Document 1 as a guide, move or delete paragraphs in CH07EX1 to match the outline topics.
6. Save the revised document, A Brief History of a Community in Action, and name it CH11PA2. Save the outline and name it CH11OUT.
7. With the cursor located in Document 1, close the window.
8. Print CH11PA2 and CH11OUT.

# CHAPTER 12

## SEARCH AND REPLACE

## *PERFORMANCE OBJECTIVES*

Upon successful completion of chapter 12, you will be able to revise text and codes in standard business letters and reports.

### SEARCH

WordPerfect's Search feature is used to locate a *string* within a document. A string may be up to 59 characters in length and it can include letters, numbers, symbols, spaces, and format codes.

With the Search key, you can

1. search for a particular word, phrase, or name;
2. search for overly used or repetitive words or phrases;
3. move the cursor quickly through a long document; and
4. search for specific format codes.

With the Search feature, you can look for a specific word or words within a document. This is helpful if you want to locate a specific name of a person or company or a particular phrase. Once WordPerfect finds the text, you can replace it with different text, delete it, or just review it.

If you compose many of your documents at the keyboard, you might find the Search feature helpful in locating words or phrases that are overused within a document. For example, if you find yourself overusing the phrase *for instance*, you can search for every occurrence of the phrase in the document. Once you find the phrase, you can leave it as it is or change it.

The Search feature can be used to quickly move to a specific location in a document. This is particularly useful in long documents. The Page Up and Page Down keys can move by page, but the Search key is faster because it can move to any location within a page.

You can also use the Search key to locate a specific format code. The code is identified at the **Search** prompt, and WordPerfect moves to the first occurrence of that code.

## Forward Search

A search begins from the location of the cursor and moves to the end of the document. To conduct a search, complete the following steps:

1. Move the cursor to the beginning of the document.
2. Access the Search key with F2.
   **M** *Click on Search, then Forward.*
3. At the **-> Srch:** prompt, key in the string you are looking for.
4. Press F2 to begin the search. WordPerfect stops at the first occurrence of the string in the document.
5. To continue the search, press F2. The Search prompt and the last string entered appear at the bottom of the screen. Press F2 again and WordPerfect moves to the next occurrence of the string.
   **M** *Click on Search, then Next.*

When WordPerfect finds no more matches for the string, the message **\* Not Found \*** appears at the bottom of the screen.

As an example, to complete a forward search for the string *as you may know*, complete the following steps:

1. Move the cursor to the beginning of the document.
2. Access the Search key with F2.
   **M** *Click on Search, then Forward.*
3. At the Search prompt, key in **as you may know**.
4. Press F2 again, and the cursor will move to the right of the first occurrence of *as you may know*.
5. To continue the search, press F2 (*as you may know* appears after the Search prompt). Press F2 to accept the string and continue the search.
   **M** *Click on Search, then Next.*
7. Continue pressing F2, F2 (**M** *Click on Search, then Next*), until WordPerfect flashes the message **\* Not Found \*** at the bottom of the screen.

## Backward Search

The Search key, F2 (**M** *Click on Search, then Forward*), searches a document in a forward direction. A search can also be conducted backward through a document with the Backward Search command, Shift + F2 (**M** *Click on Search, then Backward*). This command searches a document from the position of the cursor to the beginning of the document.

To conduct a backward search, complete the following steps:

1. Move the cursor to the end of the document.
2. Access the Backward Search command with Shift + F2.
   **M** *Click on Search, then Backward.*
3. At the **<- Srch: prompt**, key in the string you are looking for.
4. Press F2 to begin the search. The search moves backward from the location of the cursor, and WordPerfect stops at the first occurrence of the string.
5. To continue the search, press Shift + F2. The Search prompt and the last string entered appear at the bottom of the screen. Press F2 and WordPerfect moves to the next occurrence of the string.
   **M** *Click on Search, then Previous.*

When all occurrences of the string have been found, WordPerfect displays the message **\* Not Found \*** at the bottom of the screen.

As an example, to search backward through a document for *Randal Johanssen*, complete the following steps:

1. Move the cursor to the end of the document.
2. Access the Backward Search command with Shift + F2.
   **M** *Click on Search, then Backward.*
3. At the Search prompt, key in **Randal Johanssen** and press F2. The cursor stops at the first occurrence.
4. To continue the backward search, press Shift + F2. The string *Randal Johanssen* appears after the Search prompt. Press F2 to accept the string and begin the search.
   **M** *Click on Search, then Previous.*
6. Continue to press Shift + F2, F2 (**M** *Click on Search, then Previous*), until WordPerfect has found all occurrences of *Randal Johanssen*.

### Format Code Search

The Search feature searches for words, phrases, and format codes. If you need to find a format code in a document, such as margins, tabs, line spacing, boldfacing, underlining, centering, or page numbering, the Search feature can accomplish this for you quickly and easily.

To search for a format code, press F2 (**M** *Click on Search, then Forward*). At the Search prompt, press the appropriate function keys and prompts. For example, if you want to search for boldface codes, press the Boldface key, F6. (Only the code is located, not specific measurements.) Press F2 again and WordPerfect stops at the first occurrence of the Boldface format code. To see the code, access Reveal Codes with Alt + F3 or F11.

This is a quick method of locating format codes and can be quite useful in long documents where format codes may be spread throughout.

As an example, to search for a format code that changes margins, complete the following steps:

1. Move the cursor to the beginning of the document.
2. Access the Search key with F2.
   **M** *Click on Search, then Forward.*
3. At the **-> Srch:** prompt, access the Format command with Shift + F8, choose 1 or L for Line, then 6 or M for Margins.
4. Press F2 and WordPerfect moves to the first occurrence of a Margin code.
5. Press F2, F2 to continue the search.
   **M** *Click on Search, then Next.*

When all Margin codes have been located, WordPerfect displays the message **\* Not Found \*** at the bottom of the screen.

### Whole Word Search

When entering a string at the **Search** prompt, WordPerfect will stop at any occurrence of the string in the document. For example, if you told WordPerfect to search for the string *her*, it would stop at t**her**e, **her**s, rat**her** and so on.

If you want to search for a specific word such as *her*, key in a space followed by the word and then another space. This causes WordPerfect to search for the word only, skipping over anything that has a letter before or after the search text.

## Case Agreement

If the search string is entered in all lowercase letters, WordPerfect will stop at any occurrence of the string regardless of the case. If, however, the search string is entered in all uppercase letters, WordPerfect will only stop at occurrences of the string in uppercase letters.

## Character Matching Feature

If you are searching for a particular word in a document and cannot remember the exact spelling, the character matching feature, Ctrl + V, Ctrl + X, can be helpful. Ctrl + V, Ctrl + X can be used as a substitute for any character on the keyboard (excluding a blank space; also it cannot be the first character of the word or string). The character matching feature can be used in either a forward or backward search.

As an example, let us say the word *conscientious* appears in a document that you have created, but it may have been misspelled. (You think you keyed in a letter other than the *t* in *conscientious*.) To search for the word, access the Search key, F2 (**M** *Click on Search, then Forward*). At the Search prompt, key in **conscien^Xious**. (Hold the Ctrl key down and press the letters V and X to create ^X.) When you press F2, WordPerfect will stop at the correct spelling of the word and will also stop at misspellings such as *consciencious*.

## SEARCH AND REPLACE

WordPerfect's Search and Replace feature lets you look for a particular string and replace it with another string. With the Search and Replace feature you can

1.   search for a misspelled word and replace it with the correct spelling;
2.   save keystrokes by using abbreviations for common phrases, words, names, etc., and replacing them later with complete words;
3.   set up standard documents with generic names and replace them with other names to make personalized documents; and
4.   search and replace format codes.

This is just a short list of how Search and Replace can make your keyboarding job easier. As you use Search and Replace, you may find more ways that it can benefit you.

To conduct a search and replace in a document, complete the following steps:

1.   Move the cursor to the beginning of the document.
2.   Access the Replace command with Alt + F2.
     **M** *Click on Search, then Replace.*

3. At the **w/Confirm? No (Yes)** prompt, key in an **N** for No if you want WordPerfect to automatically replace all occurrences of the string without confirmation from you; or, key in a **Y** for Yes if you want to confirm each replacement.

4. At the **-> Srch:** prompt, key in the string you are looking for.

5. Press F2, and the **Replace with: _** prompt appears at the bottom of the screen. Key in the text you want as a replacement for the search string and press F2.

If you answer yes to the confirm question, WordPerfect stops at the first occurrence of the string and displays the message, **Confirm: No (Yes)**. If you want the string replaced, key in a **Y** for Yes. If you do not want the string replaced, key in an **N** for No. WordPerfect continues the search for the next occurrence of the string. This continues until there are no more occurrences.

### Search and Replace String

When you use the Search and Replace feature, the text you key in at the Search prompt is considered a string. WordPerfect will search for any occurrence of the string, no matter what comes immediately before or after.

In some situations, searching for a string can cause problems; in others, it can reduce the number of search and replaces required. Let us say you want to search for the word *bother* and replace it with *annoy*. *Bother* occurs in your document as a verb with a variety of verb endings:  -ed, -s, -ing. When you tell WordPerfect to search for *bother*, it looks for any text that matches, without concern for what comes before or after the word. When you tell WordPerfect to replace any occurrence with annoy, it will stop at *bothers, bothered*, and *bothering* and replace them with *annoys, annoyed*, and *annoying*. This saves you from having to complete three separate search and replaces.

### Whole Word Searches

In some situations, you may need to search for a whole word rather than a string. For instance, if you search for the string *rest* and replace it with *relax*, words such as *interest, crest*, and *restful* will change to inte*relax*, c*relax*, and *relax*ful. To avoid this situation, you can search for a whole word rather than a string. When asked to enter the search text, key in a space followed by the word and another space. WordPerfect searches for the word and skips over anything that has a letter before or after the search text.

When you search for a whole word only, WordPerfect will skip over any words that are followed by punctuation.

### Case Agreement

When a search and replace is conducted, WordPerfect always matches the case of the replacement text with the case of the search text. This means that if *bother* begins with a capital *B*, it will be replaced with *annoy* with a capital *A*. This happens even if you key in annoy as the replacement text. If the search string is entered in all uppercase letters, WordPerfect will match text only in uppercase letters.

## Deleting Format Codes

The Search and Replace feature can be used to delete format codes in a document. For example, if you changed the margins in a document several times and then decide to delete all Margin codes, you would complete the following steps:

1.  Move the cursor to the beginning of the document.
2.  Access the Replace command with Alt + F2.
    **M** *Click on Search, then Replace.*
3.  At the confirm question, key in an **N** for No.
4.  At the **Search** prompt, access the Format command with Shift + F8, choose 1 or L for Line, 6 or M for Margins, then press F2.
5.  At the **Replace** prompt, press F2.

When you press the F2 key at the **Replace** prompt, you are telling Word-Perfect to search for any Margin codes and replace them with nothing (because nothing was entered at the replace prompt).

## Replacing Format Codes

Search and Replace can be used to replace only some format codes. For example, you can replace superscripts, subscripts, overstrike, and more (for a complete list, see the WordPerfect reference manual). You cannot, however, replace such commonly used formats as underlining, boldfacing, or centering. If you try to replace text with boldfaced text, everything following the replaced word will be boldfaced. This is because WordPerfect inserts the beginning boldface symbol **[BOLD]** but not the ending **[bold]**.

## CHAPTER REVIEW

### Summary

- The Search feature is used to locate a string within a document. A string may be up to 59 characters in length and can include letters, numbers, symbols, spaces, and format codes.
- The Search key lets you look for particular words or phrases, repetitive words, and specific format codes, and lets you move quickly to a specific location in a document.
- A forward search is conducted from the location of the cursor to the end of the document. A backward search is conducted from the location of the cursor to the beginning of the document.
- If the search string is entered in lowercase letters, WordPerfect will find all occurrences of the string that contain lowercase or uppercase letters. If, however, the search string is entered in all uppercase letters, WordPerfect will match text only in uppercase letters.
- To search for a whole word rather than a string, enter a space, the word, and another space at the **Search** prompt.
- Ctrl + V, Ctrl + X can be used as a substitute for any character on the keyboard (except a blank space; also, Ctrl + V, Ctrl + X cannot be the first character entered).

- Search and Replace can be used to search for misspelled words and to replace them with the correct spelling, to search for abbreviations and replace with complete words, to create personalized documents, and to search for format codes and delete or replace them.
- Search and Replace can be conducted with or without confirmation. With confirmation, WordPerfect stops at each occurrence of the text you want to search for and asks before replacing. Without confirmation, WordPerfect automatically replaces text.
- Search and Replace begins at the location of the cursor and continues to the end of the document.

### Commands Review

|  | **Keyboard** | **Mouse** |
|---|---|---|
| Search key | F2 | Search, Forward |
| Backward Search command | Shift + F2 | Search, Backward |
| Replace command | Alt + F2 | Search, Replace |

## STUDY GUIDE FOR CHAPTER 12

List four uses of the Search and Replace feature.

1. _____

2. _____

3. _____

4. _____


**True/False**: Circle the letter T if the statement is true; circle the letter F if the statement is false.

1.   The maximum length of a string is 59 characters.                                      T       F

2.   Ctrl + V, Ctrl + W is the character matching feature that can be used as a           T       F
     character in a search.

3.   A string may not contain spaces.                                                      T       F

4.   The Search feature can be used to locate format codes.                                T       F

5.   If a string is entered in uppercase letters, WordPerfect will match text that is     T       F
     in uppercase and/or lowercase letters.

6.   A forward search is conducted from beginning to end of a document, no matter         T       F
     where the cursor is resting.


**Completion**: In the space provided at the right, indicate the correct symbol, term, command, or number for the explanation.

1.   Press this key (click on these choices) to access the Forward              _____
     Search feature.

2.   The search for a whole word, enter this before and after the              _____
     word at the **Search** prompt.

3.   Press these keys (click on these choices) to access the Backward           _____
     Search feature.

4.   Press these keys (click on these choices) to repeat a forward              _____
     search.

5.   Press these keys (click on these choices) to repeat a backward             _____
     search.

6.   Press these keys (click on these choices) to access the Replace            _____
     command.

## HANDS-ON EXERCISES

**Exercise One**
1. Retrieve CH07EX5 to the screen.
2. Complete a search for all occurrences of the word *Qwerty* by completing the following steps:
   A. With the cursor at the beginning of the screen, access the Search key with F2.
      **M** *Click on Search, Forward.*
   B. At the **-> Srch:** prompt, key in **qwerty** and press F2.
   C. Press F2, F2 to move to the next occurrence of qwerty.
      **M** *Click on Search, then Next.*
   D. Continue searching through the document until WordPerfect displays the
      **\* Not Found \*** message at the bottom of the screen.
3. Exit the document without saving it.


**Exercise Two**
1. At a clear screen, key in the memorandum shown in figure 12-1 in an appropriate memorandum format. Key in the misspelled words as they appear.
2. Save the memorandum and name it CH12EX2. Print CH12EX2.
3. Retrieve CH12EX2 to the screen.
4. Search for each occurrence of the string "retreiv" (without the quotations marks). As WordPerfect moves to each occurrence, delete the word and replace it with the correct spelling.
5. Save the document again as CH12EX2. Print CH12EX2.

Date: October 15, 1993; To: Heidi Schueler, Director of Sales; From: Kim Chun, Vice President; Subject: Standardized Abbreviations

A change has been recently made in our database system. In order to retreive information correctly, data entry operators must use standardized abbreviations.

With standardized abbreviations, retreiving records is quick and effecient. To run a report for the company, a systems analyst retreives records from a retreive specification screen.

Thank you for your cooperation in our efforts to effeciently and correctly retreive records.

XX:CH12EX2

Figure 12-1: Exercise Two

## Exercise Three

1. Retrieve CH03EX3 to the screen.
2. Search for every occurrence of the Boldface code. As WordPerfect stops at each occurrence, access Reveal Codes and delete the Boldface code.
3. Save the letter and name it CH12EX3. Print CH12EX3

## Exercise Four

1. Retrieve CH07EX1 to the screen.
2. Search for all occurrences of Central and replace with Northern by completing the following steps:
   A. With the cursor at the beginning of the document, access the Replace command with Alt + F2.
      **M** *Click on Search, then Replace.*
   B. At the confirm question, key in a **Y** for Yes.
   C. At the **Search** prompt, key in **central** and press F2.
   D. At the **Replace** prompt, key in **northern** and press F2.
   E. As WordPerfect moves to each occurrence of central, key in a **Y** for Yes to replace *northern* with *central*. (Because you entered central in all lowercase letters, WordPerfect will still stop at any occurrence of *central* and replace it with *northern* in the same case.)
3. Search for all occurrences of CAP and replace with NAP without confirmation.
4. Save the report and name it CH12EX4. Print CH12EX4.

## Exercise Five

1. Retrieve CH04EX3 to the screen.
2. Search for all Boldface codes and delete them by completing the following steps:
   A. With the cursor at the beginning of the document, access the Replace command with Alt + F2.
      **M** *Click on Search, then Replace.*
   B. At the confirm question, key in an **N** for No.
   C. At the **Search** prompt, press F6, then press F2.
   D. At the **Replace** prompt, press F2.
3. Save the letter and name it CH12EX5. Print CH12EX5.

## Exercise Six

1. At a clear screen, change the top margin to 2 inches and key in the legal form shown in figure 12-2. Boldface and underline text as indicated. Change the line spacing to double for the body of the form and back to single for the name under the signature line.
2. Save the legal form and name it CH12EX6. Print CH12EX6.
3. Retrieve CH12EX6 to the screen.
4. Conduct the following search and replaces without confirmation.
   A. Search for BRETT T. O'DAY and replace with NEIL A. HOFF.
   B. Search for JAN S. O'DAY and replace with MOIRA R. HOFF.
   C. Search for CARL MORIYAMA and replace with BRUCE T. COULTER.
   D. Search for KATHERINE M. and replace with ELIZABETH A.
   E. Search for MORIYAMA and replace with COULTER. (Two search and replaces are necessary for KATHERINE M. MORIYAMA because the name is split between two lines.)
5. Check the location of the right parentheses in the heading. They may need to be realigned.
6. Save the legal form again as CH12EX6. Print CH12EX6.

**IN THE SUPERIOR COURT OF THE STATE OF WASHINGTON**

**IN AND FOR KING COUNTY**

BRETT T. O'DAY and JAN S. O'DAY,    )
husband and wife,                   )
                                    )
                    Plaintiffs,     )        NO. 8320-C
                                    )
vs.                                 )        <u>NOTICE OF APPEARANCE</u>
                                    )
CARL MORIYAMA and KATHERINE M.      )
MORIYAMA, husband and wife,         )
                                    )
                    Defendants.     )
_____)

TO:  The Plaintiff(s), above named, and the attorney(s) of record:

      You and each of you will hereby please take notice that the

defendant(s) hereby enter(s) an appearance in the above-entitled

action and demand(s) and request(s) that all future pleadings,

notices, and papers herein, save and except original process, be

served upon the attorneys at their office.

      Dated at Olympia, Washington, this ___ day of _____, 19__.

                              MORENO, YAMADA, & SCHWARTZ


                              By: _____
                                  Dan Yamada
                                  Attorney for Defendants

Figure 12-2: Exercise Six

## PERFORMANCE ASSESSMENTS

### Assessment One

1. At a clear screen, key in the General Power of Attorney shown in figure 12-3. Boldface and underline text as indicated. Change the line spacing to double for the body of the agreement and back to single for the notary public acknowledgment.
2. Search for all occurrences of AIF and replace with Attorney in Fact.
3. Save the form and name it CH12PA1. Print CH12PA1.
4. Retrieve CH12PA1 to the screen.
5. Complete the following search and replaces without confirmation.
   A. Search for PETER THOMAS BORTELL and replace with DAVID EDWARD MAKI.
   B. Search for DEANNA MARIE BORTELL and replace with VERONICA ANN MAKI.
6. Save the form again as CH12PA1. Print CH12PA1.

---

### GENERAL POWER OF ATTORNEY

### WITH DURABLE PROVISIONS

KNOW ALL MEN BY THESE PRESENTS:

THAT PETER THOMAS BORTELL, THE UNDERSIGNED INDIVIDUAL, herein called the Principal, domiciled and residing in the State of Washington, as authorized by the laws of the State of Washington generally and RCW 33.00.2, <u>et</u> <u>seq</u>. specifically, hereby designates the following named person as AIF with full and complete power and authority to act for in the stead of the undersigned Principal, regardless of the later disability or incompetence of the Principal.

(1) <u>DESIGNATION</u>: DEANNA MARIE BORTELL, of 349 Rainier Boulevard, Seattle, Washington 98332, is designated as AIF for the Principal.

(2) <u>POWERS</u>: The AIF shall have full and complete power and authority to act in all matters for me and in my place and stead and for my use and benefit to ask, demand, sue for, recover, collect and receive all such sums of money, debts, dues, accounts, legacies, bequests, interests, dividends, annuities, and demands whatsoever as are now or shall hereafter become due, owing, payable, or belonging to Principal.

(3) <u>PURPOSES</u>: The AIF shall have all of the powers as are necessary or desirable to act in the stead and for and on behalf of the Principal and, in addition, to provide for the support, maintenance, health, emergencies, and urgent necessities of the Principal in the event of the Principal's subsequent disability or incompetence.

(4) <u>ACCOUNTING</u>: The AIF shall be required to account to any subsequently appointed personal representative concerning all transactions entered into in the name and stead of the Principal.

(5) <u>INDEMNITY</u>: The estate of the Principal shall defend, hold harmless and indemnify the AIF from all liability for acts done in good faith and not in fraud of the Principal.

(6) <u>EXECUTION</u>: This power of attorney is signed this _____ day of _____, 1993.

PETER THOMAS BORTELL

whose present address is:
349 Rainier Boulevard
Seattle, Washington 98332

STATE OF WASHINGTON )
                     : ss.
County of King       )

        I certify that I know or have satisfactory evidence that PETER
THOMAS BORTELL is the person who appeared before me, and said
person acknowledged that he signed this instrument and acknowledged
it to be his free and voluntary act for the uses and purposes
mentioned in the instrument.
        DATED this _____ day of _____, 1993.


NOTARY PUBLIC in and for the State
of Washington, residing at Seattle
My appointment expires: _____

**Figure 12-3: Assessment One**

**Assessment Two**
1. Retrieve CH05PA2 to the screen.
2. Search for and delete all Boldface codes.
3. Search for and delete all Underline codes.
4. Save the memorandum and name it CH12PA2. Print CH12PA2.

# CHAPTER 13

## DISK MAINTENANCE

## *PERFORMANCE OBJECTIVE*

Upon successful completion of chapter 13, you will be able to maintain standard business documents in logical sequences and directories on disks.

### FILES MAINTENANCE

Almost every company that conducts business maintains a filing system. The system may consist of documents, folders, and cabinets; or it may be a computerized filing system where information is stored on tapes and disks. Whatever kind of filing system a business uses, the daily maintenance of files is important to the company's operation. Maintaining the files can include retrieving, deleting, and archiving documents or entire files.

The disk on which you have been saving documents, like a filing system, also needs maintenance. Maintaining a disk may include such activities as deleting unnecessary documents, copying important documents into another file or onto another disk, and renaming documents.

### LIST KEY

Disk maintenance can be accomplished with selections from the directory. To access the directory, press F5 (**M** *Click on File, then List Files*), then Enter. A directory of files saved on the disk appears on the screen and may look like the sample directory in figure 13-1.

```
  12-15-92  14:25p                    Directory A:\*.*
  Document size:        0  Free:   30,4512  Used:      26,492    Files:         6

     .   Current   <Dir>                 | ..   Parent      <Dir>
     CH0EX1  .         2,345  09-29-92 10:07p | CH03EX2        2,548  09-29-92 10:35p
     CH0EX3  .         3,981  09-29-92 11:08p | CH04EX1        4,310  10-01-92 09:32p
     CH0EX4  .         4,805  10-01-92 10:11p | CH04EX3        5,768  10-01-92 10:35p
```

```
  1 Retrieve; 2 Delete; 3 Move/Rename; 4 Print; 5 Short/Long Display;
  6 Look; 7 Other Directory; 8 Copy; 9 Find; N Name Search: 6
```

Figure 13-1: Sample Directory

The current date and time, the document size (if one is displayed on the screen), the disk drive that the directory is working from, and the amount of free space available on the disk are all displayed at the top of the screen. The documents saved on the disk are listed below this area. The documents are listed in alphabetic order, reading from left to right. To the right of the document names, the amount of space that each document occupies on the disk is displayed along with the day and time that a document was created.

The cursor appears as a solid bar in the directory and can be moved with the arrow keys or other cursor movement keys. It can be moved quickly to the last document with Home, Home, Down arrow. Home, Home, Up arrow moves the cursor to the first document. You can also use the Page Up and Page Down keys. Home, Up arrow and Home, Down arrow move the cursor to the top and bottom of the screen, respectively.

At the bottom of the screen is the following prompt with 10 selections:

1 **R**etrieve; 2 **D**elete; 3 **M**ove/Rename; 4 **P**rint;
5 **S**hort/Long Display; 6 **L**ook; 7 **O**ther Directory; 8 **C**opy;
9 **F**ind; **N** Name Search: **6**.

### Retrieve

The first selection, Retrieve, is used to retrieve previously saved documents to the screen. In addition to retrieving documents with the List key, documents can also be brought to the screen for editing with the Retrieve command, Shift + F10 (**M** *Click on File, then Retrieve*). This command can be used at any time; it does not require the display of the directory. For this reason, retrieving a document with the Retrieve command may be faster. When you access the Retrieve command, the prompt **Document to be Retrieved:** _ appears at the bottom left corner of the screen.

Key in the name of the document to be retrieved and press Enter. The Retrieve command requires a good memory, because the list of documents is not displayed; you must remember the exact name of the document. If you cannot remember the document name, use the List key to display the documents that are saved on the disk.

### Delete

The disk you have been using has accumulated a number of documents, but it probably still has plenty of free space. Nevertheless, you may want to do a little "housecleaning" on the disk by deleting documents that you no longer need. If you work with WordPerfect on a regular basis, whether at home or on the job, you should establish a system for deleting documents. The system you choose depends on the work you are doing.

To delete a document, display the directory, move the cursor to the document to be deleted, choose 2 or D for Delete, and the message **Delete A:\(Document name)?** <u>No</u> **(Yes)** appears at the bottom of the screen.

The **A:** and the name of the document (without the parentheses) appear in reverse video. (The drive letter may vary.) If, after reading the question, you decide to delete the document, key in a **Y** for yes. The document is deleted from the disk and from the directory. The remaining documents are realphabetized. If you check the message and discover that you have entered the wrong document name, answer no to the delete question by keying in an **N** for No or press the Cancel key, F1.

### Move/Rename

If you decide that a document name needs to be changed, use the Rename selection from the directory. To rename a document, display the directory, move the cursor to the document to be renamed, and choose 3 or M for Move/Rename. The message **New Name: A:\(Document Name)** appears at the bottom of the screen.

Key in the new name and press Enter. The original document name disappears and is replaced by the new name in correct alphabetical order.

### Print

In chapter 2, you learned to use this selection to print documents saved on the disk.

### Short/Long Display

With the Short/Long Display selection, you can tell WordPerfect to display the long form of the directory rather than the short form, which is the default. At the long form, each file name appears on one line (rather than two on a line), and the line contains information from the Document Summary (if information was entered at the summary). The long directory displays the descriptive name of the document, the type of the document, and the file name, size, and revision date of the document. To change the display, choose 5 or S for Short/Long Display from the directory, then choose 1 or S for Short Display or 2 or L for Long Display.

## Look

The Look selection is used to view a document without bringing it to the screen for editing. This selection is useful if you are looking for a particular document but cannot remember what it was named. You can check documents with Look until you find the right one. This may save time, because you do not have to end a document to remove it from the screen.

To use this feature, move the cursor to the document to be viewed and choose 6 or L for Look. The document appears on the screen, but in a format different than the format for editing. At the top of the screen, a line in reverse video displays the disk drive on which the document is saved, the document name, and the WordPerfect version. The message **Look: 1 Next Doc; 2 Prev Doc; 0** appears at the bottom of the screen. Choose 1 or N for Next Doc to view the next document in the directory. Choose 2 or P for Prev Doc to view the previous document in the directory. This selection is used to view a document, not to edit or change its format. You can view the document by using the cursor movement keys and the commands. Press the space bar to return the cursor to the directory.

## Other Directory

The Other Directory selection is used to create and save documents in other directories or to switch from one disk drive to another. If you are working with a hard-drive system, the hard drive contains a *root* directory, which is the default directory. From this directory, you can identify other directories.

For example, on your hard drive you may have two programs stored in the root directory—WordPerfect and Super Planner (an integrated program). To enter WordPerfect, you begin at the root directory and then identify the subdirectory containing WordPerfect. Or, if you want to enter Super Planner, you identify the subdirectory containing that program. Within WordPerfect (or the other program) you can establish additional directories such as a subdirectory within WordPerfect that contains all correspondence for one department in your company and another subdirectory for a different department. Or, you may want to separate your documents by date or by type of correspondence.

When the directory is displayed, **Current <Dir>** appears at the beginning of the first column of documents, and **Parent <Dir>** appears at the beginning of the second column. If you are using a hard-drive system, the current directory may be the WordPerfect directory and the parent directory may be the root directory (this is dependent on how the computer system is set up and how you loaded WordPerfect).

To create a new directory, display the directory and choose 7 or O for Other Directory. The prompt **New Directory = A:\** appears at the bottom of the screen. (This will vary depending on your hardware configuration. It may show **C:\WP51.**).

To create a new directory on Drive A called LETTERS, key in **A:\LETT-ERS** at the new directory prompt. Press Enter and the message **Create A:\LETTERS? No (Yes)** appears at the bottom of the screen.

To create the new directory, key in a **Y** for Yes. WordPerfect temporarily removes the directory from the screen and then redisplays it with the new directory listed below the current directory.

Even though you created a new directory, you have not entered this directory, and any documents you create will be saved in the current directory. To select LETTERS as the default directory, complete the following steps:

1. With the directory displayed, move the cursor to LETTERS <Dir>.

2. Choose 7 or O for Other Directory.

3. Press Enter twice.

4. To remove the display of the LETTERS directory, press Cancel, F1 (**M** *Click on the right mouse button*).

Any documents you create will be saved in the LETTERS directory. To return to the directory you were working in before changing to LETTERS (the parent directory), complete the following steps:

1. With the LETTERS directory displayed, move the cursor to Parent <Dir> (at the top of the second column).

2. Choose 7 or O for Other Directory.

3. Press Enter twice.

4. Press Cancel, F1 (**M** *Click on the right mouse button*), to remove the display of the directory.

There is a second method that can be used to create a new directory. Press the F5 key for List (**M** *Click on File, then List Files*). At the **Dir A:\*.*** prompt, key in the equals sign (=), the drive letter (such as A: or B:), the backslash (\), and then key in the name of the new directory. To create the LETTERS directory with this method, press F5 (**M** *Click on File, then List Files*), and key in **=A:\LETTERS** (press Enter). If this is a new directory, WordPerfect displays the prompt **Create A:\LETTERS? No (Yes).**

Key in a **Y** (for Yes) and the prompt is removed from the screen. WordPerfect has created a new directory called LETTERS, but you are not working from this new directory.

When you create a new directory, it appears in the main directory as a regular document, but it has the extension **<Dir>**. Subdirectory names are not alphabetized with other documents. Instead they are displayed at the beginning of the directory.

Subdirectories can be deleted from the directory in the same manner as a regular document is deleted. First, however, the documents in the subdirectory need to be deleted. If you try to delete a subdirectory containing documents, WordPerfect displays the message **ERROR: Directory not empty**.

You can view the documents in a subdirectory by highlighting the subdirectory name and pressing Enter twice. This method does not change the default directory.

## Copy

With the Copy selection, you can make exact copies of a document and save the document either on the same disk or on another disk. Certain documents you create may be important enough to warrant a backup.

To copy a document on the same disk, display the directory and choose 8 or C for Copy. The prompt **Copy this file to: _** appears at the bottom of the screen.

Key in a name that is different from the document you are copying and press Enter. WordPerfect copies the document and includes the new document in the directory in alphabetic order.

To copy a document onto another disk in Drive B, complete the following steps:

1. Insert a formatted disk in Drive B.
2. Display the directory and move the cursor to the document to be copied to Drive B.
3. Choose 8 or C for Copy.
4. At the **Copy this file to:** prompt, key in **B:** and press Enter.

WordPerfect saves the document on Drive B with the same name. When entering the drive letter, be sure to enter the colon (:). If you do not, WordPerfect will copy the document on the same disk and name it B (or whatever drive letter you identify).

## Find

The Find selection is used to search for documents that contain a particular word or phrase. This is useful in locating certain documents when you cannot remember the document name but you can remember a unique word or words in the document. To use Find, display the directory and choose 9 or F for Find. The message **Find: 1 Name; 2 Doc Summary; 3 First Pg; 4 Entire Doc; 5 Conditions; 6 Undo: 0** appears at the bottom of the screen.

At this prompt, you can search for or find a document name, a word or words in the document summary, the first page of a document, the entire document, or you can undo a find.

The first selection, Name, lets you search for a specific document name in the directory. To search for a specific document name, complete the following steps:

1. With the directory displayed, choose 9 or F for Find.
2. Choose 1 or N for Name.
3. At the **Word pattern:** prompt, key in the document name and press Enter.

WordPerfect searches the documents in the directory, then displays the document that matches the name.

At the **Word pattern:** prompt, you can enter up to 39 characters, including the following wildcard characters and operators.

Wildcard characters:
*             = any characters up to a hard return
?             = a single character

Operators:
; (or space) = search for file containing both words
,             = search for file containing either word
-             = search for file that does not include word pattern after the dash

For example, to search for all document names that begin with CH03, you would enter CH03* at the word pattern prompt. To search for all document names from chapters 1 through 9 that end with EX1, you would enter CH0?.EX1 at the word pattern prompt. To search for documents containing the words *Weiss* and *Serosky*, you would enter Weiss;Serosky at the word pattern prompt. To search for documents containing either *Weiss* or *Serosky*, you would enter Weiss,Serosky at the word pattern prompt. To search for all documents except those that contain the word *Weiss*, you would enter -Weiss at the word pattern prompt. If the word pattern you are searching for contains an operator such as the semicolon, enclose the word pattern in quotation marks to tell WordPerfect that the semicolon is not an operator.

Complete similar steps to search for a specific document summary except choose 2 or D for Doc Summary (instead of 1 or N for Name). The Document Summary is explained later in this chapter. The First Page and Entire Doc selections let you search for a particular word, words, or word pattern in the first page of the document or the entire document. A search conducted on the first page of documents is faster than a search through entire documents.

The Conditions selection lets you establish specific conditions for completing a search. When you choose 5 or C for Conditions, the menu shown in figure 13-2 is displayed on the screen.

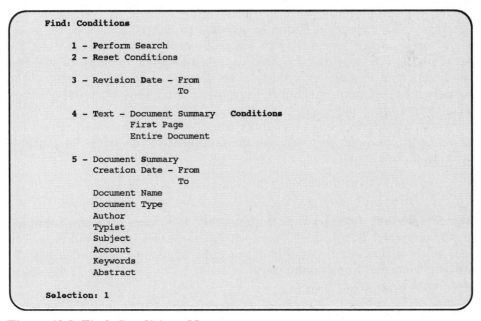

**Figure 13-2: Find: Conditions Menu**

The first selection, Perform Search, is used after all search criteria have been established. Choose 1 or P for Perform Search when all criteria have been entered and you are ready to search the documents in the directory.

The Reset Conditions selection is used to remove the information from the previous search so you can enter information for a new search.

At the Revision Date selection, you can search for documents that were edited between certain dates. For example, you can search for documents edited between January 3, 1993 and January 10, 1993 by keying in 01/03/93 at **From** after Revision Date, and keying in 01/10/93 at **To** after Revision Date.

The Text selection lets you search for specific text located in the document summary, the first page of the document, or the entire document. You can search for a word, words, or a word pattern. For example, to search for documents containing the name Janet Weiss on the first page, key in **Janet Weiss** at the First Page selection after Document Summary.

The last selection, Document Summary, lets you limit your search to specific entries in the document summary. For example, you can search for documents containing a document summary with a specific name, a specific author, a specific subject, and so on. You can also search for documents containing document summaries that were created during a certain time period. The dates entered at From and To after Creation Date find documents containing document summaries when the document summaries (not the document) were created.

When all conditions for the search have been entered, choose 1 or P for Perform Search. WordPerfect searches the documents in the directory, then displays the directory with only the documents that meet the search criteria. You can cancel a search while it is being performed or when it is complete with the Cancel key, F1.

### Name Search

The last selection from the directory is N, Name Search, which lets you search for specific documents in the directory. When you choose N, the message **(Name Search; Enter or arrows to Exit)** appears in the lower right corner of the screen. Key in the first letter of the document you are searching for in the directory. This causes the cursor to move to the first document that begins with that letter. Continue keying in letters and WordPerfect will continue highlighting documents that match the letters being keyed in.

When WordPerfect has highlighted the document you are searching for, press Enter. You can then retrieve the document to the screen or continue with other functions.

## MULTIPLE DOCUMENTS

WordPerfect has a feature that lets you work with more than one document in the directory. This feature works with delete, move, print, and copy. You can delete a series of documents at one time by using the asterisk key. To do this, complete the following steps:

1. Display the directory.
2. Move the cursor to the documents to be deleted and key in an asterisk by each name. (The asterisk appears after the numbering identifying the document's size.)
3. Choose 2 or D for Delete.
4. At the **Delete marked files? No (Yes)** prompt, key in a **Y** for Yes.
5. At the **Marked files will be deleted. Continue? No (Yes)** prompt, key in a **Y** for Yes.

WordPerfect deletes the marked documents and realphabetizes the remaining documents. The same procedure can be used to print or copy several documents. If you decide to remove an asterisk next to a document name, move the cursor to the document name and key in the asterisk again. You can quickly mark or unmark all documents with the Mark Text command, Alt + F5.

## DOCUMENT SUMMARY

A WordPerfect feature that can help you manage your documents is the Document Summary. A document summary can be created for each document that identifies important information such as the creation date and time of the document, the author, the subject, key words, and an abstract of the document.

To create a document summary, complete the following steps:

1. Display the document on the screen for which you want the summary created.

2. Access the Format: Document menu with Shift + F8, then 3 or D for Document.
   **M** *Click on Layout, then Document.*

3. At the Format: Document menu, choose 5 or S for Summary.

4. At the Document Summary menu, key in any important information then press F7 to return the cursor to the document.

The Document Summary menu shown in figure 13-3 contains a variety of selections.

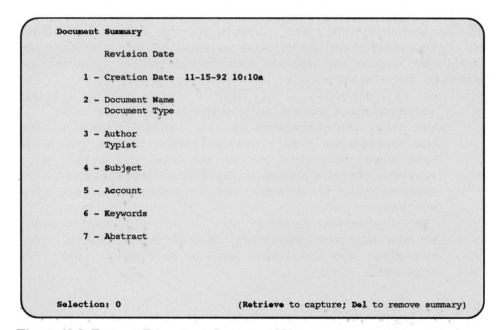

```
Document Summary


        Revision Date

  1 - Creation Date   11-15-92 10:10a


  2 - Document Name
      Document Type


  3 - Author
      Typist


  4 - Subject


  5 - Account


  6 - Keywords


  7 - Abstract




  Selection: 0                    (Retrieve to capture; Del to remove summary)
```

Figure 13-3: Format: Document: Summary Menu

The first selection, Creation Date, displays the date and time the document summary is created (not the document). The current date and time are automatically inserted after this selection when you access the Document Summary menu. To change the creation date, choose 1 or D, key in the new date and time, then press Enter. Enter the date and time in the same format as displayed by WordPerfect.

At the Document Name selection, you can enter a descriptive document name that contains up to 68 characters. At the Long Display in the directory, only the first 30 characters will display.

Enter information about the type of document at the Document Type selection. Up to 20 characters can be used to describe the type of document. At the Long Display in the directory, only the first 9 characters will display.

The Author/Typist is used to identify the author of the document as well as the typist. Up to 60 characters can be used to describe the author and up to 60 characters for the typist.

The Subject selection identifies the subject of the document. A maximum of 160 characters can be entered at this selection.

At the Account selection, you can enter up to 160 characters that might include an account name or account number.

Enter important words or phrases included in the document at the Keywords selection. Up to 160 characters can be used.

The last selection, Abstract, is a brief synopsis of the contents of the document. A maximum of 780 characters can be entered at this selection.

## Using Retrieve with the Summary

At the Document Summary menu, you can use the Retrieve command, Shift+ F10 (**M** *Click on Retrieve in the lower right corner of the Document Summary menu*), to retrieve pertinent information about the document currently displayed on the screen. When you access the Retrieve command (**M** *Click on Retrieve*), the prompt **Capture Document Summary Fields? No (Yes)** appears at the bottom of the screen. If you key in a **Y** for Yes, WordPerfect searches the document currently displayed on the screen and inserts the following information:

```
At the Subject selection, WordPerfect will search
the first 550 characters in the document looking
for the letters "RE:." Any text after RE: to the
next hard return is copied and inserted after
Subject. If the document does not contain the
letters RE:, no information is inserted after
Subject.

At the Abstract selection, WordPerfect inserts
the first 400 characters of the document after
Abstract.
```

## Maintaining the Summary

When a document containing a document summary is saved, the summary is saved also. To view and/or edit a document summary in a document, complete the following steps:

1.  Access the Format: Document menu with Shift + F8, then 3 or D for Document.
    **M** *Click on Layout, then Document.*
2.  At the Format: Document menu, choose 5 or S for Summary.
3.  Make any necessary changes to the summary.
4.  Press F7 to save the summary and return the cursor to the document.

If a document contains a summary, the summary can also be seen with the Look selection at the directory. To view the summary in a document, display the directory, move the cursor to the document containing the summary, then choose 6 or L for Look. The document summary will appear on the screen first with the prompt **Look Doc Summ: 1 Next; 2 Prev; 3 Look at text; 4 Print Summ; 5 Save to File: 0**. Choose 1 or N to view the next document in the directory. Choose 2 or P to view the previous document in the directory. If you want to see the text in the current document, choose 3 or L for Look at text. To print the summary displayed on the screen, choose 4 or R for Print Summ. The last choice, Save to File, lets you save the document summary into a separate document.

A document summary can be printed with 4 or R for Print Summ while looking at a document in the directory. Or, you can retrieve a document to the screen containing a summary, display the summary, then print with Shift + F7.

To delete a document summary, display the Document Summary menu, then press the Delete key. At the prompt, **Delete Document Summary? No (Yes)**, key in a **Y** for Yes.

## SAVE KEY

The Save key, F10 (**M** *Click on File, then Save*), lets you save a document and remain in that document to continue keying in text or to continue editing. When you use Save, the document is saved on the disk and also remains on the screen. Save can be used as a safety feature. Save a document you are creating every few minutes or every few pages; then, if the power surges or goes off, the document as it appeared when last saved will be retained on the disk.

## CHAPTER REVIEW

### Summary

- Disk maintenance features are accessed from the directory. The directory includes the following information: current date and time, size of the document (if one is in use), the current directory, the amount of free space available on the disk, an alphabetic list of documents on the disk, the amount of space occupied by each document, and the day and time that each document was created.
- When the directory appears on the screen, the prompt **1 Retrieve; 2 Delete; 3 Move/Rename; 4 Print; 5 Short/Long Display; 6 Look; 7 Other Directory; 8 Copy; 9 Find; N Name Search: 6** appears at the bottom.
- The cursor appears as a solid bar in the directory. It can be moved with the arrow keys or other cursor movement keys.
- Subdirectories can be created or selected with the Other Directory selection from the directory. Subdirectories display in the directory with the extension <Dir>. Subdirectories can be deleted from the main directory after all documents in the subdirectories have been deleted.
- Subdirectories can also be created by pressing F5 (**M** *Click on File, then List Files*), and keying in the equals sign, the drive letter and colon, the backslash, the new name, and pressing Enter.

- A document can be retrieved from the directory or with the Retrieve command, Shift + F10 (**M** *Click on File, then Retrieve*).
- The Word Search selection from the directory can be used to search for documents containing certain word patterns or documents created during a certain time period.
- The asterisk is used to identify a group of documents to be printed, deleted, or copied. The asterisk is a toggle key. The asterisks can be inserted or removed quickly with the Mark Text command.
- The Save key lets you save a document and remain in the document for further editing.
- A document summary can be created for a document that identifies the creation date and time of the summary, the document name and type, the author and typist of the document, and the subject, account name or number, keywords, and abstract of the document.
- A document summary can be viewed in a document or with the Look selection from the directory.
- Print a document summary at the Look selection or display the summary then press Shift + F7.

## Commands Review

|                        | **Keyboard**        | **Mouse**          |
|------------------------|---------------------|--------------------|
| List Key               | F5                  | File, List Files   |
| Retrieve command       | Shift + F10         | File, Retrieve     |
| Save Key               | F10                 | File, Save         |
| Format: Document menu  | Shift + F8, 3 or D  | Layout, Document   |

## STUDY GUIDE FOR CHAPTER 13

Briefly describe the ten features available from the List Files directory.

1. _____
2. _____
3. _____
4. _____
5. _____
6. _____
7. _____
8. _____
9. _____
10. _____

**True/False:** Circle the letter T if the statement is true; circle the letter F if the statement is false.

| | | | |
|---|---|---|---|
| 1. | The directory displays the time and date that a document was created. | T | F |
| 2. | In the directory, documents appear in the order in which they were created. | T | F |
| 3. | Documents can be retrieved with the Retrieve command, Shift + F10. | T | F |
| 4. | Before a document is deleted from the disk, a confirmation question must be answered. | T | F |
| 5. | When a document is retrieved with the Look selection, the cursor can be moved backward and forward. | T | F |
| 6. | A document can be copied onto another disk. | T | F |
| 7. | In the directory, the cursor appears as a solid bar. | T | F |
| 8. | The directory displays the amount of free space available on the disk. | T | F |
| 9. | The Look selection is used to edit a document. | T | F |
| 10. | Subdirectories can be created with Other Directory, from the directory. | T | F |
| 11. | Subdirectories containing documents can be deleted from the directory. | T | F |
| 12. | Access the Format: Document menu to create a document summary. | T | F |

## HANDS-ON EXERCISES

### Exercise One
1. Display the directory with F5 and Enter.
   **M** *Click on File, then List Files.*
2. Print the directory with Shift + F7.
3. Exit the directory.

**Exercise Two**

1. Display the directory.
2. Copy CH04EX1 and name it MEMO by completing the following steps:
   A. Move the cursor to CH04EX1.
   B. Choose 8 or C for Copy.
   C. Key in **MEMO** and press Enter.
3. Copy CH04EX2 and name it YAMADA.
4. Copy CH04EX3 and name it GIROUX.
5. Copy CH04EX4 and name it VONSTEIN.
6. Copy CH04EX5 and name it COBURN.
7. Print the directory with Shift + F7.
8. Exit the directory.

**Exercise Three**

1. Display the directory and delete YAMADA by completing the following steps:
   A. Move the cursor to YAMADA.
   B. Choose 2 or D for Delete.
   C. Key in a **Y** for Yes.
2. Move to each of the following documents and key in an asterisk: GIROUX, VONSTEIN, and COBURN. With the documents marked with asterisks, delete them.
3. Print the directory.
4. Exit the directory.

**Exercise Four**

1. Display the directory and rename MEMO to HERSCH by completing the following steps:
   A. Move the cursor to MEMO.
   B. Choose 3 or M for Move/Rename.
   C. Key in **HERSCH** and press Enter.
2. Print the directory.
3. Delete HERSCH.
4. Exit the directory.

**Exercise Five**

1. Create a subdirectory named MEMOS by completing the following steps:
   A. At the directory, choose 7 or O for Other Directory.
   B. Key in **A:\MEMOS** and press Enter.
   C. At the **Create A:\MEMOS?** **No** (**Yes**) prompt, key in a **Y** for Yes.
2. Copy the documents CH04EX1, CH04EX2, and CH04EX4 to the MEMOS subdirectory by completing the following steps:
   A. Move to CH04EX1 and key in an asterisk. Do the same for CH04EX2 and CH04EX4.
   B. Choose 8 or C for Copy.
   C. At the **Copy marked files?** **No** (**Yes**) prompt, key in a **Y** for Yes.
   D. At the **Copy all marked files to:** prompt, key in **A:\MEMOS** and press Enter.
3. Change to the MEMOS directory by completing the following steps:
   A. Move the cursor to MEMOS <Dir>.
   B. Choose 7 or O for Other Directory.
   C. Press Enter twice.
4. With the MEMOS directory displayed, print the directory.

5. Mark all documents in the MEMOS directory with an asterisk, then delete them.
6. Change to the parent directory by completing the following steps:
   A. Move the cursor to Parent <Dir>.
   B. Choose 7 or O for Other.
   C. Press Enter twice.
7. At the directory, move the cursor to MEMO <Dir> and delete it.
8. Print the directory.
9. Exit the directory.

**Exercise Six**
1. Find all documents containing the word *Dvorak* by completing the following steps:
   A. Display the directory.
   B. Choose 9 or F for Find.
   C. Choose 4 or E for Entire Doc.
   D. At the **Word pattern:** prompt, key in **Dvorak** and press Enter.
2. When WordPerfect displays the documents containing Dvorak, print the directory.
3. Exit the directory.

**Exercise Seven**
1. Display the directory. Copy CH07EX1 and name the new document CH13EX7.
2. Retrieve CH13EX7 to the screen.
3. Create a document summary by completing the following steps:
   A. Access the Format: Document menu with Shift + F8, then 3 or D for Document.
      **M** *Click on Layout, then Document.*
   B. At the Format: Document menu, choose 5 or S for Summary.
   C. At the Document Summary menu, choose 2 or N for Document Name. Key in **CH13EX7**, then press Enter. Key in **Report**, then press Enter.
   D. Choose 4 or S for Subject. Key in **History of CAP**, then press Enter.
   E. Retrieve the first 400 characters of the document after the Abstract selection by completing the following steps:
      (1) Access the Retrieve Command with Shift + F10.
      (2) At the prompt, **Capture Document Summary Fields? No (Yes)**, key in a **Y** for Yes.
   F. Press F7 to save the summary and return the cursor to the document.
4. Save CH13EX7 with the same name.
5. Print the document summary for CH13EX7 by completing the following steps:
   A. Display the directory.
   B. Move the cursor to CH13EX7, then choose 6 or L for Look.
   C. Choose 4 or R for Print.
6. Exit the directory.

Note: If you are using a 5 1/4-inch or 3 1/2-inch disks, you will eventually run out of disk space. In the middle of the second line of the directory, the amount of free space available on the disk is displayed. When the amount of the free space drops below 5,000 you will need to delete documents from the disk or buy a new disk.

## PERFORMANCE ASSESSMENTS

### Assessment One

1. Create a subdirectory named CAP (for Central Area Program).
2. Search for all documents containing the words Central Area Program.
3. When WordPerfect displays the documents containing Central Area Program, mark the documents and copy them to the CAP subdirectory.
4. Look in the CAP subdirectory (do not change it to the default) by moving the cursor to CAP <Dir> and pressing Enter twice.
5. With the CAP subdirectory on the screen, print the directory.
6. Exit the directory.

### Assessment Two

1. Look in the CAP subdirectory.
2. Mark all the documents in the CAP subdirectory with an asterisk, then delete the documents.
3. Exit the CAP subdirectory.
4. Display the directory and delete the CAP subdirectory.
5. Print the directory.

### Assessment Three

1. Create three subdirectories named UNIT1, UNIT2, and UNIT3.
2. Mark all documents from chapters 1, 2, 3, 4, and 5, and move them into the UNIT1 subdirectory. (Use the Move/Rename selection at the directory.)
3. Mark all documents from chapters 6, 7, 8, and 9, and move them into the UNIT2 subdirectory.
4. Mark all documents from chapters 10, 11, 12, and 13, and move them into the UNIT3 subdirectory.

*Note*: Beginning with this exercise, chapter documents are divided into unit subdirectories. Before creating new documents in following chapters, you will need to change the default directory to the appropriate unit subdirectory.

# UNIT 3
# PERFORMANCE MASTERY

## *UNIT PERFORMANCE*

In this unit, you have learned to create, revise, and maintain standard business letters and reports.

## MASTERY ASSIGNMENTS

### Assignment One

1.  Display the directory. Copy U02MA1 and name it U03MA1.
2.  Retrieve U03MA1 to the screen. Move the cursor to the end of the document and add the information shown in figure U3-1.
3.  Number the pages of the report in the bottom right corner of the page.
4.  Search for PCA and replace with Pacific Counseling Association.
5.  Complete a spell check on the report (proper names are spelled correctly).
6.  Save the revised report and name it U03MA1. Print U03MA1.

---

Treatment Program

Until 1983, there was no program differintiation within the PCA structure that encompased a range of services for the acutely, chronically mentally ill and seriously disturbed populations. Although PCA did have a modified day treatment program in the late 1970s and early 1980s, it was coordinated as part of the larger range of services. When state moneys became more focused on this population, PCA, along with all other state contracted agencies, was asked to develop treatment programs to meet the needs of this population.

A person is defined as having chronic mental illness if she or he has needed two or more psychiatric hospitalizations or has been unable to obtain or maintain self-supporting employment due to emotional problems within the year prior to service. Seriously disturbed illness is defined as being unable to provide basic care for oneself or being dangarous to oneself or to others. An individual with acute mental illness is on a conditional release from a psychatric hospital or is court-ordered to outpatient therapy.

---

**Figure U3-1: Assignment One**

**Assignment Two**

1.    Create the paragraphs shown in figure U3-2 as standardized paragraphs. Name the paragraphs as indicated in the figure.

---

SP1    Business at Cheney Manufacturing has doubled in the past year. Due to this growth, we need additional warehouse storage to meet the needs of our customers.

SP2    Last week, while driving in the Georgetown area, I noticed several signs for warehouse space with your company name and address. I am interested in talking with a representative from your company about the properties as soon as possible.

SP3    Last week, while driving in the Capitol Hill area, I noticed several For Lease signs with your company name and address. I am interested in talking with a representative from your company about the possibility of leasing warehouse space.

SP4    Last week, while driving in the Columbia District, I noticed several For Lease and For Sale signs on warehouses with your company name and address. I am interested in talking with a representative from your company about the possibility of buying or leasing warehouse space.

SP5    Please call me at my office, Monday through Friday, between 8:00 a.m. and 5:00 p.m. at 555-1700. I look forward to hearing from you soon.

SP6    Sincerely,


Charles R. Pruitt
President

---

Figure U3-2: Assignment Two


2.    Create three standardized letters with the following names and addresses and the order of the paragraphs. Name the first letter U03LTR1, name the second letter U03LTR2, and the third letter, U03LTR3. You determine the following for each letter:
A. Margins
B. Justification
C. Appropriate salutation
D. Reference initials

AB Properties
1205 Glidden Way
Suite 228
Seattle, WA 98110
SP1, SP4, SP5, SP6

Capitol Hill Property Management
3500 South Madison Street
Seattle, WA 98021

SP1, SP3, SP5, SP6


Southtown Real Estate
12035 - 34th Avenue South
Seattle, WA 98133

SP1, SP2, SP5, SP6

# UNIT 4

## ADVANCED CHARACTER AND LINE FORMATTING

In this unit, you will learn to enhance the readability of single-page business letters, legal documents, and reports, with basic typesetting features.

# CHAPTER 14

## ADVANCED CHARACTER FORMATTING

## PERFORMANCE OBJECTIVES

Upon successful completion of chapter 14, you will be able to adjust the style and size of type as well as the appearance of characters in standard office documents.

### FONTS

The text in the documents you have created so far has been printed with a default font. That font prints text with uniform appearance and spacing. For most printers, the default font is 10-pitch (12-point) Courier. Other fonts may be available depending on the printer you are using. The availability of fonts ranges from a few to several hundred. A font consists of three parts: typeface, type style, and type size.

### Typeface

A *typeface* is a set of characters with a common design and shape. Typefaces may be decorative, blocked, or plain. Courier is the WordPerfect default and the most popular typeface for typewriters. Other common typefaces include Helvetica, Times Roman, New Century Schoolbook, and Palatino.

Typefaces are either *monospaced* or *proportional*. A monospaced typeface allots the same amount of horizontal space for each letter. Courier is an example of a monospaced typeface. Proportional typefaces allow a varying amount of space for each character. For example, the lowercase letter *i* takes up less space than a capital *M*.

There are two categories of proportional typefaces: serif and sans serif. A serif is a small line at the end of a character stroke. Traditionally, a serif typeface is used with documents that are text intensive (documents that are mainly text), because the serif helps the reader's eyes travel across the page.

A sans serif typeface does not have serifs (*sans* is the French word for "without"). Sans serif typefaces are often used for headlines and advertisements that are not text intensive. The following are examples of serif typefaces:

Bookman Light
New Century Schoolbook
Palatino
Times Roman
*Zapf Chancery Medium Italic*

The following are examples of sans serif typefaces:

Avant Garde Gothic Book
Helvetica

## Type Size

Type size is divided into two categories: pitch and point size. Pitch is a measurement used for monospaced typefaces. The number of characters that can be printed in 1 inch is the pitch measurement. The default pitch for the Courier typeface is 10. This means that 10 characters can be printed in a horizontal inch. The pitch measurement can be changed to increase or decrease the size of the characters. The higher the pitch number, the smaller the characters. The lower the pitch number, the larger the characters. The following are examples of different pitch sizes in the Courier typeface.

```
12-pitch Courier
10-pitch Courier
8-pitch Courier
```

Proportional typefaces can be set in different sizes. The size of proportional type is measured vertically in units called *points*. A point is approximately 1/72 of an inch. The following are examples of different point sizes in the Helvetica typeface:

8-point Helvetica

12-point Helvetica

## 18-point Helvetica

# 24-point Helvetica

## Type Style

Within a typeface, characters may have a varying style. The standard style of the typeface is referred to as *roman* (for serif typefaces), or *book* (for serif or sans serif typefaces). There are four main categories of type styles:

1. Roman or book (standard — also called *plain, normal,* and *upright*);
2. Bold (sometimes available in different weights, such as demi);
3. Italic (called *oblique* for sans serif typefaces); and
4. Bold italic.

When a typeface is referred to without a style description, the roman or book style is assumed. Italic is a cursive form of the roman style, so sans serif typefaces do not have a true italic; the term *oblique* is correctly used for sans serif typefaces. If no style specification has been set, WordPerfect uses the roman or book style. If an italic specification is set for a sans serif typeface, WordPerfect uses the oblique style. If a bold specification is set for some typefaces, WordPerfect uses the demi style.

The following illustrates the four main type styles in 12 points:

Helvetica (book)
**Helvetica bold**
*Helvetica oblique*
***Helvetica bold oblique***

Bookman (roman)
**Bookman demi**
*Bookman light italic*
***Bookman demi italic***

The term *font* describes a particular typeface in a specific style and size. Examples of fonts are 10-pitch Courier, 12-pitch Prestige Elite, 10-point Times Roman Bold, 12-point Palatino Italic, and 14-point Bookman Demi Italic. As mentioned earlier, the fonts available to you depends on the printer you are using.

### Changing Fonts

The fonts available with your printer are displayed at the Base Font menu. Changes to the font in the document can be made at this menu. To display the Base Font menu, complete the following steps:

1. Access the Font command with Ctrl + F8.
2. Choose 4 or F for Base Font.
   **M** *Click on Font, then Base Font.*

Figure 14-1 shows the Base Font menu for a PostScript printer (your Base Font menu varies according to the printer you are using).

```
Base Font

* Courier
  Courier Bold
  Courier Bold Oblique
  Courier Oblique
  Helvetica
  Helvetica Bold
  Helvetica Bold Oblique
  Helvetica Narrow
  Helvetica Narrow Bold
  Helvetica Narrow Bold Oblique
  Helvetica Narrow Oblique
  Helvetica Oblique
  ITC Avant Garde Gothic Book
  ITC Avant Garde Gothic Book Oblique
  ITC Avant Garde Gothic Demi
  ITC Avant Garde Gothic Demi Oblique
  ITC Bookman Demi
  ITC Bookman Demi Italic
  ITC Bookman Light
  ITC Bookman Light Italic
  ITC Zapf Chancery Medium Italic

1 Select; N Name search: 1
```

**Figure 14-1: Base Font Menu**

The prompt at the bottom of the screen lets you select a new font setting or institute a name search. To use Name Search, key in a letter from the keyboard and WordPerfect highlights the first font that begins with that letter. Continue entering letters, and WordPerfect searches for a font setting that begins with the letters entered. You can also highlight fonts by pressing the Down arrow key.

The asterisk identifies the current font. To select a different font, move the cursor with the Down arrow key until the font you desire is highlighted, then choose 1 or S for Select. This selects the new font and returns the cursor to the document. (If you are using a PostScript printer, highlight the font, choose 1 or S for Select, key in the desired point size, then press Enter.) For example, to change the base font to 12-point Helvetica Bold, complete the following steps:

1.  Access the Font command with Ctrl + F8.
2.  Choose 4 or F for Base Font.
    **M** *Click on Font, then Base Font.*
3.  At the Base Font menu, move the cursor to Helvetica Bold 12 point and choose 1 or S for Select. (If you are using a PostScript printer, key in **12** and press Enter.)

WordPerfect is designed to display text in 10-pitch monospaced type. When the point size of proportional type is changed, the monitor does not display the text as it will appear when printed. When base font changes are made to a document, WordPerfect's View Document feature can be used to show how the document will look on paper before it is printed. To view a document on the screen, access the Print command with Shift + F7 (**M** *Click on File, then Print*), then choose 6 or V for View Document. Press F7 to exit View Document and return to the screen.

## SPACING PUNCTUATION

When keying in a document on a typewriter, end-of-sentence punctuation, such as the period, exclamation point, and question mark, are followed by two spaces. When creating a document in WordPerfect with a proportional typeface, space only once after end-of-sentence punctuation. Proportional type is set closer, and extra white space at the end of sentences is not needed. If extra white space is added, the text appears blotchy.

## SIZE

The type size can be selected at the Base Font menu, which lists the sizes available with each typeface, or it can be determined by the Size selection from the Font command. To use the Size selection, access the Font command with Ctrl + F8, choose 1 or S for Size and the prompt **1 Suprscpt; 2 Subscpt; 3 Fine; 4 Small; 5 Large; 6 Vry Large; 7 Ext Large: 0** appears at the bottom of the screen.

The first selection, Suprscpt, lets you create text that is raised slightly above the line. Some mathematical expressions are written with superscript numbers. For example, the mathematical expression 3 to the second power is written as $3^2$. To create a superscript character, complete the following steps:

1. Key in text to the point where the superscript character is to appear.
2. Access the Font command with Ctrl + F8.
3. Choose 1 or S for Size.
4. Choose 1 or P for Suprscript.
   **M** *Click on Font, then Superscript.*
5. Key in the superscript character.
6. Return to normal characters by pressing the Right arrow key once to move the cursor past the Superscript Off code.

Superscript can also be turned off by accessing the Font command with Ctrl+ F8 and choosing 3 or N for Normal (**M** *Click on Font, then Normal*). The Normal selection moves the cursor to the right of the Superscript code. Text will not appear in superscript form on the screen. Codes are inserted in the document and can be seen in Reveal Codes. The expression $3^2$ appears as **3[SUPRSCPT]2[suprscpt]** in Reveal Codes.

The second selection, Subscpt, lets you create text that is lowered slightly below the line. Some chemical formulas require the use of subscript characters. For example, the formula for water is written as $H_2O$. To create a subscript, complete the following steps:

1. Key in text to the point where the subscript character is to appear.
2. Access the Font command with Ctrl + F8.
3. Choose 1 or S for Size.
4. Choose 2 or B for Subscript.
   **M** *Click on Font, then Subscript.*
4. Key in the subscript character.
5. Return to normal characters by pressing the Right arrow key once to move the cursor past the Subscript Off code.

Just as with superscripts, subscripts do not appear on the screen. A code is inserted in the document and can be seen in Reveal Codes. The formula $H_2O$ appears as **H[SUBSCPT]2[subscpt]O** in Reveal Codes.

WordPerfect prints superscripts and subscripts approximately one-third of a line above and below the main line. This may vary, depending on the printer you are using. Some printers are not capable of printing superscripts and subscripts.

The remaining selections from the Size prompt are used to determine the relative size of the type based on the size of the base font in the document. The selections change the size of the current font by the following percentages:

```
3 Fine          = 60%
4 Small         = 80%
5 Large         = 120%
6 Very Large    = 150%
7 Extra Large   = 200%
```

If the base font in a document is 10-point Times Roman as displayed below, the **Fine** selection changes the size to 6 points, **Small** to 8 points, **Large** to 12 points, **Very Large** to 15 points, and **Extra Large** to 20 points.

This text is Fine or 60% of the base font.

This text is Small or 80% of the base font.

This text is the default size of the base font.

This text is Large or 120% of the base font.

This text is Very Large or 150% of the base font.

# This text is Extra Large or 200% of the base font.

Changes to the size occur when the document is printed, and only if the printer supports the point sizes. If the printer does not support the point sizes, WordPerfect chooses and prints an approximate size.

Changing point size with the Size selection from the Font command allows changes to be made easily to the document. If the size of the base font is changed, any type with size attributes attached is automatically updated. Also, if the typeface is changed, the size attribute applies to the new typeface.

To change the size of characters in a document, complete the following steps:

1.   Key in text to the point where you want the size changed.
2.   Access the Font command with Ctrl + F8.
3.   Choose 1 or S for Size.
4.   Choose the size you desire from the prompt at the bottom of the screen.
     **M** *Click on Font, then Fine, Small, Large, Very Large, or Extra Large.*
5.   Key in the characters you want at a different size.
6.   Press the Right arrow key to move the cursor past the Size Off code.

**Appearance**

The Appearance selection from the Font command is used to create a variety of character styles. When you choose 2 or A for Appearance from the Font command, the prompt **1 Bold  2 Undrln  3 Dbl Und  4 Italc  5 Outln  6 Shadw  7 Sm Cap  8 Redln  9 Stkout: 0** appears at the bottom of the screen.

The first two selections are used to boldface and underline text. In an earlier chapter, you learned to boldface text with the F6 function key and underline text with the F8 function key. These keys are probably the easiest and quickest to use. However, you can boldface and underline with the Appearance selection. To do this, complete the following steps:

1. Key in text to the point where boldface and underline characters are to appear.
2. Access the Font command with Ctrl + F8.
3. Choose 2 or A for Appearance.
4. Choose 1 or B for Bold or 2 or U for Underline.
   **M** *Click on Font, Appearance, then Bold or Underline.*
5. Press the Right arrow key once to move the cursor past the Boldface or Underline Off code.

The Double Underline selection is used to create text with a double underline such as totals in a column or words that are to be accentuated in a document. Double underline text following the steps above, except choose 3 or D for Dbl Und at step 4 (**M** *Click on Font, Appearance, then Double Underline*).

You can italicize text by choosing an italic type style from the Base Font menu or with a selection from the Appearance prompt. When text is identified as italic from the Appearance prompt, WordPerfect chooses the italic type style of the default typeface. Italicize text following the steps above, except choose 4 or I for Italic at step 4 (**M** *Click on Font, Appearance, then Italics*).

The Outline selection from the Appearance prompt prints characters with an outline. This works if the printer you are using has an outline font. Characters that have been identified for outlining will look like this:

## This is Outline Text

The Shadow selection from the Appearance prompt prints characters with a shadow. This works for some printers, including PostScript printers. Shadow characters look like this:

## This is Shadow Text

From the Appearance prompt, the Sm Cap selection lets you print small capital letters. This works for some printers, but not all. Small Capital letters look like this:

THIS IS SMALL CAPS

The Redline selection from the Appearance prompt lets you identify text that is added to a legal document. When text is added to a legal document, it prints in reverse (white text on black background) or a vertical bar appears in the left margin. The appearance of redlined text is printer dependent. How redlined text appears when printed can be changed at the Format: Document Other menu. To change the redlining method, complete the following steps:

1.  Access the Format: Document menu with Shift + F8, then choose 3 or D for Document.
    **M** *Click on Layout, then Document.*

2.  Choose 4 or R for Redline Method.

3.  From the prompt **Redline Method: 1 <u>P</u>rinter Dependent; 2 <u>L</u>eft; 3 <u>A</u>lternating: <u>1</u>**, choose 1 or P for Printer Dependent (the default); choose 2 or L for Left to tell WordPerfect to mark redlined text at the left margin; or, choose 3 or A for Alternating to tell WordPerfect to mark redlined text at the left margin on even-numbered pages and at the right margin on odd-numbered pages.

4.  Press F7 to return the cursor to the document.

The Strikeout selection from the Appearance prompt lets you show text that has been deleted from a document. Strikeout prints text with a line of hyphens running through it. This feature has practical application for some legal documents in which deleted text must be retained in the document. The hyphens indicate that the text has been deleted. Strikeout looks like this:

~~This is Strikeout Text~~

Strikeout and redlining codes can be removed quickly from a document with the Mark Text command, Alt + F5. To delete Redlining or Strikeout codes, complete the following steps:

1.  Display the document on the screen that contains redlining or strikeout.

2.  Access the Mark Text command with Alt + F5.

3.  Choose 6 or G for Generate.
    **M** *Click on Mark, then Generate.*

4.  Choose 1 or R for Remove Redline Markings and Strikeout Text from Document.

5.  At the confirmation question, key in a **Y** for Yes.

Change characters to outline, shadow, small caps, redlining, or strikeout by following steps similar to those for boldfacing and underlining.

## Character Formatting with Existing Text

The selections from the Size and Appearance prompts can be applied to existing text in a document. To do this, complete the following steps:

1.  Block the text to which you want special formatting applied.

2.  Access the Font command with Ctrl + F8.

3.  Choose 1 or S for Size, or choose 2 or A for Appearance.
    **M** *Click on Font, then Appearance, or click on a size.*

4.  Make a choice from the Size prompt or the Appearance prompt.

When a choice is made from the Size or Appearance prompt, WordPerfect inserts the On and Off codes for the feature and returns the cursor to the document.

## CHAPTER REVIEW

### Summary

- For most printers, the default font is 10-pitch (12-point) Courier. A font is a particular typeface in a specific style and size. The availability of fonts depends on the printer and ranges from a few to several hundred. Changes are made to the font at the Base Font menu.

- A font consists of three parts: typeface, type style, and type size. A typeface is a set of characters with a common general design and shape. Typefaces are either monospaced or proportional. A monospaced typeface allots the same amount of horizontal space for each character. A proportional typeface allots a varying amount of space for each character. Proportional typefaces are divided into two categories: serif and sans serif. A serif is a small line at the end of a character stroke. A sans serif typeface does not have serifs.

- Type size is divided into two categories: pitch and point size. Pitch is a measurement used for monospaced typefaces and is the number of characters that print in 1 inch. The size of a proportional typeface is measured in point sizes. A point is approximately 1/72 of an inch.

- There are four main categories of type style: roman or book, bold or demi, italic, and bold italic.

- WordPerfect is designed to display text in 10-pitch monospaced type. When the point size of proportional type is changed, use View Document to see how the document will appear when printed.

- Space once after end-of-sentence punctuation when using a proportional typeface.

- Type size can be selected at the Base Font menu or changed with the Size selection from the Font command. At the Size selection, type size can be changed to superscript, subscript, fine, small, large, very large, or extra large.

- Superscript text is printed slightly above the line, and subscript text is printed slightly below the line.

- At the Appearance prompt from the Font command, you can identify characters as bold, underline, double underline, italic, outline, shadow, small caps, redline, or strikeout. Some of the appearance selections may or may not print, depending on the printer.

- Redlining identifies text that is added to a legal document. Strikeout identifies text that has been deleted from a document. Redlining and strikeout codes can be quickly removed from a document with the Mark Text command.

- Selections from the Size and Appearance prompts can be applied to existing text. The text must first be blocked with the Block command.

### Commands

| | Keyboard | Mouse |
|---|---|---|
| Font command | Ctrl + F8 | Font |
| Mark Text command | Alt + F5 | Mark |

## STUDY GUIDE FOR CHAPTER 14

**Completion:** In the space provided at the right, indicate the correct term, command, symbol, or character for the explanation.

1.  A set of characters with a common general design and shape.     _____

2.  A small line at the end of a character stroke.     _____

3.  Measurement used for monospaced typefaces that is the number of characters that print in an inch.     _____

4.  Measurement used for proportional typefaces and is approximately 1/72 of an inch.     _____

5.  The standard style of the typeface is referred to as roman or this.     _____

6.  The bold style of a typeface is referred to as bold or this.     _____

7.  The italic style of a sans serif typeface is referred to as this.     _____

8.  A particular typeface in a specific style and size.     _____

9.  When using a proportional typeface, press the space bar this number of times after end-of-sentence punctuation.     _____

10. A character that is printed slightly above the text line.     _____

11. A character that is printed slightly below the text line.     _____

12. This selection from the Size prompt will print characters at 120% of the size of the default typeface.     _____

13. This feature prints a line of hyphens through text that is deleted from a legal document.     _____

14. This feature lets you identify text that is added to a legal document.     _____

15. This selection from the Appearance prompt lets you print small capital letters.     _____

## HANDS-ON EXERCISES

### Exercise One
1.  Create a new subdirectory named UNIT4.
2.  Change the default directory to UNIT4.

### Exercise Two
1.  Retrieve CH04EX5 to the screen. (This document is located in the UNIT1 subdirectory.)
2.  With the cursor at the beginning of the document, change the left and right margins to 1.5 inches.
3.  Change the font to 12-pitch Courier (check to see if your printer is capable of this font).
4.  Save the letter in the UNIT4 subdirectory (this should be the current directory) and name it CH14EX2. Print CH14EX2.

**Exercise Three**

1. Retrieve CH04PA2 to the screen. (This document is located in the UNIT1 subdirectory.)
2. Search for and remove all underlining codes.
3. Italicize each publication name by completing the following steps:
   A. Move the cursor to the first publication name (Psychological Bulletin) and access the Block command with Alt + F4 or F12.
      **M** *Click on Edit, then Block.*
   B. Move the cursor to the end of the publication name, then access the Font command with Ctrl + F8.
   C. Choose 2 or A for Appearance.
   D. Choose 4 or I for Italic.
      **M** *Click on Font, Appearance, then Italic.*
   E. Complete the same steps for the remainder of the publication names.
4. Save the references page and name it CH14EX3. Print CH14EX3.

**Exercise Four**

1. Retrieve CH06PA1 to the screen. (This document is located in the UNIT2 subdirectory.)
2. With the cursor at the beginning of the document, change the base font to 12-point Times Roman. (If your printer does not support Times Roman, choose a different serif, proportional typeface. If your printer does not support any proportional typefaces, choose 12-pitch Courier.)
3. Change the spacing after end-of-sentence punctuation from two spaces to one space by completing a search-and-replace with confirmation.
4. Save the letter and name it CH14EX4. Print CH14EX4.

**Exercise Five**

1. At a clear screen, change the justification to left and the left and right margins to 1.5 inches.
2. Key in the test shown in figure 14-2. Center and boldface the title and subtitle. Key in superscripts and subscripts as indicated. Use the Indent key to indent the test questions. Leave four blank lines between test questions.
3. Save the test and name it CH14EX5. Print CH14EX5.

---

### ELECTRIC CIRCUIT TEST

### Chapters 2 through 5

1. Make a table showing the values of $y$, $y^2$, $y^3$, $y^4$, $y^5$, $y^6$, $y^7$, and $y^8$. Do you notice a pattern? What is it?

2. Calculate $I_d$ in Figure 1, if $I_s = 0.02$ A and $V_d = 50$ mV and 500 mV.

3. Calculate $I_d$, if $I_s = 4$ nA.

4.  What is the torque on 1,000 turn, 1 cm x 1 cm D'Arsonval meter coil if the magnetic flux density is 0.07 Wb/m$^2$ and the coil current is 1 mA?

5.  If the torque on the coil is 1.4 x 10$^{-4}$ newton-meters, what must be the coil current?

6.  The solenoid core in Figure 2 has a cross-sectional area of 5 x 10$^{-3}$ m$^2$, and the circuit reluctance is 3 x 10$^4$ At/Wb. What must be the mmf?

7.  What is the total flux in the solenoid if the reluctance is 2.0 x 10$^6$ At/Wb?

**Figure 14-2: Exercise Five**

## Exercise Six

1.  At a clear screen, change the justification to left and the line spacing to double (2). Change the base font to 12-point Palatino. (If your printer does not support the Palatino typeface, use another serif, proportional typeface. If your printer does not support any proportional typefaces, leave the base font at the default.)
2.  Create pages 2 and 3 of a state legislative bill as shown in figure 14-3.
3.  Strike out the text as indicated by the proofreaders' marks. Insert the text as indicated and identify it with redlining.
4.  Save the bill and name it CH14EX6. Print CH14EX6.

## Exercise Seven

1.  Retrieve CH14EX6 to the screen.
2.  Remove strikeout and redlining markings from the document by completing the following steps:
    A.  Access the Mark Text command with Alt + F5.
    B.  Choose 6 or G for Generate.
        **M** *Click on Mark, then Generate.*
    C.  Choose 1 or R for Remove Redline Markings and Strikeout Text from Document.
    D.  At the confirmation question, key in a **Y** for Yes.
3.  Save the bill and name it CH14EX7. Print CH14EX7.

## Exercise Eight

1.  Retrieve CH04EX2 to the screen. (This document is located in the UNIT1 subdirectory.)
2.  Change the memorandum to all small caps by completing the following steps:
    A.  Block the entire memorandum.
    B.  Access the Font command with Control + F8.
    C.  Choose 2 or A for Appearance.
    D.  Choose 7 or C for Sm Cap.
        **M** *Click on Font, Appearance, then Small Cap.*
    E.  Check the spacing after the memorandum headings. You may need to realign the headings.
3.  Save the memorandum and name it CH14EX8. Print CH14EX8.

Sec. 2. Section 10, chapter 142, Laws of 1983 1st ex. sess. as amended by section 6, chapter 145, Laws of 1984 ex. sess. and RCW 71.03.670 are each amended to read as follows:

Nothing in this chapter shall be construed to limit the right of any person to apply voluntarily to any public or private agency or practitioner for treatment of a mental disorder, either by direct application or by referral.

Any person voluntarily admitted for inpatient treatment to any public or private agency shall orally be advised of the right to immediate release and further advised of such rights in writing as are secured to them pursuant to this chapter and their rights of access to attorneys, courts, and other legal redress.

If the _professional_ staff of any public or private agency regards a person voluntarily admitted ~~as dangerous to himself or others~~ _who requests release, presenting a likelihood of serious harm,_ or gravely disabled as defined by this act, they may detain such person for ~~a reasonable length of~~ _sufficient_ time, ~~sufficient~~ to notify the designated county health professional of such person's condition to enable such mental health professional to authorize such person being further held in custody or transported to an evaluation and treatment center pursuant to the provisions of this chapter.*

When a mental health professional designated by the county receives information alleging that a person, as a result of a mental disorder, presents a likelihood of serious harm to others or himself, or is gravely disabled, such mental health professional, after investigation and evaluation of the specific facts alleged, and of the reliability and credibility of the person or persons, if any, providing information to initiate detention, may summon such person to appear at an evaluation and treatment facility for not more than a 72-hour evaluation and treatment period.* **

\* which shall, in ordinary circumstances, be no later than one judicial day
\* \* The summons shall state whether the required 72-hour evaluation and treatment services may be delivered on an outpatient or inpatient status.

Figure 14-3: Exercise Six

## Exercise Nine

1. Retrieve CH06PA2 to the screen. (This document is located in the UNIT2 subdirectory.)
2. With the cursor at the beginning of the document, change the base font to 12-point Times Roman. (If your printer does not support Times Roman, use a serif, proportional typeface. If your printer does not support any proportional typefaces, use the default base font.)
3. Change the size of the title to Very Large by completing the following step:
   A. Block the title.
   B. Access the Font command with Control + F8.
   C. Choose 1 or S for Size.
   D. Choose 6 or V for Vry Large.
      **M** *Click on Font, then Very Large.*
4. Block the heading, THE WAR ON POVERTY YEARS: 1964-69, and change the size to Large.
5. Save the report and name it CH14EX9. Print CH14EX9.


## PERFORMANCE ASSESSMENTS

### Assessment One

1. At a clear screen, retrieve CH08EX6. (This document is located in the UNIT2 subdirectory.)
2. Change the base font to 12-pitch Courier.
3. Block the first column in the letter (the column that lists the sale items) and identify it as boldfaced text. (Each entry must be blocked individually.)
4. Block the third column (the percentage of savings) and identify it as italicized text.
5. Save the letter and name it CH14PA1. Print CH14PA1.


### Assessment Two

1. Retrieve CH07EX5 to the screen.
2. Change the base font to 12-point Palatino. (If your printer does not support Palatino, use a serif, proportional typeface. If your printer does not support any proportional typefaces, change the base font to 12-pitch Courier.)
3. Block the title and change the size to Large.
4. Delete the underline below WSBEA Quarterly and italicize the publication name.
5. Complete a search and replace with confirmation that changes the spacing after end-of-sentence punctuation from two spaces to one space.
6. Save the document and name it CH14PA2. Print CH14PA2.


### Assessment Three

1. Retrieve CH07EX1 to the screen.
2. Change the base font to 12-point New Century Schoolbook. (If your printer does not support New Century Schoolbook, use a serif, proportional typeface. If your printer does not support any proportional typefaces, change the base font to 12-pitch Courier.)
3. Block the title and change the size to Large.
4. Block the title again and identify it as shadow text.
5. Block the headings in the indented paragraphs and change them to italicized text.
6. Complete a search and replace with confirmation that changes the spacing after end-of-sentence punctuation from two spaces to one space.
7. Save the document and name it CH14PA3. Print CH14PA3.

# CHAPTER 15

## ADVANCED LINE FORMATTING

### *PERFORMANCE OBJECTIVE*

Upon successful completion of chapter 15, you will be able to manipulate the height and length of lines in finished business documents.

### HYPHENATION

In a WordPerfect document, if additions or deletions are made or the margin settings are changed, the text on the screen automatically adjusts as the cursor moves through the text. As the text adjusts, you are not allowed to hyphenate words at the end of the line. This is because hyphenation is off by default. In some situations, you may want hyphenation turned on. When it is on, you are allowed to hyphenate words at the end of lines that fall within the hyphenation zone.

#### Hyphenation Zone

To understand how hyphenation works, you must first know something about the hyphenation zone. WordPerfect automatically provides a hyphenation zone setting on the ruler line. The beginning of the hyphenation zone is called the left hyphenation zone, and the end is called the right hyphenation zone.

The default left hyphenation zone is 10 percent of the typing line before the right margin. If you are using the default margins of 1 inch, you have a typing line of 6.5 inches. The default left hyphenation zone is 10 percent of the typing line, or about .65 of an inch. (If you are using the default pitch setting of 10, you can round this off and call it about seven positions).

The default right hyphenation zone is 4 percent of the typing line after the right margin. If you are using the default margins and pitch setting, this is .25 of an inch, or approximately three positions rounded off.

If a word begins after the left hyphenation zone and goes beyond the right hyphenation zone, WordPerfect wraps it to the next line. If a word begins at or before the left hyphenation zone and extends past the right hyphenation zone, you will be asked to hyphenate if hyphenation is turned on. The illustration in figure 15-1 shows how the word *calculations* will be either wrapped to the next line or hyphenated during rewrite.

**Wrapped to next line**

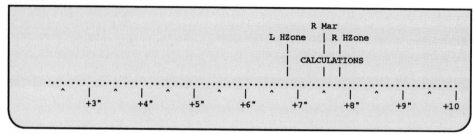

**Hyphenated During Rewrite**

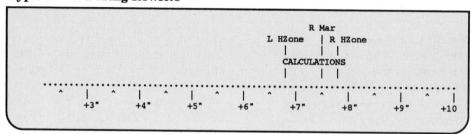

Figure 15-1: Word Wrap and Hyphenation Zone

If the hyphenation zone is shortened, you will be asked to hyphenate more words. If the hyphenation zone is lengthened, you will be asked to hyphenate fewer words. The shorter the hyphenation zone, the more words that will begin at or before the left hyphenation zone and continue past the right hyphenation zone.

You may want to change to a shorter hyphenation zone, however, if your document uses shorter margins. Many of the documents you have printed have had even left and right margins (Justification Full). WordPerfect justifies the right margin by spreading blank spaces throughout the line. If more words are hyphenated, there would be fewer blank spaces, and this improves the appearance of the printed document.

### Changing the Hyphenation Zone

If you decide to make the hyphenation zone shorter or longer, complete the following steps:

1. Access the Format command with Shift + F8, then choose 1 or L for Line.
   **M** *Click on Layout, then Line.*

2. Choose 2 or Z for Hyphenation Zone.

3. Key in a percentage number for the left hyphenation zone and press Enter.

4. Key in a percentage number for the right hyphenation zone and press Enter.

5. Press F7 to return the cursor to the document.

To check hyphenation zone settings, access Reveal Codes. A left hyphenation zone setting of 8 percent and a right hyphenation zone setting of 2 percent looks like **[HZone:8%,2%]** in Reveal Codes. If you delete a Hyphenation zone code, WordPerfect reverts to the default settings of 10 percent and 4 percent.

### Hyphenation On/Off

Before WordPerfect asks for hyphenation, hyphenation must be turned on. To turn on hyphenation, complete the following steps:

1. Access the Format command with Shift + F8, then choose 1 or L for Line.
   **M** *Click on Layout, then Line.*
2. Choose 1 or Y for Hyphenation.
3. Key in a **Y** for Yes.
4. Press F7 to return the cursor to the document.

To ensure that all text in a document is checked for possible hyphenations, press Home, Home, Down arrow key to move the cursor to the end of the document. As the cursor moves to the end of the document, WordPerfect stops and asks for hyphenation decisions.

To understand the hyphenation feature, let's look at an example. If hyphenation is on and the word *document* begins at or before the left hyphenation zone and continues past the right hyphenation zone, the following message appears in the bottom left corner of the screen:

**Position hyphen: Press ESC** docu-ment

The cursor is blinking under the hyphen in **document**. You can either hyphenate or cancel hyphenation with the Cancel key, F1. If you press the Escape key, a hyphen is inserted in the word as indicated and hyphenation continues. If you decide not to hyphenate and press F1, the word is wrapped down to the next line and hyphenation continues. Before pressing the Escape key, check where the hyphen is located in the word. WordPerfect does not always place the hyphen in the correct location. If the word is hyphenated incorrectly, move the hyphen forward or backward with the Left or Right arrow key.

To cancel hyphenation during the hyphenation process, use the Exit key, F7.

## LINE HEIGHT

WordPerfect includes a line height setting on the Line: Format menu that specifies the amount of space a line occupies. The Line Height selection from the Format: Line menu has a default setting of Auto. At this setting, WordPerfect adjusts the line height automatically when changes are made to the base font.

The auto setting can be changed to fixed, which lets you control the amount of space occupied by a line. To change the line height in a document, complete the following steps:

1.  Access the Format: Line menu with Shift + F8, then choose 1 or L for Line.
    **M** *Click on Layout, then Line.*
2.  Choose 4 or H for Line Height and the prompt **1 <u>Auto</u>; 2 <u>F</u>ixed: <u>0</u>** appears at the bottom of the screen.
3.  Choose 2 or F for Fixed.
4.  Key in the new line height measurement and press Enter.
5.  Press F7 to return the cursor to the document.

When you choose 2 or F for Fixed, the cursor moves to the setting after Line Height and the setting changes to 0.167 inches. This measurement allows approximately six lines in a vertical inch. If you key in a smaller number, more lines print per inch. If you key in a higher number, fewer lines appear in an inch.

## LINE NUMBERING

The Line Numbering selection from the Format: Line menu has a default setting of No. At this setting, no line numbers print at the left margin of the document. If Line Numbering is changed to Yes, WordPerfect numbers each line as it is being printed. This has practical applications, such as in a law office for pleading papers or for reference purposes.

To turn Line Numbering on, complete the following steps:

1.  Access the Format: Line menu with Shift + F8, then choose 1 or L for Line.
    **M** *Click on Layout, then Line.*
2.  Choose 5 or N for Line Numbering.
3.  Key in a **Y** for Yes.
4.  Make changes to the Format: Line Numbering menu.
5.  Press F7 to return the cursor to the document.

When you choose 5 or N for Line Numbering, the menu shown in figure 15-2 displays on the screen.

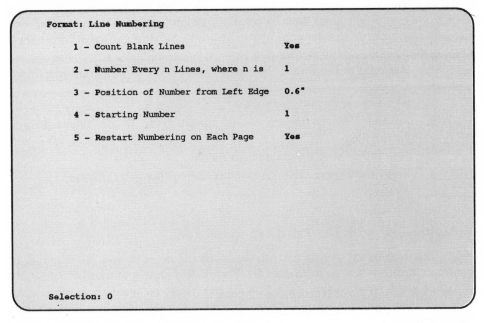

**Figure 15-2: Format: Line Numbering Menu**

Selection 1, Count Blank Lines, has a default setting of Yes. At this setting, WordPerfect counts and numbers blank lines. Change this to No if you do not want blank lines numbered.

WordPerfect lets you specify how often lines should be numbered with the second selection from the menu. For example, if you decide to have every second line numbered, choose 2 or N for Number Every n Lines, then key in a **2** over the default setting of 1.

Selection 3 identifies the location of printed line numbers on the page. The default setting prints line numbers 6/10ths of an inch from the left edge of the paper. This can be changed to any setting you desire, but you must make sure that the left margin is set to accommodate the line number.

The fourth selection lets you change the beginning starting number. If you want to begin line numbering with 6, choose 4 or S for Starting Number, then key in a **6** and press Enter.

Selection 5 causes line numbering to begin at 1 on each page. If you decide that you want consecutive line numbers, choose 5 or R for Restart Numbering on Each Page, then key in an **N** for No.

## FLUSH RIGHT

WordPerfect includes a Flush Right command that lets you create text aligned at the right margin. To use this command, access the Flush Right command with Alt + F6 (**M** *Click on Layout, Align, then Flush Right*). The cursor moves to the right margin, and the text you key in moves left. The Flush Right command is ended as soon as you press the Enter key. To align the next line at the right margin, access the Flush Right command again.

## TAB ALIGN COMMAND

With the Tab Align command, Ctrl + F6 (**M** *Click on Layout, Align, then Tab Align*), you can align text in columns around a specific character. The default character is the decimal point. This can be changed to other characters by completing the following steps:

1. Access the Format: Other menu with Shift + F8, then 4 or O for Other.
   **M** *Click on Layout, then Other.*
2. At the Format: Other menu, choose 3 or D for Decimal/Align Character.
3. Key in the new alignment character.
4. With the cursor after Thousands' Separator, press Enter.
5. Press F7.

### Entering Text with the Tab Align Command

After the alignment character has been changed, text can be aligned in columns around the new character. The Tab Align command, Ctrl + F6 (**M** *Click on Layout, Align, then Tab Align*), must be used to enter text in columns. For example, to align text around a percent symbol, first change the alignment character.

At the document, access the Tab Align command with Ctrl + F6 (**M** *Click on Layout, Align, then Tab Align*). This moves the cursor to the next tab stop to the right, and the message **Align Char = %** appears at the bottom of the screen. The text you key in moves to the left until the alignment character (in this case, the percent symbol) is pressed. This deactivates Tab Align. Other keys that turn off Tab Align include the Tab key and Enter. You must use the Tab Align command to move the cursor to the tab stop for each column and not the Tab key.

## ALIGNING COLUMNS

In chapter 5, you learned the key line method for determining tab settings for columns. This method works for text that is keyed in with a mono-spaced, 10-pitch (12-point) font. If you use a point size other than 12 or if you change to a proportional typeface, what you see on the screen is not what you get on the printed page. To accommodate the difference between the screen and the printed page, a different method for setting columns is required. The following steps are recommended for determining tab settings for columns set in a point size other than 12 or a proportional typeface:

1. Change to the desired base font.
2. Key in the longest entry of each column along with the spaces you want between columns.
3. Center the key line.
4. Print the key line with Shift + F7 (**M** *Click on File, then Print*), then choose 1 or F for Full Document.
5. Using a ruler marked with increments of 10 (the screen displays in increments of 10), measure the distance in tenths of an inch from the left margin (not the left edge of the page) to the beginning of each column.

6.  Delete the key line.
7.  Use the measurements to set tabs.
8.  Key in the text in columns.

For example, to determine tab settings for the columns shown in figure 15-3, set in 18-point Times Roman, complete the following steps:

| | |
|---|---|
| Darlene Evans | Benefits Manager |
| John White Cloud | Personnel Manager |
| Robin Simmons | Receptionist |

Figure 15-3: Aligning Columns

1.  Change the base font to 18-point Times Roman.
2.  Key in **John White Cloud**, space eight times, then key in **Personnel Manager** (these are the longest entries in each column).
3.  Access the Center command with Shift + F6.
    **M** *Click on Layout, Align, then Center.*
4.  Print the line with Shift + F7 (**M** *Click on File, then Print*), then choose 1 or F for Full Document.
5.  With a ruler marked with increments of 10, measure from the left margin (not the left edge of the page) to the first column. (The measurement is 1.0 inches.) Measure from the left margin to the second column. (The measurement is 3.5 inches.)
6.  Delete the key line.
7.  Set left tabs at +1.0 and +3.5 inches.
8.  Key in the columns using the Tab key to move to tab settings.

If the column heading is the longest line in the column, use it in the key line. Use the tab settings to key in column headings and entries below column headings. Key in the column heading at the tab setting rather than centered above the columns. Centering column headings over columns is difficult when using a font other than the default of 10-pitch (12-point), because what you see on the screen is not how the text will print. For this reason, you cannot visually center column headings.

If columns are to align at the right, centered, or at the decimal point, measure to the location of the entries where the tab is to appear. For example, if you wanted the second column in the example above to be aligned at the right, you would measure one space to the right of Personnel Manager. This measurement is then used to create a right tab.

## CHAPTER REVIEW

### Summary

- By default, hyphenation is off. The default left hyphenation zone is 10 percent and the default right hyphenation zone is 4 percent. Word wrap decisions are made in the hyphenation zone. If a word begins after the left hyphenation zone and continues past the right hyphenation zone, it is wrapped to the next line.
- With hyphenation turned on, you will be asked to hyphenate words that begin at or before the left hyphenation zone and extend past the right hyphenation zone.
- To change the length of the hyphenation zone, access the Format command with Shift + F8 (**M** *Click on Layout, then Line*), choose 1 or L for Line, then 2 or Z for Hyphenation Zone. Key in the new left hyphenation setting and press Enter. Key in the new right hyphenation setting and press Enter. Press F7 to return to the document.
- The shorter the hyphenation zone, the more words you will be asked to hyphenate.
- If a word is to be hyphenated, it is displayed at the bottom of the screen. Press the Escape key to hyphenate the word, move the cursor and press the Escape key, or press F1 for Cancel (to not hyphenate).
- Press F7, Exit, to cancel hyphenation during the hyphenation process.
- The Line Height selection from the Format: Line menu specifies the amount of space a line occupies. The default setting is Auto, which means that WordPerfect adjusts the line height automatically when a change is made to the base font. Line height can be changed to Fixed and a specific measurement can be entered.
- The Line Numbering selection from the Format: Line menu is used to number documents in the left margin. This has a practical application for some legal documents. The appearance of line numbers can be customized at the Format: Line Numbering menu.
- Access the Flush Right command with Alt + F6 (**M** *Click on Layout, Align, then Flush Right*) to align text at the right margin.
- Use the Tab Align command to align text in a column around a specific character. The alignment character can be changed at the Format: Other menu.
- When setting up columns of text with a base font other than 10-pitch (12-point), use a ruler with increments of 10 to measure the printed key line. Align a column heading at the tab setting rather than centered over the column.

### Commands

| | Keyboard | Mouse |
|---|---|---|
| Format: Line menu | Shift + F8, 1 or L | Layout, Line |
| Flush Right command | Alt + F6 | Layout, Align, Flush Right |
| Format: Other menu | Shift + F8, 4 or O | Layout, Other |
| Tab Align command | Ctrl + F6 | Layout, Align, Tab Align |

## STUDY GUIDE FOR CHAPTER 15

**Completion:** In the space provided at the right, indicate the correct symbol, term, or number for the explanation.

1.  Default setting of the left hyphenation zone.  _____

2.  Default setting of the right hyphenation zone.  _____

3.  Key used to cancel hyphenation during rewrite.  _____

4.  Key used to insert a hyphen during rewrite.  _____

5.  Key used to exit the hyphenation process.  _____

6.  Default setting for the Line Height selection of the Format: Line menu.  _____

7.  Press these keys (**M** *Click on these words*) to access the Tab Align command.  _____

**True/False:** Circle the letter T if the statement is true; circle the letter F if the statement is false.

1.  Hyphenation is off by default.  T    F
2.  The right hyphenation zone is set at the right margin.  T    F
3.  The beginning of the hyphenation zone is the left hyphenation zone.  T    F
4.  With hyphenation on, if a word begins before the left hyphenation zone and continues past the right hyphenation zone, WordPerfect wraps it to the next line.  T    F
5.  A shorter hyphenation zone causes more words to be hyphenated.  T    F
6.  If you press F1 during hyphenation, the entire word is wrapped down to the next line.  T    F
7.  Hyphenation can be turned on and off several times in a document.  T    F
8.  Line numbering is on by default.  T    F
9.  Access the Mark Text command with Alt + F6 (**M** *Click on Layout, Align, then Flush Right*).  T    F
10. When using a typeface other than 10-pitch (12-point), center column headings over column entries.  T    F
11. When determining tab settings for a document with a typeface other than 10-pitch (12-point), make measurements with a ruler marked with increments of 12.  T    F
12. The default tab alignment character is a decimal.  T    F

## HANDS-ON EXERCISES

Change the default directory to UNIT4.

### Exercise One

1.  Retrieve CH04PA1 to the screen. (This document is located in the UNIT1 subdirectory.)
2.  With the cursor at the beginning of the document change the left hyphenation zone to 6 percent and the right hyphenation zone to 0 percent and turn on hyphenation by completing the following steps:
    A. Access the Format command with Shift + F8, then choose 1 or L for Line.
       **M** *Click on Layout, then Line.*
    B. Choose 2 or Z for Hyphenation Zone.
    C. Key in **6** and press Enter.
    D. Key in **0** and press Enter.
    E. Choose 1 or Y for Hyphenation.
    F. Key in a **Y** for Yes.
    G. Press F7 to return the cursor to the document.
    H. WordPerfect will beep and ask you to hyphenate a word. Make sure the hyphen is in the correct location, then press the Escape key.
    I. Press Home, Home, Down arrow key to move the cursor to the end of the document. Make hyphenation decisions as WordPerfect stops at each location.
3.  Save the report and name it CH15EX1. Print CH15EX1.

### Exercise Two

1.  Retrieve CH07EX1 to the screen. (This document is located in the UNIT2 subdirectory.)
2.  Change the left hyphenation zone to 6 percent, leave the right hyphenation zone at 4 percent, and turn on hyphenation. Make hyphenation decisions as WordPerfect stops at each location. (To make sure WordPerfect stops at all hyphenation locations, move the cursor to the end of the document with Home, Home, Down arrow key.)
3.  Check hyphenation locations. If you hyphenated a word that should not be hyphenated (such as the last word in a paragraph), move the cursor to the hyphen, press the Delete key, then cancel hyphenation by pressing F1.
4.  Save the report and name it CH15EX2. Print CH15EX2.

### Exercise Three

1.  Retrieve CH12EX6 to the screen. (This document is located in the UNIT3 subdirectory.)
2.  With the cursor at the beginning of the document, turn on line numbering by completing the following steps:
    A. Access the Format: Line menu with Shift + F8, then choose 1 or L for Line.
       **M** *Click on Layout, then Line.*
    B. Choose 5 or N for Line Numbering.
    C. Key in a **Y** for Yes.
    D. At the Format: Line Numbering menu, press F7 to accept the default settings and return the cursor to the document.
3.  Save the legal document and name it CH15EX3. Print CH15EX3.

### Exercise Four

1.  Retrieve CH06EX2 to the screen. (This document is located in the UNIT2 subdirectory.)
2.  Change the line height for the body of the memorandum to 0.25 inches by completing the following steps:

    A. Access the Format: Line menu with Shift + F8, then choose 1 or L for Line.
       **M** *Click on Layout, then Line.*

    B. Choose 4 or H for Line Height and the prompt **1 <u>A</u>uto;  2 <u>F</u>ixed: <u>0</u>** appears at the bottom of the screen.

    C. Choose 2 or F for Fixed.

    D. Key in **0.25** and press Enter.

    E. Press F7 to return the cursor to the document.

3.   Save the memorandum and name it CH15EX4. Print CH15EX4.

## Exercise Five

1.   At a clear screen, change the base font to 14-point Helvetica. (If your printer does not support Helvetica, choose a sans serif, proportional typeface in 14-point size. If your printer does not support any sans serif typefaces, choose the default typeface in 8-pitch [14-point] size.)

2.   Create the information shown in figure 15-4. Determine the tab settings by completing the following steps:

    A. Access the Center command with Shift + F6.
       **M** *Click on Layout, Align, then Center.*

    B. Key in **Victoria Palmas**, space eight times, then key in **Research and Development** (these are the longest entries in each column).

    C. Print the line with Shift + F7 (**M** *Click on File, then Print*), then choose 1 or F for Full Document.

    D. With a ruler marked with increments of 10, measure from the left margin (not the left edge of the page) to the first column. The measurement for the first column is approximately +1.0 inches. Measure from the left margin to the second column. The measurement for the second column is approximately +3.0 inches. (Your measurements may vary slightly.)

    E. Delete the key line.

    F. Center and boldface the title and subtitle shown in figure 15-4.

    G. Triple space after the subtitle. Delete previous tabs and set new left tabs at +1.0 and +3.0 inches. (Set left tabs at your measurements if they are different from these.)

    H. Key in the column entries using the Tab key to move to tab settings.

3.   Save the table and name it CH15EX5. Print CH15EX5.

---

# PUGET SOUND SEMICONDUCTOR

## Program Directors

| | |
|---|---|
| Victoria Palmas | Finances |
| William Holley | Research and Development |
| Janet Weiss | Personnel |
| Heidi Schueler | Sales |
| Brad Majors | Facilities Management |

**Figure 15-4: Exercise Five**

**Exercise Six**

1. At a clear screen, create the letterhead shown in figure 15-5. To do this, complete the following steps:
   A. Change the base font to 14-point Avant Garde Gothic. (If your printer does not support Avant Garde Gothic, use a sans serif, proportional typeface in 14-point size. If your printer does not support proportional typefaces, use the default typeface in 8-pitch [14-point] size.)
   B. Key in the company name in all capital letters.
   C. Press Enter once, then create the underline with Shift + the hyphen key.
   D. Press Enter, then access the Flush Right command with Alt + F6 (**M** *Click on Layout, Align, then Flush Right*). Key in the street address and press Enter.
   E. Access the Flush Right command, key in the city, state, and Zip Code, then press Enter.
   F. Access the Flush Right command, key in the telephone number, then press Enter.

2. Save the letterhead and name it CH15EX6. Print CH15EX6.

---

PUGET SOUND SEMICONDUCTOR

---

1900 State Street
Tacoma, WA 98402
(206) 555-2500

---

**Figure 15-5: Exercise Six**

**Exercise Seven**

1. At a clear screen, change the left and right margins to 1.5 inches, then create the memorandum shown in figure 15-6.
2. Before keying in the columns, delete previous tabs and set left tabs at +0.5 and +3.3 inches.
3. Change the alignment character to the "at" symbol (@) by completing the following steps:
   A. Access the Format: Other menu with Shift + F8, then 4 or O for Other.
      **M** *Click on Layout, then Other.*
   B. At the Format: Other menu, choose 3 or D for Decimal/Align Character.
   C. Key in the at symbol with Shift + 2.
   D. With the cursor after Thousands' Separator, press Enter.
   E. Press F7 to change the alignment character and return the cursor to the document.
4. Move the cursor to the first tab stop with the Tab key. Move the cursor to the second tab stop with the Tab Align command, Ctrl + F6 (**M** *Click on Layout, Align, then Tab Align*).
5. Save the memorandum and name it CH15EX7. Print CH15EX7.

```
DATE:      January 3, 1993

TO:        Supply Department

FROM:      John White Cloud, Personnel Manager

SUBJECT:   Supplies


Please  send  the  following  supplies  to  the  Personnel
Department.   We would  like  the  order  filled by January
10, 1993. Bill account number 023-1234.

        Bond paper          3 reams @ $3.59 per ream
        Ballpoint pens      2 dozen @ $1.50 per dozen
        Paper clips         5 boxes @ $1.29 per box
        Scissors            3 pair @ $5.49 per pair
        No. 10 envelopes    5 cts. @ $2.75 per ct.
        File folders        2 dozen @ $3.55 per dozen

   xx:CH15EX7
```

Figure 15-6: Exercise Seven


## PERFORMANCE ASSESSMENTS

### Assessment One
1.  Retrieve CH04EX5 to the screen. (This document is located in the UNIT1 subdirectory.)
2.  Change the left hyphenation zone to 5 percent and the right hyphenation zone to 0 percent and turn on hyphenation. Make appropriate hyphenation decisions.
3.  Save the document and name it CH15PA1. Print CH15PA1.


### Assessment Two
1.  At a clear screen, change the line height to 0.2 inches and turn on line numbering.
2.  Key in the contract shown in figure 15-7. Center and boldface the title. Boldface the introductory words of the paragraphs as indicated in the figure. Indent the paragraphs after the numbers with the Indent key. Use the Flush Right command at the end of the document to align DATE: and the signature line at the right margin.
3.  Move the cursor to the beginning of the document and change the left hyphenation zone to 6 percent and the right hyphenation zone to 2 percent and turn on hyphenation. Move the cursor to the end of the document and make appropriate hyphenation decisions.
4.  Save the contract and name it CH15PA2. Print CH15PA2.

## BUILDING CONSTRUCTION CONTRACT

**THIS AGREEMENT** made this _____ day of _____,
1993, between _____ hereinafter called Owner,
and _____, hereinafter called Contractor,
whose address is 2300 Grand Avenue, Gig Harbor, WA 98322.

In consideration of the covenants and agreements herein
contained, the parties hereto agree as follows:

1. Contractor agrees to construct and complete in good
   workmanlike and substantial manner, upon the real
   property hereinafter described, furnishing all labor,
   materials, tools, and equipment therefor.

2. The structure is to be constructed and completed in
   substantial conformance with the plans and specifications
   for the same signed by the parties hereto.

3. In consideration of the covenants and agreements hereof
   being substantially performed and kept by Contractor,
   including the supplying of all labor, material and
   services required by this Contract, and the construction
   and completion of the structure, Owner agrees to pay to
   Contractors, the sum of *Ninety-nine Thousand Nine Hundred
   and Eighty Two Dollars* ($99,982).

4. The Contractor shall pay all valid bills and charges for
   materials, labor, or otherwise in connection with or
   arising out of the construction of the structure and will
   hold the Owner of the property free and harmless against
   all liens and claims of lien for labor and materials, or
   either of them, filed against the property.

5. The plans and specifications are intended to supplement
   each other, so that any works exhibited in either and not
   mentioned in the other are to be executed the same as if
   they were mentioned and set forth in both.

6. The Contractor shall not be responsible for any damage
   occasioned by the Owner or the Owner's agent, acts of
   God, earthquake, or other causes beyond the control of
   the Contractor, unless otherwise herein provided or
   unless he is obligated by the terms hereof to provide
   insurance against such hazard or hazards.

7. The Owner agrees to procure at his own expense and prior
   to the commencement of any work hereunder, fire insurance. Such insurance to be in a sum equal to the total
   cost of the improvements as set forth in Paragraph 3
   hereof, with loss, if any, payable to any mortgages or
   beneficiary, under any deed of trust, such insurance to
   be written to protect the Owner and Contractor, and
   lienholder.

8. The Contractor shall at his own expense carry all
   workers' compensation insurance and public liability
   insurance necessary for the full protection of Contractor
   and Owner during the progress of the work. Certificates

of such insurance shall be filed with Owner and the first
lienholder if Owner and first lienholder so require.

9.   Contractor has the right to subcontract any part, or all,
of the work herein agreed to be performed.

**IN WITNESS WHEREOF**, the parties hereunto set their hands and
seal the day and year first above written.

OWNER: _____     DATE: _____

CONTRACTOR: _____     DATE: _____

---

Figure 15-7: Assessment Two

## Assessment Three

1.   At a clear screen, change the base font to 14-point Helvetica. (If your printer does not
support the Helvetica typeface, use a sans serif, proportional typeface. If your printer does
not support proportional typefaces, use the default typeface in 8-pitch.)
2.   Determine the tab settings for the columns shown in figure 15-8.
3.   Change the line height to 0.25 inches.
4.   Center and boldface text as indicated in figure 15-8.
5.   Save the document and name it CH15PA3. Print CH15PA3.

---

### MORENO, YAMADA, & SCHWARTZ

### Attorneys at Law

| **Name** | **Position** |
|---|---|
| Anita M. Moreno | Partner |
| Dan S. Yamada | Partner |
| James D. Schwartz | Partner |
| Karen L. Sonneson | Associate |
| Thomas T. Lambert | Associate |
| Andy R. Boskovich | Associate |
| Marilyn Alosio | Intern |
| David G. Lemke | Intern |

---

Figure 15-8: Assessment Three

# CHAPTER 16

## LINE DRAW AND CODE FEATURES

## *PERFORMANCE OBJECTIVES*

Upon successful completion of chapter 16, you will be able to generate special features of business documents, such as organizational charts; you will also be able to enhance document maintenance with pre-coded features.

### LINE DRAW

WordPerfect's Line Draw feature lets you create boxes and figures that you would not normally be able to produce with the regular keys. Line Draw can be used to create boxes, graphs, figures, pictures, and other types of graphic highlights.

   You may want to experiment with Line Draw to find out whether your printer can support Line Draw characters. You may see lines on the screen, but the printer may use different characters when printing.

   To use Line Draw, complete the following steps:

1.   Access the Screen command with Ctrl + F3, then choose 2 or L for Line Draw.
     **M** *Click on Tools, then Line Draw.*

2.   At the **1 |; 2 ||; 3 \*; 4 Change; 5 Erase; 6 Move: 0** prompt, choose **1** to draw lines with a single line, choose 2 to draw lines with a double line, or choose 3 to draw lines with an asterisk.

3.   In Line Draw, use the arrow keys — up, down, left, and right — to move the cursor. You will see an arrow at the beginning of the line draw and an arrow indicating the direction of the cursor. When you move the cursor back to the beginning of the line draw, the two arrows disappear.

4.   When you are finished with Line Draw, press the Cancel key, F1, to exit Line Draw.

When you are in Line Draw, Insert mode is turned off and you are in Typeover. If you are drawing lines in existing text, any text you move the cursor through will be replaced by a line.

### Erasing Lines

If you make a mistake while you are using Line Draw, or if you want to change the lines, choose 5 or E for Erase, from the Line Draw prompt. Erase works like an eraser on a pencil. Any line that you move the cursor through is deleted (erased). When you want to resume drawing lines, select the number of the character with which you were drawing.

### Changing Line Draw Characters

The Change selection from the Line Draw prompt is used to change the Line Draw character. When you choose 4 or C for Change, the Line Draw prompt disappears and is replaced by a prompt that gives you eight different characters and a ninth option that allows you to select your own character. You can select from a variety of clear boxes and shaded boxes or thicker vertical lines. Depending on the printer you are using, these Line Draw characters may or may not print.

### Moving the Cursor in Line Draw

The last selection from the Line Draw prompt, Move, lets you move the cursor without drawing lines. This selection is useful in situations in which you are drawing several different figures or you want to move to a different part of the figure and continue drawing. After you have moved the cursor, key in the number of the character with which you were drawing and continue line drawing.

### Moving Rectangles

The Block and Move commands can be used to move figures that have been drawn with Line Draw. When blocking figures, the Rectangle selection from the Move command lets you specify a beginning and an ending point. With this selection, you can block a box that has been drawn with Line Draw and move or copy it to a different location in the document.

To block a figure or box, complete the following steps:

1.  Move the cursor to the top left corner of the box and access the Block command with Alt + F4 or F12.
    **M** *Click on Edit, then Block.*

2.  Move the cursor to the bottom right corner of the box and access the Move command with Ctrl + F4.

3.  From the prompts that display at the bottom of the screen, choose 3 or R for Rectangle. The block highlighting changes and only the rectangle is highlighted.

4.  From the prompt that displays at the bottom of the screen, choose 1 or M for Move, 2 or C for Copy, 3 or D for Delete, or 4 or A for Append.

5. If you are moving or copying the rectangle, move the cursor to the location where you want the rectangle to appear and press Enter. If you are appending the rectangle to a document, key in the name of the document, then press Enter.

## DOCUMENT COMPARISON

WordPerfect includes a feature that compares two documents and inserts redlining and strikeout codes in the document on the screen where there are differences between the two documents.

To compare strikeout and redlining between two documents, complete the following steps:

1. Retrieve to the screen the document you want to compare.
2. Access the Mark Text command with Alt + F5.
3. From the prompts that display at the bottom of the screen, choose 6 or G for Generate.
   **M** *Click on Mark, then Generate.*
4. At the Mark Text: Generate menu, choose 2 or C for Compare Screen and Disk Documents and Add Redline and Strikeout.
5. At the **Other Document:** prompt, key in the name of the document on the disk that you want to compare to the document on the screen, then press Enter.

WordPerfect compares the two documents and inserts redline codes around text that does not appear in the document on the disk and inserts strikeout codes and a copy of the text that is in the document on the disk but not in the document on the screen.

## CODED SPACE

As you key in text in a document, WordPerfect makes line-end decisions and automatically wraps text to the next line. Word Wrap is a time-saving feature that can increase your keyboarding speed.

Even though Word Wrap is helpful, there may be times when Word Wrap breaks up words or phrases that should remain together. For example, a name such as *Fredrick K. Wienstein* can be broken after the initial *K.* but should not be broken before. The phrase *World War II* can be broken between *World* and *War* but should not be broken between *War* and *II*.

To control what text is wrapped to the next line, a coded space can be inserted between words. When a coded space is inserted, WordPerfect considers the words as one unit and will not divide them.

To insert a coded space, press Home and then press the space bar. This inserts a code in the document that can be seen in Reveal Codes. A coded space is a space enclosed by brackets ([ ]).

## INSERTING THE DATE

When you go through the WordPerfect loading process, you enter the current date at the date prompt. This date is kept in temporary memory and can be used to insert the current date quickly in a document.

To use the date entered when you loaded WordPerfect, complete the following steps:

1.   Access the Date/Outline command with Shift + F5.

2.   At the **1 Date Text; 2 Date Code; 3 Date Format; 4 Outline; 5
     Para Num; 6 Define: 0** prompt, choose 1 or T for Date Text, and
     WordPerfect will insert the current date.
     **M** *Click on Tools, then Date Text.*

The date is entered as month, date, and year. For example, if today's date is
February 15, 1993, it will be inserted as **February 15, 1993**. The style of
display for the date can be changed to accommodate other needs. To change
the display style, access the Date/Outline command with Shift + F5, and
choose 3 or F for Date Format (**M** *Click on Tools, then Date Format*). The
document disappears and is replaced by the Date Format menu shown in
figure 16-1.

```
Date Format

     Character    Meaning
         1        Day of the Month
         2        Month (number)
         3        Month (word)
         4        Year (all four digits)
         5        Year (last two digits)
         6        Day of the Week (word)
         7        Hour (24-hour clock)
         8        Hour (12-hour clock)
         9        Minute
         0        am / pm
        %,$       Used before a number, will:
                     Pad numbers less than 10 with a leading zero or space
                     Abbreviate the month or day of the week

     Examples:  3 1, 4        = December 25, 1984
                %6 %3 1, 4    = Tue Dec 25, 1984
                %2/%1/5 (6)   = 01/01/85 (Tuesday)
                $2/$1/5 ($6) =  1/ 1/85 (Tue)
                8:90          = 10:55am


Date format: 3 1, 4
```

Figure 16-1: Date Format Menu

The default setting for the date format is 3 1, 4. These numbers are described in the menu and indicate what will appear on the screen. The
selections from this menu are self-explanatory. The examples at the bottom
of the screen show a variety of methods for entering the date as well as the
time.

The cursor is located under the 3 at the bottom of the screen. To change
to a different date format, enter the new numbers and press F7 to return
the cursor to the document. For example, to change to a military style of
date, key in **1 3 4**. This prints the day of the month first, followed by the
month and then the year (all four digits).

At the Date/Outline prompt **1 Date Text; 2 Date Code; 3 Date Format;
4 Outline; 5 Para Num; 6 Define: 0**, the first selection, Date Text, inserts
the current date, while the second selection, Date Code, inserts the date as
a code. With the second selection, the current date changes as the document
is updated. The date does not change if the first selection is used.

## CHAPTER REVIEW

### Summary

- Line Draw can be used to create boxes, graphs, and other figures. Access Line Draw with Ctrl + F3, then choose 2 or L for Line Draw (**M** *Click on Tools, then Line Draw*).

- A single vertical line, a double vertical line, or an asterisk can be selected as the Line Draw character. WordPerfect also has a selection to change to a variety of other characters.

- Line Draw text can be erased by choosing 5 or E for Erase from the Line Draw prompt and moving the cursor through the text to be removed.

- Line Draw boxes or figures can be moved, copied, deleted, or appended with the Block and Move commands. To block a figure, move the cursor to the upper left corner of the figure and access the Block command with Alt + F4 (**M** *Click on Edit, then Block*). Move the cursor to the lower right corner of the figure and access the Move command, Ctrl + F4. From the prompts that display at the bottom of the screen, choose 3 or R for Rectangle.

- A document on the screen can be compared with a document on the disk. WordPerfect inserts redline codes around text that does not appear in the document on the disk and inserts strikeout codes and a copy of the text that is in the document on the disk but not in the document on the screen.

- A coded space can be inserted between words to keep words and phrases together. A coded space is inserted by pressing Home and then the space bar.

- The current date can be entered at the screen with the Date/Outline command, Shift + F5 (**M** *Click on Tools, then Date Text*). This command lets you determine your own display style, enter the date, or enter a Date code.

### Commands Review

| | Keyboard | Mouse |
|---|---|---|
| Screen command | Ctrl + F3 | |
| Date/Outline command | Shift + F5 | |
| Line Draw | Ctrl + F3, 2 or L | Tools, Line Draw |
| Coded space | Home, space bar | |

## STUDY GUIDE FOR CHAPTER 16

**True/False:** Circle the letter T if the statement is true; circle the letter F if the statement is false.

1. Access line draw with Ctrl + F3, then choose 2 or L for Line Draw (**M** *Click on*          T          F
   *Tools, then Line Draw*).

2. When using Line Draw, the Insert mode is on.                                                    T          F

3. The Line Draw feature includes a selection to move the cursor without drawing          T          F
   lines.

4. A coded space keeps words and phrases together.                                                  T          F

5. Access the Date/Outline command with Shift + F5.                                                 T          F

6. The default setting for the date is month, day, and year, in figures.                            T          F


**Completion:** In the space provided at the right, indicate the correct term, command, or symbol for the explanation.

1. At the Line Draw prompt, you can choose to draw lines with a          _____
   single line, double lines, or this character.

2. Press these keys to insert a coded space between words.               _____

3. At the Line Draw prompt, choose this selection to delete lines.       _____

4. Document comparison compares two documents and inserts               _____
   redlining codes and these codes on the screen where there are
   differences between the two documents.

5. Choose this selection from the Mark Text command to compare          _____
   two documents.

6. This is the default setting for the date format.                     _____

7. This selection from the Date/Outline command inserts the date        _____
   as a code in the document.

8. This selection from the Date/Outline command inserts the             _____
   current date.

## HANDS-ON EXERCISES

Change the default directory to UNIT4.

**Exercise One**

1.  At a clear screen, access Line Draw with Ctrl + F3, then choose 2 or L for Line Draw (**M** *Click on Tools, then Line Draw*). Key in a **2** to draw with a double line. Create the box shown in figure 16-2. Use Erase to correct any mistakes.

2.  When the box is created, exit Line Draw, then save the box with the Save key, F10 (**M** *Click on File, then Save*). Name the document CH16EX1. (Save the document now so if mistakes are made you can exit the document without saving and retrieving it again.)

3.  Turn Insert off (typeover) and key in the company name, the employee name, and position title inside the box.

4.  Save the document again with the same name. Print CH16EX1.

```
╔══════════════════════════════════════╗
║                                      ║
║     PUGET SOUND SEMICONDUCTOR        ║
║                                      ║
║           JANET WEISS                ║
║                                      ║
║        DIRECTOR OF PERSONNEL         ║
║                                      ║
╚══════════════════════════════════════╝
```

**Figure 16-2: Exercise One**

**Exercise Two**

1.  At a clear screen, access Line Draw and create the boxes shown in figure 16-3. Use the double line to draw the boxes and the single line to draw the lines connecting the boxes. Use Erase to correct any mistakes.

2.  Exit Line Draw and save the document with the Save key. Name the document CH16EX2.

3.  Turn Insert off (typeover) and key in the information in the boxes as shown in figure 16-3.

4.  Save the document again. Print CH16EX2.

EVOLUTION OF WORD PROCESSING

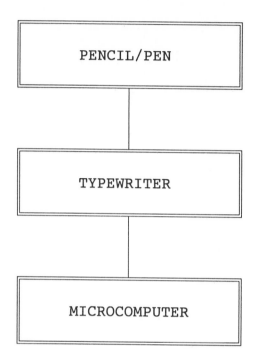

Figure 16-3: Exercise Two

## Exercise Three

1. At a clear screen, access Line Draw, then create the boxes shown in figure 16-4. Use Erase to correct mistakes and use Move to move to different locations on the page.
2. Exit Line Draw and save the document with the Save key. Name the document CH16EX3.
3. Turn Insert off (typeover) and key in the job titles in the boxes as shown in figure 16-4.
4. Save the document again. Print CH16EX3.

**ORGANIZATIONAL CHART**

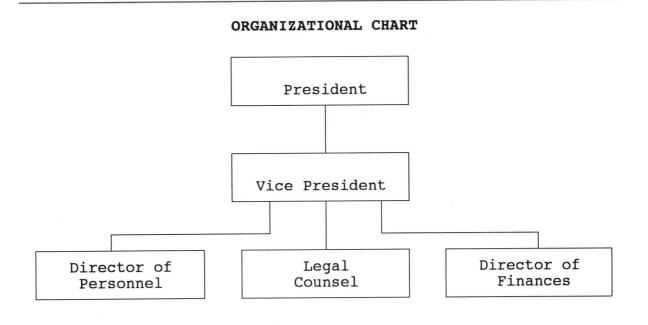

**Figure 16-4: Exercise Three**

### Exercise Four

1. Retrieve CH16EX3 to the screen.
2. Make the changes indicated in figure 16-5.
3. Save the document and name it CH16EX4. Print CH16EX4.

**ORGANIZATIONAL CHART**

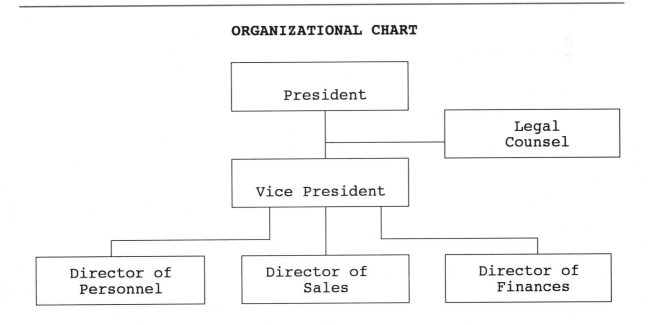

**Figure 16-5: Exercise Four**

**Exercise Five**

1. At a clear screen, change the left and right margins to 1.5 inches. Create the memorandum shown in figure 16-6 in an appropriate memorandum format. Insert coded spaces between the commands in the memorandum, for example, between Ctrl + F8. (Insert a coded space between Ctrl and the plus symbol and between the plus symbol and F8.)

2. Use the **Date/Outline** command to insert the current date. To do this, complete the following steps:
   A. Key in **DATE:** and press the Tab key.
   B. Access the Date/Outline command with Shift + F5.
   C. Choose 1 or T for Date Text.
      **M** *Click on Tools, then Date Text.*

3. Save the memorandum and name it CH16EX5. Print CH16EX5. (When the memorandum is printed, none of the commands should be divided by Word Wrap.)

---

```
DATE:        (Current date)
TO:          Harold Vonstein
FROM:        Devon McKenna
SUBJECT:     WordPerfect Features
```

The WordPerfect program includes a variety of special features that you can use to enhance documents. Some special features are created with the Font command, Ctrl + F8.

To create a superscript, key in text to the point where the superscript text is to be inserted and access Ctrl + F8. From the prompts that appear at the bottom of the screen, choose 1 or S for Size, then 1 or P for Suprscpt.

Other print features include Strikeout and Redline. To identify Strikeout text, access the Font command, Ctrl + F8 and choose 2 or A for Appearance, then 9 or S for Stkout.

Certain text inserted in a legal document may need to be identified. This is called redlining. To identify text for redlining, access the Font command with Ctrl + F8, and choose 2 or A for Appearance, then 8 or R for Redln.

---

**Figure 16-6: Exercise Five**

**Exercise Six**

1. At a clear screen, change the line spacing to double (2), then key in the text in figure 16-7. (This is the state legislative bill you created in chapter 14, without the redlining and strikeout text.)

2. Save the bill and name it CH16EX6.

3. Compare CH16EX6 with CH14EX7 by completing the following steps:
   A. Retrieve CH16EX6 to the screen.
   B. Access the Mark Text command with Alt + F5.

C. From the prompts that display at the bottom of the screen, choose 6 or G for Generate.
**M** *Click on Mark, then Generate.*

D. At the Mark Text: Generate menu, choose 2 or C for Compare Screen and Disk Documents and Add Redline and Strikeout.

E. At the **Other Document:** prompt, key in **CH14EX7**, then press Enter.

4.   After the comparison is complete, save the document again as CH16EX6. Print CH16EX6.


Sec. 2.  Section 10, chapter 142, Laws of 1983 1st ex. sess. as amended by section 6, chapter 145, Laws of 1984 ex. sess. and RCW 71.03.670 are each amended to read as follows:

Nothing in this chapter shall be construed to limit the right of any person to apply voluntarily to any public or private agency or practitioner for treatment of a mental disorder, either by direct application or by referral.

Any person voluntarily admitted for inpatient treatment to any public or private agency shall orally be advised of the right to immediate release and further advised of such rights in writing as are secured to them pursuant to this chapter and their rights of access to attorneys, courts, and other legal redress.

If the staff of any public or private agency regards a person voluntarily admitted as dangerous to himself or others or gravely disabled as defined by this act, they may detain such person for a reasonable length of time, sufficient to notify the designated county health professional of such person's condition to enable such mental health professional to authorize such person being further held in custody or transported to an evaluation and treatment center pursuant to the provisions of this chapter.

When a mental health professional designated by the county receives information alleging that a person, as a result of a mental disorder, presents a likelihood of serious harm to others or himself, or is gravely disabled, such mental health professional,

after investigation and evaluation of the specific facts alleged,

and of the reliability and credibility of the person or persons, if

any, providing information to initiate detention, may summon such

person to appear at an evaluation and treatment facility for not

more than a 72-hour evaluation and treatment period.

**Figure 16-7: Exercise Six**

## PERFORMANCE ASSESSMENTS

### Assessment One

1.  At a clear screen, create an organizational chart with Line Draw. Create boxes for the following job titles:
    President
    Vice President, Support
    Vice President, Operations
    Director of Sales
    Director of Personnel
    Director of Finances
    Create the two vice president boxes at the same level. Create the three director boxes at the same level.
2.  Save the organizational chart and name it CH16PA1. Print CH16PA1.

### Assessment Two

1.  At a clear screen, key in the memorandum shown in figure 16-8. Insert coded spaces between the first name and middle initial of each name. Also, insert a coded space between the month and the day.
2.  Use the Date/Outline command to insert the date.
3.  Save the memorandum and name it CH16PA2. Print CH16PA2.

```
DATE:      (Current Date)
TO:        Leslie Duvall
FROM:      Sally Ramsey
SUBJECT:   Report
```

The background report you are preparing for Moreno, Yamada & Schwartz is a great idea.  I am happy to provide the names and beginning employment dates of the firm's senior partner, partners, associates, and interns. Anita M. Moreno, senior partner, began the law firm on August 1, 1983.  She started in a small business office in Southeast Seattle.  As business increased, she hired Dan S. Yamada as an associate.  Within two years, Dan was promoted to partner.  In 1985, Anita and Dan hired James D. Schwartz as an associate.  James became a partner on May 1, 1988.

At this time, the associates are Karen L. Sonneson, Andy R. Boskovich, and Thomas T. Lambert.  Karen was hired on May 15, 1990; Andy was hired on August 15, 1991; and Thomas was hired on January 1, 1992.

The current law interns, Marilyn Alosio and David G. Lemke, both began their employment with our firm on April 15, 1992.

If you need further information about the firm employees, please let me know.

**Figure 16-8: Assessment Two**

# PERFORMANCE MASTERY

## UNIT PERFORMANCE

In this unit, you have learned to enhance the readability of single-page business letters, legal documents, and reports, with basic typesetting features.

## MASTERY ASSIGNMENTS

**Assignment One**

1. Display the directory. Copy U03MA1 and name the new copy U04MA1.
2. Retrieve U04MA1 to the screen.
3. Make the following changes to the document:
   A. Change the base font to 12-point Times Roman. (Use a 12-point serif typeface if your printer does not support Times Roman.)
   B. Change the size of the title and subtitle of the report to Very Large.
   C. Change the size of the headings within the report to Large.
   D. Move the cursor to the beginning of the report, change the left hyphenation zone to 6% and the right hyphenation zone to 2%, and turn on hyphenation. Move the cursor to the end of the document and make appropriate hyphenation decisions.
4. Save the revised report and name it U04MA1. Print U04MA1.

**Assignment Two**

1. At a clear screen, create the Community Property Agreement shown in figure U4-1. You determine the following:
   A. Base font
   B. Boldfacing
   C. Margins
   D. Justification
   E. Hyphenation
2. Save the Agreement and name it U04MA2. Print U04MA2.

---

## COMMUNITY PROPERTY AGREEMENT

**THIS AGREEMENT**, made and entered into this _____ day of _____, 19--, by and between STEVEN J. LAWSON and CAROLYN A. LAWSON, husband and wife.

**WITNESSETH:**

**WHEREAS**, STEVEN J. LAWSON and CAROLYN A. LAWSON are husband and wife and reside at 13205 - 132nd Street, Olympia, in Thurston County, Washington; and

**WHEREAS**, it is the intention of STEVEN J. LAWSON and CAROLYN A. LAWSON that all of the property now owned or hereafter acquired by them or either of them shall be community property and shall vest in the survivor upon the death of them;

**NOW, THEREFORE**, for and in consideration of the covenants herein contained and the mutual benefits to be derived therefrom, STEVEN J. LAWSON and CAROLYN A. LAWSON hereto covenant and agree that every piece, parcel, and item of property, whatever its nature and wherever situated, now owned or hereafter acquired by either or both of them, shall be and have the status of community property and all of such property is hereby conveyed by each and both to themselves as a marital community, and upon the death of either party, title to such property shall immediately pass to, and become vested in, the survivor as his or her sole and separate property.

**IN WITNESS WHEREOF,** STEVEN J. LAWSON and CAROLYN A. LAWSON hereto have set their hands and seals the day and year first above written.

_____
STEVEN J. LAWSON

_____
CAROLYN A. LAWSON

STATE OF WASHINGTON     )
                        ss.
County of Thurston      )

On this day personally appeared before me STEVEN J. LAWSON and CAROLYN A. LAWSON, to me known to be the individuals described in and who executed the within and foregoing instrument, and acknowledged that they signed and sealed the same as their free and voluntary act and deed, for the uses and purposes therein mentioned.

**GIVEN** under my hand and official seal this _____ day of _____, 19--.

_____
**NOTARY PUBLIC** in and for the State of Washington, residing at Olympia.

Figure U4-1: Assignment Two

**Assignment Three**

1.   At a clear screen, use Line Draw to create an organizational chart for the staff members of the Personnel Department. Title the document ORGANIZATIONAL CHART and subtitle it Personnel Department. Enclose the names and positions in boxes with line draw in the order they appear in figure U4-2.

2.   Save the chart and name it U04MA3. Print U04MA3.


```
                          Janet Weiss
                          Director of Personnel

          John White Cloud              Darlene Evans
          Personnel Manager             Benefits Manager

                          Maria Valdez
                          Recruitment Coordinator

                          Brett Weinstein
                          Compensations Specialist

          Duardo Carollo               Ann Watanabe
          Administrative Assistant     Administrative Assistant

                          Robin Simmons
                          Receptionist
```

**Figure U4-2: Assignment Three**

# UNIT 5

In this unit, you will learn to enhance the readability of business forms and multiple-page reports.

# CHAPTER 17

## FORMS

## *PERFORMANCE OBJECTIVES*

Upon successful completion of chapter 17, you will be able to define and adjust structures for business forms that require standardized data input and print options.

### FORMS

When a printer is installed with WordPerfect, a standard form is also installed. This form prints text on regular-sized stationery—8.5 by 11 inches. The standard form also contains commands specifying where the text prints on the page. In addition to the standard form, an ALL OTHERS form may be included. Some printers may have several forms installed; others may have just one.

Additionally, some printers can accept and print many types of forms and other printers can print text in only a few forms. A form is created for special printing needs. For example, many legal documents need to be printed on legal-sized paper (8.5 by 14 inches). Other documents may need to be printed on half-sized or executive-sized stationery.

### Inserting a Form

WordPerfect has a number of predesigned forms that can be inserted in a document. For example, a legal-sized form may already be available that can be inserted in a document that is to be printed on legal paper. To insert a form in a document, complete the following steps:

1. Access the Format: Page menu with Shift + F8, then 2 or P for Page.
   **M** *Click on Layout, then Page.*
2. At the Format: Page menu, choose 7 or S for Paper Size/Type, and the Format: Paper Size/Type menu shown in figure 17-1 appears on the screen.

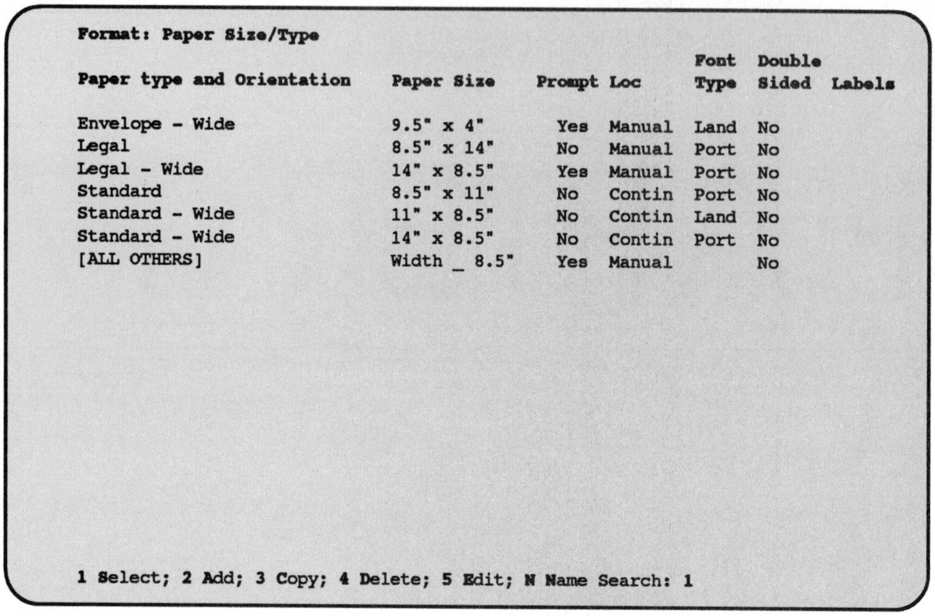

```
Format: Paper Size/Type
                                                            Font  Double
Paper type and Orientation      Paper Size   Prompt Loc    Type  Sided  Labels

Envelope - Wide                 9.5" x 4"     Yes  Manual  Land  No
Legal                           8.5" x 14"    No   Manual  Port  No
Legal - Wide                    14" x 8.5"    Yes  Manual  Port  No
Standard                        8.5" x 11"    No   Contin  Port  No
Standard - Wide                 11" x 8.5"    No   Contin  Land  No
Standard - Wide                 14" x 8.5"    No   Contin  Port  No
[ALL OTHERS]                    Width _ 8.5"  Yes  Manual        No




1 Select; 2 Add; 3 Copy; 4 Delete; 5 Edit; N Name Search: 1
```

Figure 17-1: Format: Page: Paper Size/Type

> (The forms displayed in this menu are for a popular laser printer. The forms installed with your printer may vary. You should have at least a standard form (8.5" x 11") and an ALL OTHERS form.)

3.  If the form size you are using appears in this menu, move the cursor to the form desired and choose 1 or S for Select.

4.  Press F7 to insert the form and return the cursor to the document.

If the form size Legal is inserted in a document, the code [Paper Sz/Typ:8.5" x 14",Legal] appears in Reveal Codes. When a form is inserted in a document, it should be the very first code.

## Adding a Form

If you want to change the form in a document and the form is not included in the Format: Paper Size/Type menu, it can be added. To add a form, complete the following steps:

1.  Access the Format: Page menu with Shift + F8, then 2 or P for Page.
    **M** *Click on Layout, then Page.*

2.  At the Format: Page menu, choose 7 or S for Paper Size/Type.

3.  At the Format: Paper Size/Type menu, choose 2 or A for Add.

4.  At the Format: Paper Type menu shown in figure 17-2, choose the type of paper. (The selections from this menu are meant to be used as a description of the type of stationery to be used. For example, choose 3 or H for Letterhead, when you add a form that should be printed with letterhead stationery.)

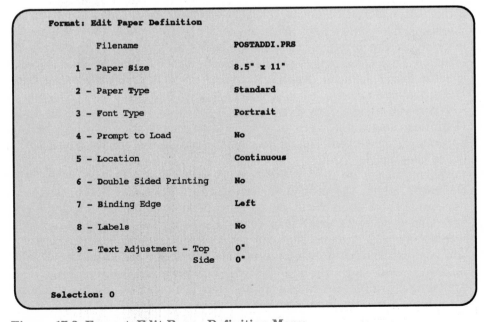

```
Format: Paper Type

    1 - Standard

    2 - Bond

    3 - Letterhead

    4 - Labels

    5 - Envelope

    6 - Transparency

    7 - Cardstock

    8 - [ALL OTHERS]

    9 - Other




Selection: 1
```

**Figure 17-2: Format: Paper Type Menu**

5.  After a selection is made from the Format: Paper Type menu, the Format: Edit Paper Definition menu shown in figure 17-3 displays on the screen. Make any necessary changes at this menu.

6.  Press F7 three times to add the new form and return the cursor to the document.

```
Format: Edit Paper Definition

        Filename                POSTADDI.PRS

    1 - Paper Size              8.5" x 11"

    2 - Paper Type              Standard

    3 - Font Type               Portrait

    4 - Prompt to Load          No

    5 - Location                Continuous

    6 - Double Sided Printing   No

    7 - Binding Edge            Left

    8 - Labels                  No

    9 - Text Adjustment - Top   0"
                         Side   0"

Selection: 0
```

**Figure 17-3: Format: Edit Paper Definition Menu**

## Format: Edit Paper Definition Menu

The selections from the Format: Edit Paper Definition menu let you customize the form for your specific printing needs.

The first selection, Paper Size, is used to identify the width and length of the form. When you choose 1 or S for Paper Size, the Format: Paper Size menu shown in figure 17-4 appears on the screen.

```
Format: Paper Size            Width  Height

    1 - Standard              (8.5" x 11")

    2 - Standard Landscape    (11" x 8.5")

    3 - Legal                 (8.5" x 14")

    4 - Legal Landscape       (14" x 8.5")

    5 - Envelope              (9.5" x 4")

    6 - Half Sheet            (5.5" x 8.5")

    7 - US Government         (8" x 11")

    8 - A4                    (210mm x 297mm)

    9 - A4 Landscape          (297mm x 210mm)

    o - Other

Selection: 0
```

Figure 17-4: Format: Paper Size Menu

At the Format: Paper Size menu, you can select the size of paper you will be using—for example, standard, legal, envelope, government, and so on. Standard Wide and Legal Wide are settings to be used if the paper is inserted in the printer sideways, the width of the paper first. The last selection, Other, lets you establish a specific paper length. When a selection is made from this menu, WordPerfect returns you to the Format: Edit Paper Definition menu.

When you choose 2 or T for Paper Type from the Format: Edit Paper Definition menu, the Format: Paper Type menu shown in figure 17-2 appears on the screen. This is the same menu as the one described earlier in the chapter.

When you choose 3 or F for Font Type, from the Format: Edit Paper Definition menu, the prompt **Orientation: 1 Portrait; 2 Landscape: 0** appears at the bottom of the screen. Portrait fonts print text across the page and landscape fonts print text down the page. The Landscape selection works only with printers that can rotate fonts (such as laser printers). If you are using a laser printer and select a paper definition in which a landscape (wide) form is selected, choose Landscape as the Font Type. If you are using a printer that cannot rotate fonts, such as a dot matrix or character printer, leave the Font Type set at Portrait.

The fourth selection from the Format: Edit Paper Definition menu, Prompt to Load, has a default setting of No. At this setting, WordPerfect prints a document without prompting you. If you change the setting to Yes,

WordPerfect causes a beep to sound and a message telling you to insert paper appears at the Print: Control Printer menu.

The Location selection from the Format: Edit Paper Definition menu identifies how the paper is fed into the printer. When you choose 5 or L for Location, the prompt **Location: 1 <u>C</u>ontinuous; 2 <u>B</u>in Number; 3 <u>M</u>anual: <u>0</u>** appears at the bottom of the screen. Choose 1 or C for Continuous if your paper is tractor-fed into the printer. Choose 2 or B for Bin Number if your printer has more than one paper bin from which paper is inserted in the printer. When you choose 2 or B, the prompt **Bin Number:** appears at the bottom of the screen. Key in the bin number from which you want the paper drawn, then press Enter. Choose 3 or M for Manual if your paper is hand-fed into the printer.

The sixth selection, Double Sided Printing, from the Format: Edit Paper Definition menu, lets you print on both sides of the paper. This selection works only with printers that are capable of double-sided (called *duplex*) printing, such as an HP Series IID. (Check your printer manuals to see whether your printer is capable of double-sided printing.)

The Binding Edge selection from the Format: Edit Paper Definition menu lets you select Top or Left as the binding edge. To identify a binding edge on the page, you must also select Binding Edge at the Print menu.

You can identify mailing labels for printing with the Labels selection from the Format: Edit Paper Definition menu. When you choose 8 or A for Labels, then key in a Y for Yes, the Format: Labels menu shown in figure 17-5 appears on the screen.

```
Format: Labels

    1 - Label Size
                    Width           2.63"
                    Height          1"

    2 - Number of Labels
                    Columns         3
                    Rows            10

    3 - Top Left Corner
                    Top             0.5"
                    Left            0.188"

    4 - Distance Between Labels
                    Column          0.125"
                    Row             0"

    5 - Label Margins
                    Left            0.113"
                    Right           0.113"
                    Top             0"
                    Bottom          0"

Selection: 0
```

Figure 17-5: Format: Labels Menu

At the Format: Labels menu, make changes to the menu as needed to accommodate the size and type of labels you are using. At the default settings, WordPerfect assumes you are using a sheet of labels that has 3 columns across the page and 10 rows down the page. If you are using single-column labels, make changes in the Number of Labels selection. You may want to measure the labels you are using to determine whether the measurements at this menu are appropriate and to make changes, if necessary.

The last selection from the Format: Edit Paper Definition menu is Text Adjustment. When you choose 9 or E for Text Adjustment, the prompt **Adjust Text: 1 Up; 2 Down; 3 Left; 4 Right: 0** appears at the bottom of the screen. Use this selection if you are inserting paper manually into a dot matrix or character printer. For example, you can adjust text up 1 inch to compensate for the amount of the paper already inserted in the printer.

## DELETING AND EDITING FORMS

Any forms that display at the Format: Paper/Size Type menu can be deleted or edited. To delete a form, move the cursor (which appears as a solid bar) until the form you want to delete is highlighted, choose 4 or D for Delete, and the prompt **Delete paper definition? No (Yes)** appears at the bottom of the screen. Key in a Y for Yes to delete the form. Press F7 twice to return to the document.

To edit a form, display the Format: Paper/Size Type menu, select the form to be edited, then choose 5 or E for Edit. The Format: Edit Paper Definition menu displays on the screen. Make necessary changes to paper specifications listed in this menu, then press F7 three times to return the cursor to the document.

### Creating Envelopes

Envelopes can be printed with WordPerfect by selecting an envelope form at the Format: Paper Size/Type menu. If an envelope form is not available at the Format: Paper Size/Type menu, complete the following steps to add one:

1. Access the Format: Page menu with Shift + F8, then 2 or P for Page.
   **M** *Click on Layout, then Page.*

2. At the Format: Page menu, choose 7 or S for Paper Size/Type.

3. At the Format: Paper Size/Type menu, choose 2 or A for Add.

4. At the Format: Paper Type menu, choose 5 or E for Envelope.

5. At the Format: Edit Paper Definition menu, choose 1 or S for Paper Size.

6. At the Format: Paper Size menu, choose 5 or E for Envelope.

7. At the Format: Edit Paper Definition menu, choose 4 or P for Prompt to Load, then key in a **Y** for Yes.

8. At the Format: Edit Paper Definition menu, choose 5 or L for Location. From the prompts that display at the bottom of the screen, choose 3 or M for Manual.

9. If you are using a laser printer, choose 3 or F for Font Type, at the Format: Edit Paper Definition menu, then choose 2 or L for Landscape.

10. Press F7 three times to add the form and return the cursor to the document.

After an envelope form has been added to the Format: Paper Size/Type menu, it can be selected. Select an envelope in the same manner in which you select other forms.

Once an envelope form is selected in a document, the margins must be changed. If you are using letterhead envelopes (with a preprinted company address in the upper left corner), change the top margin to 2 inches and the left margin to 4 inches. Key in the name and address, then print the envelope in the same manner as any other document. If you changed the Prompt to Load to Yes, a beep will sound, indicating that the envelope is to be inserted in the printer. With the envelope inserted, access the Print: Control Printer with Shift + F7 (**M** *Click on File, then Print*), 4 or C for Control Printer, then press the letter G (for Go) to tell the printer to begin.

If you are printing an envelope with a laser printer, insert the envelope in the slot at the top of the letter tray, face up, with the top of the envelope at the left.

### Creating Mailing Labels

Mailing label forms can be added at the Format: Paper Size/Type menu. Add a mailing label form for each type of mailing label you use, such as a full sheet of labels with 3 columns and 10 rows, or single labels on a continuous roll.

To add a mailing label form for a full sheet of labels (3 columns and 10 rows), complete the following steps:

1.  Access the Format: Page menu with Shift + F8, then 2 or P for Page.
    **M** *Click on Layout, then Page.*
2.  At the Format: Page menu, choose 7 or S for Paper Size/Type.
3.  At the Format: Paper Size/Type menu, choose 2 or A for Add.
4.  At the Format: Paper Type menu, choose 4 or L for Labels.
5.  At the Format: Edit Paper Definition menu, choose 8 or A for Labels, then key in a **Y** for Yes.
6.  At the Format: Labels menu, press F7. (The default settings are appropriate for a full sheet of labels.)
7.  At the Format: Edit Paper Definition menu, choose 4 or P for Prompt to Load, then key in a **Y** for Yes. (If you are using a laser printer and the labels sheet is fed into the printer from the printer tray, keep the Prompt to Load setting at No.)
8.  At the Format: Edit Paper Definition menu, choose 5 or L for Location. From the prompts that display at the bottom of the screen, choose 3 or M for Manual. (If you are using a laser printer and the labels sheet is fed into the printer from the printer tray, change the Location to Bin Number, then identify the number of the bin containing the labels.)
9.  Press F7 three times to add the form and return the cursor to the document.

After a labels form has been added to the Format: Paper Size/Type menu, it can be selected. Select a label form in the same manner in which you select other forms.

When creating mailing labels, insert the Form code at the beginning of the document, then key in the names and addresses you want printed on the labels. When entering addresses for mailing labels, end each address with a hard page command, Ctrl + Enter. The Hard Page code tells WordPerfect to move to the next label.

## FORMS CONSIDERATION

When a paper size is changed in an existing document, the soft page breaks are affected. For example, if you change the paper size in a document from standard (8.5 by 11 inches) to legal-sized (8.5 by 14 inches), the soft page break will occur after every 12 inches of text instead of after every 9 inches.

The code to change the paper size and type should be the very first code in a document. If you are inserting the code in a document containing other codes, access Reveal Codes and move the cursor before any codes.

## CHAPTER REVIEW

### Summary

- When a printer is installed with WordPerfect, a standard form is generally included in the printer definition menu. In addition, an ALL OTHERS form may also be included.
- The standard form is used to print text on stationery that is 8.5 by 11 inches. The ALL OTHERS form may be used to print text that is 8.5 inches wide or less and 11 inches long or less.
- If you want to print text on stationery that does not fit the standard or ALL OTHERS forms, additional forms must be added to the printer definition.
- When adding a form to the printer definition, WordPerfect offers several predefined forms such as legal, half sheet, and government. You can also create a specialized form with the Others selection.
- At the Format: Edit Paper Definition menu, identify the paper size, paper type, font type, whether WordPerfect prompts to load paper, the location of the paper, if you want printing on both sides of the paper, change the binding edge, identify mailing labels, or adjust the text up, down, left, or right.
- A form can be edited or deleted at the Format: Paper Size/Type menu.
- When entering names and addresses for mailing labels, insert a Hard Page command with Ctrl + Enter, after each address.
- When the paper size is changed in a document containing text, the soft page breaks are affected.
- The code to change the paper size and type should be the very first code in a document.

**Adding a Form Review**

Complete the following steps to add a form to the Format: Paper Size/Type menu:

1. Access the Format: Page menu with Shift + F8, then 2 or P for Page.
   **M** *Click on Layout, then Page.*

2. At the Format: Page menu, choose 7 or S for Paper Size/Type.

3. At the Format: Paper Size/Type menu, choose 2 or A for Add.

4. At the Format: Paper Type menu, select the type of paper.

5. At the Format: Edit Paper Definition menu, make any necessary changes, then press F7 three times to add the new form and return the cursor to the document.

**Inserting a Form Review**

Complete the following steps to insert a form in a document:

1. Access the Format: Page menu with Shift + F8, then 2 or P for Page.
   **M** *Click on Layout, then Page.*

2. At the Format: Page menu, choose 7 or S for Paper Size/Type.

3. At the Format: Paper Size/Type menu, move the cursor to the desired form and choose 1 or S for Select.

4. Press F7 to insert the form and return the cursor to the document.

## STUDY GUIDE FOR CHAPTER 17

**Completion:** In the space provided at the right, indicate the correct symbol, term, or number for the explanation.

1. Width and length, in inches, of standard-sized stationery.                    _____

2. Width and length, in inches, of legal-sized stationery.                       _____

3. Selection number and letter from the Format: Paper Size/Type                  _____
   menu to add a form.

4. Orientation of the font that causes text to print down the page              _____
   (with a laser printer).

5. Selection number and letter from the Format: Paper Size/Type                  _____
   menu to delete a form.

6. When keying in names and addresses for mailing labels, insert               _____
   this code after each address.

**True/False:** Circle the letter T if the statement is true; circle the letter F if the statement is false.

1. Once a form is added to the Format: Paper Size/Type menu, it cannot be edited.       T       F

2. A form can be deleted from the printer definition.                                   T       F

3. A code to change the paper size and type should be the very first code in a          T       F
   document.

4. A paper size and type code can be deleted in Reveal Codes.                           T       F

5. When all information about a form has been entered at the Format: Edit Paper         T       F
   Definition menu, press Cancel, F1.

6. When a code is entered in an existing document changing the paper size, the soft     T       F
   page breaks are affected.

## HANDS-ON EXERCISES

Create a new subdirectory named UNIT5. Change the default directory to UNIT5.

**Exercise One**
1. At a clear screen, add a legal-sized form by completing the following steps: (If you already
   have a legal-sized form added, skip these steps.)
   A. Access the Format: Page menu with Shift + F8, then 2 or P for Page.
      **M** *Click on Layout, then Page.*
   B. At the Format: Page menu, choose 7 or S for Paper Size/Type.
   C. At the Format: Paper Size/Type menu, choose 2 or A for Add.
   D. At the Format: Paper Type menu, choose 9 or O for Other. Key in **Legal**, then press
      Enter.
   E. At the Format: Edit Paper Definition menu, choose 1 or S for Paper Size.
   F. At the Format: Paper Size menu, choose 3 or L for Legal.
   G. Press F7 three times to add the form and return the cursor to the document.
2. Complete the following steps to add a half-sized form that measure 8.5 by 5.5 inches:
   A. Access the Format: Page menu with Shift + F8, then 2 or P for Page.
      **M** *Click on Layout, then Page.*

B. At the Format: Page menu, choose 7 or S for Paper Size/Type.

C. At the Format: Paper Size/Type menu, choose 2 or A for Add.

D. At the Format: Paper Type menu, choose 9 or O for Other.  Key in **Half**, then press Enter.

E. At the Format: Edit Paper Definition menu, choose 1 or S for Paper Size.

F. At the Format: Paper Size menu, choose O for Other.

G. Key in **8.5** and press Enter.

H. Key in **5.5** and press Enter.

I. Press F7 three times to add the form and return the cursor to the document.

## Exercise Two

1. Retrieve CH07EX1 to the screen.

2. Access Reveal Codes and make sure the cursor is located on the very first code, then change the form to legal sized by completing the following steps:

   A. Access the Format: Page menu with Shift + F8, then 2 or P for Page.
   **M** *Click on Layout, then Page*.

   B. At the Format: Page menu, choose 7 or S for Paper Size/Type.

   C. At the Format: Paper Size/Type menu, move the cursor to the legal form and choose 1 or S for Select.

   D. Press F7 to insert the code and return the cursor to the document.

3. Save the document and name it CH17EX2. Print CH17EX2.

## Exercise Three

1. At a clear screen, change the form size to half-size (8.5 by 5.5 inches).

2. Key in the memorandum shown in figure 17-6 in an appropriate memorandum style.

3. Save the memorandum and name it CH17EX3. Print CH17EX3.

---

```
DATE:  December 21, 1992
TO:  Heidi Schueler
FROM:  Terry Preston
SUBJECT:  Directors' Meeting


The January directors' meeting has been scheduled for January 22,
1993. I will be out of town that day and I would like you to chair
the meeting.

Brad Majors is scheduled to talk about the impending remodeling in
the personnel area. Please call him and find out how much time he
needs during the meeting.

In addition, there are some quarterly reports that need to be
shared with the directors.  Stop by my office and I will give you
a copy of the reports.

xx:CH17EX3
```

---

Figure 17-6: Exercise Three

**Exercise Four**

1.  At a clear screen, create a form for envelopes by completing the following steps (skip these steps if an envelope form is already available at the Format: Paper Size/Type menu):

    A.  Access the Format: Page menu with Shift + F8, then 2 or P for Page.
        **M** *Click on Layout, then Page.*

    B.  At the Format: Page menu, choose 7 or S for Paper Size/Type.

    C.  At the Format: Paper Size/Type menu, choose 2 or A for Add.

    D.  At the Format: Paper Type menu, choose 5 or E for Envelope.

    E.  At the Format: Edit Paper Definition menu, choose 1 or S for Paper Size.

    F.  At the Format: Paper Size menu, choose 5 or E for Envelope.

    G.  At the Format: Edit Paper Definition menu, choose 4 or P for Prompt to Load, then key in a **Y** for Yes.

    H.  At the Format: Edit Paper Definition menu, choose 5 or L for Location. From the prompts that display at the bottom of the screen, choose 3 or M for Manual.

    I.  If you are using a laser printer, choose 3 or F for Font Type, at the Format: Edit Paper Definition menu, then choose 2 or L for Landscape. (If you are using a dot-matrix or character printer, skip this step.)

    J.  Press F7 three times to add the form and return the cursor to the document.

2.  At a clear screen, create a form for full-sheet labels by completing the following steps (skip these steps if a labels form is already available at the Format: Paper Size/Type menu):

    A.  Access the Format: Page menu with Shift + F8, then 2 or P for Page.
        **M** *Click on Layout, then Page.*

    B.  At the Format: Page menu, choose 7 or S for Paper Size/Type.

    C.  At the Format: Paper Size/Type menu, choose 2 or A for Add.

    D.  At the Format: Paper Type menu, choose 4 or L for Labels.

    E.  At the Format: Edit Paper Definition menu, choose 8 or A for Labels, then key in a **Y** for Yes.

    F.  At the Format: Labels menu, press F7. (The default settings are appropriate for a full sheet of labels.)

    G.  At the Format: Edit Paper Definition menu, choose 4 or P for Prompt to Load, then key in a **Y** for Yes. (If you are using a laser printer and the labels sheet is fed into the printer from the printer tray, keep the Prompt to Load setting at No.)

    H.  At the Format: Edit Paper Definition menu, choose 5 or L for Location. From the prompts that display at the bottom of the screen, choose 3 or M for Manual. (If you are using a laser printer and the labels sheet is fed into the printer from the printer tray, change the Location to Bin Number, then identify the number of the bin containing the labels.)

    I.  Press F7 three times to add the form and return the cursor to the document.

**Exercise Five**

1.  At a clear screen, select the envelope form.

2.  Change the top margin to 2 inches and the left margin to 4 inches.

3.  Key in the name and address shown in figure 17-7.

4.  Save the envelope and name it CH17EX5. Print CH17EX5.

```
Noreen Glascow, M.D.
Evergreen Medical Clinic
1200 South Cedar Street
Olympia, WA 98011
```

Figure 17-7: Exercise Five

## Exercise Six

1.  At a clear screen, select the labels form.
2.  Key in the names and addresses shown in figure 17-8. After entering the name and address for each person, insert a hard page command with Ctrl + Enter.
3.  When all the names and addresses are entered, access View Document to see whether the names and addresses will print in the proper location. (Even though the names and addresses are displayed down the screen, they will print from left to right on the labels sheet as shown in View Document.)
4.  Save the names and addresses and name the document CH17EX6. Print CH17EX6. (The names and addresses will not fill the entire page.)

```
Mr. John Sabo          Mr. August Boyer        Mrs. Renee Zundel
2801 Rosedale          20322 101st East        224 Cherry Street
Santa Fe, NM 50934     Santa Fe, NM 50934      Santa Fe, NM 50932


Mr. Fred Leitz         Ms. Nina Tucker         Mr. and Mrs. Rory Heyer
4900 Jenkins Street    National Software       13022 McCutcheon Road
Santa Fe, NM 50932     120 Meridian Drive      Santa Fe, NM 50932
                       Santa Fe, NM 50934


Roberta Lee, M.D.      Mrs. Cathy Tomlin       Mr. Michael Salatino
Lee Medical Center     5413 South 52nd         6606 66th Avenue
500 South Fifth        Santa Fe, NM 59034      Santa Fe, NM 59032
Santa Fe, NM 59034
```

Figure 17-8: Exercise Six

## PERFORMANCE ASSESSMENTS

## Assessment One

1.  At a clear screen, add a half-sized form that measures 5.5 by 8.5 inches.
2.  With the cursor at the beginning of the document, select the half-sized form at the Format: Paper Size/Type menu.
3.  Key in the memorandum shown in figure 17-9 in an appropriate memorandum format.
4.  Save the memorandum and name it CH17PA1. Print CH17PA1.

Date: December 27, 1992; To: Terry Preston; From: Heidi Schueler; Subject: Director's Meeting

Thank you for the opportunity to chair the January Director's meeting. Brad Majors feels he will need approximately 30 minutes to present the information about the construction.

I talked with the other directors about agenda items and, after my conversations with them, created the enclosed agenda.

If you have further items to be added to the agenda, please contact me before you go out of town. The agenda will be sent to the directors by January 7, 1993.

XX:CH17PA1
Enclosure

**Figure 17-9: Assessment One**

**Assessment Two**

1. Print the addresses in figure 17-10 as envelopes. You determine the form needed, the margins, and the name of the document or documents.

---

```
Mr. and Mrs. Theodore Leonard
12003 Hilton Avenue
Boise, ID 80732

Mrs. Rachelle Nettleton
2270 Graham Street Northwest
Boise, ID 80732

Ms. Danielle Edison
7403 Lakewood Circle
Boise, ID 80732
```

Figure 17-10: Assessment Two

---

**Assessment Three**

1. At a clear screen, add a labels form that prints 1 column and 10 rows of labels. (*Hint*: Follow the same steps for creating full-sheet labels described earlier in the chapter, except change the Number of Labels at the Format: Labels menu to 1 Column.)
2. Select the single-column labels form you just added.
3. Key in the addresses shown in figure 17-11. (Insert a hard page code after each address.)
4. Save the label document and name it CH17PA3. Print CH17PA3.

---

```
Mr. Kenneth Sager
10432 120th Street East
Renton, WA 98044

Mr. and Mrs. Gerald Lehfeldt
1908 North Lexington
Renton, WA 98044

Ms. Lois Fischer
1204 North Pine Street
Renton, WA 98044

Mrs. Lois Gianni
8322 32nd Avenue South
Renton, WA 98044
```

Figure 17-11: Assessment Three

# CHAPTER 18

## PERFORMANCE OBJECTIVES

Upon successful completion of chapter 18, you will be able to define and adjust structures for business tables according to a variety of format and size considerations.

### TABLES

WordPerfect's Tables feature can be used to create columns and rows of information that are surrounded by horizontal and vertical lines. With Tables, a form can be created with boxes of information, called *cells*, with customized lines surrounding each cell. A cell is the intersection between a row and a column. It can contain text, characters, numbers, data, or formulas. Text within a cell can be left, right, center, or decimal aligned and can be boldfaced, italicized, or underlined. The formatting choices available with Tables are quite extensive and allow you to create a wide variety of forms.

### Creating a Table

To create a table, complete the following steps:

1. Access the Columns/Table command with Alt + F7, choose 2 or T for Tables, then 1 or C for Create.
   Ⓜ *Click on Layout, Tables, then Create.*

2. The prompt **Number of Columns: 3** displays at the bottom of the page. Columns run vertically down the page. WordPerfect allows a maximum of 32 columns. Press Enter to accept the default number of three columns, or key in a different number and press Enter.

3. When you press Enter, the prompt changes to **Number of Rows: 1**. Rows run horizontally across the page. WordPerfect allows a maximum of 32,767 rows. Press Enter to accept the default number of 1 row, or key in a different number and press Enter.

When the number of columns and rows has been entered, WordPerfect displays the table on the screen. If a table was created with three columns and three rows, it would display as shown in figure 18-1 (without the cell names).

```
+-------------------------------------------------------------------+
| +------------------------------------------------------------+    |
| | Cell A1      |     Cell B1      |     Cell C1       |       |    |
| |-------------+------------------+-------------------|        |    |
| | Cell A2      |     Cell B2      |     Cell C2       |       |    |
| |-------------+------------------+-------------------|        |    |
| | Cell A3      |     Cell B3      |     Cell C3       |       |    |
| +------------------------------------------------------------+    |
|                                                                   |
|                                                                   |
|                                                                   |
|                                                                   |
|                                                                   |
|                                                                   |
|  Table Edit:  Press Exit when done      Cell A1 Doc 1 Pg 1 Ln 1.14" Pos 1.75" |
| ---------------------------------------------------------------   |
|  Ctrl-Arrows Column Widths; Ins Insert; Del Delete; Move Move/Copy;|
|  1 Size; 2 Format; 3 Lines; 4 Header; 5 Math; 6 Options; 7 Join; 8 Split: 0 |
+-------------------------------------------------------------------+
```

**Figure 18-1: Table with Three Columns and Three Rows**

When the columns are displayed, the cursor is located in the upper left corner of the table in cell A1. Columns are lettered from left to right, beginning with A, and rows are numbered from top to bottom, beginning with 1. The cell to the right of A1 is B1, the cell to the right of B1 is C1, and so on. The cells below A1 are A2, A3, A4, and so on. The cell in which the cursor is located is displayed in the status line in the lower right corner of the screen.

When the table first displays, you are in what is called the table editing mode. In this mode, changes are made to the structure of the table. In the table editing mode, the cursor displays as a solid bar, filling the entire cell. This mode can be changed to the normal editing mode to enter text in the cells.

To change to the normal editing mode, press F7. The lines of information at the bottom of the screen disappear, and the cursor within the cell displays as a normal cursor. Key in and edit text in the cells as you would normal text. Press the Tab key to move to the next cell, and press Shift + Tab to move to the previous cell. If the text you key in does not fit on one line, it wraps to the next line within the same cell. The cell vertically lengthens to accommodate the text, and all cells in that row also lengthen. To insert a Tab code within a cell, press Home + Tab. The Home + Tab command tells WordPerfect to insert a Tab code in the cell rather than to move the cursor to the next cell.

When all information has been entered in the cells, move the cursor below the table and continue keying in the document, or save the document in the normal manner. If you want to return to the table editing mode, make sure the cursor is located within the table, and press Alt + F7.

## Table-Editing Mode

In the table-editing mode, the last two lines at the bottom of the screen, shown in figure 18-2, provide a wide variety of selections for customizing the table.

```
Table Edit:  Press Exit when done        Cell A1 Doc 1 Pg 1 Ln 1.14" Pos 1.12"
------------------------------------------------------------------------------
Ctrl-Arrows Column Widths; Ins Insert; Del Delete; Move Move/Copy;
1 Size; 2 Format; 3 Lines; 4 Header; 5 Math; 6 Options; 7 Join; 8 Split: 0
```

Figure 18-2: Table-Editing Selections

### *Control + Arrow*

The Control key plus the right or left arrow keys make a row or column of cells wider or narrower. To use these commands, complete the following steps:

1.  Move the cursor to the row or column of cells to be changed.
2.  Hold down the Ctrl key and press the arrow key in the direction you want the cells to expand or contract.

For example, press Ctrl + right arrow to widen the column of cells to the right; press Ctrl + left arrow to contract the column of cells to the left.

### *Insert*

The Insert key is used to insert a row or column. To insert rows or columns, complete the following steps:

1.  At the table-editing mode, press the Insert key.
2.  At the prompt **Insert: 1 <u>R</u>ows; 2 <u>C</u>olumns**, choose 1 or R to insert rows or 2 or C to insert columns.
3.  Key in the number of rows or columns to be inserted and press Enter.

The row or column is inserted at the location of the cursor.

### *Delete*

The Delete key is used to delete a row or column. To delete rows or columns, complete the following steps:

1.  At the table-editing mode, press the Delete key.
2.  At the prompt **Delete: 1 <u>R</u>ows; 2 <u>C</u>olumns**, choose 1 or R to delete rows or 2 or C to delete columns.

The row or column is deleted at the location of the cursor.

### *Move*

The Move command, Ctrl + F4, can be used to move or copy the complete table or portions of it.

### Size

The Size selection is used to add or delete rows or columns from the end of a table. To change the number of rows or columns, complete the following steps:

1. At the table-editing mode, choose 1 or S for Size.
2. At the prompt **Table Size: 1 Rows; 2 Columns**, choose 1 or R to change the number of rows or 2 or C to change the number of columns.
3. Key in the total number of rows or columns desired and press Enter.

For example, if the table contains four rows and you want to add three more, enter 7 at the **Number of Rows** prompt. If the table contains eight columns and you want to delete three, enter 5 at the **Number of Columns** prompt.

### Format

The Format selection can be used to format a single cell, a column of cells, or a row of cells in a table. Some formatting can be done with the Format selection in the table-editing mode or with normal formatting keys in the normal editing mode. For example, text within a cell can be centered with Shift + F6 or with a choice from the Format selection. When the Format selection is used, no codes are inserted in the cell. If text within a cell is formatted in the normal editing mode, a code is inserted in the cell. Both methods produce the same appearance.

When you choose 2 or F for Format at the table-editing mode, the information at the bottom of the screen changes. A prompt is inserted identifying the choices you have for formatting. In addition, a prompt displays at the bottom right corner of the screen that identifies the width of the cell where the cursor is located, the alignment of the cell, and any attributes that are applied to the cell. At the default settings, this prompt displays as **Col: 2.17 ";Left;Normal**, which means that the column width is 2.17 inches, the alignment is Left, and the attributes are normal.

To format a cell or a row or column of cells, complete the following steps:

1. At the table-editing mode, choose 2 or F for Format.
2. At the prompt **Format: 1 Cell; 2 Column; 3 Row Height**, choose 1 or C for Cell, 2 or L for Column, or 3 or R for Row.

With the Cell and Column selections from this prompt, columns, rows, or individual cells can be formatted. To format an entire row of cells, block all the cells to be formatted and then choose 2 or F for Format. From the prompts that display at the bottom of the screen, choose 1 or C for Cell, and all cells in the block are formatted. Choose 2 or L for Column, and each column in the block is formatted.

#### Cell

To format a cell, complete the following steps:

1. At the-table editing mode, choose 2 or F for Format.
2. Choose 1 or C for Cell.

3.  At the prompt **Cell: 1 _T_ype; 2 _A_ttributes; 3 _J_ustify; 4 _V_ertical Alignment; 5 _L_ock**, make changes to the cell with the selections in the prompt as described below.

### Type

When you choose 1 or T for Type, the prompt **Cell Type: 1 _N_umeric; 2 _T_ext** appears at the bottom of the screen. By default, entries within a cell are considered to be numbers and will be included in mathematical calculations. To identify the cell entry as text, choose 2 or T for Text.

### Attributes

The Attributes selection lets you use the Size and Appearance options usually available from the Font command, Ctrl + F8 (**M** _Click on Font, then Base Font_). When you select Attributes, the prompt **1 _S_ize; 2 _A_ppearance; 3 _N_ormal; 4 _R_eset** appears at the bottom of the screen. With Size and Appearance you can format individual entries within a cell, or block several cells and apply the size or appearance attributes to all cells within the block. When an attribute is turned on, it stays on unless it is turned off or the Normal or Reset selections are used. Normal returns all attributes to the normal base font, while Reset causes cells to take on the attributes of the column.

### Justify

When you select Justify, the prompt **Justification: 1 _L_eft; 2 _C_enter; 3 _R_ight; 4 _F_ull; 5 _D_ecimal Align; 6 _R_eset; _1_** appears at the bottom of the screen. From this prompt, cell entries can be aligned left, center, right, full, or on a decimal point. The default setting for Justify is Left.

### Vertical Alignment

When you select Vertical Alignment, the prompt **Vertical Alignment: 1 _T_op; 2 _B_ottom; 3 _C_enter: _1_** appears at the bottom of the screen. By default, cell entries are aligned at the top of the cell. WordPerfect leaves one-tenth of an inch between the top ruled line of the cell and the top of the text characters. This vertical alignment of cell entries can be changed to Bottom or Center.

### Lock

When you select Lock, the prompt **Lock: 1 _O_n; 2 O_f_f: _0_** appears at the bottom of the screen. With the On selection, a cell can be locked so that no further text can be entered; text may not be edited, and the cell cannot be moved or copied. If a cell has been locked, it can be unlocked by choosing 2 or F for Off.

### Column

To format a column, complete the following steps:
1.  At the table-editing mode, choose 2 or F for Format.
2.  Choose 2 or L for Column.
3.  At the prompt **Column: 1 _W_idth; 2 _A_ttributes; 3 _J_ustify; 4 _#_ Digits**, make changes to the column with the selections in the prompt as described in the following text.

### Width

With the Width selection, the column size can be increased. If a column size is increased, any columns to the right will be decreased, if necessary, to ensure that the table fits within the margins. To use this feature, complete the following steps:

1. At the table-editing mode, choose 2 or F for Format.
2. Choose 2 or L for Column.
3. Choose 1 or W for Width.
4. At the prompt **Column width: 2.17"**, key in the width desired (in inches or inch increments), then press Enter.

### Attributes and Justify

The Attributes and Justify options from the Column selection are the same as the Attributes and Justify for the Cell selection, except they do not contain the Reset choice. The difference is that the attribute or justification will apply to all entries in the column rather than an individual cell.

### # Digits

The # Digits selection lets you specify the number of digits you want to appear after the decimal point. This selection has a default setting of 2. If changes are made to this option, all entries within the column are affected.

### Row Height

The Row Height option from Format is used to determine the line height and whether the line height will fit single or multiple lines. To determine the line height, complete the following steps:

1. At the table-editing mode, choose 2 or F for Format.
2. Choose 3 or R for Row.
3. At the prompt **Row Height -- Single line: 1 Fixed; 2 Auto; Multi-line: 3 Fixed; 4 Auto: 4** make changes to the row height with the selections as described below.

### Multi-line Auto

The default setting for the row height prompt is Multi-line, Auto. At this setting, the row height can be more than one line, and the line height is automatically determined by WordPerfect to accommodate such changes as the base font.

### Single-line

At the Single line setting of Fixed or Auto, only one line is allowed in a cell. If more than one line of characters is being keyed in, pressing Enter will not start a new line, but instead will cause the cursor to move to the next cell.

### Editing an Existing Table

With the Tables selection from the Columns/Table command, a table can be edited as well as created. To edit the table structure while you are inside the table, access the edit menu with Alt + F7. To edit a table you have saved earlier, complete the following steps:

1. Access the Columns/Table command with Alt + F7.
2. Choose 2 or T for Tables, then 2 or E for Edit.
   **M** *Click on Layout, Tables, then Edit.*

WordPerfect searches backward through the document until a Table Definition code is found. If no code is found searching backward, then WordPerfect searches forward through the document. When a code is found, the table is displayed on the screen for editing.

## CHAPTER REVIEW

### Summary

- The Tables feature is used to create columns and rows of information surrounded by horizontal and vertical lines. Columns run vertically down the page. WordPerfect allows a maximum of 32 columns in a table. Rows run horizontally across the page. WordPerfect allows a maximum of 32,767 rows in a table. The intersection between a column and row is called a cell.

- When a table is first displayed, the table-editing mode is in effect. This mode is used to customize the structure of the table. Press F7 to change to the normal editing mode. This mode is used to enter information in the cells in the table. The Tab key moves the cursor to the next cell, and Shift + Tab moves the cursor to the previous cell. Use Home + Tab to insert a Tab code in the cell. To return to the table-editing mode, make sure the cursor is located within the table, and press Alt + F7.

- At the table-editing mode, the last two lines at the bottom of the screen contain selections to customize a table. With selections from the first line you can use the Ctrl key plus the left and right arrow keys to make cells wider or narrower. The Insert and Delete keys are used to insert or delete rows or columns. The Move command is used to move or copy portions of the table.

- At the table-editing mode, the last line contains selections to customize a table. The Size selection lets you change the size of rows or columns. The Format selection contains a variety of formatting choices as follows:

```
2 Format
     1 Cell
          1 Type
               1 Numeric
               2 Text
          2 Attributes
               1 Size
               2 Appearance
               3 Normal
               4 Reset
          3 Justify
               1 Left
               2 Center
               3 Right
               4 Full
               5 Decimal Align
               6 Reset
          4 Vertical Alignment
               1 Top
               2 Bottom
               3 Center
          5 Lock
               1 On
               2 Off
     2 Column
          1 Width
          2 Attributes
               1 Size
               2 Appearance
               3 Normal
          3 Justify
               1 Left
               2 Center
               3 Right
               4 Full
               5 Decimal Align
          4 # Digits
     3 Row Height
          Single line
          1 Fixed
          2 Auto
          Multi-line
          3 Fixed
          4 Auto
```

## Commands Review

|                       | **Keyboard** | **Mouse**      |
|-----------------------|--------------|----------------|
| Columns/Table command | Alt + F7     | Layout, Tables |

## STUDY GUIDE FOR CHAPTER 18

**Completion:** In the space provided at the right, indicate the correct term, symbol, or command for the explanation.

1. Access the Columns/Table command.                                    _____

2. Maximum number of rows allowed by WordPerfect.                        _____

3. Maximum number of columns allowed by WordPerfect.                     _____

4. The intersection between a row and a column.                          _____

5. In this mode, you customize the appearance of the table.              _____

6. In this mode, you enter text into a table.                           _____

7. The default justification for a cell.                                 _____

8. Press this key to move the cursor to the next cell.                   _____

9. Press this key to move the cursor to the previous cell.               _____

10. Press these keys to move the cursor to a tab stop within a cell.      _____

**True/False:** Circle the letter T if the statement is true; circle the letter F if the statement is false.

1. Columns run horizontally across the page.                                            T     F

2. In the table-editing mode, Ctrl + right arrow makes the cell contract.                T     F

3. In the table-editing mode, the Insert key can be used to insert a row or a            T     F
   column.

4. The # Digits selection has a default setting of 0.                                    T     F

5. A table can be edited.                                                                T     F

6. The default setting for cell type is Text.                                            T     F

7. Press F7 to change from the table-editing mode to the normal editing mode.            T     F

## HANDS-ON EXERCISES

Change the default directory to UNIT5.

### Exercise One

1. At a clear screen, create the table shown in figure 18-3 by completing the following steps:
   A. Access the Center command with Shift + F6 (**M** *Click on Layout, Align, then Center*), key in **PROGRAM PLANNING SHEET**, then press Enter three times.
   B. Access the Columns/Table command with Alt + F7, choose 2 or T for Tables, then 1 or C for Create.
      **M** *Click on Layout, Tables, then Create.*
   C. At the prompt **Number of Columns: 3**, press Enter to accept the default setting of 3.
   D. At the prompt **Number of Rows: 1**, key in **5**, then press Enter.
   E. With the table displayed on the screen and the cursor located in cell A1, widen the cell by holding down the Ctrl key and pressing the right arrow key 13 times.
   F. Press the Tab key to move the cursor to cell B1. Press Ctrl + right arrow three times to widen the column.

G. Press Shift + Tab to move the cursor back to cell A1.

H. Press F7 to switch to the normal editing mode.

I. With the cursor in cell A1, access the Center command with Shift + F6 (**M** *Click on Layout, Align, then Center*), then key in **Course Title**.

J. Press the Tab key to move the cursor to cell B1. Access the Center command and key in **Course Number**.

K. Press the Tab key to move the cursor to cell C1. Access the Center command and key in **Credits**.

2. Save the table and name it CH18EX1. Print CH18EX1.

---

## PROGRAM PLANNING SHEET

| Course Title | Course Number | Credits |
|---|---|---|
|  |  |  |
|  |  |  |
|  |  |  |
|  |  |  |

---

**Figure 18-3: Exercise One**

## Exercise Two

1. At a clear screen, create the table shown in figure 18-4 by completing the following steps:

A. Access the Columns/Table command with Alt + F7, choose 2 or T for Tables, then 1 or C for Create.
**M** *Click on Layout, Tables, then Create.*

C. At the prompt **Number of Columns: 3**, press Enter to accept the default setting of 3.

D. At the prompt **Number of Rows: 1**, key in **5**, then press Enter.

E. With the table displayed on the screen and the cursor located in cell A1, widen the cell by holding down the Ctrl key and pressing the right arrow key four times.

F. Press the Tab key to move the cursor to cell B1. Press Ctrl + right arrow six times to widen the column.

E. Press F7 to switch to the normal editing mode.

F. With the cursor in cell A1, access the Center command with Shift + F6 (**M** *Click on Layout, Align, then Center*), then key in **Name**.

G. Press the Tab key to move the cursor to cell B1. Access the Center command and key in **Department**.

H. Press the Tab key to move the cursor to cell C1. Access the Center command and key in **Ext**.

I. Key in the text in the columns as shown in figure 18-4. Use the Tab key to move the cursor from cell to cell. When entering the names in column A, press Home + Tab before keying in the name.

2. Save the table and name it CH18EX2. Print CH18EX2.

| Name | Department | Ext. |
|------|------------|------|
| Victoria Palmas | Finances | 355 |
| William Holley | Research & Development | 208 |
| Janet Weiss | Personnel | 120 |
| Heidi Schueler | Sales | 226 |

**Figure 18-4: Exercise Two**

## Exercise Three

1. Retrieve CH18EX2 to the screen.
2. Move the cursor within the table.
3. Press Alt + F7 to access the table-editing mode.
4. Change the alignment of the numbers in cells C2 through C5 by completing the following steps:
   A. Move the cursor to cell C2 and access the Block command.
   B. Move the cursor to cell C5.
   C. With cells C2 through C5 blocked, choose 2 or F for Format.
   D. Choose 1 or C for Cell.
   E. Choose 3 or J for Justify.
   F. Choose 2 or C for Center.
   G. Press F7 to return to the normal editing mode.
5. Save the revised table and name it CH18EX3. Print CH18EX3.

## Exercise Four

1. At a clear screen, create the table shown in figure 18-5 by completing the following steps:
   A. Center and boldface the title, **SALES DEPARTMENT**.
   B. Center and boldface the subtitle, **Gross Sales, April and May**.
   C. Triple space after the subtitle, then create a table that contains 3 columns and 8 rows.
   D. With the table displayed on the screen and the cursor located in cell A1, widen the cell by holding down the Ctrl key and pressing the right arrow key 7 times.
   E. Press F7 to switch to the normal editing mode.
   F. With the cursor in cell A1, center and boldface the heading, Name. Move the cursor to cell B1 and center and boldface the heading, April. Move the cursor to cell C1 and center and boldface the heading, May.
   G. Key in the text in the columns as shown in figure 18-5. Use the Tab key to move the cursor from cell to cell. When entering the names in column A, press Home + Tab before keying in the name.
2. Save the table and name it CH18EX4. Print CH18EX4.

## SALES DEPARTMENT

## Gross Sales, April and May

| Name | April | May |
|:---:|:---:|:---:|
| Nona Lancaster | $ 5,231.50 | $ 6,302.44 |
| Carl Gasperez | 4,320.18 | 5,394.57 |
| Deanna Dimico | 3,459.23 | 4,593.24 |
| Greg Acosta | 10,834.20 | 9,431.30 |
| Sue Yi | 11,234.39 | 12,394.32 |
| Faye Youngchild | 8,334.00 | 9,234.88 |
| Claire Rozell | 12,435.45 | 13,204.66 |

Figure 18-5: Exercise Four

**Exercise Five**

1. Retrieve CH18EX4 to the screen.
2. Move the cursor within the table.
3. Press Alt + F7 to access the table-editing mode.
4. Change the alignment of the numbers in cells B2 through B8 and cells C2 through C8 by completing the following steps:
   A. Move the cursor to cell B2 and access the Block command.
   B. Move the cursor to cell C8.
   C. With cells B2 through C8 blocked, choose 2 or F for Format.
   D. Choose 1 or C for Cell.
   E. Choose 3 or J for Justify.
   F. Choose 5 or D for Decimal Align.
   G. Press F7 to return to the normal editing mode.
5. Save the revised table and name it CH18EX5. Print CH18EX5.

**Exercise Six**

1. Retrieve CH18EX3 to the screen.
2. Move the cursor within the table.
3. Press Alt + F7 to access the table-editing mode.
4. Insert another row in the table by completing the following steps:
   A. Choose 1 or S for Size.
   B. At the prompt **Table Size: 1 Rows; 2 Columns: 0**, choose 1 or R for Rows.
   C. At the prompt **Number of Rows:**, key in **6**, then press Enter.
5. Press F7 to return to the normal editing mode.
6. Key in the following information in the last row:
   Name = Brad Majors

Department = Facilities Management
Extension = 531

7.  Save the revised table and name it CH18EX6. Print CH18EX6.

## PERFORMANCE ASSESSMENTS

**Assessment One**

1.  At a clear screen, create the table shown in figure 18-6. Customize the table to make it match the table in the figure.
2.  After the table is customized, return to the normal editing mode and key in the text shown in figure 18-6.
3.  Save the table and name it CH18PA1. Print CH18PA1.

**PERSONNEL DEPARTMENT**

**Staff Members**

| Name | Position | Grade |
|---|---|---|
| Janet Weiss | Director of Personnel | Step 6 |
| John White Cloud | Personnel Manager | Step 5 |
| Darlene Evans | Benefits Manager | Step 5 |
| Maria Valdez | Recruitment Coordinator | Step 4 |
| Brett Weinstein | Compensation Specialist | Step 3 |
| Duardo Carollo | Administrative Assistant | Step 2 |

**Figure 18-6: Assessment One**

**Assessment Two**

1.  Retrieve CH18PA1 to the screen.
2.  Add two more rows to the bottom of the table. Enter the following information in the rows:

    Name = Ann Watanabe
    Position = Administrative Assistant
    Grade = Step 2

    Name = Robin Simmons
    Position = Receptionist
    Grade = Step 1

3.  Change the alignment of cells B2 through B9 to Center.
4.  Change the alignment of cells C2 through C9 to Center.
5.  Save the revised table and name it CH18PA2. Print CH18PA2.

# CHAPTER 19

## MORE TABLES

## PERFORMANCE OBJECTIVE

Upon successful completion of chapter 19, you will be able to customize tables you have created to illustrate different business situations, including the mathematical analysis.

### TABLES

In chapter 18 you learned to use WordPerfect's Tables feature and to customize tables with a variety of formatting selections. In this chapter, you will learn about the remaining table-editing selections.

### Table Editing Mode

When you create a table, you are in table-editing mode, where you can customize the appearance of the table. In this mode, two lines appear at the bottom of the screen, as shown in figure 19-1.

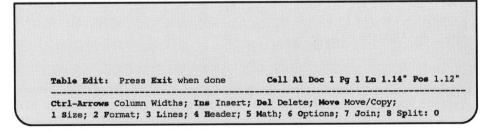

```
Table Edit:  Press Exit when done          Cell A1 Doc 1 Pg 1 Ln 1.14" Pos 1.12"
-----------------------------------------------------------------------------
Ctrl-Arrows Column Widths; Ins Insert; Del Delete; Move Move/Copy;
1 Size; 2 Format; 3 Lines; 4 Header; 5 Math; 6 Options; 7 Join; 8 Split: 0
```

Figure 19-1: Table-Editing Selections

In chapter 18, you learned about the selections from the first line, as well as the Size and Format selections from the second line. In this chapter you will learn about the remaining selections: Lines, Header, Math, Options, Join, and Split.

### Lines

The Lines selection lets you specify the type of lines used to form cells in the table. All lines in the table can be customized the same way box outlines are customized.

When you select Lines, the prompt **Lines: 1 Left; 2 Right; 3 Top; 4 Bottom; 5 Inside; 6 Outside; 7 All; 8 Shade** appears at the bottom of the screen. At this prompt, you specify which lines in the cell or blocked cells are to be changed. Select Left, Right, Top, or Bottom to customize that specific line in the cell. The Inside choice indicates that cell borders inside the block are to be customized. The Outside choice indicates that all cells outside the blocked cells are to be customized. The All choice customizes all lines in the cell or all lines in blocked cells. The last choice, Shade, is used to turn on gray shading in a cell. If shading is turned on, the default shading is 10%. This can be changed at the Options selection.

When a selection is made from this prompt (except Shade), the prompt changes to **1 None; 2 Single; 3 Double 4 Dashed; 5 Dotted; 6 Thick; 7 Extra Thick**. The line of information just above this prompt is important because it indicates the current status of each line of the cell where the cursor is located. When the cursor is located in a cell, the lines affected are the top and left side. The rules at the bottom and right side actually belong to other cells. Be sure to remember this when customizing lines for individual cells.

For example, to change the lines in cells A1 through B8 to double, complete the following steps:

1. In the table-editing mode, block cells A1 through B8.
2. With the cells blocked, choose 3 or L for Lines.
3. At the prompt **Lines: 1 Left; 2 Right; 3 Top; 4 Bottom; 5 Inside; 6 Outside; 7 All; 8 Shade**, choose 7 or A for All.
4. At the prompt **1 None; 2 Single; 3 Double 4 Dashed; 5 Dotted; 6 Thick; 7 Extra Thick**, choose 3 or D for Double, and all lines within the block are changed to double lines.

### Header

The Header selection from the table-editing mode is used to create header rows that are repeated at the top of every page of the table. When you choose Header, WordPerfect prompts you for the number of rows. If you enter 3, the first three rows of the table will be the header rows. Header rows are displayed in the document only on the first page, but they will print at the top of all pages. To see how the table and the header rows will print, use View Document.

### Math

You can calculate numbers in rows or columns in a table with the Math selection. Cells within a table can include a formula to calculate data. For example, the formula A2-A3 (A2 minus A3) can be inserted in Cell A4, which tells WordPerfect to insert the difference of A2 and A3. If changes are made to the numbers in Cells A2 or A3, the difference in A4 can be recalculated. This option lets the Tables feature operate like a spreadsheet.

Four operators can be used when writing formulas: the plus sign for addition, the minus sign (hyphen) for subtraction, the asterisk for multiplication, and the forward slash for division. Examples of how formulas can be written are shown in figure 19-2.

---

**Cell E4 is the total price of items.**
Cell B4 contains the quantity of items, and Cell D4 contains the unit price. The formula for Cell E4 is B4*D4. (This formula multiplies the quantity of items in Cell B4 by the unit price in Cell D4.)

**Cell D3 is the percentage of increase
of sales from the previous year.**
Cell B3 contains the amount of sales for the previous year, and Cell C3 contains the amount of sales for the current year. The formula for Cell D3 is C3-B3/C3*100. (This formula subtracts the amount of sales last year by the amount of sales this year. The remaining amount is divided by the amount of sales this year and then multiplied by 100 to display the product as a percentage.)

**Cell F5 is the average of test scores.**
Cells F1 through F4 contain test scores. The formula to calculate the average score is (F1+F2+F3+F4)/4. (This formulas adds the scores from cells F1 through F4, then divides that sum by 4.)

---

**Figure 19-2: Example Formulas**

If there are two or more operators in a calculation, WordPerfect calculates from left to right. If you want to change the order of calculation, use parentheses around the part of the calculation to be performed first.

The Math selection also contains an option that copies a formula to other cells. This selection saves you time when you are inserting formulas. For example, suppose in a table you create, cell E3 contains the formula A3 + D3. You want the same formula copied to cells E4, E5, and E6, except you want the correct column letter in the formula. To create and copy the formula, you would complete the following steps:

1.  Move the cursor to cell E3 and insert the formula A3 + D3 by completing the following steps:
    A. With the cursor in cell E3, choose 5 or M for Math.
    B. At the prompt **Math: 1 Calculate; 2 Formula; 3 Copy Formula; 4 +; 5 =; 6 *: 0**, choose 2 or F for Formula.
    C. At the **Enter formula:** prompt, key in **A3 + D3**, then press Enter.
2.  Copy the formula to cells E4 through E6 by completing the following steps:
    A. With the cursor in cell E3, choose 5 or M for Math.
    B. Choose 3 or P for Copy Formula.
    C. Choose 2 or D for Down.
    D. At the **Number of times to copy formula** prompt, key in **3**, then press Enter.

WordPerfect copies the formula three times to cells E4, E5, and E6.

When changes are made to numeric entries in a table containing a formula or formulas, the numbers must be recalculated. To do this, complete the following steps:

1.  In the table-editing mode (with the cursor located anywhere in the table), choose 5 or M for Math.

2.  At the prompt **Math: 1 Calculate; 2 Formula; 3 Copy Formula; 4 +; 5 =; 6 \*: 0**, choose 1 or C for Calculate.

When the calculation is complete, the answer to the formula is inserted in the cell.

In addition to writing formulas, the operators +, =, and * can be used to calculate subtotals, totals, and grand totals. The plus sign (+) totals all numeric entries in a column. The equal symbol (=) totals all subtotals. The asterisk symbol (*) calculates the grand total. When these symbols are inserted in a cell, any numeric entry in the column will be calculated. There is no need to identify the specific cells.

## Options

The Options selection is used to further customize cells. When Options is selected from the table-editing mode, the menu in figure 19-3 displays on the screen.

```
Table Options

     1 - Spacing Between Text and Lines
              Left                    0.083"
              Right                   0.083"
              Top                     0.1"
              Bottom                  0"

     2 - Display Negative Results     1
              1 = with minus signs
              2 = with parentheses

     3 - Position of Table            Left

     4 - Gray Shading (% of black)    10%




Selection: 0
```

Figure 19-3: Table Options Menu

Selection 1 from this menu is used to determine the amount of space between the text in a cell and the ruled lines.

Selection 2 provides two options for displaying negative results in a cell: either preceded by a minus sign or surrounded by parentheses. The default setting is the minus sign.

The Position of Table selection lets you either align the table at the left margin, the right margin, between the margins, or adjust the full table width from left to right margins. This selection has a default setting of Left, which means that the table will align at the left margin.

The last selection is used to determine the amount of gray shading in a cell that has been formatted for shading. The default setting is 10%; it can be changed to any percentage from 0% to 100%.

### *Join/Split*

The last two selections available when creating a table are Join and Split. The Join selection is used to join several cells together. To use this selection, complete the following steps:

1. Block the cells to be joined with the Block command.
2. Choose 7 or J for Join.
3. Key in a **Y** for Yes at the confirmation question.

The Split selection is used to split one cell into two or more cells. To use this selection, complete the following steps:

1. Move the cursor to the cell to be split, then choose 8 or S for Split.
2. At the prompt **Split: 1 <u>R</u>ows; 2 <u>C</u>olumns**, choose 1 or R to split rows or 2 or C to split columns.
3. Key in the number of rows or columns you want created.

To split several cells at one time, block the cells before choosing 8 or S for Split.

### Table Formatting Options

A variety of selections can be used to format a table. To help you customize and format your table, refer to figure 19-4 for a quick summary of the selections available from the last line in the table-editing mode.

1 Size
    1 Rows
    2 Columns
2 Format
    1 Cell
        1 Type
            1 Numeric
            2 Text
        2 Attributes
            1 Size
            2 Appearance
            3 Normal
            4 Reset
        3 Justify
            1 Left
            2 Center
            3 Right
            4 Full
            5 Decimal Align
            6 Reset
        4 Vertical Alignment
            1 Top
            2 Bottom
            3 Center
        5 Lock
            1 On
            2 Off
    2 Column
        1 Width
        2 Attributes
            1 Size
            2 Appearance
            3 Normal
        3 Justify
            1 Left
            2 Center
            3 Right
            4 Full
            5 Decimal Align
        4 # Digits
    3 Row Height
        Single line
        1 Fixed
        2 Auto
        Multi-line
        3 Fixed
        4 Auto

3 Lines
    1 Left
    2 Right
    3 Top
    4 Bottom
    5 Inside
    6 Outside
    7 All
        1 None
        2 Single
        3 Double
        4 Dashed
        5 Dotted
        6 Thick
        7 Extra Thick
    8 Shade
        1 On
        2 Off
4 Header
5 Math
    1 Calculate
    2 Formula
    3 Copy
    4 +
    5 =
    6 *
6 Options
    1 Spacing Between Text
      and Lines
    2 Display Negative Results
    3 Position
    4 Gray Shading
7 Join
8 Split
    1 Rows
    2 Columns

**Figure 19-4: Table Formatting Options**

## CHAPTER REVIEW

### Summary

- In the table-editing mode, the Line selection lets you customize the left, right, top, or bottom lines in a cell; lines inside a block and outside a block; and all lines in the cell or blocked cells. With the Lines selection you can also shade cells.
- When customizing lines, you can choose None, Single, Double, Dashed, Dotted, Thick, or Extra Thick.
- With the Header selection, you can create header rows that repeat at the top of every page of the table.
- The Math selection lets you calculate numbers in rows and columns. Cells within a table can include a formula to calculate data.
- Four operators can be used to write a formula: the plus sign for addition, the minus sign (hyphen) for subtraction, the asterisk for multiplication, and the forward slash for division.
- WordPerfect calculates a formula from left to right. To change the order of the calculation, use parentheses around the part of the calculation to be performed first.
- The operators +, =, and * can be used to calculate subtotals, totals, and grand totals, respectively. The plus sign totals all numeric entries in a column. The equal sign totals all subtotals. The asterisk calculates the grand total.
- Cells within a table can be further customized at the Table Options menu. At the Table Options menu, you can change the spacing between text and lines, display negative results with a minus sign or parentheses, change the position of the table, and change the gray shading.
- The Join selection lets you join several cells together. The Split selection lets you split one cell into two or more cells.

### Commands Review

| | Keyboard | Mouse |
|---|---|---|
| Columns/Table command | Alt + F7 | Layout, Tables |

## STUDY GUIDE FOR CHAPTER 19

List the seven styles of lines that can be selected to customize lines in the table-editing mode.

1. _____

2. _____

3. _____

4. _____

5. _____

6. _____

7. _____

**Completion:** In the space provided at the right, indicate the correct symbol, command, or character for the explanation.

1.  Default gray shading percentage.                                    _____

2.  Choose this selection at the **Lines** prompt to change lines of all   _____
    cells within the block.

3.  This selection in the table-editing mode is used to calculate       _____
    numbers in rows or columns.

4.  In a cell, this operator totals all numeric entries in a column.     _____

5.  In a cell, this operator calculates the grand totals.                _____

6.  When writing a formula in a cell, this symbol subtracts.             _____

7.  When writing a formula in a cell, this symbol divides.               _____

8.  When writing a formula in a cell, this symbol multiplies.            _____

9.  To change the order of calculation in a formula, enclose part of     _____
    the formula to be calculated first in these symbols.

## HANDS-ON EXERCISES

Change the default directory to UNIT5.

**Exercise One**
1.  Retrieve CH18EX3 to the screen.
2.  Change the lines at the top of cells A2 through C2 to double by completing the following steps:
    A.  Move the cursor within the table and press Alt + F7.
    B.  Move the cursor to cell A2 and access the Block command.
    C.  Move the cursor to cell C2.
    D.  With cells A2 through C2 blocked, choose 3 or L for Lines.
    E.  Choose 3 or T for Top.
    F.  Choose 3 or D for Double.

3. Remove the lines inside cells A2 through C5 by completing the following steps:
   A. Move the cursor to cell A2 and access the Block command.
   B. Move the cursor to cell C5. (This should block all cells except the top row.)
   C. Choose 3 or L for Line.
   D. Choose 5 or I for Inside.
   E. Choose 1 or N for None.
4. Press F7 to change to the normal editing mode.
5. Save the revised table and name it CH19EX1. Print CH19EX1.

**Exercise Two**

1. At a clear screen, create the table shown in figure 19-5 by completing the following steps:
   A. Center and boldface the title, **COMPARISON OF PROGRAM FEATURES**.
   B. Create a table that contains six columns and five rows.
   C. With the cursor in cell A1, widen column A by pressing Ctrl + right arrow four times.
   D. Press F7 to return to the normal editing mode. Fill in the cells with the information displayed in figure 19-5.
   E. With the cursor located within the table, press Alt + F7 to return to the table-editing mode.
   F. Move the cursor to cell B1, access the Block command, then move the cursor to cell F1. With the column headings blocked, change the justification to center by completing the following steps:
      (1) Choose 2 or F for Format.
      (2) Choose 1 or C for Cell.
      (3) Choose 3 or J for Justify.
      (4) Choose 2 or C for Center.
   G. Move the cursor to cell A1 and remove the lines by completing the following steps:
      (1) Choose 3 or L for Lines.
      (2) Choose 7 or A for All.
      (3) Choose 1 or N for None.
   H. Change the gray shading at the Options menu from 10% to 50% by completing the following steps:
      (1) Choose 6 or O for Options.
      (2) Choose 4 or G for Gray Shading.
      (3) Key in **50**, then press Enter twice.
   I. Insert gray shading in the cells as shown in figure 19-5. To do this, move to each cell individually and complete the following steps:
      (1) Choose 3 or L for Lines.
      (2) Choose 8 or S for Shade.
      (3) Choose 1 or O for On. (Gray shading displays only in View Document.)
   J. Press F7 to return to the normal editing mode.
2. Save the table and name it CH19EX2. Print CH19EX2.

## COMPARISON OF PROGRAM FEATURES

| | Graphics | Styles | Glossary | Macros | Merge |
|---|---|---|---|---|---|
| Words Galore | ▓ | | ▓ | | ▓ |
| Write Way | | | ▓ | | ▓ |
| Word Magic | | ▓ | | ▓ | ▓ |
| PowerWriter | ▓ | ▓ | | ▓ | ▓ |

Figure 19-5: Exercise Two

## Exercise Three

1. Retrieve CH18EX5 to the screen.
2. Add a row to the bottom of the table.
3. Move the cursor to cell B9 and insert a formula to add the column entries by completing the following steps:
   A. Choose 5 or M for Math.
   B. Choose 2 or F for Formula.
   C. Key in the formula **B2+B3+B4+B5+B6+B7+B8**, then press Enter.
4. Move the cursor to cell C9 and insert a formula to add the column entries by completing the following steps:
   A. Choose 5 or M for Math.
   B. Choose 2 or F for Formula.
   C. Key in the formula **C2+C3+C4+C5+C6+C7+C8**, then press Enter.
5. Press F7 to return to the editing mode.
6. Move the cursor to cell A9 and key in **TOTAL**.
7. Save the revised table and name it CH19EX3. Print CH19EX3.

## Exercise Four

1. At a clear screen, create the table shown in figure 19-6 by completing the following steps:
   A. Create a table with three columns and eight rows.
   B. Join cells A1, B1 and C1 by completing the following steps:
      (1) With the cursor in cell A1, access the Block command.
      (2) Move the cursor to cell C1.
      (3) Choose 7 or J for Join.
      (4) Key in a **Y** for Yes.
   C. Join cells A2 through C2.
   D. Move the cursor to any cell in column A and increase the size of the column by pressing Ctrl + right arrow eight times.
   E. Press F7 to return to the normal editing mode.
   F. Move the cursor to cell A1 and center and boldface the heading OFFICE PRODUCTS SALE ITEMS.
   G. Move the cursor to cell A2 and center and boldface the subheading February 1993.
   H. Move the cursor to cell A3, access the Bold key with F6, then key in the column heading, **Product**.

I. Move the cursor to cell B3, access the Bold key, then key in **Current Price**.

J. Move the cursor to cell C3, access the Bold key, then key in **Sale Price**.

K. Fill in the remaining cells with the information shown in figure 19-6. Use Home + Tab to indent the products.

L. With the cursor located anywhere within the table, press Alt + F7 to return to the table-editing mode.

M. Move the cursor to any cell in column B and change the justification to Decimal Align by completing the following steps:

    (1) Choose 2 or F for Format.

    (2) Choose 2 or L for Column.

    (3) Choose 3 or J for Justify.

    (4) Choose 5 or D for Decimal Align.

N. Move the cursor to any cell in column C and change the justification to Decimal Align by completing the preceding steps.

O. Move the cursor to cell A3 and center the column heading, Product, by completing the following steps:

    (1) Choose 2 or F for Format.

    (2) Choose 1 or C for Cell.

    (3) Choose 3 or J for Justify.

    (4) Choose 2 or C for Center.

P. Complete the same steps for cells B3 and C3.

Q. Center the entire table between the left and right margins by completing the following steps:

    (1) Choose 6 or O for Options.

    (2) Choose 3 or P for Position of Table.

    (3) Choose 3 or C for Center.

    (4) Press F7 to return to the table.

R. Press F7 to return to the normal editing mode.

2. Save the table and name it CH19EX4. Print CH19EX4.

| OFFICE PRODUCTS SALE ITEMS | | |
|---|---|---|
| February 1993 | | |
| Product | Current Price | Sale Price |
| Ergonomic Chair | $275.00 | $179.99 |
| 3-Drawer Cabinet | 195.00 | 159.99 |
| 4-Drawer Cabinet | 249.00 | 199.99 |
| Executive Desk | 950.00 | 829.99 |
| Computer Table | 245.00 | 199.99 |

**Figure 19-6: Exercise Four**

**Exercise Five**

1.  Retrieve CH19EX4 to the screen.
2.  Add a column to the table by completing the following steps:
    A.  With the cursor located anywhere in the table, press Alt + F7 to change to the table-editing mode.
    B.  Choose 1 or S for Size.
    C.  Choose 2 or C for Columns.
    D.  Key in **4**, then press Enter.
3.  Adjust the columns so they are more evenly spaced (and the column headings fit on one line).
4.  Join cells A1 and D1.
5.  Join cells A2 and D2.
6.  Move the cursor to cell D4 and insert a formula by completing the following steps:
    A.  Choose 5 or M for Math
    B.  Choose 2 or F for Formula.
    C.  Key in **B4-C4**, then press Enter.
7.  With the cursor in cell D4, copy the formula to cells D5, D6, D7, and D8 by completing the following steps:
    A.  Choose 5 or M for Math.
    B.  Choose 3 or P for Copy Formula.
    C.  Choose 2 or D for Down.
    D.  At the prompt **Number of times to copy formula:**, key in **4**, then press Enter.
8.  Press F7 to change to the normal editing mode.
9.  Move the cursor to cell D3. Center and boldface the column heading, Savings.
10. Save the revised table and name it CH19EX5. Print CH19EX5.

**Exercise Six**

1.  At a clear screen, create the invoice shown in figure 19-7 by completing the following steps:
    A.  Create a table with four column and eight rows.
    B.  At the table-editing mode, increase the size of column A by pressing Ctrl + right arrow 14 times.
    C.  Join cells A1 through D1.
    D.  Block cells A2 through D2 and change the top line to Double.
    E.  Block cells A3 through D3 and change the top line to Double.
    F.  Block cells B3 through D6 and change the justification to Decimal Align by completing the following steps:
        (1)  Choose 2 or F for Format.
        (2)  Choose 1 or C for Cell.
        (3)  Choose 3 or J for Justify.
        (4)  Choose 5 or D for Decimal Align.
    G.  Press F7 to change to the normal editing mode.
    H.  Move the cursor to cell A1, press Enter, then key in the headings shown in figure 19-7. Use Home + Tab to indent items to tab stops.
    I.  Move the cursor to cell A2 and boldface and center Description.
    J.  Move the cursor to cell B2 and boldface and center Qty.
    K.  Move the cursor to cell C2 and boldface and center Price.
    L.  Move the cursor to cell D2 and boldface and center Total.
    M.  Key in the remainder of the information shown in figure 19-7.
2.  Save the invoice and name it CH19EX6. Print CH19EX6.

| Puget Sound Semiconductor<br>1900 State Street<br>Tacoma, WA 98402<br>(206) 555-2599 | | Invoice #:<br>Date:<br>Clerk: | |
|---|---|---|---|
| Description | Qty. | Price | Total |
| Parallel printer cable | 25 | $ 29.99 | |
| Serial mouse | 75 | 35.00 | |
| Printer cartridge | 30 | 95.50 | |
| Computer monitor | 20 | 199.00 | |
| | | | |
| | | | |

Figure 19-7: Exercise Six

**Exercise Seven**
1. Retrieve CH19EX6 to the screen.
2. With the cursor located anywhere in the table, press Alt + F7 to change to the table-editing mode.
3. Move the cursor to cell D3 and insert the formula **B3*C3**.
4. With the cursor in cell D3, copy the formula to cells D4, D5, and D6 by completing the following steps:
   A. Choose 5 or M for Math.
   B. Choose 3 or P for Copy Formula.
   C. Choose 2 or D for Down.
   D. Key in **3**, then press Enter.
5. Block cells A3 through D8 and remove the inside lines by completing the following steps:
   A. Choose 3 or L for Lines.
   B. Choose 5 or I for Inside.
   C. Choose 1 or N for None.
6. Save the revised table and name it CH19EX7. Print CH19EX7.

## PERFORMANCE ASSESSMENTS

**Assessment One**
1. At a clear screen, create the table shown in figure 19-8.
2. Determine the number of rows and columns for the table.
3. Make changes to the lines as shown in figure 19-8.
4. Change the alignment of cells B4 through D15 to Decimal Align.

5. In the normal editing mode, enter the information as shown in figure 19-8. Center and boldface headings as indicated.

6. Save the table and name it CH19PA1. Print CH19PA1.

| CHENEY MANUFACTURING | | | |
|---|---|---|---|
| Sales Comparisons, 1991 and 1992 | | | |
| **Month** | **1991** | **1992** | **Increase** |
| January | $125,440.55 | $134,255.00 | |
| February | 133,220.56 | 142,344.57 | |
| March | 142,334.65 | 143,220.45 | |
| April | 153,223.66 | 153,678.90 | |
| May | 143,227.55 | 150,456.32 | |
| June | 150,345.86 | 151,345.22 | |
| July | 142,345.76 | 145,678.45 | |
| August | 139,456.32 | 137,456.33 | |
| September | 143,245.78 | 145,678.43 | |
| October | 151,345.90 | 154,356.97 | |
| November | 158,543.24 | 160,345.33 | |
| December | 160,345.22 | 162,345.70 | |

Figure 19-8: Assessment One

**Assessment Two**

1. Retrieve CH19PA1 to the screen.

2. With the cursor located anywhere in the table, press Alt + F7 to access the table-editing mode.

3. Move the cursor to cell D4 and insert the formula **C4-B4**.

4. Copy the formula in cell D4 to cells D5 through D15.

5. Block the entire table, then remove all lines by completing the following steps:
   A. With the entire table blocked, choose 3 or L for Lines.
   B. Choose 7 or A for All.
   C. Choose 1 or N for None.

6. Save the revised table and name it CH19PA2. Print CH19PA2.

# CHAPTER 20

## PARAGRAPH NUMBERING/OUTLINES

### PERFORMANCE OBJECTIVE

Upon successful completion of chapter 20, you will be able to enhance the organization of business reports and speech outlines automatically.

The WordPerfect program includes a feature that lets you create numbered paragraphs and outlines in a document. The Date/Outline command can be used to automatically insert numbers before paragraphs or to insert outlining numbers. When the Date/Outline command is used to number paragraphs or create outlines, text can be inserted or deleted and WordPerfect automatically renumbers the remaining text.

### PARAGRAPH NUMBERING

The style of numbers WordPerfect uses to automatically number paragraphs is determined by tab positions. The default paragraph numbering style that WordPerfect uses is an outlining style that includes eight levels of numbers, as shown in figure 20-1.

```
         I. Level 1 = Left Margin

            A. Level 2 = First Tab

               1. Level 3 = Second Tab

                  a. Level 4 = Third Tab

                     (1) Level 5 = Fourth Tab

                        (a) Level 6 = Fifth Tab

                           i) Level 7 = Sixth Tab

                              a) Level 8 = Seventh Tab
```

Figure 20-1: Default Paragraph Numbering Style

If the cursor is positioned at the left margin and the command to number paragraphs is accessed, paragraphs are numbered with Roman numerals (I., II., III., etc.). With the cursor positioned at the first tab stop, paragraphs are numbered with capital letters (A., B., C., etc.). Each successive tab stop causes numbering to occur as shown in figure 20-1. This numbering style is the WordPerfect default. Later in this chapter you will learn that you can change the numbering style of paragraphs.

## Creating Paragraph Numbers in a Document

Paragraph numbering can be included in a document as the document is being keyed in, or paragraph numbering can be inserted in existing text. To insert paragraph numbering at the left margin in a document as it is being keyed in, position the cursor at the left margin of the line where you want numbering to appear and complete the following steps:

1. Access the Date/Outline command with Shift + F5.

2. At the prompt **1 Date Text; 2 Date Code; 3 Date Format; 4 Outline; 5 Para Num; 6 Define: 0**, choose 5 or P for Para Num.
   **M** *Click on Tools, then Paragraph Number.*

3. At the **Paragraph Level (Press Enter for Automatic):** prompt, press Enter and WordPerfect inserts a Roman numeral I.

WordPerfect inserts the code **[Par Num:Auto]** in the document, which can be seen in Reveal Codes. After the number is inserted, press the space bar or the Tab key to separate the number from the text, then begin keying in text.

To insert a number at the first tab stop, move the cursor to the tab stop and repeat the steps listed above. You must access the Date/Outline command before each paragraph to be numbered.

To insert paragraph numbering into existing text, move the cursor to the margin or tab stop where numbering is to occur and proceed as described above. If you need to indent text to a particular tab stop to obtain a certain level of paragraph numbering, make sure Insert is on.

### Deleting a Paragraph Number

Delete paragraph numbering in a document as you would any other text. Move the cursor to the number and press the Delete key. When the number is deleted, the code is also removed from the document. If you delete an entire paragraph that includes paragraph numbering, WordPerfect automatically renumbers any remaining paragraphs.

### Changing the Paragraph Numbering

The style of number used to number paragraphs can be changed in a document. You may want to move text to a different tab stop or change the style of numbering.

If, after creating numbered paragraphs, you decide you want numbering at a different tab stop, move the cursor to the paragraph and press the Tab key. Insert the text to the tab stop level you desire and WordPerfect automatically changes the paragraph number style.

The methods described so far cause paragraph numbering styles to be determined by the tab position or left margin. The levels of the style used to number paragraphs can be changed. For example, to number paragraphs at the left margin with Arabic numbers rather than Roman numerals, complete the following steps:

1.   Access the Date/Outline command with Shift + F5.
2.   Choose 5 or P for Para Num.
     **M** *Click on Tools, then Paragraph Number.*
3.   At the prompt **Paragraph Level (Press Enter for Automatic):** **0**, key in **3** (to identify level 3 numbering style — 1., 2., 3., etc.), then press Enter.

### Changing the Numbering Style

The preceding paragraph describes the method for changing the paragraph numbering style for certain paragraphs within a document. WordPerfect also has a selection that lets you change the default level numbering style. To change the numbering style, complete the following steps:

1.   Access the Date/Outline command with Shift + F5.
2.   Choose 6 or D for Define and WordPerfect displays the Paragraph Number Definition menu shown in figure 20-2.
     **M** *Click on Tools, then Define.*

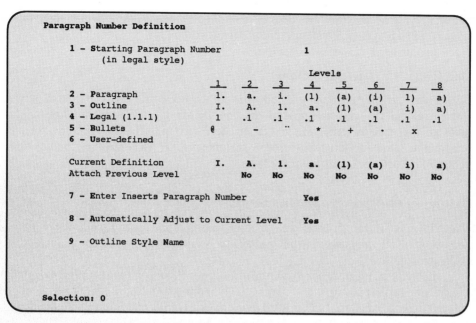

```
Paragraph Number Definition

     1 - Starting Paragraph Number              1
         (in legal style)
                                          Levels
                              1    2    3    4    5    6    7    8
     2 - Paragraph           1.   a.   i.  (1)  (a)  (i)  1)   a)
     3 - Outline             I.   A.   1.   a.  (1)  (a)  i)   a)
     4 - Legal (1.1.1)       1   .1   .1   .1   .1   .1   .1   .1
     5 - Bullets             @    -    ··   *    +    ·    x
     6 - User-defined

     Current Definition      I.   A.   1.   a.  (1)  (a)  i)   a)
     Attach Previous Level        No   No   No   No   No   No   No

     7 - Enter Inserts Paragraph Number         Yes

     8 - Automatically Adjust to Current Level   Yes

     9 - Outline Style Name


Selection: 0
```

Figure 20-2: Paragraph Number Definition Menu

The first selection from this menu, Starting Paragraph Number, lets you begin numbering paragraphs with a number other than 1. To identify a new beginning number, complete the following steps:

1. At the Paragraph Number Definition menu, choose 1 or S for Starting Paragraph Number.

2. Key in the new beginning number (in Arabic numbers), and press Enter.

WordPerfect begins numbering paragraphs with this new number in the style for the appropriate level. For example, if you keyed in 5 as the new starting number, a Roman numeral V appears in the document at level 1.

Selections 2 through 6 are used to change the paragraph numbering style. Selection 3, Outline, is the default style. The Current Definition selection displays the levels of numbers and the current settings. To change the current definition from Outline to one of the other selections, key in a new number. For example, to change the numbering style to paragraph numbering, choose 2 or P for Paragraph, at the Paragraph Number Definition menu. This causes the settings after Current Definition to change and reflect the numbering levels of the Paragraph style.

Selection 5, Bullets, is used to identify paragraphs with symbols rather than numbers. Selection 6, User-defined, lets you specify your own level of numbering styles. When you choose 6 or U for User-defined, the cursor moves to the first selection after Current Definition (Level 1), and the information shown in figure 20-3 is displayed at the bottom of the menu.

```
Paragraph Number Definition

      1 - Starting Paragraph Number              1
          (in legal style)
                                            Levels
                               1    2    3    4    5    6    7    8
      2 - Paragraph           1.   a.   i.  (1)  (a)  (i)  1)   a)
      3 - Outline             I.   A.   1.   a.  (1)  (a)  i)   a)
      4 - Legal (1.1.1)       1   .1   .1   .1   .1   .1   .1   .1
      5 - Bullets             @    -    ..   *    +    .    x
      6 - User-defined

      Current Definition      I.   A.   1.   a.  (1)  (a)  i)   a)
      Attach Previous Level        No   No   No   No   No   No   No

      7 - Enter Inserts Paragraph Number         Yes

      8 - Automatically Adjust to Current Level   Yes

      9 - Outline Style Name

   1 - Digits, A - Uppercase Letters, a - Lowercase Letters
   I - Uppercase Roman, i - Lowercase Roman
   X - Uppercase Roman/Digits if Attached, x - Lowercase Roman/Digits if Attached
   Other character - Bullet or Punctuation
```

Figure 20-3: User-defined Selections

If you enter a 1, digits are used for that paragraph level. If you enter an A, capital letters are used for that paragraph level. An I numbers the paragraph level with uppercase Roman numerals, and an i numbers the paragraph level with lowercase Roman numerals.

If you enter an X, the paragraph is numbered with an uppercase Roman numeral unless the level is attached to the previous level. If the level is attached to the previous level, then the paragraph level numbering is a digit (Arabic number). For example, in some documents, you may want your paragraphs numbered in the following manner:

$$I = Level\ 1$$
$$I.1 = Level\ 2$$
$$I.1.i = Level\ 3$$

The last three selections from the Paragraph Number Definition menu pertain to outlining and are described later in this chapter.

When all changes to the Paragraph Number Definition menu have been made, press F7 to return to the Date/Outline prompt. Press F7 again to return to the document, or turn paragraph numbering on by choosing 5 or P for Para Num.

The Paragraph Number Definition menu can be used to allow several groups of paragraphs, each beginning with the number 1. If your document includes numbered paragraphs and later in the document you want to begin a new set of numbered paragraphs, you must use the Paragraph Number Definition menu to start the numbering with 1. If you do not use this menu, WordPerfect continues paragraph numbering with the next number from the previous series of paragraphs.

## OUTLINE NUMBERING

The WordPerfect outline numbering style is the same as paragraph numbering style (I., A., 1., etc.). Outlining, however, operates differently than paragraph numbering. When you include paragraph numbering in a document, you must access the Date/Outline command before each paragraph. When using the outlining feature, you access the Date/Outline command just once and WordPerfect automatically inserts outlining numbers.

To turn on outlining, complete the following steps:

1.  Position the cursor on the blank line above where outlining is to occur and access the Date/Outline command with Shift + F5.

2.  Choose 4 or O for Outline.

3.  At the prompt **Outline: 1 On; 2 Off; 3 Move Family; 4 Copy Family; 5 Delete Family: 0**, choose 1 or O for On.
    **M** *Click on Tools, Outline, then On.*

When outlining is turned on, WordPerfect displays the message **Outline** at the bottom left of the screen. With this message displayed, the Enter key, Tab key, and Indent keys cause the following to occur:

Enter                    = Moves the cursor down to the left margin or the tab setting of the previous level and inserts the appropriate level numbering.

Tab                      = Moves the cursor to the next tab stop and inserts the level of numbering for that tab stop.

Indent (F4),             = Inserts a "hard tab" and moves the cursor
Indent (Shift + F4),     to the next tab stop without changing the
Home + Tab               paragraph level numbering.

When all outline information is entered, you must exit outline. To do this, complete the following steps:

1.  With the cursor below the outline, access the Date/Outline command with Shift + F5.

2.  Choose 4 or O for Outline.

3.  Choose 2 or F for Off.
    **M** *Click on Tools, Outline, then Off.*

The steps to create the outline shown in figure 20-4 are described after the figure.

```
I.   Font

     A.   Typeface
          1.  Proportional spaced
              a.  Serif
              b.  Sans serif
     B.   Type Style
```

**Figure 20-4: Example Outline**

Complete the following steps to key in the outline:

1. To align the text properly after each number, delete previous tabs and set new left tabs at +0.4, +0.8, +1.2, and +1.6 inches.

2. On the blank line above the outline, access the Date/Outline command with Shift + F5, choose 4 or O for Outline, then 1 or O for On.
   **M** *Click on Tools, Outline, then On.*

3. Press the Enter key. This moves the cursor to the left margin and inserts Roman numeral *I*.

4. Press Home + Tab to move the cursor to the next tab stop (without changing the level numbering) and key in **Font**. Press Enter twice.

5. Press the Tab key, and a capital *A*. is inserted in the document. Press Home + Tab to move the cursor to the tab stop without inserting a new level number and key in **Typeface**. Press Enter to move to the next line.

6. Press the Tab key once to move the cursor to the second tab stop. This causes a number *1*. to be inserted. Press Home + Tab, then key in **Proportional spaced**. Press Enter to move the cursor to the next line.

7. Press the Tab key once to move the cursor to the next tab stop and insert a lowercase *a*. Press Home + Tab, then key in **Serif**.

8. Press Enter to move the cursor to the next line and WordPerfect automatically inserts a lowercase *b*. Press Home + Tab, key in **Sans Serif**, then press Enter.

9. Press the Margin Release command, Shift + Tab, twice to move the cursor back two tab settings and change the paragraph level numbering.
   **M** *Click on Layout, Align, then Margin Rel.*

10. Press Home + Tab then key in **Type Style**.

11. Turn off outlining by accessing the Date/Outline command with Shift + F5, choose 4 or O for Outline, then 2 or F for Off.
    **M** *Click on Tools, Outline, then Off.*

**Customizing the Outline**

When creating an outline, the Enter key moves the cursor down to the left margin or to the tab setting of the previous level. A change can be made at the Paragraph Number Definition menu that will cause the Enter key to move the cursor to the left margin and insert level-one numbering. To make this change, complete the following steps:

1.  Access the Paragraph Number Definition with Shift + F5, then choose 6 or D for Define.
    **M** *Click on Tools, then Define.*

2.  At the Paragraph Number Definition menu, choose 8 or A for Automatically Adjust to Current Level.

3.  Key in an **N** for No, then press F7.

4.  Press F1 to remove the Date/Outline prompt from the bottom of the screen.

With the Automatically Adjust to Current Level selection changed to No, the Enter key causes the cursor to move to the left margin of the next line. For example, when creating the outline in figure 20-4, the Enter key pressed after **Typeface** would move the cursor to the left margin and insert a Roman numeral *II* (instead of moving the cursor to the first tab setting and inserting a capital *B*).

The Enter Inserts Paragraph Number selection from the Paragraph Number Definition menu has a default setting of Yes. At this setting, the Enter key causes a paragraph level number to be inserted in the document. If this selection is changed to No, the Enter key moves the cursor to the next line but does not insert paragraph numbering. Paragraph numbering must be inserted manually with the Date/Outline command.

The last selection from the Paragraph Number Definition menu, Outline Style Name, is discussed in the chapter on styles.

## Editing Outline

If you delete a line from an outline, WordPerfect automatically renumbers the remaining lines. Several selections from the Date/Outline prompt can be used to move, copy, or delete an outline family. When you access the Date/Outline command and choose 4 or O for Outline, the prompt **Outline: 1 On; 2 Off; 3 Move Family; 4 Copy Family; 5 Delete Family: 0** appears at the bottom of the screen.

The Move Family, Copy Family, and Delete Family selections are used to edit a family. A family is the current level where the cursor is located in an outline plus any sublevels within that level. For example, in the outline shown in figure 20-4, if the cursor was located on **Typeface**, the outline family would include the following:

    A.    Typeface
        1.    Proportional spaced
            a.    Serif
            b.    Sans serif

With the outline family selections from the Outline prompt, you can move an outline family, copy an outline family, or delete an outline family. For example, to move the outline family beginning with **Typeface** in the outline shown in figure 20-4 below **Type Size**, complete the following steps:

1.  Move the cursor so it is located on the line containing **Typeface**.

2.  Access the Date/Outline command with Shift + F5.

3.  Choose 4 or O for Outline.

4. Choose 3 or M for Move family.
   **M** *Click on Tools, Outline, then Move Family.*

5. WordPerfect highlights the entire outline family and inserts the prompt **Press Arrows to Move Family; Enter when done** at the bottom of the screen. Press the Down arrow key once to move the outline family below Type Size, then press Enter.

When the outline family is moved to a new location in the outline, WordPerfect automatically renumbers the remainder of the outline. Follow similar steps to copy an outline family. The difference is that the outline family remains in its original position and a copy is inserted in a new location.

An outline family can also be deleted from an outline. For example, to delete the outline family beginning with Typeface in the outline shown in figure 20-4, complete the following steps:

1. Move the cursor so it is located on the line containing Typeface.

2. Access the Date/Outline command with Shift + F5.

3. Choose 4 or O for Outline.

4. Choose 5 or D for Delete family.
   **M** *Click on Tools, Outline, then Delete Family.*

5. WordPerfect highlights the entire outline family and inserts the prompt **Delete Outline Family? No (Yes)** at the bottom of the screen. Key in a **Y** for Yes.

### Changing the Outline Numbering Style

The outline default level numbering style can be changed in the same manner as the paragraph default level numbering style. To change the outline numbering style, access the Paragraph Number Definition menu and select a new numbering style or create your own.

### Outlining Considerations

If you use the default tab settings to create an outline, the outlining numbers may not align correctly. Setting tabs every .4 inches instead of .5 inches may allow some of the outlining numbers and letters to align correctly in the document.

Changing the tab stops, however, will not help to correctly align the Roman numerals. If alignment of the Roman numerals is important, you may need to manually insert spaces.

## CHAPTER REVIEW

### Summary

- Paragraph numbering can be inserted in a document with the Date/Outline command, Shift + F5. When the Date/Outline command is used, paragraphs are automatically renumbered if paragraphs are inserted or deleted.

- The default paragraph numbering style is an outline style. Numbers are determined by the location of the cursor at a tab stop or left margin.

- The default levels are I. for left margin; A. for first tab stop; 1. for second tab stop; a. for third tab stop; (1) for fourth tab stop; (a) for fifth tab stop; i) for sixth tab stop; and, a) for seventh tab stop.

- To number paragraphs with the Date/Outline command, position the cursor at the left margin or a tab stop and access the Date/Outline command with Shift + F5, then choose 5 or P for Para Num (**M** *Click on Tools, then Para Num*). Press Enter or key in the level numbering style you desire and press Enter.

- Paragraph numbering can be inserted in a document as it is being keyed in, or it can be inserted afterwards.

- Paragraphs and paragraph numbering can be deleted. WordPerfect automatically renumbers existing paragraphs.

- The default level numbering style can be changed at the Paragraph Number Definition menu.

- To display the Paragraph Number Definition menu, access the Date/Outline command with Shift + F5, then choose 6 or D for Define (**M** *Click on Tools, then Define*).

- To turn on the outline feature, access the Date/Outline command with Shift + F5, choose 4 or O for Outline, then 1 or O for On (**M** *Click on Tools, Outline, then On*). With the outline feature on, WordPerfect automatically inserts outline numbers. Text can be inserted or deleted from an outline, and WordPerfect will renumber existing text.

- An outline family is the current level where the cursor is located in an outline plus any sublevels within that level. An outline family can be moved, copied, or deleted.

- The outline default level numbering style can be changed at the Paragraph Number Definition menu.

## Command Review

**Keyboard**

| | |
|---|---|
| Insert paragraph number | Shift + F5, 5 or P |
| Turn on outline | Shift + F5, 4 or O, 1 or O |
| Turn off outline | Shift + F5, 4 or O, 2 or F |
| Paragraph Number Definition menu | Shift + F5, 6 or D |
| Hard tab | Home + Tab |
| Margin release | Shift + Tab |

**Mouse**

| | |
|---|---|
| Insert paragraph number | Tools, Paragraph Number |
| Turn on outline | Tools, Outline, On |
| Turn off outline | Tools, Outline, Off |
| Paragraph Number Definition menu | Tools, Define |
| Margin release | Layout, Align, Margin Rel |

## STUDY GUIDE FOR CHAPTER 20

**Completion:** In the space provided at the right, indicate the correct symbol, term, or number for the explanation.

1. Insert paragraph numbering. _____

2. Turn on the outline feature. _____

3. Default Level 2 paragraph number. _____

4. Default tab stop that numbers paragraphs with a lowercase letter followed by a period. _____

5. With the Outline feature on, this key moves the cursor down to the left margin or the tab setting of the previous level. _____

6. Default Level 7 paragraph number. _____

7. Access the Paragraph Number Definition Menu. _____

8. Default Level 3 paragraph number. _____

9. The three functions you can perform with an outline family at the Outline prompt. _____

**True/False:** Circle the letter T if the statement is true; circle the letter F if the statement is false.

1. Level 1 numbering is inserted at the first tab stop. T    F

2. Paragraph numbering can be inserted in existing text. T    F

3. If a paragraph number is deleted, WordPerfect automatically renumbers the remaining paragraphs. T    F

4. To number paragraphs, the Date/Outline command must be accessed at each paragraph. T    F

5. At the Paragraph Number Definition menu, the default level numbering style is paragraph numbering. T    F

6. The Date/Outline command must be accessed before each line in an outline. T    F

7. Text can be inserted in an outline. T    F

## HANDS-ON EXERCISES

Change the default directory to UNIT5.

### Exercise One

1. At a clear screen, create the business letter shown in figure 20-5 by completing the following steps:
    A. Change the numbering style from outline to paragraph by completing the following steps:
       (1) Access the Date/Outline command with Shift + F5, then choose 6 or D for Define.
          **M** *Click on Tools, then Define.*

        (2)  At the Paragraph Number Definition menu, choose 2 or P for Paragraph, then Press F7.

        (3)  Press F1 to remove the Outline prompt from the bottom of the screen.

  B.  Delete previous tabs and set a new left tab at +0.4 inches.

  C.  Key in the business letter shown in figure 20-5. To number the paragraphs, complete the following steps:

        (1)  Access the Date/Outline command with Shift + F5, then choose 5 or P for Para Num.

           **M** *Click on Tools, then Paragraph Number.*

        (2)  Press Enter to insert the default level numbering.

  D.  Use the Indent key to indent the text after the numbers.

2.  When the letter is complete, save it and name it CH20EX1. Print CH20EX1.

March 24, 1993


Mr. Frank Calucci
1203 Northside Avenue
Renton, WA 98033

Dear Mr. Calucci:

The product you mentioned in your letter of March 10 sounds interesting. Depending on the availability of similar products, the current market, and the production cost of a product, our law firm may be interested in helping you obtain a patent.

Before the process of applying for the patent can begin, I need to gather information about you and your product. As soon as you can, please provide me with the following information:

1.  Your full legal name.
2.  Addresses of your business and residence.
3.  Name and address of another company or business where you are employed, if applicable.
4.  Name or names you have considered for your product.
5.  Research you have completed on marketing opportunities for your product.
6.  Any products on the market that are similar to yours.
7.  Approximate cost of producing your product.

After I receive this information and study it carefully, I will contact you with my suggestions.

Sincerely,

MORENO, YAMADA, & SCHWARTZ


Dan Yamada
Attorney-at-Law

**Figure 20-5: Exercise One**

**Exercise Two**

1.  Retrieve CH20EX1 to the screen and make the following changes:
    A. Insert the sentence **Spouse's full legal name.** after the first numbered paragraph by completing the following steps:
       (1) Move the cursor to the end of the first numbered paragraph and press Enter.
       (2) Access the Date/Outline command with Shift + F5, then choose 5 or P for Para Num.
           **M** *Click on Tools, then Paragraph Number.*
       (3) Press Enter to accept the default numbering level.

(4) Access the Indent key with F4 (**M** *Click on Layout, Align, then Indent, F4*), then key in **Spouse's full legal name.**

    B. Move the cursor to the end of the fourth numbered paragraph and press Enter. Insert the sentence **Name and address of the company or business where your spouse is employed.** as the fifth item by following the steps listed above.

    C. Delete the sentence **Name or names you have considered for your product.** and the number in front of it.

2. Save the revised letter and name it CH20EX2. Print CH20EX2.

**Exercise Three**

1. At a clear screen, create the agenda shown in figure 20-6 by completing the following steps:

    A. Change the left and right margins to 2 inches.

    B. Delete previous tabs and set new left tabs at +0.5 and +0.8 inch.

    C. Center and boldface the title and subtitles.

    D. Triple-space below the date, then center, boldface, and capitalize the word *AGENDA*.

    E. Double space after *AGENDA* and turn on the Outline feature by completing the following steps:

        (1) Access the Date/Outline command with Shift + F5, then choose 4 or O for Outline.

        (2) At the prompt **Outline: 1 On; 2 Off; 3 Move Family; 4 Copy Family; 5 Delete Family: 0**, choose 1 or O for On.

           **M** *Click on Tools, Outline, then On.*

    F. Press Enter and WordPerfect inserts the Roman numeral I. Press Home + Tab (or F4) to move the cursor to the next tab stop without changing the outline number, then key in **Welcome.**

    G. Key in the remainder of the outline. When necessary, use the Margin Rel command, Shift + Tab (**M** *Click on Layout, Align, then Margin Rel*) to move the cursor to a previous tab setting and change the outline number.

    H. When the outline is complete, turn off the Outline feature. To do this, access the Date/Outline command with Shift + F5, choose 4 or O for Outline, then 2 or F for Off (**M** *Click on Tools, Outline, then Off*).

2. Save the agenda and name it CH20EX3. Print CH20EX3.

**PUGET SOUND SEMICONDUCTOR**
Department Meeting
February 12, 1993


**AGENDA**


I.   Welcome

II.  Approval of minutes from January 11, 1993

III. Introduction of new staff members

     A. Personnel Department, John White Cloud
     B. Sales Department, Heidi Schueler

IV.  New Business

     A. Construction site, Brad Majors
     B. Company slogan, Terry Preston
     C. Recruitment campaign, Maria Valdez
     D. Equipment purchases, Kim Chun

V.   Old Business

     A. Personnel selection, Janet Weiss
     B. Employee benefits, Darlene Evans
     C. Business forms, Terry Preston
     D. Company newsletter, Terry Preston
     E. Marketing strategies, Pat Serosky

VI.  Adjournment

---

Figure 20-6: Exercise Three

**Exercise Four**
1. Retrieve CH20EX3 to the screen.
2. Delete item D under Old Business (Company newsletter, Terry Preston) by completing the following steps:
   A. Block the line containing item D with the Block command.
   B. With the line blocked, press the Delete key.
   C. At the confirmation question, key in a **Y** for Yes.
3. Move the New Business outline family below Old Business by completing the following steps:
   A. Locate the cursor on the New Business line.
   B. Access the Date/Outline command with Shift + F5, choose 4 or O for Outline, then 3 or M for Move family.
      **M** *Click on Tools, Outline, then Move Family.*

      C. Press the Down arrow key once (to move the family below Old Business) and press
         Enter.
    4. Save the revised agenda and name it CH20EX4. Print CH20EX4.

**Exercise Five**
    1. At a clear screen, create the business letter shown in figure 20-7 by completing the
       following steps:
      A. Access the Paragraph Number Definition menu and change the numbering style to
         Legal.
      B. Delete previous tabs and set new left tabs at +0.3, and +0.8 inches.
      C. Key in the letter shown in figure 20-7 in an appropriate business letter format.
    2. Save the letter and name it CH20EX5. Print CH20EX5.

---

March 20, 1993

Ms. Elaine Kilpatrick
General Manager
Catamaran Properties
2174 South Milton Way
Federal Way, WA 94935

Dear Ms. Kilpatrick:

Re:  Apartment Rental Agreement

I have reviewed the draft of the Monthly Rental Agreement you sent
earlier this week.  As a whole, the Agreement looks fine.  There
are some changes, however, that should be made.  The second section
of the Agreement should include the following paragraphs:

1  Sublet:  Tenant agrees not to sublet said premises nor assign
   this agreement nor any part thereof without the prior written
   consent of Landlord.

2  Agreement:  The Tenant agrees to the following conditions:

   2.1  To keep said premises in a clean and sanitary condition;
   2.2  To properly use and operate all electrical, gas, heating,
        plumbing facilities, fixtures, and appliances;
   2.3  To not intentionally or negligently destroy, deface, or
        damage the premises, their appurtenances, facilities,
        equipment, furniture, furnishings and appliances.

3  Access:  Landlord shall have the right to place and maintain
   "For Rent" signs in a conspicuous place on said premises for
   thirty days prior to the vacation of said premises.  Landlord
   reserves the right of access to the premises for purposes of:

   3.1  Inspection;
   3.2  Repairs, alterations or improvements;
   3.3  To supply services; or

3.4   To exhibit or display the premises to prospective or actual purchasers, mortgagees, tenants, workers, or contractors.

I would like to see the following paragraphs added to the last section of the Agreement.  These paragraphs help to spell out specific information on security deposits, vacation of property, and responsibilities of both parties.

4   Security Deposit:  The Tenant agrees to deposit the sum of _____ dollars, receipt of which is hereby acknowledged. All or a portion of such deposit may be retained by Landlord and refund of any portion of such deposit is conditioned as follows:

4.1   Tenant shall fully perform obligations hereunder;
4.2   Tenant shall occupy said premises for _____ months or longer from date hereof;
4.3   Tenant shall surrender to Landlord the keys to premises.

5   Notice to Vacate:  Tenant shall give the Landlord twenty (20) days written notice of intention to vacate the premises. Landlord shall give twenty (20) days' notice to Tenant of intention to terminate the tenancy hereunder.

After you have reviewed these paragraphs, call me at the office number and let me know whether you want them added to the Agreement.  With luck, the Monthly Rental Agreement can be completed by next week.

Very truly yours,

MORENO, YAMADA, & SCHWARTZ

Anita M. Moreno
Attorney-at-Law

---

Figure 20-7: Exercise Five

**Exercise Six**
1.   Retrieve CH20EX5 to the screen and make the following changes:
    A. Move the cursor to the end of the first paragraph, **Sublet** and press Enter twice to create a blank line. Key in the paragraph shown in figure 20-8. (Use the Date/Outline command to create the paragraph number.)

2       Inspection of Premises:   Tenant agrees that he has made
        inspection of the premises and accepts the conditions of the
        premises in its present state, and that there are no repairs,
        changes, or modifications to said premises to be made.

**Figure 20-8: Exercise Six**

      B. Delete paragraphs 3.2 and 4.2.
      C. Move the cursor to the end of paragraph 5.3. Press Enter twice to create a blank line
         and key in the paragraph shown in figure 20-9. (Use the Date/Outline command to
         create the paragraph number.)

  2.  Save the document and name it CH20EX6.  Print CH20EX6.

6       Alterations:   Tenant agrees not to make alterations or do or
        cause to be done any painting or wallpapering to said premises
        without the prior written consent of Landlord.

**Figure 20-9: Exercise Six**

## PERFORMANCE ASSESSMENTS

**Assessment One**
  1.  At a clear screen, key in the outline shown in figure 20-10 using the outline feature. Set
     appropriate tabs to align the information correctly.
  2.  Save the outline and name it CH20PA1. Print CH20PA1.

I.    Computer Equipment

    A.   Monitor
    B.   Central Processing Unit
    C.   Disk Drive
       1.   Floppy drive
       2.   Hard drive
    D.   Keyboard
    E.   Printer
       1.   Dot matrix
       2.   Laser
       3.   Character
    F.   Mouse

II.   Loading Instructions

    A.   Hard drive
    B.   Floppy drive

III. Cursor Movement

    A.   Character
    B.   Word
    C.   Screen
    D.   Page

IV. Deletion

    A.   Character
        1.   Del
        2.   Backspace
    B.   Word
    C.   Line
    D.   Page

V. Margins

    A.   Default settings
    B.   Format: Line menu

VI. Tabs

    A.   Delete tabs
    B.   Set tabs
        1.   Left
        2.   Right
        3.   Decimal
        4.   Center
        5.   Preceding leaders

---

Figure 20-10: Assessment One

**Assessment Two**
1.   Retrieve CH20PA1 to the screen and make the following changes:
    A. Move the cursor to the blank line below **B. Floppy drive**. Press the Enter key and key in the text in figure 20-11.

---

III. Directory

    A.   Retrieve document
    B.   Print document

---

Figure 20-11: Assessment Two

    B. Delete the lines of text pertaining to margins.
2.   Save the revised outline and name it CH20PA2. Print CH20PA2.

**Assessment Three**

1.  At a clear screen, create the legal document shown in figure 20-12. Double-space the body of the document and use the legal style for paragraph numbering.
2.  Save the legal document and name it CH20PA3. Print CH20PA3.

---

## IN THE SUPERIOR COURT OF THE STATE OF WASHINGTON

## IN AND FOR KING COUNTY

```
In the Matter of the Estate of  )
                                )
      MOLLY A. KINGSTON,        )   NO.  2132-W
                                )
                    Deceased.   )   ORDER APPROVING FINAL ACCOUNT
                                )
_____ )
```

1    HEARING

1.1 <u>Date</u>.  April 2, 1993.

1.2 <u>Appearance</u>.  The executor-personal representative appeared personally and by attorney.

1.3 <u>Guardian ad Litem</u>.  Amanda M. Andersen, as guardian ad litem, appeared in person and filed her report, representing Molly A. Kingston.

1.4 <u>Purpose</u>.  The purpose of the hearing was to consider the final account and petition for distribution.

1.5 <u>Evidence</u>.  The final account and petition for distribution, the report of the guardian ad litem, if any, and all other documents and papers on file in this proceeding were considered.

2    FINDINGS

On the basis of the files and records, and the testimony of the witnesses, the Court finds:

2.1  <u>Death</u>.  The decedent died on April 2, 1993, was a resident of Lincoln County, Idaho, and left property in the state of Idaho subject to probate.

2.2  <u>Will</u>.  The decedent executed a Will which was admitted to probate.

2.3  <u>Ex PR</u>.  The person named in the Will qualified as Ex PR to serve without bond.

2.4  <u>Report of Guardian ad Litem</u>.  The report of the guardian ad litem should be approved.

2.5  <u>Creditors</u>.  Notice to creditors was filed and published as required by law.  The time for filing claims has expired.  All claims presented and filed have been allowed and paid.

2.6  <u>Taxes</u>.  All inheritance taxes due to the state of Idaho have been paid, and any federal estate tax has been paid.

3   DECREE OF DISTRIBUTION

3.1  <u>Final Account</u>.  The final account is approved.

3.2  <u>Discharge</u>.  When receipts are filed showing that all payments and distributions have been made, the Ex PR shall be discharged and the estate shall be closed.

DONE IN OPEN COURT this ____ day of _____, 1993.

_____
JUDGE

Presented and approved:

MORENO, YAMADA, & SCHWARTZ

By: _____
    James D. Schwartz
    Attorney for Ex PR

**Figure 20-12: Assessment Three**

**Assessment Four**

1. Retrieve CH20PA3 to the screen.
2. Move the cursor to the beginning of the line that reads **2.4 Report of Guardian ad Litem** and press the Enter key to insert a hard return. Move the cursor between the paragraphs and key in the text shown in figure 20-13.
3. Delete the paragraph **2.8 Taxes**.
4. Save the revised legal document and name it CH20PA4. Print CH20PA4.

---

2.4   <u>Notices</u>.   All notices have been given, as required by law, including the notice of this hearing.

2.5   <u>Assets</u>.   The assets remaining are as described in the annexed schedule with a total value of $85,000.00.

---

**Figure 20-13: Assessment Four**

# CHAPTER 21

## TEXT COLUMNS

## PERFORMANCE OBJECTIVES

Upon successful completion of Chapter 21, you will be able to create business documents, such as newsletters, with different column styles. You will also be able to adjust and manipulate columns you have created.

WordPerfect offers a text Columns feature that lets you create attractive documents containing columns of text. Two types of text columns can be created: newspaper-style and parallel. The Columns/Table command is used to identify the type of column and specify the number of columns. When you create either newspaper-style or parallel columns, you complete the following four steps:

1. Define the columns.
2. Turn on the column feature.
3. Key in the text.
4. Turn off the column feature.

You can turn text columns on and off as often as you like in a document. Text columns can fill the entire document or they may be contained in part of the document, on a partial page, or on several pages. You must define the columns only once. After that you can turn the Column feature on and off wherever you want in the document.

### CREATING NEWSPAPER-STYLE COLUMNS

Newspaper-style columns let you create text that flows up and down through columns. This feature is useful for creating documents such as newsletters, brochures, and pamphlets. When the first column of text is completed on the page, WordPerfect moves the cursor to the top of the page in the second column. Text flows from the bottom of one column to the top of the next column.  When the last column on a page is entered, WordPerfect inserts a page break and moves the cursor to the beginning of the first column on the next page.

To understand newspaper-style columns, let us look at an example. Suppose you want to create three newspaper-style columns that are separated by 0.25 inches. To create these columns, complete the following steps:

1. Move the cursor to the location where you want the columns to begin and access the Columns/Table command with Alt + F7.

2. At the prompt **1 Columns; 2 Tables; 3 Math: 0**, choose 1 or C for Columns.

3. At the **Columns** prompt, choose 3 or D for Define. The text on the screen disappears and is replaced with the Text Columns Definition menu shown in figure 21-1.
   **M** *Click on Layout, Columns, then Define.*

```
Text Column Definition

    1 - Type                         Newspaper

    2 - Number of Columns            2

    3 - Distance Between Columns

    4 - Margins

    Column   Left    Right    Column   Left    Right
      1:     1"      4"        13:
      2:     4.5"    7.5"      14:
      3:                       15:
      4:                       16:
      5:                       17:
      6:                       18:
      7:                       19:
      8:                       20:
      9:                       21:
     10:                       22:
     11:                       23:
     12:                       24:

Selection: 0
```

Figure 21-1: Text Column Definition Menu

The first selection from this menu, Type, lets you establish three types of columns—newspaper-style, parallel, and parallel with block protection. The default setting is Newspaper. Since Newspaper-style columns is the type of columns you want, leave it at the default setting.

The second selection, Number of Columns, has a default setting of 2. WordPerfect assumes that you want two columns down the page. To change this number to 3, choose 2 or N for Number of Columns, key in 3, then press Enter. (WordPerfect allows a minimum of two columns and a maximum of 24.)

By default, WordPerfect separates columns by 0.5 inches. To change this to 0.25 inches, choose 3 or D for Distance Between Columns, key in 0.25 and press Enter. When you change the distance, WordPerfect automatically changes the column margins.

The last selection, Margins, is used to establish your own margin settings. WordPerfect automatically sets margins for columns and spaces them evenly across the page. (If you want to create different settings, choose 4 or M for Margins. The cursor moves to the number after Column 1. Key in the number you desire over the WordPerfect number and press Enter. Continue in this manner until all settings have been entered.)

4.  When all change have been made to Text Column Definition menu, press F7.

5.  At the Columns prompt, choose 1 or O for On. WordPerfect removes the prompt and inserts a **[Col on]** code in the document and also a Column Define code that identifies the left and right margin settings for the columns. Both codes can be seen in Reveal Codes.

6.  With the column feature on, key in the text. Make sure that the cursor is located to the right of the **[Col on]** code in Reveal Codes. If the cursor is resting before the code, the Columns feature will not work.

7.  When all columnar text is entered, turn the Column feature off by accessing the Columns/Table command with Alt + F7, choose 1 or C for Columns, then 2 or F for Off.
    **M** *Click on Layout, Columns, then Off.*

The columns need to be defined only once. After that the Column feature can be turned on and off within a document as many times as necessary.

## CREATING PARALLEL COLUMNS

With parallel columns you can create text that moves horizontally across columns. Parallel columns can be used to create documents such as a script, itinerary, address list, or other text that is to be read horizontally.

Parallel columns are defined in a manner similar to newspaper-style columns. To create three parallel columns with 0.5 inches between columns, complete the following steps:

1.  Move the cursor to the location where you want the columns to begin and access the Columns/Table command with Alt + F7.

2.  At the prompt **1 Columns; 2 Tables; 3 Math: 0**, choose 1 or C for Columns.

3.  At the **Columns** prompt, choose 3 or D for Define.
    **M** *Click on Layout, Columns, then Define.*

4.  At the Text Column Definition menu, choose 1 or T for Type and the prompt **Column Type: 1 Newspaper; 2 Parallel; 3 Parallel with Block Protect: 0** appears at the bottom of the screen.

5.  Choose 2 or P for Parallel, or choose 3 or B for Parallel with Block Protect. The Parallel selection is used to establish parallel columns, and the Parallel with Block Protect selection is used to create parallel columns that will not be split by a page break. The block protect feature keeps WordPerfect from inserting a soft page break in the middle of the column entry.

6.  Press F7 to accept the default setting of the remaining selection.

7.  At the **Columns** prompt, choose 1 or O for On.

8.  Key in the columnar information.

9.  Turn off the column feature by accessing the Columns/Table command with Alt + F7, choose 1 or C for Columns, then 2 or F for Off.
    🅼 *Click on Layout, Columns, then Off.*

## Entering Text in Parallel Columns

The procedure for entering text in parallel columns is different from the procedure for entering text in newspaper-style columns. After a group of text is entered, a Hard Page command must be inserted in the document to tell WordPerfect to move to the next column. A Hard Page code is entered with Ctrl + Enter. End each columnar entry with this command.

To understand how parallel columns work, look at the itinerary shown in figure 21-2.

| | | |
|---|---|---|
| 9:00 - 10:00 a.m. | Meeting of marketing personnel to discuss new division | Alyssa Pisetzner, Marketing Director, Room 320 |
| 10:00 - 10:20 a.m. | Coffee break | Cafeteria, Room 200 |
| 10:20 - 12:00 p.m. | Seminar on new marketing techniques | Ricardo Jimenez, President, NEW Techniques, Inc., Room 104. |

**Figure 21-2: Itinerary**

After keying in the first columnar entry, the time, a Hard Page code must be inserted with Ctrl + Enter. This tells WordPerfect to end the first column and move to the second column.

At the second column, the information about the meeting is entered. Let word wrap end the lines. When all information for the meeting is keyed in, insert a Hard Page code with Ctrl + Enter.

The cursor moves to the beginning of the third column where the name and room number are keyed in. After keying in the text, press Ctrl + Enter to end the columnar entry. This moves the cursor to the first column one blank line below the columns above. Parallel columns are separated by a blank line. If you want more space separating columns, you can enter extra blank lines in the last column before pressing the Hard Page command.

## EDITING COLUMNAR TEXT

To edit text established in columns, use the cursor movement keys and commands. When moving the cursor in columnar text, you will be moving either within or between columns.

### Moving the Cursor Within Columns

When you move the cursor within columns, the cursor movement keys—up, down, left and right arrows—cause the cursor to move in the direction indicated. If you press the up or down arrow, the cursor moves up or down within the column. If the cursor is located on the last line of a column on a page, the down arrow will cause the cursor to move to the beginning of the same column on the next page. If the cursor is located on the beginning of a line of columnar text, pressing the Up arrow key will cause the cursor to move to the end of the same column on the previous page.

The Left and Right arrow keys move the cursor in the direction indicated within the column. When the cursor gets to the end of the line within the column, it moves down to the beginning of the next line within the same column.

### Moving the Cursor Between Columns

To move the cursor between columns, you must access the Go To command with Ctrl + Home (**M** *Click on Search, then Go To*). The information shown in figure 21-3 illustrates what is accomplished with the Go To command.

| | |
|---|---|
| **Go to, Right Arrow** | Moves cursor to the next column. |
| **Go to, Left Arrow** | Moves cursor to the previous column. |
| **Go to, Home, Left Arrow** | Moves cursor to the first column. |
| **Go to, Home, Right Arrow** | Moves cursor to the last column. |

**Figure 21-3: Cursor Movement Between Columns**

Deleting and inserting text is done in the same manner as in regular text. Special features such as boldfacing, underlining, and centering can also be used in columnar text. When text is centered, WordPerfect centers it between the left and right margins of the column, not on the page.

## COLUMN CONSIDERATIONS

Once you have defined columns in a document, you can turn the Column feature on and off as often as you like. This lets you have columns in several locations in the document.

You can also have several different column definitions in a document. To establish a new column setting, access the Columns/Table command and identify new columns.

### Retrieving Text Into Columns

Text can be retrieved into newspaper-style columns. Before retrieving the text, turn on the Column feature and define the columns. Make sure that the cursor is located after the **[Col on]** code before the text is retrieved.

Parallel columns are created with Hard Page codes identifying the column group. For this reason, text cannot be retrieved into parallel columns.

### Realigning Columns

Text that is established in columns can be redefined. If you decide, after creating columns, that you want more or less space between columns or you want the columns shortened or widened, you can redefine the columns. Access Reveal Codes and move the cursor to the right of the Column-Define code. Access the Columns/Table command and redefine the columns. Press the down arrow key to adjust the columns. After the columns are adjusted, access Reveal Codes and delete the original Column Define code.

### Blocking Columnar Text

The Block command can be used to block text in columns. The Block command operates the same way in columnar text as it does in regular text.

When blocking parallel columns with block protection, access Reveal Codes and make sure that the cursor is located on or before the **[Col On]** and **[Block Pro:On]** codes before accessing the Block command. If the Column On and Block Protect codes are not included in the block, the columns will not align correctly in the new location.

## CHAPTER REVIEW

### Summary

- With WordPerfect you can create two types of columns — newspaper-style and parallel.
- Text in newspaper-style columns flows up and down through columns. Parallel columns establish text in horizontal columns.
- When creating columns, you complete four steps: (1) define the columns, (2) turn on the Column feature, (3) key in the text, and 4) turn off the Column feature.
- When entering text in columns, make sure the cursor is located after the **[Col On]** code.
- By default WordPerfect establishes column margin settings. A minimum of 2 columns and a maximum of 24 can be defined.
- Once columns are defined, the Column feature can be turned on and off in a document as many times as necessary.
- After entering text in a parallel column, insert a Hard Page code with Ctrl + Enter to move the cursor to the next column. Parallel columns are separated horizontally by a blank line.
- The cursor movement keys move the cursor in the direction indicated within columns. Use the Go To command to move the cursor between columns.
- Text can be retrieved into newspaper-style columns but not parallel columns.
- Text in columns can be realigned by redefining the column definition.
- The Block command can be used to highlight text in columns. When blocking parallel columns, make sure the cursor is located on or before the Column On and Block Protect codes before accessing the Block command.

**Commands Review**

|  | **Keyboard** |
| --- | --- |
| Columns/Table command | Alt + F7 |
| Define columns | Alt + F7, 1 or C, 3 or D |
| Turn on columns | Alt + F7, 1 or C, 1 or O |
| Turn off columns | Alt + F7, 1 or C, 2 or F |
| Go To | Ctrl + Home |
| Move cursor to next column | Go To, right arrow |
| Move cursor to previous column | Go To, left arrow |
| Move cursor to first column | Go To, Home, left arrow |
| Move cursor to last column | Go To, Home, right arrow |
|  | **Mouse** |
| Define columns | Layout, Columns, Define |
| Turn on columns | Layout, Columns, On |
| Turn off columns | Layout, Columns, Off |
| Go To | Search, Go To |

## STUDY GUIDE FOR CHAPTER 21

**Completion:** In the space provided at the right, indicate the correct symbol, term, or number for the explanation.

1.    Access the Columns/Table command.                                          _____

2.    Move the cursor to next columm.                                            _____

3.    Move the cursor to first column.                                           _____

4.    Selection from the **Columns** prompt to define columns.                   _____

5.    Move the cursor to the previous column.                                    _____

6.    Selection from the **Columns** prompt to turn the column feature
      on and off.                                                                _____

7.    Maximum number of columns allowed by WordPerfect.                          _____

8.    Move the cursor to the last column.                                        _____

9.    After a group of text is entered in a parallel column, press this
      to tell WordPerfect to move to the next column.                            _____

**True/False:**  Circle the letter T if the statement is true; circle the letter F if the statement is false.

1.    Text in parallel columns flows up and down on the page.                              T       F

2.    The Column feature can be turned on and off as often as needed in documents.         T       F

3.    By default, WordPerfect automatically set margins for text columns at the Text       T       F
      Column Definition menu.

4.    Make sure the cursor is to the left of the **[Col On]** code before entering          T       F
      columnar text.

5.    WordPerfect allows a minimum of three columns.                                       T       F

6.    When newspaper-style columns are created, WordPerfect inserts Block Protect          T       F
      codes in the document.

7.    WordPerfect separates parallel columns horizontally by a blank line.                 T       F

8.    Access the Go To command to move the cursor within columns.                          T       F

9.    Centering, boldfacing, and underlining can be used in columnar text.                 T       F

10.   A document can contain only one column definition.                                   T       F

11.   Text can be retrieved into newspaper-style columns.                                  T       F

12.   Columnar text can be realigned by redefining the columns.                            T       F

## HANDS-ON EXERCISES

Change the default directory to UNIT5.

### Exercise One

1. At a clear screen, create the newsletter shown in figure 21-4 by completing the following steps:

    A. Change the base font to 18-point Helvetica. Capitalize and boldface the organization name, CENTRAL AREA PROGRAM. Access the Flush Right command and key in **NEWSLETTER**. (If your printer does not support Helvetica, use a sans serif typeface in 18 point. If your printer does not support a sans serif typeface, use the default typeface.)

    B. After keying in **NEWSLETTER**, change the base font to 10-point Helvetica, press Enter, then key in the line with Shift + hyphen key.

    C. Press Enter then key in **Vol. 3, No. 4**. Access the Flush Right command, then key in **Summer, 1993**.

    D. Press Enter twice, then change the base font to 12-point Courier (or use your default typeface). Boldface should be off.

    E. Define two newspaper-style columns by completing the following steps:

    1) Access the Columns/Table command with Alt + F7.
    2) At the prompt **1 Columns; 2 Tables; 3 Math: 0**, choose 1 or C for Columns.
    3) At the Columns prompt, choose 3 or D for Define.
       **M** *Click on Layout, Columns, then Define.*
    4) At the Text Column Definition menu, press F7.
    5) At the **Columns** prompt, choose 1 or O for On.

    F. Center and boldface the heading, **Basketball Champions**.

    G. Press Enter twice, then change the base font to 10-point Courier (or use your default typeface).

    H. Delete all previous tabs and set left tabs at +0.3 and +3.8 inch.

    I. Key in the remainder of the newsletter. Set the headings in 12-point Courier (or the default typeface) and the body text in 10-point Courier.

2. When the newsletter is complete, move the cursor to the beginning of the document. Change the left hyphenation zone to 6%, the right hyphenation zone to 2%, and turn on hyphenation. Move the cursor to the end of the document, making appropriate hyphenation decisions.

3. Save the newsletter and name it CH21EX1. Print CH21EX1.

## Basketball Champions

"We are winners!" say Jason Maraire and Dumi Jasper, team players for CAP Wildcats, the West Coast Regional Champions. This great WCA team of 13 and under boys won four games on Memorial Day weekend in Boise, Idaho. Head coach Ronald Preston was impressed with the confidence of the team as they "experienced a new environment and emerged as disciplined, strong young men."

CAP Magic, undefeated girls WCA team (ages 13-18) will compete in the WCA National Invitational Tournament in Tampa, Florida in August. Magic is coached by Jean Weston. Takiyah Johnson, one of the starting players, says "I'm looking forward to the trip. We have team unity and we'll do well in national competition."

CAP Mustangs, another WCA team, will also be in Tampa in August. This team of undefeated 11 year old boys is coached by Nick Adolphis. "We are great!" says guard Adolphis Moore. "My team practice makes me tough--my grades went up and I'm going to Florida with a number one team."

The CAP Bears, Pacific Northwest Regional Champions (16 year old boys), will travel to Dallas, Texas mid-August to compete in the National WCA Championships. Parent Coordinator Millie Jackson says, "This is our third appearance in the WCA Nationals and our youth have matured. I think we will win!"

Being winners takes hard work, plus a "winning" attitude and plenty of support from all of us. CAP Wildcat team member Seth Larson sums it all up by saying, "CAP makes me feel good about myself, and we are having fun as a team."

## A Tradition of Excellence

We are still doing a great tradition that is cited in the ancient folk song of Homer's *Odyssey*. The tradition is of "being a Mentor." In the epic legend, the man called Mentor, was friend and advisor to the hero Odysseus. When Odysseus went to fight in the Trojan War, he entrusted Mentor to educate his son Telemachus. Mentor was a wise, faithful counselor for the youth Telemachus. With the guidance of this strong role model, Telemachus matured, traveled, and faced up to the challenges of life.

Now the word mentor still means a wise, devoted advisor. Today we are proud of CAP mentors who have committed their time to the tradition of serving as career role models, friends and advisors of our youth. We commend our new mentors:

Telma Reitman, Northwest Bank
Jim Nather, Sea Corporation
Gerald Ijioma, Lyons Construction
Matthew White, Whitemore College

You can sign up now for CAP Mentorship Program. Please call Cathy Black at 555-2231 for more information. As a mentor, you can be part of a legend!

## Cheers to Miss CAP

We welcome you and your family to join us at the Emerald Fair events to cheer on our beautiful Miss CAP, Lanie Wong, as she competes for the title of Miss Emerald Fair 1993.

Gifted with talent and pizazz, Lanie Wong is a trained dancer who has performed with the Northwest Ballet's performance of the "Nutcracker" and in TV commercials. Winner of the Academic Achievement Award, she earned a 3.6 GPA at the University of Washington.

## Summer with CAP

During the summer, CAP offers a variety of support groups and activities for people of all ages.

Girls and women are welcome to attend CAP aerobics class on Saturdays from 9:00 a.m. to 11:00 a.m. at CAP.

If you are interested in coaching football, soccer, or baseball, please call CAP at 555-2231

The CAP Teen Parenting Housing Program will conduct support group meetings and field trips for participants all during the summer, especially during the month of August.

Figure 21-4: Exercise One

**Exercise Two**

1. Retrieve CH21EX1.

2. Access Reveal Codes and move the cursor one position to the right of the Column Definition code. Access the Text Column Definition menu and change the definition to two newspaper-style columns that are 0.3 inch apart. (Let WordPerfect establish the column margins for you.)

3. Move the cursor to the end of the document to allow columns to adjust. Make hyphenation decisions. Move the cursor to the beginning of the document, access Reveal Codes, and delete the Column Definition code that you created in Exercise One.

4. Save the newsletter and name it CH21EX2. Print CH21EX2.

**Exercise Three**

1. At a clear screen, create the directory shown in figure 21-5 by completing the following steps:

   A. Change the base font to 10-point Courier.

   B. Change the justification to Left.

   C. Key in the heading **PUGET SOUND SEMICONDUCTOR**, boldfaced, capitalized and centered.

   D. Double-space, then key in the subheading, **Directory**, boldfaced and centered.

   E. Triple-space after the subheading and create three parallel columns that are 0.5 inch apart by completing the following steps:

      1) Access the Columns/Table command with Alt + F7.

      2) At the prompt **1 Columns; 2 Tables; 3 Math: 0** , choose 1 or C for Columns.

      3) At the **Columns** prompt, choose 3 or D for Define.
      **M** *Click on Layout, Columns, then Define.*

      4) At the Text Column Definition menu, choose 1 or T for Type and the prompt **Column Type: 1 Newspaper; 2 Parallel; 3 Parallel with Block Protect: 0** appears at the bottom of the screen.

      5) Choose 2 or P for Parallel.

      6) Choose 2 or N for Number of Columns; key in **3**, then press Enter.

      7) Press F7 to accept the default setting of the remaining selections.

      8) At the **Columns** prompt, choose 1 or O for On.

   F. Key in the columnar information as shown in figure 21-5. Use the Hard Page command, Ctrl + Enter, to end each columnar entry.

   G. When all the information is keyed in, turn off the column feature by accessing the Columns/Table command with Alt + F7, choosing 1 or C for Columns, then 2 or F for Off.
   **M** *Click on Layout, Columns, then Off.*

2. Save the directory and name it CH21EX3. Print CH21EX3.

**PUGET SOUND SEMICONDUCTOR**

**Directory**

| | | |
|---|---|---|
| Pat Serosky, President | Corporate Headquarters<br>1900 State Street<br>Tacoma, WA 98402 | (206) 555-2500<br>Extension 1 |
| Kim Chun, Vice<br>President, Operations | Corporate Headquarters<br>1900 State Street<br>Tacoma, WA 98402 | (206) 555-2500<br>Extension 12 |
| Terry Preston, Vice<br>President, Support<br>Services | Corporate Headquarters<br>1900 State Street<br>Tacoma, WA 98402 | (206) 555-2500<br>Extension 17 |
| Heidi Schueler,<br>Director of Sales | Sales Division<br>230 Miller Avenue<br>Fife, WA 98522 | (206) 555-2500<br>Extension 32 |
| Janet Weiss, Director<br>of Personnel | Sales Division<br>230 Miller Avenue<br>Fife, WA 98522 | (206) 555-2500<br>Extension 43 |
| Victoria Palmas,<br>Director of Finances | Sales Division<br>230 Miller Avenue<br>Fife, WA 98522 | (206) 555-2500<br>Extension 51 |
| Brad Majors, Director<br>of Facilities<br>Management | Corporate Headquarters<br>1900 State Street<br>Tacoma, WA 98402 | (206) 555-2500<br>Extension 28 |
| William Holley,<br>Director of Research<br>and Development | Corporate Headquarters<br>1900 State Street<br>Tacoma, WA 98402 | (206) 555-2500<br>Extension 37 |
| John White Cloud,<br>Personnel Manager | Sales Division<br>230 Miller Avenue<br>Fife, WA 98522 | (206) 555-2500<br>Extension 67 |
| Darlene Evans,<br>Benefits Manager | Corporate Headquarters<br>1900 State Street<br>Tacoma, WA 98402 | (206) 555-2500<br>Extension 40 |
| Maria Valdez,<br>Recruitment<br>Coordinator | Sales Division<br>230 Miller Avenue<br>Fife, WA 98522 | (206) 555-2500<br>Extension 55 |
| Brett Weinstein,<br>Compensations<br>Specialist | Corporate Headquarters<br>1900 State Street<br>Tacoma, WA 98402 | (206) 555-2500<br>Extension 84 |

Figure 21-5: Exercise Three

## Exercise Four

1. Retrieve CH21EX3 to the screen.
2. Move the three columns pertaining to Victoria Palmas between Terry Preston and Heidi Schuler by completing the following steps:
   A. Move the cursor to the **V** in **Victoria**. Access Reveal Codes and move the cursor so it is located on the **[Block Pro;On]** code.
   B. Turn on the Block command and block the three columns pertaining to Victoria Palmas.
   C. Access the Move command with Ctrl + F4, choose 1 or B for Block, then 1 or M for Move.
      **M** *Click on Edit, then Move.*
   D. Move the cursor to the **H** in **Heidi**. (Access Reveal Codes and make sure the cursor is located on the **[Block Pro;On]** code.)
   E. Press Enter to retrieve the columns in the new location.
3. Block the columns for Darlene Evans and delete them from the directory.
4. Save the directory and name it CH21EX4. Print CH21EX4.

## Exercise Five

1. Display the directory. Copy CH07EX5 and name it CH21EX5.
2. Retrieve CH21EX5 to the screen.
3. Move the cursor to the beginning of the first paragraph and create two newspaper-style columns by completing the following steps:
   A. Access the Columns/Table command with Alt + F7.
   B. Choose 1 or C for Columns.
   C. Choose 3 or D for Define.
      **M** *Click on Layout, Columns, then Define.*
   D. At the Text Column Definition menu, press F7.
   E. At the **Columns** prompt, choose 1 or O for On.
   F. Move the cursor to the end of the document to adjust the text.
   G. With the cursor at the end of the document, turn off the Column feature by completing the following steps:
      (1) Access the Columns/Table command with Alt + F7.
      (2) Choose 1 or C for Columns.
      (3) Choose 2 or F for Off.
4. Move the cursor to the beginning of the document. Change the left hyphenation zone to 5% and the right hyphenation zone to 3% and turn on hyphenation. Move the cursor to the end of the document and make appropriate hyphenation decisions.
5. Save the document with the name CH21EX5. Print page 1 of CH21EX5.

## PERFORMANCE ASSESSMENTS

**Assessment One**

1.  Display the directory. Copy CH07EX1 and name it CH21PA1.
2.  Retrieve CH21PA1 to the screen and make the following changes:
    A.  Delete the **[Ln Spacing:2]** code.
    B.  Move the cursor to the left margin of the first heading (THE WAR ON POVERTY YEARS: 1964-1969) and change the base font to 10-point Courier.
    C.  Delete all previous tabs and set left tabs at +0.2 and +3.6.
    D.  Move the cursor through the document and delete the Indent code (**[->Indent]**) before each indented paragraph and insert a Tab code instead.
    D.  Move the cursor back to the left margin of the first heading and create two news-paper-style columns with 0.3 inch between. (Let WordPerfect establish the margin settings.)
    E.  Move the cursor to the end of the document to adjust the text into columns.
    F.  Move the cursor to the beginning of the document. Change the left hyphenation zone to 5% and the right to 2% and turn on hyphenation. Move the cursor to the end of the document and make appropriate hyphenation decisions.
3.  Save the document with the name CH21PA1. Print page 1 of CH21PA1.

**Assessment Two**

1.  At a clear screen, create the agenda shown in figure 21-6. Change the justification to Left. Boldface and center the text as indicated. With the cursor a triple space below Agenda, create two parallel columns with the following margins:
    Column 1: Left = 1", Right = 3.5"
    Column 2: Left = 4", Right = 7.5"
2.  Save the agenda and name it CH21PA2. Print CH21PA2.

**PUGET SOUND SEMICONDUCTOR**
Directors' Meeting
March 14, 1993

**AGENDA**

| Time | Activity and Location |
|------|------------------------|
| 8:00 a.m. - 8:15 a.m. | Welcome and refreshments, cafeteria, main level |
| 8:15 a.m. - 8:30 a.m. | Adoption of minutes from February 10, 1993, meeting, conference room number 3 |
| 8:30 a.m. - 9:30 a.m. | Directors' reports, conference room number 3 |
| 9:30 a.m. - 10:30 a.m. | Report on old business, conference room number 3 |
| 10:30 a.m. - 10:45 a.m. | Break, cafeteria, main level |
| 10:45 a.m. - 12:00 noon | Sales Department, video presentation, room 225 |
| 12:00 noon - 1:00 p.m. | New business, conference room number 3 |
| 1:00 p.m. | Adjournment, conference room number 3 |

**Figure 21-6: Assessment Two**

# CHAPTER 22

## PERFORMANCE OBJECTIVE

Upon successful completion of chapter 22, you will be able to add figures and text boxes to business documents, such as seminar announcements; and to edit them for style.

### GRAPHICS

With WordPerfect's Graphics feature, clip art images provided by WordPerfect Corporation or created with a graphics program can be inserted into a box. With the Graphics feature, you can create four different box types. Into these boxes you can insert graphic images or text or you can leave the box empty. If you insert one of the box types in a document containing text, the text will flow around the box. You can also create horizontal and vertical lines on pages.

To fully utilize the Graphics feature, a graphics card should be installed in your computer. If you do not have a graphics card, you can still create graphics, but you will be able to see only a rough picture of the image on the screen. To be able to print graphics, you need a printer that supports graphics. Check your printer manual to determine whether it is capable of printing graphic images.

The Graphics feature operates more smoothly with a hard-drive system. If you are using a floppy-drive system, you may be limited in the graphics functions you can perform. Also you will need to move disks in and out of disk drives.

When you purchase WordPerfect, you receive several disks. One of these disks is labeled Fonts/Graphics and contains several predesigned graphic images. (If you are using WordPerfect on a hard-drive or network system, the graphic images should be located in the WP51 directory.) You will be using some of these predesigned pictures in this chapter and the next. Graphic images can also be brought in from other programs. Check the WordPerfect reference manual to determine what programs are compatible with the Graphics feature.

## CREATING BOXES IN WORDPERFECT

In WordPerfect, four types of boxes can be created to enclose graphics or text, including boxes for figures, tables, text, and user instructions. The method for creating and editing all four boxes is very similar. Use a figure box for graphic images, charts and diagrams; a table box for statistical data, maps, and tables of numbers; a text box for quotes or other special text to be set off; and a user box for specific needs not addressed by the first three.

WordPerfect includes the four box types so that separate lists can be generated with the Mark Text command. In a long document containing figure, table, text, or user boxes, a list can be generated for each type of box. To create a box, complete the following steps:

1. Access the Graphics command with Alt + F9 and choose 1 or F for a figure box, 2 or T for a table box, 3 or B for a text box, or 4 or U for a user box.

2. After choosing the type of box, choose 1 or C for Create.
   **M** *Click on Graphics, Figure, Table Box, Text Box, or User Box, then Create.*

3. The menu in figure 22-1 is displayed on the screen (the menu name varies according to the type of box).

4. Make changes as needed to the menu, then press F7 to return the cursor to the document, and insert the box.

```
Definition: Figure

     1 - Filename

     2 - Contents            Empty

     3 - Caption

     4 - Anchor Type         Paragraph

     5 - Vertical Position   0"

     6 - Horizontal Position Right

     7 - Size                3.25" wide x 3.25" (high)

     8 - Wrap Text Around Box Yes

     9 - Edit




  Selection: 0
```

Figure 22-1: Definition: Figure Menu

The selections available on the Definition: Figure menu are described below.

### Filename

When creating a figure, table, text, or user box, enter a file name to indicate what will be set in the box. This file name can be the name of a document that contains text or it may be the name of a graphics file.

## Contents

The Contents selection identifies what is contained in the box. If a graphic file is inserted, the message after **Contents** is **Graphic**; if text is inserted, the message is **Text**.

## Caption

The Caption selection is used to create a caption for the box and is optional. If you create a caption, it will print below the box and outside the border for figure, text, and user boxes and above the box and outside the border for table boxes.

When you select Caption, the menu is removed from the screen and is replaced by a clear screen. At this screen, key in the caption you want, then press F7.

## Anchor Type

The Anchor Type selection has a default setting of Paragraph. This setting indicates that the box will move with the paragraph surrounding it. This setting can be changed to Page or Character. At the Page setting, the box will remain at a fixed location on the page; at the Character setting, it will be treated as part of the text on a line.

In many situations, the Paragraph setting is appropriate because you want the box to stay with the paragraph to which it refers. In other situations, such as a newsletter, banner, or mailer, you may want the box fixed at a particular location on the page and not tied to a specific paragraph.

To change the Anchor Type setting, choose 4 or T for Anchor Type and the prompt **Type: 1 Paragraph; 2 Page; 3 Character: 0** appears at the bottom of the screen.

Choose the anchor type you want, and WordPerfect will change the setting. When you change to either Page or Character, the default settings for the vertical and horizontal position are changed. If the Anchor Type is changed to Page, the image must be set on the first page of the document, then Word-Perfect asks for the number of pages to be skipped. This prompt lets you specify on what page the box is to appear. If you want the box to print on page 4, key in 3 when prompted for the number of pages to skip. If you want the image to print on the first page of the document, press Enter to accept the default of zero.

## Vertical Position

The vertical position of the box varies according to the anchor type selected. At the Paragraph Anchor Type setting, the vertical position indicates the offset measurement from the first line of the paragraph. With a vertical position setting of 0", the top of the figure aligns with the first line of the paragraph. Enter higher numbers to move the figure down, relative to the paragraph.

If the Anchor Type is changed to Page, the box can be aligned with the top or bottom of the page, or centered on the page. You can also enter your own offset measurement from the top of the page or identify the box as full page. With the full-page vertical position, the box fills the entire page within the margins.

If the Anchor Type is changed to Character, the figure can be aligned with the top, middle, or bottom of the text on the line.

## Horizontal Position

The horizontal position of the box varies according to the Anchor Type selected. At the Paragraph Anchor Type setting, the box can be aligned at the left or right, or it can be centered within the paragraph. You can also choose to have the box fill the paragraph area from left to right.

If the Anchor Type is changed to Page, the box can be aligned at margins, columns, or at a set position. The Margin setting lets you align the box at the left or right margin, or fill the page from the left to the right margin. The Columns setting lets you align the box with the left, right, or center of one or more columns. To use this feature, enter the column number or numbers, then select how you want to align the box with those columns. The Set Position setting lets you enter an offset measurement from the left edge of the page.

If the Box Anchor Type is changed to Character, you cannot enter a horizontal position. The box will be located after the character to its left.

## Size

The Size selection establishes the height and width of the box. When you select Size, the prompt **1 Set Width/Auto Height; 2 Set Height/Auto Width; 3 Set Both; 4 Auto Both: 0** appears at the bottom of the screen. The first selection, **Set Width/Auto Height**, lets you set the width, and the height is automatically determined to preserve the original dimensions of the image. The second selection, **Set Height/Auto Width**, lets you set the height, and the width is automatically determined. The third selection, **Set Both**, lets you set the width and the height with no automatic settings. The last selection, **Auto Both**, sets the width and height of the box according to the default dimensions.

## Wrap Text Around Box

The default setting for the selection Wrap Text Around Box is Yes. At this setting, WordPerfect flows text around the box. This setting can be changed to No, which causes WordPerfect to ignore the box and continue printing text from margin to margin.

## Edit

If you choose **Edit** for a graphic image, you can rotate, scale, and move a graphic image in a figure box. When you choose 9 or E, the menu is replaced by the graphic image (if you inserted one in the figure and you have a graphics card installed in your computer). A list of selections appears at the bottom of the screen, letting you customize the image. If you choose Edit for a table, text, or user box, you can key in new text or change existing text within the box.

## INSERTING GRAPHIC IMAGES IN A BOX

To insert a graphic image in a WordPerfect document, move the cursor to the location where the image is to appear if the anchor type is Paragraph or Character. If the anchor type is Page, move the cursor to the beginning of the document. To insert the image in the document, complete the following steps:

1. Access the Graphics command with Alt + F9.
2. Choose 1 or F for Figure.
3. Choose 1 or C for Create.
   **M** *Click on Graphics, Figure, then Create.*
4. Choose 1 or F for Filename. (If necessary, you can press F5 and Enter to see the directory.)
5. Key in the name of the graphics file and press Enter.
6. Change any of the other selections to customize the image or the box around the image.
7. Press F7 to return the cursor to the document.

When a graphic image is inserted in a figure box, the image can be edited with the Edit selection from the Definition: Figure menu. For example, to edit the BALLOONS.WPG graphic image, complete the following steps:

1. Access the Graphics command with Alt + F9.
2. Choose 1 or F for Figure.
3. Choose 1 or C for Create.
   **M** *Click on Graphics, Figure, then Create.*
4. Choose 1 or F for Filename.
5. Key in **BALLOONS.WPG** and press Enter.
6. Choose 9 or E for Edit, and the image of the balloons appears on the screen as shown in figure 22-2.

Figure 22-2: Graphic Image

The arrow keys — up, down, left, and right — let you move the graphic image in the box. The arrow keys move the image in the direction indicated on the key. The **10%** in the lower right corner of the screen is the default percentage of change. If you press the up arrow one time, the image moves up approximately 10 percent of the screen depth.

Page Up and Page Down keys scale the image either larger or smaller. Each time you press the Page Up or Page Down key, the image is scaled by 10 percent. The plus and minus keys let you rotate the image. Again, the rotation is 10 percent each time one of the keys is pressed.

The Ins key can be used to change the percentage of change from the default setting of 10% to 1%, 5%, or 25%. As you press Ins, the number in the right corner of the screen changes.

The last selection from the top line of prompts is Go to. The Go to command, Ctrl + Home, causes the image to return to its original size.

The prompts that display in the last line on the screen let you move, scale, rotate, or invert the picture. If you choose 1 or M for Move, you are asked for a horizontal and vertical position. Enter a positive number to move the image up or to the right. Enter a negative number to move the image down or to the left.

The second selection from the last line at the bottom of the screen is Scale. WordPerfect automatically scales the image based on the space available in the box. With the Scale selection you can change the amount of scaling for the x axis, which is horizontal, and for the y axis, which is vertical. The normal scaling is 100 percent. If you change the x axis to a smaller number, the image appears thinner. If you change the x axis to a higher number, the image appears wider. At the y axis, a smaller number makes the image appear shorter, and a higher number makes the image appear taller.

The third selection, Rotate, lets you enter a number of degrees for rotating the image. For example, if you wanted to turn an image upside down, you would enter 180 (for 180 degrees). After you enter a number of degree for rotation, WordPerfect asks you if you want a mirror image. Key in a Y for Yes or an N for No. A mirrored image changes the dots in an image so they display from right to left rather than from left to right. For example, if you had an image of an airplane displayed with the airplane facing left, selecting a mirrored image would cause the airplane to face right.

The Invert selection lets you change each color in the image to its complementary colors. For example, white is replaced with black, black with white, green with red, red with green, and so on. Most printers are not capable of printing images in color. Inverting gives the appearance of a negative image.

The last selection, Black & White, lets you print and display an image in black and white.

When a graphic image is inserted in a document, only the figure box displays on the screen. The lines of the figure box appear on the screen as text, or hard returns are entered. The number of the figure box appears in the upper left corner of the box. Use View Document to see how the image appears in the figure box. Access View Document with Shift + F7 (**M** *Click on File, then Print*), then choose 6 or V for View.


### Figure Example

To better understand the Graphics feature, the steps to insert the balloons graphic file that has a horizontal position of Full and is 2 inches wide and 3 inches high in a document are described below:

    1.    Retrieve to the screen the document where the balloon image is to be inserted.

2.  Move the cursor to the beginning of the paragraph where you want the balloons to appear.

3.  Access the Graphics command with Alt + F9. (On a floppy-drive system, take your work disk out of Drive B and insert the Fonts/Graphics disk and then access the Graphics command.)

4.  Choose 1 or F for Figure.

5.  Choose 1 or C for Create.
    **M** *Click on Graphics, Figure, then Create.*

6.  At the Definition: Figure menu, choose 1 or F for Filename.

7.  Key in **BALLOONS.WPG** and press Enter. (You may have to identify the directory where the image is located. If you are using a floppy-drive system, key in **B:BALLOON.WPG** and then press Enter.)

8.  At the Definition: Figure menu, choose 6 or H for Horizontal Position. Then choose 4 or F for Full.

9.  At the Definition: Figure menu, choose 7 or S for Size, then 3 or B for Both. At the **Width** = prompt, key in **2** and press Enter. At the **Height** = prompt, key in **3** and press Enter.

10. Leave all other settings at the default. Press F7 to return the cursor to the document. (On a floppy-drive system, take the Fonts/Graphics disk out of Drive B and insert your work disk, then press Exit, F7.)

## CREATING A TABLE OR TEXT BOX

Creating a table or box is similar to creating a figure. The only difference is the type of box you select at the Graphics command prompt. WordPerfect numbers tables with Roman numerals and text boxes with Arabic numbers. For example, the first table is named "Table I" and the first text box is labeled "1" (without the quotations marks).

If you want to create a box that contains text, there are two methods for inserting the text. With the first method, create the text at a clear screen and then save it as you would any other document. At the document where you want the text box inserted, complete the following steps:

1.  Access the Graphics command with Alt + F9, then choose the type of box you want.
    **M** *Click on Graphics, then Figure, Table Box, Text Box, or User Box, then Create.*

2.  At the Definition menu, choose 1 or F for Filename, key in the name you gave the document containing text, then press Enter. This retrieves the document into the box.

3.  Press F7 to return the cursor to the document.

The other method is to access the Graphics command with Alt + F9, choose the type of box desired, then choose 9 or E for Edit at the Definition menu. Because a file name has not been identified, WordPerfect takes you to an editing screen where you can key in text. Press F7 twice to return the cursor to the document.

## EDITING A BOX

A box that has been created in a document can be edited. To make changes, retrieve the document containing the box and complete the following steps:

1. Access the Graphics command with Alt + F9.

2. From the prompt that displays at the bottom of the screen, identify the box that you want to edit—figure, table, text box, or user box—then choose 2 or E for Edit.
**M** *Click on Graphics, then Figure, Table Box, Text Box, or User Box, then Edit.*

3. WordPerfect asks which box you want to edit and displays a number. If the number displayed is the number of the box you want to edit, press Enter. If you want to edit a different box number, key in the new number, then press Enter.

4. WordPerfect searches through the document, finds the box that corresponds with the number, and retrieves the Definition menu to the screen. After changes have been made to this menu, press F7 to return the cursor to the document.

## CHANGING A BOX NUMBER

When a box such as a figure or table is created, WordPerfect automatically numbers the boxes, beginning with 1. If you want a box to have a different number than the default, complete the following steps:

1. Access the Graphics command with Alt + F9, then choose the type of box you created (figure, table, text box, or user box).
**M** *Click on Graphics, then Figure, Table Box, Text Box, or User Box, then New Number.*

2. Choose 3 or N for New Number.

3. Key in the new box number and press Enter.

## VIEW DOCUMENT

The View Document selection from the Print command is very useful in documents containing boxes. With View Document you can see how the document will appear before it is printed. View a document to determine whether the figure, table, or text box appears in the correct location and whether or not the text flows correctly around the box.

## CHAPTER REVIEW

**Summary**

- WordPerfect's Graphics feature can be used to create figure boxes, table boxes, text boxes, and user boxes. Use figure boxes for graphic images, charts, and diagrams; table boxes for statistical data, maps, and tables of numbers; text boxes for quotes or other special text to be set off; and user boxes for specific needs not addressed by the first three.

- When you access the Graphics command and identify the type of box, you can create a box, edit a box, or establish a new number for the box.

- When a box is created, the Definition menu displays with the following nine selections:

1 **Filename** — Enter the name of the document to be created in the box.

2 **Contents** — Identifies what is contained in the box.

3 **Caption** — Include a title or description of the box.

4 **Anchor Type** — Default setting is Paragraph, which attaches the box to a particular paragraph. This can be changed to Page or Character.

5 **Vertical Position** — Displays the vertical position, in inches, of the box in relation to the Anchor Type that is selected. The default setting is 0", which means that the box will align with the first line of the paragraph where it was created.

6 **Horizontal Position** — Displays the horizontal position of the box in relation to the Anchor Type that is selected. The default setting is Right, which inserts a box at the right margin of the paragraph.

7 **Size** — Displays the width and height of the box.

8 **Wrap Text Around Box** — At the default setting Yes, text flows around the box.

9 **Edit** — Move, scale, rotate, or invert a graphic image.

- WordPerfect numbers figures with Arabic numbers and tables with Roman numerals.

- To insert text in a box, either key in the name of a document containing text at the **Filename** prompt from the Definition menu, or choose 9 or E for Edit, then key in the text.

- To edit a figure, table box, text box, or user box, access the Graphics command, identify the type of box, then choose 2 or E for Edit.

- To create a new number for a box, access the Graphics command, identify the type of box, and choose 3 or N for Number. Key in the new number and press Enter.

- Use View Document to see how the document will appear when printed. This lets you determine whether the box is located in the correct position and whether text flows properly around boxes.

## Commands Review

|  | **Keyboard** | **Mouse** |
|---|---|---|
| Graphics Command | Alt + F9 | Graphics |
| View Document | Shift + F7, 6 or V | File, Print, 6 or V |

## STUDY GUIDE FOR CHAPTER 22

List the steps necessary to create a figure box in a document attached to the second paragraph that contains the graphics file CHECK.WPG and changes the graphics image to 1 inch wide and 2 inches high.

_____

_____

_____

_____

_____

Name the four types of boxes that can be created with the Graphics command.

1. _____

2. _____

3. _____

4. _____

**Completion:** In the space provided at the right, indicate the correct term, symbol, or command for the explanation.

1. Access the Graphics command.                                        _____

2. Selection from the Graphics command to create a table.              _____

3. The default Anchor Type setting at the Definition menu.             _____

4. At the Edit menu, this command resets the graphic image back        _____
   to its original size and scale.

5. At the Edit menu, these two keys scales the image.                   _____

6. At the Edit menu, these two keys rotates the image.                  _____

**True/False:** Circle the letter T if the statement is true; circle the letter F if the statement is false.

1. WordPerfect numbers tables with Arabic numbers.                              T      F

2. Five types of boxes can be created with the Graphics command.               T      F

3. Boxes can be edited.                                                          T      F

4. By default, text flows around a box created in a document.                   T      F

5. At the Edit menu, you can invert a graphic image.                            T      F

6. After all changes have been made to the Definition menu, press Exit, F7, to  T      F
   return to the document.

## HANDS-ON EXERCISES

### Exercise One

1. At a clear screen, create a figure box that includes the graphic image BUTTRFLY.WPG, with a horizontal position of Full by completing the following steps:
   A. Access the Graphics command with Alt + F9.
   B. Choose 1 or F for Figure.
   C. Choose 1 or C for Create.
      **M** *Click on Graphics, Figure, then Create.*
   D. Choose 1 or F for Filename.
   E. At the **Filename:** prompt, key in **BUTTRFLY.WPG** and press Enter. (You may need to enter the directory path or the disk drive. Check with your instructor.)
   F. Choose 6 or H for Horizontal Position.
   G. From the prompts that display at the bottom of the screen, choose 4 or F for Full.
   H. Press F7.
2. Save the document and name it CH22EX1. Print CH22EX1.

### Exercise Two

1. Retrieve CH05EX5 to the screen.
2. Block the columns in the memorandum. (Be sure to include the tab set code.)
3. With the columns blocked, access the Save command with F10 (**M** *Click on File, then Save*), key in **TABLE**, and press Enter.
4. Exit CH05EX5 without saving it.
5. At a clear screen, create a table box with a horizontal position of Full that contains the document Table by completing the following steps:
   A. Access the Graphics command with Alt + F9.
   B. Choose 2 or T for Table.
   C. Choose 1 or C for Create.
      **M** *Click on Graphics, Table Box, then Create.*
   D. Choose 1 or F for Filename.
   E. At the **Filename:** prompt, key in **TABLE** and press Enter.
   F. Choose 6 or H for Horizontal Position.
   G. From the prompts that display at the bottom of the screen, choose 4 or F for Full.
   H. Press F7.
6. Save the table and name it CH22EX2. Print CH22EX2.

### Exercise Three

1. At a clear screen, create a text box that contains the document CH02EX2, has an anchor type of Page, a vertical position of Center, and a horizontal position of Margins, Center by completing the following steps:
   A. Access the Graphics command with Alt + F9.
   B. Choose 3 or B for Text Box.
   C. Choose 1 or C for Create.
      **M** *Click on Graphics, Text Box, then Create.*
   D. Choose 1 or F for Filename.
   E. At the **Filename:** prompt, key in **CH02EX2** and press Enter.
   F. Choose 4 or T for Anchor Type. At the prompt, choose 2 or A for Page. At the **Number of pages to skip** prompt, press Enter.
   G. Choose 5 or V for Vertical Position. From the prompts that display at the bottom of the screen, choose 3 or C for Center.

H. Choose 6 or H for Horizontal Position. From the prompts that display at the bottom of the screen, choose 1 or M for Margins, then 3 or C for Center.
I. Press F7.
2. Save the document and name it CH22EX3. Print CH22EX3.

## Exercise Four

1. Retrieve CH22EX1 to the screen.
2. Rotate and scale the butterfly image by completing the following steps:
A. Access the Graphics command with Alt + F9.
B. Choose 1 or F for Figure.
C. Choose 2 or E for Edit.
   **M** *Click on Graphics, Figure, then Edit.*
D. At the **Figure number?** prompt, key in a **1** and press Enter.
E. With the Definition: Figure menu displayed on the screen, choose 9 or E for Edit.
F. At the edit screen, press Page Dn four times to scale the butterfly smaller.
G. Press the Plus key twice to rotate the butterfly to the right.
H. Press F7 to return the cursor to the Definition: Figure menu.
I. Press F7 to return the cursor to the document.
2. Save the document and name it CH22EX4. Print CH22EX4.

## Exercise Five

1. Retrieve CH22EX2 to the screen. Include the caption, Net Profits, by completing the following steps:
A. Access the Graphics command with Alt + F9.
B. Choose 2 or T for Table Box.
C. Choose 2 or E for Edit.
   **M** *Click on Graphics, Table Box, then Edit.*
D. At the **Table Box number?** prompt, key in a **1** and press Enter.
E. With the Definition: Table Box menu displayed on the screen, choose 3 or C for Caption.
F. At the caption screen, key in a colon (:), then press the space bar twice. Key in **Net Profits.**
G. Press F7 to return the cursor to the Definition: Table Box menu.
H. Press F7 to return the cursor to the document.
2. Save the document and name it CH22EX5. Print CH22EX5.

## Exercise Six

1. At a clear screen, create the sign shown in figure 22-3 by completing the following steps:
A. Change the base font to 18-point Helvetica Bold (or a sans serif typeface if your printer does not support Helvetica).
B. Key in the workshop heading as indicated in figure 22-3.
C. With the cursor a double space below the heading, create the arrow image by completing the following steps:
   (1) Access the Graphics command with Alt + F9.
   (2) Choose 1 or F for Figure.
   (3) Choose 1 or C for Create.
       **M** *Click on Graphics, Figure, then Create.*
   (4) Choose 1 or F for Filename.
   (5) At the **Filename:** prompt, key in **ARROW-22.WPG** and press Enter. (You may need to enter the directory path or the disk drive. Check with your instructor.)

       (6)  Choose 6 or H for Horizontal Position.

       (7)  From the prompts that display at the bottom of the screen, choose 3 or C for Center.

       (8)  Press F7.

    D.  Press Enter enough times to move the cursor below the figure box, then key in the workshop times below the arrow.

  2.    Save the document and name it CH22EX6. Print CH22EX6.

---

# FUNDAMENTALS OF DESKTOP PUBLISHING
# WORKSHOP

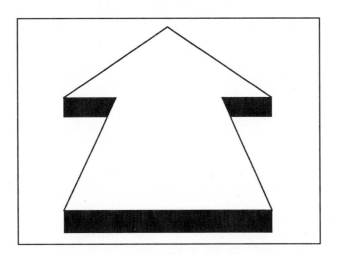

# 1:00 p.m. to 5:00 p.m.
# Room 130

---

Figure 22-3: Exercise Six

**Exercise Seven**

  1.    Retrieve CH22EX6 to the screen.

  2.    Edit the arrow and make it point to the right by completing the following steps:

    A.  Access the Graphics command with Alt + F9.

    B.  Choose 1 or F for Figure.

    C.  Choose 2 or E for Edit.

       **M** *Click on Graphics, Figure, then Edit.*

    D.  At the **Figure number?** prompt, key in a **1** and press Enter.

    E.  With the Definition: Figure menu displayed on the screen, choose 9 or E for Edit.

    F.  At the edit screen, rotate the arrow 90 degrees by completing the following steps:

       (1)  Choose 3 or R for Rotate.

       (2)  At the **Enter number of degrees (0-360)** prompt, key in **90** and press Enter.

       (3)  At the **Mirror image? No (Yes)** prompt, key in a **Y** for Yes.

    G.  Scale the arrow by completing the following steps:

       (1)  Choose 2 or S for Scale.

       (2)  At the **Scale X: 100** prompt, key in **140** and press Enter.

(3) At the **Scale Y: _1_00** prompt, key in **60** and press Enter.

    H. Press F7 to return to the Definition: Figure menu.

    I. Press F7 to return the cursor to the document.

3. Save the document and name it CH22EX7. Print CH22EX7.

## PERFORMANCE ASSESSMENTS

**Assessment One**

1. At a clear screen, change the left and right margins to 1.5 inches, then create the memorandum shown in figure 22-4.

2. Insert the text box with the horizontal position at Full. Key in the text at the editing screen.

3. Save the memorandum and name it CH22PA1. Print CH22PA1.

---

```
DATE:      May 3, 1993

TO:        All Directors

FROM:      Kim Chun, Vice President

SUBJECT:   New Slogan


Puget  Sound  Semiconductor  is  continuing  the  public
relations  campaign  that  started  earlier  this  year.   The
new  company  logo  was  unveiled  at  the  Board  of  Trustees
meeting  last  month.   To  go  along  with  the  logo,  the  media
department  has  created  this  slogan:
```

> **QUALITY CUSTOMERS--QUALITY PRODUCTS**

```
The  slogan  will  begin  to  appear  within  the  month  in
company  publications  such  as  brochures  and  pamphlets.
Business  cards  will  be  issued  in  June  that  will  contain
the  new  logo  and  slogan.

Information  on  ordering  business  cards  will  be  circulated
next  week.

xx:CH22PA1
```

---

Figure 22-4: Assessment One

## Assessment Two

1. Retrieve CH21EX1 to the screen.
2. Move the cursor to the paragraph that begins "We are still doing a great tradition . . ." and insert the graphic image HANDS-3.WPG with the default settings at the Figure: Definition menu, except change the size to 1 inch wide and 0.789 inches high.
3. Save the newsletter and name it CH22PA2. Print page 1 of CH22PA2.

## Assessment Three

1. Retrieve CH22PA2 to the screen.
2. Move the cursor to the paragraph that begins, "We welcome you and your family to join us . . ." and insert the graphic image TROPHY.WPG with the default settings at the Figure: Definition menu, except change the horizontal position to Left.
3. Save the newsletter and name it CH22PA3. Print page 1 of CH22PA3.

# CHAPTER 23

## GRAPHICS, LINES, AND EQUATIONS

## *PERFORMANCE OBJECTIVES*

Upon successful completion of chapter 23, you will be able to enhance graphic features you have generated and add mathematical equations to many types of standard business documents.

When you created the figure, table, and text box in chapter 22, did you notice that they had different borders? The figure had a thin line on all sides; the table box had thick lines above and below the table but not on the sides; and the text box had thick lines above and below, and the box was shaded.

With the varying styles of borders, you can easily identify the type of box that was created. The default settings for the boxes are appropriate for most occasions. The default settings can be changed to customize the border, change the shading and the caption, and make other modifications.

### FIGURE OPTIONS

If you determine that changes need to be made to a figure, complete the following steps:

1.  Access the Graphics command with Alt + F9.
2.  Choose 1 or F for Figure.
3.  Choose 4 or O for Options.
    **M** *Click on Graphics, Figure, then Options.*
4.  Make changes to the Options: Figure menu.
5.  Press F7.

The Options: Figure menu shown in figure 23-1 has a variety of selections.

```
Options: Figure

    1 - Border Style
            Left                          Single
            Right                         Single
            Top                           Single
            Bottom                        Single
    2 - Outside Border Space
            Left                          0.167"
            Right                         0.167"
            Top                           0.167"
            Bottom                        0.167"
    3 - Inside Border Space
            Left                          0"
            Right                         0"
            Top                           0"
            Bottom                        0"
    4 - First Level Numbering Method      Numbers
    5 - Second Level Numbering Method     Off
    6 - Caption Number Style              [BOLD]Figure 1[bold]
    7 - Position of Caption               Below box, Outside borders
    8 - Minimum Offset from Paragraph     0"
    9 - Gray Shading (% of black)         0%

    Selection: 0
```

Figure 23-1: Options: Figure Menu

## Border Style

The first selection, Border Style, has a single line as the default setting for the left, right, top, and bottom of the figure. When you choose 1 or B for Border Style, the prompt **1 None; 2 Single; 3 Double; 4 Dashed; 5 Dotted; 6 Thick; 7 Extra Thick: 0** appears at the bottom of the screen. To change the border style, key in the number of the type of line desired.

## Outside Border Space

The outside borders of a figure have the default settings of 0.167 inches. This measurement is the distance from the border of the figure to the surrounding text. This can be widened or shortened by keying in different measurements for the left, right, top, and bottom of the figure.

## Inside Border Space

The third selection, Inside Border Space, has default measurements of 0 inches for all sides of the figure. At these settings, there may not be any space between the graphic image and the figure box. These settings can be changed by choosing 3 or I for Inside Border, then entering the new measurements.

## First and Second Level Numbering Method

When a figure is created, WordPerfect automatically numbers it with Arabic numerals. This is the default setting for the First Level Numbering Method selection from the Options: Figure menu. The default setting for the Second Level Numbering Method selection is Off (or none). When you choose either of these selections, the prompt **1 O_ff; 2 _Numbers; 3 _Letters; 4 Roman Numerals: _0** appears at the bottom of the screen.

The default numbering style for figures can be turned off or changed to letters or Roman numerals. To change the style, key in the number you desire. You can establish second-level numbering for figures, such as Figure 1-1, or Figure 1-A.

### Caption Number Style

The caption number style is **Figure 1**, boldfaced. You can change this by choosing 6 or C for Caption Number Style at the Options: Figure menu. WordPerfect displays the current caption style at the bottom of the screen. You can use codes and other features at this prompt. Key in the style you desire and press Enter.

### Position of Caption

The position of a caption in a figure is below the box, outside the borders. This can be changed to above the box or inside the border.

### Minimum Offset from Paragraph

The Minimum Offset from Paragraph selection lets you establish how far a figure can be moved up into the paragraph when the offset measurement needs to be reduced. The offset measurement may need to be reduced if the paragraph containing a figure is too close to the bottom of the page and the figure cannot fit. If the paragraph is close to the bottom, WordPerfect reduces the offset measurement to try to keep the text and paragraph together. The offset measurement entered tells WordPerfect how far the measurement can be reduced. If the figure still cannot fit at the bottom of the page, it is inserted at the top of the next page.

### Gray Shading (Percentage of Black)

The last selection from the Options: Figure menu lets you shade a figure box. The default setting is 0%, which means there is no shading. Change this to a higher number to shade the figure. A shading of 100% makes the figure box black.

When all changes have been made to the Options: Figure menu, press F7 to return to the document and save the changes. WordPerfect inserts the code **[Fig Opt]** in the document. Changes can be made in the Options menu as often as needed in a document. The changes made at the Options menu are in effect from the location of the code to the end of the document or until another Options change code is encountered. Therefore, if you want a figure to print with the changes, make sure the Figure Options code is located before the figure.

## OTHER BOX OPTIONS

Options for the other types of boxes that can be created—table box, text box, and user box—are similar to the figure options. The border style for table boxes and text boxes is no left and right lines and thick top and bottom lines. If you want to change the lines, the same selections are available as the ones from the Options: Figure menu. The default border style for user boxes is no lines. Again, this can be changed with the same selections as provided in the Options: Figure menu.

The first-level numbering method for boxes varies. The default for figure boxes is Arabic numerals, the default for table boxes is Roman numerals, and the default for text boxes and user boxes is numbers. The location of the caption for text boxes and user boxes is the same as for figures — below box, outside border. The default location of the caption for table boxes is above the box, outside borders.

All boxes have no shading except text boxes. The default setting for text boxes is 10%.

## HORIZONTAL AND VERTICAL LINES

The Line selection from the Graphics command lets you create horizontal and vertical lines in a document. This feature is different from Line Draw. You can adjust the width and shading of graphic lines, and create graphic lines in a document with a proportional font. You cannot do this with Line Draw.

Horizontal and vertical lines can be used in a document to separate sections, create a focal point, separate columns, or add visual appeal.

To insert a horizontal or vertical line in a document, complete the following steps:

1. Access the Graphics command with Alt + F9.
2. Choose 5 or L for Line.
3. Choose 1 or H for Horizontal or 2 or V for Vertical.
   **M** *Click on Graphics, Line, Create Horizontal, or Create Vertical.*
4. At the Graphics: Horizontal Line or Graphics: Vertical Line menu, make changes as needed, then press F7.

The Graphics: Horizontal Line and Graphics Vertical Line menus contain the same selections, but the default settings vary as shown in figure 23-2.

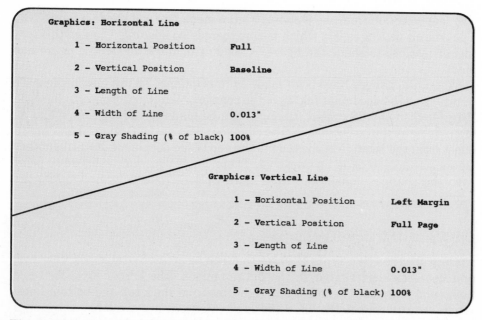

**Figure 23-2: Graphics: Horizontal Line and Graphics Vertical Line**

## CUSTOMIZING HORIZONTAL LINES

Using the default settings from the Graphics: Horizontal Line menu, a horizontal line prints from the left to the right margin at the baseline of the line where the cursor is located and is 0.013 inches wide. Changes can be made to the default settings of the Graphics: Horizontal Line menu to customize the line.

### Horizontal Position

If you select Horizontal Position from the Graphics: Horizontal Line menu, the prompt **Horizontal Pos: 1 <u>L</u>eft; 2 <u>R</u>ight; 3 <u>C</u>enter: 4 <u>F</u>ull; 5 <u>S</u>et Position: 0** appears at the bottom of the screen.

The Left selection draws a horizontal line from the left margin, and the Right selection draws a horizontal ruled line from the right margin. The Center selection begins a horizontal ruled line at the center point of the margins. Full is the default setting and draws a horizontal line from the left to the right margin. The Set Position selection is used to begin the line at a specific distance from the left edge of the page.

### Vertical Position

The Vertical Position selection on the Graphics: Horizontal Line menu has a default setting of Baseline. At this setting, the horizontal line is drawn at the baseline of the text where the cursor is located. This can be changed to Set Position, which is used to begin the line at a specific distance from the top of the page.

### Length of Line

If the Horizontal Position selection is set at the default of Full, then changes cannot be made to the Length of Line selection. If the Horizontal Position selection is changed to Left, Right, Center, or Set Position, then a measurement can be entered after the Length of Line selection. For example, if you change the horizontal position to Left and you want a line drawn 3 inches beginning at the left margin, then enter 3 at the Length of Line selection.

### Width of Line

The thickness of a line, in WordPerfect, is called the width. The width is measured in inches and is 0.013 inches. The width can be changed to make the line thinner or thicker. The following illustration shows how a ruled line appears at different widths.

= 0.013 inches

= 0.1 inches

= 0.25 inches

## Gray Shading

The last selection on the Graphics: Horizontal Line menu is Gray Shading. By default, all lines are 100% black. This percentage can be decreased to produce a lighter line. The lower the percentage, the lighter the shading. The ruled lines below have a width of 0.1 inches with varying gray shading.

= 10% gray shading

= 25% gray shading

= 50% gray shading

= 100% gray shading

## CUSTOMIZING VERTICAL LINES

The settings for the Graphics: Vertical Line menu are similar to the settings on the menu for horizontal lines. By default, a vertical line prints at the left margin, from the top margin to the bottom margin, and is 0.013 inches wide. Changes can be made to the default settings of the Graphics: Vertical Line menu to customize the line.

### Horizontal Position

If you select Horizontal Position from the Graphics: Vertical Line menu, the prompt **Horizontal Position: 1 Left; 2 Right; 3 Between Columns; 4 Set Position; 0** appears at the bottom of the screen.

The Left selection draws a vertical line at the left margin, and the Right selection draws a vertical line at the right margin. The Between Columns selection lets you insert a line between columns. When selected, WordPerfect displays the prompt **Place line to right of column: 1**. If you want a vertical line between the first and second columns, press Enter. If you want a line between the second and third columns, key in a 2 and press Enter. If you want a line between all columns in the document, you must create separate lines for each column. The Set Position selection lets you draw a line at a precise distance from the left edge of the page.

### Vertical Position

If you select Vertical Position from the Graphics: Vertical Line menu, the prompt **Vertical Position: 1 Full Page; 2 Top; 3 Center; 4 Bottom; 5 Set Position: 0** appears at the bottom of the screen.

The Full Page selection is the default and draws a line from the top margin to the bottom margin. A line can be drawn from the top margin with the Top selection, from the center of the page with the Center selection, and from the bottom of the page with the Bottom selection. The Set Position selection lets you draw a line at a precise distance from the top of the page.

### Length of Line

The length of the line can be determined with the Length of Line selection from the Graphics: Vertical Line menu. If the Vertical Position selection is changed to Top, Center, Bottom, or Set Position, then a measurement can be entered after the Length of Line selection. For example, if the Vertical

Position is changed to Top and you want a 4-inch line beginning at the top margin, then key in 4 at the Length of Line selection.

### Width of Line

The Width of Line selection on the Graphics: Vertical Line menu operates the same as this setting on the Graphics: Horizontal Line menu. This selection lets you determine the exact width of the line.

### Gray Shading

The Gray Shading selection on the Graphics: Vertical Line menu operates the same as this setting on the Graphics: Horizontal Line menu. Gray shading can be 1 to 100 percent.

## VERTICAL LINE EXAMPLE

To better understand how the line feature works with the Graphics command, the steps to insert a vertical line between two columns in a document are described below:

1. Move the cursor to beginning of the first paragraph and access the Graphics command with Alt + F9.
2. Choose 5 or L for Line.
3. Choose 2 or V for Vertical.
   **M** *Click on Graphics, Line, then Create Vertical.*
4. At the Graphics: Vertical Line menu, choose 1 or H for Horizontal Position.
5. From the prompts that display at the bottom of the screen, choose 3 or B for Between Columns.
6. At the prompt **Place line to right of columns: 1**, press Enter.
7. At the Graphics: Vertical Line menu, choose 2 or V for Vertical Position.
8. From the prompts that display at the bottom of the screen, choose 5 or S for Set Position, then press Enter. (This changes the beginning of the line to the location of the cursor rather than the beginning of the document.)
9. Press F7 to return the cursor to the document.

With the changes made to the Graphics: Vertical Line menu, the vertical line prints between the columns from the location of the cursor to the bottom of the page (excluding the 1-inch bottom margin).

## EQUATIONS

The Equation selection from the Graphics command, lets you write mathematic and scientific equations that can be printed on a dot matrix or laser printer without any special fonts.

WordPerfect uses conventions from the mathematic and scientific community when creating equations. For example, numbers are printed in a normal font, and variables such as x and y are printed in italics.

To create an equation, complete the following steps:

1. Access the Graphics command with Alt + F9.
2. Choose 6 or E for Equation.
3. Choose 1 or C for Create.
   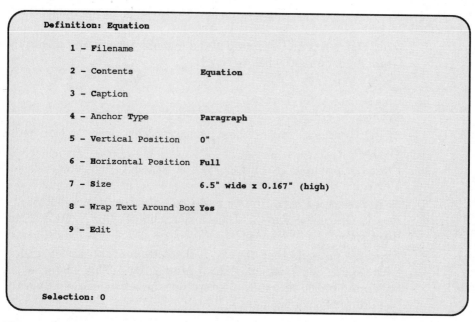 *Click on Graphics, Equation, then Create.*
4. At the Definition: Equation menu, choose 9 or E for Edit.
5. At the Equation Editor, key in your equation.
6. Press Ctrl + F3 or F9 to view the equation.
7. Press F7 to save the equation and return the cursor to the Definition: Equation menu.
8. Press F7 to return the cursor to the document.

The Definition: Equation menu, shown in figure 23-3, has the same selections as the Definition menu for a figure, table box, text box, or user box.

```
Definition: Equation

    1 - Filename

    2 - Contents          Equation

    3 - Caption

    4 - Anchor Type        Paragraph

    5 - Vertical Position  0"

    6 - Horizontal Position Full

    7 - Size               6.5" wide x 0.167" (high)

    8 - Wrap Text Around Box Yes

    9 - Edit




Selection: 0
```

Figure 23-3: Definition: Equation Menu

Make changes to these selections in the same manner as you would in the Definition menu for a figure, table box, text box, or user box.

When you choose 9 or E for Edit from the Definition: Equation menu, WordPerfect displays the Equation Editor as shown in figure 23-4.

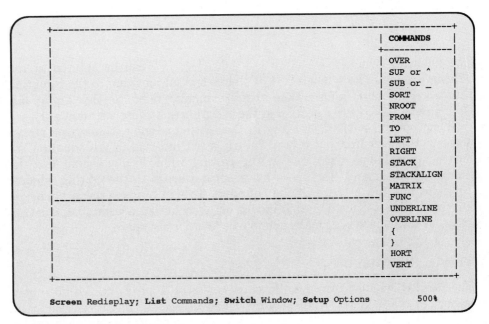

+-----------------------------------------------------+----------------+
|                                                     | **COMMANDS**   |
|                                                     +----------------+
|                                                     | OVER           |
|                                                     | SUP or ^       |
|                                                     | SUB or _       |
|                                                     | SORT           |
|                                                     | NROOT          |
|                                                     | FROM           |
|                                                     | TO             |
|                                                     | LEFT           |
|                                                     | RIGHT          |
|                                                     | STACK          |
|                                                     | STACKALIGN     |
|                                                     | MATRIX         |
|----------------------------------------------------| FUNC           |
|                                                     | UNDERLINE      |
|                                                     | OVERLINE       |
|                                                     | {              |
|                                                     | }              |
|                                                     | HORT           |
|                                                     | VERT           |
+-----------------------------------------------------+----------------+
**Screen** Redisplay; **List** Commands; **Switch** Window; **Setup** Options          500%

**Figure 23-4: Equation Editor**

The Equation Editor contains three sections: the display window, the editing window, and the equation palette. The display window is the upper left section of the editor. This section displays equations as they will appear when printed (at 500% view). The editing window is the lower left corner of the editor and is the section where the equation is keyed in. The cursor is located in this section. The section to the right is the equation palette and contains a variety of commands and symbols that can be used when writing an equation.

## Writing an Equation

With the cursor located in the editing window, key in the equation using special commands and symbols. A wide variety of commands and symbols can be used when keying in an equation. (For more information, please refer to pages 186-208, and Appendix D, pages 785-795, in the WordPerfect 5.1 reference manual.)

For example, to write the equation $a + b$ $over$ $c$, key in the following at the editing window:

{a~+~b} over c

Key in the braces ({}) around $a + b$ to tell WordPerfect that both are to appear over the $c$. Key in a tilde (~) to insert a space after the $a$ and before the $b$. To see how the equation will appear in the document, press Ctrl + F3 or F9 and WordPerfect displays the following equation in the display window (at 500% view).

$$\frac{a + b}{c}$$

The following symbols: + - * / = < > ! ? . | @ , ; : can be entered at the editing window. The symbols ' " { } ( ) have special meaning to the Equation Editor. (For more information about symbols, refer to the *Equations, Commands and Symbols* section in the WordPerfect reference manual.)

When you press the Enter key in the editing window, the cursor moves down to the next line, but a hard return is not inserted in the equation. To create multiple-line equations in the editing window, you would use the Stackalign command. The space bar inserts a space in the editing window but does not add a space in the equation. To add a space to an equation, key in a tilde (~) for a normal space or a backward accent (`) for a thin space. A thin space is equal to one-fourth of a normal space.

### Viewing the Equation

The display window displays the equation as it appears in the document (except at 500% view). To display an equation, access the Screen command with Ctrl + F3 or press F9. Press Ctrl + F3 again to redisplay an equation after making changes.

If you have made a syntax error when writing the formula, the equation will not display in the display window. Instead, an **Incorrect Format** message will appear on the screen and the cursor will be positioned at the location in the equation where the error occurs.

### Selecting from the Equation Palette

To move the cursor from the Equation Editing menu to the equation palette, press F5. In the palette, use the up and down arrow keys to move the cursor to a specific symbol or command. Press Page Up or Page Down to display the next menu in the palette.

With the cursor positioned on the command or symbol you want to insert in the equation, press Enter or Ctrl + Enter. Some commands are represented by text as well as a character. With these symbols, press Enter to insert the text or press Ctrl + Enter to insert the character.

To exit the equation palette without selecting a symbol or command, press F7 or F1.

### Aligning the Equation

With the Equation Editor on the screen, you can change the alignment of the equation by accessing the Setup command with Shift + F1. When you press Shift + F1 the menu shown in figure 23-5 displays on the screen.

```
Equation: Options

    1 - Print as Graphics        Yes

    2 - Graphical Font Size       Defalt

    3 - Horizontal Alignment      Center

    4 - Vertical Alignment        Center




Selection: 0
```

Figure 23-5: Equation: Options Menu

The first selection, Print as Graphics, prints the equation as graphics. This can be changed to Text if your printer does not print graphics (such as a daisy wheel printer).

The Graphical Font Size selection has a setting of Default. At this setting, equations are printed with the font size of the document. If you want equations to print with a different font size, enter the size at the Graphical Font Size selection.

The Horizontal Alignment selection lets you position the equation at the left, center, or right in the equation box. The Vertical Alignment selection lets you position the equation at the top, center, or bottom of the equation box.

### Creating an Equation

The steps to create the equation shown in figure 23-6 are listed below.

$$\frac{Q_3 - Q_1}{2}$$

Figure 23-6: Equation

1. Access the Graphics command with Alt + F9.
2. Choose 6 or E for Equation.
3. Choose 1 or C for Create.
   **M** *Click on Graphics, Equation, then Create.*
4. At the Definition: Equation menu, choose 9 or E for Edit.

5. At the Equation Editor, key in **{Q_3~-~Q_1} over 2**. (The braces, {}, tell WordPerfect that what is between the braces is to be positioned over the 2. The underline symbols create subscripts. The tilde inserts a space. The word *over* inserts the line and moves the 2 below the first part of the equation.)

6. Press Ctrl + F3 or F9 to view the equation.

7. Press F7 to save the equation and return the cursor to the Definition: Equation menu.

8. Press F7 to return the cursor to the document.

The steps to create equations in the exercises at the end of this chapter will be provided. For information on writing more extensive equations, please refer to the WordPerfect reference manual.

### Inserting an Options Code

The box containing the equation can be customized in the same manner as figure, table, text, or user boxes are customized. To make changes to the equation box, complete the following steps:

1. Access the Graphics command with Alt + F9.
2. Choose 6 or E for Equation.
3. Choose 4 or O for Options.
   **M** *Click on Graphics, Equation, then Options.*
4. At the Options: Equation menu, make any necessary changes.
5. Press F7 to return the cursor to the document.

The selections from the Options: Equation menu are the same as the Options: Figure, Options: Table Box, Options: Text Box; and Options: User Box menus.

### VIEW DOCUMENT

As described in chapter 22, View Document is useful in documents containing boxes, lines or equations. Before printing, view the document to determine whether the boxes are in the correct location and text flows properly around boxes.

### CHAPTER REVIEW

### Summary

* Changes to be made to figure, table, text, or user boxes can be made at the Options menu. The Options menu contains several selections: Border Style, Outside Border Space, Inside Border Space, First Level Numbering Method, Second Level Numbering Method, Caption Number Style, Position of Caption, Minimum Offset from Paragraph, and Gray Shading.

* The default settings of the selections at the Options menu vary according to whether you are changing a figure, table, text box, or user box.

- Horizontal and vertical lines can be inserted in a document with the Graphics command to create separate sections, act as a focal point, separate columns, or add visual appeal.
- The Line feature is different from Line Draw. When inserting lines with the Graphics command, you can adjust the width and darkness of lines.
- Horizontal and vertical lines can be created and customized at the Graphics: Vertical Line or Graphics: Horizontal Line menu. Each menu contains selections to change the Horizontal Position, Vertical Position, Length of Line, Width of Line, and Gray Shading.
- Mathematic and scientific equations can be written at the Equation Editor. An equation is created in a box that has no lines around the borders and no gray shading. The box around the equation can be customized in the same manner as boxes around figures, tables, or text.
- The Equation Editor contains three sections: the display window, the editing window, and the equation palette. Equations are written in the editing window, the equation is viewed in the display window, and commands and symbols are inserted in an equation at the equation palette.
- While in the Equation Editor, the Setup command, Shift + F1, displays the Equation: Options menu. Customize the appearance and location of the equation at this menu.

## Commands Review

|  | **Keyboard** | **Mouse** |
|---|---|---|
| Graphics command | Alt + F9 | Graphics |
| View Document | Shift + F7, 6 or V | File, Print, 6 or V |

## STUDY GUIDE FOR CHAPTER 23

Describe the necessary steps to change the border style to double lines, the caption style to letters, and the gray shading to 75% in a document containing a figure.

_____

_____

_____

_____

_____

_____

_____

**Completion:** In the space provided at the right, write in the correct term, symbol, or command for the explanation.

1. Access the Graphics command.                                                      _____

2. Selection from the Graphics command to insert a horizontal or vertical line.                                                                    _____

3. The default border style for figures.                                             _____

4. The default border style for user boxes.                                          _____

5. The default gray shading for figures.                                             _____

6. The default position of captions in tables.                                       _____

7. The default gray shading for text boxes.                                          _____

8. The default Width of Line setting at Graphics: Vertical Line.                      _____

9. The default Gray Shading setting at Graphics: Vertical Line.                       _____

10. The three sections of the Equation Editor are the display window, the equation palette, and this section.                      _____

11. Use this symbol to indicate a space when writing an equation.                     _____

12. In the display window of the Equation Editor, the equation is displayed at this percentage of normal.                              _____

## HANDS-ON EXERCISES

Change the default directory to UNIT5.

### Exercise One
1. Retrieve CH22EX6 to the screen.
2. Remove the lines around the arrow by completing the following steps:
   A. With the cursor at the beginning of the document, access the Graphics command with Alt + F9.
   B. Choose 1 or F for Figure.

    C. Choose 4 or O for Options.
       **M** *Click on Graphics, Figure, then Options.*
    D. At the Options: Figure menu, choose 1 or B for Border Style.
    E. Press **1** or **N** four times to change the lines to None.
    F. Press F7 to return the cursor to the document.
3. Save the document and name it CH23EX1. Print CH23EX1.

## Exercise Two

1. Retrieve CH22EX5 to the screen.
2. Change the lines around the table to double lines and move the caption below the box by completing the following steps:
    A. With the cursor at the beginning of the document, access the Graphics command with Alt + F9.
    B. Choose 2 or T for Table Box.
    C. Choose 4 or O for Options.
       **M** *Click on Graphics, Table Box, then Options.*
    D. At the Options: Table Box menu, choose 1 or B for Border Style.
    E. Press **3** or **D** four times to change the lines to Double.
    F. Choose 7 or P for Position of Caption, then choose 1 or B for Below Box.
    G. Choose 1 or O for Outside of Border.
    H. Press F7 to return the cursor to the document.
3. Save the document and name it CH23EX2. Print CH23EX2.

## Exercise Three

1. Retrieve CH22PA3 to the screen.
2. Change the lines around the figure boxes to double and the gray shading to 10% by completing the following steps:
    A. With the cursor at the beginning of the document, access the Graphics command with Alt + F9.
    B. Choose 1 or F for Figure.
    C. Choose 4 or O for Options.
       **M** *Click on Graphics, Figure, then Options.*
    D. At the Options: Figure menu, choose 1 or B for Border Style.
    E. Press **3** or **D** four times to change the lines to Double.
    F. Choose 9 or G for Gray Shading, key in **10**, then press Enter.
    G. Press F7 to return the cursor to the document.
3. Save the newsletter and name it CH23EX3. Print page 1 of CH23EX3.

## Exercise Four

1. Retrieve CH21EX1 to the screen.
2. Insert a vertical line between the two columns by completing the following steps:
    A. Move cursor to the beginning of the heading "Basketball Champions" and access the Graphics command with Alt + F9.
    B. Choose 5 or L for Line.
    C. Choose 2 or V for Vertical.
       **M** *Click on Graphics, Line, then Create Vertical.*
    D. At the Graphics: Vertical Line menu, choose 1 or H for Horizontal Position.
    E. From the prompts that display at the bottom of the screen, choose 3 or B for Between Columns.
    F. At the **Place line to right of columns: 1** prompt, press Enter.
    G. At the Graphics: Vertical Line menu, choose 2 or V for Vertical Position.

H. From the prompts that display at the bottom of the screen, choose 5 or S for Set Position, then press Enter. (This changes the beginning of the line to the location of the cursor rather than the beginning of the document.)

I. Press F7 to return the cursor to the document.

3. Save the newsletter and name it CH23EX4. Print CH23EX4.

**Exercise Five**

1. At a clear screen, create the letterhead shown in figure 23-7, by completing the following steps:

A. Change the base font to 18-point Helvetica Bold (use a sans serif typeface if your printer does not support Helvetica).

B. Key in **OMEGA TECH**, then change the base font to 12-point Helvetica bold.

C. Press Enter, then create a horizontal line that is 0.2 inches wide and has a gray shading of 50% by completing the following steps:

(1) Access the Graphics command with Alt + F9.

(2) Choose 5 or L for Line.

(3) Choose 1 or H for Horizontal.
    **M** *Click on Graphics, Line, then Create Horizontal.*

(4) At the Graphics: Horizontal Line menu, choose 4 or W for Width of Line, key in **0.2**, then press Enter.

(5) Choose 5 or G for Gray Shading, key in **50**, then press Enter.

(6) Press F7 to return the cursor to the document.

D. Press Enter twice, then access the Flush Right command with Alt + F6.
   **M** *Click on Layout, Align, then Flush Right.*

E. Key in the street address, **250 Center Street**. Key in the remainder of the address and telephone number using the Flush Right command as indicated in figure 23-7.

2. Save the letterhead and name it CH23EX5. Print CH23EX5.

# OMEGA TECH

250 Center Street

Spokane, WA 99302

(509) 555-1255

Figure 23-7: Exercise Five

**Exercise Six**

1. At a clear screen, create the memorandum shown in figure 23-8 in an appropriate memorandum format. To create the equation, complete the following steps:

A. Access the Graphics command with Alt + F9.

B. Choose 6 or E for Equation.

    C. Choose 1 or C for Create.
       **M** *Click on Graphics, Equation, then Create.*
    D. At the Definition: Equation menu, choose 9 or E for Edit.
    E. At the Equation Editor, key in **SUM d^2~=~1 over N [N SUM X^2~-~( SUM X)^2]**.
       (Be sure to key in the equation exactly as shown, including spaces and tildes.)
    F. Press Ctrl + F3 or F9 to view the equation.
    G. Press F7 to save the equation and return the cursor to the Definition: Equation menu.
    H. Press F7 to return the cursor to the document.
  2. When the memorandum is complete, save it and name it CH23EX6. Print CH23EX6.

---

DATE:  April 23, 1993; TO:  Rhonda Napier; FROM:  William Holley;
SUBJECT:  Statistical Analysis

I received the statistical analysis of the market research you
performed on the new electronic component. The statistics seem
complete, but I would like you to recompute the standard deviation
using the following formula:

$$\sum d^2 = \frac{1}{N}[N\sum X^2 - (\sum X)^2]$$

Please have the computations to me by the end of next week. I will
be presenting the statistics at the next department meeting.
xx:CH23EX6

---

**Figure 23-8: Exercise Six**

**Exercise Seven**
  1. Retrieve CH23EX6 to the screen.
  2. Create lines around the equation by completing the following steps:
    A. With the cursor at the beginning of the document, access the Graphics command with
       Alt + F9.
    B. Choose 6 or E for Equation.
    C. Choose 4 or O for Options.
       **M** *Click on Graphics, Equation, then Options.*
    D. At the Options: Equation menu, choose 1 or B for Border Style, then key in a **2 or S** for
       single four times for single line borders.
    E. Press F7 to return the cursor to the document.
  3. Save the memorandum and name it CH23EX7. Print CH23EX7.

## PERFORMANCE ASSESSMENTS

**Assessment One**
  1. Retrieve CH22PA1 to the screen.
  2. With the cursor at the beginning of the document, insert a Text Box Options code that
    changes the border style to single for the right and top and extra thick for the left and
    bottom lines and changes the gray shading to 0 percent.
  3. Save the document and name it CH23PA1. Print CH23PA1.

**Assessment Two**

1. At a clear screen, create the letter shown in figure 23-9 by completing the following steps:
   A. Access the Options: Figure menu and change the border to extra thick for the top and bottom and thick for the left and right lines. Change the gray shading to 10%. Exit the Options: Figure menu with F7.
   B. With the cursor positioned after the Options code, insert the graphic file, PC-1.WPG. At the Definition: Figure menu, change the horizontal position to left, and change the size to 3 inches wide by 2 inches high.
   C. Key in the letter as shown in figure 23-9.
2. Save the letter and name it CH23PA2. Print CH23PA2.

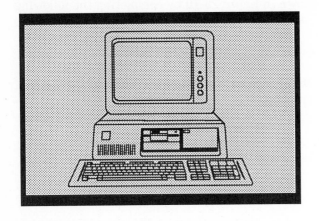

**OMEGA TECH**
**250 Center Street**
**Spokane, WA 99302**
**(509) 555-1255**

January 10, 1993


Mr. and Mrs. Floyd Stoltz
21993 - 32nd Street East
Spokane, WA 99302

Dear Mr. and Mrs. Stoltz:

You made a wise choice when you purchased a Rontech III computer.
The Rontech III is a powerful and versatile microcomputer that
includes the latest technological advances.  Thank you for letting
us help you make your computer selection.

Omega Tech will continue to provide support to you as you learn to
operate the Rontech III.  We offer training sessions regularly
during the month.  These training sessions are free to new owners
of the Rontech III.  If you are interested in attending a training
session, call our store and we will be happy to schedule a time for
both of you.

In the future, when we are offering special prices on peripheral
equipment and software programs, we will notify you by flyer.  In
the meantime, if there is anything we can do for you, just give us
a call.

Sincerely,


Devon McKenna
Manager

xx:CH23PA2

Figure 23-9: Assessment Two

## Assessment Three

1. At a clear screen, create the letterhead shown in figure 23-10 by completing the following steps (the vertical line in your letterhead will extend to the bottom of the page, except the last inch):

   A. Change the base font to 14-point Times Roman Bold (use a serif typeface if your printer does not support Times Roman).

   B. Create a vertical line with the default settings at the Graphics: Vertical Line menu, except change the width of line to 0.05 inches.

   C. Use the Flush Right command to key in the company name, address, and telephone number.

2. Save the letterhead and name it CH23PA3.  Print CH23PA3.

**CHENEY MANUFACTURING**
**625 Parkway Plaza**
**Seattle, WA 98116**
**(206) 555-1700**

Figure 23-10: Assessment Three

## Assessment Four

1. At a clear screen, create the memorandum displayed in figure 23-11 in an appropriate memorandum format.

2. When creating the equation, key in the following at the editing window:

   **X^2~=~SUM {(O~-~E )^2} over E~=~6.908**

3. Access the Options: Equation menu, and change the Border Style to Double for all sides. (Make sure the options code is inserted before the equation.)

4. Save the memorandum and name it CH23PA4. Print CH23PA4.

Date : April 27, 1993 ; To: William Holley ; From: Rhonda Napier ; Subject : Chi Square

When I ran the statistical analysis on the market research you received last week, I used the following formula to determine the chi square by summing the resulting quotients.

$$X^2 = \sum \frac{(0 - E)^2}{E} = 6.908$$

If you need anything further, please contact me by 5:00 p.m. tomorrow. I will be out of town the rest of the week.

XX: CH23PA4

Figure 23-11: Assessment Four

# PERFORMANCE MASTERY

## *UNIT PERFORMANCE*

In this unit, you have learned to enhance the readability of business forms and multiple-page reports.

## MASTERY ASSIGNMENTS

**Assignment One**

1. At a clear screen, create a table with the information shown in figure U5-1. Calculate the yearly totals row.
2. You determine the following:
   A. Base font
   B. Alignment of cells
   C. Types of lines in the cells
   D. Boldfacing
3. Save the table and name it U05MA1. Print U05MA1.

PACIFIC COUNSELING ASSOCIATION

Statement of Revenues, 1992

|  | 1st Half | 2nd Half | Yearly |
|---|---|---|---|
| Contributions | $18,543 | $17,324 |  |
| Foundations | 9,325 | 10,432 |  |
| Special Events | 8,345 | 10,219 |  |
| United Funds | 23,432 | 25,543 |  |
| Government Fees | 40,345 | 51,498 |  |
| Government Grants | 75,394 | 77,094 |  |
| Program Fees | 23,903 | 25,342 |  |

Figure U5-1: Assignment One

**Assignment Two**

1. At a clear screen, create the legal document shown in figure U5-2 with the following specifications:
   A. Change the paper size to legal.
   B. Turn on line numbering.
   C. Change the paragraph numbering style at the Paragraph Number Definition menu to Paragraph.
2. Use automatic paragraph numbering to enter the paragraph numbers in figure U5-2.
3. You determine the following;
   A. Base font
   B. Margins
   C. Justification

      D. Indentions
      E. Spacing
      F. Page numbering
      G. Page breaks
      H. Correct spelling (use Speller)
      I. Correct grammar and usage
  4. Save the legal document and name it U05MA2. Print U05MA2.

---

## POLICY OF TITLE INSURANCE

### Conditions and Stipulations

1. Defenition of Terms
The following terms when used in this policy mean:
   a. <u>insured</u>: the insured named in Schedule A and subject to any rights or defenses.
   b. <u>insured</u> claimant: an insured claiming loss or damage.
   c. <u>land</u>: the land described or refered to in Schedule A.
   d. <u>mortgage</u>: mortgage, deed of trust, trust deed, or other security instrument.

2. Defense and Prosection of Actions
   a. Upon written request by the insured, the Company, shall provide for the defense of an insured in litigation but only as to those stated causes of action alleging a defect, lien or emcumbrance.
   b. The Company shall have the right to institute and prosecute any action or proceding to prevent or reduce loss or damage to the insured.
   c. Whenever the Company shall have brought an action, the Company may pursue any litigation to final determination by the court.
   d. In all cases where this policy permits or requires the Company to prosecute, the ensured shall secure to the Company the right to so prosecute.

3. Determination of Liability
   a. The liability of the Company under this policy shall not exceed the least of:
     i. the amount of insurance stated in Scedule A; or
     ii. the difference between the value of the insured estate or interest.
   b. In the even the Amount of Insurance stated in Scedule A is less than 80 percent of the value of the insured estate, this Policy is subject to the following:
     i. where no subsequent improvement has been made, as to any partial loss, the Company shall only pay the loss pro rata; or
     ii. where a subsequent improvment has been made, the Company shall only pay the loss pro rata in the proportion of 120 percent.
   c. The Company will pay only those costs, attorneys' fees and expenses incured in accordance with section four of Schedule A.

4.   Limitation of Liability
     a.   If the Company establishes the title, or removes the
          alledged defect or lien, it shall have fully performed
          its obligations with respect to that matter and shall not
          be liable for any loss or damage caused thereby.
     b.   In the event of any litigation, the Company shall have no
          liability for loss or damage until there has been a final
          determination by the Court.
     c.   The Company shall not be liable for loss or damage to any
          insured for liability voluntarly assumed by the insured.
5.   Reduction of Insurance
     All payments under this policy, except payments made for
     costs, attorneys' fees and expenses shall reduce the amount of
     the insurance pro rata.

**Figure U5-2: Assignment Two**

## Assignment Three

1.   Create the position description form shown in figure U5-3 using WordPerfect's outline
     feature. Change the paragraph numbering style at the Paragraph Number Definition menu
     to Paragraph.
2.   You determine the following:
     A. Margins
     B. Justification
     C. Spacing
     D. Boldfacing
     E. Page numbering
     F. Page breaks
     G. Correct spelling (use Speller)
     H. Correct grammar and usage
3.   Save the position description and name it U05MA3. Print U05MA3.

PUGET SOUND SEMICONDUCTOR
1900 State Street
Tacoma, WA 98402

POSITION TITLE:  Manager

DIRECTLY RESPONSIBLE TO:  Vice President

MAJOR FUNCTIONS AND RESPONSIBILITIES:

1.   Moniters and identifies financial needs of the department.
     a.   Monitors department revenues, salaries, and other
          expenses to meet program budget.
     b.   Is knowledgable about all parts of monthly financial and
          productivity reports.
2.   Supervises department staff.
     a.   Is knowledgable about organizational procedures for
          hiring, disciplining, and terminating employees.

    b.    Performs employee evaluations using proper format within 14 days of designated evaluation date.

    c.    Holds regular staff meetings for the department.

3.    Maintains satisfactery level of service as detailed in organizational and program policies.

    a.    Evaluates, develops, and implements any needed changes in paperwork or other organizational policies.

    b.    Develops and maintains quality asurance plan.

    c.    Ensures that all staff are trained in emergency procedures.

4.    Support organizational objectives.

    a.    Actively participates in organizational commitees.

    b.    Maintains effective communication with peer managers.

5.    Demonstrates effective leadership style.

    a.    Delegates tasks appropriatly so that program goals are accomplished.

    b.    Demonstrates a consistant ability to communicate clearly and maintain a rapport with staff.

    c.    Demonstrates willingness and ability to improve management style by accepting feedback in a cooperative manner.

6.    Completes reports and paperwork as required.

    a.    Maintains 90 percent accuracy and compliance with company requirements.

        i.    Personnel evaluations performed within 14 days of employee anniversery date.

        ii.   Required consultations are documented.

7.    Attendance

    a.    Begins shift promptly.

    b.    Absenteeism does not exceed agency policy of 6.5 days per year.

    c.    Notifies director when absent from work according to policy.

**Figure U5-3: Assignment Three**

## Assignment Four

1. At a clear screen, create a newsletter with the information shown in figure U5-4. Set the body of the newsletter in two newspaper-style columns.

2. You determine the following:
   A. Base font
   B. Appearance of the title
   C. Boldfacing
   D. Tab settings for indented paragraphs
   E. Margins
   F. Justification
   G. Correct spelling (use Speller)
   H. Correct grammar and usage
   I. Hyphenation

3. Insert the graphics file BICYCLE.WPG by the paragraph on bicycling adventures. You determine the position and size of the image.

4. Save the newsletter and name it U05MA4. Print page 1 of U05MA4.

## TAHOMA SUMMER CAMP

### Summer, 1993

### Discover New Adventures
Tahoma Summer Camp provide many opportunities to widen horizons, increase self-awareness, experience individual and group decision making, accept responsibility, learn new skills and build self-confidence. We, the counselors at Tahoma Summer Camp, believe that the potential for personal growth is unlimited and acheive this by providing campers a well balanced approach to programing. Campers experience choosing some of their own activities, planning activities with their cabin mates, and participating in larger unit or all camp events.

A variety of activities is offered including, instructional swimming, recreational swimming, bicycling, canoeing, sailing, archery, hiking, and kayaking.

### Bicycling Adventures
The Vashon Island Bicycle Adventure takes you to beautiful Vashon Island for six days of bicycle touring and camping. Explore quiet beaches, cook your own group meals, and watch the sun set over the waters. This is a popular adventure for beginning bicyclists.

If you want a longer adventure, try the San Juan Islands Bicycle Adventure. This ten-day tour will include all the islands in the San Juan group. Previous bicycle touring experience is required for this intermediate adventure.

### Location and Facilities
The Tahoma Summer Camp is locate on 250 acres of quiet, country land on the Key Peninsula, 40 miles West of Tacoma. The camp features over a mile of shoreline along the Puget Sound. Facilities include a health center, outdoor swimming pool, nature ecology center, archery range, and a separate program lodge. Campers are housed in cabins, which have there own bathrooms. There are shower facilities and a complete dining hall.

### A Typical Day at Camp
Campers rise daily by 7:15 a.m. Morning activities, after breakfast, include cabin and camp cleanup. Two hour-long "camptivity" instructional classes are held daily on Monday, Wednesday, and Friday--one hour just prior to lunch, the other in mid-afternoon. Campers are asked to select from a list of offered activities for these camptivity times and remain in those activities for the week. After lunch, campers experience a short rest period, followed by a cabin activity time, their second camptivity period, and a late afternoon free time, where they can choose daily an activity in which they wish to participate. After dinner activities include those planned by their age-grouped units or an all-camp activity.

Many days end with our exceptional campfires. Lights are out at
9:30 p.m.

---

Figure U5-4: Assignment Four

## Assignment Five

1.  At a clear screen, create a sign directing students to a WordPerfect class that contains the following information:

BEGINNING WORDPERFECT

DAILY, 9:00 - 9:50

Room 110

2.  Insert the ARROW-22.WPG in the sign pointing to the left.
3.  You determine the following:
    A. Form size
    B. Positioning of elements on the page.
    C. Base font
    D. Boldfacing
4.  Save the sign and name it U05MA5. Print U05MA5.

# UNIT 6

## ADVANCED DOCUMENT FORMATTING

In this unit, you will learn to finish multiple-page reports with reference attributes, standardize features of multiple-page reports, and utilize the database features of WordPerfect for maintaining records.

# CHAPTER 24

---

## HEADERS AND FOOTERS

## PERFORMANCE OBJECTIVE

Upon successful completion of chapter 24, you will be able to finish pages in multiple-page business reports with specific page characteristics.

### HEADERS AND FOOTERS

WordPerfect includes a feature that lets you create text that appears at the top or bottom of each page. Text that appears at the top of each page is called a *header*, and text that appears at the bottom of each page is called a *footer*. When text is identified as a header or footer, it needs to be keyed in only one time after that, WordPerfect prints the text on each page. Headers and footers are common in textbooks and are also used in term papers, manuscripts, articles, and other publications.

### Considerations for Headers and Footers

WordPerfect allows up to two headers and two footers on the same page. WordPerfect refers to them as Header A, Header B, Footer A, and Footer B. (A document does not have to contain that many headers or footers; this is the maximum.) A header or footer may contain as many lines as you wish, up to a page. Generally, however, most headers and footers are only one to two lines long.

### Types of Headers and Footers

WordPerfect headers and footers can be created in various forms. They can appear on every page or can be identified as alternating headers or footers. With alternating headers or footers, text is printed only on even-numbered or odd-numbered pages.

A header or footer can be turned off or discontinued in a document. For example, you can have a header printed on pages 1 and 2 of a document and not printed on the remaining pages. You can also turn a header or footer off on specific pages.

## CREATING A HEADER OR FOOTER

To create a header in a document that prints on every page, complete the following steps:

1. Access the Format command with Shift + F8.
2. Choose 2 or P for Page.
   **M** *Click on Layout, then Page.*
3. At the Format: Page menu, choose 3 or H for Headers.
4. At the prompt **1 Header A; 2 Header B**, choose 1 or A for Header A.
5. At the prompt **1 Discontinue; 2 Every Page; 3 Odd Pages; 4 Even Pages; 5 Edit: 0**, choose 2 or P for Every Page.
6. When you choose 2 or P for Every Page, the Format: Page menu is removed from the screen and replaced by an editing screen. At this screen, key in the header text. Most WordPerfect features can be used in the header document. These features include underlining, boldfacing, indenting, and centering.
7. After the header text is keyed in, press F7 twice to return the cursor to the document.

The steps to create a footer are similar, except you choose 4 or F for Footers in step 3.

### Printing Headers and Footers

Headers and footers take the place of regular text lines. By default, 9 inches of text are printed on a standard piece of paper. WordPerfect automatically assigns a blank line after a header or a blank line before a footer. Therefore, if you create a header of 2 lines, WordPerfect prints the header (2 lines), leaves one line blank, and then prints 8.5 inches of text.

A footer prints in a similar manner. WordPerfect prints a footer on the last line of printed text and leaves a blank line between the footer and the text. If, however, a footer is more than one line long, the additional lines are printed in the bottom margin of the document.

### Creating Two Headers or Footers

If two headers or footers are created in the same document, they must be separated by either spaces or blank lines to ensure that they do not print on top of each other. For example, you can create Header A at the left margin and Header B at the right margin. Or you can create Header A on the first line of the header or footer document and Header B on the second or third line.

### Viewing Headers and Footers

Header or footer text does not appear in the main document. When a header or footer is created, a special code is inserted in the document that can be seen in Reveal Codes. If you create the name of this program, WordPerfect, as Header A to print at the left margin on every page, it appears as **[Header A:2;WordPerfect]** in Reveal Codes.

If the header or footer text is quite long, or if you create the header or footer at the right margin, WordPerfect does not display all the text; instead, you see the beginning of the code and as much of the header or footer text as possible, followed by three leaders (...). The leaders indicate that there is more text that is not visible. If you want to see how the document will print on the paper before actually printing, access View Document from the Print command.

### Editing Headers and Footers

If you have a header or footer saved in the document and decide to change it, you must bring the header or footer to the screen. To do this, complete the following steps:

1. Access the Format: Page menu with Shift + F8, then choose 2 or P for Page.
   **M** *Click on Layout, then Page.*

2. At the Format: Page menu, choose 3 or H for Headers or 4 or F for Footers.

3. At the prompt, identify which header or footer you are searching for (A or B).

4. Choose 5 or E for Edit.

5. At the header or footer screen, edit the header or footer document, then press F7.

6. At the Format: Page menu, press F7 to return the cursor to the document.

### Formatting Changes in Headers and Footers

Most formatting codes can be inserted in header or footer text, such as left and right margins, justification, and font changes. If you do not enter a margin setting in a header or footer, the margin setting of the document when the header or footer was created is used. If you later change the left and right margins in a document containing headers or footers, the margin change does not affect header or footer text. To change margins in headers or footers to match the margins in the document, you must retrieve each header or footer to the screen and change the margins.

### Extended Search or Search-and-Replace

If you conduct a search-and-replace in a document, WordPerfect does not search header or footer text. To include header or footer text in a search or in a search-and-replace, conduct an extended search or search-and-replace. To do this, press the Home key before the Search key, F2, or Replace, Alt + F2, and then conduct the search or search-and-replace in the normal manner.

### Example

To better understand how headers and footers work within a document, let us look at an example. Suppose you have a three-page document and you want to create a header at the left margin that prints the words Desktop Publishing on every page and a footer at the right margin that prints the word Typography on every page. To create the header and footer, complete the following steps:

1.  Key in the document. Move the cursor to the beginning of the document.

2.  Access the Format: Page menu with Shift + F8, then choose 2 or P for Page.
    **M** *Click on Layout, then Page.*

3.  Choose 3 or H for Headers.

4.  Choose 1 or A for Header A.

5.  Choose 2 or P for Every Page.

6.  At the header screen, key in **Desktop Publishing** at the left margin.

7.  Press F7 to return the cursor to the Format: Page menu.

8.  Choose 4 or F for Footers.

9.  Choose 1 or A for Footer A.

10. Choose 2 or P for Every Page.

11. At the footer screen, access the Flush Right command with Alt + F6 (**M** *Click on Layout, Align, then Flush Right*), and key in **Typography**.

12. Press F7 twice to return the cursor to the document.

When this document is printed, Desktop Publishing appears at the left margin at the top of each page, and Typography appears at the right margin at the bottom of each page.

## Beginning Headers and Footers on Specific Pages

If the cursor is positioned at the beginning of the document when headers or footers are created, the header or footer prints on every page. Headers and footers can also begin on a page other than 1. You determine where they begin by positioning the cursor on the appropriate page before accessing the Format: Page menu.

For example, if you want a header to begin printing on page 1, the cursor must be located on page 1, line 1 inch, before you access the Format: Page menu. If the cursor is located on any other line, the header will not begin printing until the next page. To print a header that begins on page 3, position the cursor anywhere on page 2, except line 1 inch or on page 3, line 1 inch.

A footer prints at the bottom of the page in which it is created. The cursor does not have to be located on line 1 inch. If a footer is created on line 5.5 inches of page 4, it begins printing at the bottom of page 4.

## Hard Page Breaks

Header and footer text occupy lines of your printed document. Therefore, when a header or footer is created in a document, it affects the position at which WordPerfect inserts a soft page break. WordPerfect usually inserts a soft page break after every 9 inches of text, but when a header or footer is entered, the page break occurs a few lines earlier.

If a header or footer is created at the beginning of the document and is the only header or footer in the document, you do not have to be concerned about page breaks. However, if you want to include more than one header and one or two footers, and you want them to begin on different pages, you must watch the page breaks.

For example, suppose you want a footer to begin at the bottom of page 2 and a header to begin at the top of page 4. First, key in all the text so that you know where page breaks occur. Move the cursor to page 2 (anywhere on the page), and create the footer.

Next, move the cursor to the end of the document so that WordPerfect can repaginate (adjust the soft page breaks). The footer takes up at least two lines, and WordPerfect has to compensate for that on all pages, beginning with page 2. After pagination, move the cursor to line 1 inch on page 4 and key in the header. Once again, move the cursor through the document so that soft page breaks can be shifted to accommodate the header.

The location of page breaks becomes even more important when you want to discontinue a header or footer or suppress one on a particular page. If necessary, you can insert hard page breaks in place of the soft page breaks to ensure that headers and footers will be printed or not printed on the correct pages. (A hard page break is inserted with Ctrl + Enter.)

### Page Numbers in Headers and Footers

In a previous chapter, you learned how to number pages with the Page Numbering selection from the Format: Page menu. You can also number pages within a header or footer with the command Ctrl + B. When WordPerfect prints the document, a page number is inserted where the ^B code occurred.

### Suppressing and Discontinuing Headers and Footers

Header or footer text can appear at the top or bottom of each page, beginning with the first page of the document, or it can appear on certain pages and be suppressed or discontinued on others.

To discontinue a header or footer, complete the following steps:

1.  Move to the page where the header or footer is to be discontinued and access the Format: Page menu with Shift + F8, then choose 2 or P for Page.
    **M** *Click on Layout, then Page.*

2.  Choose 3 or H for Headers or 4 or F for Footers, then identify the header or footer (A or B).

3.  From the prompt that displays at the bottom of the screen, choose 1 or D for Discontinue.

4.  Press F7 to return the cursor to the document.

The header or footer will be discontinued from the position of the cursor to the end of the document.

A header or footer can also be suppressed on a specific page. To suppress a header or footer, complete the following steps:

1.  Access the Format: Page menu with Shift + F8, then choose 2 or P for Page.
    **M** *Click on Layout, then Page.*

2.  At the Format: Page menu, choose 8 or U for Suppress (this page only), and the menu shown in figure 24-1 appears on the screen.

3. At the Format: Suppress (this page only) menu, choose 2 or S to suppress all headers and footers, choose 5 or H to suppress Header A, choose 6 or E to suppress Header B, choose 7 or F to Suppress Footer A, or choose 8 or O to Suppress Footer B.
4. Press F7 to return the cursor to the document.

```
Format: Suppress (this page only)

    1 - Suppress All Page Numbering, Headers and Footers

    2 - Suppress Headers and Footers

    3 - Print Page Number at Bottom Center   No

    4 - Suppress Page Numbering               No

    5 - Suppress Header A                      No

    6 - Suppress Header B                      No

    7 - Suppress Footer A                      No

    8 - Suppress Footer B                      No




Selection: 0
```

Figure 24-1: Format: Suppress (this page only) Menu

## EXAMPLES OF HEADERS AND FOOTERS

To better understand how headers and footers work within a document, let us look at an example. Suppose you have created a 10-page document and decide to include the following header and footers:

1. The header Types of Printers to print on every page, beginning with page 2.
2. The footer Laser Printers to print on all odd-numbered pages, beginning with page 3.
3. The footer Laser Printers to be suppressed on page 7.
4. The header Types of Printers to be discontinued after page 8.

Before entering any headers or footers, key in the text. After keying in the text, complete the following steps to create the header, Types of Printers:

1. Move the cursor to the beginning of page 2, line 1 inch.
2. Access the Format: Page menu with Shift + F8, then choose 2 or P for Page.
   **M** Click on Layout, then Page.
3. Choose 3 or H for Headers.
4. Choose 1 or A for Header A.
5. Choose 2 or P for Every Page.
6. Key in **Types of Printers**, then press F7.
7. Press F7 again to return the cursor to the document.

Because the header text occupies two extra lines on each page, move the cursor to the end of the document to adjust the soft page breaks. Once the page breaks are adjusted, complete the following steps to create the footer Laser Printers:

1. Move the cursor to page 3, line 1 inch.
2. Access the Format: Page menu with Shift + F8, then choose 2 or P for Page.
   **M** *Click on Layout, then Page.*
3. Choose 4 or F for Footers.
4. Choose 1 or A for Footer A.
5. Choose 3 or O for Odd Pages.
6. Key in **Laser Printers**, then press F7.
7. Press F7 again to return the cursor to the document.

Move the cursor to the end of the document to adjust the soft page breaks (the footer takes up additional lines on the pages). To suppress the footer on page 7, complete the following steps:

1. Move the cursor to page 7, line 1 inch.
2. Access the Format: Page menu with Shift + F8, then choose 2 or P for Page.
   **M** *Click on Layout, then Page.*
3. At the Format: Page menu, choose 8 or U for Suppress (this page only).
4. At the Format: Suppress (this page only) menu, choose 7 or F for Suppress Footer A, then key in a **Y** for Yes.
5. Press F7 to return the cursor to the document.

Move the cursor to the end of the document to readjust the last few page breaks. To discontinue the header Types of Printers after page 8, complete the following steps:

1. Move the cursor to page 9, line 1 inch.
2. Access the Format: Page menu with Shift + F8, then choose 2 or P for Page.
   **M** *Click on Layout, then Page.*
3. Choose 3 or H for Headers.
4. Choose 1 or A for Header A.
5. From the prompt that displays at the bottom of the screen, choose 1 or D for Discontinue.
6. Press F7 to return the cursor to the end of the document.

After all header footer text is entered, you may want to change the soft page breaks to hard page breaks. To do this, move the cursor to each soft page break and press Ctrl + Enter.

# CHAPTER REVIEW

## Summary

- Text that appears at the top of every page is called a header; text that appears at the bottom of every page is called a footer.
- WordPerfect allows up to two headers and two footers on the same page. WordPerfect calls them Header A, Header B, Footer A, and Footer B.
- A header or footer can contain as many lines as you need, up to a page.
- A header or footer is created at a separate screen from the main document.
- To search or search-and-replace text in a document containing headers or footers, use the extended search or search-and-replace feature.
- To format a header or footer document with the margin settings of the main document, edit the header or footer and change the margin settings.
- When a document is printed, header or footer text occupies the place of regular text lines. A blank line separates the header or footer from the main text.
- Header or footer text can be edited by retrieving the header or footer to the screen.
- When a header or footer is created, a special code is inserted in the document; this can be viewed in Reveal Codes.
- Header or footer text can begin on a page other than page 1. Determine where a header or footer begins by positioning the cursor appropriately before accessing the Format: Page menu.
- For a header to begin on a specific page, the cursor must be positioned on line 1 inch, position 1 inch, of that page (or on any line of the previous page except line 1 inch). If the cursor is positioned on any other line of the page, the header will not begin until the following page.
- A footer will be printed at the bottom of the page on which it was created.
- If a document contains headers or footers that begin and end on specific pages, you will want to paginate the document.
- A hard page break can be inserted with Ctrl + Enter.
- Page numbers can be inserted in header or footer text with the command Ctrl + B.
- Header or footer text can be suppressed on specific pages or discontinued in the document.

## STUDY GUIDE FOR CHAPTER 24

In the space provided at the right, indicate the correct term, command, symbol, or character for the explanation.

1.  Maximum number of headers that can be created in the same document.

2.  Text that appears at the bottom of every page is referred to as this.

3.  Insert a Page Numbering code in a header or footer with this command.

4.  Insert a Hard Page code with this command.

5.  If a footer is created on page 6, line 4 inches, it will begin on this page.

**True/False:** Circle the letter T if the statement is true; circle the letter F if the statement is false.

1.  A footer can be printed on even pages only.                                                    T    F

2.  Text that appears at the top of every page is called a header.                                 T    F

3.  A header or footer can contain a maximum of two lines.                                          T    F

4.  When a document is printed, header or footer text occupies the place of regular                T    F
    text lines.

5.  Header or footer text is separated from regular text by two blank lines.                        T    F

6.  When a header or footer is created, a code is inserted in the document.                         T    F

7.  Headers always begin on page 1.                                                                 T    F

8.  The page at which header or footer text begins is determined by the location of                 T    F
    the cursor before accessing the Format: Page menu.

9.  When a header or footer is inserted in a document, the position of soft page                    T    F
    breaks is affected.

## HANDS-ON EXERCISES

Create a new subdirectory named UNIT6. Change the default directory to UNIT6.

### Exercise One

1.  Display the directory. Copy CH07EX1 and name it CH24EX1.
2.  Retrieve CH24EX1 to the screen.
3.  Create the footer History of CAP at the right margin that prints on every page, by completing the following steps:
    A.  With the cursor at the beginning of the document, access the Format: Page menu with Shift + F8, then choose 2 or P for Page.
        **M** *Click on Layout, then Page.*
    B.  Choose 4 or F for Footers.
    C.  Choose 1 or A for Footer A.
    D.  Choose 2 or P for Every Page.

E. At the footer screen, access the Flush Right command with Alt + F6 (**M** *Click on Layout, Align, then Flush Right*), and key in **History of CAP**.

F. Press F7 twice to return the cursor to the document.

4. Save the document with the same name (CH24EX1). Print CH24EX1.

## Exercise Two

1. Retrieve CH24EX1.

2. Create the header, **A Community in Action**, that prints on every page but the first page at the left margin by completing the following steps:

A. Move the cursor to the beginning of page 2.

B. Access the Format: Page menu with Shift + F8, then choose 2 or P for Page. **M** *Click on Layout, then Page.*

C. Choose 3 or H for Headers.

D. Choose 1 or A for Header A.

E. Choose 2 or P for Every Page.

F. At the header screen, key in **A Community in Action**.

G. Press F7 twice to return the cursor to the document.

3. Save the document and name it CH24EX2. Print CH24EX2.

## Exercise Three

1. Retrieve CH24EX2 to the screen.

2. Discontinue the footer from page 3 to the end of the document by completing the following steps:

A. Move the cursor to the beginning of page 3.

B. Access the Format: Page menu with Shift + F8, then 2 or P for Page. **M** *Click on Layout, then Page.*

C. Choose 4 or F for Footers.

D. Choose 1 or A for Footer A.

E. Choose 1 or D for Discontinue.

F. Press F7 to return the cursor to the document.

3. Save the document and name it CH24EX3. Print CH24EX3.

## Exercise Four

1. Retrieve CH24EX3 to the screen.

2. Suppress Header A on page 3 by completing the following steps:

A. Move the cursor to the beginning of page 3.

B. Access the Format: Page menu with Shift + F8, then 2 or P for Page. **M** *Click on Layout, then Page.*

C. Choose 8 or U for Suppress (this page only).

D. At the Format: Suppress (this page only) menu, choose 5 or H for Suppress Header A, then key in a **Y** for Yes.

E. Press F7 to return the cursor to the document.

3. Save the document and name it CH24EX4. Print CH24EX4.

## Exercise Five

1. Retrieve CH11POL1 to the screen. Access Reveal Codes and delete the page numbering code.

2. Create Footer A, **LIFE INSURANCE POLICY**, at the left margin that prints on every page, by completing the following steps:

    A. With the cursor at the beginning of the document, access the Format: Page menu with Shift + F8, then choose 2 or P for Page.
       **M** *Click on Layout, then Page.*

    B. Choose 4 or F for Footers.

    C. Choose 1 or A for Footer A.

    D. Choose 2 or P for Every Page.

    E. At the footer screen, key in **LIFE INSURANCE POLICY**.

    F. Press F7 twice to return the cursor to the document.

3.  Create Footer B, Page ^B, that prints at the right margin on every page but the first by completing the following steps:

    A. Move the cursor to the beginning of page 2.

    B. Access the Format: Page menu with Shift + F8, then choose 2 or P for Page.
       **M** *Click on Layout, then Page.*

    C. Choose 4 or F for Footers.

    D. Choose 2 or B for Footer B.

    E. Choose 2 or P for Every Page.

    F. At the footer screen, access the Flush Right command with Alt + F6 (**M** *Click on Layout, Align, then Flush Right*). Key in **Page**, then access the page numbering command with Ctrl + B.

    G. Press F7 twice to return the cursor to the document.

4.  Save the policy and name it CH24EX5. Print CH24EX5.

## Exercise Six

1.  Retrieve CH24EX2 to the screen.

2.  Retrieve Header A to the editing screen by completing the following steps:

    A. Access the Format: Page menu with Shift + F8, then 2 or P for Page.
       **M** *Click on Layout, then Page.*

    B. Choose 3 or H for Headers.

    C. Choose 1 or A for Header A.

    D. Choose 5 or E for Edit.

    E. With the header **A Community in Action** displayed on the screen, delete the header. Key in **Page**, press the space bar, then access the command to insert a Page Numbering code with Ctrl + B. (Your new header should look like this: **Page ^B**.)

3.  Save the document and name it CH24EX6. Print CH24EX6.

## PERFORMANCE ASSESSMENTS

### Assessment One

1.  Display the directory. Copy CH07EX5 and name it CH24PA1.

2.  Retrieve CH24PA1 to the screen. Access Reveal Codes and delete the code for line spacing 2. Insert a code that changes the line spacing to 3.

3.  Create Footer A, **EVOLUTION OF THE TYPEWRITER**, at the left margin on every page.

4.  Create Footer B, **DVORAK KEYBOARD**, at the right margin beginning with page 3.

5.  Save the document and name it CH24PA1. Print CH24PA1.

**Assessment Two**

1.  Retrieve CH11POL2 to the screen. Access Reveal Codes and delete the page numbering code.

2.  Access Reveal Codes and delete the code for double spacing and insert a code that changes the line spacing to triple.

3.  Create Footer A, **POLICY AGREEMENT**, that prints at the left margin on every page.

4.  Create Header A, **Page ^B**, that prints at the right margin of every page except the first page.

5.  Suppress Footer A on page 3.

6.  Save the policy and name it CH24PA2. Print CH24PA2.

# CHAPTER 25

## FOOTNOTES AND ENDNOTES

## *PERFORMANCE OBJECTIVE*

Upon successful completion of chapter 25, you will be able to amend a researched business report with properly formatted references and footnotes.

### FOOTNOTES AND ENDNOTES

A research paper or report contains information from a variety of sources. To give credit to these sources, a footnote can be inserted in the document. A footnote is an explanatory note or reference that is printed at the bottom of the page.

A footnote notation appears in the body of the document as a superscript number. This number identifies the footnote at the bottom of the page that contains information identifying the source.

Creating footnotes on a typewriter requires some calculating. The typist needs to determine how many footnote notations are made on a particular page and how many lines are required at the bottom of the page for the footnotes. The typist needs to leave enough room at the bottom of the page for the footnotes and still allow a 1-inch bottom margin.

WordPerfect simplifies this task. The typist simply identifies the location of the footnote notation and keys in the footnote reference. WordPerfect determines the number of lines needed at the bottom of the page and adjusts the page endings accordingly.

An endnote is similar to a footnote, except that endnote reference information appears at the end of a document rather than on the page where the reference was made. Endnotes and footnotes are created in a similar manner with WordPerfect.

## Creating a Footnote

A typist using WordPerfect to create a research paper or report can include a footnote and reference while keying in the document or after the document is completed.

To create a footnote, complete the following steps:

1. Move the cursor to the location in the document where the notation is to appear and access the Footnote command with Ctrl + F7.

2. At the prompt **1 Footnote; 2 Endnote; 3 Endnote Placement: 0**, choose 1 or F for Footnote.

3. At the **Footnote: 1 Create; 2 Edit; 3 New Number; 4 Options: 0** prompt, choose 1 or C for Create.
   **M** *Click on Layout, Footnote, then Create.*

4. When you choose Create, WordPerfect takes you to a special editing screen that displays the first footnote number and the cursor in the upper left corner of the screen indented five spaces from the left margin. Key in the footnote reference information at this screen. When the footnote is keyed in, press F7 to return the cursor to the document, and insert the footnote reference number.

A footnote can be up to 16,000 lines long. You can use many WordPerfect features in this special editing screen, including Block, Move, and Speller.

## Creating an Endnote

To create an endnote, complete the following steps:

1. Move the cursor to the location in the document where the notation is to appear and access the Footnote command with Ctrl + F7.

2. At the prompt **1 Footnote; 2 Endnote; 3 Endnote Placement: 0**, choose 2 or E for Endnote.

3. At the **Endnote: 1 Create; 2 Edit; 3 New Number; 4 Options: 0** prompt, choose 1 or C for Create.
   **M** *Click on Layout, Endnote, then Create.*

4. When you choose Create, WordPerfect takes you to a special editing screen that displays the first endnote number followed by a period and the cursor. Press the Tab key once or the space bar a couple of times to separate the endnote reference information from the number. Key in the endnote reference information at this screen, then press F7 to return the cursor to the document.

An endnote can be up to 16,000 lines long. You can use many WordPerfect features in this special editing screen, including Block, Move, and Speller.

## Editing a Footnote

Changes can be made to footnotes that have previously been entered in a document. To edit an existing footnote, complete the following steps:

1. Access the Footnote command with Ctrl + F7, choose 1 or F for Footnote, then 2 or E for Edit.
   **M** *Click on Layout, Footnote, then Edit.*

2. At the prompt **Footnote number?** <u>1</u>, key in the number of the footnote you want to edit and press Enter. WordPerfect searches through the document, retrieves the footnote, and displays it in the special editing screen.

3. Make any necessary changes to the footnote reference information, then press F7 to return the cursor to the document.

### Editing an Endnote

Editing an endnote is similar to editing a footnote. To edit an endnote, complete the following steps:

1. With the cursor resting anywhere in the document, access the Footnote command with Ctrl + F7, choose 2 or E for Endnote, then 2 or E for Edit.
   **M** *Click on Layout, Endnote, then Edit.*

2. At the prompt **Endnote number?** <u>1</u>, key in the number of the endnote you want to edit, then press Enter.

3. Make any necessary changes to the endnote reference information, then press F7 to return the cursor to the document.

### Deleting a Footnote/Endnote

A footnote or endnote can be removed from a document by moving the cursor to the footnote or endnote number and pressing either the Delete key or the Backspace key. To use the Delete key, position the cursor under the footnote or endnote number. To use the Backspace key, position the cursor to the right of the number.

When either the Backspace key or the Delete key is pressed, the following prompt appears at the bottom of the screen: **Delete [Note]?** <u>N</u>o (<u>Y</u>es). Key in a Y for Yes and WordPerfect deletes the number as well as the footnote or endnote reference from the document. In addition, WordPerfect automatically renumbers the remaining footnotes or endnotes.

### Printing a Footnote

When a document containing footnotes is printed, WordPerfect automatically reduces the number of text lines on a page by the number of lines in the footnote along with two lines for spacing between the text and the footnote. If there is not enough room on the page, the footnote number and footnote are taken to the next page. WordPerfect separates the footnotes from the text with a 2-inch line beginning at the left margin.

The footnote number in the document as well as the footnote number before the reference information prints as superscript numbers above the line.

### Printing an Endnote

When endnotes are created in a document, WordPerfect prints all endnote references at the end of the document beginning with the last page. If you want the endnotes printed on a separate page at the end of the document, insert a Hard Page code with Ctrl + Enter at the end of the text.

You can also have endnotes placed in other locations in the document. To do this, complete the following steps:

1. Access the Footnote command with Ctrl + F7, then choose 3 or P for Endnote Placement.
   **M** *Click on Layout, Endnote, then Placement.*

2. WordPerfect displays the prompt **Restart endnote numbering? Yes (No)**. If you are inserting endnotes in different locations in the document, you may either want to restart numbering at each location or let WordPerfect number the endnotes consecutively. If you want endnote numbering to restart, press Enter. If you want endnotes numbered consecutively, key in an N for No.

When the above steps are completed, WordPerfect inserts the following comment in the document.

---

Endnote Placement
It is not known how much space endnotes will occupy here.
Generate to determine.

---

To see how much space the endnotes will occupy on the page, the endnotes must be generated. To do this, complete the following steps:

1. Access the Mark Text command with Alt + F5.

2. Choose 6 or G for Generate.
   **M** *Click on Mark, then Generate.*

3. At the Mark Text: Generate menu, choose 5 or G for Generate Tables, Indexes, Cross-References, etc.

4. At the prompt **Existing tables, lists, and indexes will be replaced. Continue? Yes (No)**, key in a Y for Yes.

When the endnotes are generated, the comment on the screen changes to the following.

---

Endnote Placement

---

The amount of space taken up by the endnotes is determined by WordPerfect and accounted for on the screen (even though the code appears to be small).

### Entering a New Footnote/Endnote Number

When a footnote or endnote is created in a document, the numbering begins with 1 and continues sequentially. The beginning footnote or endnote number can be changed to whatever you need. For example, if you want the footnote or endnote numbering to begin with 4, complete the following steps:

1. Access the Footnote command with Ctrl + F7, choose 1 or F for footnote or 2 or E for Endnote, then choose 3 or N for New Number.
   **M** *Click on Layout, Footnote, then New Number; or, click on Layout, Endnote, then New Number.*

2.  WordPerfect displays the prompt **Footnote number?** or **Endnote number?** at the bottom of the screen. Key in a **4** and press Enter.

## FOOTNOTE OPTIONS MENU

The Options selection from the Footnote prompt is used to change the format of a footnote. When you access the Footnote command with Ctrl + F7, choose 1 or F for Footnote, then 4 or O for Options (**M** *Click on Layout, Footnote, then Options*), the text disappears and is replaced by the Footnote Options menu shown in figure 25-1.

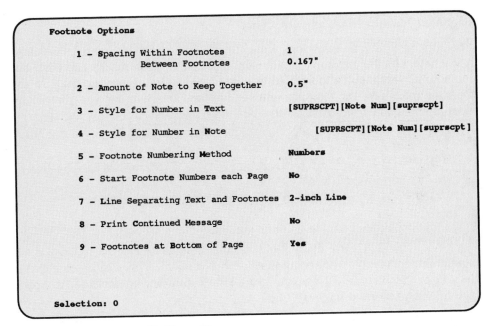

```
Footnote Options


       1 - Spacing Within Footnotes          1
                Between Footnotes             0.167"

       2 - Amount of Note to Keep Together    0.5"

       3 - Style for Number in Text           [SUPRSCPT][Note Num][suprscpt]

       4 - Style for Number in Note                   [SUPRSCPT][Note Num][suprscpt]

       5 - Footnote Numbering Method          Numbers

       6 - Start Footnote Numbers each Page   No

       7 - Line Separating Text and Footnotes 2-inch Line

       8 - Print Continued Message            No

       9 - Footnotes at Bottom of Page        Yes



  Selection: 0
```

Figure 25-1: Footnote Options Menu

### Spacing Within and Between Footnotes

The first selection lets you determine the spacing within footnotes and endnotes. The default setting is 1, single spacing. To have more line spacing within footnotes or endnotes, complete the following steps:

1.  At the Footnote Options menu, choose 1 or S for Spacing Within Footnotes, and the cursor moves to the location of the number 1. Key in the line spacing you desire and press Enter.

2.  With the cursor located on 0.167" after Between Footnotes, key in the line spacing you desire and press Enter.

3.  Press F7 to return the cursor to the document.

The default setting for Between Footnotes is 0.167 inches. By default, WordPerfect inserts a blank line between footnotes or endnotes. If you want more line spacing between your footnotes or endnotes, key in the inch measurement of the line spacing you desire, and press Enter. For example, if you want footnotes to be separated by a triple space, key in .5 after Between Footnotes.

## Amount of Note to Keep Together

The Amount of Note to Keep Together selection from the Footnote Options menu tells WordPerfect to keep at least 0.5 inches (approximately three lines) of a footnote or endnote together on a page. If you want more or fewer lines kept together, complete the following steps:

1. At the Footnote Options menu, choose 2 or A for Amount of Note to Keep Together.

2. Key in the inch measurement of the number of lines you want kept together and press Enter.

3. Press F7 to return the cursor to the document.

## Style for Number in Text and Note

The third and fourth selections from the Footnote Options menu show how a footnote number appears in the text and in the footnote. In the text, the footnote appears as a superscript number immediately after the text. In the footnote reference, the footnote number appears as a superscript number indented five spaces. To change these settings, complete the following steps:

1. At the Footnote Options menu, choose 3 or T for Style for Number in Text or 4 or N for Style for Number in Note.

2. At the **Replace with:** prompt, key in the new style you desire, then press Enter.

3. Press F7 to return the cursor to the document.

## Footnote Numbering Method

The default footnote numbering method is Numbers. This can be changed to letters or characters. To change the footnote numbering method, complete the following steps:

1. At the Footnote Options menu, choose 5 or M for Footnote Numbering Method.

2. At the prompt **1 Numbers; 2 Letters; 3 Characters: 0**, key in the new selection and press Enter.

3. Press F7 to return the cursor to the document.

## Start Footnote Numbers on Each Page

The WordPerfect default is to number footnotes consecutively throughout the document. If you want footnote numbers to start with 1 at the beginning of each new page, complete the following steps:

1. At the Footnote Options menu, choose 6 or P for Start Footnote Numbers on each Page.

2. Key in a Y for Yes.

3. Press F7 to return the cursor to the document.

## Line Separating Text and Footnotes

When a document containing footnotes is printed, the text is separated from the footnote references with a 2-inch line, which is the default setting for the Line Separating Text and Footnotes selection from the Footnote Options menu. To change this default setting, complete the following steps:

1.  At the Footnote Options menu, choose 7 or L for Line Separating Text and Footnotes.

2.  At the prompt **1 <u>N</u>o Line; 2 2-inch Line; 3 <u>M</u>argin to Margin: <u>0</u>**, choose 1 or N for No Line if you do not want a line to print between the text and the footnotes; choose 2 for 2-inch Line if you want the default of a 2-inch line; choose 3 or M for Margin to Margin if you want a line to print from the left margin to the right margin.

3.  Press F7 to return the cursor to the document.

### Print Continued Message

When WordPerfect encounters a long footnote that does not fit at the bottom of the page, the remainder of the footnote is taken over to the bottom of the next page. A "continued" message can be inserted at the bottom of the first page to indicate that the footnote continues to the next.

The default setting for the Print Continued Message selection from the Footnote Options menu is No. To change this to Yes, complete the following steps:

1.  At the Footnote Options menu, choose 8 or C for Print Continued Message.

2.  Key in a Y for Yes.

3.  Press F7 to return the cursor to the document.

### Footnotes at Bottom of Page

When footnotes appear on a page containing a small amount of text, WordPerfect inserts blank lines between the end of the text and the beginning of the footnotes to ensure that there is a 1-inch margin at the bottom of the page. The Footnote at Bottom of Page selection from the Footnote Options menu has a default setting of Yes. If you do not want blank lines inserted between the end of text and the beginning of footnotes, complete the following steps:

1.  At the Footnote Options menu, choose 9 or B for Footnotes at Bottom.

2.  Key in an N for No.

3.  Press F7 to return the cursor to the document.

## ENDNOTE OPTIONS MENU

The Endnote Options menu is similar to the Footnote Options menu. It contains selections to change the format of an endnote. When you choose 4 or O for Options from the **Endnote** prompt, the text disappears and is replaced by the Endnote Options menu shown in figure 25-2.

```
Endnote Options

     1 - Spacing Within Endnotes          1
                Between Endnotes           0.167"

     2 - Amount of Endnote to Keep Together   0.5"

     3 - Style for Numbers in Text         [SUPRSCPT][Note Num][suprscpt]

     4 - Style for Numbers in Note         [Note Num].

     5 - Endnote Numbering Method          Numbers

     Selection: 0
```

Figure 25-2: Endnote Options Menu

The selections from this menu are similar to the selections from the Footnote Options menu. The only difference is that the default style for numbers in a note is to display the number at the left margin followed by a period.

Make changes to this menu in the same manner as you make changes to the Footnote Options menu.

## FOOTNOTE CONSIDERATIONS

Footnotes and endnotes assume the default 1-inch left and right margins no matter what margins are set in the document. If you want footnotes or endnotes to print with a different margin setting, you must change the settings at the footnote or endnote editing screen. You can do this as you create the footnote or endnote for the first time. Or, you can change the margins in existing footnotes or endnotes by retrieving them to the screen with the edit selection.

If line spacing is changed in a document containing footnotes or endnotes, the footnotes or endnotes do not assume the new line spacing. Line spacing in footnotes or endnotes is separate from the main document and is controlled at the Footnote or Endnote Options menu.

## CHAPTER REVIEW

### Summary

- A footnote is an explanatory note or reference that is printed at the bottom of the page. An endnote is an explanatory note or reference that is printed at the end of a document.

- Footnotes and endnotes are created at a special editing screen. A footnote or endnote may be up to 16,000 lines long. Special Word-Perfect features such as Block, Move, and Speller can be used.
- To create a footnote, access the Footnote command with Ctrl + F7, choose 1 or F for Footnote, then 1 or C for Create (**M** *Click on Layout, Footnote, then Create*). To create an endnote, access the Footnote command with Ctrl + F7, choose 2 or E for Endnote, then 1 or C for Create (**M** *Click on Layout, Endnote, then Create*).
- To edit a footnote, access the Footnote command with Ctrl + F7, choose 1 or F for Footnote, then 2 or E for Edit. (**M** *Click on Layout, Footnote, then Edit.*) To edit an endnote, access the Footnote command with Ctrl + F7, choose 2 or E for Endnote, then 3 or E for Edit. (**M** *Click on Layout, Endnote, then Edit.*)
- To delete a footnote or endnote, move the cursor to the footnote or endnote number, press the Delete key, and answer Yes to the delete question. The Backspace key can also be used to delete a footnote or endnote when the cursor is resting one space to the right of the number.
- When a footnote is printed, WordPerfect reduces the number of text lines on a page by the number of lines in the footnote along with two lines for spacing between the text and the footnote.
- Endnotes are printed at the end of a document. To print endnotes on a separate page, enter a Hard Page command with Ctrl + Enter at the end of the text.
- Endnotes can be inserted anywhere in the document by accessing the Footnote command with Ctrl + F7, then choosing 3 or P for Endnote Placement.
- Footnotes or endnotes can be numbered with a beginning number other than 1.
- By default, footnotes and endnotes are single spaced within notes.
- By default, WordPerfect inserts a blank line between footnotes or endnotes.
- WordPerfect tries to keep 0.5 inches (approximately three lines) of a footnote or endnote together on a page. By default, footnotes and endnotes are numbered. This can be changed to letters or characters.
- When a document containing footnotes is printed, footnotes are separated from text by a 2-inch line. This can be changed to no line, or a line from the left to right margins.
- WordPerfect inserts blank lines between the end of text and the foot-note line to ensure a 1-inch bottom margin. This can be turned off.
- If margin changes are made to a document containing footnotes or endnotes, the footnotes or endnotes do not accept the new settings. To adjust footnotes or endnotes to new margin settings, bring each footnote or endnote to the screen and change the margins.
- Line spacing changes in a document containing footnotes or endnotes do not affect spacing in footnotes or endnotes.

**Commands Review**

**Keyboard**

| | |
|---|---|
| Footnote command | Ctrl + F7 |
| Create a footnote | Ctrl + F7, 1 or F, 1 or C |
| Create an endnote | Ctrl + F7, 2 or E, 1 or C |
| Edit a footnote | Ctrl + F7, 1 or F, 2 or E |
| Edit an endnote | Ctrl + F7, 2 or E, 2 or E |
| Endnote Placement | Ctrl + F7, 3 or P |
| Footnote new number | Ctrl + F7, 1 or F, 3 or N |
| Endnote new number | Ctrl + F7, 2 or E, 3 or N |
| Footnote Options menu | Ctrl + F7, 1 or F, 4 or O |
| Endnote Options menu | Ctrl + F7, 2 or E, 4 or O |

**Mouse**

| | |
|---|---|
| Create a footnote | Layout, Footnote, Create |
| Create an endnote | Layout, Endnote, Create |
| Edit a footnote | Layout, Footnote, Edit |
| Edit an endnote | Layout, Endnote, Edit |
| Endnote Placement | Layout, Endnote, Placement |
| Footnote new number | Layout, Footnote, New Number |
| Endnote new number | Layout, Endnote, New Number |
| Footnote Options menu | Layout, Footnote, Options |
| Endnote Options menu | Layout, Endnote, Options |

## STUDY GUIDE FOR CHAPTER 25

**True/False:** Circle the letter T if the statement is true; circle the letter F if the statement is false.

1. Footnote numbering starts with 1 at the beginning of each page.　　　T　　F

2. All footnotes in a document are printed on the last page.　　　T　　F

3. When the endnote reference information has been entered, press Exit, F7, to return to the document.　　　T　　F

4. You must be in Reveal Codes to delete a footnote.　　　T　　F

5. When an endnote is deleted, WordPerfect automatically renumbers the remaining endnotes.　　　T　　F

6. By default, WordPerfect separates footnotes from the text by a line across the entire length of the page.　　　T　　F

7. If margin settings are changed in a document containing footnotes or endnotes, the footnotes or endnotes automatically assume the new margin settings.　　　T　　F

8. To edit a footnote or endnote, the cursor must be positioned at the beginning of the document before accessing the Footnote command.　　　T　　F

9. If line spacing is changed in a document containing footnotes or endnotes, the footnotes or endnotes do not assume the new line spacing.　　　T　　F

**Completion:** In the space provided at the right, indicate the correct symbol, term, or number for the explanation.

1. Access the Footnote command.　　　_____

2. Default spacing within endnotes.　　　_____

3. The WordPerfect default character for endnotes or footnotes.　　　_____

4. Default spacing between footnotes.　　　_____

5. Maximum number of lines a footnote or endnote may contain.　　　_____

6. Access the Footnote Options menu.　　　_____

## HANDS-ON EXERCISES

Change the default directory to UNIT6.

**Exercise One**

1. At a clear screen, change the line spacing to double. Key in the information in figure 25-3. Boldface and center the heading.

2. Insert footnote numbers as indicated. Key in the footnote reference information displayed in figure 25-4.

3. Save the document and name it CH25EX1. Print CH25EX1.

## WORDPERFECT OUTSELLING THEM ALL

Nestled in the foothills of the Rocky Mountains in the state of Utah is the town of Orem, twin city to Provo. During the last few years, this town has gained nationwide attention as the home of the popular word processing program, WordPerfect.[1]

What has caused this word processing program to take the nation by storm? What is it about the program that causes national as well as international sales to skyrocket? To understand the popularity of the program, one must look to the development of the company, now called WordPerfect Corporation.

WordPerfect Corporation began in 1976 with two men--Alan Ashton, a science professor at Brigham Young University, and Bruce Bastian, a student at the University. They found they had common interests in music and computers. In 1978 these two men formed a company they called Satellite Systems, Inc. They wrote a word processing program they named SSI*WP that was designed to run on Data General Equipment.[2]

In 1979 they changed the name of the company to Satellite Software, Inc., and began marketing their SSI*WP program. The company started slowly but began picking up momentum in the early 1980s. Many new employees joined the company. In 1982 the SSI*WP program was written to operate on IBM personal computers. During the rewriting of the program, Ashton and Bastian enlisted the help of the secretaries for the City of Orem who were using SSI*WP on Data General Equipment. The program designed for microcomputers was named "WordPerfect."[3]

In 1983, WordPerfect nudged ahead of other word processing programs that had been popular and became the top-selling word processing program for microcomputers.[4]

In 1986, Satellite Software, Inc., officially changed its name to WordPerfect Corporation. A company that started out with just two men now boasts over 500 employees. The WordPerfect program continues to be the top-selling word processing program and is moving into the international market.[5]

Figure 25-3: Exercise One

Footnote #1:  Cruz, Margaux, "Word Processing with WordPerfect," Information Systems, September, 1988, page 49.

Footnote #2:  Mosetti, Brian R., "WordPerfect--The Beginning," Software News, August, 1988, pages 78-79.

Footnote #3:  Cruz, Margaux, "Word Processing with WordPerfect," Information Systems, September, 1988, page 50.

```
Footnote #4:   Zandt-Myer, Toni, and Rhea G. Nichols, "Top-Selling
Word Processing Programs," Computers, Inc., November, 1988, page
23.

Footnote #5:   Mosetti, Brian R., "WordPerfect--The Beginning,"
Software News,   August, 1988, page 81.
```

**Figure 25-4: Exercise One**

## Exercise Two

1. Retrieve CH25EX1 to the screen.
2. Delete all footnotes.
3. Create endnotes for this document in the same location as the footnotes. Use the reference information in figure 25-4.
4. Insert a hard page break at the end of the document. This causes the endnotes to print on a separate page.
5. Save the document and name it CH25EX2. Print CH25EX2.

## Exercise Three

1. Retrieve CH25EX2 to the screen.
2. Change the left and right margins to 1.5 inches. Retrieve each endnote and change the margins to 1.5 inches.
3. Save the document and name it CH25EX3. Print CH25EX3.

## Exercise Four

1. Retrieve CH25EX1 to the screen. (This document contains footnotes.)
2. Begin footnotes with number 4 rather than the default of 1 by completing the following steps:
   A. Access the Footnote command with Ctrl + F7.
   B. Choose 1 or F for Footnote.
   C. Choose 3 or N for New Number.
      **M** *Click on Layout, Footnote, then New Number.*
   D. Key in a **4** and press Enter.
3. Change the line separating the footnotes from the body of the text by a line that runs from margin to margin rather than the 2-inch line. To do this, complete the following steps:
   A. Access the Footnote command with Ctrl + F7.
   B. Choose 1 or F for Footnote.
   C. Choose 4 or O for Options.
      **M** *Click on Layout, Footnote, then Options.*
   D. At the Footnote Options menu, choose 7 or L for Line Separating Text and Footnotes.
   E. At the **1 No Line; 2 2-inch Line; 3 Margin to Margin: 0** prompt, choose 3 or M for Margin to Margin.
   F. Press F7 to return the cursor to the document.
4. Save the document and name it CH25EX4. Print CH25EX4.

## PERFORMANCE ASSESSMENTS

**Assessment One**

1.  Display the directory. Copy CH07EX5 and name it CH25PA1.
2.  Retrieve CH25PA1 to the screen.
3.  Insert footnote reference numbers and information in the document as follows:
    A.  Move the cursor to the space after the period at the end of the third paragraph and create the following footnote: Brooks, Norma L., "The Typewriter Then and Now," *Information Processing in Today's World*, Second Edition. Rutherford Publishing, 1983, pages 45-47.
    B.  Move the cursor to the space after the period at the end of the fourth paragraph and create the following footnote: Ryerson, Jonathon, "The Development of the Typewriter," *Business Education for the 80's*, Ashanti & Sons Publishing, 1980, pages 24-29.
    C.  Move the cursor to the space after the period at the end of the ninth paragraph and create the following footnote: Manley, Eugene E., and Dinah McNally, "Dvorak Keyboard Efficiency," *Computers Unlimited*, August, 1988, pages 20-23.
    D.  Move the cursor to the space after the period at the end of the tenth paragraph and create the following footnote: Shearson, Cecilia, "The Dvorak Keyboard," *WSBEA Quarterly*, September/October, 1988, page 54.
4.  With the cursor at the beginning of the document, change the beginning footnote number to 5.
5.  Change the line separating the footnotes from the text with a line from margin to margin.
6.  Save the report as CH25PA1. Print CH25PA1.

**Assessment Two**

1.  Retrieve CH25PA1 to the screen and make the following changes:
    A.  Change the base font to 10-point Courier (or 10-point in your default typeface).
    B.  Delete the [Just:Left] code.
    C.  Delete all footnote notations.
    D.  Insert endnotes in the document. Use the reference information from Assessment One and insert endnotes in the same location as the footnotes were inserted.
    E.  Move to the end of the document and insert a Hard Page code with Ctrl + Enter. (This causes the endnotes to print on a separate page.)
2.  Save the report and name it CH25PA2. Print CH25PA2.

# CHAPTER 26

## MACROS

## PERFORMANCE OBJECTIVE

Upon successful completion of chapter 26, you will be able to automate keystrokes, such as the closing to a business letter, you may repeat in many different business documents.

## MACROS

WordPerfect has a time-saving feature called *macros*. With macros, you can save a series of keystrokes under a particular name and bring those keystrokes back to the screen at any time. WordPerfect's macro feature lets you record and play back (called *executing*) keystrokes.

A macro can contain letters, words, terms, or commands. Macros can contain frequently used

- terms and phrases
- formats
- commands

If you spend a little time creating macros, you can save time and effort later.

### Defining a Macro

To *define* a macro, you must perform five basic steps. *Define* is the term WordPerfect attaches to the process of identifying text or commands to be saved. The five steps are:

1. Access the Macro Define command with Ctrl + F10.
   **M** *Click on Tools, Macro, then Define.*
2. Name the macro.
3. Provide a description of the macro.
4. Define the macro by entering the keystrokes.
5. End by accessing the Macro Define command with Ctrl + F10.

As keystrokes are entered for the macro in step 4, editing changes can be made. WordPerfect, however, records all keystrokes, including keystrokes to correct an error. Once the macro is defined, you cannot change it unless you redefine the macro or go to a special editing screen. Macro files cannot be retrieved to the regular editing screen.

### Naming a Macro

Three types of macros can be created. They are a named macro, an Alt key macro, and a temporary macro. A named macro is one to which you assign a unique name. Macro names follow the same rules as naming a document. A macro name can be from one to eight characters long, including letters, numbers, and symbols. Do not use the period (.) when naming a macro. WordPerfect adds a period and the extension WPM (for WordPerfect Macro) to a macro name. When you name a macro, name it with something that is easy to remember and gives you an idea of what is saved in the macro.

There can be up to 26 Alt key macros. An Alt key macro is similar to a named macro, except that it uses the Alt key in combination with one of the 26 letters of the alphabet to define macros that can be quickly executed. If a macro was named with Alt + S, it would appear as ALTS.WPM in the directory.

While creating or editing a WordPerfect document, you may want to create a temporary macro. A temporary macro stays in effect only as long as you are working in the current document. As soon as you exit the document, the macro is deleted. WordPerfect allows only one temporary macro at a time. The temporary macro is named with the Enter key.

### Describing a Macro

The macro description is a brief explanation of what the macro contains and can be a maximum of 39 characters long. The description can contain letters, numbers, and spaces. The macro description is entered when the macro is being defined.

### Executing a Macro

After a macro has been defined, it can be executed in the document. To execute a named macro, complete the following steps:

1. Key in the text to the point where the macro is to be executed and access the Macro command with Alt + F10.
   **M** *Click on Tools, Macro, then Execute.*
2. Key in the name assigned to the macro, then press Enter.

The information saved in the macro will be brought to the screen. Or, if the macro was a command (or series of commands), it will be executed.

To execute an Alt key macro, complete the following steps:

1. Key in the text to the point where the macro is to be executed.
2. Hold down the Alt key and press the letter you assigned to the macro.

### Canceling a Macro

The Cancel key, F1, can be used to cancel a macro when it is being executed. Macros execute quickly, so the macro may be executed before the Cancel key can take effect. During the define process, you can end a macro by accessing the Macro Define command with Ctrl + F10 (**M** *Click on Macro, then Define*). This ends and saves the macro. If the macro is not needed, it can be deleted from the directory or redefined.

### Deleting a Macro

When a macro is created, it displays in the directory with the extension .WPM. A macro can be deleted from the directory in the same manner as a regular document.

## LOCATION OF MACRO FILES

When a macro is defined, more than likely it will be saved in the WP51 directory. (This is the default during setup.) In some situations, you may want to change where WordPerfect saves macro files. For example, in a school setting, you may want to change the location of macro files to Drive A or Drive B (the drive that contains your student disk). This lets you create macros and save them on your disk.

To change the location of macro files, complete the following steps:

1. Access the Setup command with Shift + F1.
2. At the Setup menu, choose 6 or L for Location of Files.
   **M** *Click on File, Setup, then Location of Files.*
3. At the Setup: Location of Files menu, choose 2 or K for Keyboard/-Macro Files.
4. With the cursor at **Location of Keyboard/Macro Files,** key in the letter of the drive where you want macro files saved and press Enter.
5. Press F7 to return the cursor to the document.

Changes made to this menu will remain in effect even after you exit Word-Perfect.

## MACRO EXAMPLES

The following examples illustrate how to define macros that contain frequently used terms, frequently used formats, and frequently used commands.

### Frequently Used Terms

In a law office, the term *plaintiff* is used often in legal documents. To create *plaintiff* as an Alt key macro named Alt + P, complete the following steps:

1. Access the Macro Define command with Ctrl + F10.
   **M** *Click on Tools, Macro, then Define.*
2. At the **Define macro:** prompt, hold the Alt key down and press the letter P (for Plaintiff).
3. At the **Description:** prompt, key in **Enter plaintiff**, then press Enter.

4.  With **Macro Def** flashing in the lower left corner of the screen, key in **Plaintiff**.

5.  End by accessing the Macro Define command with Ctrl + F10.

## Frequently Used Formats

You can save time formatting a document by including frequently used formats in a macro. For example, the steps to change the left and right margins to 1.5 inches can be defined in a macro named MAR by completing the following steps:

1.  Access the Macro Define command with Ctrl + F10.
    **M** *Click on Tools, Macro, then Define.*

2.  At the **Define macro:** prompt, key in **MAR** and press Enter.

3.  At the **Description:** prompt, key in **Change margins to 1.5 inches**, then press Enter.

4.  With **Macro Def** flashing in the lower left corner of the screen, complete the following steps:
    A.  Access the Format: Line menu with Shift + F8, then choose 1 or L for Line.
        **M** *Click on Layout, then Line.*
    B.  At the Format: Line menu, choose 7 or M for Margins.
    C.  Key in **1.5** and press Enter.
    D.  Key in **1.5** and press Enter.
    E.  Press F7 to return the cursor to the document.

5.  End the macro by accessing the Macro Define command with Ctrl + F10.

The formats are saved in the macro and are also inserted in the document. If you do not want the format changes in the current document, delete them in Reveal Codes.

## Frequently Used Commands

Commands that you use on a regular basis can be saved in a macro. You can define the steps needed to print the document on the screen and save the steps in a macro named PR by completing the following steps:

1.  Access the Macro Define command with Ctrl + F10.
    **M** *Click on Tools, Macro, then Define.*

2.  At the **Define macro:** prompt, key in **PR** and press Enter.

3.  At the **Description:** prompt, key in **Print current document**, and press Enter.

4.  With **Macro Def** flashing in the bottom left corner of the screen, access the Print command with Shift + F7.
    **M** *Click on File, then Print.*

5.  Choose 1 or F for Full Document.

6.  End the macro by accessing the Macro Define command with Ctrl + F10.

## MACRO CHAINING

You can execute a macro that executes another macro that executes yet another macro. WordPerfect calls this macro *chaining*. When defining a macro, you can key in text, commands, formats, or another macro. WordPerfect allows only one macro to be defined within another macro. You can, however, insert a macro within a second macro and insert that combination within a macro, and so on. When chaining macros, WordPerfect executes the first macro before executing the macro within.

For example, you can define a macro to change the margin settings and then define a macro that changes the top margin and also executes the macro for margin settings. Then you can define a macro that changes the paper size and type and executes the macro that includes the margin top and the macro for changing margins.

To understand how macro chaining works, suppose you wanted to include the MAR macro in a macro named LS that changes line spacing to double. To do this, complete the following steps:

1. Access the Macro Define command with Ctrl + F10.
   **M** *Click on Tools, Macro, then Define.*

2. At the **Define macro:** prompt, key in **LS** (for line spacing) and press Enter.

3. At the **Description:** prompt, key in **Change margins and line spacing**, and press Enter.

4. With **Macro Def** flashing in the bottom left corner of the screen, change the line spacing by completing the following steps:
   A. Access the Format: Line menu with Shift + F8, then choose 1 or L for Line.
      **M** *Click on Layout, then Line.*
   B. Choose 6 or S for Spacing.
   C. Key in a **2** and press Enter.
   D. Press F7.

5. Execute the MAR macro by completing the following steps:
   A. Access the Macro command with Alt + F10.
   B. At the **Macro:** prompt, key in **MAR**, and press Enter.

6. End the macro by accessing the Macro Define command with Ctrl + F10.

When the LS macro is executed, the line spacing and the margin settings are changed.

## MACRO NESTING

Macro nesting is similar to macro chaining. The difference is that when a macro is nested, WordPerfect executes the macro at the location where the macro was inserted, not at the end, as it does when chaining. The only macros that can be nested are macros saved with the Alt key.

In the example shown in figure 26-1, the law firm name, NELSON & FREEMAN, is contained in a macro named Alt + N. The paragraph containing the law firm name is a macro named PARA (for paragraph). The Alt + N macro is nested in the PARA macro. To create the PARA macro, complete the following steps:

1. Define a macro named Alt + N that contains the law firm name NELSON & FREEMAN.

2. Define the PARA macro by completing the following steps:
   A. Access the Macro Define command with Ctrl + F10.
      **M** *Click on Tools, Macro, then Define.*

B. At the **Define macro:** prompt, key in **PARA** and press Enter.
C. At the **Description:** prompt, key in **Insert billing paragraph**, and press Enter.
D. With **Macro Def** flashing in the bottom left corner of the screen, key in the paragraph shown in figure 26-2 up to the law firm name.
E. With the cursor located where the law firm name is to appear, execute the firm name macro by pressing Alt + N. This inserts the names in the paragraph.
F. Key in the remainder of the paragraph.
G. End the macro by accessing the Macro Define command with Ctrl + F10.

---

This letter confirms your retention of NELSON & FREEMAN to render legal services on your behalf. Attached are our general billing policies and procedures. Please read the attachment carefully. The policies and procedures set forth in the attachment are subject to change.

---

Figure 26-1: An Example of Macro Nesting

Another example of a nested macro is a situation in which you are creating a partial document as a macro that contains listed items. You decide that you want the paragraphs within the partial document single spaced but the lines for the listed items spaced at 1.5. First, you would create a macro that changes line spacing to 1.5 and another macro that changes the line spacing to single. Each macro would be named with the Alt key. Next, you would create the macro for the partial document. While creating the macro, you would execute the Alt key macro, changing line spacing to 1.5 above the listed items, then execute the Alt key macro, changing the line spacing to single after the listed item.

## REPLACING OR EDITING A MACRO

When a macro has been defined and you decide you want to change it, you either replace the macro or edit it. If you replace the macro, you will need to redefine each keystroke. To replace a macro, complete the following steps:

1. Access the Macro Define command, Ctrl + F10.
   **M** *Click on Tools, Macro, then Define.*
2. Key in the name of an existing macro, press Enter, and the prompt **<Name of Macro>.WPM is Already Exists: 1 <u>R</u>eplace; 2 <u>E</u>dit; 3 <u>D</u>escription: <u>0</u>** displays at the bottom of the screen.
3. Choose 1 or R for Replace to replace the existing macro, and redefine it in the usual manner.

If you want to edit an existing macro, choose 2 or E for Edit. For example, to edit a macro named DS that changes the line spacing to double, access the Macro Define command with Ctrl + F10, key in **LS**, and press Enter. At the **Replace** or **Edit** prompt, choose 2 or E for Edit, and the Macro: Action menu as shown in figure 26-2 appears on the screen. (This macro displays the keystrokes using mnemonic keys rather than number choices.)

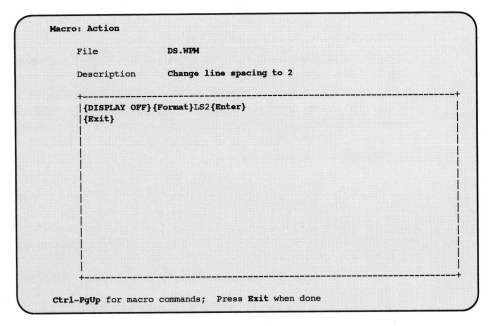

```
Macro: Action

     File            DS.WPM

     Description     Change line spacing to 2

+---------------------------------------------------------------------+
|{DISPLAY OFF}{Format}LS2{Enter}                                      |
|{Exit}                                                               |
|                                                                     |
|                                                                     |
|                                                                     |
|                                                                     |
|                                                                     |
|                                                                     |
|                                                                     |
|                                                                     |
|                                                                     |
|                                                                     |
+---------------------------------------------------------------------+

   Ctrl-PgUp for macro commands;   Press Exit when done
```

**Figure 26-2: Macro: Action Menu**

The Macro: Action menu identifies the name of the macro file, LS.WPM; indicates the description of the macro; and, in the box, shows what actions were taken to originally define the macro. The cursor is located within the box. In this example, the first line indicates that the macro display is off. The word *Format* indicates that the Format command, Shift + F8, was accessed. The letters *LS* are the mnemonic keys to access Line and Line Spacing. The number 2 indicates double spacing. The *Enter* in brackets indicates that Enter was pressed, and Exit indicates that the F7 key was pressed.

If you want this macro to change the line spacing from double to triple, move the cursor to the 2, delete it, and key in a 3. Leave the remaining codes as they are. Press F7 to save the change. Press F7 again to return the cursor to the document. When major changes are needed in a macro, you might find it easier to redefine the macro rather than edit it.

The macro feature with WordPerfect is very powerful. In addition to the methods described in this chapter, you can create repeating macros, program your own macro, and create pauses in macros for keyboard entry. Refer to Appendix K of the WordPerfect reference manual for information about these advanced features.

## CHAPTER REVIEW

### Summary

- A series of keystrokes can be saved in a macro. A macro can contain letters, words, terms, formats, or commands.
- *Define* is the term WordPerfect uses to refer to the process of identifying text or commands to be saved. There are three types of

macros that can be defined: a named macro, an Alt key macro, and a temporary macro. To create a temporary macro, name it with the Enter key.

* A macro name can contain between one and eight characters. When a macro is defined, the name given to the macro appears in the directory with the extension .WPM.

* A macro description is a brief explanation of what the macro contains and can be a maximum of 39 characters long.

* To execute a named macro, access the Macro command with Alt + F10, key in the name of the macro, and press Enter. To execute an Alt key macro, move the cursor to the location where you want the macro inserted, hold down the Alt key, and key in the letter you assigned to the macro.

* Use the Cancel key, F1, to cancel a macro while it is being executed. Use the Macro Define command, Ctrl + F10, to cancel a macro while it is being defined.

* A macro displays in the directory with the extension .WPM. A macro can be deleted from the directory in the same manner as any other document.

* The location of macro files can be changed at the Setup: Location of Files menu.

* A macro can execute another macro. This is called macro chaining or nesting. A chained macro is executed after the first macro. A nested macro is executed where it is located in the macro. Only macros named with the Alt key can be nested.

* You can change a macro by replacing it or editing it. When you key in the name of an existing macro at the Macro Define command, WordPerfect displays a prompt to either replace or edit. Choose 1 or R to replace or choose 2 or E for edit to edit the macro. When you edit a macro, WordPerfect displays the Macro: Action menu where changes can be made.

## Commands Review

To define a macro, complete the following steps:
1. Access the Macro Define command, Ctrl + F10.
2. Key in a name for the macro, then press Enter.
3. Key in a description of the macro, then press Enter.
4. Key in the text or enter commands for the macro.
5. End the macro with the Macro Define command, Ctrl + F10.

To execute a named macro, complete the following steps:
1. Key in text to the point where the macro is to be executed.
2. Access the Macro command, Alt + F10.
3. Key in the macro name and press Enter.

To execute an Alt key macro, complete the following steps:
1. Key in text to the point where the macro is to be executed.
2. Hold down the Alt key and key in the letter assigned to the macro.

## STUDY GUIDE FOR CHAPTER 26

List the steps necessary to define a macro that changes the justification to Left. Name the macro JLEFT.

---

---

---

---

---

---

List the steps necessary to execute the JLEFT macro defined above.

---

---

---

---

**True/False:** Circle the letter T if the statement is true; circle the letter F if the statement is false.

1. A macro can contain letters, words, terms, or commands.      T      F

2. A macro name can contain 1 to 10 characters.      T      F

3. If you define a macro with the name LN, it appears in the directory as LN.MAC.      T      F

4. The Alt key followed by a letter can be used to name macros.      T      F

5.  A macro is executed with the Macro Define command, Ctrl + F10 (**M** *Click on*     T     F
    *Tools, Macro, then Define*).

6.  A temporary macro can be created by naming the macro with the Enter key.      T     F

7.  A macro cannot be edited.                                                     T     F

8.  A macro can be executed within another macro.                                 T     F

9.  A macro can be deleted from the directory.                                    T     F


## HANDS-ON EXERCISES

Change the default directory to UNIT6.


### Exercise One

1.  At a clear screen, create a macro named CM that includes the company name of Cheney
    Manufacturing by completing the following steps:
    A.  Access the Macro Define command with Ctrl + F10.
        **M** *Click on Tools, Macro, then Define.*
    B.  At the **Define macro:** prompt, key in **CM**, and press Enter.
    C.  At the **Description:** prompt, key in **Enter company name**, then press Enter.
    D.  With **Macro Def** flashing in the lower left corner of the screen, key in **Cheney Manu-
        facturing**.
    E.  End the macro by accessing the Macro Define command with Ctrl + F10.
2.  Define a macro named Alt + S for the signature block shown in figure 26-3 by completing
    the following steps:
    A.  Access the Macro Define command with Ctrl + F10.
        **M** *Click on Tools, Macro, then Define.*
    B.  At the **Define macro:** prompt, hold down the Alt key and key in the letter **S**.
    C.  At the **Description:** prompt, key in **Enter signature block**, then press Enter.
    D.  With **Macro Def** flashing in the lower left corner of the screen, key in the text shown
        in figure 26-3. Space the text correctly.
    E.  End the macro by accessing the Macro Define command with Ctrl + F10.

---

```
Very truly yours,

MORENO, YAMADA, & SCHWARTZ



Dan S. Yamada
Attorney at Law
```

---

**Figure 26-3: Exercise One**


3.  Define a macro named MAR15 that changes the left and right margins to 1.5 inches by
    completing the following steps:
    A.  Access the Macro Define command with Ctrl + F10.
        **M** *Click on Tools, Macro, then Define.*

B. At the **Define macro:** prompt, key in **MAR15** and press Enter.

C. At the **Description:** prompt, key in **Change margins to 1.5 inches,** then press Enter.

D. With **Macro Def** flashing in the lower left corner of the screen, complete the following steps:

    (1) Access the Format: Line menu with Shift + F8, then choose 1 or L for Line.

       **M** *Click on Layout, then Line.*

    (2) At the Format: Line menu, choose 7 or M for Margins.

    (3) Key in **1.5** and press Enter.

    (4) Key in **1.5** and press Enter.

    (5) Press F7 to return the cursor to the document.

E. End the macro by accessing the Macro Define command with Ctrl + F10.

4. Define a macro named JL that changes the justification to Left by completing the following steps:

A. Access the Macro Define command with Ctrl + F10.

   **M** *Click on Tools, Macro, then Define.*

B. At the **Define macro:** prompt, key in **JL** and press Enter.

C. At the **Description:** prompt, key in **Change justification to left,** then press Enter.

D. With **Macro Def** flashing in the lower left corner of the screen, complete the following steps:

    (1) Access the Format: Line menu with Shift + F8, then choose 1 or L for Line.

       **M** *Click on Layout, then Line.*

    (2) At the Format: Line menu, choose 3 or J for Justification.

    (3) Choose 1 or L for Left.

    (4) Press F7 to return the cursor to the document.

E. End the macro by accessing the Macro Define command with Ctrl + F10.

5. Define a macro named Alt + D that changes the line spacing to double by completing the following steps:

A. Access the Macro Define command with Ctrl + F10.

   **M** *Click on Tools, Macro, then Define.*

B. At the **Define macro:** prompt, hold down the Alt key, and key in the letter **D**.

C. At the **Description:** prompt, key in **Change to double spacing,** then press Enter.

D. With **Macro Def** flashing in the lower left corner of the screen, complete the following steps:

    (1) Access the Format: Line menu with Shift + F8, then choose 1 or L for Line.

       **M** *Click on Layout, then Line.*

    (2) At the Format: Line menu, choose 6 or S for Spacing.

    (3) Key in a **2** and press Enter.

    (4) Press F7 to return the cursor to the document.

E. End the macro by accessing the Macro Define command with Ctrl + F10.

6. When all macros are defined, exit from the current document without saving it.

7. Display the directory and print the directory with Shift + F7.

### Exercise Two

1. At a clear screen, create the letter shown in figure 26-4 in an appropriate business letter format with the following changes:

A. At the beginning of the document, execute the MAR15 macro by completing the following steps:

    (1) Access the Macro command with Alt + F10.

       **M** *Click on Tools, Macro, then Execute.*

    (2) Key in **MAR15** and press Enter.

B. Execute the JL macro.

C. When keying in the letter, execute the CM macro to insert the company name.

    D. With the cursor a double space below the last paragraph, execute the signature block
       macro by pressing Alt + S.

  2.  Save the letter and name it CH26EX2. Print CH26EX2.

---

```
April 14, 1993

Mr. Charles Pruitt
CM
625 Parkway Plaza
Seattle, WA 98116

Dear Mr. Pruitt:
Re: CM, Articles of Incorporation

Thank you for sending the information I need to prepare the
Articles of Incorporation for CM.

There are a few minor questions that remain unanswered.  Please
call me as soon as possible.  I am sure we can take care of this
business over the phone.

(Execute the Alt + S macro here.  Include reference initials and
file name.)
```

---

Figure 26-4: Exercise Two

## Exercise Three

  1.  At a clear screen, execute the MAR15 and JL macros, then create the memorandum shown
     in figure 26-5 in an appropriate memorandum format. Use the CM macro to insert the
     name of the corporation.

  2.  Save the memorandum and name it CH26EX3. Print CH26EX3.

DATE: April 22, 1993
TO: Anita Moreno
FROM: Dan S. Yamada
SUBJECT: CM, Articles of Incorporation


Please look over the attached Articles of Incorporation
I have prepared for CM. I will be out of town next
week and want to get the Articles filed as soon as
I get back.


xx: CH26EX3
Enclosure

**Figure 26-5: Exercise Three**

**Exercise Four**

1. At a clear screen, execute the MAR15 and JL macros, then create the letter shown in figure 26-6 in an appropriate business letter format. Use the CM macro to insert the company name, and use the Alt + S macro to insert the signature block.

2. Save the letter and name it CH26EX4. Print CH26EX4.

April 30, 1993

Mr. Charles Pruitt
CM
625 Parkway Plaza
Seattle, WA 98116

Dear Mr. Pruitt:
Re:  CM, Articles of Incorporation

The Articles of Incorporation for CM are prepared.  I have enclosed
a copy of the Articles.  Please read them and let me know if you
find any errors.

Please call my secretary this week to make an appointment to sign
the Articles.

(Execute the Alt + S macro here.  Include reference initials and
file name.)

Figure 26-6: Exercise Four

**Exercise Five**

1.  At a clear screen, create a macro named Alt + T that changes the top margin to 1.5 inches and executes the Alt + D macro by completing the following steps:
    A.  Access the Macro Define command with Ctrl + F10.
        **M** *Click on Tools, Macro, then Define.*
    B.  At the **Define macro:** prompt, hold down the Alt key and key in the letter **T**.
    C.  At the **Description:** prompt, key in **Change top margin and spacing**, then press Enter.
    D.  With **Macro Def** flashing in the lower left corner of the screen, complete the following steps:
        (1)  Access the Format: Page menu with Shift + F8, then choose 2 or P for Page.
             **M** *Click on Layout, then Page.*
        (2)  At the Format: Page menu, choose 5 or M for Margins.
        (3)  Key in a **1.5** and press Enter.
        (4)  Press Enter again at the bottom margin.
        (5)  Press F7 to return the cursor to the document.
    E.  Execute the double spacing macro with Alt + D.
    F.  End the macro by accessing the Macro Define command with Ctrl + F10.
2.  Exit the document without saving it.
3.  At a clear screen, execute the Alt + T macro, then create the legal form shown in figure 26-7. Execute the CM macro to insert the company name.  Change the line spacing to 1 before keying in the signature lines and names.
4.  Save the legal document and name it CH26EX5. Print CH26EX5.

## ARTICLES OF INCORPORATION

The undersigned, for the purpose of forming a corporation under the laws of the State of Washington, RCW 24.01, hereby adopt the following Articles of Incorporation.

### ARTICLE I

The name of the corporation shall be CM.

### ARTICLE II

The term of existence of CM shall be perpetual.

### ARTICLE III

The purpose for which CM is organized is to manufacture computer hardware and components related thereto.

### ARTICLE IV

The name of the Registered Agent of CM is Charles R. Pruitt. The street address of the Registered Office is CM, 625 Parkway Plaza, Seattle, WA 98116.

### ARTICLE V

There shall be four directors serving as the initial Board of Directors for CM.   Their names and addresses are as follows:

Charles R. Pruitt, 5227 Olympic Drive, Renton, WA 98504
Jamie N. Monier, 12665 - 143rd Avenue, Lynnwood, WA 98733
Lawrence D. Souza, 12689 - 132nd Street, Woodinville, WA 98763
Brenda Han, 12411 South 43rd Street, Auburn, WA 98012

### ARTICLE VI

In the event of dissolution of CM, the net assets and all liabilities and obligations of CM shall first be paid, satisfied and discharged.   Any remaining assets shall be divided equally among the Board of Directors.

**IN WITNESS WHEREOF,** each incorporator has affixed his/her signature on this _____ day of _____, 19--.


CHARLES R. PRUITT                        JAMIE N. MONIER

LAWRENCE D. SOUZA                        BRENDA HAN

Figure 26-7: Exercise Five


## PERFORMANCE ASSESSMENTS


### Assessment One

1.  At a clear screen, create the following macros:
    A. Macro named Alt + M that includes the firm name MORENO, YAMADA, & SCHWARTZ.
    B. Macro named Alt + A that includes the name Anita M. Moreno.
    C. Macro named Alt + Y that includes the name Dan S. Yamada.

D. Macro named Alt + K that inclues the name Karen L. Sonneson.

E. Macro named BILL1 that includes the paragraph shown in figure 26-8 with the Alt + M macro nested within.

```
This letter confirms your retention of (execute Alt + M macro
here), to render legal services on your behalf. Attached are our
general billing policies and procedures. Please read the attachment
carefully. The policies and procedures set forth in the attachment
are subject to change.
```

**Figure 26-8: Assessment One**

F. Macro named BILL2 that includes the paragraph shown in figure 26-9 with the Alt + Y and Alt + K macro nested within.

```
The primary responsibility for your case will be handled by
(execute Alt + Y macro here) and (execute Alt + K macro here) will
be assisting. Services will be rendered at the hourly rate of
$125.00 for (execute Alt + Y macro here) and $90.00 for (execute
Alt + K macro here).
```

**Figure 26-9: Assessment One**

2. Exit the document without saving it.

**Assessment Two**

1. At a clear screen, create the business letter shown in figure 26-10 in an appropriate business letter format. Execute the macros as indicated in the letter.

2. Save the letter and name it CH26PA2. Print CH26PA2.

March 23, 1993

Mr. Bernard Cho
342 St. Helens
Federal Way, WA 98002

Dear Mr. Cho:

(Execute the BILL1 macro here.)

(Execute the BILL2 macro here.)

In the event that it is necessary to use other attorneys or legal assistants not specifically mentioned herein due to the size and scope of this matter, any time constraints which may arise, or for any other reason, we will staff as appropriate.

If you have any further questions or comments regarding the contents of this letter, please contact me at your earliest convenience.

(Execute the Alt + S macro here.)

**Figure 26-10: Assessment Two**

**Assessment Three**

1.  At a clear screen, create the Verification by Attorney document shown in figure 26-11. Before keying in the document, execute the Alt + T macro. Execute other macros as indicated in the document.
2.  Save the verification document and name it CH26PA3. Print CH26PA3.

---

### VERIFICATION BY ATTORNEY

I, the undersigned, declare:

I am an attorney-at-law duly admitted to practice before all courts of the State of Washington, and I have my office at 800 Fourth Avenue, Suite 350, Seattle, Washington, 98002.

I am (execute the Alt + A macro here) of (execute the Alt + M macro here), attorneys for the defendant in the matter.

The defendant is absent from the country in which I have my office and for that reason I make this Verification on behalf of said defendant.

I have read the foregoing Complaint and know the contents thereof, and am informed and believe that the matters therein are true and on that ground allege that the matters stated therein are true.

I declare under penalty of perjury, under the laws of the State of Washington, that the foregoing is true and correct.

Executed this _____ day of _____, 19___.

```
                              _____
                              (execute Alt + A macro here), of
                              (execute Alt + M macro here)
```

---

Figure 26-11: Assessment Three

# CHAPTER 27

## STYLES

## PERFORMANCE OBJECTIVE

Upon successful completion of chapter 27, you will be able to maintain consistency within all similar business documents using the styles feature.

### STYLES

Some documents, such as company newsletters, reports, or brochures, may be created on a regular basis. These documents should maintain a consistency in formatting each time they are created. For example, a company newsletter should maintain a consistency from issue to issue, and a company report should contain consistent formatting each time one is created.

Formatting that is applied to a variety of documents on a regular basis or that maintains a consistency within a publication can be applied to text using a *style*. In WordPerfect, a style can include formatting codes, text, or a combination of both.

The Style and Macro features are similar in that both are used to automate functions. A *macro* inserts the actual formatting codes in a document, while a style inserts the style code that contains the formatting codes. Because formatting codes are contained within a style, a style can be edited, automatically updating any text to which that style has been applied.

For example, let us say that, for subheadings in a newsletter, you create a style that changes the base font to 14-point Helvetica Bold. After using the style several times in the document, you decide the subheadings will look better if they are set in 12-point Helvetica Bold. To change all the subheadings at once in the document, you access the Style command and edit the style containing the base font change. When the style is edited, all occurrences of that style in the document are automatically changed to the new base font.

The style feature includes several options. You can create a style, turn a style on and off in a document, edit a style, save and retrieve a style document, and delete styles.

## Creating a Style

A style can be created at a blank screen or in a document that contains text. To create a style, you would complete the following steps:

1.  Access the Style command with Alt + F8.
    **M** *Click on Layout, then Styles.*
2.  Choose 3 or C for Create.
3.  At the Styles: Edit menu, make changes as needed, then press F7 twice.

The Styles: Edit menu, shown in figure 27-1, contains the selections Name, Type, Description, Codes, and Enter.

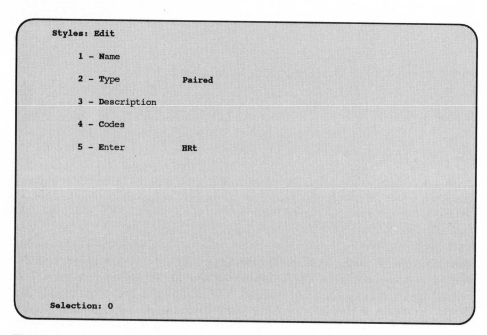

```
Styles: Edit

    1 - Name

    2 - Type            Paired

    3 - Description

    4 - Codes

    5 - Enter           HRt




    Selection: 0
```

Figure 27-1: Styles: Edit Menu

The Name selection is used to name the style. The style name can contain a maximum of 12 characters, including spaces.

The second selection, Type, can be either paired or open, with paired the default. A paired style contains formats that are turned on and off, such as underlining and boldfacing. An open style contains formats that are turned on but not off. An open style is useful in formatting an entire document, such as changing the base font, line spacing, justification, or other formats.

The Description selection lets you describe the contents of the style. The maximum length of a description is 54 characters, which can contain spaces.

The fourth selection, Codes, is used to enter the desired formats or text in the style. When you choose 4 or C for Codes, the Style: Edit menu disappears and is replaced by the paired styles editing screen, shown in figure 27-2.

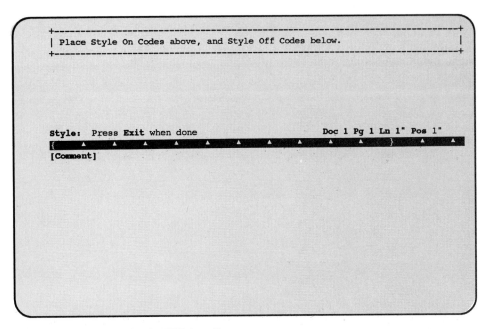

**Figure 27-2: Paired Style Editing Screen**

The top of the screen displays a rectangular box with the message **Place Style On Codes above, and Style Off Codes below.** The cursor is blinking above this box. In the middle of the screen is the ruler line with the message **Press Exit when done** above it. Below the ruler line is the code [Comment]. You specify formats or key in text at this screen. Follow the same steps you would follow to create formats or text in a document.

The message in the box tells you to create Style On codes above the comment and Style Off codes below. To create Style Off codes below the line, move the cursor past the [Comment] code with the right or down arrow keys.

To create an open style, change the Type to Open, then choose 4 or C for Codes. The open style editing screen shown in figure 27-3 is displayed.

At the open style screen, the message to place Style On codes above and Style Off codes below is not included.

The last selection from the Styles: Edit menu is Enter. When you choose 5 or E for Enter, the prompt **Enter: 1 Hrt; 2 Off; 3 Off/On: 0** appears at the bottom of the screen. With the first choice, 1 or H, the Enter key is used to turn the style on or off. Choose 2 or F if you want the Enter key to turn a style off, and choose 3 or O if you want the Enter key to turn the style off and on.

When all selections are made at the Styles: Edit menu, press F7 to return to the Styles menu. This menu displays a list of styles that have been created. Press F7 again to return the cursor to the document.

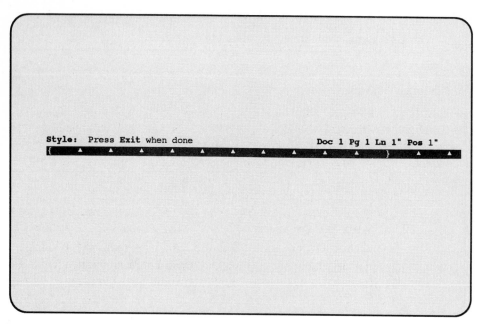

**Style:** Press **Exit** when done          Doc 1 Pg 1 Ln 1" Pos 1"

Figure 27-3: Open Style Editing Screen

To understand how to create a style, let us look at an example. Suppose you want to create a paired style named SUB1 (for subheading 1) that changes the base font to 14-point Times Roman, then changes the base font to 12-point Times Roman for subheadings in a report. To create this paired style, complete the following steps:

1. Access the Styles command with Alt + F8.
   **M** *Click on Layout, then Styles*.
2. Choose 3 or C for Create.
3. At the Styles: Edit menu, choose 1 or N for Name, key in **SUB1**, and press Enter.
4. Choose 3 or D for Description, key in **Change base font for subheading**, then press Enter.
5. Choose 4 or C for Codes. At the paired style editing screen, insert the Font Change code by completing the following steps:
   A. Access the Font command with Ctrl + F8.
   B. Choose 4 or F for Base Font.
      **M** *Click on Font, then Base Font*.
   C. At the Base Font menu, move the cursor to 14-point Times Roman and choose 1 or S for Select. (If you are using a PostScript printer, move the cursor to Times Roman, choose 1 or S for Select, key in **14**, then press Enter.)
6. Press the right arrow key once to move the cursor past the Comment code, then insert the Font Change code by completing the following steps:
   A. Access the font command with Ctrl + F8.
   B. Choose 4 or F for Base Font.
      **M** *Click on Font, then Base Font*.

      C.  Move the cursor to 12-point Times Roman, and choose 1 or S for Select. (If you are using a PostScript printer, move the cursor to Times Roman, choose 1 or S for Select, key in **12**, then press Enter.)

   7.  Press F7 three times to return the cursor to the document.

## Applying a Style

After a style has been created, it can be applied in a document. To apply a paired style to text or characters in a document, complete the following steps:

1. Position the cursor at the location in the document where you want the paired style applied, and access the Style command with Alt + F8.
   **M** *Click on Layout, then Styles.*
2. Select the desired style, then choose 1 or O for On from the prompts that display at the bottom of the screen.
3. Key in the characters to which you want the style applied.
4. To turn off the style, access the Style command with Alt + F8, (**M** *Click on Layout, then Style*), highlight the style, then choose 2 or F for Off.

The steps to apply an open style in a document are similar to the steps for a paired style. To apply an open style in a document, complete the following steps:

1. Position the cursor at the location in the document where the open style is to be applied, then access the Style command with Alt + F8.
   **M** *Click on Layout, then Styles.*
2. Select the desired style, then choose 1 or O from the prompts that display at the bottom of the screen.

A paired style can be applied to existing text or characters in a document. To do this, complete the following steps:

1. Block the text with Alt + F4 or F12.
   **M** *Click on Edit, then Block*
2. Access the Style command with Alt + F8.
   **M** *Click on Layout, then Styles.*
3. Select the desired style, then choose 1 or O for On.

When these steps are completed, a Style On code is inserted before the blocked text, and a Style Off code is inserted after the blocked text.

## Editing a Style

One of the advantages of using styles within a document is that a style can be edited, and all occurrences of that style are automatically updated. For example, let us say you applied the SUB1 style to several subheadings in a newsletter you created. After printing the newsletter, you decide that the subheadings would look better set in Helvetica. To quickly change the formatting of the subheadings, edit the SUB1 style by completing the following steps:

1. Access the Style command with Alt + F8.
   **M** *Click on Layout, then Styles.*
2. Select SUB1, then choose 4 or E for Edit.
3. With the Styles: Edit menu displayed on the screen, choose 4 or C for Codes. The Styles: Edit menu is removed from the screen and replaced by the paired style editing screen that displays all the format codes for the style.
4. Delete the Font Change code for 14-point Times Roman and insert a Font Change code for 14-point Helvetica.
5. When the change has been made, press F7 three times to return the cursor to the document.

When the cursor is returned to the document, the styles applied to each subheading in the newsletter are automatically updated to reflect the new font code. This is the major advantage of using a style to format text over a macro. Changes that automatically update every occurrence of the style can be easily made to styles.

## Saving Styles

When a style is created in a document, the style is saved with the document. If you access the Style command in a document in which styles were previously created, the styles are listed in the Styles menu.

Styles can also be saved into a separate document. This lets you use a style in different documents. To save styles in a separate document, complete the following steps:

1. Access the Style command with Alt + F8.
   **M** *Click on Layout, then Styles.*
2. Choose 6 or S for Save.
3. Key in the name for the style document and press Enter. (The rules for naming a style document are the same as rules for a regular document.

To help you remember that the document contains styles, you may want to add an extension to the style document name such as .STL or .STY. The styles are saved in the document in which they were created, as well as in the new style document.

## Retrieving Styles

Styles that have been saved in a separate document can be retrieved at any time. If you want to retrieve a style document into the document currently displayed on the screen, complete the following steps:

1. Access the Style command with Alt + F8.
   **M** *Click on Layout, then Styles.*
2. Choose 7 or R for Retrieve.
3. Key in the name you gave the style document, then press Enter.

### Updating a Style Library

WordPerfect, Version 5.1, contains a default style library with a number of predefined styles. If the Styles command is accessed in a document that does not have styles defined, the default styles in the style library are retrieved. If the document already contains styles, the styles from the style library can be added by choosing 8 or U for Update from the Styles menu. If there are styles with the same names, the style library styles will replace the existing styles without confirmation.

### Deleting a Style

A style applied to text in a document can be deleted from the text by accessing Reveal Codes and deleting the Style On or Style Off code with the Delete key.

Styles can also be deleted from the Styles menu. To do this, complete the following steps:

1. Access the Style command with Alt + F8.
   **M** *Click on Layout, then Styles.*
2. Select the style to be deleted, choose 5 or D for Delete, and the prompt **Deleting Codes: 1 Leaving Codes; 2 Including Codes; 3 Definition Only** appears at the bottom of the screen.
3. Choose 1 or L to delete the style, but leave the codes. Choose 2 or I to delete the style as well as all codes contained in the style from the document. This option is useful if you want to return the document to the original format (before styles were applied). Choose 3 or D to delete the style definition from the menu and leave the style codes in the document.
4. Press F7 to return the cursor to the document.

### Changing Location of Style Documents

When a style document is saved, it is saved in the WP51 directory (unless otherwise specified during installation). The default style library is also located in the WP51 directory and is named LIBRARY.STY.

Style documents and the style library can be saved to a different directory, subdirectory, or drive, and the style library name can be changed with a selection from the Setup menu. To change the location of style documents, style library, or style library name, complete the following steps:

1. Access the Setup command with Shift + F1, and choose 6 or L for Location of Files.
   **M** *Click on File, Setup, then Location of Files.*
2. At the Setup: Location of Files menu, choose 5 or S for Style Files.
3. Key in the new directory, subdirectory, or drive and press Enter. If you want to change the directory, subdirectory, drive, or name of the style library, key in the new path or name, and press Enter.
4. Press F7 to return to the document.

This feature can be useful in a situation in which more than one person uses the computer terminal with WordPerfect. The style documents and style library path can be changed so style documents are saved and retrieved from a disk in Drive A or B, or a subdirectory path can be entered so personal styles are saved and retrieved to a specific directory or subdirectory.

For example, in a school setting, the style files and style library selections can be changed to Drive A (or Drive B), which contains students' disks. With the settings changed, styles created by students are saved to and retrieved from their own disk.

## OUTLINE STYLES

In chapter 20, you learned to create numbered paragraphs and outlines. When you created numbered paragraphs or outlines, WordPerfect automatically inserted level numbering. When numbering paragraphs or creating an outline, you can use the default level numbering or you can access the Paragraph Number Definition menu and change the style of numbering.

Even though you can change the outlining style at the Paragraph Number Definition menu, you still have to apply any special formatting to the paragraph number or outline as it is being keyed in. For example, you may want to boldface paragraph or outline numbers, or boldface the number and the heading that follows. You may want to create an outline containing paragraphs at each level and have those paragraphs indented with the Indent key.

The formatting changes can be made to paragraph numbering or an outline as it is being keyed in, or you can create an outline style that contains formatting for each level of the paragraph number or outline, saving you time.

### Creating an Outline Style

An outline style is created in much the same way as a regular style. The difference is that you access the Outline Style menu through the Date/Outline command rather than the Styles command. Complete the following steps to create an outline style:

1.  Access the Date/Outline command with Shift + F5.
2.  Choose 6 or D for Define.
    **M** *Click on Tools, then Define.*
3.  At the Paragraph Number Definition menu, choose 9 or N for Outline Style Name, and the Outline Styles menu shown in figure 27-4 displays on the screen.
4.  At the Outline Styles menu, choose 2 or C for Create to create a new outline style, and the Outline Styles: Edit menu shown in figure 27-5 displays on the screen.

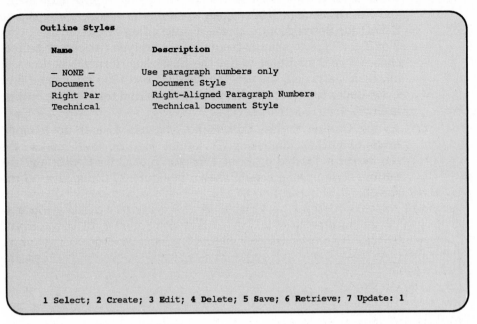

```
Outline Styles

   Name                   Description

   — NONE —               Use paragraph numbers only
   Document               Document Style
   Right Par              Right-Aligned Paragraph Numbers
   Technical              Technical Document Style
```

```
1 Select; 2 Create; 3 Edit; 4 Delete; 5 Save; 6 Retrieve; 7 Update: 1
```

**Figure 27-4: Outline Styles Menu**

```
Outline Styles: Edit

   Name:

   Description:


   Level   Type      Enter

      1     Open
      2     Open
      3     Open
      4     Open
      5     Open
      6     Open
      7     Open
      8     Open
```

```
1 Name; 2 Description; 3 Type; 4 Enter; 5 Codes: 0
```

**Figure 27-5: Outline Styles: Edit Menu**

5.  The Outline Styles: Edit menu contains selections similar to those at the Styles: Edit menu. At the Outline Styles: Edit menu, you can choose 1 or N for Name to name the outline style; choose 2 or D for Description to create a description of the outline style; 3 or T for Type to change the outline style type to open or paired; choose 4 or E for Enter to use the Enter key to turn a style on or off, turn a style off, or turn the style off and then on; choose 5 or C for Codes to insert the formatting codes and text for the outline level.

6.  At the Outline Styles: Edit menu, you can format up to eight levels of outline numbering. To format the first level, make sure the cursor is located on level 1, choose 5 or C for Codes, and the outline style editing screen shown in figure 27-6 displays on the screen.

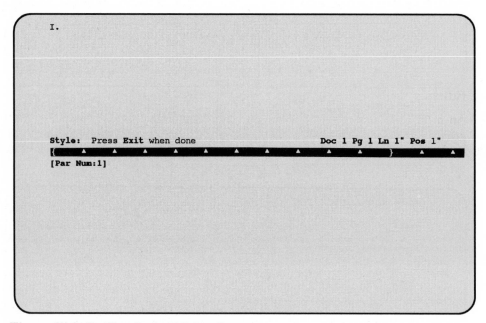

**Figure 27-6: Outline Style Editing Screen**

7.  At the outline style editing screen, insert the formatting that you want applied to level 1 numbering.

8.  When all formatting codes are inserted, press F7, and you are returned to the Outline Styles: Edit menu (shown in figure 27-5).

9.  At the Outline Styles: Edit menu, move the cursor to level 2 and choose 5 or C for Codes. Insert formatting codes for level 2 numbering, then press F7.

10. At the Outline Styles: Edit menu, insert formatting codes for the remaining levels (if needed).

11. When you are done inserting formatting codes for each level, press F7 and you are returned to the Outline Styles menu (shown in figure 27-4).

12. At the Outline Styles menu, press F7 three times to return the cursor to the document.

### Selecting an Outline Style

Once an outline style (or several outline styles) has been created, it can be selected at the Paragraph Number Definition menu and used in paragraph numbering or outlining. To select an outline style, complete the following steps:

1. Access the Date/Outline command with Shift + F5.
2. Choose 6 or D for Define.
   **M** *Click on Tools, then Define.*
3. At the Paragraph Number Definition menu, choose 9 or N for Outline Style Name.
4. At the Outline Styles menu, move the cursor to the desired outline style, and choose 1 or L for Select.
5. At the Paragraph Number Definition menu, press F7.
6. From the prompts that display at the bottom of the screen, choose 4 or O for Outline, or 5 or P for Para Num.
7. If you chose 4 or O for Outline in the step above, choose 1 or O for On. If you chose 5 or P for Para Num in the step above, press Enter, or key in the level numbering desired, then press Enter.
8. Key in the remainder of the outline or paragraphs.

### Editing an Outline Style

An outline style can be edited in the same manner as a regular style. The advantage to editing an outline style is that any occurrence of the outline style in the document is automatically updated to reflect the changes (edits). To edit an outline style, complete the following steps:

1. Access the Date/Outline command with Shift + F5.
2. Choose 6 or D for Define.
   **M** *Click on Tools, then Define.*
3. At the Paragraph Number Definition menu, choose 9 or N for Outline Style Name.
4. At the Outline Styles menu, move the cursor to the desired outline style, then choose 3 or E for Edit.
5. At the Outline Styles: Edit menu, move the cursor to the level number to be edited and choose 5 or C for Codes. Edit the styles, then press F7. Edit the other levels as needed. When all changes are made, press F7.
6. At the Outline Styles menu, press F7.
7. At the Paragraph Definition menu, press F7 twice to return the cursor to the document.

When the cursor is returned to the document, all occurrences of the outline style in the document are automatically updated.

### Saving Outline Styles

Outline styles are saved with the document in which they are created. If you want to use outline styles in other documents, you can save the outline styles in a separate document. To save outline styles in a separate document, complete the following steps:

1.  Access the Date/Outline command with Shift + F5.
2.  Choose 6 or D for Define.
    **M** *Click on Tools, then Define.*
3.  At the Paragraph Number Definition menu, choose 9 or N for Outline Style Name.
4.  At the Outline Styles menu, choose 5 or S for Save.
5.  At the prompt **Filename:**, key in a name for the outline style document, then press Enter. (Outline style document names follow the same naming rules as regular documents. You may want to add the extension .STL or .STY to the document name to identify that it contains styles.)
6.  Press F7 three times to return the cursor to the document.

### Retrieving Outline Styles

Outline styles that have been saved in a separate document can be retrieved to the current document by completing the following steps:

1.  Access the Date/Outline command with Shift + F5.
2.  Choose 6 or D for Define.
    **M** *Click on Tools, then Define.*
3.  At the Paragraph Number Definition menu, choose 9 or N for Outline Style Name.
4.  At the Outline Styles menu, choose 6 or R for Retrieve.
5.  At the prompt **Filename:**, key in the name of the outline style document you want retrieved, then press Enter. (The outline styles in the document are retrieved to the screen and display at the Outline Styles menu.
6.  Press F7 three times to return the cursor to the document.

### Outline Style Example

To better understand how to create and select an outline style, let us look at an example. Suppose you create an agenda for a company meeting once a week. You determine that you need three number levels, and you want the agenda levels formatted in the following manner:

Level 1 =   Boldfaced Roman numerals indented to the first tab stop with the Decimal Tab command (to align the numerals at the right), then the Tab key used to indent the cursor to the next tab stop.

Level 2 =   Boldfaced capital letters indented to the second tab stop, then the Tab key used to indent the cursor to the next tab stop.

Level 3 =   Boldfaced Arabic numbers indented to the third tab stop, then the Tab key used to indent the cursor to the next tab stop.

To create an open outline style named AGENDA that applies this level formatting, complete the following steps:

1.  Access the Date/Outline command with Shift + F5.

2.  Choose 6 or D for Define.
    **M** *Click on Tools, then Define.*

3.  At the Paragraph Number Definition menu, choose 9 or N for Outline Style Name.

4.  At the Outline Styles menu, choose 2 or C for Create to create the new outline style.

5.  At the Outline Styles: Edit menu, choose 1 or N for Name, key in **AGENDA**, then press Enter.

6.  At the Outline Styles: Edit menu, choose 2 or D for Description, key in **Agenda Outline**, then press Enter.

7.  At the Outline Styles: Edit menu, choose 5 or C for Codes.

8.  At the outline style editing screen, complete the following steps to format level 1:
    A.  Access the Tab Align command with Ctrl + F6 to insert the **[DEC TAB]** code.
    B.  Press F6 to insert the **[BOLD]** code.
    C.  Press the right arrow key once time to move the cursor past the **[Par Num:1]** code.
    D.  Press F6 again to insert the **[bold]** code.
    E.  Press the Tab key to insert the **[Tab]** code.
    F.  Press F7 to return the cursor to the Outline: Styles Edit menu.

9.  Move the cursor to level 2, then choose 5 or C for Codes.

10. At the outline style editing screen, complete the following steps to format level 2:
    A.  Press the Tab key twice to insert two Tab codes.
    B.  Press F6 to insert the **[BOLD]** code.
    C.  Press the right arrow key once to move the cursor past the **[Par Num:2]** code.
    D.  Press F6 again to insert the **[bold]** code.
    E.  Press the Tab key to insert the **[Tab]** code.
    F.  Press F7 to return the cursor to the Outline: Styles Edit menu.

11. Move the cursor to level 3, then choose 5 or C for Codes.

12. At the outline style editing screen, complete the following steps to format level 3:
    A.  Press the Tab key three times to insert three Tab codes.
    B.  Press F6 to insert the **[BOLD]** code.
    C.  Press the right arrow key once to move the cursor past the **[Par Num:3]** code.
    D.  Press F6 again to insert the **[bold]** code.
    E.  Press the Tab key to insert the **[Tab]** code.
    F.  Press F7 to return the cursor to the Outline: Styles Edit menu.

13. Press F7 four times to save the outline style and return the cursor to the document.

To select the AGENDA outline style to be used in an outline for an agenda, complete the following steps:

1.  Access the Date/Outline command with Shift + F5.

2.  Choose 6 or D for Define.
    **M** *Click on Tools, then Define.*

3.  At the Paragraph Number Definition menu, choose 9 or N for Outline Style Name.

4.  At the Outline Styles menu, move the cursor to the AGENDA outline style, then choose 1 or L for Select.

5.  At the Paragraph Definition menu, press F7.

6.  From the prompts that display at the bottom of the screen, choose 4 or O for Outline, then 1 or O for On.

7.  Key in the agenda, then turn outlining off by completing the following steps:

    A.  Access the Date/Outline command with Shift + F5.

    B.  Choose 4 or O for Outline.

    C.  Choose 2 or F for Off.

        **M** *Click on Tools, Outline, then Off.*

## CHAPTER REVIEW

### Summary

- The Style feature automates functions. A style can be created that includes formats, text, or a combination of both. With the Styles feature, you can create a style, turn a style on and off in a document, edit a style, delete a style, and save and retrieve a style document.

- When a style is edited, all occurrences of that style in a document are automatically changed.

- A style can be created at a blank screen or in a document containing text.

- A style can be open or paired. A paired style contains formats that are turned on and then off. An open style contains formats that are turned on but not off.

- At the Styles: Edit menu, a style can be named, a description written, the Enter key used to turn the style on or off, and any codes identified. A style name can contain a maximum of 12 characters, and the description a maximum of 54 characters, including spaces.

- A style can be applied in a document as text is being keyed in or applied to existing text. To apply a style to existing text, the text must first be blocked with the Block command.

- When a style is created in a document, it is saved with the document. Styles can also be saved into a separate document that lets you use a style in many different documents.

- A style applied to text can be deleted in Reveal Codes, or a style can be deleted at the Styles menu.

- When a style document is saved, by default it is saved in the WP51 directory. The location of style documents can be changed at the Setup: Location of Files menu.

- An outline style can be created to format paragraphs created with automatic paragraph numbering or outlines created with automatic outlining.

- An outline style is created in a manner similar to a regular style. Create an outline style at the Outline Styles menu.

- At the Outline Styles: Edit menu, an outline style can be named, a description written, the type changed to either paired or open, the Enter key used to turn the style on or off, and any codes identified. An outline style name can contain a maximum of 12 character and the description a maximum of 54 characters, including spaces.

- Once an outline style has been created, it can be selected and used when numbering paragraphs or when keying in an outline with the Date/Outline command.

- An outline style can be edited, and any occurrences of that outline style in the document will be automatically updated.

- When an outline style is created in a document, it is saved with the document. Outline styles can also be saved into a separate document that lets you use an outline style in many different documents.

## Commands Review

**Keyboard**

| | |
|---|---|
| Style command | Alt + F8 |
| Date/Outline command | Shift + F5 |
| Paragraph Number Definition menu | Shift + F5, 6 or D |
| Block command | Alt + F4 or F12 |

**Mouse**

| | |
|---|---|
| Style command | Layout, Styles |
| Paragraph Number Definition menu | Tools, Paragraph Number |
| Block command | Edit, Block |

## STUDY GUIDE FOR CHAPTER 27

Describe the steps necessary to create a paired style that boldfaces text.

_____

_____

_____

_____

_____

_____

**Completion:** In the space provided at the right, indicate the correct term, command, symbol, or character for the explanation.

1.  Access the Style command.                                              _____

2.  Maximum number of characters that can be used in a style               _____
    name.

3.  Maximum number of characters that can be used in a style               _____
    description.

4.  Default style type at the Styles: Edit menu.                           _____

5.  When a style document is saved, it is saved in this directory          _____
    (unless otherwise specified during installation).

6.  Access the Paragraph Number Definition menu.                           _____

7.  Maximum number of characters that can be used in an outline            _____
    style name.

**True/False:** Circle the letter T if the statement is true; circle the letter F if the statement is false.

1.  A style can be created at a blank screen or in a document containing text.      T      F

2.  A style created in a document is deleted when the document is saved.            T      F

3.  A style cannot be edited.                                                       T      F

4.  A style can be applied to existing text.                                        T      F

5.  An open style contains formatting that is turned on and off.                    T      F

6.  A style can be deleted at the Styles menu.                                      T      F

7.   An outline style is created at the Styles: Edit menu.                    T      F

8.   An outline style can be edited.                                          T      F

9.   An outline style can be saved into a separate document.                  T      F

## HANDS-ON EXERCISES

Change the default directory to UNIT6.

### Exercise One

1.  At a clear screen, create a paired style named HEADING that turns boldfacing and under-
    lining on and off by completing the following steps:
    A. Access the Styles command with Alt + F8.
       **M** *Click on Layout, then Styles.*
    B. Choose 3 or C for Create.
    C. At the Styles: Edit menu, choose 1 or N for Name, key in **HEADING**, and press Enter.
    D. Choose 3 or D for Description, key in **Format headings**, then press Enter.
    E. Choose 4 or C for Codes. At the paired style editing screen, insert the boldface and un-
       derline codes by completing the following steps:
       (1) Press the boldface key, F6.
           **M** *Click on Font, Appearance, then Bold.*
       (2) Press the underline key, F8.
           **M** *Click on Font, Appearance, then Underline.*
    F. At the paired style editing screen, press the right arrow key once to move the cursor
       past the Comment code, then turn off boldfacing and underlining by completing the
       following steps:
       (1) Press the boldface key, F6.
           **M** *Click on Font, Appearance, then Bold.*
       (2) Press the underline key, F8.
           **M** *Click on Font, Appearance, then Underline.*
    G. At the paired style editing screen, press F7 twice to save the style and return the cursor
       to the Styles menu.
    H. At the Styles menu, save the heading style in a document named **HEADING.STY** by
       completing the following steps:
       (1) At the Styles menu, choose 6 or S for Save.
       (2) At the **Filename:** prompt, key in **HEADING.STY**, then press Enter.
2.  Press F7 to return the cursor to the document.
3.  Exit the document without saving it.

### Exercise Two

1.  Retrieve CH21EX1 to the screen.
2.  Delete the boldfacing codes around the headings within the document (not the title) by com-
    pleting the following steps:
    A. Access the Replace command with Alt + F2.
       **M** *Click on Search, then Replace.*
    B. At the confirmation questions, key in a **Y** for Yes.
    C. At the **-> Srch:** prompt, press the F6 function key.
    D. Press F2.
    E. At the **Replace with:** prompt, press F2.

F. As WordPerfect stops at each occurrence of a Boldface code, press **Y** to delete the code or **N** to leave the code. (Leave the Boldface codes at the title, but remove them from the headings within the newsletter.)

3. Retrieve the HEADING.STY style document by completing the following steps:
   A. Access the Styles command with Alt + F8.
      **M** *Click on Layout, then Styles.*
   B. At the Styles menu, choose 7 or R for Retrieve.
   C. At the **Filename:** prompt, key in **HEADING.STY** and press Enter.
   D. Press F7 to return the cursor to the document.

4. Apply the HEADING style to the headings within the document by completing the following steps:
   A. Block the first heading (Basketball Champions) with the Block command.
   B. With the heading blocked, access the Styles command with Alt + F8.
      **M** *Click on Layout, then Styles.*
   C. At the Styles menu, make sure the cursor is located on **HEADING** then choose 1 or O for On.
   D. Repeat the same steps for the remaining headings.

5. When the HEADING style has been applied to all headings in the newsletter, save the newsletter and name it CH27EX2. Print CH27EX2.


**Exercise Three**

1. After looking at the printing of CH27EX2, you decide that the headings would look better boldfaced and italicized rather than boldfaced and underlined. To edit the style to make the changes, complete the following steps:
   A. Retrieve CH27EX2 to the screen.
   B. Access the Style command with Alt + F8.
      **M** *Click on Layout, then Styles.*
   C. At the Styles menu, make sure the cursor is located on **HEADING**, then press 4 or E for Edit.
   D. At the Styles: Edit menu, choose 4 or C for Codes.
   E. With the paired style codes displayed, delete the **[UND]** code (the **[und]** will automatically be removed). With the cursor before the Comment code, insert a code for italics by completing the following steps:
      (1) Access the Font command with Ctrl + F8.
      (2) Choose 2 or A for Appearance.
      (3) Choose 4 or I for Italic.
         **M** *Click on Font, Appearance, then Italics.*
   F. Move the cursor after the Commend code and insert the code to turn italics off by completing the following steps:
      (1) Access the Font command with Ctrl + F8.
      (2) Choose 2 or A for Appearance.
      (3) Choose 4 or I for Italic.
         **M** *Click on Font, Appearance, then Italics.*
   G. Press F7 three times to save the edited style and return the cursor to the document.

2. Save the edited newsletter and name it CH27EX3. Print CH27EX3. (When the newsletter is printed, the headings will be boldfaced and italicized.)


**Exercise Four**

1. At a clear screen, create two styles for formatting a newsletter. First, create an open style named NEWSLETTER that inserts the top portion of a newsletter by completing the following steps:

A. Access the Styles command with Alt + F8.
  **M** *Click on Layout, then Styles.*
B. Choose 3 or C for Create.
C. At the Styles: Edit menu, choose 1 or N for Name, key in **NEWSLETTER**, and press Enter.
D. Choose 3 or D for Description, key in **Format Newsletter**, then press Enter.
E. Choose 2 or T for Type, then 2 or O for Open.
F. Choose 4 or C for Codes. At the open style editing screen, insert the Font Change code by completing the following steps:
  (1) Access the Font command with Ctrl + F8.
  (2) Choose 4 or F for Base Font.
    **M** *Click on Font, then Base Font.*
  (3) At the Base Font menu, move the cursor to 18-point Helvetica and choose 1 or S for Select. (If you are using a PostScript printer, move the cursor to Helvetica, choose 1 or S for Select, key in **18**, then press Enter. If your printer does not support Helvetica, chose a sans serif typeface.)
G. At the open style editing screen, key in **CAP RESEARCH CENTER** at the left margin, access the Flush Right command with Alt + F6 (**M** *Click on Layout, Align, then Flush Right*), then key in **NEWSLETTER**.
H. Press Enter then create a horizontal line by completing the following steps:
  (1) Access the Graphics command with Alt + F9.
  (2) Choose 5 or L for Line.
  (3) Choose 1 or H for Horizontal.
    **M** *Click on Graphics, Line, then Create Horizontal.*
  (4) Choose 4 or W for Width, key in **0.025**, then press Enter.
  (5) Press F7 to return the cursor to the open styles editing screen.
I. At the open style editing screen, change the base font to 12-point Times Roman by completing the following steps:
  (1) Access the Font command with Ctrl + F8.
  (2) Choose 4 or F for Base Font.
    **M** *Click on Font, then Base Font.*
  (3) At the Base Font menu, move the cursor to 12-point Times Roman and choose 1 or S for Select. (If you are using a PostScript printer, move the cursor to Times Roman, choose 1 or S for Select, key in **12**, then press Enter. If your printers does not support Times Roman, choose a serif typeface.)
J. At the open style editing screen, press Enter twice.
K. Press F7 three times to save the style and return the cursor to the document.

2. Create a paired style, named SUBHEADINGS, that turns boldfacing and italics on and off by completing the following steps:
  A. Access the Styles command with Alt + F8.
    **M** *Click on Layout, then Styles.*
  B. Choose 3 or C for Create.
  C. At the Styles: Edit menu, choose 1 or N for Name, key in **SUBHEADINGS**, and press Enter.
  D. Choose 3 or D for Description, key in **Format subheadings**, then press Enter.
  E. Choose 4 or C for Codes. At the paired style editing screen, insert the Boldface and Italics codes by completing the following steps:
    (1) Press the boldface key, F6.
      **M** *Click on Font, Appearance, then Bold.*
    (2) Access the Font command with Ctrl + F8, choose 2 or A for Appearance, then 4 or I for Italic.
      **M** *Click on Font, Appearance, then Italics.*

F. At the paired style editing screen, press the right arrow key once to move the cursor past the Comment code, then turn off boldfacing and italics by completing the following steps:

    (1)  Press the boldface key, F6.

        **M** *Click on Font, Appearance, then Bold.*

    (2)  Access the Font command with Ctrl + F8, choose 2 or A for Appearance, then 4 or I for Italic.

        **M** *Click on Font, Appearance, then Italics.*

G. At the paired style editing screen, press F7 twice to save the style and return the cursor to the Styles menu.

3. At the Styles menu, save the styles in a separate document named NEWSLTR.STY by completing the following steps:

    A. At the Styles menu, choose 6 or S for Save.

    B. At the **Filename:** prompt, key in **NEWSLTR.STY**, then press Enter.

4. Press F7 to return the cursor to the document.

5. Exit the document without saving it.

## Exercise Five

1. At a clear screen, retrieve the document NEWSLTR.STY by completing the following steps:

    A. Access the Style command with Alt + F8.

       **M** *Click on Layout, then Styles.*

    B. At the Styles menu, choose 7 or R for Retrieve.

    C. At the **Filename:** prompt, key in **NEWSLTR.STY**, then press Enter.

2. At the Styles menu, move the cursor to the NEWSLETTER style and choose 1 or O for On.

3. Access the Flush Right command with Alt + F6 (**M** *Click on Layout, Align, then Flush Right*), then key in **Summer, 1993**.

4. Press Enter twice, then create two newspaper-style columns with the default settings.

5. Key in the text shown in figure 27-7. (The text appears in a single column; your text will appear in two newspaper-style columns.)

6. When all the text is keyed in, apply the SUBHEADING style to each of the subheadings in the newsletter by completing the following steps:

    A. Block the first heading, Services to Minorities, with the Block command.

    B. With the heading blocked, access the Styles command with Alt + F8.

       **M** *Click on Layout, then Styles.*

    C. At the Styles menu, move the cursor to SUBHEADING, then choose 1 or O for On.

    D. Repeat the same steps for the remaining subheadings.

7. Save the newsletter and name it CH27EX5. Print page 1 of CH27EX5.

---

## Services to Minorities

In the last two decades, there has been a movement in the mental health field toward improved services to children and families who are members of minority populations. Recognized as at-risk and underserved, families of minority populations have repeatedly been the subjects of research and demonstration projects. Mental health professionals serving these children and families today are faced with the nagging question, "What constitutes appropriate services for minority clients?"

Fortunately the cumulative results of twenty years of work in this area are now becoming apparent. The knowledge base has grown, and models for working cross-culturally have been developed and reviewed in the literature.

Sound cross-cultural practice begins with a commitment from the worker to provide culturally competent services. To succeed, workers need an awareness and acceptance of cultural differences, an awareness of their own cultural values, an understanding of the "dynamics of difference" in the helping process, basic knowledge about client's culture, and the ability to adapt practice skills to fit the client's cultural context.

As we learn more about improving services to minority children, services to all children will be improved.

## Implementing Family Goals

The CAP Research and Training Center sponsored a workshop May 6-12, which provided an in-depth look at the process of developing and implementing family involvement and support goals for area providers. The training was facilitated by the CAP Research and Training Director, Dorothy Jackson.

Each participant completed a pretraining questionnaire that was used to focus the training on the particular needs of the area provider. A significant portion of the training was devoted to specific strategy development within an area. The training provided a unique opportunity for participants to share their experiences and knowledge using a peer-consultation process. At the end of the training participants agreed to continue in informal sharing of experiences with each other as they progress in their program planning to provide improved systems of care for children with serious emotional disabilities and their families.

## Conference a Success

Over one hundred Indian and non-Indian mental health practitioners, professionals, and advocates interested in Indian children with serious emotional disorders met in Spokane, Washington, at a conference entitled "Mental Health Issues for the North American Indian Child and Adolescent." Initiated by Washington's Child and Adolescent Services Program, the June conference was the first ever to focus on this population and is unique in its international scope. Representatives of the Canadian government were on hand to share the experience.

The conference was planned with the goal of sharing concerns, knowledge, and strategies to assist in efforts to provide the best possible continuum of care to a population highly at risk and greatly underserved. Through building networks and coordination, the quality of services for Indian children with serious emotional handicaps will be improved.

Written conference proceedings will be available in late August. If you are interested in obtaining the proceedings, please contact the CAP Research and Training Center.

Figure 27-7: Exercise Five

**Exercise Six**

1. Retrieve CH27EX5 to the screen. Edit the NEWSLETTER open style and add codes that change the justification to Left and change tab settings by completing the following steps:
   A. Access the Styles command with Alt + F8.
      **M** *Click on Layout, then Styles.*
   B. At the Styles menu, move the cursor to NEWSLETTER, choose 4 or E for Edit, then 4 or C for Codes.
   C. At the open style editing screen, move the cursor to the end of text and format codes. Insert a code that changes the justification to Left.
   D. At the open style editing screen, delete all previous tabs, and set new left tabs at +0.3 and +3.8 inches.
   E. Press F7 three times to save the edited style and return the cursor to the document.

2. Edit the SUBHEADINGS paired style, and remove the code for italics. To do this, complete the following steps:
   A. Access the Styles command with Alt + F8.
      **M** *Click on Layout, then Styles.*
   B. At the Styles menu, move the cursor to SUBHEADINGS, choose 4 or E for Edit, then 4 or C for Codes.
   C. At the paired style editing screen, delete the Italics codes.
   D. Press F7 three times to save the edited style and return the cursor to the document.

3. Save the edited newsletter and name it CH27EX6. Print page 1 of CH27EX6.

**Exercise Seven**

1. At a clear screen, create an open outline style that formats the first three levels as follows:

   Level 1 = Roman numerals indented to the first tab stop with the Decimal Tab command (to align the numerals at the right), the Indent key used to indent the cursor to the next tab stop.

   Level 2 = Capital letters indented to the second tab stop, the Indent key used to indent the cursor to the next tab stop.

   Level 3 = Arabic numbers indented to the third tab stop, the Indent key used to indent the cursor to the next tab stop.

   To create an open outline style named DEPT AGENDA that applies this level formatting, complete the following steps:
   A. Access the Date/Outline command with Shift + F5.
   B. Choose 6 or D for Define.
      **M** *Click on Tools, then Define.*
   C. At the Paragraph Number Definition menu, choose 9 or N for Outline Style Name.
   D. At the Outline Styles menu, choose 2 or C for Create to create the new outline style.
   E. At the Outline Styles: Edit menu, choose 1 or N for Name, key in **DEPT AGENDA**, then press Enter.
   F. At the Outline Styles: Edit menu, choose 2 or D for Description, key in **Department Agenda Outline**, then press Enter.
   G. At the Outline Styles: Edit menu, choose 5 or C for Codes.
   H. At the outline style editing screen, complete the following steps to format level 1:
      (1) Access the Tab Align command with Ctrl + F6 to insert the **[DEC TAB]** code.
      (2) Press the right arrow key one time to move the cursor past the **[Par Num:1]** code.
      (3) Press the Indent key, F4 (**M** *Click on Layout, Align, then Indent, F4*).
      (4) Press F7 to return the cursor to the Outline: Styles Edit menu.

    I. Move the cursor to level 2, then choose 5 or C for Codes.

    J. At the outline style editing screen, complete the following steps to format level 2:

       (1) Press the Tab key twice to insert two Tab codes.

       (2) Press the right arrow key once to move the cursor past the **[Par Num:2]** code.

       (3) Press the Indent key, F4 (**M** *Click on Layout, Align, then Indent, F4*).

       (4) Press F7 to return the cursor to the Outline: Styles Edit menu.

    K. Move the cursor to level 3, then choose 5 or C for Codes.

    L. At the outline style editing screen, complete the following steps to format level 3:

       (1) Press the Tab key three times to insert three Tab codes.

       (2) Press the right arrow key once to move the cursor past the **[Par Num:3]** code.

       (3) Press the Indent key, F4 (**M** *Click on Layout, Align, then Indent, F4*).

       (4) Press F7 to return the cursor to the Outline: Styles Edit menu.

    M. Press F7 to return the cursor to the Outline Styles menu. At this menu, save the DEPT AGENDA outline style as a separate document by completing the following steps:

       (1) Choose 5 or S for Save.

       (2) At the prompt **Filename:**, key in **AGENDA.STY**, then press Enter.

    N. Press F7 three times to save the outline style and outline style document and return the cursor to the document.

2. Key in the heading and subheadings of the agenda shown in figure 27-8.

3. With the cursor a double space below the subheading AGENDA, delete previous tabs and set new left tabs at +0.5, +0.7, +1.1, and +1.5.

4. With the cursor a double space below the subheading, AGENDA, select the DEPT AGENDA outline style to be used in the agenda by completing the following steps:

    A. Access the Date/Outline command with Shift + F5.

    B. Choose 6 or D for Define.

      **M** *Click on Tools, then Define.*

    C. At the Paragraph Number Definition menu, choose 9 or N for Outline Style Name.

    D. At the Outline Styles menu, move the cursor to the DEPT AGENDA outline style, then choose 1 or L for Select.

    E. At the Paragraph Definition menu, press F7.

    F. From the prompts that display at the bottom of the screen, choose 4 or O for Outline, then 1 or O for On.

    G. Press Enter, then key in the remainder of the agenda shown in figure 27-8.

5. When the agenda is completed, turn outlining off by completing the following steps:

    A. Access the Date/Outline command with Shift + F5.

    B. Choose 4 or O for Outline.

    C. Choose 2 or F for Off.

      **M** *Click on Tools, Outline, then Off.*

6. Save the agenda and name it CH27EX7. Print CH27EX7.

## PUGET SOUND SEMICONDUCTOR

### Sales Department Meeting, May 11, 1993

### AGENDA

I.   Approval of minutes from the April 14, 1993, Sales Department meeting.

II.  Old Business
     A.   Follow-up report on sales figures for the first quarter of 1993.
     B.   Update on sales strategies for new electronic components.

III. New Business
     A.   Update on conference entitled "Excellence in Sales" sponsored by the State of Washington.
     B.   Expansion of sales department including new offices and equipment.
     C.   Sales promotions for the month of June.

IV.  Committee Reports
     A.   Sales task force
          1.   Summer conferences
          2.   Sales strategies
          3.   Promotion ideas
     B.   Construction committee
          1.   Office configuration
          2.   Task lighting
          3.   Computer stations

V.   Adjournment

Figure 27-8: Exercise Seven

## PERFORMANCE ASSESSMENTS

### Assessment One

1.   At a clear screen, create an open style named FORMAT that includes the following formats:
     A.  Base font of 12-point Times Roman (or a serif typeface if your printer does not support Times Roman).
     B.  Paper size and type of standard legal (8.5" x 14").
     C.  Justification changed to Left.
     D.  Top margin of 1.5 inches.
     E.  Double spacing.

2. Create a paired style named HEADING A that turns boldfacing on and off and changes the base font to 14-point Times Roman. (Insert the Boldface On code before the Comment code and the Boldface Off code after the Comment code. You do not need to change the base font back to 12-point Times Roman. WordPerfect will do that automatically.)

3. Create a paired style named HEADING B that turns boldfacing and italics on and off.

4. Save the three styles in a styles document named LEGAL.STY.

5. Exit from the document without saving it.

## Assessment Two

1. At a clear screen, retrieve the LEGAL.STY document. (Do this through the Styles menu.)

2. Access the Styles menu and turn on the FORMAT style.

3. Key in the legal text shown in figure 27-9. Turn the HEADING A style on before the title and turn it off after the title. Turn the HEADING B style on and off for the following paragraph headings:

    A. Know All Men by These Presents:

    B. Giving and Granting

    C. In Witness Whereof,

    You can turn on the styles, key in the text, then turn off the styles; or you can key in the entire document then go back and block the headings and turn on the styles.

4. Save the legal document and name it CH27PA2. Print CH27PA2.

SPECIAL POWER OF ATTORNEY

Know All Men by These Presents: That _____
has made, constituted and appointed, and by these presents does
make, constitute and appoint _____ the true and
lawful attorney for him/her and in his/her name, place, and stead,
and for the use and benefit described below:



Giving and Granting unto his said attorney full power and
authority to do and perform all and every act and thing whatsoever
requisite and necessary to be done in and about the premises, as
fully to all intents and purposes as he might or could do if
personally present, hereby ratifying and confirming all that his
said attorney shall lawfully do or cause to be done by virtue of
these presents.

In Witness Whereof, we have hereunto set our hands and seals
the _____ day of _____, 19 __.

_____(SEAL)
_____(SEAL)
_____(SEAL)
_____(SEAL)

**Figure 27-9: Assessment Two**

**Assessment Three**
1.  Retrieve CH27PA2 to the screen.
2.  Edit the FORMAT style by deleting the code that changes justification to Left.
3.  Edit the HEADING B style by deleting the Italics codes.
4.  Save the legal document and name it CH27PA3. Print CH27PA3.

**Assessment Four**
1.  At a clear screen, key in the title and subtitle of the outline shown in figure 27-10.
2.  With the cursor a double space below the subheading, Corporate Report, delete previous tabs and set new left tabs at +0.5, +0.7, +1.1, and +1.5.
3.  With the cursor a double space below the subheading Corporate Report, retrieve the AGENDA.STY outline style document, and select the DEPT AGENDA outline style.
4.  Key in the outline as shown in figure 27-10.
5.  When the outline is complete, save it and name it CH27PA4. Print CH27PA4.

## PUGET SOUND SEMICONDUCTOR

### Corporate Report

I.  Industrial and technological growth in the Puget Sound region from North Seattle to South Tacoma.
    A. Industrial growth in the Puget Sound region
        1.  Industrial growth before 1940
        2.  Industrial growth during World War II
        3.  Industrial growth between 1945 and 1950
        4.  Industrial growth since the 1950s
    B. Technological growth in the Puget Sound region
        1.  Before the 1950s
        2.  After the 1950s

II.  Formation of Puget Sound Semiconductor
    A. Founding members of Puget Sound Semiconductor
    B. Corporate goals for the new company
        1.  Financial
        2.  Growth
        3.  Product

III.  Impact of the computer revolution
    A. Changes in manufacturing
    B. Product development
    C. Regional economy

IV.  Current status of Puget Sound Semiconductor
    A. Product development
    B. Financial situation
    C. Expansion

V.  Future of Puget Sound Semiconductor
    A. Diversification
    B. Research and development
    C. Changes in manufacturing techniques
    D. Regional corporate sites

Figure 27-10: Assessment Four

# CHAPTER 28

## MERGE DOCUMENTS

## PERFORMANCE OBJECTIVES

Upon successful completion of chapter 28, you will be able to format and merge separate files to create a series of similar business documents, such as personalized form letters.

### MERGE FEATURE

Have you ever received a letter from a company marketing a new product? The letter seems to be addressed to you personally. Your name and address are listed on the letter, the salutation includes your name, and the body of the letter may mention something about you: the city in which you live, your state, or other personal information. Even though the letter seems to be addressed just to you, it was probably sent to hundreds or thousands of other households.

This form letter has a personal touch because it probably was created on a word processor with a merge capability. WordPerfect has a powerful and easy-to-operate Merge feature. With it you can create form letters, mailing labels, reports, lists, and much more, all with personalized information.

### CREATING A PERSONALIZED FORM LETTER

Creating a personalized form letter requires two documents. One document contains the form letter with identifiers showing where variable information (information that changes with each letter) is to be inserted. WordPerfect calls this the *primary file*. The other document, which WordPerfect calls the *secondary file*, contains the variable information.

To better understand how these two documents work together, let us look at an example. Suppose the law firm Moreno, Yamada, & Schwartz wants to send a letter to all their clients inviting them to an open house.

To create a primary and secondary file for this example, several steps need to be completed. The first step is to design the letter, a task that includes determining variable information. Look at the example letter in figure 28-1 to see one way to organize the letter.

April 3, 1993


Name
Address
City, State  ZIP

Dear (Name):

In the past several years, our law firm has
experienced a steady growth in clients and
personnel.

This growth has necessitated an increase in office
space. For the past six months, we have been
remodeling our offices and expanding our size.

We are proud of the look of our new offices and
would like to invite you to come and see us.
Please be our guests at an open house on Thursday,
April 22, from 7:00 to 9:00 p.m.

Sincerely,

MORENO, YAMADA, & SCHWARTZ



Anita M. Moreno
Senior Partner

---

**Figure 28-1: Sample Letter**

---

The date, body of the letter, and the signature block are standard. The
variable information — information that will change with each letter — is
the name, address, city, state, Zip Code, and salutation.


## Determining Fields

In this form letter, the variable information must be broken into sections
called *fields* and identified with a special command. To determine the
variable fields, you must decide how the information will be used and in
what form. As an example, let's look at a client of the law firm.

> Mr. Joshua Greenburg
> 12004 South 43rd Street
> Renton, WA 98344

The name, "Mr. Joshua Greenburg" could be identified as an entire field,
but the salutation for this client should read "Dear Mr. Greenburg." If the
name is left as one field, the salutation would read "Dear Mr. Joshua

Greenburg" (which sounds okay but is not correct). In this example, then, the name should be broken into three fields: title (Mr.), first name, and last name.

There is no need for the street address to be broken into smaller parts. Therefore, it can be identified as one field.

The city, state, and Zip Code in this example can also be considered as one field. However, if you decide that you need the city or state name separated, you need to make separate fields for each item.

After all fields have been determined, the next step is to determine field numbers. WordPerfect inserts variable data based on field numbers. There is no limit to how many field numbers a document can contain. Let us look at one way the field names in this example can be assigned numbers.

| | |
|---|---|
| Title | = Field 1 |
| First name | = Field 2 |
| Last name | = Field 3 |
| Street address | = Field 4 |
| City, state, zip code | = Field 5 |

You may want to write this information on a piece of paper. When you create documents with a large number of fields, remembering what is contained in each can be difficult.

### Merge Codes Command

Creating a field within a document requires the use of the Merge Codes command. To create fields in a primary file, complete the following steps:

1. Key in text to the point where variable text is to be inserted and access the Merge Codes command with Shift + F9.

2. At the prompt **1 Field; 2 End Record; 3 Input; 4 Page Off; 5 Next Record; 6 More: 0**, choose 1 or F for Field.
   **M** *Click on Tools, Merge Codes, then Field.*

3. The prompt **Field:** _ appears at the bottom of the screen. At this prompt, key in the number you assigned to the field, press Enter, and WordPerfect inserts the code {**FIELD**}1~ in the document.

Continue in this manner until all fields are inserted in their appropriate positions within the document. Space between the fields as you want the text to be spaced when it is inserted in the letter. The same field number can be inserted in many different locations throughout the document.

### Primary File

Now that you understand how to insert codes to identify fields, you can create the primary file. At a clear screen, you would key in the letter as shown in figure 28-2 (using the Merge Codes command to insert the field numbers).

April 3, 1993


{FIELD}1~ {FIELD}2~ {FIELD}3~
{FIELD}4~
{FIELD}5~

Dear {FIELD}1~ {FIELD}3~:

In the past several years, our law firm has
experienced a steady growth in clients and
personnel.

This growth has necessitated an increase in office
space. For the past six months, we have been
remodeling our offices and expanding our size.

We are proud of the look of our new offices and
would like to invite you to come see us. Please
be our guests at an open house on Thursday, April
22, from 7:00 to 9:00 p.m.

Sincerely,

MORENO, YAMADA, & SCHWARTZ



Anita M. Moreno
Senior Partner

**Figure 28-2: Primary File**

Notice that there is a space between the fields. You space the fields the
same way you would space text. Fields 1 and 3 were used again in the
salutation. As mentioned before, you can use fields in a primary document
as often as you need to.

Save a primary file in the same manner as any other document. To help
you remember that it is a primary file, you may want to add an extension to
the document name. For example, you may want to call this document
OPENHS.PF (for open house letter, primary file).


**Secondary File**

After the primary file is created, you need to create another document
consisting of a record for each client. WordPerfect calls this the secondary
file.

Variable information in a secondary file is saved as a record. A record
contains all the information for one unit (for example, a person, family, or
business). A series of fields make one record. In our example, each record

will contain five fields of information — title; first name; last name; address; and the city, state and Zip Code.

Each record in a secondary file must contain the same number of fields. If the number of fields is not consistent, information will not be correctly inserted during the merge.

### End Field and End Record

Each field of information for a record is created on a separate line or lines. After the information for the field is keyed in, you press the End Field key, F9. This key inserts the code {**END FIELD**} on the screen and also inserts a hard return. Continue in this manner until all fields for the record have been entered. To end the record, access the Merge Codes command with Shift + F9 and choose 2 or E for End Record (**M** *Click on Tools, Merge Codes, then End Record*). This inserts the code {**END RECORD**} in the document and also inserts a hard page break. This identifies the end of one record and the beginning of the next.

When all records have been entered, save the secondary file in the same manner as any other document. To identify it as a secondary file, you may want to add an extension — for instance, SF (for secondary file) at the end of the document name.

To create a secondary file for the open house letter, a few more clients are needed. The following four people are clients of the law firm Moreno, Yamada, & Schwartz.

Mr. Joshua Greenburg
12004 South 43rd Street
Renton, WA 98344

Mrs. Raylene Whidden
3255 South J Street
Tacoma, WA 98431

Mr. and Mrs. Mark Tison
8433 Lakewood Drive
Fife, WA 98522

Ms. Sylvia Berg
4300 Narrows Avenue
Tacoma, WA 98409

To create the secondary file, start with a blank screen and key in a record for each family. Each record will contain the five fields identified earlier.

The names and addresses shown in figure 28-3 illustrate how the secondary file will look when completed. The {**END FIELD**} code is created with the End Field key, F9. The {**END RECORD**} code is created by accessing the Merge Codes command with Shift + F9 and choosing 2 or E for End Record (**M** *Click on Tools, Merge Codes, then End Record*).

```
Mr.{END FIELD}
Joshua{END FIELD}
Greenburg{END FIELD}
12004 South 43rd Street{END FIELD}
Renton, WA 98344{END FIELD}
{END RECORD}
==================================================
Mrs.{END FIELD}
Raylene{END FIELD}
Whidden{END FIELD}
3255 South J Street{END FIELD}
Tacoma, WA 98431{END FIELD}
{END RECORD}
==================================================
Mr. and Mrs.{END FIELD}
Mark{END FIELD}
Tyson{END FIELD}
8433 Lakewood Drive{END FIELD}
Fife, WA 98522{END FIELD}
{END RECORD}
==================================================
Ms.{END FIELD}
Sylvia{END FIELD}
Berg{END FIELD}
4300 Narrows Avenue{END FIELD}
Tacoma, WA 98409{END FIELD}
{END RECORD}
==================================================
```

**Figure 28-3: Secondary File Records**

When all the records have been entered, the document needs to be saved. Name it something that tells you what is contained in the document, for example — OPENHS.SF, for open house, secondary file.

### Merging the Files

Once the primary and secondary documents are saved on the disk, they can be merged. To merge the documents, complete the following steps:

1.  Access the Merge/Sort command with Ctrl + F9.

2.  At the prompt **1 Merge; 2 Sort; 3 Convert Old Merge Codes: 0**, choose 1 or M for Merge.
    **M** *Click on Tools, then Merge.*

3.  At the **Primary file:_** prompt, key in the name of the primary file and press Enter. (In the open house example, you would key in OPENHS.PF and press Enter.)

4.  At the **Secondary file:** prompt, key in the name of the secondary file and press Enter. (In the open house example, you would key in OPENHS.SF and press Enter.)

WordPerfect flashes the message **\* Merging \*** on the screen. When the merge process is complete, the merged letters display on the screen. The number of letters is determined by the number of records in the secondary file. To print, save the merged letters as you would any other document and print with the method you prefer.

### Canceling a Merge

If, during the merge, you want to stop the merge process, press the Cancel key, F1. You may need to clear the screen. To begin the merge again, you will need to repeat the steps for completing a merge.

## CHAPTER REVIEW

### Summary

- The WordPerfect Merge feature is used to create form documents with personalized text.
- The merge process requires two documents. WordPerfect calls these the primary and secondary files.
- The primary file contains the form document, with identifiers that show where variable information is to be inserted. The secondary file contains the variable information.
- Variable information must be broken into fields. Fields are identified by numbers. There is no limit to the number of fields that may be contained in a document.
- The same field number can be used in many different locations throughout a document. Fields are spaced in the same manner that text is spaced.
- Primary and secondary files are saved in the same manner as any other document.
- A secondary file contains records. A record contains all the information for one unit (a person, family, or business).
- Each field for a record is created on a separate line. To end a field, access the End Field key, F9.
- When a primary and secondary file are merged, the merge occurs at the screen. To print, save the merged document, then print with the method your prefer.
- Use the Cancel key, F1, to stop a merge.

### Commands Review

| | **Keyboard** |
|---|---|
| End Field key | F9 |
| Merge Codes command | Shift + F9 |
| Merge/Sort command | Ctrl + F9 |
| | **Mouse** |
| Merge Codes command | Tools, Merge Codes |
| Merge command | Tools, Merge |

## STUDY GUIDE FOR CHAPTER 28

**Completion:** In the space provided at the right, indicate the correct symbol, term, or number for the explanation.

1.  An amount of information.                                                    _____

2.  Ends a field.                                                               _____

3.  Ends a record.                                                             _____

4.  File containing form letter with identifiers showing where
    variable information is to be inserted.                                     _____

5.  All the information for one unit (person, family, business, etc.).          _____

6.  File containing records.                                                   _____

7.  Access the Merge/Sort command.                                             _____

**True/False:** Circle the letter T if the statement is true; circle the letter F if the statement is false.

1.  A field number can be used only once in a form document.                          T     F

2.  A primary file is saved in the same manner as any other document.                 T     F

3.  Each field for a record is created on a separate line.                             T     F

4.  The primary file contains records.                                                T     F

5.  When a primary and secondary file are merged, the merge occurs at the printer.    T     F

6.  Fields in a form document are spaced in the same manner as text.                   T     F

## HANDS-ON EXERCISES

Change the default directory to UNIT6.

### Exercise One

(In this exercise, you will be creating the open house letter used as an example in this chapter.)

1.  At a clear screen, create the letter shown in figure 28-4 in an appropriate business letter
    format. Make the following changes:
    A. Change the left and right margins to 1.5 inches.
    B. Change the justification to Left.
    C. To create the fields in the letter, complete the following steps:
       (1) Key in text to the point where the field code is to appear. Access the Merge Codes
           command with Shift + F9, then choose 1 or F for Field.
           **M** *Click on Tools, Merge Codes, then Field.*
       (2) Key in the appropriate field number and press Enter.
2.  When the letter is complete, save it and name it OPENHS.PF. Print OPENHS.PF.

April 3, 1993


{FIELD}1~ {FIELD}2~ {FIELD}3~
{FIELD}4~
{FIELD}5~

Dear {FIELD}1~ {FIELD}3~:

In the past several years, our law firm has experienced
a steady growth in clients and personnel.

This growth has necessitated an increase in office
space.  For the past six months, we have been remodeling our offices and expanding our size.

We are proud of the look of our new offices and would
like to invite you to come and see us.  Please be our
guests at an open house on Thursday, April 22, from
7:00 to 9:00 p.m.

Sincerely,

MORENO, YAMADA, & SCHWARTZ



Anita M. Moreno
Senior Partner

---

Figure 28-4: Exercise One


## Exercise Two

1. At a clear screen, create a secondary file with the records shown in figure 28-5. Use the **End Field** key, F9, at the end of each field. End each record by completing the following steps:
   A. Access the Merge Codes command with **Shift + F9.**
   B. Choose 2 or E for End Record.
      **M** *Click on Tools, Merge Codes, then End Record.*
2. When the records are entered, save the document and name it OPENHS.SF. Print OPEN-HS.SF.

```
Mr.{END FIELD}
Joshua{END FIELD}
Greenburg{END FIELD}
12004 South 43rd Street{END FIELD}
Renton, WA 98344{END FIELD}
{END RECORD}
=====================================================================
Mrs.{END FIELD}
Raylene{END FIELD}
Whidden{END FIELD}
3255 South J Street{END FIELD}
Tacoma, WA 98431{END FIELD}
{END RECORD}
=====================================================================
Mr. and Mrs.{END FIELD}
Mark{END FIELD}
Tyson{END FIELD}
8433 Lakewood Drive{END FIELD}
Fife, WA 98522{END FIELD}
{END RECORD}
=====================================================================
Ms.{END FIELD}
Sylvia{END FIELD}
Berg{END FIELD}
4300 Narrows Avenue{END FIELD}
Tacoma, WA 98409{END FIELD}
{END RECORD}
=====================================================================
```

Figure 28-5: Exercise Two

## Exercise Three

1.  At a clear screen, merge the OPENHS.PF primary file with the OPENHS.SF secondary file by completing the following steps:
    A.  Access the Merge/Sort command with Ctrl + F9.
    B.  Choose 1 or M for Merge.
        **M** *Click on Tools, then Merge.*
    C.  Key in **OPENHS.PF** and press Enter.
    D.  Key in **OPENHS.SF** and press Enter.
2.  When the primary and secondary file are merged, save the merged document and name it CH28EX3. Print CH28EX3.

## Exercise Four

1.  At a clear screen, create the primary file shown in figure 28-6 in an appropriate business letter format. Make the following changes:
    A.  Change the left and right margins to 1.5 inches.
    B.  Change justification to Left.
    C.  Use the Merge Codes command to create the fields.
2.  Save the primary file and name it REVIEW.PF. Print REVIEW.PF

March 31, 1993


{FIELD}1~ {FIELD}2~ {FIELD}3~
{FIELD}4~
{FIELD}5~

Dear {FIELD}1~ {FIELD}3~:

The employees of Quality Life Insurance are committed
to improving the quality of life for our clients during
their retirement years.  To ensure that you have
financial stability during retirement, we would like to
review your present and future financial situation on a
regular basis.

The customer service representative in your area would
like to visit you at your home, {FIELD}1~ {FIELD}3~, to
perform a financial review.  Please call our company at
555-7435 to schedule an appointment.

Very truly yours,



Margaret Streek
Vice President

xx:REVIEW.PF

---

**Figure 28-6: Exercise Four**


## Exercise Five

1.  At a clear screen, create a secondary file with the records shown in figure 28-7. Use the End Field key, F9, at the end of each field. End each record by completing the following steps:
    A.  Access the Merge Codes command with Shift + F9.
    B.  Choose 2 or E for End Record.
    **M** *Click on Tools, Merge Codes, then End Record.*

2.  When the records are entered, save the document and name it REVIEW.SF. Print REVIEW.SF.

```
Mr. and Mrs.{END FIELD}
Bryce{END FIELD}
Heymann{END FIELD}
3306 - 124th Avenue East{END FIELD}
Portland, OR 96034{END FIELD}
{END RECORD}
=================================================================
Mrs.{END FIELD}
Cynthia{END FIELD}
Jonville{END FIELD}
3002 Steele Street{END FIELD}
Portland, OR 96026{END FIELD}
{END RECORD}
=================================================================
Mr. and Mrs.{END FIELD}
Steven{END FIELD}
Baretto{END FIELD}
3201 South Graham{END FIELD}
Portland, OR 96422{END FIELD}
{END RECORD}
=================================================================
Ms.{END FIELD}
Dori{END FIELD}
Walston{END FIELD}
520 Meridian Avenue{END FIELD}
Portland, OR 96329{END FIELD}
{END RECORD}
=================================================================
```

**Figure 28-7: Exercise Five**

**Exercise Six**

1. At a clear screen, merge the **REVIEW.PF** primary file with the **REVIEW.SF** secondary file by completing the following steps:
   A. Access the Merge/Sort command with Ctrl + F9.
   B. Choose 1 or M for Merge.
      **M** *Click on Tools, then Merge.*
   C. Key in **REVIEW.PF** and press Enter.
   D. Key in **REVIEW.SF** and press Enter.
2. When the primary and secondary file are merged, save the merged document and name it CH28EX6. Print CH28EX6.

## PERFORMANCE ASSESSMENTS

**Assessment One**

1.  At a clear screen, create the letter shown in figure 28-8 as a primary file in an appropriate business letter format. You determine the margins and justification as well as the fields and field numbers.

2.  When the primary file is complete, save it and name it SOFTWARE.PF. Print SOFTWARE.PF.

---

April 14, 1993


(Name)
(Address)
(City, State, Zip Code)

(Salutation):

We hope you are having great success with your (program name) program. As you may have discovered, (program name) is a powerful and versatile (type of software) software program.

Just recently, the company that manufactures (program name) has updated the program. The new version includes additional features not previously available.

You are currently using (program name), Version (version #). The update of (program name) is Version (new version #). We feel confident that you will be pleased with the new features.

Please come into our store for a free demonstration of the new software, or give us a call at our toll-free number, 1-800-555-2345. We look forward to hearing from you.

Very truly yours,


Devon McKenna
Manager

xx:SOFTWARE.PF

---

Figure 28-8: Assessment One

**Assessment Two**

1.  At a clear screen, key in the records shown in figure 28-9 as a secondary file. Arrange the fields and records in the correct format.
2.  Save the secondary file and name it SOFTWARE.SF. Print SOFTWARE.SF.
3.  Merge SOFTWARE.PF with SOFTWARE.SF and name the merged file CH28PA2. Print CH28PA2.

---

Mr. Edward Snead
4917 Bennett Court
Hayford, WA 99422
Program name: Quick File
Type of software:  database
Version #:  2.0
New Version #:  3.0

Ms. Karen Stearns
4211 Yakima Street
Glenrose, WA 99626
Program name:  CalcPlus
Type of software:  spreadsheet
Version #:  2.0
New Version #:  3.0

Mrs. Donna Almadi
11304 - 142nd Avenue
Hayford, WA 99422
Program name:  Writer's Edge
Type of software:  word processing
Version #:  2.1
New Version #:  2.2

Mrs. Allan Metcalfe
122 Callow Drive
Hayford, WA 99422
Program name:  Powerhouse
Type of software:  integrated
Version #:  2.0
New Version #:  2.1

Ms. Patricia Gumbel
7002 Tenth Avenue
Four Lakes, WA 99201
Program name: Right Writer
Type of software: word processing
Version #:  3.0
New version #:  3.1

Mr. Judd Dougherty
3987 Montgomery Street
Four Lakes, WA 99201
Program name:  Enhancer
Type of software:  integrated
Version #:  1.0
New Version #:  2.0

Mr. Arthur Gallagher
7332 Willow Road
Glenrose, WA 99626
Program name:  Super File
Type of software:  database
Version #:  2.0
New Version #:  2.2

Mr. Scott Belzona
1305 Randolph Road
Glenrose, WA 99626
Program name:  Word's Galore
Type of software:  word processing
Version #:  3.2
New Version #:  3.3

---

**Figure 28-9: Assessment Two**

# CHAPTER 29

## PERFORMANCE OBJECTIVES

Upon successful completion of chapter 29, you will be able to perform merges that input variable information from the keyboard or another file. You will also be able to send merged documents directly to the printer.

### MERGE CODES

In the previous chapter, you learned to create primary and secondary files and merge the two on the screen to create personalized form letters. To print the letters, you had to save the merged letters as separate documents and print with any method you desired.

This method is simple enough, but it can be cumbersome with long secondary files. If your secondary file contained hundreds of records, WordPerfect might not be able to merge all records on the screen. There might not be enough memory available to hold all that information at one time. To avoid this situation, you can insert commands in the primary file that tell WordPerfect to send the merged documents directly to the printer. With this method, you will not see the merged documents on the screen.

### Direct Printing

WordPerfect's merge feature contains numerous commands that can be inserted in a primary or secondary file. To see a list of the commands available, access the Merge Codes command with Shift + F9 and choose 6 or M for More (**M** *Click on Tools, Merge Codes, then More*). WordPerfect inserts a window in the upper right corner of the screen containing the Merge commands. Appendix K in the WordPerfect 5.1 reference manual explains each command.

To merge a primary and secondary file at the printer, the codes {**PAGE OFF**} and {**PRINT**} need to be inserted at the end of the primary file. The {**PAGE OFF**} code tells WordPerfect not to insert an extra hard page break, and the {PRINT} command merges the primary and secondary file at the printer.

To insert the commands, complete the following steps:

1.  Retrieve the primary file to the screen. Move the cursor to the end of the document and access the Merge Codes command with Shift + F9.

2.  Choose 4 or P for Page Off. This causes WordPerfect to insert the {PAGE OFF} code in the document.
    **M** *Click on Tools, Merge Codes, then Page Off.*

3.  Access the Merge Codes command again with Shift + F9 and choose 6 or M for More.
    **M** *Click on Tools, Merge Codes, then More.*

4.  WordPerfect displays a window containing Merge codes in the upper right corner of the screen. Move the cursor to {PRINT} and press Enter. This inserts the {PRINT} code in the document and removes the window of codes.

In the steps above, the Page Off selection from the Merge Codes command was used to insert the {PAGE OFF} code. This code can also be inserted in the document through the window of Merge codes. To do this, complete the following steps:

1.  Access the Merge Codes command with Shift + F9 and choose 6 or M for More.
    **M** *Click on Tools, Merge Codes, then More.*

2.  With the cursor located in the window of Merge codes, move the cursor to {PAGE OFF} and press Enter.

### Keyboard Entry

Situations may arise in which you do not need to keep variable information in a secondary file. WordPerfect lets you input variable information directly from the keyboard so you do not have to create a secondary file. You can create a form letter with fields *and* with keyboard entry, or you can create a document that requires just keyboard entry.

Keyboard entry in a document requires the {KEYBOARD} command. To insert the {KEYBOARD} command in a document, complete the following steps:

1.  Key in the document to the point where you want keyboard entry and access the Merge Codes command with Shift + F9, then choose 6 or M for More.
    **M** *Click on Tools, Merge Codes, then More.*

2.  With the cursor in the window of codes, move the cursor to {KEYBOARD} and press Enter.

During the merge, the primary file appears on the screen with the cursor positioned where the first {KEYBOARD} is located. Key in the information and press the End Field key, F9. This continues the merge to the next {KEYBOARD} code or the next record.

The {INPUT} code can also be used for keyboard entry. The advantage to the {INPUT} code over the {KEYBOARD} code is that the {INPUT} code lets you insert a message identifying what information is to be entered at the keyboard. For example, you can create an {INPUT} code for keyboard entry after the DATE: heading in a memorandum and include the message **Enter the current date**. When the document is merged, the message appears at the bottom of the screen, telling you what to enter. A message can contain a maximum of 59 characters.

To include an **{INPUT}** code in a document with the message **Enter the current date**, complete the following steps:

1.  Key in the document to the point where the **{INPUT}** code is to be inserted and access the Merge Codes command with Shift + F9.

2.  Choose 3 or I for Input.
    **M** *Click on Tools, Merge Codes, then Input.*

3.  At the prompt **Enter Message:**, key in **Enter the current date** and press Enter.

WordPerfect inserts the code **{INPUT}Enter current date~** in the document. When the document is merged, the merge stops at the location of the **{INPUT}** and the message **Enter the current date** is displayed at the bottom of the screen.

### Next Record

The Next Record selection from the Merge Codes command is used to tell WordPerfect to skip a particular record in a secondary file and move to the next one. For example, if you want the primary file merged with records 1, 2, 4, and 5 in the secondary file but not record 3, you would insert the **{NEXT RECORD}** code before the third record. To do this, complete the following steps:

1.  Display the secondary file on the screen.
2.  Move the cursor to the beginning of Field 1 in the third record.
3.  Access the Merge Codes command with Shift + F9
4.  Choose 5 or N for Next Record.
    **M** *Click on Tools, Merge Codes, then Next Record.*

When this secondary file is merged with a primary file, WordPerfect merges through record two, sees the code to move to the next record, and skips the third record. This might be useful in a situation in which you do not want all records merged with the primary file.

### Canceling a Keyboard Merge

A keyboard merge can be canceled with the Merge Codes command. To do this, complete the following steps:

1.  During the merge, access the Merge Codes command with Shift + F9.
2.  Choose 1 or Q for Quit.

## OTHER MERGE CODES

When you access the Merge Codes command with Shift + F9 and choose 6 or M for More, several options appear in the window in the upper right corner of the screen. Some of these Merge codes are explained below. (For more information about the codes, refer to Appendix K in the WordPerfect 5.1 reference manual.)

### Date

The Merge code {DATE} can be used to insert the current date into a document. This works only if the correct date was entered when the computer was started. To insert the Date code in a document, complete the following steps:

1. Access the Merge Codes command with Shift + F9, then choose 6 or M for More.
   **M** *Click on Tools, Merge Codes, then More.*
2. Move the cursor to the {DATE} code and press Enter.

This inserts the code {DATE} in the document. The current date is inserted in this location when the document is merged.

### Macro Name

A macro can be executed within a merge by including the {CHAIN MACRO}**macroname~** code. To use this, complete the following steps:

1. Access the Merge Codes command with Shift + F9, then choose 6 or M for More.
   **M** *Click on Tools, Merge Codes, then More.*
2. Move the cursor on to the {CHAIN MACRO}**macroname~** code and press Enter.
3. At the **Enter Macro Name:** prompt, key in the name of the macro and press Enter.

This inserts the code {CHAIN MACRO}**macroname~** in the document, and when the document is merged the macro is executed.

### Stopping the Merge

In a lengthy secondary file, the {QUIT} code can be very useful. To use {QUIT}, complete the following steps:

1. Retrieve a secondary file to the screen and move the cursor to the location where you want the merge stopped. Access the Merge Codes command with Shift + F9, then choose 6 or M for More.
   **M** *Click on Tools, Merge Codes, then More.*
2. Move the cursor to the {QUIT} codes and press Enter.

This inserts the code {QUIT} in the document. When merging the secondary file with the primary file, the merge will stop at the record containing the {QUIT} code. For this command to operate correctly, the {QUIT} code must be inserted in front of the {END RECORD} code for the last record to be printed.

## MERGE CONSIDERATIONS

### Varying Field Lines

In the exercises you completed in chapter 28, the records in the secondary files contained the same number of lines. When names and addresses contain a varying number of lines, some thought has to go into the preparation of the primary and secondary file. For example, suppose you created a primary file with the following fields:

```
{FIELD}1~ {FIELD}2~ {FIELD}3~
{FIELD}4~
{FIELD}5~
{FIELD}6~
```

The first field, {FIELD}1~, is title; {FIELD}2~ is first name; {FIELD}3~ is last name; {FIELD}4~ is company name; {FIELD}5~ is street address; and {FIELD}6~ is city, state, and Zip Code.

When entering the records in the secondary file, you discover that not all records contain a company address. You cannot simply leave out the line for the company address, because each record in a secondary file must contain the same number of fields. To remedy this situation, a question mark can be inserted in the primary file in any field that may not always contain information in the secondary file. The fields for the primary file in the example above should then be entered like this:

```
{FIELD}1~ {FIELD}2~ {FIELD}3~
{FIELD}4?~
{FIELD}5~
{FIELD}6~
```

The question mark in Field 4 tells WordPerfect that if there is no information to merge at this field, do not insert a blank line; instead, delete the blank line. Information in a secondary file would be entered in this manner:

```
Mrs.{END FIELD}
Jane{END FIELD}
Greenbaum{END FIELD}
Masterfield Unlimited{END FIELD}
345 South Third Street{END FIELD}
Sacramento, CA  90345{END FIELD}
{END RECORD}
==================================
Mr.{END FIELD}
Sampson{END FIELD}
Delaney{END FIELD}
{END FIELD}
12453 North 4th Street{END FIELD}
Sacramento, CA  90345{END FIELD}
```

Each record contains the same number of fields. The second record does not contain a company name, but an **{END FIELD}** code must still be inserted. Because the primary file contains a question mark within Field 4, WordPerfect does not create a blank line when printing the name and address for Mr. Delaney.

Fields in a secondary file can contain more than one line. For example, the record for Mrs. Greenbaum may include the following:

```
Mrs.{END FIELD}
Jane{END FIELD}
Greenbaum{END FIELD}
Masterfield Unlimited{END FIELD}
345 South Third Street
Suite 540{END FIELD}
Sacramento, CA  90345{END FIELD}
```

The fifth field, the street address, contains an extra line for the suite number. Only the last line of the field should contain the **{END FIELD}** code.

## Creating Envelopes

When you create a personalized form letter, you may also want to address an envelope for each letter. To print envelopes, you need two documents—the primary file identifying the fields, and the secondary file containing the records.

To create a primary file for envelopes, complete the following steps:

1.  At a clear screen, select an envelope form (9.5 by 4 inches at the Format: Paper Size/Type menu).
2.  Change the top margin to 2 inches and the left margin to 4 inches.
3.  Key in the fields in the appropriate locations.
4.  Save the envelope. Add the extension, .PF, to the document name.

If you are creating a primary file to print the names and addresses of the clients of the law firm, the fields would look like this:

```
{FIELD}1~ {FIELD}2~ {FIELD}3~
{FIELD}4~
{FIELD}5~
```

To print the envelopes, merge the envelope primary file with a secondary file containing records.

## Creating Mailing Labels

In chapter 17, you created forms for mailing labels. A mailing label form can be used in a primary file to merge with records in a secondary file.

To create a mailing label as a primary file, key in the fields that are to be merged, then save the document. At a clear screen, merge the newly created primary file with a secondary file. The merged names and addresses will appear on the screen followed by a page break. After the primary and secondary files are merged, move the cursor to the beginning of the primary file and insert the labels code. Access View Document to ensure that the names and addresses adjusted correctly. (Be sure to insert the labels code *after* the merge has occurred.)

For example, to create a mailing label for the records REVIEW.SF secondary file, complete the following steps:

1. At a clear screen, create the primary file by keying in the code at the left margin.

   {FIELD}1~ {FIELD}2~ {FIELD}3~
   {FIELD}4~
   {FIELD}5~

2. Save the primary file and name it LABELS.PF.
3. Merge LABEL.PF with REVIEW.SF by completing the following steps:
   a. Access the Merge/Sort command with Ctrl + F9.
   b. At the prompt **1 Merge; 2 Sort; 3 Convert Old Merge Codes: 0**, choose 1 or M for merge.
      **M** *Click on Tools, then Merge.*
   c. At the prompt **Primary file:_**, key in **LABELS.PF** and press enter.
   d. At the prompt **Secondary file:_** key in **REVIEW.SF** and press enter.
4. With the records merged on the screen, move the cursor to the beginning of the document and insert the labels code by completing the following steps:
   a. Access the Format: Page menu with Shift + F8, then 2 or P for Page.
      **M** *Click on Layout, then Page.*
   b. At the Format: Page menu, choose 7 or F for Paper Size/Type.
   c. At the Format: Paper Size/Type menu, move the cursor to the labels form and choose 1 or S for Select.
   d. Press F7 to insert the labels form and return the cursor to the document.
5. Access View Document and make sure the names and addresses appear in the correct location.
6. Save the document and print it.

Another code can be inserted in the primary file to adjust how the names and addresses print within the labels. By default, the name and address will print at the top of the label. If the address is only a few lines long, this will make the address on the label appear off-centered. To remedy this situation, a Center Page code can be entered at the beginning of a primary file *before* it is merged with a secondary file. With the code inserted in the document before performing the merge, the code will be inserted before each label.

The Center Page code tells WordPerfect to center text vertically on the page. With the Center Page code in a document containing the Labels code, text will be centered within each label rather than on the entire page. After merging the primary and secondary files, insert the Labels code before the Center Page code. Insert the Center Page code as the very first step when creating the primary file. In the example above, insert the Center Page code before Step 1.

# CHAPTER REVIEW

## Summary

- A primary and secondary file can be merged at the printer. To merge at the printer, the codes {PAGE OFF} and {PRINT} need to be inserted at the end of the primary file.

- When documents are merged and sent directly to the printer, the merge does not appear on the screen.

- Variable information can be obtained from a secondary file, directly from the keyboard, or from a combination of both methods. Insert an {INPUT} or {KEYBOARD} code in a document where keyboard entry is to occur.

- The Next Record selection from the Merge Codes command tells WordPerfect to skip a particular record in a secondary file.

- To cancel a keyboard merge, access the Merge Codes command with Shift + F9, then choose 1 or Q for Quit.

- The {DATE} code can be inserted in a document, and when the document is merged the current date is inserted at the code.

- A macro can be executed within a merge with the {CHAIN MACRO}macroname~ code.

- The {QUIT} code can be inserted in a secondary file and tells WordPerfect to quit the merge when the code is encountered.

- Records in a secondary file must contain the same number of fields.

- Fields in a secondary file can be more than one line. Only the last line of the field contains the ({END FIELD} code.

- Use a question mark within a field in a primary file to tell Word-Perfect to delete the blank line if there is no information for that field in the secondary file.

- A primary file can be created to print envelopes.

- To create a primary file for mailing labels, create the primary file (without the Labels code), merge it with a secondary file and then insert the Labels code at the beginning of the merged document.

### Commands Review

| | **Keyboard** |
|---|---|
| End Field | F9 |
| Merge Codes | Shift + F9 |
| Merge/Sort command | Ctrl + F9 |
| Insert field | Shift + F9, 1 or F |
| End Record | Shift + F9, 2 or E |
| Insert Input code | Shift + F9, 3 or I |
| Insert Page Off code | Shift + F9, 4 or P |
| Insert Next Record code | Shift + F9, 5 or N |
| Display window of codes | Shift + F9, 6 or M |

| | **Mouse** |
|---|---|
| Merge Codes | Tools, Merge Codes |
| Merge | Tools, Merge |
| Insert field | Tools, Merge Codes, Field |
| End Record | Tools, Merge Codes, End Record |
| Insert Input code | Tools, Merge Codes, Input |
| Insert Page Off code | Tools, Merge Codes, Page Off |
| Insert Next Record code | Tools, Merge Codes, Next Record |
| Display window of codes | Tools, Merge Codes, More |

## STUDY GUIDE FOR CHAPTER 29

**Completion:** In the space provided at the right, fill in the correct term, symbol, character, or command for the explanation.

1.   Insert these two codes at the end of a primary file to merge a          _____
     primary and secondary file at the printer.

2.   Either the {**KEYBOARD**} code or this code can be used for             _____
     keyboard entry.

3.   Maximum length of a message.                                           _____

4.   During a merge, this code inserts the current date.                    _____

5.   Insert this code in a secondary file to tell WordPerfect to quit        _____
     the merge.

6.   This symbol, inserted in a field, tells WordPerfect to delete the       _____
     blank line if there is no information for that field.

**True/False:** Circle the letter T if the statement is true; circle the letter F if the statement is false.

1.   Variable information can be input at the keyboard.                                      T     F

2.   When a primary file is merged with a secondary file, information cannot be              T     F
     entered at the keyboard.

3.   When a document (without keyboard entry) is merged and sent directly to the            T     F
     printer, it does not appear on the screen.

4.   Each record in a secondary file must contain the same number of fields.                T     F

5.   When a document contains commands for keyboard entry, it displays on the               T     F
     screen during the merge.

6.   Fields in a secondary file can be more than one line long.                             T     F

7.   Insert the Labels code in the primary file before merging with a secondary file.       T     F

## HANDS-ON EXERCISES

Change the default directory to UNIT6.

**Exercise One**
1.   Retrieve REVIEW.PF to the screen. Make the changes to the second paragraph of the letter
     as indicated in figure 29-1. Make the editing changes to the second paragraph in the letter
     as indicated in figure 29-1, then insert the {**INPUT**} code by completing the following steps:
     A. Move the cursor to the beginning of the second paragraph, access the Merge Codes com-
        mand with Shift + F9, and choose 3 or I for Input.
        **M** *Click on Tools, Merge Codes, then Input.*
     B. At the prompt **Enter Message:**, key in **Enter representative's name**, and press
        Enter.
2.   Insert {**PAGE OFF**} and {**PRINT**} codes to tell WordPerfect to merge at the printer. To do
     this, complete the following steps:

A. Move the cursor to the end of the document and access the Merge Codes command with Shift + F9.

B. Choose 4 or P for Page Off.
   **M** *Click on Tools, Merge Codes, then Page Off.*

C. Access the Merge Codes command again with Shift + F9, then choose 6 or M for More.
   **M** *Click on Tools, Merge Codes, then More.*

D. In the window of codes, move the cursor to {**PRINT**} and press Enter.

3. Save the document as REVIEW2.PF. Print REVIEW2.PF

---

```
{INPUT}Enter representative's name~, the customer service represen-
tative in your area, would like to visit you at your home,
{FIELD}1~ {FIELD}3~, to perform a financial review.  Please call
our company at 555-7435 to schedule an appointment.
```

---

**Figure 29-1: Exercise One**

## Exercise Two

1. Retrieve REVIEW.SF to the screen and add the records shown in figure 29-2. (When adding the record for Mr. and Mrs. Rowe, be sure to include an {**END FIELD**} code where the first name should appear.)

---

```
Mrs. Alice Ferrell              Mr. and Mrs. Rowe
23104 North Mildred             5496 South Park
Portland, OR 96422              Portland, OR 96329


Mr. Neal Hoskins                Mr. and Mrs. John Carter
12033 - 112th Street            4931 North Bristol
Portland, OR 96034              Portland, OR 96026
```

---

**Figure 29-2: Exercise Two**

2. Save the secondary file and name it REVIEW2.SF. Print REVIEW2.SF.

3. Merge REVIEW2.PF with REVIEW2.SF by completing the following steps:

A. At a clear screen, access the Merge/Sort command with Ctrl + F9, then choose 1 or M for Merge.
   **M** *Click on Tools, then Merge.*

B. Key in **REVIEW2.PF** and press Enter.

C. Key in **REVIEW2.SF** and press Enter.

D. When the merge stops for the representative's name, key in the representative name listed after the client's last name as indicated below:

Heymann - Joseph Carron
Jonville - Rebecca Welles
Baretto - Laurie Rossman
Walston - Michael Milam
Ferrell - Laurie Rossman
Rowe - Michael Milam
Hoskins - Joseph Carron
Carter - Rebecca Welles

## Exercise Three

1. Retrieve SOFTWARE.PF to the screen. Insert the paragraph shown in figure 29-3 between the third and fourth paragraphs of the letter.

---

```
For the next two weeks, we are offering the new version
of your software for the low price of {INPUT}Enter
price~.  We are confident that you will not find a lower
price anywhere in town.
```

---

Figure 29-3: Exercise Three

2. Move the cursor to the end of the document and insert the {PAGE OFF} and {PRINT} codes so the merge will occur at the printer.
3. Save the revised primary file and name it SFTWARE2.PF.
4. Merge SFTWARE2.PF and SOFTWARE.SF. When the merge stops for the software price, key in the price shown below after the customer's last name:

Edward Snead - $75.00
Patricia Gumbel - $40.00
Karen Stearns - $25.95
Judd Dougherty - $69.95
Donna Almadi - $50.00
Arthur Gallagher - $39.95
Allan Metcalfe - $85.00
Scott Belzona - $35.00

## Exercise Four

1. At a clear screen, key in the memorandum shown in figure 29-4. Complete the following steps to insert the {DATE} code in the memorandum:
   A. With the cursor positioned after DATE:, access the Merge Codes command with Shift + F9, then choose 6 or M for More.
      **M** *Click on Tools, Merge Codes, then More.*
   B. Move the cursor to the {DATE} code and press Enter.
2. Complete the following steps to insert the first {INPUT} code in the memorandum:
   A. With the cursor positioned after TO:, access the Merge Codes command with Shift + F9, then choose 3 or I for Input.
      **M** *Click on Tools, Merge Codes, then Input.*
   B. At the prompt **Enter Message:**, key in **Enter name** and press Enter.
3. Complete similar steps to insert the other {INPUT} codes in the memorandum. Key in the appropriate message when prompted.

4. Move the cursor to the end of the memorandum and insert the {**PRINT**} code.
5. Save the memorandum and name it MEMO.PF. Print MEMO.PF.

---

DATE:       {DATE}

TO:         {INPUT}Enter name~

FROM:       William Holley, Director, Research and Development

SUBJECT:    New Products


The Research and Development Department of Puget Sound Semiconductor has developed several new products, which I would like to
preview for you at the next meeting of the {INPUT}Enter department
name~ Department.

Please contact me, {INPUT}Enter Director's name~, and let me know
if I can be put on your agenda. I think you will be excited about
the potential for these new products.

---

**Figure 29-4: Exercise Four**


**Exercise Five**

1. Merge the memorandum with the information shown in figure 29-5 by completing the
   following steps:
   A. At a clear screen, access the Merge/Sort command with Ctrl + F9, then choose 1 or M
      for Merge.
      **M** *Click on Tools, then Merge.*
   B. At the **Primary file:** prompt, key in **MEMO.PF** and press Enter.
   C. At the **Secondary file:** prompt, press Enter. (There is no secondary file. Variable
      information will be entered at the keyboard.)
   D. When the memorandum appears on the screen, the cursor is located at the first
      {**INPUT**} code. Enter the information prompted by the message at the bottom of the
      screen, then press F9. The cursor moves to the location of the next {**INPUT**} code.
      Continue in this manner until all information is entered. When all information is
      entered, the memo will print.
   E. Merge the memorandum again with the Merge/Sort command and key in the informa-
      tion for the next memo.

Print four memoranda with the information shown in figure 29-5. You must access the Merge/Sort
command for each printing.

First memorandum:
    Director's name and department: Victoria Palmas, Director
    of Finance
    Department name: Finance
    Director's first name: Victoria

Second memorandum:
    Director's name and department: Janet Weiss, Director of
    Personnel
    Department name: Personnel
    Director's first name: Janet

Third memorandum:
    Director's name and department: Heidi Schueler, Director
    of Sales
    Department name: Sales
    Director's first name: Heidi

Fourth memorandum:
    Director's name and department: Brad Majors, Director of
    Facilities Management
    Department name: Facilities Management
    Director's first name: Brad

**Figure 29-5: Exercise Five**

## Exercise Six

1. Retrieve REVIEW.SF to the screen.

2. Insert a {**NEXT RECORD**} code before the first record by completing the following steps:
   A. Move the cursor to the M in Mr. in the first record.
   B. Access the Merge Codes command with Shift + F9, then choose 5 or N for Next Record.
   **M** *Click on Tools, Merge Codes, then Next Record.*

3. Insert a {**NEXT RECORD**} code before the third record by completing steps similar to those listed above.

4. Save the revised secondary file and name it REVIEW3.SF.

5. Retrieve REVIEW.PF to the screen. Move to the end of the document and insert {**PAGE OFF**} and {**PRINT**} codes to merge at the printer. Save the primary file and name it REVIEW3.PF.

6. Merge REVIEW3.PF with REVIEW3.SF. (Only the letters for Mrs. Cynthia Jonville and Ms. Dori Walston should print.)

## Exercise Seven

1. Create a primary file (for labels), named CH29ML.PF, and merge it with SOFTWARE.SF by completing the following steps:
   A. At a clear screen, insert the Center Page (top to bottom) code by completing the following steps:
   (1) Access the Format: Page menu with Shift + F8, then 2 or P for Page.
   **M** *Click on Layout, then Page.*

(2) At the Format: Page menu, choose 1 or C for Center Page (top to bottom), then key in **Y** for Yes.

B. Key in the following fields at the left margin.

**{FIELD}1~ {FIELD}2~ {FIELD}3~**
**{FIELD}4~**
**{FIELD}5~**

C. Save the primary field and name it CH29ML.PF.

D. Merge CH29ML.PF with REVIEW2.SF.

E. At the merged document, make sure the cursor is located at the beginning of the document and insert the labels form that prints labels in 3 columns and 10 rows. (This label form was created in chapter 17.)

F. Access View Document and make sure the labels appear in the correct location.

2. Save the merged document and name it CH29EX7. Print CH29EX7.

## PERFORMANCE ASSESSMENTS

**Assessment One**

1. At a clear screen, create the business letter shown in figure 29-6 as a primary file in an appropriate business letter format. You determine the margins and justification as well as the fields and field numbers. Insert the **{DATE}** and **{INPUT}** codes as indicated.

2. Insert the **{PAGE OFF}** and **{PRINT}** codes at the end of the letter.

3. When the letter is complete, save it as a primary file and name it SITE.PF. Print SITE.PF

```
{DATE}


Name
Address
City, State, Zip Code

Dear (Salutation):

Puget Sound Semiconductor is a company located in the Pacific
Northwest that manufactures electronic components. In recent years,
our business has grown in the Southwest region of the United
States. As the vice president for Operations, I am responsible for
locating possible sites for new construction.

We are in the initial stages of planning a new facility to be
located in a Southwestern state. We have chosen (city name) as a
possible location for a manufacturing plant. I would like informa-
tion on your city as well as the outlying area of {INPUT}Enter area
name~. Please include information on the availability of commercial
land, approximate price of commercial land per acre, and zoning
restrictions for a manufacturing company.

Thank you for your time. After I have received the information, I
will meet with the president of the company and department
directors to make the final site selection.

Very truly yours,



Kim Chun
Vice President, Operations
```

**Figure 29-6: Assessment One**

## Assessment Two

1. At a clear screen, key in the records shown in figure 29-7 as a secondary file. Arrange the fields and records in the correct format.
2. Save the secondary file and name it SITE.SF. Print SITE.SF.

Mr. Dale Jorgensen                    Ms. Anne Wickstrom
San Diego Chamber of Commerce         Phoenix Chamber of Commerce
13220 South Park Drive                3500 Palmdale Drive
San Diego, CA 95322                   Phoenix, AZ 94110

Ms. Toni Harai                        Mrs. Linda Carras
Houston Chamber of Commerce           Las Vegas Chamber of Commerce
400 South Industrial Way              5330 North Fourth Street
Houston, TX 78332                     Las Vegas, NV 72235

Figure 29-7: Assessment Two

3. Merge SITE.PF with SITE.SF. When the merge stops for the area name, key in the following:

   Mr. Dale Joregensen:
        Area name - Escondido
   Ms. Anne Wickstrom:
        Area name - Scottsdale
   Ms. Toni Harai:
        Area name - Angelton
   Mrs. Linda Carras
        Area name - Incline Village

## Assessment Three

1. Create a primary file for an envelope (9.5 x 4 inches).
2. Merge the envelope primary file with the secondary file, SITE.SF.
3. Name the merged document CH29PA3. Print CH29PA3.

# CHAPTER 30

## TABLES, INDEXES, AND LISTS

## PERFORMANCE OBJECTIVES

Upon successful completion of chapter 30, you will be able to specify information in a document to be included in a table of contents, index, or table and to generate the final list.

A book, textbook, report, or manuscript often includes sections such as a table of contents, index, and lists of tables or figures in the document. Creating these sections can be tedious when done by hand. With WordPerfect's Mark Text command, the functions can be automated to make the generating of sections quick and easy.

In this chapter you will learn the steps to mark text for a table of contents, index, list, and table of authorities, and then generate the table, index, or list. You will find that the steps involved in identifying and generating tables, indexes, and lists are similar and include the following:

1. Locate the reference and mark it with the Block command.
2. Identify whether it is to be included in a table of contents, list, index, or table of authorities.
3. Define the table, list, or index.
4. Generate the table, list, or index.

## CREATING A TABLE OF CONTENTS

A table of contents appears at the beginning of a book, manuscript, or report and contains headings and subheadings with page numbers. To create a table of contents, you need to mark the text that is to be included in the table.

### Marking Text

Generally, when you create a table of contents you are working in an existing document — one that already has the headings and subheadings included. To mark text for the table of contents, complete the following steps:

1.  Move the cursor to the heading or subheading and block it with the Block command, Alt + F4 or F12.
    **M** *Click on Edit, then Block.*

2.  Access the Mark Text command with Alt + F5.

3.  At the **Mark for: 1 ToC; 2 List; 3 Index; 4 ToA: 0** prompt, choose 1 or C for ToC.
    **M** *Click on Mark, then Table of Contents.*

4.  At the **ToC Level: -** prompt, key in the level number and press Enter.

Text to be included in a table of contents is identified by level numbering. The first level is generally reserved for headings, the second level for subheadings, and other levels for subheadings within subheadings. Word-Perfect allows a maximum of five levels. When text is marked for a table of contents, codes are inserted before and after the text, which can be seen in Reveal Codes. For example, if you identified the heading INDUSTRIAL REVOLUTION for a table of contents as level 1, the heading and codes appear as follows in Reveal Codes:

```
[Mark:ToC,1]INDUSTRIAL REVOLUTION[End Mark:ToC,1]
```

The codes identify the beginning and end of the marked text as well as the level numbering. Continue blocking headings and subheadings in a document and identifying the level numbering. When all headings and subheadings have been marked for the table of contents, the table needs to be defined and generated in the document.

## Defining the Table of Contents

Before defining the table of contents, move the cursor to the location in the document where the table is to appear (generally at the beginning of the document), and insert a Hard Page code with Ctrl + Enter. To define the table of contents, complete the following steps:

1.  Move the cursor above the hard page break. Access the Mark Text command with Alt + F5, choose 5 or D for Define, then 1 or C for Define Table of Contents.
    **M** *Click on Mark, Define, then Table of Contents.*

2.  Make any necessary changes to the Table of Contents Definition menu.

3.  Press F7 to return to the document.

The Table of Contents Definition menu shown in figure 30-1 contains a number of selections. The first selection, Number of Levels, tells WordPer-fect how many levels of headings are contained in the table. If a document contains one main heading and three subheadings, four levels are identified. When a level number higher than 1 is keyed in, WordPerfect identifies each level page numbering as Flush right with leader. A maximum of five levels can be identified.

```
┌─────────────────────────────────────────────────────────────────┐
│   Table of Contents Definition                                  │
│                                                                 │
│       1 - Number of Levels               1                      │
│                                                                 │
│       2 - Display Last Level in          No                     │
│           Wrapped Format                                        │
│                                                                 │
│       3 - Page Numbering - Level 1    Flush right with leader   │
│                            Level 2                              │
│                            Level 3                              │
│                            Level 4                              │
│                            Level 5                              │
│                                                                 │
│                                                                 │
│                                                                 │
│                                                                 │
│                                                                 │
│                                                                 │
│                                                                 │
│   Selection: 0                                                  │
└─────────────────────────────────────────────────────────────────┘
```

**Figure 30-1: Table of Contents Definition Menu**

The second selection, Display Last Level in Wrapped Format, has a default setting of No. At this setting, each entry appears on a line by itself. If this is changed to Yes, the entry for the lowest level is displayed as a unit, and entries are separated by semicolons instead of being placed on a separate line.

The last selection, Page Numbering, has a default setting of Flush right with leaders. To change the Page Numbering style, choose 3 or P for Page Numbering, and the prompt **1 None; 2 Pg # Follows; 3 (Pg #) Follows; 4 Flush Rt; 5 Flush Rt with Leader: 0** appears at the bottom of the screen. From this prompt, choose the page numbering style desired, and the settings after the levels will change.

### Generating the Table of Contents

After defining the table of contents, generate it by completing the following steps:

1.  Access the Mark Text command with Alt + F5.
2.  Choose 6 or G for Generate.
    **M** *Click on Mark, then Generate.*
3.  At the Mark Text: Generate menu, choose 5 or G for Generate Tables, Indexes, Cross-References, etc.
4.  At the **Existing tables, lists, and indexes will be replaced. Continue? Yes (No)** prompt, press Enter to start the generation.

When generated, the table of contents is displayed on the screen. WordPerfect does not include a title for the table of contents, nor does it number the pages. To include a title, move the cursor to the beginning of the page where the table will appear, and insert formatting codes and a heading.

Pages in a table of contents are generally numbered with Roman numerals. To number the pages of a table of contents, turn page numbering on and change the numbering style to Roman numeral. If you want the body of the book, report, or manuscript to begin with an Arabic numeral 1, change the numbering back from Roman.

Some headings and subheadings may include special features such as boldfacing and underlining. If you do not want the headings and subheadings to include boldfacing and underlining in the table of contents, access Reveal Codes, make sure the cursor is positioned after the codes, and then block the text.

## CREATING A LIST

A list is created in a manner similar to that for the table of contents. A list of illustrations or tables contains the captions of the illustrations and tables used in the documents. A list is created in a manner similar to that for the table of contents. A list can consist of illustrations, tables, figures, or other data, and is inserted at the beginning of the document. To create a list, complete the following steps:

1.  Block each item to be included in the list with Alt + F4 or F12.
    **M** *Click on Edit, then Block.*

2.  Access the Mark Text command with Alt + F5, and choose 2 or L for List.
    **M** *Click on Mark, then List.*

3.  At the **List Number:_** prompt, key in the number of the list in which the item is to be included, and press Enter.

When these steps are completed, beginning and ending codes are inserted before and after the blocked text. A maximum of 10 lists may be created in a document.

### Defining and Generating the List

Generally, a list appears at the beginning of the document. Before defining the list, move the cursor to the beginning of the document and insert a Hard Page code with Ctrl + Enter. Move the cursor above the hard page break and create an appropriate heading for the list. Press Enter two or three times, then define the list. To define marked text for a list, complete the following steps:

1.  Access the Mark Text command with Alt + F5.

2.  Choose 5 or D for Define.

3.  Choose 2 or L for Define List.
    **M** *Click on Mark, Define, then List.*

4.  A the **List Number (1-10)** prompt, key in the number of the list to be defined, and press Enter. The List # Definition (where # indicates the list number identified) menu shown in figure 30-2 is displayed.

5.  At the List # Definition menu, choose the numbering style for the list.

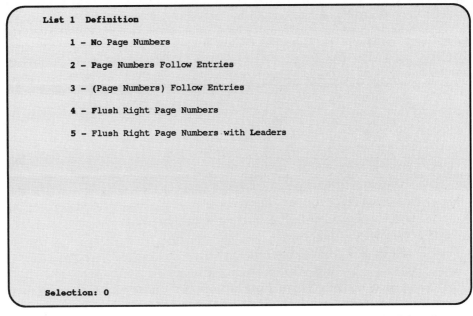

**Figure 30-2: List Definition Menu**

If you are defining a list of figure captions, key in 6 at the **List Number:_** prompt. Key in 7 if you are defining table box captions, 8 if you are defining user box captions, and 10 if you are defining equation captions. After choosing the numbering style for the list, the cursor is returned to the document and a definition code is inserted.

After defining the list, generate it by completing the following steps:

1. Access the Mark Text command with Alt + F5, then choose 6 or G for Generate.
   **M** *Click on Mark, then Generate.*

2. At the Mark Text: Generate menu, choose 5 or G for Generate Tables, Indexes, Cross-References, etc.

3. At the **Existing tables, lists, and indexes will be replaced. Continue? (Y/N):** **Yes** prompt, press Enter.

When you key in Y at the prompt, the list is generated and displayed on the screen.

## CREATING AN INDEX

An index is a list of topics contained in the publication, along with the pages where those topics are discussed. WordPerfect lets you automate the process of creating an index in a manner similar to that used for creating a list or a table of contents. When creating an index, you can mark the word the cursor is positioned under, or you can block the text and add it to an index. Creating an index takes some thought and consideration. The author of the book, manuscript, or report must determine the headings desired and what subheadings will be listed under headings.

**Marking Text**

After the decision has been made about the appearance of headings and subheadings in an index, the text to be included can be identified. The text can be marked by locating the cursor on a word to be included in the index, or by blocking text. To mark text with the first method, complete the following steps:

1.  Locate the cursor on the word to be marked.
2.  Access the Mark Text command with Alt + F5.
3.  Choose 3 or I for Index.
    **M** *Click on Mark, then Index.*

To mark text with the second method, complete the following steps:

1.  Block the text with Alt + F4 or F12.
    **M** *Click on Edit, then Block.*
2.  Access the Mark Text command with Alt + F5.
3.  Choose 3 or I for Index.
    **M** *Click on Mark, then Index.*

The first method is limited to one word (the word under which the cursor is positioned). The second method allows more than one word to be marked at the same time.

After choosing 3 or I for Index, the prompt **Index heading: [word(s)]** (the word or words identified appear in the brackets) appear at the bottom of the screen. If the word(s) are to be a heading in an index, press Enter. If, however, the word or words identified are a subheading, key in the appropriate heading under which they will appear, and press Enter. The prompt **Subheading:** is then displayed at the bottom of the screen. If a heading different from the text identified is keyed in, the blocked text will be displayed at the **Subheading:** prompt. The text displayed can be accepted as the subheading or different text can be keyed in. When the correct text is displayed, press Enter. WordPerfect inserts codes before and after the text marked for the index.

WordPerfect displays a heading with the first letter capitalized whether or not the text marked had a capital letter. Subheadings, however, are not capitalized. This default can be accepted or the text can be rekeyed as desired.

As an example of how to mark text for an index, suppose that a publication included the terms **Delete**, **Character**, **Word**, and **End of Line**. **Delete** is to be a heading in the index, and **Character**, **Word**, and **End of Line** are to be subheadings under **Delete**. To include these words in the index, complete the following steps:

1.  Move the cursor to the word **Delete** and access the Mark Text command with Alt + F5.
2.  Choose 3 or I for Index.
    **M** *Click on Mark, then Index.*
3.  At the heading prompt, press Enter to accept Delete as a heading.
4.  At the subheading prompt, no text is displayed. Press Enter to accept this default.
5.  Move the cursor to **Character** and access the Mark Text command with Alt + F5.

6. Choose 3 or I for Index.
   **M** *Click on Mark, then Index.*

7. At the heading prompt, key in **Delete** (over **Character**), and press Enter.

8. At the subheading text, **Character** is displayed. Accept this as the subheading by pressing Enter.

Complete the same steps for **Word** and **End of Line**. When marking **End of Line** for the index, block the three words before accessing the Mark Text command.

### Creating a Concordance File

Words or phrases that appear frequently in a document can be saved in a concordance file, which saves you from having to mark each reference in the document. A concordance file is a regular WordPerfect document that contains words or phrases to be included in an index. Each word or phrase is created on a separate line.

To create a concordance file, start at a clear screen and key in the common words or phrases for the index. Put each word or phrase on a separate line followed by a hard return. When WordPerfect generates the index, it checks the document for any occurrence of the word or phrases in the concordance file and includes them in the index.

Each word or phrase in the concordance file is treated as a heading. If you want some of the words or phrases to be treated as subheadings, you must mark them as you would mark regular text in a document and identify to WordPerfect what heading you want and then identify the text as the subheading. When creating an index, text can come from a concordance file or it may be marked in the document. The concordance file does not limit you to just the file.

When all entries have been made to the concordance file, save it as you would any other document. (Depending on the length of the concordance file, WordPerfect may not have enough available memory during the generation of the index. If this should occur, WordPerfect displays a message on the screen.)

### Defining the Index

An index should appear at the end of a document. Before defining the index, move the cursor to the end of the document and insert a hard page code with Ctrl + Enter. Move the cursor below the hard page break, create an appropriate heading for the index, then define the index. To define the index, complete the following steps:

1. Access the Mark Text command with Alt + F5, then choose 5 or D for Define.

2. From the Mark Text: Define menu, choose 3 or I for Define Index.
   **M** *Click on Mark, Define, then Index.*

3. At the **Concordance Filename (Enter=none)** prompt, press Enter if a concordance file has not been created, or key in the name of the concordance file, and press Enter.

4. At the Index Definition menu, choose the numbering style for the index.

WordPerfect displays the Index Definition menu, which contains the same page numbering selections as the List 1 Definition menu. Select the style of numbering desired for the index.

### Generating the Index

To generate the index, complete the following steps:

1.  Access the Mark Text command with Alt + F5, then choose 6 or G for Generate.
    **M** *Click on Mark, then Generate.*

2.  From the Mark Text: Generate menu, choose 5 or G for Generate Tables, Indexes, Cross-References, etc.

3.  Press Enter to start the generation. When the index is generated, it is displayed on the screen.

## REGENERATING A TABLE, LIST, OR INDEX

A table of contents, list, or index can be edited after it has been generated. If you notice that you made a mistake when blocking text or you make changes to text, reblock the text and then regenerate the table, list, or index by completing the following steps:

1.  Access the Mark Text command with Alt + F5, then choose 6 or G for Generate.
    **M** *Click on Mark, then Generate.*

2.  From the Mark Text: Generate menu, choose 5 or G for Generate Tables, Indexes, Cross-References, etc.

3.  Press Enter to start the generation.

You do not need to define the table, list, or index again because the document still contains the definition code inserted before the table, list, or index was generated the first time.

If, after you generate a table, list, or index, you decide you do not like the appearance, you can redefine the document. Before redefining, you must delete the old definition codes. Access Reveal Codes and delete the **[DefMark]** code and the **[EndDef]** code. If the codes are not properly deleted, WordPerfect displays an error message when you regenerate.

## TABLE OF AUTHORITIES

A table of authorities is a list of citations for a legal brief that lists the pages of sources where the citings occur. The table is divided into sections and can include cases, statutes, regulations, and miscellaneous categories. A table of authorities can be defined and generated in a document in a similar manner to a table of contents, index, or list.

Some thought goes into planning a table of authorities. Before marking any text in a legal brief, you need to determine what section headings you want, the number of each section, and what should be contained in the sections. For example, sections may include headings for Supreme Court cases, state court cases, other cases, and statutes. WordPerfect allows a maximum of 16 sections.

### Marking the Text

When marking text for a table of authorities, you need to find the first occurrence of the authority, mark it as a *long form* with the complete name, case or statute, and then any other occurrence of that case or statute can be identified with a *short form*.  Using a short form once the long form has been established saves time.

To create a table of authorities, complete the following steps:

1.   Move the cursor to each item in a legal brief that is to be included, and block the item with the Block command, Alt + F4 or F12.
     Ⓜ *Click on Edit, then Block.*

2.   With the item blocked, access the Mark Text command with Alt + F5, then choose 4 or A for ToA.
     Ⓜ *Click on Mark, Table of Authorities, then Mark Full.*

3.   WordPerfect inserts the prompt **ToA Section Number (Press Enter for Short Form only):** at the bottom of the screen. Key in the section number where the text is to appear and press Enter.

4.   WordPerfect moves into a special editing screen and displays the blocked text. Edit the text, if necessary, so the text displays as you want it to appear in the table of authorities, including any special print features such as boldfacing and underlining.

5.   When the full form is edited, press Exit, F7.

6.   WordPerfect displays the message **Short Form: _** and displays the long form after the prompt. If the text appears elsewhere in the document, include a short form name. Shorten the long form to a significant word or words to clearly identify the case or statute, and press Enter.

When Enter is pressed, the cursor is returned to the document and a code is inserted identifying the section of the table where the marked text will be inserted along with the short form name.

Move through the document (legal brief) and locate all occurrences of the same authority; mark each with the short form. To do this, complete the following steps:

1.   Move the cursor to the short form name and access the Mark Text command with Alt + F5. From the prompts at the bottom of the screen, choose 4 or A for ToA Short Form.
     Ⓜ *Click on Mark, Table of Authorities, then Mark Short.*

2.   WordPerfect displays the last short form created. Press Enter if this is the correct short form, or key in a different short form name and press Enter.

### Defining the Table of Authorities

A table of authorities should be placed at the beginning of a document. Before defining the table of authorities, move the cursor to the beginning of the document, insert a Hard Page code with Ctrl + Enter, then move the cursor above the command. Key in the table of authorities heading.

When defining a table of authorities, you need to define each section in the table. After keying the heading, press Enter twice and key in the first section heading and then define this section. To define the first section, complete the following steps:

1.  Access the Mark Text command with Alt + F5, then choose 5 or D for Define.

2.  At the Mark Text: Define menu, choose 4 or A for Define Table of Authorities.
    **M** *Click on Mark, Define, then Table of Authorities.*

3.  At the **Section Number (1-16)_** prompt, key in the section number and press Enter. WordPerfect displays the Definition for Table of Authorities 1 menu shown in figure 30-3 on the screen. At this menu, determine whether or not you want leaders, underlining, and blank lines between authorities. In most cases, you will want to use Yes for all three settings.

4.  After any changes are made to the Definition for Table of Authorities 1 menu, press F7 to return the cursor to the document.

At the document, press Enter to space between the sections and then define the remaining sections by completing the same steps.

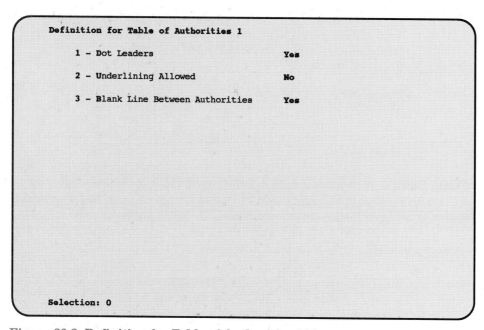

**Definition for Table of Authorities 1**

1 - Dot Leaders                                       Yes

2 - Underlining Allowed                               No

3 - Blank Line Between Authorities                    Yes

Selection: 0

Figure 30-3: Definition for Table of Authorities 1 Menu

## Generating the Table of Authorities

Before generating the table of authorities, you will need to include a new page numbering code in the document. The table should be numbered with Roman numerals and the beginning of the document should include a New Page Numbering code to start numbering at 1 and to change the numbering style back to Arabic numbers. If you do not insert the New Page Numbering code at the beginning of the document (after the table of authorities), the page numbers generated in the table will be incorrect.

Once all the sections of the table of authorities have been defined and the New Page Numbering codes have been inserted, generate the table by completing the following steps:

1.  Access the Mark Text command with Alt + F5, then choose 6 or G for Generate.
    **M** *Click on Mark, then Generate.*
2.  At the Mark Text: Generate menu, choose 5 or G for Generate Tables, Indexes, Cross-References, etc.
3.  At the prompt **Existing tables, lists, and indexes will be replaced. Continue? Yes (No)**, key in a **Y** to start the generation.

When the table of authorities is generated, it is displayed on the screen.

### Editing a Table of Authorities

If changes need to be made to a full form, move the cursor to the first occurrence of the authority and access Reveal Codes. Make sure the cursor is to the right of the ToA code, and complete the following steps:

1.  Access the Mark Text command with Alt + F5, then choose 5 or D for Define.
2.  At the Mark Text: Define menu, choose 5 or E for Edit Table of Authorities Full Form.
    **M** *Click on Mark, Table of Authorities, then Edit Full.*
3.  WordPerfect displays the full form authority. Make the necessary changes, then press F7 to save the changes. WordPerfect prompts you for a section number. Key in the section number and press Enter. This takes you back to the document.

## CHAPTER REVIEW

### Summary

- WordPerfect includes a feature to help automate the creation of a table of contents, list, index, and table of authorities in a document.
- When creating a table of contents, list, index, or table of authorities, four steps are completed: (1) Locate the reference in the document and mark it with the Block command; (2) identify whether it is to be included in a table of contents, list, index, or table of authorities; (3) define the table of contents, list, index, or table of authorities; and 4) generate the table of contents, list, index, or table of authorities.
- A table of contents, list, and table of authorities appear at the beginning of the document; an index appears at the end.
- To insert a table of contents, list, or table of authorities in the beginning of the document, move the cursor to the beginning of the document and insert a Hard Page code with Ctrl + Enter. Move the cursor above the hard page break and create a heading for the table or list. Turn page numbering on and identify the numbering style as Roman numeral. Change the numbering style back to Arabic after the table, or list and enter a new starting number.
- WordPerfect allows a maximum of five levels in a table of contents.
- When blocking text in a document, make sure special codes such as underlining and boldfacing are not included in the block unless you want them to appear in the table, list or index.
- A list can be created that contains tables, figures, or other data. WordPerfect allows a maximum of ten lists in one document.

- When marking text for inclusion in an index, you need to determine whether it is a heading or a subheading. By default, WordPerfect capitalizes the first letter of a heading but not of a subheading. You can accept these defaults or rekey the text with the capitalization preferred.
- A concordance file can be created that includes words or phrases that appear often in the document. In the concordance file, key in each heading or subheading on a separate line with a hard return. WordPerfect considers each line a heading. You must mark subheading text.
- A table of contents, list, index, or table of authorities must be defined before it can be generated.
- During the definition process, the location and page numbering style are established.
- A table of contents, index, or list can be regenerated if changes have been made to the document.
- The Mark Text command can be used to automate the process of creating a table of authorities, which is a list of citations for a legal brief.
- When planning a table of authorities, the sections to be included in the table need to be determined before text is marked. WordPerfect allows a maximum of 16 sections in a table of authorities.
- When marking text for a table of authorities, if a citation occurs often in a document, mark it once as a full form and after that mark it as a short form.
- Before generating a table of authorities, each section in the table needs to be defined.
- Text in a table of authorities can be edited.

## Commands Review

### Keyboard

| | |
|---|---|
| Mark Table of Contents | Alt + F4 or F12, then Alt + F5, 1 or C |
| Mark List | Alt + F4 or F12, then Alt + F5, 2 or L |
| Mark Index | Alt + F5, 3 or I |
| Mark Table of Authorities | Alt + F4 or F12, then Alt + F5, 4 or A |
| | |
| Define Table of Contents | Alt + F5, 5 or D, 1 or C |
| Define List | Alt + F5, 5 or D, 2 or L |
| Define Index | Alt + F5, 5 or D, 3 or I |
| Define Table of Authorities | Alt + F5, 5 or D, 4 or A |
| | |
| Generate tables, lists and indexes | Alt + F5, 6 or G, 5 or G |

### Mouse

| | |
|---|---|
| Mark Table of Contents | Mark, Table of Contents |
| Mark List | Mark, List |
| Mark Index | Mark, Index |
| Mark Table of Authorities | Mark, Table of Authorities |

|                                   | **Mouse**                               |
| --------------------------------- | --------------------------------------- |
| Define Table of Contents          | Mark, Define, Table of Contents         |
| Define List                       | Mark, Define, List                      |
| Define Index                      | Mark, Define, Index                     |
| Define Table of Authorities       | Mark, Define, Table of Authorities      |
| Generate tables, lists and indexes | Mark, Generate, 5 or G                 |

## STUDY GUIDE FOR CHAPTER 30

List the four steps to be completed when creating a table of contents, list, index, or table of authorities.

1. _____

2. _____

3. _____

4. _____


**Completion:** In the space provided at the right, indicate the correct term, symbol, or command for the explanation.

1.   Access the Mark Text command.                                    _____

2.   Maximum number of levels in a table of contents.                 _____

3.   Insert a Hard Page code.                                         _____

4.   Maximum number of lists allowed in a document.                   _____

5.   Page numbering style for a table of contents.                    _____

6.   Name of a file that can be created which contains headings for    _____
     an index.

7.   Maximum number of sections in a table of authorities.            _____


**True/False:** Circle the letter T if the statement is true; circle the letter F if the statement is false.

1.   An index generally appears at the beginning of a document.                    T     F

2.   A table of contents generally appears at the beginning of a document.         T     F

3.   By default, WordPerfect capitalizes the first letter of a heading in an index. T     F

4.   Before generating a table of authorities, each section needs to be defined.   T     F

5.   A table of contents contains a list of citations in a legal brief.            T     F

6.   A table of contents, list, index, or table of authorities must be defined before it   T     F
     can be generated.

7.   Once a table of contents has been generated, it cannot be changed.            T     F


List the steps required to generate a table of contents, list, index, or table of authorities:


_____


_____


_____

## HANDS-ON EXERCISES

Change the default directory to UNIT6.

### Exercise One

1.  At a clear screen, create the textbook chapter shown in figure 30-4. Center, boldface, and italicize text as indicated.

2.  Move the cursor to the beginning of the chapter and turn on page numbering at the bottom center of each page. Turn on Widow/Orphan Protection. Create hanging paragraphs for the paragraphs in figure 1-2.

3.  Save the chapter and name it CH30EX1.

## CHAPTER 1: ORAL QUESTIONING TECHNIQUES

### BACKGROUND

Most experts agree that students learn better by doing or in active participation. Active participation, however, goes beyond simply doing. It includes the consistent involvement of the minds as well as the bodies of the learners. The easiest way to achieve this mental engagement is through questions that require the learner to think. The value of such thinking is that as it is being rehearsed in short-term memory, it is being retained and transferred to long-term memory.

Active participation increases true learning. Active participation also provides the instructor with a tool for determining the degree to which students are meeting performance outcomes. Finally, it is an efficient way to monitor learner progress and adjust lessons accordingly.

### LEVELS OF QUESTIONS

An understanding of Bloom's Taxonomy of Educational Objectives is a classification system for the various levels of the thinking processes. An understanding of this taxonomy is indispensable for any effective instructor. It guides instructors in specifying performance outcomes, and it leads them to ask more effective questions, resulting in increased learning. The taxonomy has six levels, which are shown in figure 1-1.

```
Level 1 = Knowledge
Level 2 = Comprehension
Level 3 = Application
Level 4 = Analysis
Level 5 = Synthesis
Level 6 = Evaluation
```

**Figure 1-1: Taxonomy Levels**

## Knowledge

The knowledge level is the first stage of the taxonomy. It is essentially a recall of facts, definitions, or other memorized information. Knowledge is associated with remembering and it is the simplest form of the thinking process.

## Comprehension

Comprehension is the second level of the taxonomy. This stage of the thinking processes is slightly broader than the knowledge level; it requires the learner to select among facts, organize those facts, and restate them in the learner's own words. Comprehension connotes understanding.

## Application

This third level of the taxonomy is application. At this stage the learner must use information or skills learned. The operative word is *apply*, and the verbs often found with this level include *translate, interpret, employ, illustrate, schedule, solve*, and *show*. Simply stated, this level emphasizes the application of facts, rules, and principles to other situations.

## Analysis

The fourth level of the taxonomy is analysis, which is characterized by classification and sorting. Analysis-type questions use verbs such as *categorize, differentiate, compare, contrast*, and *criticize*. These questions involve the separation of the whole into its various parts.

## Synthesis

The fifth level of Bloom's taxonomy is synthesis. At this level the learner combines ideas from previous learning to create a new whole. Synthesis is characterized by bringing together a variety of ideas or concepts. Verbs often found in synthesis-type questions include *compose, assemble, construct, organize, design, develop*, and *create*.

## Evaluation

The sixth and final level of the taxonomy is evaluation. At this level of the thinking process the learner develops opinions, judgments or decisions based upon previously known facts or opinions. Verbs found in evaluation-type questions include *appraise*, *evaluate*, *prioritize*, *assess*, *decide*, *choose*, *select*, *justify*, and *recommend*.

## EXAMPLE QUESTIONS

Questions or directions can be written to relate to the six levels of the thinking processes. The questions in figure 1-2 show examples of questions written at different levels.

---

Knowledge:    1. What dramatic event caused the United States to enter Word War II?  2. Define marketing.

Comprehension:  1. Describe the damage that the Japanese caused to the U.S. Navy at Pearl Harbor.  2. Describe the basic purposes of a marketing system.

Application:   1. How is Pearl Harbor an example of the need for preparedness?  2. How is the "lite" beer phenomenon an example of market segmentation?

Analysis:    1. Compare and contrast the relative strengths of the U.S. Navy and the Japanese Navy immediately following Pearl Harbor.   2. Compare the views of a typical marketing director with those of a quality assurance director in terms of marketing's effect on product quality.

Synthesis:    1. Given the facts of Pearl Harbor, design an overall strategic defense that will avoid such an attack in the future.   2. Given the statistical data in the enclosed report, prepare an overall marketing plan for the company;  include strategies and tactics.

Evaluation:   1. Would you have dropped the bomb on Hiroshima? Why or why not?   2. Given these two strategic marketing plans for our company, determine which would be more effective. Why?

---

**Figure 1-2: Example Questions**

---

Figure 30-4: Exercise One

**Exercise Two**

  1.  Retrieve CH30EX1 to the screen. Mark the title, headings, and subheadings in the chapter for inclusion in a table of contents. To do this, complete the following steps:

  A. Move the cursor to the title, heading or subheading and block it with the Block command, Alt + F4 or F12. (Before blocking text, access Reveal Codes and make sure the cursor is positioned after the Boldface code. Exit Reveal Codes and then block the text. You do not want to include the Boldface code in the table of contents.)
  **M** *Click on Edit, then Block.*

  B. Access the Mark Text command with Alt + F5.

C. At the prompt **Mark for: 1 ToC; 2 List; 3 Index; 4 ToA: 0**, choose 1 or C for ToC.
   **M** *Click on Mark, then Table of Contents.*

D. At the prompt, **ToC Level: -**, key in the level number as indicated below:

| | |
|---|---|
| CHAPTER 1: ORAL QUESTIONING TECHNIQUES | Level 1 |
| BACKGROUND | Level 2 |
| LEVELS OF QUESTIONS | Level 2 |
| Knowledge | Level 3 |
| Comprehension | Level 3 |
| Application | Level 3 |
| Analysis | Level 3 |
| Synthesis | Level 3 |
| Evaluation | Level 3 |
| EXAMPLE QUESTIONS | Level 2 |

2. After identifying all headings and subheading to be included in the table of contents, move the cursor to the beginning of the document and complete the following steps:

   A. Access Reveal Codes and move the cursor on the Page Numbering code.  Exit Reveal Codes.

   B. Insert a Hard Page code with Ctrl + Enter and move the cursor above the page break.

   C. Turn page numbering on at the bottom center of each page and change the page numbering style to lowercase Roman numerals.

   D. Center and boldface the title TABLE OF CONTENTS and press Enter three times.

   E. Define the table of contents by completing the following steps:

      (1) Access the Mark Text command with Alt + F5, choose 5 or D for Define, then 1 or C for Define Table of Contents.
          **M** *Click on Mark, Define, then Table of Contents.*

      (2) At the Table of Contents Definition menu, choose 1 or N for Number of Levels, then key in a **3**.

      (3) Press F7 to return to the document and insert a Table of Contents Definition code in the document.

   F. Move the cursor to the beginning of the title page, access the Page: Format menu and change the beginning page to 1 in Arabic numbers.

3. Generate the table of contents by completing the following steps:

   A. Access the Mark Text command with Alt + F5.

   B. Choose 6 or G for Generate.
      **M** *Click on Mark, then Generate.*

   C. At the Mark Text: Generate menu, choose 5 or G for Generate Tables, Indexes, Cross-References, etc.

   D. At the prompt **Existing tables, lists, and indexes will be replaced. Continue? Yes (No)**, press Enter to start the generation.

4. Save the chapter and name it CH30EX2. Print CH30EX2. (The first page of the document should be the table of contents.)


## Exercise Three

1. Retrieve CH30EX2 to the screen. Mark the figure captions for inclusion in a list (there are two) by completing the following steps:

   A. Block the figure caption, Figure 1-1: Taxonomy Levels, with Alt + F4 or F12. (Make sure you do not include the Boldface codes.)
      **M** *Click on Edit, then Block.*

   B. Access the Mark Text command with Alt + F5, and choose 2 or L for List.
      **M** *Click on Mark, then List.*

   C. At the prompt **List Number: _**, key in a 1, and press Enter.

   D. Mark the second figure caption following the same steps.

2. After marking the figure captions, move the cursor to the beginning of the chapter title page (on the Page Numbering code) and complete the following steps:

A. Insert a Hard Page code with Ctrl + Enter.

B. Move the cursor above the page break.

C. Center and boldface the title FIGURES, then press Enter three times.

D. Define the list by completing the following steps:

    (1) Access the Mark Text command with Alt + F5.

    (2) Choose 5 or D for Define.

    (3) Choose 2 or L for Define List.
       **M** *Click on Mark, Define, then List.*

    (4) At the **List Number (1-10)** prompt, key in a **1**, and press Enter.

    (5) At the List 1 Definition menu, choose 5 or L for Flush Right Page Numbers with Leaders.

E. Block the title FIGURES (without boldfacing) and identify it as text to be included in the Table of Contents, Level 1.

3. Generate the list (and regenerate the table of contents) by completing the following steps:

A. Access the Mark Text command with Alt + F5.

B. Choose 6 or G for Generate.
   **M** *Click on Mark, then Generate.*

C. At the Mark Text: Generate menu, choose 5 or G for Generate Tables, Indexes, Cross-References, etc.

D. At the prompt **Existing tables, lists, and indexes will be replaced. Continue? Yes (No)**, press Enter to start the generation.

4. Save the chapter and name it CH30EX3. Print CH30EX3. (When printed, the first page should be the table of contents and the second page should be the list of figures.)

## Exercise Four

1. Retrieve CH30EX3 to the screen. Mark the following text for inclusion in an index:

    Active participation (heading)

    Bloom's Taxonomy (heading)

    Knowledge (subheading; Taxonomy Levels, heading)

    Comprehension (subheading; Taxonomy Levels, heading)

    Application (subheading; Taxonomy Levels, heading)

    Analysis (subheading; Taxonomy Levels, heading)

    Synthesis (subheading; Taxonomy Levels, heading)

    Evaluation (subheading; Taxonomy Levels, heading)

For example, mark Active participation for the index by completing the following steps:

A. Block Active participation with the Block command, Alt + F4 or F12.
   **M** *Click on Edit, then Block.*

B. Access the Mark Text command with Alt + F5.

C. Choose 3 or I for Index.
   **M** *Click on Mark, then Index.*

D. At the prompt **Index heading: Active participation**, press Enter.

E. At the **Subheading:** prompt, press Enter.

2. To mark Knowledge for inclusion in the index, complete the following steps:

A. Locate the cursor on the word Knowledge.

B. Access the Mark Text command with Alt + F5.

C. Choose 3 or I for Index.
   **M** *Click on Mark, then Index.*

D. At the **Index heading: Knowledge** prompt, key in **Taxonomy Levels**, and press Enter.

E. At the prompt, **Subheading: Knowledge**, press Enter.

Mark the other words for the index as indicated in the parentheses following similar steps.

3.   After marking all text for the index, move the cursor to the end of the chapter and complete the following steps:

A.   Insert a Hard Page code with Ctrl + Enter.

B.   Center and boldface the title INDEX and press Enter three times.

C.   Define the index by completing the following steps:

(1)   Access the Mark Text command with Alt + F5, then choose 5 or D for Define.

(2)   From the Mark Text: Define menu, choose 3 or I for Define Index.
    **M** *Click on Mark, Define, then Index.*

(3)   At the prompt **Concordance Filename (Enter=none)**, press Enter.

(4)   At the Index Definition menu, choose 2 or P for Page Numbers Follow Entries.

D.   Block the title INDEX (without boldfacing) and identify it as text to be included in the table of contents, Level 1.

4.   Generate the index (and regenerate the table of contents and list of figures) by completing the following steps:

A.   Access the Mark Text command with Alt + F5.

B.   Choose 6 or G for Generate.
    **M** *Click on Mark, then Generate.*

C.   At the Mark Text: Generate menu, choose 5 or G for Generate Tables, Indexes, Cross-References, etc.

D.   At the prompt **Existing tables, lists, and indexes will be replaced. Continue? Yes (No)**, press Enter to start the generation.

5.   Save the chapter and name it CH30EX4. Print CH30EX4. (The last page of the chapter will be the index.)


**Exercise Five**

1.   At a clear screen, turn page numbering on at the bottom center of each page, execute the Alt + D macro, and turn on Widow/Orphan Protection. Key in the legal brief shown in figure 30-5.

2.   Save the legal brief and name it CH30EX5. Print CH30EX5.

---

A.   <u>STATEMENT OF THE CASE</u>

This lawsuit is the result of a pedestrian/automobile accident that occurred on January 5, 1992, while Plaintiff Sonya Webb was walking with her four-year-old daughter, Sylvana, in a northerly direction, facing traffic, along Elm Street in Everett, Washington.

Elm Street is maintained by Snohomish County. There is no sidewalk or paved shoulder along the two-lane rural road. However, there is a grassy shoulder next to the road that is approximately 30 inches wide.

Just before the accident, as Sylvana and Mrs. Webb were walking along Elm Street, Sylvana bent to tie her shoe. Her mother saw an oncoming car driven by Steve Abbot approaching from the distance and told Sylvana to stand up because she wanted to make sure the driver of the car could see them. Mrs. Webb at this point was standing in front (on the north side) of Sylvana. It is disputed that she and Sylvana were both standing on the grassy area <u>off</u> the paved road and as close as possible to the ditch.

The Abbot vehicle was traveling in a southerly direction. There were no other vehicles on the road in the vicinity of the plaintiffs at the time of the accident. Specifically, there was no oncoming traffic to the Abbot vehicle. Elm Street, at the site of the accident, is approximately 16 feet wide.

After telling Sylvana to stand up, Mrs. Webb turned <u>left</u> in order to make a three-quarter turn so that she could face Sylvana and hear what she was saying.

While in the process of turning, both Mrs. Webb and Sylvana were struck by the Abbot vehicle. At the time of impact, Mrs. Webb was not looking at the vehicle. She did not realize that the vehicle was going to hit her and Sylvana until the accident occurred.

The driver of the vehicle, Steve Abbot, maintains that he was blinded by the sun and did not see Mrs. Webb and Sylvana at all before impact and thought he had hit a dog.

Mrs. Webb testified that the ditch was shallow enough and narrow enough that she could have stepped <u>over</u> and <u>into</u> the ditch with Sylvana.

Melrose Irrigation Company does not own the land through which the ditch runs; rather it operates by way of an easement from the property owners. Plaintiffs have recovered from the driver of the vehicle and have brought this suit against Defendant Melrose Irrigation Company.

B.    <u>REPLY ARGUMENT</u>

The appellants are desperately trying to show that an issue of material fact exists when one does not. Melrose Irrigation Company, by the mere maintenance of an irrigation ditch, as a matter of law is not liable for injuries suffered when a vehicle leaves the roadway and strikes pedestrians.

1.    <u>Melrose Owed No Duty of Care to Appellants</u>.

Appellant mistakenly maintains that Melrose owes a duty of care to pedestrians walking on the shoulder of a public highway. <u>Johnson v. Tiegert</u>, 15 Wn.2d 119, 129 P.2d 790 (1959), cited by appellants, is wholly inapplicable in their contention. <u>Johnson</u> deals with the obstruction of a sidewalk next to a street. In the instant case, no sidewalk or walkway existed along the rural road.

In <u>Bergland v. Spokane Co.</u>, 4 Wn.2d 309, 103 P.2d 355 (1951), the leading case regarding liability of a municipality for pedestrian injury, the Washington State Supreme Court stated that a <u>municipality</u>:

> . . . may in the first instance leave such ways unopened, without liability for not having improved them. But if they choose to improve them, they must exercise reasonable care to keep them in safe condition.

RCWA 46.43.250, requires that pedestrians move to the shoulder when a vehicle is approaching to guarantee the safe and free flow of traffic. This requirement in no way extends an invitation to pedestrians to use the shoulder as a public walkway.

Certainly, if Snohomish County has no obligation to provide a walkway, Melrose likewise had no such obligation.

Moreover, appellants' reliance on <u>Harcourt v. Sinclair</u>, 62 Wash. 398, 113 P. 1115 (1923), is similarly misplaced. <u>Harcourt</u> deals with liability, not for personal injury, but for diversion of water to one landowner from another.

While foreseeability of injury is an <u>element</u> of common law negligence, foreseeability, without a breach of duty <u>and</u> proximate cause between the breach and the resulting injury is insufficient to establish negligence (<u>Ibsen v. Washington Natural Gas Co.</u>, 93 Wn.2d 755, 532 P.2d 439 (1984)). Foreseeability is directed to causation and not to whether a duty actually exists.

    2.   <u>Whether Melrose Breached a Duty to Pedestrians is an Appropriate Question for the Trial Court on a Summary Judgment Motion.</u>

<u>Closson v. Rock River Valley Users' Association</u>, 456 P.2d 483 (Ariz. Ct. App. 1975), which appellants cited at length for the proposition that Melrose owes a duty of care to pedestrians and that a breach of that duty is a jury question was <u>vacated</u> in <u>Closson v. Rock River Valley Users' Association</u>, 208 Ariz. 513, 475 P.2d 371 (1976). In the later proceeding, the trial court's decision of no liability on the part of the ditch owner was affirmed by the Arizona Supreme Court.

Finally, while appellants are correct in their position that the public has a right to unobstructed use of a highway, the unpaved shoulder of a roadway is <u>not</u> considered part of the highway (<u>Benetti v. Selma Transit</u>, 49 Wn.2d 855, 321 P.2d 573 (1963)). Since the irrigation ditch did not inhibit the use of the paved highway, Melrose has breached no duty of care.

C.   <u>CONCLUSION</u>

Melrose, being neither a municipality nor having invited the public to use the shoulder as a walkway, has no duty of care to pedestrians. Secondly, the existence of a breach of duty is a question of law and was correctly decided by the trial court.

For these reasons, the respondents respectfully urge this court to deny the appellants' appeal and to uphold the trial court's summary judgment for respondents; and award costs pursuant to RAP 15.3.

---

**Figure 30-5: Exercise Five**

**Exercise Six**

   1.  Retrieve CH30EX5 to the screen. Mark the authorities for inclusion in a table of authorities by completing the following steps:

      A.  Move the cursor to each citation in the legal brief that is to be included and block it with the Block command, Alt + F4 or F12.
         **M** *Click on Edit, then Block.*

      B.  With the citation blocked, access the Mark Text command with Alt + F5, then choose 4 or A for ToA.
         **M** *Click on Mark, Table of Authorities, then Mark Full.*

      C.  WordPerfect inserts the prompt **ToA Section Number (Press Enter for Short Form only):_** at the bottom of the screen. Key in the section number where the text is to appear and press Enter. (The level number is indicated below, after the citation.)

    D. WordPerfect moves into a special editing screen and displays the blocked text. Edit the text, if necessary, so the text displays as you want it to appear in the table of authorities, including any special print features such as boldfacing and underlining.

    E. When the full form is edited, press Exit, F7.

    F. WordPerfect displays the message **Short Form:** _ and displays the long form after the prompt. If the text appears elsewhere in the document, include a short form name. (The short form is indicated below after the citation.) Shorten the long form to a significant word or words to clearly identify the case or statute and press Enter.

Mark the following citations for inclusion in the table of authorities. (Be sure to include the Underlining code in the block because you want it to appear in the table of authorities.) The authority levels are identified along with the short form, if needed:

    Johnson v. Tiegert, 15 Wn.2d 119, 129 P.2d 790 (1959)
        Level 1; Short form, Johnson

Move to the next occurrence of Johnson and mark it as a short form:

    Bergland v. Spokane Co., 4 Wn.2d 309,103 P.2d 355 (1951)
        Level 1; no short form

    RCWA 46.43.250
        Level 3; no short form

    Harcourt v. Sinclair, 62 Wash. 398, 113 P. 1115 (1923)
        Level 1; Short form, Harcourt

Move to the next occurrence of Harcourt and mark it as a short form:

    Ibsen v. Washington Natural Gas Co., 93 Wn.2d 755, 532 P.2d 439 (1984)
        Level 1; no short form

    Closson v. Rock River Valley Users' Association, 456 P.2d 483 (Ariz. Ct. App. 1975)
        Level 2; no short form

    Closson v. Rock River Valley Users' Association, 208 Ariz. 513, 475 P.2d 371 (1976)
        Level 2; Short form, Closson

    Benetti v. Selma Transit, 49 Wn.2d 855, 321 P.2d 573 (1963)
        Level 1; no short form

2. After identifying all citations to be included in the table of authorities, move the cursor to the beginning of the document and complete the following steps:

    A. Access Reveal Codes and move the cursor on the Page Numbering code. Exit Reveal Codes.

    B. Insert a Hard Page code with Ctrl + Enter and move the cursor above the page break.

    C. Turn page numbering on and change the page numbering style to lowercase Roman numerals.

    D. Center and boldface the title TABLE OF AUTHORITIES and press Enter three times.

    E. Key in the subheading **Washington Cases**, underlined, at the left margin.
       Press Enter twice.

    F. Define the first section of the table of authorities by completing the following steps:
       (1) Access the Mark Text command with Alt + F5, then choose 5 or D for Define.
       (2) At the Mark Text: Define menu, choose 4 or A for Define Table of Authorities.

**M** *Click on Mark, Define, then Table of Authorities.*
(3) At the prompt **Section Number (1-16)_**, key in **1**, and press Enter.
(4) At the Definition for Table of Authorities 1 menu, choose 2 or U for Underlining Allowed, then key in a **Y** for Yes.
(5) Press F7 to return the cursor to the document.
G. Press Enter and key in the subheading **Other Cases**, underlined, at the left margin. Press Enter twice.
H. Define Section 2 following the same steps for Section 1.
I. Press Enter and key in the subheading **Statutes**, underlined, at the left margin. Press Enter twice.
J. Define Section 3 following the same steps for Section 1.
K. Move the cursor to the beginning of the legal brief, access the Page: Format menu and change the beginning page to 1 in Arabic numbers.
3. Generate the table of authorities by completing the following steps:
A. Access the Mark Text command with Alt + F5, then choose 6 or G for Generate.
**M** *Click on Mark, then Generate.*
B. At the Mark Text: Generate menu, choose 5 or G for Generate Tables, Indexes, Cross-References, etc.
C. At the prompt **Existing tables, lists, and indexes will be replaced. Continue? Yes (No)**, key in a **Y** to start the generation.
4. Save the legal brief and name it CH30EX6. Print CH30EX6. (The first page of the document should be the table of authorities.)

## PERFORMANCE ASSESSMENTS

**Assessment One**
1. At a clear screen, create the chapter shown in figure 30-6.
2. Save the chapter and name it CH30PA1. Print CH30PA1.

---

## CHAPTER 2: MODE OF INSTRUCTION

**LECTURE**

The lecture is among the most widely used, and abused, modes of instruction. To deliver a lecture effectively, instructors must be completely familiar with the material. They must speak loudly and clearly, and they must be careful that the pace of the lesson flows smoothly. An effective lecturer is enthusiastic and dramatic and watches for nonverbal responses from the audience. The lecturer must be natural without relying excessively on notes. Moving around the room is often a helpful technique to use while delivering the lecture. Advantages of the lecture mode are shown in figure 2-1.

---

1. The lecture is an efficient way to deliver a broad range of material in a brief amount of time.
2. The instructor has complete control over the content and sequencing of information.
3. The lecture provides the opportunity to use a wide variety of supplementary verbal illustrations and visual aids to assist in making a point.

4.    An effective lecturer has a unique opportunity to get the
      attention of and inspire an audience.

## Figure 2-1: Advantages of the Lecture

Though lecture is an effective mode of instruction, there are some
disadvantages to lectures that are shown in figure 2-2.

1.    The lecture is a large-group activity, whereas most learning
      takes place individually.
2.    The lecture is essentially one-way communication, unless it is
      combined with another mode of instruction.
3.    The lecture does not allow active involvement of students.
      Long spans of passivity are detrimental to learning.
4.    In lectures there is a heavy reliance on self-instruction,
      because the instructor merely presents the material.
5.    Transfer of learning relies totally upon the instructor.
6.    Other than for short segments, the lecture is largely inappro-
      priate for skill-type lessons.

## Figure 2-2: Disadvantages of the Lecture

## SMALL GROUPS

Using small groups in a classroom setting is a second mode of
instruction frequently used by skilled instructors. This mode of
instruction can be extremely effective if implemented appropriately.

Typically, the instructor selects a topic for group discussion. The
instructor then orients the students to the topic, provides time
limitations, gives guidelines for the activity, and allows the
groups to go to work. While the groups are discussing the topic or
problem, the instructor circulates through the room to keep groups
on task, encourage interaction, ask leading questions, clarify
problems, and assess the degree to which the performance outcome is
being met. After reaching consensus, the groups may report to the
entire class. Some advantages to the small group mode of instruction are listed in figure 2-3.

1.    Small groups are versatile; they can be used for a variety of
      topics and material.
2.    Small groups can be effective in solving problems and handling
      controversial issues.
3.    Small groups require active participation.
4.    Small groups help develop interpersonal and leadership skills.
5.    Small groups allow students to become involved in the transfer
      of learning.

## Figure 2-3: Advantages of the Small Group

Disadvantages to the small group mode of instruction are listed in figure 2-4.

---

1.   Groups can be sidetracked easily.
2.   Groups are usually unable to deal with a breadth of material.
3.   Groups are easily dominated by a few students, thus elminating the benefit of active participation on the part of all students.
4.   Group activity is time-consuming.
5.   Some questions may be left unanswered.

---

**Figure 2-4: Disadvantages of the Small Group**

**DEMONSTRATION**

Demonstration is the third frequently used mode of instruction. An effective demonstration requires careful planning; it must flow in a logical order with key points emphasized throughout. The demonstration is an appropriate technique for showing students how to perform a task or for explaining a concept. The keys to a good demonstration are the questioning that takes place and the opportunity students have to practice the modeled behavior. Advantages of the demonstration mode of instruction are listed in figure 2-5.

---

1.   Demonstrations are appropriate for explaining a concept or showing how to perform a task.
2.   The demonstration is an effective method for getting students to think at the application level of thinking skills.
3.   Demonstrations can be thought-provoking, particularly if done in a discovery fashion.
4.   The demonstration allows active participation.
5.   Demonstrations provide an opportunity for excellent transer of learning if effective questioning accompanies them.

---

**Figure 2-5: Advantages to the Demonstration**

Disadvantages to the demonstration mode of instruction are listed in figure 2-6.

---

1.   Time and expense involved in preparing and giving the demonstration are often significant.
2.   Materials and equipment are often in limited supply (especially for subsequent student practice).
3.   Unless the instructor combines the demonstration with effective questioning and student practice, there is no opportunity to check for understanding.
4.   Demonstrations require extensive planning and organization so that crucial steps are not skipped.

---

**Figure 2-6: Disadvantages of the Demonstration**

## LABORATORY

A fourth mode of instruction used frequently in discovery or skill-type classes is the laboratory. An effective laboratory class is usually preceded by some other mode of instruction — for example, lecture or demonstration. Following this introduction, the teacher provides written instructions to the students; then the students perform in the lab. Throughout the lab, the instructor moves around the room to the various individuals or groups and provides assistance, asks and answers questions, and gives feedback. Provision of appropriate materials is a key to a successful lab. Advantages to the laboratory mode of instruction are listed in figure 2-7.

1. Students are actively involved and learn by doing.
2. The laboratory can be individualized to the interests and abilities of each student.
3. Laboratories can be thought-provoking and allow students to engage in discovery activities.
4. Instructors are able to assess student understanding as they circulate through the room.
5. Instructors have the opportunity to encourage students to transfer learning in the lab to previously learned material.

**Figure 2-7: Advantages to the Laboratory**

Disadvantages to the laboratory mode of instruction are listed in figure 2-8.

1. Frequently, equipment and supplies are unavailable or insufficient.
2. The breadth of material that can be covered is limited.
3. The time involved in planning and delivering a lab can be considerable.
4. The lab requires self-directed students who are capable of handling the freedom inherent in a lab setting.
5. A lab can be extremely disorganized if instructions are unclear.

**Figure 2-8: Disadvantages of the Laboratory**

Figure 30-6: Assessment One

**Assessment Two**

1. Retrieve CH30PA1 to the screen.
2. Create, define, and generate a table of contents.
3. Create, define, and generate a list of figures.
4. Create, define, and generate an index. You determine the words to be indexed along with the heading or subheading.
5. Save the chapter and name it CH30PA2. Print CH30PA2.

# CHAPTER 31

SORT AND SELECT

## PERFORMANCE OBJECTIVES

Upon successful completion of chapter 31, you will be able to sort information in a properly prepared file and select specified groups of information from a larger group.

WordPerfect is a word processing program that includes some basic database features. Database programs include features that let you alphabetize information or arrange numbers numerically. In addition, with a database program you can select specific files or records from a larger file.

With WordPerfect's Sort and Select features you can perform basic database functions such as sorting lines, records, or paragraphs alphabetically or numerically or selecting specific lines or records from a document.

### SORT

With the Sort feature, text can be sorted alphabetically or numerically by lines within columns, by records in a secondary file, or by paragraphs in a document.

### Line Sorting

Line sorting requires text to be set up in columns with tab settings on the tab ruler line. Columns need to be set up as described in chapter 5. Text is sorted alphabetically, beginning with A and ending with Z. This order can be reversed if desired. Numbers are sorted in ascending order, beginning with the lowest and continuing to the highest. This order can also be reversed.

To sort text in columns, move the cursor to the first column and access the Merge/Sort command with Ctrl + F9. The following prompt appears at the bottom of the screen:

1 **M**erge; 2 **S**ort; 3 **C**onvert Old Merge Codes: **0**

Choose 2 or S for Sort, and the prompt changes to the following:

**Input file to sort: (Screen)**

This message is asking for the name of the file you want to have sorted. The WordPerfect default is to sort the file currently displayed on the screen. If you decide to sort a different file, key in its name and press Enter. To sort the text displayed on the screen, press Enter, and the prompt changes to the following:

**Output file for sort: (Screen)**

This message is asking for the name of a file in which to save the sorted material. The default is for the sorted material to be saved in the document currently displayed on the screen. If you decide to save the material in another document, key in its name and press Enter. To save the sorted material to the document displayed on the screen, just press Enter.

The Sort by Line menu shown in figure 31-1 appears on the screen. Ten lines of the document are displayed at the top of the screen and the Sort by Line menu displays at the bottom. (The tab ruler line separates the document from the menu.)

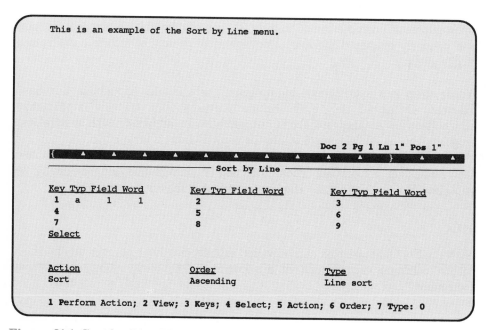

Figure 31-1: Sort by Line Menu

At the top of this menu is an area to identify nine different keys by type, field, and word. A key is essentially a field of information. For example, a key can be a particular word within a field or it can be a column of text. To identify a key, choose 3 or K for Keys.

When you choose Keys, the cursor moves to Key 1. Key 1 has a default setting, which indicates that the first key is to be sorted alphabetically by the first word in the first field. Key 1 is considered the primary key, and text is sorted by this key first.

Two settings can be identified under Typ—alphabetic ("a") or numeric ("n"). The default setting is alphabetic. If this is the setting you want, press Enter. If you want to do a numeric sort, key in an N, then press Enter.

The cursor moves to the next heading, Field. When working with columns, the left margin is considered Field 1, the first tab stop is Field 2, the second tab stop is Field 3, and so on. (If no text is keyed in at the left margin, it is still considered a field.) Key in a field number, then press Enter.

The cursor moves to the last selection in Key 1, Word. The default setting is 1 (for the first word). If a column contains only one word, or if you want to sort on the first word of the column, press Enter. If, however, you want to sort on a word other than the first word, you must change the number to reflect the position of that word. WordPerfect reads words from left to right in the field. When all keys have been identified, press F7.

The last three headings—Action, Order, and Type—describe the type of sort that is to be completed.

After the keys have been identified, choose 1 or P for Perform Action to perform the sort. WordPerfect searches the column entries and rearranges them in alphabetic or numeric order. When sorting is complete, the Sort by Line menu disappears from the screen.

To understand how line sorting works, let us look at an example. In the columns shown in figure 31-2, the first and second columns are keyed in with left tabs set at +1.0 and +3.0 inches. The third column is keyed in with a decimal tab set at +5.5 inches.

```
Masterson          September              $432.65
Austin             October                 237.84
Weinstein          April                   645.23
Karson             February                763.45
```

Figure 31-2: Columns

To sort the first column alphabetically, complete the following steps:

1. Access the Merge/Sort command with Ctrl + F9.
2. Choose 2 or S for Sort.
   **M** *Click on Tools, then Sort.*
3. At the prompt **Input file to sort: (Screen)**, press Enter
4. At the prompt **Output file for sort: (Screen)**, press Enter.
5. At the Sort by Line menu, choose 3 or K for Keys.
6. With the cursor located below the a under Typ, press Enter.
7. With the cursor located to the right of the 1 under Field, key in a **2** and press Enter. (Even though you want to sort the first column, WordPerfect considers it the second field; the left margin is the first field.)
8. With the cursor located to the right of the 1 under Word, press Enter.
9. With the cursor located beneath the a after Key 2, press F7. (You do not want to identify any further keys.)
10. Choose 1 or P for Perform Action to perform the sort.

When the sort is complete, the column entries will be arranged alphabetically by last name and will appear as shown in figure 31-3.

| | | |
|---|---|---|
| Austin | October | 237.84 |
| Karson | February | 763.45 |
| Masterson | September | $432.65 |
| Weinstein | April | 645.23 |

Figure 31-3: Sorted Columns

## Sorting with the Block Command

Sorting by line works for a document containing only columns. If there is other text in the document, WordPerfect tries to sort that information as well, which can result in a mess. If you want to sort columns in a document containing other text, block the columns with the Block command and then perform the sort. (Make sure you include the Tab code for the columns in the block.)

## Merge Sorting

A Merge sort is accomplished in the same manner as a Line sort. A Merge sort lets you alphabetically or numerically rearrange the records in a secondary file. For example, you can arrange all the records alphabetically by last name, or you can arrange all records numerically by Zip Code.

To complete a sort with a secondary file, the sort menu must be changed. By default, the Sort by Line menu appears on the screen. To sort a secondary file, choose 7 or T for Type from the Sort by Line menu. From the prompts that display at the bottom of the menu, choose 1 or M for Merge.

The Sort Secondary Merge File menu that appears on the screen is very similar to the Sort by Line menu. There are nine keys that can be identified, and in each key there are four headings instead of three. A key can be identified by type (alpha or numeric), line, field, or word. With the addition of the Line feature, you can identify a specific line within a field for sorting.

To understand merge sorting, let us sort the records shown in figure 31-4 in a secondary file alphabetically, by last name.

```
     Mr. Eugene Zager
     11239 South 93rd Street
     Rochester, NY 10232{END FIELD}
     {END RECORD}
     ====================================
     Ms. Marilyn Donaldson
     15422 North 23rd Avenue
     Syracruse, NY 12312{END FIELD}
     {END RECORD}
     ====================================
     Mrs. Rebecca Kauffman
     21883 - 145th Street East
     Albany, NY 13122{END FIELD}
     {END RECORD}
     ====================================
```

Figure 31-4: Records

To sort the records alphabetically by last name, complete the following steps:

1. With the secondary file displayed on the screen, access the Merge/Sort command with Ctrl + F9.

2. Choose 2 or S for Sort.
   **M** *Click on Tools, then Sort.*

3. At the prompt **Input file to sort: (Screen)**, press Enter

4. At the prompt **Output file for sort: (Screen)**, press Enter.

5. At the Sort by Line menu, choose 7 or T for Type, then choose 1 or M for Merge.

6. At the Sort Secondary Merge File menu, choose 3 or K for Keys.

7. With the cursor located below the a under Typ, press Enter.

8. With the cursor located to the right of the 1 under Field, press Enter.

9. With the cursor located to the right of the 1 under Line, press Enter.

10. With the cursor located to the right of the 1 under Word, key in a 3 and press Enter. (The last name is the third word in the first field.)

11. With the cursor located below the a after Key 2, press F7. (You do not want to identify any further keys.)

12. Choose 1 or P for Perform Action to perform the sort.

When the records are sorted alphabetically by last name, they appear as shown in figure 31-5.

```
    Ms. Marilyn Donaldson
    15422 North 23rd Avenue
    Syracruse, NY 12312{END FIELD}
    {END RECORD}
    ====================================
    Mrs. Rebecca Kauffman
    21883 - 145th Street East
    Albany, NY 13122{END FIELD}
    {END RECORD}
    ====================================
    Mr. Eugene Zager
    11239 South 93rd Street
    Rochester, NY 10232{END FIELD}
    {END RECORD}
    ====================================
```

**Figure 31-5: Sorted Records**


### Merge Sort by Zip Code

The secondary file records shown in figure 31-4 can be sorted by Zip Code by completing the following steps:

1. With the secondary file displayed on the screen, access the Merge/Sort command with Ctrl + F9.

2. Choose 2 or S for Sort.
   **M** *Click on Tools, then Sort.*

3. At the prompt **Input file to sort: (Screen)**, press Enter

4. At the prompt **Output file for sort: (Screen)**, press Enter.

5. At the Sort by Line menu, choose 7 or T for Type, then choose 1 or M for Merge.

6. At the Sort Secondary Merge File menu, choose 3 or K for Keys.

7. With the cursor located below the a under Typ, key in an **n** (for numeric).

8. With the cursor located to the right of the 1 under Field, press Enter.

9. With the cursor located to the right of the 1 under Line, key in a **3** and press Enter. (The Zip Code is located in the third line of the first field.)

10. With the cursor located to the right of the 1 under Word, key in a **3** and press Enter. (The Zip Code is the third word in the third line field.)

11. With the cursor located below the a after Key 2, press F7. (You do not want to identify any further keys.)

12. Choose 1 or P for Perform Action to perform the sort.


### Paragraph Sorting

A paragraph sort lets you arrange paragraphs alphabetically or numerically. Paragraphs that are to be sorted need to follow certain formats. The paragraphs must be single spaced, each paragraph should end in at least one hard return, and no paragraph should be longer than a page. Paragraphs to be sorted in a document should be entered in a consistent manner. Enter the same number of hard returns after each paragraph, or enter all paragraphs indented or flush left.

Before performing a paragraph sort, be sure to change the type of sort to Paragraph. To do this, choose 7 or T for Type at the Sort by Line (or Sort Secondary Merge File menu), then choose 3 or P for Paragraph. The Sort by Paragraph menu is similar to the Sort Secondary Merge File menu. The difference is that the key headings are Type, Line, Field, and Word rather than Type, Field, and Line Word.

When sorting paragraphs, there are only two fields. Identify Field 1 if the paragraphs were entered at the left margin, and identify Field 2 if the paragraphs are indented to the first tab stop.

**Paragraph Sort Example**

Paragraph sorts can be helpful in many documents, but one of the most useful is alphabetizing bibliographic entries. For example, the bibliographic entries shown in figure 31-6 can be sorted by paragraphs if each paragraph is entered in the same manner. The entries shown in figure 31-6 each begin at the left margin and end in two hard returns. Two hard returns are also entered after the last paragraph to make it consistent with the others. To alphabetize these entries, complete the following steps:

1. With the entries displayed on the screen, access the Merge/Sort command with Ctrl + F9.
2. Choose 2 or S for Sort.
   **M** *Click on Tools, then Sort.*
3. At the prompt **Input file to sort: (Screen)**, press Enter
4. At the prompt **Output file for sort: (Screen)**, press Enter.
5. At the Sort by Line menu (or Sort Secondary Merge File menu), choose 7 or T for Type, then choose 3 or P for Paragraph.
6. The default settings for Key 1 are the settings you want to sort the entries alphabetically, so leave the settings as they are and choose 1 or P for Perform Action to perform the sort.

```
Wang, Christine, "Desktop Publishing in the 90s," Desktop Designs,
Northern Publishing, 1991.

Norris, Leonard, "Printing with Style," Publishing Weekly, Jameson
Publishing, 1992.

Bradford, Charles, "Desktop Publishing Applications," Personalized
Computing, 1993.
```

Figure 31-6: Paragraphs

When the paragraphs are sorted, they appear as shown in figure 31-7.

Bradford, Charles, "Desktop Publishing Applications," *Personalized Computing*, 1993.

Norris, Leonard, "Printing with Style," *Publishing Weekly*, Jameson Publishing, 1992.

Wang, Christine, "Desktop Publishing in the 90s," *Desktop Designs*, Northern Publishing, 1991.

**Figure 31-7: Sorted Paragraphs**

If you are going to sort paragraphs in a document containing other text, block the paragraphs first and then perform the sort. To sort indented paragraphs, identify the key as an alphabetic sort on the first line of the first word of the *second* field. The tab to indent paragraphs is what causes it to be the second field.

## Sorting With More Than One Key

So far, the examples of sorting have been done on only one key. For example, sorting was done alphabetically by last name, and in another example, sorting was done numerically by Zip Code. WordPerfect allows up to nine sorting keys. Records in a secondary file can be sorted alphabetically by state, then sorted alphabetically by city within each state and, finally, sorted numerically by Zip Code for each city.

Sorting on more than one key can also be used to correctly order text. For example, you can identify Key 1 to sort by last name, and Key 2 to sort by first name. Then, if the document contains several people with the same last name, WordPerfect puts them in correct alphabetic order by also alphabetizing by the first name.

WordPerfect sorts first by Key 1, which is considered the primary key, and then proceeds to the next keys, in the order in which they are entered at the Sort menu.

## Sorting Considerations

The Sort feature can be used to sort words within fields. WordPerfect reads words within a field from left to right. A word is considered one space to the next. In some situations, some text may not be sorted by word correctly unless precautions are taken. For example, if records in a secondary file contain a field with the city, state, and Zip Code and you want to sort on the state, you identify the field number and then the second word (the city is first and the state is second). The records containing one-word cities would sort correctly, but records containing two-word cities would not. The records containing one-word cities sort on the state, but records containing two-word cities sort on the second word. A record containing Fife, Washington would sort on Washington, but a record containing Los Angeles, California would sort on Angeles.

There are two methods that can be used to ensure that sorting occurs correctly. The first method is to enter two-word cities (or states) with a coded space between the names. For example, when keying in Los Angeles, press Home + space bar between Los and Angeles (rather than a regular space).

The second method is to identify the word in a field reading the field from right to left. If the field contains the city, state, and Zip Code, you can tell WordPerfect to sort on the second word from the right and this would sort the state correctly. To use this method, key in a hyphen before the number under the Word category in the Sort menu. The hyphen tells WordPerfect to reverse the order in which words are determined.

## SELECT

The Select feature lets you select specific items or records from a document. Select can be useful when you want to merge specific records in a secondary file or retrieve specific lines from a column.

With Select, you can select specific records from a secondary file for printing. For example, you can create a form letter for a software firm to be sent only to customers living in a certain Zip Code area or only those customers using a specific software program.

### Select Conditions

The symbols +(OR), *(AND), =, <>, >, <, >=, <= are used to establish select conditions. The plus sign specifies records that match one of two conditions and describes "or" situations. For example, with the plus sign, you can retrieve all customers who live in San Francisco or Los Angeles. The asterisk symbol specifies two conditions and describes "and" situations. With this symbol, the record must contain both conditions — for example, all customers living in a specific state and having a specific area code.

The other symbols are mathematical symbols, with the following conditions:

```
=     Equal to
<>    Not equal to
>     Greater than
<     Less than
>=    Greater than or equal to
<=    Less than or equal to
```

The conditions available in Select offer a wide range of choices. You can be quite specific in the items you want to have selected.

### Using Select

Select operates in the same manner as Sort. At the Sort menu, you enter a select equation that identifies the specific records you want. The examples in figure 31-8 show how select equations are written for specific situations.

1. Suppose Key 1 is the committee assignment and you want to retrieve records of individuals serving on the Publicity committee. The select equation you would key in is Key1=Publicity.

2.   Suppose Key 1 is the software program and you want to retrieve all records except those customers using Enhancer software. The select equation you would key in is Key1<>Enhancer.

3.   Suppose Key 1 is the company name and Key 2 is the state and you want to select records of individuals working for CompuPlace in the state of Oregon. The selection equation you would key in is Key1=CompuPlace * Key2=Oregon.

4.   Suppose Key 1 is the social security number and you want to retrieve records of individuals with numbers higher than 125-55-7980. The select equation you would key in is Key1>125-55-7980.

**Figure 31-8: Examples of Select Equations**

When keying in a select equation, space before and after the asterisk (*) or the plus (+) sign, but do not space within the key. If you space within a key or enter other incorrect text, WordPerfect displays the message **Incorrect Format** and moves the cursor to the equation.

### Select Example

To understand how Select operates, suppose that you wanted to select the records of people with the Zip Code 13122 shown in figure 31-4. To do this, complete the following steps:

1.   With the secondary file displayed in the screen, access the Merge/Sort command with Ctrl + F9.

2.   Choose 2 or S for Sort.
     **M** *Click on Tools, then Sort.*

3.   At the prompt **Input file to sort: (Screen)**, press Enter

4.   At the prompt **Output file for sort: (Screen)**, press Enter.

5.   At the Sort by Line menu, choose 7 or T for Type, then choose 1 or M for Merge.

6.   At the Sort Secondary Merge File menu, choose 3 or K for Keys.

7.   With the cursor located below the a under Typ, key in an **n** (for numeric).

8.   With the cursor located to the right of the 1 under Field, press Enter.

9.   With the cursor located to the right of the 1 under Line, key in a **3** and press Enter. (The Zip Code is located in the third line of the first field.)

10.  With the cursor located to the right of the 1 under Word, key in a **3** and press Enter. (The Zip Code is the third word in the third line field.)

11.  With the cursor located to the right of the a after Key 2, press F7. (You do not want to identify any further keys.)

12.  Choose 4 or S for Select. With the cursor located below Select, key in the select equation **Key1=13122**, then press Enter.

13.  Choose 1 or P for Perform Action to perform the sort and select.

When the records are selected, the only record to appear on the screen is that of Mrs. Rebecca Kauffman. Her record was the only one that matched the select equation.

## Selecting from Two Keys

Information can be selected from two different fields. In the columns shown in figure 31-9, complete the following steps to select people with the last name of Smith living in the city of Seattle.

```
Jerome Smith          Tacoma, WA
Rindetta Smith        Seattle, WA
Ryan Smith            Renton, WA
Monica Pournelle      Seattle, WA
Phyllis Smith         Seattle, WA
Raymond Smith         Tacoma, WA
```

Figure 31-9: Columns

1.	With the columns displayed on the screen, access the Merge/Sort command with Ctrl + F9.
2.	Choose 2 or S for Sort.
	**M** *Click on Tools, then Sort.*
3.	At the prompt **Input file to sort: (Screen)**, press Enter
4.	At the prompt **Output file for sort: (Screen)**, press Enter.
5.	At the Sort by Line menu, choose 3 or K for Keys. (Check to make sure the Sort by Line menu is displayed on the screen. If it is not, change the type to Line.)
6.	With the cursor located below the a under Typ, press Enter. (If the letter under Typ is an n, key in an **a**.)
7.	Key in a **2** below Field, then press Enter.
8.	Key in a **2** below Word, then press Enter.
9.	With the cursor located below the a after Key 2 and below Typ, press Enter.
10.	Key in a **3** below Field, then press Enter.
11.	Key in a **1** below Word, then press Enter.
12.	With the cursor located below the A after Key 3 and below Typ, press F7.
13.	Choose 4 or S for Select. With the cursor located below Select, key in the select equation **Key1=Smith * Key2=Seattle**, then press Enter.
14.	Choose 1 or P for Perform Action to perform the sort and select.

When the sort and select is complete, the lines for Rindetta Smith and Phyllis Smith display on the screen.

**Menu Selections**

When either the Sort by Line menu or one of the other two sort menus (Sort Secondary Merge File or Paragraph) is displayed on the screen, the prompt **1 Perform Action; 2 View; 3 Keys; 4 Select; 5 Action; 6 Order; 7 Type: 0** appears at the bottom of the screen.

The first selection, Perform Action, performs the sort or sort and select. The View selection causes the cursor to move to the document displayed above the menu, where you can scroll through the document. The Keys selection is used to identify keys for sorting or selecting. The fourth selection is used to write a select equation.

The fifth selection, Action, lets you perform a select and sort or a select only. By default, WordPerfect performs a select and also sorts the selected lines or records alphabetically or numerically. This can be changed to Select Only, which causes only the select to be performed and the selected lines or records will not be sorted. To make changes to Action, choose 5 or A for Action, and the prompt **Action 1 Select and Sort; 2 Select Only: 0** appears at the bottom of the screen. Choose 1 or S to select and sort, or choose 2 or O to select only.

When you choose 6 or O for Order from the Sort menu, the prompt **Order 1 Ascending; 2 Descending: 0** appears at the bottom of the screen. The default sorting order is Ascending. This can be changed to Descending by choosing 2 or D for Descending.

The last selection from the Sort menu is Type. This selection lets you sort or sort and select lines, paragraphs, or records in a secondary file.

**Saving to a New Document**

In the examples in this chapter, the lines and records that have been sorted and selected have been saved in the document that was displayed on the screen. In some situations, you may want to save the sorted or selected information in a new document. This allows the document to remain in its original form and a new document to be created with the sorted or selected information.

In some of the exercises at the end of this chapter, you will be sorting lines and records to be saved in a new document. To do this, enter a new document name at the **Output file for sort** prompt.

When the sort or sort and select is completed, the original document reappears on the screen. The new document is saved on the disk and can be retrieved from the directory or with the Retrieve command.

## CHAPTER REVIEW

### Summary

- Text can be sorted either alphabetically or numerically, by line, paragraph, or records in a secondary file. Text is sorted alphabetically, beginning with A and ending with Z. Numbers are sorted in ascending order, from the lowest number to the highest.
- Line sorting requires text to be established in columns, with tab settings on the tab ruler line.
- Nine different keys can be identified in a sort. A key is a field of

information. The first key is considered the primary key and sorting is done first with that key. From the Sort menu, the Keys selection is used to identify the type, field, line, or word for sorting.

* From the Sort menu, the Perform Action selection performs the sort. The View selection moves the cursor to the document displayed above the Sort menu. The Keys selection is used to identify the type, field, line, or word for sorting or selecting. Select lets you write a select equation to select specific lines, records, or paragraphs. With the Action selection, you can sort only or sort and select. The Order selection lets you change the order in which numbers or letters are sorted from ascending to descending. The last selection, Type, lets you change the type of sort.

* Paragraphs to be sorted must be single spaced, contain at least one hard return at the end, and be keyed in with the same format.

* WordPerfect reads fields in a record from left to right. That order can be reversed by entering a hyphen before the number under the Word category at the Sort menu.

* Enter a coded space between some words in fields to ensure proper sorting.

* When writing a select equation, the plus symbol (+) is used to specify information that matches one of two conditions. The asterisk symbol (*) is used to specify two conditions. Mathematical operators that can be used are =, <>, >, <, >=, and <=.

* To save sorted or sorted and selected lines, paragraphs, or records to a new document, key in the new document name at the **Output file for sort** prompt.

**Commands Review**

| | **Keyboard** | **Mouse** |
| --- | --- | --- |
| Sort menu | Ctrl + F9, 2 or S | Tools, Sort |

## STUDY GUIDE FOR CHAPTER 31

Describe the steps necessary to sort the following columns alphabetically by state.

| | |
|---|---|
| Sanderson | Boise, Idaho |
| Hobart | Denver, Colorado |
| Lee | Helena, Montana |
| Reinhold | Anchorage, Alaska |

_____

_____

_____

_____

_____

In the space provided below each selection, write the necessary select equation.

1.  Key 1 is identified as the last name. Select records of all individuals with the last name of Anderson.

    _____

2.  Key 1 is identified as the Zip Code. Select records of individuals with a Zip Code higher than 78344.

    _____

3.  Key 1 is identified as the city. Select records of individuals who do not live in Miami.

    _____

4.  Key 1 is identified as the state, and Key 2 is identified as the last name. Select records of individuals who live in Virginia and have the last name of Jones.

    _____

5.  Key 1 is identified as the city, and Key 2 is identified as the Zip Code. Select records of individuals who live in Sacramento and have the Zip Code of 97233.

    _____

**True/False:** Circle the letter T if the statement is true; circle the letter F if the statement is false.

| | | | |
|---|---|---|---|
| 1. | Sorting can be done by line, paragraph, or page. | T | F |
| 2. | By default, an alphabetic sort is performed from A to Z. | T | F |
| 3. | When sorting columns, the first column is considered Field 1. | T | F |
| 4. | Text can be sorted on more than one key. | T | F |
| 5. | By default, numbers are sorted in descending order (from highest to lowest). | T | F |
| 6. | A word within a field can be identified for sorting. | T | F |

7.  Information can be selected from two different fields.     T    F

8.  The asterisk is used to specify "or" conditions.          T    F

9.  Selected information can be saved in a new document.       T    F

## HANDS-ON EXERCISES

Change the default directory to UNIT6.

### Exercise One

1.  At a clear screen, key in the columns shown in figure 31-10. You determine the tab settings.
2.  Save the document with the Save key, F10 (**M** *Click on File, then Save*), and name it CH31EX1.

---

```
Pat Serosky           President
Kim Chun              Vice President, Operations
Terry Preston         Vice President, Support Services
Victoria Palmas       Director of Finances
Janet Weiss           Director of Personnel
William Holley        Director of Research and Development
Brad Majors           Director of Facilities Management
Heidi Schueler        Director of Sales
```

---

**Figure 31-10: Exercise One**

3.  Sort the last names in the first column alphabetically by completing the following steps:
    A.  Access the Merge/Sort command with Ctrl + F9, then choose 2 or S for Sort.
        **M** *Click on Tools, then Sort.*
    B.  At the prompt **Input file to sort: (Screen)**, press Enter.
    C.  At the prompt **Output file for sort: (Screen)**, press Enter.
    D.  At the Sort by Line menu, choose 3 or K for Keys.
    E.  With the cursor located below the a under Typ, press Enter.
    F.  With the cursor located to the right of the 1 under Field, key in a **2** and press Enter. (Even though you want to sort the first column, WordPerfect considers it the second field.)
    G.  With the cursor located to the right of the 1 under Word, key in a **2**, then press Enter.
    H.  With the cursor located under the a after Key 2, press F7. (You do not want to identify any further keys.)
    I.  Choose 1 or P for Perform Action to perform the sort.
4.  Save the sorted document with the same name (CH31EX1). Print CH31EX1. (If for some reason the sort does not work correctly, exit from the document without saving it. You can then retrieve the document to the screen in its original form and try the sort again.)

### Exercise Two

1.  At a clear screen, create the columns shown in figure 31-11. You determine the tab settings.
2.  Save the document with the Save key, F10 (**M** *Click on File, then Save*), and name it CH31EX2.

Scheyer, Margaret        Boulder, CO        643-23-8977
Graf, David              Santa Fe, NM       879-31-9833
Bigelow, Jill            Cheyenne, WY       562-84-1234
Ledford, Donald          Santa Fe, NM       790-22-5764
Powers, Anita            Cheyenne, WY       542-54-1229
Woodruff, Arthur         Boulder, CO        680-43-7845
Akioka, Joseph           Santa Fe, NM       794-93-4933
Maddock, George          Cheyenne, WY       590-34-8594
O'Shea, Daniel           Santa Fe, NM       834-22-8754

**Figure 31-11: Exercise Two**

3.  Sort the third column numerically by social security number. To do this, complete the following steps:
    A. Access the Merge/Sort command with Ctrl + F9, then choose 2 or S for Sort.
       **M** *Click on Tools, then Sort.*
    B. At the prompt **Input file to sort: (Screen)**, press Enter.
    C. At the prompt **Output file for sort: (Screen)**, press Enter.
    D. At the Sort by Line menu, choose 3 or K for Keys.
    E. Key in an **n** below Typ.
    F. Key in a **4** below Field, then press Enter.
    G. Key in a **1** below Word, then press Enter.
    H. With the cursor located below the a after Key 2, press F7.
    I. Choose 1 or P for Perform Action to perform the sort.
4.  Save the document with the same name (CH31EX2). Print CH31EX2.

**Exercise Three**
1.  Retrieve CH31EX2 to the screen.
2.  Sort the second column alphabetically by state and the third column numerically by Social Security Number. To do this, complete the following steps:
    A. Access the Merge/Sort command with Ctrl + F9, then choose 2 or S for Sort.
       **M** *Click on Tools, then Sort.*

B. At the prompt **Input file to sort: (Screen)**, press Enter.

C. At the prompt **Output file for sort: (Screen)**, press Enter.

D. At the Sort by Line menu, choose 3 or K for Keys.

E. Key in an **a** below Typ.

F. Key in a **3** below Field, then press Enter.

G. Key in a **-1** below Word, then press Enter. (The -1 tells WordPerfect to read the words from right to left.)

H. With the cursor located below the a after Key 2, key in an **n**.

I. Key in a **4** below Field, then press Enter.

J. Key in a **1** below Word, then press Enter.

K. With the cursor located below the a after Key 3, press F7.

L. Choose 1 or P for Perform Action to perform the sort.

3. When the sort is complete, the lines are alphabetized by state and the social security numbers are in numeric order *within* each state. Save the document as CH31EX3. Print CH31EX3.

## Exercise Four

1. Retrieve REVIEW.SF to the screen.

2. Sort the records alphabetically by last name by completing the following steps:

A. Access the Merge/Sort command with Ctrl + F9, then choose 2 or S for Sort.
   **M** *Click on Tools, then Sort.*

B. At the prompt **Input file to sort: (Screen)**, press Enter.

C. At the prompt **Output file for sort: (Screen)**, press Enter.

D. At the Sort by Line menu, choose 7 or T for Type, then 1 or M for Merge.

E. At the Sort Secondary Merge File menu, choose 3 or K for Keys.

F. Key in an **a** below Typ.

G. Key in a **3** below Field, then press Enter.

H. Key in a **1** below Line, then press Enter.

I. Key in a **1** below Word, then press Enter.

J. With the cursor located below the a after Key 2, press F7. (If you just completed exercise 3, press the delete key to remove everything after Key 2 except the a below Typ, then press F7.)

K. Choose 1 or P for Perform Action to perform the sort.

3. Save the sorted records and name the document CH31EX4. Print CH31EX4.

## Exercise Five

1. Retrieve CH05EX2 to the screen.

2. Block the columns within the memorandum with the Block command. (Make sure you include the Tab Set code in the block.)

3. With the columns blocked, sort the first column alphabetically by last name by completing the following steps:

A. Access the Merge/Sort command with Ctrl + F9.
   **M** *Click on Tools, then Sort.*

B. At the Sort Secondary Merge File menu, choose 7 or T for Type, then 2 or L for Line.

C. At the Sort by Line menu, choose 3 or K for Keys.

D. Key in an **a** below Typ.

E. Key in a **2** below Field, then press Enter.

F. Key in a **2** below Word, then press Enter.

G. With the cursor located below the a after Key 2, press F7.

H. Choose 1 or P for Perform Action to perform the sort.

4. When the sort is complete, save the memorandum and name it CH31EX5. Print CH31EX5.

**Exercise Six**

1. At a clear screen, key in the paragraphs shown in figure 31-12.
2. Save the paragraphs with the Save key, F10 (**M** *Click on File, then Save*), and name the document CH31EX6.
3. Sort the paragraphs alphabetically by last name by completing the following steps:
   A. Access the Merge/Sort command with Ctrl + F9, then choose 2 or S for Sort.
      **M** *Click on Tools, then Sort.*
   B. At the prompt **Input file to sort: (Screen)**, press Enter.
   C. At the prompt **Output file for sort: (Screen)**, press Enter.
   D. At the Sort by Line menu, choose 7 or T for Type, then choose 3 or P for Paragraph.
   E. At the Sort by Paragraph menu, choose 3 or K for Keys.
   F. Key in an **a** below Typ.
   G. Key in a **1** below Line, then press Enter.
   H. Key in a **1** below Field, then press Enter.
   I. Key in a **1** below Word, then press Enter.
   J. With the cursor located below the a after Key 2, press F7.
   K. Choose 1 or P for Perform Action to perform the sort.
4. Save the sorted paragraphs with the same name (CH31EX6). Print CH31EX6.

---

Porter, L. W., & Smith, F. J. (1970). "Racism and Mental Health" (pp. 269-298). *Pittsburgh: University of Pittsburgh Press.*

Wheeler, W. H., & Thomas, P. (1980). "Value Orientation and Role Conflict" (pp. 329-332). *American Sociological Review.*

Berry, J. W. (1990). "Social Psychology of Cross-Cultural Relations" (pp. 65-72). *A Manual of Intergroup Relations.*

Heller, F. A. (1992). "Organization Development and Change" (pp. 121-130). *Annual Review of Psychology.*

---

**Figure 31-13: Exercise Six**

**Exercise Seven**

1. Retrieve CH31EX1 to the screen.
2. Select the lines of those individuals who are directors by completing the following steps:
   A. Access the Merge/Sort command with Ctrl + F9.
   B. Choose 2 or S for Sort.
      **M** *Click on Tools, then Sort.*
   C. At the prompt **Input file to sort: (Screen)**, press Enter.
   D. At the prompt **Output file for sort: (Screen)**, press Enter.
   E. At the Sort by Paragraph menu, choose 7 or T for Type, then 2 or L for Line.
   F. At the Sort by Line menu, choose 3 or K for Keys.
   G. Key in an **a** below Typ.
   H. Key in a **3** below Field, then press Enter.
   I. Key in a **1** below Word, then press Enter.
   J. With the cursor located below the a after Key 2, press F7.
   K. Choose 4 or S for Select. With the cursor located below **Select**, key in the select equation **Key1=Director**, then press Enter.

       L.  Choose 1 or P for Perform Action to perform the sort and select.

  3.  When the lines are selected, save the document and name it CH31EX7. Print CH31EX7.


## Exercise Eight

1. Retrieve CH31EX2 to the screen.
2. Select the lines of those individuals living in New Mexico with a social security number higher than 800-00-000 by completing the following steps:
   A. Access the Merge/Sort command with Ctrl + F9.
   B. Choose 2 or S for Sort.
      **M** *Click on Tools, then Sort.*
   C. At the prompt **Input file to sort: (Screen)**, press Enter.
   D. At the prompt **Output file for sort: (Screen)**, press Enter.
   E. At the Sort by Line menu, choose 3 or K for Keys.
   F. Key in an **a** below Typ.
   G. Key in a **3** below Field, then press Enter.
   H. Key in a **-1** below Word, then press Enter.
   I. With the cursor located below the a after Key 2, key in an **n**.
   J. Key in a **4** below Field, then press Enter.
   K. Key in a **1** below Word, then press Enter.
   L. With the cursor located to the right of the a after Key 3, press F7.
   M. Choose 4 or S for Select. With the cursor located below **Select**, key in the select equation **Key1=NM \* Key 2>800-00-0000**, then press Enter. (Before keying in the equation, you may need to delete the previous equation.)
   K. Choose 1 or P for Perform Action to perform the sort and select.
3. When the lines are selected, save the document and name it CH31EX8. Print CH31EX8.


## Exercise Nine

1. Retrieve REVIEW2.SF to the screen.
2. Select the records of those individuals who do not have the Zip Code 96026, and save them in a separate document named ZIP by completing the following steps:
   A. Access the Merge/Sort command with Ctrl + F9, then choose 2 or S for Sort.
      **M** *Click on Tools, then Sort.*
   B. At the prompt **Input file to sort: (Screen)**, press Enter.
   C. At the prompt **Output file for sort: (Screen)**, key in **ZIP**, then press Enter.
   D. At the Sort by Line menu, choose 7 or T for Type, then 1 or M for Merge.
   E. At the Sort Secondary Merge File menu, choose 3 or K for Keys.
   F. Key in an **n** below Typ.
   G. Key in a **5** below Field, then press Enter.
   H. Key in a **1** below Line, then press Enter.
   H. Key in a **3** below Word, then press Enter.
   L. With the cursor located below the a after Key 2, press F7. (If you just completed exercise 8, press the Delete key to remove everything after Key 2 except the a, then press F7.)
   M. Choose 4 or S for Select. With the cursor located below Select, key in the select equation **Key1<>96026**, then press Enter. (Before keying in the equation, you may need to delete the previous equation.)
   K. Choose 1 or P for Perform Action to perform the sort and select.
3. Exit from REVIEW2.SF without saving it.
4. Display the directory and print ZIP.

## PERFORMANCE ASSESSMENTS

**Assessment One**
1.  Retrieve CH31EX2 to the screen.
2.  Sort the lines alphabetically by last name.
3.  When the lines are sorted, save the document and name it CH31PA1. Print CH31PA1.

**Assessment Two**
1.  Retrieve CH05EX5 to the screen.
2.  Block the columns in the memorandum, then sort the second column numerically.
3.  Save the sorted memorandum and name it CH31PA2. Print CH31PA2.

**Assessment Three**
1.  Retrieve SOFTWARE.SF to the screen.
2.  Sort the records alphabetically by last name.
3.  When the records are sorted, save the document and name it CH31PA3. Print CH31PA3.

**Assessment Four**
1.  Retrieve CH31EX2 to the screen.
2.  Select the lines of those individuals with a social security number higher than 600-00-0000. Save the selected lines in a separate document named SSN.
3.  Exit from CH31EX2 without saving it.
4.  Display the directory and print SSN.

**Assessment Five**
1.  Retrieve SOFTWARE.SF to the screen.
2.  Select the records of those individuals living in Hayford with database type of software. Save the selected records into a separate document named DATABASE.
3.  Exit from SOFTWARE.SF without saving it.
4.  Display the directory and print DATABASE.

# PERFORMANCE MASTERY

## UNIT PERFORMANCE

In this unit, you have learned to finish multiple-page reports with reference attributes, standardize features of multiple-page reports, and utilize the database features of WordPerfect for maintaining records.

## MASTERY ASSIGNMENTS

**Assignment One**
1. Retrieve CH30EX1 to the screen.
2. Move the cursor to the end of the document, insert a hard page code, move the cursor below the hard page break, then retrieve CH30PA1.
3. Create an open style to format the document. Include formatting codes in the open style such as the following:
   A. Base font
   B. Margins
   C. Justification
   D. Widow/orphan protection
4. Create paired styles to format the chapter titles, headings, and subheadings. You decide on the type of formatting you want applied to titles, headings, and subheadings.
5. Turn on page numbering and number pages in the upper right corner of every page.
6. Create Footer A, Chapter 1: Oral Questioning Techniques, at the left margin that prints on every page of chapter 1, except the first page.
7. Create Footer B, Chapter 2: Mode of Instruction, at the left margin that prints on every page of chapter 2, except the first page.
8. Mark titles, headings, and subheadings in the chapters for inclusion in a table of contents. Define and generate the table of contents.
9. Mark the figure captions for inclusion in a list. Define and generate the list.
10. Save the document and name it U06MA1. Print U06MA1.

**Assignment Two**
1. At a clear screen, create a primary file named U06MA2.PF, with the information shown in figure U6-1. You determine the following:
   A. Margins
   B. Justification
   C. Correct spelling (use Speller)
   D. Correct grammar and usage
   E. Date
   F. Fields for inside address
   G. Fields for salutation
   H. Complimentary close
2. Create a secondary file, named U06MA2.SF, with the information shown in figure U6-2.
3. Merge U06MA2.PF with U06MA2.SF at the printer.

Create a primary file with the following information in the body of the letter.

As the president of Cheney Manufacturing, I want to thank you, (name), for your business this past year. Providing quality products to our customers is our primary goal.

Business at Cheney Manufacturing far exceeded our corporate goals for last year. In light of this increased business, we have sped up production of all products.

Currently, our warehouse is filled to capacity. We are in the process of looking for additional warehouse space. In the meantime, however, we need to make room for new products.

We are offering all our products to you, (name), at twenty percent off wholesale prices. I am sure you realize the incredible savings we are passing on to you, a valued customer.

The sale prices will remain in effect for the next 30 days. Please call our customer service number, 1-800-555-1122, to place your order. Thank you again for your support of Cheney Manufacturing.

Charles R. Pruitt
President

**Figure U6-1: Assignment Two**

Ms. Sarah Stone
Armin Associates
8114 199th Avenue East
Seattle, WA 98112

Mr. David Sorenson
Future Computing
13724 24th Street
Seattle, WA 98420

Mr. Arnold Dahl
8515 Church Lake Drive
Seattle, WA 98112

Mr. Richard Merrill
Merrill Computers
9923 Woodland Avenue
Seattle, WA 98421

Mrs. Blaire McFadden
5422 Rainier Avenue
Seattle, WA 98112

Ms. Carole Vaughn
Fife Computing
3205 Pioneer Avenue
Seattle, WA 98420

**Figure U6-2: Assignment Two**

**Assignment Three**

1.  Retrieve U06MA2.SF to the screen.
2.  Select all records of those customers with the Zip Code 98112 and save the selected records into a new document named U06MA3.SF.
3.  At a clear screen, create a primary file for an envelope and name the document U06MA3.PF.
4.  Merge U06MA3.PF with U06MA3.SF at the screen.
5.  Name the new document U06ENV. Print U06ENV.

# APPENDIX A

## MOUSE INSTRUCTIONS

WordPerfect, Version 5.1, can be operated using just a keyboard or it can be operated with the keyboard and a special piece of equipment called a *mouse* (see figure A-1). A mouse is a small device that sits on a flat surface next to the computer. It is operated with one hand and works best if sitting on a mouse pad. The mouse may have two or three buttons on top, which are pressed to execute specific functions and commands.

Standard                                          Trackball

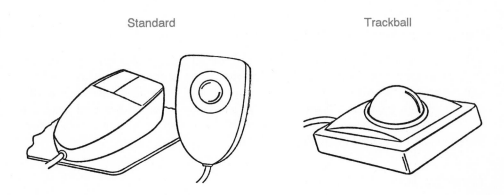

**Figure A-1: Standard and Trackball Mice**

Before a mouse can be used with WordPerfect, it must be installed according to the instructions in the mouse documentation. Once the mouse is
installed, changes can be made to the mouse setup in WordPerfect. To
display the Setup: Mouse menu, complete the following steps:

1.   Access the Setup menu with Shift + F1.
2.   At the Setup menu, choose 1 or M for Mouse.
     **M** *Click on File, Setup, then Mouse.*
3.   At the Setup: Mouse menu, customize the mouse as needed then
     press F7 to save the changes and return the cursor to the docu-
     ment.

The Setup: Mouse menu contains a variety of selections that let you customize mouse support. Refer to the Mouse Setup section of the WordPerfect,
Version 5.1, reference manual for information about this menu.

## USING A MOUSE

To use a standard mouse, rest it on a flat surface or a mouse pad and put
your hand over it with your palm resting on the table surface. Extend two
fingers to the buttons on top of the mouse. As you move the mouse on the
flat surface, a cursor that displays as a rectangle in reverse video (called the
*mouse pointer*) moves on the screen. It takes some practice to coordinate
the moves on the surface with where you want to position the mouse pointer
on the screen. (With the trackball mouse, cursor movement is controlled
with the palm of your hand. The trackball mouse does not move on the
surface of the table.)

To operate the mouse, there are three terms you need to be familiar
with—click, double-click, and drag. *Click* means to press a button on the
mouse and then release it. *Double-click* means to press the button twice in
quick succession. The term *drag* means to press a button and move the
mouse pointer to a specific location before releasing the button.

The mouse can be used to perform three functions: cursor movement,
blocking text, and selecting features and options from menus.

### Cursor Movement and Scrolling with the Mouse

The mouse can be used to move the WordPerfect cursor to a specific location
in a document. To do this, position the mouse pointer at the location where
you want the WordPerfect cursor to appear and click the left button. To
scroll through parts of a document, hold the right button down and drag the
mouse cursor to the end of the screen in the direction you want to scroll.
Release the right button to stop scrolling.

### Blocking Text with the Mouse

The mouse can be used to block text on the screen. To block text, move the
mouse pointer to the beginning of the block and hold down the left button.
With the button down, drag the mouse pointer until it is located at the end
of the block and then release the left button. The text the mouse passes
through will be highlighted. With the text blocked, you can apply any
WordPerfect feature desired. If, after blocking text, you change your mind
and want to turn off the block, click the left button on the mouse one time.

### Selecting from Menus with the Mouse

The mouse can be used to select features and options from WordPerfect menus and prompts. The mouse can be used exclusively or it may be used together with keys from the keyboard. In addition to the menus displayed with the function keys, you can also display pull-down menus with the mouse. To display the mouse menu bar, click the right button once. The pull-down menu displays as a bar at the top of the screen. Click the right button again to remove the display of pull-down menus. (The menu bar can be set up to display at all times at the Setup: Menu Options menu.) The selections from the pull-down menus are shown in figure A-2.

If you do not have a mouse, you can display the menu bar at the top of the screen with Alt + =. The same command, Alt + =, will remove the menu bar.

Menu selections from the pull down menus that display with brackets ([]) cannot be used unless Block is on. If Block is on and you display a pull-down menu, selections that cannot be used with Block are displayed in brackets.

To select an option from a regular menu or a pull-down menu, move the mouse pointer to an option and click the left button. You can also click the left button on a prompt and the action from the prompt will occur. To exit out of a menu, click the right button once.

Double-clicking the left button in a regular menu or pull-down menu, performs the same actions as clicking the left button once and pressing Enter.

If you are using a mouse with three buttons, the center button will perform the same function as the Cancel key, F1. If you are using a mouse with two buttons, press either of the buttons, keep it down, click the other button, and then release the first button.

For more information on mouse support, refer to the Mouse Setup, Mouse Support, and Pull-Down Menus sections of the WordPerfect, Version 5.1, reference manual.

## MOUSE INSTRUCTIONS IN THE TEXTBOOK

WordPerfect commands can be executed from the keyboard or with a mouse. The directions for each method are contained in this text. The mouse directions in this textbook are preceded by the icon, **M**, and are set in italics. When formatting documents with WordPerfect commands either from the keyboard or the mouse, the same menus are eventually encountered. When this happens, the directions use the word *choose* to indicate that the number or letter can be used or the mouse can be clicked on that selection. For example, the steps to display the Format: Line menu and select Justification would be written in this manner:

1. Access the Format command with Shift + F8.
2. Choose 1 or L for Line.
   **M** *Click on Layout, then Line.*
3. Choose 3 or J for Justification.

Step 3 can be executed from the keyboard by pressing 3 or J, or can be executed with the mouse by moving the mouse cursor to the selection and clicking the left button.

To exit from a menu, the instructions in the textbook will say to press the Exit key, F7, to insert the formatting code and return the cursor to the document. If you are using a mouse, you can press the right button on the mouse to return the cursor to the document and insert the formatting code.

File
    Retrieve
    Save
    Text In
    Text Out
    Password
    List Files
    Summary
    Print
    Setup
    Goto Shell
    Exit

Edit
    Move (Cut)
    Copy
    Paste
    Append
    Delete
    Undelete
    Block
    Select
    Comment
    Convert Case
    Protect Block
    Switch Document
    Window
    Reveal Codes

Search
    Forward
    Backward
    Next
    Previous
    Replace
    Extended
    Goto

Layout
    Line
    Page
    Document
    Other
    Columns
    Tables
    Math
    Footnote
    Endnote
    Justify
    Align
    Styles

Mark
    Index
    Table of Contents
    List
    Cross-References
    Table of Authorities
    Define
    Generate
    Master Documents
    Subdocument
    Document Compare

Tools
    Spell
    Thesaurus
    Macro
    Date Text
    Date Code
    Date Format
    Outline
    Paragraph Number
    Define
    Merge Codes
    Merge
    Sort
    Line Draw

Font
    Base Font
    Normal
    Appearance
    Superscript
    Subscript
    Fine
    Small
    Large
    Very Large
    Extra Large
    Print Color
    Characters

Graphics
    Figure
    Table Box
    Text Box
    User Box
    Equation
    Line

Help
    Help
    Index
    Template

**Figure A-2: Pull-Down Menus and Selections**

The right button on the mouse can also be used instead of the Enter key. For example, to display the directory using the mouse, complete the following steps:

**M**    1.   *Click on File.*

2.   *Click on List Files.*

3.   *Click the right button once.*

When you click on List Files in step 2, the prompt **Dir: C:\WP51** (your path may display differently) displays at the bottom of the screen. Clicking the right button in step 3 accomplishes the same thing as pressing the Enter key. You are telling WordPerfect that you want to see a list of files displayed in the directory.

# APPENDIX B

## DISK FORMATTING

Before a disk can be used to save WordPerfect documents, it must be formatted. Formatting is the process that prepares the surface of a disk for the particular disk operating system you are using. A disk can be formatted using the Format command from the Disk Operating System (DOS).

During the formatting process, any information on the disk is erased. Before formatting, make sure you do not have anything on the disk that you want to save.

Complete the following steps to format a disk:

1.  Turn on the computer.
2.  In a few seconds, a prompt appears asking you to enter the date. Enter the date as mm/dd/yy. For example, if today is October 1, 1991, enter 10/09/91. After keying in the date, press Enter.
3.  A prompt appears asking you to enter the time. You must use military time. For example, if the time is 1:30 in the afternoon, enter 13:30. After keying in the time, press Enter.
4.  When the date and time have been entered, a **C>** appears on the screen. At the **C>**, key in **FORMAT A:** and press Enter.
5.  The message **Insert new diskette in drive A: and strike Enter when ready** appears on the screen. Insert a blank disk in Drive A, close the door, and press Enter.
6.  The formatting process begins. The message **Formatting ...** appears on the screen and the disk light comes on. Do not remove the disk as the disk is being formatted. Formatting takes approximately 1 minute.
7.  When the disk is formatted, you will see the message **Format Complete, Format another (Y/N)?_**. If you do not want to format another disk, key in an **N** and press Enter. The **C>** appears on the screen.
8.  Take out the disk and turn off the computer.

# APPENDIX C

| Proofreaders' Mark | Example | Revised |
|---|---|---|
| # Insert space | letter to the | letter to the |
| Delete | the commands is | the command is |
| lc / Lowercase | he is Branch Manager | he is branch manager |
| uc Uppercase | Margaret simpson | Margaret Simpson |
| ¶ New paragraph | ¶ The new product | The new product |
| No ¶ No paragraph | the meeting. Bring the | the meeting. Bring the |
| ^ Insert | pens, clips | pens, and clips |
| ⊙ Insert period | a global search | a global search. |
| ] Move right | With the papers | With the papers |
| [ Move left | access the code | access the code |
| ][ Center | Chapter Six | Chapter Six |
| ∪ Transpose | It is raesonable | It is reasonable |
| SP Spell out | 475 Mill Ave. | 475 Mill Avenue |
| ... Stet (do not delete) | I am very pleased | I am very pleased |
| Close up | regret fully | regretfully |

| | | | |
|---|---|---|---|
| SS | Single-space | SS The margin top<br>is 1 inch. | The margin top<br>is 1 inch. |
| ds | Double-space | ds Paper length is<br>set for 11 inches. | Paper length is<br><br>set for 11 inches. |
| ts | Triple-space | ts The F8 function<br><br>key contains commands | The F8 function<br><br>key contains commands |

# APPENDIX D

There are many business letter styles. This appendix includes two: block style and modified block style. The following two pages show their proper placement and spacing. Both letters have been created with standard punctuation. Standard punctuation includes a colon after the salutation and a comma after the complimentary close.

A business letter can be printed on letterhead stationery, or the company name and address can be keyed in at the top of the letter. For the examples in this textbook, you should assume that all business letters you create will be printed on letterhead stationery.

*2 inches*

December 8, 19--

*5 returns*

Ms. Genevieve Alexander
Park Medical Center
4500 Park Boulevard
Tacoma, WA  98405
*ds*
Dear Ms. Alexander:
*ds*
During the entire month of January, our laser printer, Model No.
34-454, will be on sale.  We are cutting the original price by 33
percent!
*ds*
When you purchased your computer system from our store last month,
you indicated an interest in a laser printer.  Now is your chance,
Ms. Alexander, to purchase a high-quality laser printer at a rock-
bottom price.
*ds*
Once you have seen the quality of print produced by a laser
printer, you will not be satisfied with any other type of printer.
*ds*
Visit our store at your convenience and see a demonstration of this
incredible printer.  We are so confident you will purchase the
printer that we are enclosing a coupon for a free printer cartridge
worth over $100.
*ds*
Very truly yours,

*4 returns*

Roland Prasad, Manager
*ds*
xx:BLOCKLTR
*ds*
Enclosure

**BLOCK-STYLE BUSINESS LETTER**

*2 inches*

December 8, 19--

*5 returns*

Ms. Genevieve Alexander
Park Medical Center
4500 Park Boulevard
Tacoma, WA  98405

*ds*

Dear Ms. Alexander:

*ds*

Re:  Laser Printer Sale

*ds*

During the entire month of January, our laser printer, Model No. 34-454, will be on sale.  We are cutting the original price by 33 percent!

*ds*

When you purchased your computer system from our store last month, you indicated an interest in a laser printer.  Now is your chance, Ms. Alexander, to purchase a high-quality laser printer at a rock-bottom price.

*ds*

Once you have seen the quality of print produced by a laser printer, you will not be satisfied with any other type of printer.

*ds*

Visit our store at your convenience and see a demonstration of this incredible printer.  We are so confident you will purchase the printer that we are enclosing a coupon for a free printer cartridge worth over $100.

*ds*

Very truly yours,

*ds*

ACE COMPUTER SUPPLIES

*4 returns*

Roland Prasad, Manager

*ds*

xx:BLOCKLTR

*ds*

Enclosure

MODIFIED BLOCK-STYLE BUSINESS LETTER

# APPENDIX E

## MEMORANDUM

↓ | inch

DATE:     September 29, 19--

TO:       Lonnie Parlette, Vice President

FROM:     Carla Mendoza, Manager

SUBJECT:  New Employees


Two new employees have been hired to work in the Word Processing Department.  Miguel Sandiago will begin work on October 1 and Chris Ossinger will begin on October 15.

Mr. Sandiago has worked for three years as a word processing operator for another company.  Due to his previous experience, he was hired as a Word Processing Operator I.

Ms. Ossinger has just completed a one-year training program at a local community college.  She was hired as a Word Processing Trainee.

I would like to introduce you to the new employees.  Please schedule a time for a short visit.

xx:MEMO

# APPENDIX F

## ADDITIONAL WORDPERFECT FEATURES

WordPerfect is a powerful word processing program that contains a wide range of sophisticated features. Most of the features have been presented in the chapters of this textbook.

This appendix briefly describes the following WordPerfect features not addressed in the main body of the book:

> Shell, Ctrl + F1 (**M** *Click on File, then Go to DOS*)
>
> Setup, Shift + F1 (**M** *Click on File, then Setup*)
>
> Text In/Out, Ctrl + F5 (**M** *Click on File, then Text In or Text Out*)

### SHELL

The Shell command, Ctrl + F1 (**M** *Click on File, then Go to DOS*) lets you return to DOS while WordPerfect remains in resident memory. In DOS you can perform DOS functions and then return to the WordPerfect program.

If you are using WordPerfect Library (a program separate from WordPerfect), you can use the Shell command to retrieve the clipboard.

### SETUP

WordPerfect contains many program defaults or preset standards. WordPerfect defaults are determined by the individuals who designed the program. With the Setup command, however, you can tailor WordPerfect for your specific needs. When changes are made to WordPerfect with the Setup command, they remain in effect each time you load WordPerfect.

Access the Setup command with Shift + F1 (**M** *Click on File, then Setup*), and the Setup menu shown in figure F-1 appears on the screen (if you are using the mouse, the choices display as a pull-down menu):

```
  Setup

     1 - Mouse

     2 - Display

     3 - Environment

     4 - Initial Settings

     5 - Keyboard Layout

     6 - Location of Files













  Selection: 0
```

**Figure F-1: Setup Menu**

To make changes to this menu, choose the letter or number next to the
selection, make any changes necessary and press Exit, F7, the number of
times it takes to return to the document. Changes made to the Setup menu
are in effect each time you load WordPerfect. A brief description of the
menu selections is described below. Figure F-2 on the next page shows a full
listing of the Setup menu selections and submenus.

## Mouse

With the Mouse selection from the Setup menu, you can select the type of
mouse, the port where it is attached and the response time of the mouse.

## Display

The Display selection from the Setup menu contains a number of choices
that can be used to determine how text is displayed on the screen. When
you choose 2 or D for Display from the Setup menu, the Setup: Display
menu appears on the screen with eight choices.

The first choice from the Setup: Display menu, Colors/Font/Attributes,
lets you determine the appearance on the screen of characters with attributes. If you are using a color monitor, you can use this selection to change
the color of text that is identified for underlining, boldfacing, centering, and
so on. If you are using a monochrome monitor, your choice of appearances
is limited.

With the second choice, Graphics Screen Type, you can select the style of
monitor that you are using. With the third choice, Text Screen Type, you
can change the number of characters and lines that display on the screen.
The number of choices available depends on the monitor installed.

1 Mouse
  1 Type
  2 Port
  3 Double-Click Interval
  4 Submenu Delay Time
  5 Acceleration Factor
  6 Left-Handed Mouse
  7 Assisted Mouse Pointer Movement

2 Display
  1 Colors/Fonts/Attributes
  2 Graphics Screen Type
  3 Text Screen Type
  4 Menu Options
    1 Menu Letter Display
    2 Pull-Down Letter Display
    3 Pull-Down Text
    4 Alt Key Selects Pull-Down Menu
    5 Menu Bar Letter Display
    6 Menu Bar Text
    7 Menu Bar Separator Line
    8 Menu Bar Remains Visible
  5 View Document Options
    1 Text in Black & White
    2 Graphics in Black & White
    3 Bold Displayed with Color
  6 Edit-Screen Options
    1 Automatically Format and Rewrite
    2 Comments Display
    3 Filename on the Status Line
    4 Hard Return Display Character
    5 Merge Codes Display
    6 Reveal Codes Window Size
    7 Side-by-Side Columns Display

3 Environment
  1 Backup Options
    1 Timed Document Backup
    2 Original Document Backup
  2 Beep Options
    1 Beep on Error
    2 Beep on Hyphenation
    3 Beep on Search Failure
  3 Cursor Speed
  4 Document Management/Summary
    1 Create Summary on Save/Exit
    2 Subject Search Text
    3 Long Document Names
    4 Default Document Type
  5 Fast Save (unformatted)

6 Hyphenation
7 Prompt for Hyphenation
8 Units of Measure
9 Alternate Keyboard

4 Initial Settings
  1 Merge
    1 Field Delimiters
    2 Record Delimiters
  2 Date Format
  3 Equations
    1 Print as Graphics
    2 Graphical Font Size
    3 Horizontal Alignment
    4 Vertical Alignment
    5 Keyboard for Editing
  4 Format Retrieved Doc. for Default Printer
  5 Initial Codes
  6 Repeat Value
  7 Table of Authorities
    1 Dot Leaders
    2 Underlining Allowed
    3 Blank Line Between Authorities
  8 Print Options
    1 Binding Offset
    2 Number of Copies
      Multiple Copies Generated by
    3 Graphics Quality
    4 Text Quality
    5 Redline Method
    6 Size Attribute Ratios

5 Keyboard Layout

6 Location of Files
  1 Backup Files
  2 Keyboard/Macro Files
  3 Thesaurus/Spell/Hyphenation
  4 Printer Files
  5 Style Files
    Library Filename
  6 Graphics Files
  7 Documents
  8 Spreadsheet Files

**Figure F-2: Setup Menus and Submenus**

When you choose 4 or M from the Setup: Display menu, the Setup: Menu Options menu displays on the screen. At this menu, you can determine how the mnemonic keys in menus display, the display of the pull-down menu, and the display of the menu bar.

The fifth choice from the Setup: Display menu, View Document Options, lets you change the display of text and graphics to black and white if you have a color monitor. The advantage of changing the display to black and white is that the screen will provide a more accurate representation of how the text and graphics will appear when printed.

At the Edit-Screen Options you can determine what and how information at the WordPerfect screen displays. With the Edit-Screen Options you can change the automatic format and rewrite, comments display, display of the file name on the status line, and display of side-by-side columns to yes or no. In addition, you can enter a character to display when the Enter key is pressed, and change the size of the Reveal Codes screen.

## Environment

When you choose 3 or E for Environment from the Setup menu, the Setup: Environment menu is displayed on the screen.

With the first choice from the Setup: Environment menu, Backup Options, you can choose to have WordPerfect automatically backup the document in which you are working at specific time intervals. The time interval is entered as minutes. Or you can chose to have WordPerfect automatically create a backup of a document when you save it a second or subsequent time. WordPerfect saves the backup document with the same name as the original but adds the extension .BK!. To retrieve a backup file, it must first be renamed to remove the .BK! extension.

With the Beep choice, you can have WordPerfect beep when a hyphenation decision needs to be made, when an error occurs, or when a search is completed. Or, you can turn the beep off for these situations.

The Cursor Speed choice lets you determine the speed of the cursor as you are entering text, scrolling, or deleting characters. The default setting is 50 characters per second. This can be changed from 50 to 15, 20, 30, or 40.

With the Document Management/Summary choice, you can tell WordPerfect to create a document summary automatically when a document is saved, change the subject search text, or change the display of documents in the directory to long display.

The Fast Save choice from the Setup: Environment menu has a default setting of Yes. This means that WordPerfect saves a document in an unformatted state, which takes less time. When a document is saved unformatted, however, printing a document from the disk takes a little longer. The Fast Save choice can be changed to No.

The Hyphenation choice has a default setting of External Dictionary/Rules. By default, WordPerfect uses the spelling dictionary to make hyphenation decisions. This can be changed to internal rules, which uses an algorithm for making hyphenation decisions.

By default, WordPerfect prompts for hyphenation when required. This is the setting at the Prompt for Hyphenation choice from the Setup: Environment menu. It can be changed to Always or Never.

At the Units of Measure choice, you can change the units of measurements used by WordPerfect. The default units of measurement are inches. This can be changed to centimeters, points, or lines and columns.

The last choice from the Setup: Environment menu, Alternate Keyboard, lets you change the function of the F1, Esc, and F3 keys. If you change the setting after Alternate Keyboard to Yes, the F1 key becomes the Help key, the Esc key becomes the Cancel key, and the F3 key becomes the Repeat key.

## Initial Settings

The Initial Settings selection from the Setup menu contains choices that lets you customize documents. When you choose 4 or I for Initial Settings from the Setup menu, the Setup: Initial Settings menu displays on the screen. Changes made to this menu stay in effect even if WordPerfect is exited.

With the Merge choice from the Setup: Initial Settings menu, you can establish the field and record delimiters for DOS files that you are using in a merge.

The Date selection from the Setup: Initial Settings menu is used to change the format of the current date. Earlier in this textbook, you learned that the current date can be inserted in a document using the Date/Outline command. You also learned that the format of the date can be changed at the Date Format menu. When you select Date from the Setup: Initial Settings menu, you are presented with the same Date Format menu. When you make changes to this menu, the changes remain in effect every time you load WordPerfect. When you make changes with the Date/Outline command, the date format remains until WordPerfect is exited and then it reverts to the default.

With the third selection from the Setup: Initial Settings menu, Document Summary, you can have WordPerfect prompt you for a document summary when you save or exit the document. You can also change the default character used to search for text in a document.

The Equations choice from the Setup: Initial Settings menu lets you customize how equations will print. This choice can be useful if you are using a printer that cannot print graphics.

By default, WordPerfect formats a document with the printer file that was in effect when the document was saved. At the Format Retrieved Documents for Default Printer choice, you can tell WordPerfect to format the document for the current printer.

Initial Codes from the Setup: Initial Settings menu lets you change the default setting for most WordPerfect initial settings. This lets you tailor document formats for your particular needs. When you choose 5 or C for Initial Codes from the Setup: Initial Settings menu, WordPerfect presents you with a Reveal Codes screen. At this screen, insert formatting codes to customize documents. For example, you could change justification to Left, change the left and right margins, change the top margin, and so on.

The Esc key can be used as a repeat value key. When you press Esc, the message **Repeat Value = 8** appears in the lower left corner of the screen. With selection 5, Repeat Value, from the Setup: Initial Settings menu, you can change the default repeat number from 8 to any number you desire.

The Table of Authorities choice from the Setup: Initial Settings menu is used to change the default settings of Table of Authorities. You can make changes to this menu when you define the Table of Authorities. Those changes remain in effect until WordPerfect is exited. When you make changes to this menu through the Setup: Initial Settings menu, the changes remain in effect every time WordPerfect is loaded.

With the Print Options choice from the Setup: Initial Settings menu, you can make permanent changes to the options that are available in the lower half of the Print menu.

**Keyboard Layout**

With the Keyboard Layout selection from the Setup menu, you can define different keyboards. For example, you can use this selection to create the Dvorak keyboard, or any other arrangement of keys that you desire.

**Location of Files**

When you choose 6 or L for Location of Files at the Setup menu, WordPerfect displays the Setup: Location of Files menu on the screen. At this menu, you can identify where certain files such as styles and macro files are saved. In addition, the path for Thesaurus, Speller, and graphics files is identified at this menu, telling WordPerfect where to find the files. You can customize the location of files at this menu.

## TEXT IN/OUT

The Text In/Out command contains several selections that let you save a document with another format and insert nonprinting comments. Access the Text In/Out command with Ctrl + F5, and the prompt **1 DOS Text; 2 Password; 3 Save As; 4 Comment; 5 Spreadsheet: 0** appears at the bottom of the screen.

**DOS Text**

The first selection, DOS Text, lets you save a document as a DOS text file or retrieve a DOS text file into WordPerfect. Use this selection when you want to take a WordPerfect document to another program or when you want to bring a text file from a different program into WordPerfect.

**Password**

If, for any reason, you want to lock a file for security purposes, use the Password selection from the Text In/Out command. With this selection you can add, change, or remove a password from a document. A password can be a maximum of 76 characters. When you create a password for a document, WordPerfect has you enter it twice. When you enter the password, you do not see it on the screen.

   When you have added a password to a document, WordPerfect will ask for the password when you try to retrieve the document. If you enter the wrong password, WordPerfect displays a file-locked error message.

**Save As**

The Save As selection from the Text In/Out command is used to save a WordPerfect document as a generic word processing document, a WordPerfect, Version 5.0 document, or a WordPerfect, Version 4.2 document.

**Comment**

The Comment selection from the Text In/Out command can be used to insert a comment at any location in the document. When you use this feature, the comment is inserted in the document surrounded by a double-lined box. A comment may contain a maximum of 1,024 characters. With the Comment selection, a comment can be created or edited, or you can block text within a document and convert it to a comment.

## Spreadsheet

With the Spreadsheet selection, you can import or create a link to a spreadsheet document from PlanPerfect, Excel, or Lotus 1-2-3.

# INDEX

# WORDPERFECT, VERSION 5.1
## COMMAND CARD

| | |
|---|---|
| Backspace . . . . . . . . . . . . | Backspace Key |
| Base Font . . . . . . . . . . . . | Ctrl + F8,4 |
| Binding . . . . . . . . . . . . | Shift + F7,B |
| Block . . . . . . . . . . . | Alt + F4 or F12 |
| Block Move/Copy (Block on) . . . . . | Ctrl + F4 |
| Bold . . . . . . . . . . . . . | F6 |
| Bottom Margin . . . . . . . . . | Shift + F8,2 |
| Cancel . . . . . . . . . . . . | F1 |
| Cancel Hyphenation . . . . . . . . | F1 |
| Cancel Print Job(s) . . . . . . | Shift + F7,4,1 |
| Case Conversion (Block on) . . . . | Shift + F3 |
| Center . . . . . . . . . . . | Shift + F6 |
| Center Page Top to Bottom . . . . | Shift + F8,2 |
| Coded Space . . . . . . . . . | Home, Space bar |
| Column, Move/Copy (Block on) . . . . | Ctrl + F4 |
| Columns, Text . . . . . . . . . | Alt + F7 |
| Conditional End of Page . . . . . | Shift + F8 |
| Copy (List Files) . . . . . . | F5,Enter,8 |
| Date/Outline . . . . . . . . . | Shift + F5 |
| Decimal/Align Character . . . . . | Shift + F8,4 |
| Delete . . . . . . . . . . . . | Del Key |
| Delete to End of Line (EOL) . . . . | Ctrl + End |
| Delete to End of Page (EOP) . . . . | Ctrl + Pg Dn |
| Delete (List) . . . . . . . . . | F5,Enter,2 |
| Delete Word . . . . . . | Ctrl + Backspace |
| Delete Word (cursor to beginning) | Home, Backspace |
| Delete Word (cursor to end) . . . | Home, Del |
| Display All Print Jobs . . . . | Shift + F7,4,3 |
| Display Pitch . . . . . . . . . | Shift + F8,3 |
| End Field . . . . . . . . . . . | F9 |
| Endnote . . . . . . . . . . . | Ctrl + F7 |
| Escape . . . . . . . . . . . | Esc Key |
| Exit . . . . . . . . . . . . . | F7 |
| Find . . . . . . . . . . . . | F5,Enter,9 |
| Flush Right . . . . . . . . . . | Alt + F6 |
| Force Odd/Even Page . . . . . . | Shift + F8,2 |
| Font . . . . . . . . . . . . | Ctrl + F8 |
| Footnote . . . . . . . . . . . | Ctrl + F7 |
| Format: Document menu . . . . . . | Shift + F8,3 |
| Format: Line menu . . . . . . . | Shift + F8,1 |
| Format: Other menu . . . . . . | Shift + F8,4 |
| Format: Page menu . . . . . . . | Shift + F8,2 |
| Full Document (Print) . . . . . . | Shift + F7,1 |
| Go (Start Printing) . . . . . . | Shift + F7,4,4 |
| Graphics . . . . . . . . . . . | Alt + F9 |
| Hard Page . . . . . . . . . . . | Ctrl + Enter |
| Hard Return . . . . . . . . . . | Enter |
| Headers or Footers . . . . . . | Shift + F8,2 |
| Help . . . . . . . . . . . . . | F3 |
| Hyphenation On/Off . . . . . . | Shift + F8,1 |
| Hyphenation Zone . . . . . . . | Shift + F8,1 |
| ->Indent . . . . . . . . . . . | F4 |
| ->Indent<- . . . . . . . . . . | Shift + F4 |
| Index . . . . . . . . . . . | Alt + F5 |
| Initial Codes/Font . . . . . . | Shift + F8,3 |
| Justification . . . . . . . . . | Shift + F8,1 |
| Line Draw . . . . . . . . . . | Ctrl + F3,2 |
| Line Height . . . . . . . . . | Shift + F8,1 |
| Line Numbering . . . . . . . . | Shift + F8,1 |
| Line Spacing . . . . . . . . . | Shift + F8,1 |
| List (Block on) . . . . . . . . | Alt + F5 |
| List directory . . . . . . . . | F5,Enter |
| Look . . . . . . . . . . . | F5,Enter,6 |
| Macro . . . . . . . . . . . | Alt + F10 |
| Macro Def . . . . . . . . . . | Ctrl + F10 |
| Margin Release . . . . . . . . | Shift + Tab |
| Margins . . . . . . . . . . . | Shift + F8,1 |
| Mark Text . . . . . . . . . . | Alt + F5 |
| Math . . . . . . . . . . . . | Alt + F7 |
| Merge . . . . . . . . . . . . | Ctrl + F9 |

| | |
|---|---|
| Merge Codes . . . . . . . . . . | Shift + F9 |
| Move . . . . . . . . . . . . | Ctrl + F4 |
| Move/Rename (List) . . . . . . . | F5,Enter,3 |
| Name Search . . . . . . . . . | F5,Enter,N |
| New Page Number . . . . . . . | Shift + F8,2 |
| Number of Copies . . . . . . . | Shift + F7,N |
| Other Directory . . . . . . . . | F5,Enter,7 |
| Overstrike . . . . . . . . . . | Shift + F8,4 |
| Page Numbering . . . . . . . . | Shift + F8,2 |
| Page (Print) . . . . . . . . . | Shift + F7,2 |
| Paper Size/Type . . . . . . . | Shift + F8,2 |
| Print Block (Block on) . . . . . | Shift + F7 |
| Print: Control Printer menu . . . . | Shift + F7,4 |
| Print a Document . . . . . . . | Shift + F7,3 |
| Print (List) . . . . . . . . . | F5,Enter,4 |
| Print menu . . . . . . . . . | Shift + F7 |
| Redline . . . . . . . . . . | Ctrl + F8,2,8 |
| Replace . . . . . . . . . . . | Alt + F2 |
| Retrieve . . . . . . . . . . | Shift + F10 |
| Retrieve (List) . . . . . . . . | F5,Enter |
| Reveal Codes . . . . . . . . . | Alt + F3 |
| Rush Print Job . . . . . . . | Shift + F7,4,2 |
| Save . . . . . . . . . . . . . | F10 |
| Screen . . . . . . . . . . . | Ctrl + F3 |
| Search (Backward) . . . . . . . | Shift + F2 |
| Search (Forward) . . . . . . . | F2 |
| Select Printer . . . . . . . . | Shift + F7,S |
| Setup . . . . . . . . . . . | Shift + F1 |
| Shell . . . . . . . . . . . | Ctrl + F1 |
| Sort . . . . . . . . . . . | Ctrl + F9 |
| Spacing . . . . . . . . . . . | Shift + F8,1 |
| Spell . . . . . . . . . . . | Ctrl + F2 |
| Stop Printing . . . . . . . . | Shift + F7,4,5 |
| Strikeout (Block on) . . . . . | Ctrl + F8,2,9 |
| Style . . . . . . . . . . . | Alt + F8 |
| Super/Subscript . . . . . . . . | Ctrl + F8,1 |
| Suppress . . . . . . . . . . | Shift + F8,2 |
| Switch . . . . . . . . . . . | Shift + F3 |
| Tab Align . . . . . . . . . . | Ctrl + F6 |
| Tab Set . . . . . . . . . . . | Shift + F8,1 |
| Table of Authorities (Block on) . . . | Alt + F5 |
| Table of Contents (Block on) . . . . | Alt + F5 |
| Text In/Out . . . . . . . . . | Ctrl + F5 |
| Thesaurus . . . . . . . . . . | Alt + F1 |
| Top Margin . . . . . . . . . . | Shift + F8,2 |
| Typeover . . . . . . . . . . . | Ins Key |
| Type-thru . . . . . . . . . . | Shift + F7,5 |
| Undelete . . . . . . . . . . . | F1 |
| Underline . . . . . . . . . . . | F8 |
| Underline Style . . . . . . . . | Shift + F8,4 |
| Widow/Orphan . . . . . . . . . | Shift + F8,1 |
| Word Count . . . . . . . . . . | Ctrl + F2 |

## CURSOR MOVEMENT COMMANDS

| | |
|---|---|
| Word Left . . . . . . . . . . | Ctrl + Left Arrow |
| Word Right . . . . . . . . | Ctrl + Right Arrow |
| End of Line . . . . . . . . . . . . . | End |
| Screen Left . . . . . . . . | Home, Left Arrow |
| Screen Right . . . . . . . | Home, Right Arrow |
| Screen Down . . . . . . . | Home, Down Arrow |
| Screen Up . . . . . . . . | Home, Up Arrow |
| Page Down . . . . . . . . . | Page Down Key |
| Page Up . . . . . . . . . . | Page Up Key |
| Specific Page . . . . . . | Ctrl + Home, #, Enter |
| Beginning of Text . . . . | Home, Home, Up Arrow |
| End of Text . . . . . . | Home, Home, Down Arrow |